CHARLES DICKENS

CHARLES DICKENS, AGED 27
by Daniel Maclise, R.A.

" Here we have the real identical man Dickens "

W. M. THACKERAY

CHARLES DICKENS

1812-1870

UNA POPE-HENNESSY

THE REPRINT SOCIETY
LONDON

FIRST PUBLISHED 1945
THIS EDITION FIRST PUBLISHED BY THE REPRINT SOCIETY LTD
BY ARRANGEMENT WITH CHATTO & WINDUS
1947

PRINTED IN GREAT BRITAIN BY
R. & R. CLARK, LIMITED, EDINBURGH

TO

RICHARD

Acknowledgements

I OWE a deep debt of gratitude to the late Mr. Walter Dexter, editor of *The Dickensian* and prime authority on every aspect and detail of the life of Charles Dickens. He lent me books, he showed me unpublished letters, and, more valuable than any other form of help, discussed with me the problems that inevitably arose in dealing with the novelist's relations with his family and his contemporaries. All my questions were replied to unequivocally and with patience. It is a source of great regret to me that he is not alive to read the book he saw in typescript.

My warm thanks are due to Mr. William Maxwell of R. & R. Clark, Ltd., Edinburgh, for lending me for four years a copy of *The Letters of Charles Dickens* (edited by Walter Dexter for the Nonesuch Press). It is a book I could neither buy nor borrow from a library, and as my work is for the most part based on these *Letters* it will be understood how vital and important was this loan.

In these days of austerity it would be waste of paper and labour to print the very long list of books I have read or consulted. I must, however, mention the comprehensive bibliography included in *Charles Dickens*, by William Dibelius (1916), as being extremely helpful, and add that I have made use of Mr. Ellis Gummer's book, *Dickens's Works in Germany* (1940) with appreciation. Fresh light is thrown on Dickens's family life in *Mr. and Mrs. Dickens*, by Walter Dexter (1935), and in *Dickens and Daughter* (a record of conversations with Mrs. Perugini), by Gladys Storey (1939).

For help over photographs I wish to thank Sir Eric Maclagan and Mr. Carl Winter of the Victoria and Albert Museum; Mr. A. Hind of the British Museum; Dr. Wittkower of the Warburg Institute; and Lord Glenconner. I must also express my gratitude to the Earl of Lytton for showing me over Knebworth, the cradle of the Guild of Literature and Art. Special thanks go to my kind friend Mr. C. F. Bell for reading through both typescript and proofs, and to my son, John Pope-Hennessy, for constructive criticism.

U. P.-H.

Ladbroke Grove, 1945

List of Contents

List of Illustrations

INTRODUCTION

No Life of Charles Dickens has been written since his collected letters were published by the Nonesuch Press in 1938.[1] These letters not only provide new biographical material, but throw light on the difficult temperament of a writer who said of himself that his inventive faculty must be allowed to master his whole existence. Owing to his unusual psychological make-up Charles Dickens has been the subject of several mutually contradictory appreciations. One biographer has seen in him a satirist and a woman-hater, another a man living his life in a trauma, another an exemplar of applied Christianity, another a neurotic and highly disagreeable sentimentalist, another a social reformer with a tendency towards Marxian views, while to the commonalty the mere name of Dickens conjures up the cosy fireside, the joys of home, glowing hearts and Christmas largess.

Dickens was an adept in what he called laying his hand upon the time, and in doing this became the recognised exponent of the English character to Victorian England, and not to Victorian England only, but to the world. He revealed the masses to the classes in one country and the people of all lands understood what he had to say. In trite and truthful words Bagehot summed up the universality of his appeal:

> The penetrating power of this remarkable genius among all classes at home is not inferior to its diffusive energy abroad. The phrase 'household book' has, when applied to the works of Mr. Dickens, a peculiar propriety. There is no contemporary English writer whose works are read so generally through the whole house, who can give pleasure to the servant as well as to the mistress, to the children as well as to the master.

Dickens was a purely instinctive writer and the creator of the democratic novel. He was the first novelist to give the

[1] *The Letters of Charles Dickens*, edited by Walter Dexter. Nonesuch Press. 3 vols. 1938.

common people of Europe the sentiment of a contagious democratic fraternity. *Cor ad cor loquitur*, for it is heart alone that can speak to heart.

The first and greatest book on Charles Dickens was written seventy years ago.[1] John Forster, its author, apologised for making the letters he had received from his friend, 'letters of unexampled candour and truthfulness', the basis of his narrative, but it turned out to be an excellent method of presentation. The book is readable and as interesting as its prototype, *The Life and Works of Goethe*, by George Lewes, another masterpiece of Victorian biography. The value of Forster's record is in no way diminished by the German criticism that it is not so much a biography as an analytical collection of letters and memoranda, nor is it invalidated by the fact that he eliminated certain people and certain episodes from his story with the aim of presenting a Dickens so consistently great and good as to compel the homage of posterity. Despite its planned limitations, the book remains and must remain the indispensable monument to friendship and genius that it was constructed to be.

Until his own marriage in 1856 Forster, for twenty years, had been Dickens's close companion and the recipient of his confidences. After that date a comparative estrangement developed between them, and as the friendship dwindled in intensity, Forster's account of Dickens flags both in intimacy and accuracy. He says himself that for the last years he had to draw on *The Uncommercial Traveller* for detailed information. The *Letters* printed by the Nonesuch Press (between eight and nine thousand in number) supplement the material provided for us by Forster. They reveal Dickens's motive for speech and action, throw light on the composition of his books and show the great emotional strain under which many of them were written. They also dispel the illusion that their author was a merely insular humorist and prove that the handicap of a defective education did not prevent his becoming a continentally-minded man. He liked and understood

[1] *The Life of Charles Dickens*, by John Forster. 3 vols. 1872–4.

foreigners, learnt to talk French and Italian fluently and felt as much at home in France and Italy as he did in England. When he died Genoese newspapers carried the headline *Il nostro Carlo Dickens è morto*.

Conscious of possessing great reserves of power, Dickens was so responsive to stimulus from without and to inspiration from within that he surprised people by his capacity for adaptation. His spontaneity was amazing, he was for ever bursting out in new directions and it is doubtful whether anyone of his own day really took the measure of his personality. He was something of an enigma to his contemporaries and he remains something of an enigma to us. It does not make him less of one to know how widespread was his influence abroad, how Tolstoi condemned parliamentary government on the strength of his books and how Moltke and his staff officers based their appreciations of the English character on *Pickwick* and *Little Dorrit*.

Pervasive in influence, Dickens is embedded deep in our national mind. We cannot ignore him even if we would, and, liking or disliking him, we have to admit that he is one of the great pivotal authors of England. Nothing has ever been quite the same for English folk since Dickens published his novels, for he faced the stupefying platitude of anonymous human fates and gave them value, humour and incident. More than this, his letters and his speeches make it clear that in Dickens we have to reckon with a seer as well as a very great novelist. No one of his day understood the condition of England better or saw more plainly how the dead weight of conservatism for its own sake tended not to preserve, but to stifle the essential genius of our people. As we read of his lifelong crusade against illiteracy, vile industrial conditions and slumdom, of his contempt for the misuse by rich men of parliamentary opportunities of procrastination, we see how inevitable it was that in the end he should appeal to the people to educate themselves for self-government by means of the Mechanics' Institutes, Polytechnics and Athenaeums that they through their own thrift and intelligence had brought into being. By the classes he was regarded, with few exceptions, as an entertainer, by the masses as a social reformer. To a class-ridden country he gave the watchword, 'Men must get together in good citizenship'; to a class-conscious community he preached class fusion as the best corrective to the confusion of class warfare.

Other great writers, Victor Hugo for example, have found themselves instinctively in opposition to the society of their day and for one reason or another have been thrown out from the country of their birth. Dickens, in spite of his fights for humanity and justice, alienated no one among his compatriots, earned the worship of countless thousands of readers and was taken to all hearts. The people of England responded to the fiery radiation of a soul which in some mysterious way expressed their being in a manner they recognised as their very own. Such an achievement is as inexplicable as it is unique.

Chapter 1
THE FAMILY BACKGROUND

A man, a personal ascendency, is the only great phenomenon.
R. W. EMERSON

In *Bleak House* it is laid down as 'a melancholy truth' that 'even great men have their poor relations'. To be a great man and to have none but poor relations was the lot of Charles Dickens, who lived in a day when a family background, in so far as it connoted a station in society, was apt to tether a boy for life. Though neither poverty nor lowliness of birth can any longer be viewed as social fixatives, they must still be reckoned with in sizing up the influences that go to the conditioning of personality. In the case of Charles Dickens they were of basic significance, for his horror of patronage and distrust of the aristocratic system masquerading as representative government in the England of his day was probably as much due to the fact that his father had been brought up in the servants' quarters of that typical source of place and power—a political country house—as that he himself had a hard and lonely fight to win a niche in the temple of privilege.

His grandfather, William Dickens, began life as a footman, and after marrying Lady Blandford's housemaid, Elizabeth Ball,[1] became steward at Crewe Hall, the seat of John Crewe, M.P. for Chester. This couple had two sons, William and John, and in the year of John's birth (1785) William Dickens died. For thirty-five years his widow remained on at the Hall as housekeeper. When pensioned in 1820, she settled in lodgings in Oxford Street, and there, as in the 'room' at Crewe Hall, this vivacious little woman spun stories for the children who visited her. Among these children was her grandson, Charles, who was to keep her memory for ever green in the wise and kindly figure who moves through the pages of *Bleak*

[1] See Register, St. George's, Hanover Square.

House as Mrs. Rouncewell, housekeeper to Lady Dedlock at Chesney Wold.

The Crewes interested themselves in Mrs. Dickens's boys, saw to their education, placed William in the world, and obtained for John, through their friend Mr. Canning, a clerk-ship in the Navy Pay Office. This was an advantageous start in life, as it raised the young man to what would now be called a post in the Civil Service and assured him of £70 a year. Just about the time John Dickens took up his job (1805) another young man, Thomas Culliford Barrow, was nomin-ated to a clerkship in the same office through the interest of his father, Charles Barrow, a senior supervisor in the department. The two young men became friends, John Dickens was intro-duced to Thomas Barrow's family and in due course fell in love with his sister, Elizabeth, whom he married in 1809 at St. Mary-le-Strand. One gets the impression that the Barrows did not care much about the alliance and it may be supposed that as members, however humble, of the bureau-cracy running England, they considered themselves a cut above the housekeeper's son. Anyway when Charles Dickens many years later announced to this maternal uncle his own engagement, he expressed regret that family loyalty prevented him from bringing his young bride to a house in which his father was not received. In later years he was to condemn 'the accursèd gentility' and 'subserviousness' that had eaten the heart out of the body politic of England, by which he meant its social structure in his day. Had the shoe not pinched his own foot in his tender years he might not, so early, have been made aware how badly it fitted the England into which he was born.

We will now look at the other side of the genealogical picture and see whether the Barrows had reason to be proud of their station. Possibly their relationship to Sir John Barrow,[1] second secretary of the Admiralty from 1804 to 1845,

[1] It has been suggested that Mrs. Micawber's references to her 'influential relations' and their ignoring of repeated requests may have originated in Mrs. Dickens's appeals to Sir John Barrow.

may have invested them with a sense of importance, but this must to some extent have been weakened by the conduct of Charles Barrow, John Dickens's father-in-law, who, at the time of his marriage, was 'Chief Conductor of Money in Town', a responsible appointment carrying with it a salary of £350 a year. Part of Mr. Barrow's work was to dispatch money under armed guard to the out-ports, Plymouth, Portsmouth, Sheerness and Chatham, which money he obtained by means of imprest bills for £900 each. These bills were granted upon an account signed by himself as Chief Conductor and endorsed by the Paymaster to the Navy Board. Some two years after his daughter's marriage, Mr. Barrow made up his account in the usual way and handed it to the Paymaster who, as usual, endorsed it and forwarded it to the Navy Board. It was a horrifying surprise for Mr. Barrow when, instead of the cash indented for, a Writ of Extent arrived with the official explanation that, as the Chief Conductor was suspected of having money in hand, an inquiry into previous accounts had been carried out with the result that a debit balance, to the tune of nearly four thousand pounds, was found to exist against him. Further investigation showed that as Mr. Barrow since 1803 had on every application for an imprest bill stated a false balance, the deficiency was even larger than was at first calculated. Mr. Barrow at once resigned his appointment and in extenuation pleaded ten children and ill-health. When criminal proceedings were instituted against him he left England.[1] Though it was a shaming business to his family it does not seem to have affected their careers adversely. His third son, John Henry, was already a barrister of Gray's Inn and law-reporter for the *Times*, and Thomas, his eldest son, clerk in the Prize Branch of the Navy Pay Office, was allowed to qualify for the considerable pension of £710 a year. His second son, Edward, married to Janet Ross the miniaturist,

[1] For details of the Barrow inquest see Admiralty Navy Pay Office correspondence. Public Record Office. Quoted in *Dickens and Daughter* by Miss Gladys Storey.

may not have made good as we find Charles Dickens ruefully paying a £57 debt for him in 1838. One daughter, Mary, was married to a naval lieutenant, Allen, and the other, Elizabeth, with whom we are directly concerned, to the navy pay clerk, John Dickens. These facts, though not of any intrinsic interest, give atmosphere and perspective to the family background and show that it comprised a social position from which it was possible to slip down. We can find no excuse in this ancestral record for the failure of Charles Dickens's father to keep his own head above water or submerge his children in a sea of poverty. His circumstances were not so very good, but they were not so bad as inevitably to bring him to destitution or his family to neglect. The clue to his misfortune must have lain in his own habits or character.

John Dickens had married on £200 a year and had taken his wife to live at Landport.[1] A daughter, Fanny, was born in 1810 and a son, Charles, in 1812. Both were christened at St. Mary's, Portsea. No foursquare account of John Dickens exists. He is alluded to by a woman friend of the family as 'an old buck' who dressed well and was always fingering the large bunch of seals attached to his watch. Charles sometimes spoke of him with an admiring affection he never extended to his mother, and at other times groaned at the financial handicap imposed on him by his father's irresponsible running-up of bills. He seems to have been a jovial opportunist without money sense, who borrowed from anyone foolish enough to make him cash advances. Unlike little Nell's grandfather in *The Old Curiosity Shop*, he does not seem to have been a gambler though he indulged a taste for expensive wines. The debt that landed him in the Marshalsea in 1834 for the second time was incurred to a wine merchant, but what the nature of the debt was that caused his first arrest in 1824 is not revealed. There was never a time in young Charles's life when he did not hear of money difficulties, never a time when he could believe his feet were planted on a rock,

[1] 387 Commercial Road, Portsmouth, once Mile End Terrace.

and the memory of the shifting sands through which he as a child had stumbled made him desperately anxious in later years to secure that solid foothold which a steady income alone can ensure.

Naval pay clerks had no fixed residence and were liable to be pushed about the country at short notice. In 1814 John Dickens was transferred to Somerset House and lodged himself and family at 10 Norfolk Street, near the Middlesex Hospital. In 1817 he was shifted to Chatham. Their house was 11 Ordnance Terrace [1] on the border-line between Chatham and Rochester, where (according to the Rate Book) he lived till Lady Day 1821. Mrs. Allen, Mrs. Dickens's widowed sister, lived with them and shared expenses. Her Commander husband had been drowned at Rio, but by 1821 she had engaged herself to marry Surgeon Lamert of the Chatham Hospital who is supposed to be Dr. Slammer in *Pickwick*. When she re-married, the John Dickens family, father, mother and five children, moved for the remainder of the assignment to Chatham (1822–3) into a cheaper house, 18 St. Mary's Place, The Brook, where James Lamert, Mrs. Allen's stepson, boarded with them. *A Child's Dream of a Star* is said to be a reminiscence of childhood at St. Mary's Place.

No one can hope to reconstruct the family circumstances precisely, nor indeed would it be interesting to do so, but it is something of a clue to know that when Charles was eight years old his father was earning £350 a year, more than the equivalent of £700 a year to-day, and that when they first got to Chatham, he with his sister Fanny attended a day school. Their nurse, Mary Weller, described Charles as 'a terrible boy to read . . . his custom was to sit with his book in his left hand, holding his wrist with his right, and constantly moving it up and down and at the same time sucking his tongue'.[2] In spite of chronic shortness of cash John Dickens managed to acquire

[1] Now No. 2. Harriet Ellen (1819) and Frederick William (1820) born here.
[2] *Childhood and Youth of Charles Dickens*, by R. Langton.

a collection of cheaply-produced novels including *Roderick Random*, *Peregrine Pickle*, *Humphrey Clinker*, *Tom Jones*, *The Vicar of Wakefield*, *Robinson Crusoe*, *The Arabian Nights*, *The Tales of the Genii* and *Don Quixote*. It was Smollett's translation of *Gil Blas* that introduced Charles to the greatest of the picaresque stories. In one of the many true passages in *David Copperfield* he speaks of the company of this 'glorious host'. 'They kept alive my fancy and my hope of something beyond that place and time', and he could console himself in trouble by impersonating from out this host his favourite characters. '... I have been Tom Jones for a week together, I have sustained my own idea of Roderick Random for a month at a stretch.' When he thought of these books in later years, the picture always came into his mind 'of a summer evening, the boys at play in the churchyard and I sitting on my bed reading as if for life'. And he was reading for life. Read and re-read by this alert, sensitive boy, these books opened up for him a limitless world of adventure and romance.

One of Charles Dickens's happiest recollections was of trips down the Medway to Sheerness on the Navy Pay Office yacht *Chatham*, a high-sterned, cutter-rigged craft pierced with circular ports, dating from the time of the Commonwealth, a sluggish boat except in a stiff breeze. In view of the part it was to play in *Great Expectations*, the convict hulk, 'roofed like a Noah's Ark', that lay off the dockyard must also be mentioned. Another early memory was that of a visit to the theatre in London to see the great clown Grimaldi, whose *Memoirs* he was as an adult to edit. Yet another was the 'Lines' review of the 43rd and 52nd Light Infantry described in *Pickwick*. But the best memory of all was that of his schooling with William Giles, son of the Baptist minister, William Giles, of Providence Chapel on The Brook. Young Giles's school was made up of his own brothers and sisters and the children of officers and naval employees, and he established it in a largish house on the corner of Rhode Street and Best Street adjoining Clover Lane. Giles, who had been at Oxford and was an 'accomplished scholar', recognised

Charles's unusual aptitudes and did his best to train the boy's mind and taste, pointing out in particular how pure and flowing was Goldsmith's English. When he parted with his pupil in 1823, he gave him a set of *The Bee* (a miniature periodical of eight weeks' life edited and written by Oliver Goldsmith[1]) as a keepsake. *The Bee* was a Saturday miscellany, containing 'a select collection of essays on the most interesting and entertaining subjects'. There were three, four, or five essays in a number with titles such as 'Remarks on Theatres', 'Travellers' Letters', 'Charles XII', 'Dress', 'M. Maupertuis', 'Happiness dependent on Constitution', 'Use of Language', 'A City Nightpiece'. It must have been his great enjoyment of *The Bee* that gave Dickens his enduring passion for the miscellany with which he experimented at different periods of his life under the title of *Master Humphrey's Clock*, *Household Words* and *All the Year Round*. *The Bee*, he used to say, always called up in his mind the past and made him wonder whether he had himself 'ever fledged any little bees whose humming had been heard abroad'.

In the winter of 1822–3 John Dickens was transferred to Somerset House again, still at the same salary, and before moving he arranged with Mr. Giles that Charles should continue being educated at his school. The young pedagogue, of twenty-four, was delighted to be left in charge of so unusually bright and eager a learner. Living at Chatham, the boy naturally came to know every cranny of Rochester. It was the first place he wrote about in the opening chapters of *Pickwick*: it was the last place he wrote about in *Edwin Drood*. And in his last will and testament he directed that his body should be laid near Rochester.

John Dickens and his family moved to London by coach, sending their heavy goods by water, and settled themselves at 16 Bayham Street,[2] Camden Town, on the outer fringe of the

---

[1] October 6–November 24, 1759.
[2] Apart from basement, garret and outhouse, a four-roomed house. Probably the home of the Micawbers and the Cratchits.

city, close to the arboured tea-gardens at Chalk Farm. Most writers on Dickens describe it as a squalid neighbourhood, but no railway building had as yet scarred the district and country roads linked the newly-built blocks of little town houses. James Lamert, who was awaiting a commission in the army, moved with the Dickens family to London as did a sharp little maid from Chatham Workhouse—the 'Marchioness' of *The Old Curiosity Shop*. Fanny, the eldest girl, turned out to be musical and somehow, through the family friend Tomkisson, a piano-maker of 77 Dean Street, Soho, obtained a nomination[1] as 'a pupilage-boarder' to the Royal Academy of Music where she spent four happy years and won distinctions.

John Dickens arranged for his son to leave Mr. Giles's Academy in the spring of 1823, 'the end of the winter term'. Charles was put into the stage-coach Commodore, and never forgot during all the years of his life the smell of the damp straw in which he was packed, 'like game, carriage paid'. 'There was no other inside passenger, and I consumed my sandwiches in solitude and dreariness, and it rained hard all the way, and I thought life sloppier than I expected to find it.' It was a painful shock to the lad to find on arriving in Bayham Street that he was expected to do house-work, clean boots and brush clothes; he had counted on going to school again, but the family seemed to have no idea of paying any more school fees. Boy-like and insatiably curious, he set out to examine the adjacent streets and soon knew every corner of the three little towns of Camden, Kentish and Somers as well as every path leading to Chalcot and Chalk farms. The whole neighbourhood appears and reappears in his books. Bob Cratchit lived in Camden Town, so did Jemima Evans: Traddles lodged there with Micawber: the Toodles family lived in Staggs's Garden, 'Camberling' Town: Heyling in *Pickwick* ran down his victim in Little College Street, Camden Town, 'a desolate place surrounded by fields and ditches'.

Often the boy went further afield, getting James Lamert, or

[1] April 23, 1823.

anyone else available, to pilot him to Seven Dials, a locality that fascinated him on account of its name, its wickedness and its squalor. He liked, too, going to see his godfather, Christopher Huffam, at Limehouse Hole.[1] Huffam was an oar- and block-maker and 'Rigger to His Majesty's Navy'.[2] He had come to the notice of the Regent for fitting out a privateer against the French, and was said to have been offered an honour for this service. Charles also explored the nearer region of Soho, where his mother's eldest brother, Thomas Barrow, lodged over Manson's, the bookshop in Gerrard Street. To this sick uncle the boy became a 'little companion and nurse'. Through this association he found material for subsequent *Sketches*, notably his uncle's barber, a very old man who talked of Napoleon's campaigns, and he also depicted, on the pattern of Gil Blas' housekeeper, the deaf old woman who waited on Mr. Barrow. Miscellaneous reading, too, came his way, as Mrs. Manson, widow of the bookseller, let him see the *Tatler* and *Spectator*, and lent him Miss Porter's *Scottish Chiefs*, George Colman's *Broad Grins* and Holbein's *Dance of Death*.

The happiness he derived from these contacts was dimmed by the poverty at home. At Michaelmas 1823 Mrs. Dickens, who had the rather scrambling notion of making money by running a small school for the children of parents living in the Indies, rented number 4 Gower Street, North, in her own name with money said to have been guaranteed by Christopher Huffam.[3] Partly furnishing the house and fixing a brass plate upon the door with the words 'Mrs. Dickens's Establishment', she caused handbills to be printed for distribution in the neighbourhood. Charles and the other children were called on to push them into letter-boxes. None of them drew custom and no pupil appeared. Her son was to crystallise the venture in 'Mrs. Micawber's Boarding Establishment for Young Ladies'.

[1] *Our Mutual Friend* has scenes in Limehouse.

[2] Cuttle, Peggotty and the seafaring characters are said to have had their origin in Huffam.

[3] Michaelmas 1823 to Lady Day 1824 at £50 per annum.

Things went so badly that even the well-fingered library of fiction had to be taken down from the chiffonier to be sold to a bookseller in the Hampstead Road. Possessions other than books went to the pawn-shop where Charles was pleased to find that the pawnbroker's assistant liked to listen to him conjugating Latin verbs and declining his *musa* and *dominus*. One day when things were looking hopeless and arrest for debt unavoidable, James Lamert turned up with an offer of employment for Charles. James, having given up his prospective commission to a younger brother, had gone into partnership with his cousin George Lamert who was running Warren's Blacking Factory at Hungerford Stairs near Charing Cross. When he said he could give Charles six or seven shillings a week, Mrs. Dickens jumped at the offer, and even John Dickens, dearly as he wished his son to be educated, felt the circumstances to be so desperate that acceptance was necessary. This blow fell on Charles's twelfth birthday, February 7, 1824. So many children were in harness in those days that James Lamert may have thought he was doing the boy a kindness as he promised him instruction and a 'station', but to the boy, knowing himself to be 'of good ability, quick, eager, delicate', it was a shattering blow to be cast away at such an age with all early hopes of learning and distinction crushed. He describes himself as sunk in 'a deep sense of abandonment'. The worst pang of all was that his parents seemed pleased to have him off their hands. With despair in his heart he realised that they frankly welcomed his being entered to servitude. He says himself that they could not have appeared more satisfied had he had a 'distinguished career at a grammar-school' and had qualified to go to Cambridge.

In the fragment of autobiography he dredged out of himself before deciding to sublimate his experience in *David Copperfield* he says:

The blacking warehouse was the last house on the left-hand side of the way at old Hungerford Stairs. It was a crazy, tumble-down old house, abutting of course, on the river and literally over-run with rats. Its wainscotted rooms and its rotten floors and stair-case, and the old grey rats swarming down in the cellars, and the sound of their squeaking and scuffling coming up the stairs at all times, and the dirt and decay of the place rise up visibly before me.

As day succeeded day, never to be redeemed, the boy had the sensation of being utterly neglected and without hope:

My whole nature was so penetrated with the grief and humiliation of such considerations, that even now, famous and caressed and happy, I often forget in my dreams that I have a dear wife and children; even that I am a man; and wander desolately back to that time of my life.

A fortnight after poor Charles had become a wage-drudge the long-expected blow fell and John Dickens, at the suit of James Karr, was arrested for a £40 debt and incarcerated at the Marshalsea.[1] His entire property was sworn at £10 and Charles had to go before an appraiser, 'near the Obelisk', to have the clothes on his back and the silver watch in his pocket valued. Mrs. Dickens in her hand-to-mouth fashion still tried to carry on by pawning brooches and spoons, but eventually gave up the struggle and, gathering up her brood of young children, at Lady Day she also moved into the Marshalsea. The maid who accompanied her found a lodging near the gates and the family confessed to each other that they felt more comfortable and unmolestable there than they ever had at home.

Charles, being already employed at Warren's Blacking Factory, was not included in the Marshalsea party but lodged by his mother's arrangement in Little College Street, Camden Town, with a Mrs. Roylance, to become famous as Mrs. Pipchin in *Dombey and Son*. At the factory he received a shilling a day on which to support himself. The weekly

[1] Copy of register at Record Office. Admitted Friday, February 20, 1824; discharged May 28, 1824. See Facsimile *Dickensian*, 1932, p. 227.

pittance did not go far. When he had no money for food he 'took a turn in Covent Garden and stared at the pineapples'. His work was simple; it consisted of tying bottles up neatly and sticking labels on to them, a task at which he soon became expeditious. To begin with, the boy walked daily from Camden Town to the Strand and back at night. On Sundays he would call at the Royal Academy of Music for his sister Fanny and take her to spend the day at the Marshalsea which lay beyond St. George's Church, Southwark. Camden Town, however, soon proved so distant and so unbearably lonely that he got his father's consent to move to Lant Street, on the south side of the river, the street 'near Guy's and handy for me' in which he was to lodge Bob Sawyer. Charles occupied a back attic looking on to 'the pleasant prospect of a timber-yard' and found the situation 'a Paradise'. The land-lord of his lodging had a quiet wife and a lame son. They were all very good to him and they live on as the Garland family in *The Old Curiosity Shop*. He now breakfasted and supped at the Marshalsea and in the evenings explored the creeks and jetties by the river, discovering all sorts of water-side secrets. Sometimes he went to a shabby public-house, the Fox-under-the-Hill, and on the bench there would eat his sandwiches and watch its patrons, the coal-heavers, dance. At the outside he could not have slept in Lant Street for more than six or seven weeks, but into these weeks was packed a gamut of experience.

Another boy, Robert Browning (just Charles's age), was also living south of the Thames at this time, imbibing a different set of experiences in a garden in Camberwell. In this garden was an old laburnum tree, the haunt of nightin-gales, and Robert, as he listened to their song, was imbued with a positive conviction that in these birds were reincarnated the spirits of two great poets, Keats and Shelley, who had settled in leafy Camberwell to sing to the only person in all suburbia who would understand their song. Yet another boy (six months older than Charles), an Anglo-Indian boy, William Makepeace Thackeray, was living north of the river in Chiswick in the house known in *Vanity Fair* as Miss Pinkerton's Academy. Both these boys had incomparably better starts in life's race than Charles Dickens, but in the long run he was to out-distance them.

One of the odd facts of the Marshalsea situation is that all the time that John Dickens and family were incarcerated there, they were in receipt of over £6 a week income, but made no effort to clear themselves of debt. 'They had no want of bodily comforts', and being tucked safely away from creditors they felt free from care, and were not anxious to be released. Outside agencies, however, were at work to return them to normal life.

When Mrs. William Dickens, John Dickens's mother, died in April 1824, her elder son arranged that the funeral service should take place at St. George's Church where she had been married. During retirement she had lived quietly in London on the interest of her savings and the pension granted by the family she had served. On her death £500 of the £750 invested savings went to William and the remainder to John, who had from time to time extracted gifts of money from her. William at once paid £40 into court for James Karr and thus effected his brother's discharge from the Marshalsea.

After an absence of three months, John Dickens resumed work at the Navy Pay Office despite the fact that he had from the Marshalsea respectfully solicited the Hon. William Huskisson to recommend him for a superannuation grant on the grounds of ill-health.[1] The family, like homing pigeons, returned to Camden Town, this time to Little College Street. Charles still went daily to the factory, now transferred to Chandos Street, but was suddenly withdrawn when his father had 'words' with James Lamert. Mrs. Dickens did her best to patch the quarrel and get James to take the boy back. 'I never afterwards forgot, I never shall forget, I never can forget that my mother was warm for my being sent back', records

---

[1] He enclosed a medical certificate stating that he had a chronic affection of the urinary organs.

Charles. His father would have none of it, nor hear of his return, and set out to find his son a school. By June 1824 the whole family had transferred from Little College Street to 29 (later 13) Johnson Street, Somers Town, a small house in an even poorer locality rented in the name of Mrs. Dickens.[1]

In due course the case of Mr. John Dickens passed from the hands of the Treasurer of the Navy to those of Mr. Croker, Secretary to the Admiralty, who had to lay it before the Commissioners and the First Lord, Viscount Melville. Mr. Croker was informed by Mr. Huskisson[2] that John Dickens having taken advantage of the Insolvent Debtors Act, could not continue to be employed in the Navy Pay Office. In consideration of his twenty years of service and six children he would, however, on compassionate grounds, be granted 'a retired allowance' of £145 a year.

Bracing himself to meet the fall in income, John Dickens at once applied to his brother-in-law, J. H. Barrow, editor of the *Mirror of Parliament*, for work as a political reporter. He had already dabbled in journalism at Chatham, but his proficiency in shorthand is such a surprising development that one wonders whether he may not have practised it in prison. However it came about, stout, active, anecdotic John Dickens, aged forty, by January 1825 was an established parliamentary reporter for the *British Press*, a newspaper with which S. C. Hall was connected.[3] This enabled him to continue paying fees at 'the very superior school' to which he had entered Charles six months previously. The dear boy had had a bad educational break of a year, but now he could study as much as he pleased. S. C. Hall, who saw him at this time, said he was 'a handsome lad gleaning intelligence in the byeways of the metropolis'. A new life now dawned for Charles Dickens. His youth hitherto had been characterised by sharp suffering and bitter disappointment. The crumbling of his private world had made such terrible inroads into his sensibility that he buried all remembrance of it fathoms deep

---

[1] Tenant from July 1824 to July 1827.   [2] December 1, 1824.
[3] *Memories of S. C. Hall*, p. 456.

in his subconsciousness. His own children were grown up before he could summon the resolution needed to disinter and face up to his own childhood. Delving into a past which he had never disclosed even to his wife, he twenty-five years later drew from it material for the romanticised autobiography which is the distinguishing and touching feature of *David Copperfield*.

Mr. Jones's Classical and Commercial Academy, otherwise Wellington House, was situated at the corner of Granby Street, Hampstead Road. The subjects taught there were Latin, mathematics, history and the hornpipe. For at least two years Charles attended the classes there as a day-boy, and it is probable that he worked there for nine months more.[1] He described the school later on for *Household Words*,[2] dwelling specially on the pets kept by the boys, who contrived 'to drill their white mice much better than the master trained the boys'. They were very strong in theatricals and mounted small stage-sets for themselves. A school-fellow, Owen Thomas, remembered him as a healthy-looking boy with a general air of smartness, but with nothing to indicate that he would ever 'become a literary celebrity'.

Though there is nothing remarkable to record about the years at school, they did enable Charles to recover and improve on the teaching given him by Mr. Giles at Chatham. Education was almost entirely classical in those days and we can form a good notion of what the boy studied by glancing at the curriculum of Salem House in *David Copperfield*. The gap in his schooling that prevented him from competing with boys who had had no break in their education did not hinder him from picking up a great deal of information which he at once put to operative use.

When John Dickens was asked by a prospective employer where his son Charles had been educated he replied, 'Why, indeed sir, (ha! ha!) he may be said to have educated himself!' The high value of that form of education is to be found in the

[1] June 1824 to June 1826 and probably stayed on till April 1827.
[2] October 11, 1851.

quality of observation embodied in the thousands of pages
of Charles Dickens's novels. No other education could
possibly have formed the intellectual background to his interpretation of the very peculiar England of which he knew the
under-side, and we may be thankful that his knowledge of
the upper-side was so long deferred as to enable him
thoroughly to understand the point of view of the disinherited.

While Charles was still at school his father's elder brother,
William, died suddenly at the age of forty-three, leaving his
whole estate of £1300 to be shared, after his wife's demise,
equally between his nephews and nieces. The prospect of
some day becoming owners of capital rejoiced the hearts of
Charles and his sister Fanny, who realised only too clearly by
this time that they could not look to their father for a living.

Chapter 2

CLERK AND REPORTER

These years, the usefullest of my life.
CHARLES DICKENS

ON leaving school just before Easter 1827 Charles Dickens
became office-boy to Charles Molloy, solicitor, of 6
Symonds Inn.[1] He could only have been there for six or
seven weeks, but it was long enough for him to display his
peculiar fearlessness and his even more peculiar faculty of
incorporating the people with whom he came in daily contact
into the texture of his life. A fellow clerk, Thomas Mitton,
became his 'dear Tom' and first business agent: he even
managed to make use of his employer as legal adviser. Remarkable in Charles Dickens is a kind of octopus quality of
absorbing into himself human material of every variety, good,
bad, and indifferent. To begin with it was an instinctive
technique and was developed by degrees into a method which
served him very well in writing his novels, and is proof, if
proof were needed, of the quiddity of his genius.

By May in this year John Dickens had managed, through
his wife's aunt, Mrs. Charlton, who kept a boarding house at
16 Berners Street, to obtain for Charles a clerkship in the firm
of Ellis and Blackmore, solicitors, of 1 Raymond Buildings,
Gray's Inn. Edward Blackmore, one of the partners, lodged
with Mrs. Charlton, whose son, Thomas, was a reporter in
Doctors' Commons. Charles worked for Ellis and Blackmore till November 1828, and was paid after the first month
15s. a week. He lived with his parents at 17 The Polygon,
Somers Town, a place of tenuous literary affiliations in so far
as Mary Wollstonecraft had died there thirty years earlier in
giving birth to the daughter who was to marry Shelley.[2] In

[1] Later of 4 New Square, Lincoln's Inn.
[2] December 30, 1816. Cassell's *Old and New London*. Dickens housed
Skimpole in The Polygon.

his off-time Charles learnt shorthand, possibly from his father, possibly from his uncle, John Henry Barrow. What he calls 'the intensity' of his nature prevented him from doing things by halves and eighteen months of persistent application to 'Mr. Gurney's Half-guinea Brachygraphy' gave him confidence to hand in his notice to Ellis and Blackmore in order to join his cousin, Thomas Charlton, as a reporter in the Consistory Court of Doctors' Commons. It was his intention eventually to follow his father to the gallery of the House of Commons, but as he was still very young he had to make do for the time being with legal reporting, which gave him opportunity to gain speed, self-reliance and experience. In partnership therefore with Thomas Charlton he rented a box in Doctors' Commons where, to begin with, he sat waiting for custom. He also shared in the expense of a room or transcribing office[1] where the longhand copies of his notes could be made.

As he went about he absorbed varied impressions which composed themselves into pictures in his mind. Doctors' Commons with its many courts and its aloof, robed personnel of doctors and proctors struck him strangely, for it had so little relation with the tide of life that flowed down Ludgate Hill to the Strand. He was later to describe its ways in a 'Sketch', and make play with its activities in *David Copperfield*. 'What is a proctor?' David asks Steerforth and is told,

> He is a sort of monkish attorney . . . a functionary whose existence, in the natural course of things would have terminated about two hundred years ago. I can tell you best what he is by telling you what Doctors' Commons is. It's a little out-of-the-way place, where they administer what is called ecclesiastical law and play all kinds of tricks with obsolete old monsters of Acts of Parliament. . . . It's a place that has an ancient monopoly in suits about people's wills and people's marriages and disputes among ships and boats.

[1] 5 Bell Yard, Paul's Chain.

Doctors' Commons[1] lay on the south side of St. Paul's and was approached by a street called 'Paul's Chain'. Paul's Chain led to an archway which gave on to 'a quiet shady courtyard paved with stone', and frowned upon by old red brick houses. One of its doors, a green-baize one studded with brass nails, admitted visitors to the Court of Doctors' Commons, all the other doors were painted in white letters with the names of learned civilians. Here the noise of the city was muffled and seemed to melt as if by magic into a softened distance. Attached to Doctors' Commons were various sinecure appointments in the gift of the Lord Chancellor. The poet James Thomson had held one of them, the Secretaryship for Briefs. In these ghostly precincts Dickens became familiar with the many types of legal gentlemen that thread the pages of his novels—Vholes, Heep, Dodson and Fogg, Sampson Brass, Spenlow, Jorkins, Tulkinghorn and the rest. As a body of men they were probably more real to him than the men of other educated professions—such as medicine or the church. Doctors and clergy when they have to be called in to fill up a chink in a narrative are never more than lay figures.

The term Doctors' Commons covered an agglomeration of 'courts' using the same premises and the same officials. There was the Court of Arches, the provincial court of the Archbishop of Canterbury, whose Dean was President of Doctors' Commons: and there was the Consistory Court, the diocesan court of the Bishop of London, in which Dickens chose to work. There was the Prerogative Court dealing with testamentary matters in the dioceses: the Prerogative Office in which wills were registered and filed, and then the Admiralty Court which occasioned David Copperfield's protest to Steerforth that there could be no affinity between ecclesiastical and nautical matters and the explanation that there was no affinity, but that all courts were managed and all cases decided by the same set of people.

[1] Doctors' Commons abolished as such in 1857 when its jurisdiction was taken over by the new Probate Court. The land on which it stood was then sold.

You go there one day and find them blundering through the nautical terms in Young's Dictionary and you go there another day and find the judge going through evidence respecting a clergyman who has misbehaved himself.

The unfavourable impression made on Charles Dickens's mind by wandering in and out of courts of law was imparted by him years after to Mr. Frederick Pollock:[1]

I have that high opinion of the law of England generally, which one is likely to derive from the impression that it puts all the honest men under the diabolical hoofs of all the scoundrels.

The cases Charles Dickens was called on to report were heard and argued in a large room resembling a dissenters' chapel. In *David Copperfield* he describes this place in a manner that presents a lively visual image:

The upper part of this room was fenced off from the rest; and there on the two sides of a raised platform of the horse-shoe form, sitting on easy old-fashioned dining-room chairs, were sundry gentlemen in red gowns and grey wigs, whom I found to be the Doctors. Blinking over a little desk like a pulpit desk, in the curve of the horse-shoe, was an old gentleman, whom if I had seen him in an aviary I should certainly have taken for an owl, but who I learned was the presiding judge. In the space within the horse-shoe about the level of the floor, were sundry other gentlemen . . . dressed . . . in black gowns with white fur upon them sitting at a long green table.

We may in this connection remind ourselves that Charles Dickens was not alone in his opinion of the anachronistic character of the Law Courts of his day for at the very same time Mr. Macaulay, the nominee of the East India Company in the House of Commons, was charging Parliament with failing to keep in order the machinery of justice and of winking at the tangle of procedures kept up for the good of the lawyers.

[1] May 2, 1870.

'Look,' he said, 'at that series of penal statutes the most bloody and the most inefficient in the world, at the puerile fictions which make every declaration and every plea unintelligible both to the plaintiff and the defendant, at the chaos of precedents, and *the bottomless pit of Chancery*. . . . Place the people and the Government side by side and you will see barbarism belongs to the Government, civilisation to the people.'

The legal profession, distinguished by its 'costiveness', was in no way, Macaulay alleged, controlled by Parliament, the reverse in fact being true. In his opinion one great reform remained to be satisfied—a rational system of private law.

It was into a strange, crabbed, dusty world that Charles Dickens had entered himself and in the beginning he had leisure to observe it in all its convolutions, for patrons were few and custom 'wearily uncertain'. If not called on by the proctors to report, he occupied himself in reading or learning parts in plays. Conscious that he had a great deal of leeway to make up both educationally and culturally, he secured (on the day after he was eighteen) a reader's ticket for the British Museum[1] and there set himself to make good some of the gaps in his accomplishment. He was extremely thorough in anything he undertook, and once it was discovered by clients how reliable and rapid was the young clerk's reporting, commissions poured in and in middle life he would sometimes say that the two years spent in Doctors' Commons were 'the usefullest of my life'.

The home background although still set in lodging-houses was at this time pleasant enough, for his sister Fanny and her musical friends clustered round the piano of an evening. Charles sang and so did John Hullah and J. P. Harley, ex-pupils at the College of Music. Henry Austin, an artist, and Henry Kolle, a calico-printer with a voice, formed part of the circle. Between them they produced the Covent Garden

---

[1] February 8, 1830. Vouched for by Mrs. Charlton of 16 Berners Street.

success of some years earlier, *Clari, the Maid of Milan*,[1] with its popular song 'Home, Sweet Home'.

For a time Charles, partly from love of the stage and partly with the idea of becoming, if other trades failed, a professional actor, spent all his spare evenings at the theatre, 'always studying the bills first, always seeing the best plays', and following Charles Mathews in all his impersonations. Prescribing for himself 'a kind of Hamiltonian system' for learning parts he memorised a good number, took lessons from the actor Robert Keeley, and practised at home before a mirror how to enter a room, how to sit down on a chair, how to bow. He went so far as to apply for an audition to Mathews and to approach the comedian George Bartley, manager of Covent Garden. Owing to 'disfiguring illness', in other words a swollen face, he could not keep his appointment with these gentlemen and before he could ask for another, success as a political journalist had made a theatrical career out of the question. The training for the stage was not wasted, nothing ever was wasted in Dickens's life; he managed to make good use of every experience, and the self-assurance acquired in this way stood him in good stead when making his debut in the salon of Lady Blessington and in the Holland House circle.

Henry Kolle, the young man with the voice, idolised Charles and insisted, when he engaged himself to Anne, daughter of George Beadnell, a bank manager in the city,[2] on taking him to the Beadnell home in Lombard Street. This was probably the first family circle to which Dickens had been introduced and he enjoyed it, even taking a fancy to Mrs. Beadnell, who treated him almost as a servant and addressed him as 'Mr. Dickin'. Anne turned out to be a lute-player and one of three musical sisters, the youngest of whom, Maria, was a harpist. Extremely pretty, Maria asked nothing better than to flirt with the good-looking, charming boy produced by Kolle. No one in the family could regard him as a

[1] See *Sketches by 'Boz'* for skit on rehearsals.
[2] Of Smith, Payne, Smith.

possible suitor, he was just a penniless reporter who could laugh and sing; but negligible and innocuous as he appeared to the prosperous Beadnells, he fell head and ears in love with their daughter. For Maria's album[1] Charles constructed an acrostic of the thirteen letters of her name, and just adored her 'every minute, day and night' since the first moment he saw her. His friend, Henry Austin, also adored Maria, and painted her and her little brother George in *gouache* as Dido and Ascanius. He did a tinted drawing of her, too, for Charles as 'The Milkmaid', depicting her under a tree with dangling sun-bonnet and bucket at her side. As go-between for letters, Kolle became party to the development of a clandestine romance. One assumes there must have been the encouragement of a secret engagement for, for Maria's sweet sake, Dickens slaved to raise himself from the rut of family circumstance. He worked harder than ever in Doctors' Commons, he read harder than ever in the British Museum, and was lifted by his passion for Maria out of black memories of suffering and humiliation. By this stiff struggle against poverty and obscurity he laid the foundation of his future success.

Maria played with his devotion and extracted all the fun there was to be got out of the situation, little knowing that one day she and her pet, 'Daphne', immortalised as 'Dora' and 'Jip', would wring the hearts of thousands. The game went on for some two years, but after Henry Kolle's marriage to Anne, at which Charles was best man, the Beadnell parents whisked their youngest daughter off to 'a finishing establishment' in Paris. For Charles, out of sight was not out of memory; Maria still 'pervaded every corner and crevice' of his mind and this love affair went as deep as his blacking factory experience in shaping his attitude to life. When Maria spurned his suit, he told her roundly that 'whatever of fancy, romance, passion, aspiration and determination belong to me I never have separated and never shall separate from that hard-hearted little woman—you'. Again he wrote:

[1] Maria's album is preserved in the Huntington Library (U.S.A.).

I can claim for myself and *feel* that I deserve the merit of having ever throughout our intercourse acted fairly, intelligently and honourably, under kindness and encouragement one day and a cold change of conduct the next. . . . I have ever acted without reserve. . . . I have never loved and I never can love any human creature breathing but yourself.

When he could no longer stand her ridicule, he returned her presents and set his teeth, determining 'to ride on, rough-shod if need be, smooth-shod if that will do, but ride on'.

In the pages of *David Copperfield* the story of Charles's love for Maria lives for ever. Twenty years on, Lady Olliffe asked the famous Mr. Dickens when he was dining with her in Paris whether it was really true that he used to love Maria Beadnell so very, very, very much. And Mr. Dickens replied that there was no woman in the world and very few men who could ever imagine how much. He paused and then said reflectively, 'When we were falling off each other I came from the House of Commons many a night at two or three o'clock in the morning only to wander past the place she was asleep in.'

When years later Maria dined as a married woman with Mr. and Mrs. Charles Dickens at Tavistock House she was fat and middle-aged, and her host saw fit to turn her into Flora Finching of *Little Dorrit*. But even the realisation that she was stupid, commonplace and had never cared, did not kill within him the image he had once made of her because his original perception was stored like a sun-picture in his mind.

Charles celebrated his twentieth birthday with a quadrille party. His always nomadic parents were at the time living in furnished lodgings at 70 Margaret Street.[1] Tom Beard of the Gallery came to the feast and congratulated his friend, who had at last, owing to the expenditure of his 'celestial or diabolical energy', qualified as 'a first-class parliamentary re-

[1] 10 Norfolk Street, Fitzroy Square, over a grocer's shop, 1831; 70 Margaret Street, February 1832; 13 Fitzroy Street, July 1832; 18 Bentinck Street, over an upholsterer's shop, June 1838.

porter' and was to join him in the House of Commons almost immediately. Most cheerfully Charles reconciled himself to forgoing plays, announcing to a friend that he would now have no certain night at his disposal. To have qualified for the Gallery at twenty was a minor triumph, but could anyone have guessed that it could be a way of catching up with those unknown competitors in life's race, Robert Browning and William Makepiece Thackeray? Most people, it may be assumed, would at this time have backed both these promising young men against an unknown journalist. Prosperous Robert Browning with *Pauline* written and *Paracelsus* planned, and Thackeray, a student at the Middle Temple, with a good working knowledge of French and German to his credit and a *Wanderjahr* behind him. What had young Mr. Dickens to show against such achievements?

Joining the staff of the *True Sun* (a sevenpenny evening paper owned by Murdo Young and edited by Laman Blanchard) on the first day of its publication, March 5, 1832, Charles Dickens got to the House of Commons just in time to take down the last speeches made during the Committee stage of the Reform Bill.

Chapter 3

THE GALLERY

I wallow in words. Britannia, that unfortunate female, is always before me like a trussed fowl: skewered through and through with office pins and bound hand and foot with red tape. I am sufficiently behind the scenes to know the worth of political life. I am quite an Infidel about it and shall never be converted. 'DAVID COPPERFIELD'

IT has been well said that the Reform debates may be reckoned as the first term in the education of most Englishmen in politics. So eager was the man in the street to read the speeches in full that every morning paper engaged at least ten reporters, at a cost of something like £3000 a year, to satisfy this craving. A sevenpenny newspaper taken twenty miles out of London was readily snapped up for a shilling. The thirst for political information was really a new thing, so new that up till this time no official effort had been made to meet the demand, no formal permission given to reporters either to note down or to publish debates, no facilities such as seats or tables provided for their use. This keen intelligent group of men were in the House, as it were, on sufferance, for many legislators, including of course the Duke of Wellington, steadily refused to admit that the people of England had any right, through the medium of the press, to know what was said in Parliament.

The Committee stage of the Reform Bill ended a few days after Dickens had begun regular work in the Gallery. Passing its third reading on March 23, it was sent up to the Lords on March 26 and read there for the second time on April 9 when it was carried by nine votes. Lord Grey then moved the adjournment of the debate and fixed May 10 for further consideration of the Bill. This interval was wasted on the Lords, who in May 1832 put up as sharp an opposition as they had done in October 1831. Lord Grey at once tendered his resignation, which was accepted by the King. As neither Lord Lyndhurst nor the Duke of Wellington were able to form an administration and Sir Robert Peel refused to make himself responsible for an anti-reform cabinet, the King had to recall Lord Grey and consent to grant the measures necessary for pushing the Bill through, even if it involved the creation of peers. What Macaulay termed 'our glorious ten days' was now breathlessly experienced by the members of both Houses and by the pressmen of the Gallery. When the Bill finally became law it set bells ringing and flags flying throughout the country.

Charles Dickens was neither excited nor impressed by the enthusiasm of those who supported reform or the anger of those who opposed it. One might be inclined to put this down to ignorance of politics and parliamentary history if he had not left behind him the skit on the 'Howsa Kummauns' in which the lovely odalisque, 'Reefawm', is shown as an illusory phantom of delight. Instinctively he realised that the Bill had changed nothing for the great bulk of the working classes, though it certainly had made the State a partnership between two great powers instead of the monopoly of one. As Dickens began so he ended. After four years' work in the Gallery, involving as it did an intensive political and administrative education, he wholeheartedly condemned and despised the activities that went on in what he was apt to designate 'the great dustheap of Westminster'.

During the first session of the reformed parliament Charles Dickens looked down from his Gallery on an assembly that appeared, and in fact was, a little older than the average in the unreformed parliament. Its members worked harder than their predecessors and, in token of earnestness, met at noon and seldom rose before midnight. A Tory Speaker presided in a House in which the Whigs outnumbered the Tories by nearly three to one. Among the new faces he observed was that of William Cobbett of the *Two-penny Postbag*, the first journalist to sit in the House of Commons. Cobbett took his seat on the Treasury bench, and when gently squeezed

from there sat down next to Sir Robert Peel on the front
Opposition bench, to the amusement of his colleagues up
above. The leaders of the old parliament were leaders of the
new, beginning with Lord Grey as Prime Minister and continuing with the veterans of the Reform debates, Lord
Althorp, Lord John Russell and Mr. Stanley, whose brilliant,
nimble powers of dialectic had supplied and were still to
supply the vigour lacking in his colleagues. Dickens got to
know the look of many famous people as they filed from lobby
to chamber. Among them were Macaulay, Gladstone,
Grote, Edward Bulwer, James Silk Buckingham as well as
O'Connell and Grattan. If personalities make a good House
of Commons this should have been a specially remarkable
one.

Dickens was kept hard at work, for it fell to him to report
three important measures, the Peace Preservation Bill (Ireland), the Abolition of Slavery (British Colonies) and a
measure for the administration of British India by which the
East India Company was turned by charter into a trustee for
the Crown. Having resigned from the *True Sun* in the
autumn of 1832, he reported all these debates for a kind of
Hansard, specialising in exact transcription, called the *Mirror
of Parliament*.[1] The *Mirror* was produced at 3 Abingdon
Street and was both owned and edited by his uncle, John
Henry Barrow.[2] Charles, it seems, had now earned favour
with his mother's family, for we find one uncle offering him a
job and the wife of another uncle painting his miniature. It
was at last recognised that this young nephew was someone
to be encouraged, even to be proud of. John Henry Barrow,
author of *The Battle of Talavera*, an epic poem, of the type
made fashionable by Scott and Southey, was well up in Indian
affairs and still on the staff of the *Times*, in connection with
which he had earned a great reputation at the time of the

[1] Superseded October 1841.
[2] J. H. Barrow, member of Gray's Inn, 1823. Third son of Charles
Barrow. Died Stoke Newington, March 30, 1858 (it is said in poverty).

Queen's Trial. The grey paper covers of his *Mirror of Parliament*, in shape and size like a blue book, contain very well printed reports. They are verbally accurate and carefully punctuated with 'No! No!' 'Slight laughter' and so on. All this in spite of the prohibition which still in form existed against the publishing of debates. As reward for his conscientious work on the *Mirror* Charles was often invited to accompany his uncle at week-ends to his house at Norwood, a house that was to figure as the home of Mr. Spenlow in *David Copperfield*.

Sixteen years later we find Charles Dickens writing to Tom Beard from his fine house in Devonshire Terrace, 'John Henry Barrow dines here next Sunday at half-past five for a quarter to six. Will you come and meet the little man?'[1] Could the tables of patronage be more completely turned? A testimonial to Barrow, which incidentally reflects credit on his nephew, was spoken by Gladstone in the House of Commons in 1877. He said, 'At the time of the Reform Bill an attempt was made by a gentleman of the name of Barrow to produce verbatim reports of the debates in that House. . . . Barrow's work was done in the highest degree of perfection.'[2]

In February 1833 Dickens was reporting speeches on the Bill for the Suppression of Disturbances in Ireland and curiously enough by so doing was brought into direct contact with the Chief Secretary himself, Mr. Stanley. This Coercion Bill had been drafted in Mr. Stanley's office in Dublin and was approved by Lord Grey. It embodied the usual features proper to such measures, including the replacing of trials by jury by courts-martial. In fact it was the application to Leinster peasants of the dragooning of the Scottish lowlands under Charles II and of the Cevennes under Louis XV, a more severe measure than any passed by Tories. It is a tribute both to O'Connell's eloquence and to Dickens's sensibility that when taking down a speech describing a scene

[1] 20. II. L.   [2] *Daily News*, April 21, 1877.

at an Irish anti-tithe riot the reporter had to abandon his pencil
and weep. When moving the second reading of the Bill Mr.
Stanley spoke at great length. *Mirror* reporters, working
for three-quarters of an hour each, were on the job, and Charles
Dickens who reported the first part of the speech also reported
the last part. When it appeared in print Mr. Stanley found all
except the beginning and the end full of mistakes; he therefore
requested the editor of the *Mirror* to send across the reporter
of the first and last sections to take down the whole speech as
it was to be printed for circulation in Ireland. Barrow instructed John Dickens to fetch Charles up from the country
whither he had gone for a rest, and dispatched the lad to
Carlton House Terrace. Shown into a room the tables of
which were covered with newspapers, young Mr. Dickens
awaited the minister who had summoned him. Mr. Stanley
walked in and eyeing him suspiciously said, 'I beg pardon,
but I had hoped to see the gentleman who had reported part
of my speech.' 'I am that gentleman,' said Dickens, redden-
ing. 'Oh indeed,' responded Mr. Stanley, looking down to
conceal a half smile. Sir James Graham coming in at this
moment, Mr. Stanley began to walk up and down the room
declaiming his speech. Sir James followed his words with
the newspaper version and occasionally intervened. The
ordeal over, Mr. Stanley wrote a highly complimentary note
to Barrow thanking him for sending so smart a stenographer,
while in the hall his private secretary, Richard Earle, praised
Dickens to his face. This encouraged him to write to Earle
explaining that as he was entirely unemployed during the
recess he would be thankful to be recommended as shorthand
writer to a Commission or Board. First and last things
sometimes meet. When dining, as a famous man, with Mr.
Gladstone many years later, Dickens found himself in the
very room in which he had taken down Mr. Stanley's speech.
The scene flashed back and he spoke to his host about the
incident, whereupon Lord Derby who was present told his
version of the story. Another witness to Dickens's excellence as a reporter is William Harness, who says that when

Joseph Hume in 1834 complained that his speeches on the Repeal of the Corn Laws were not faithfully reported in the *Times*, the editor of the *Mirror* put his young nephew on to him and the dissatisfied member very soon called 'Peccavi'.[1]

As soon as Mr. Stanley had seen the Coercion Bill become law he ceased to be Irish Secretary and went to the Colonial Office, where he at once framed a Bill for the Abolition of Slavery in the British Colonies, a measure certain of success in the reformed House. It was Dickens's duty to record the debates on this measure which include the maiden speech of Mr. Gladstone, the young hope of the Conservative party, whose (family) fortunes were partially derived from Demerara and who was forced to his feet when Lord Howick during the course of the discussion accused the administrator of the family estates of being a 'murderer of slaves'. He also reported Bulwer, whose rhetorical speech about keeping faith with the negro went down so well with the House that O'Connell tore his speech-notes in half, saying, 'There is nothing to add, the House must divide!' During the same session (1833) Dickens was on duty in the Gallery for the India Act debates in which Silk Buckingham and Macaulay played so large a part. Macaulay, who had been brought up by his father (at one time Governor of Sierra Leone) to respect coloured people, was all for the equality of races and warm-hearted for the employment of natives in official positions. When the Governing Corporation of India was forced to abandon its commercial monopolies and trading activities and was limited to administration and patronage, Macaulay was appointed to the Supreme Council of India and went out to work under that ardent reformer, Lord William Bentinck, the first Governor-General under the new Constitution. Reformers differ from improvers in being guided by faith and imagination to the discernment of things possible. Discernment and hope were needed then in full measure if the customs of the dwellers in India (even with regard to Lord William's special

[1] L'Estrange, *Life of W. Harness*, p. 169.

bugbears suttee and thuggee) were to be in any degree modified.

It is important in assessing Dickens's career to stress the character of the education he absorbed while working in the Gallery. There is too great a tendency among biographers to regard him in a parochial way as a man only acquainted with English middle and lower class life, who, owing to circumstances, was shut out from the affairs of the great world until the great world, discovering him in his amazingly successful books, took him up and made him into an idol. Of course we see in reading his novels that he was always emotionalising his personal experience and dealing with examples of private suffering in a way that the humblest understood, but this did not mean that he himself was not fully alive to wider social issues. Always anxious that the people, so uninterested in their own interests, should be made aware that they were quite needlessly living a disinherited life, he addressed himself to the common folk and the generality of the humble. Never after his experience in the House of Commons would he have thought it worth while to appeal to legislators as such. Conscious of the power within him of stirring men to laughter or tears, he knew that if he could move them enough they must themselves seek to remedy their condition. The manner in which he worked on society was almost stealthy; it was as if he felt that it would invalidate the magic in his books, if it ever became generally known that he was a philanthropist at heart working for the abolition of slums, the founding of Ragged Schools and the reclaiming of girls from the streets. These activities for years remained a secret between himself and Miss Burdett Coutts. Some native instinct made him wise and caused him to realise that his real magic was vested in the wand, Romance, with which he could stir men powerfully to achieve their own salvation.

Impressed by his nephew's ability and by the testimonials to his efficiency furnished by Mr. Stanley and Mr. Hume, John

Henry Barrow spoke to his friend Payne Collier, then in charge of parliamentary reporting on the *Morning Chronicle*,[1] about the young man's future. He called him 'an extremely clever youth' and said he would have liked, had there been a vacancy, to get him on to the staff of the *Times*. Was it possible for Payne Collier to introduce him to the new stockbroker proprietor of the *Morning Chronicle*, Mr. John Easthope? Payne Collier at once asked where the nephew had been educated and what his record was, for it was more than his place was worth to recommend an unknown person to an employer so irascible and so disagreeable to employees as to be nicknamed 'Blasthope'. The reply he received to his question being ambiguous, he said he must see the candidate himself. Barrow arranged for them to meet at dinner at his house at Norwood. Charles disarmed criticism by chattering merrily and, after a good deal of pressure, singing two comic songs. Payne Collier was charmed with the young man and readily wrote out an introduction to the editor of the *Chronicle*, John Black, who had been commissioned by the new proprietor to look for a staff good enough to compete with the *Times*. Black had already engaged Eyre Crowe as Paris correspondent and George Hogarth as theatrical and musical critic. Thackeray had offered himself as sub-editor, but was not wanted, as Payne Collier and Charles Mackay, both of whom had greater experience, were preferred before him and later on he was engaged by the *Times*. Tom Beard, one of Black's parliamentary reporters, vouched for his friend, Charles Dickens, as 'the fastest and most accurate man in the Gallery'. This chit in the end got him the job. He was engaged at five guineas a week, a salary which (unlike that of the *Mirror*) was to be paid session or no session. With this team the *Morning Chronicle* after one year became, according to Charles Mackay, the commercial and literary rival of the *Times*.[2]

[1] The *Morning Chronicle* was established (1769) twenty years before the *Times*. It had declined in circulation and Easthope bought it for £17,000 to turn into a Liberal paper.

[2] C. Mackay, *Through the Long Day*, 1887.

The *Morning Chronicle* had its office at 332 Strand and John Black his private residence above it. The account of Pott and Slurk, the Eatanswill editors in *Pickwick*, may be taken as Edward Sterling rolling out thunder from Printing House Square and Black discharging answering bolts from the Strand.[1] This was in accordance with the Dickens method. In the opening chapter of *Pickwick* a quarrel between the founder of the Club and a member called Blotton is recorded. This was undoubtedly suggested by a famous House of Commons scene in which Brougham and Canning were the chief figures.[2] Brougham had described Canning's accession to a divided cabinet as an incredible specimen of monstrous trickery for the sake of obtaining office. Canning at once interrupted with the words 'That is false!' The two political rivals were about to be committed to the Serjeant-at-Arms when Sir Robert Wilson suggested the explanation that Brougham's offensive words were applied to Canning not in his personal, but in his official character. Thirteen years later, when *Pickwick* was at the height of its renown, Fonblanque, referring to the adroitness with which the disturbance had been quelled, commented, 'In fact Brougham and Canning only called each other liars in the Pickwickian sense, just as in the story Blotton said he had merely considered Mr. Pickwick a humbug in the Pickwickian sense'.

We get a further side-light on Dickens at this time from James Grant of the *Morning Advertiser*. He says that of the eighty or ninety men in the Gallery young Dickens not only occupied the highest rank for rapidity and accuracy of transcription but that 'a more talented reporter never sat in the Gallery'. The 'faithful stenographer' as they called him was described as 'exceedingly reserved in manners, courteous, but personally intimate only with Thomas Beard also reporting for the *Morning Chronicle*'. As soon as Dickens began drawing his salary from the *Chronicle*,[3] Payne Collier noted a remarkable smartening-up of his appearance which made him

[1] T. H. S. Escott, *Masters of Journalism*, p. 160. [2] April 17, 1823.
[3] August 1834.

wonder whether his uncle might not have been underpaying him. The young fellow was now to be seen wearing a new hat and a handsome blue cloak with black velvet facings 'which he threw over his shoulders *à l'Espagnole*'.

For the *Chronicle* Dickens was called on to report the debates on the Poor Law Bill with its hundred and more clauses on guardians, parishes and paupers. It was a racking but deeply interesting spell of duty, a duty by execution of which he may be said to have qualified himself forcefully to attack the conditions created by the new legislation. Critics reviewing *Oliver Twist* thought it impertinent for a young new author to write in this vein, for how could so young a novelist possibly know what he was talking about? But then few, if any, critics of that day realised in what school 'Boz' had graduated.

As the House of Commons was burnt out in October 1834 Dickens had the experience of reporting both in the old Chamber and in the House of Lords where the Commons were accommodated after the fire. He says he wore out his knees by writing on them in the old House and wore out his feet in the temporary House by standing to write in 'a preposterous pen where we used to be huddled together like so many sheep kept in waiting say—until the wool-sack might need restuffing'.

To Dickens the attitude of the House towards common-sense reforms was perfectly epitomised in the origin of the fire that had destroyed it. Had there been no mania for preserving outworn customs there would have been no fire. It pleased him to tell the story of how in ages past a savage method of keeping accounts, Crusoe-wise on notched sticks, was introduced into the Court of Exchequer. These notched sticks were treated by officials as pillars of the Constitution and it was ordained that Exchequer accounts should always be kept on splints of elm-wood called 'tallies'. In the reign of George III some revolutionary spirit suggested that the tallies should be replaced by accounts kept in pen and ink on paper. A long wrangle ensued ending in the abolition of tallies in 1826. Eight years later someone noticed an accumulation of splints, some of them worm-eaten and perished, and suggested that they should be disposed of. Instead of being given to the poor as firewood, an order went forth that they were to be destroyed 'privately and confidentially'. Crammed into a stove in the House of Lords, they set fire to the panelling and the panelling to the House itself. At the height of the blaze a stickler for etiquette and precedent presented himself in the shape of Joseph Hume who watched the Guards coming in to fight the flames and addressed their commanding officer thus: 'There ought to be ten pioneers to each regiment. I see only eight. How is this, Lord Hill?' Bulwer writing to Lady Blessington next day said, 'Only think of burning down the two Houses! I am so delighted we shall now be able to breathe, I hope![1] And the moral drawn by Dickens from the occurrence was that 'all obstinate adherence to rubbish which the time has long outlived is certain to have in the soul of it more or less what is pernicious and destructive and will one day set fire to something or other'.

Rarely did Dickens comment on anything he had seen in the House, but a short post-fire account by him of what the place looked like appears in a *Sketch*. He tells of the little stair leading to the 'first gallery ever allocated to reporters' from which a fair view of the House could be obtained. As the eyes accustomed themselves to the misty atmosphere and the glare of the gas chandeliers, and the ears attuned themselves to the confused sound of voices, it might be possible to distinguish the words of the speaker 'to whom nobody listens'. He describes the body of the House and the side galleries full of members, some with legs on backs of seats, some with them stretched full length, all laughing, coughing, oh-ing, groaning, questioning, in short presenting to an onlooker 'a conglomeration of noise and confusion to be met with in no other place in existence not even excepting Smith-

[1] Earl of Lytton, *Life of Edward Bulwer Lytton*, vol. ii. p. 461.

field on a market-day or a cock-pit in its glory'. 'Talk of mobs!' said William Hazlitt after his year's experience as a reporter for the *Morning Chronicle*. 'See how few who have distinguished themselves in the House of Commons have ever done anything else.' To Carlyle the sight of members 'sitting in their hats and talking to one another' during speeches was almost as provoking as it was to Dickens. How was it possible to believe, much less to think, that in the Commons was rooted the strength of England and not its weakness?

Such allusions as Dickens makes in his novels to Parliament and its members are not complimentary. In the *Sketches* we meet Cornelius Brook Dingwall, M.P., solemn and portentous, drawing up a Bill for the better observance of Easter Monday. In *Pickwick* the account of the Eatanswill election leaves us with the impression that parliamentary government is deep-rooted in stupidity, chicanery and corruption. In *Nicholas Nickleby* we make acquaintance with Gregsbury, M.P., a mere windbag, and in *Dombey and Son* with Warming Pan Adams who is keeping a place warm for a minor. In *Hard Times* we meet Gradgrind, M.P., and in *Our Mutual Friend* Boots and Brewer. Then in *Bleak House* we are taken to Chesney Wold and shown how governments are formed by Lord Boodle with his followers Coodle, Doodle and Foodle, or by an opposition under the Right Honourable William Buffy with his retinue of Cuffy, Duffy and Fuffy. No other leaders are so much as mentioned. Either the Boodles or the Buffys act the play, Administration, and the stage is always reserved for these great performers who from time to time address audiences known as 'the People' and evoke shouts, choruses and general applause. Nothing favourable to the House or its members was ever said or suggested in any of the Dickens novels.

Between sessions Dickens was sent to report speeches by political leaders all over the country. For instance, in September 1834 he and Tom Beard were ordered to Edinburgh to cover the banquet given to Lord Grey on his retirement from office. The young men went by sea to Leith and it delighted Dickens to see a bagman on the boat reading *The Bloomsbury Christening* with chuckles of laughter. Nat Willis was also in Edinburgh on a similar errand and noted 'Lord Grey's statesman-like head, as it bowed industriously from the platform' and the expression on Lord Brougham's ugliest and shrewdest of human faces'. To the American it was an amusing occasion.

The *Morning Chronicle* of Wednesday, September 17, printed a bright half column from 'Our own correspondent', describing Edinburgh in festal mood:

> The Earl of Durham is here and the Lord Chancellor arrived at three o'clock this afternoon. . . . I obtained a view of the temporary banqueting hall (the Grey Pavilion as it is called) this morning. It is erecting in the High School grounds on Calton Hill and . . . capable of dining 1500 individuals. The room is square with seven entrances: it has no ventilation. . . . Earl Grey staying with Sir John Dalrymple at Oxenford will receive a deputation en route at Dalkeith.

The correspondent goes on to tell of the arrival at Dalkeith of four carriages and four escorted by bands, of the stage opposite the church where Earl Grey received addresses, of Edinburgh crowds and a progress to the Waterloo Hotel where the Guilds met the statesman to make him a freeman of the city.

Dickens waited inside the Grey Pavilion 'which with chandeliers borrowed from the Theatre Royal, armorial designs, gilt laurels and crimson pillars' had been made to look quite gay. Earl Grey, due to arrive at five-thirty, did not come till six. At five-thirty people began to consume the food on the tables. Owing to the absence of the Duke of Hamilton, Lord Rosebery took the chair and Dickens, pencil poised, set himself to report what the big-wigs had to say.

And who among the distinguished guests gathered in the Grey Pavilion that evening could have guessed that an insignificant young reporter, at that moment on duty, would in seven years' time be going through the identical experience of Lord Grey in being made a freeman of the city of Edinburgh?

The *Times* by its new system of 'extraordinary expresses', costing £290 a journey, was able to print, by delaying for four hours the publication of the paper, a full report of the speeches on Wednesday, September 17. The *Morning Chronicle* printed the speeches on the day following, and the *Times* of September 19 jeered at the editor for labelling his report 'By Express'. This was a lesson Dickens did not forget and from henceforth we shall find him too making use of 'extraordinary expresses'.

In October Dickens took lodgings in Cecil Street, Strand, so as to be near his newspaper office, and shortly afterwards moved to 15 Buckingham Street in the same neighbourhood. These lodgings were so unsatisfactory that he began to consider taking unfurnished rooms and setting up house for himself. Rooms, however, were by no means his only worry at this time, as we may gather from his letters to Henry Kolle in which he alludes to his father's borrowing habits as 'the damnable shadow' cast over his life. The shadow at this time was lengthening. To Tom Mitton he wrote, 'my father went out yesterday accompanied by Alfred to endeavour to get some money as Burr refused to wait beyond last evening. He sent the boy [Alfred] home to say he had been unsuccessful and has not made his appearance all night or forwarded a message of any kind.'[1] Next day the news of John Dickens's arrest by 'Shaw and Maxwell the quondam wine people' reached him, and a much-harassed Charles had to rush off to Sloman's sponging-house before taking his turn of duty for the *Morning Chronicle*. In *Pickwick* we shall find a description of this half-way house to prison. Cash had to be found at once to provide 'the Governor' with his keep, so Tom Mitton was asked to advance £5 against the 'money order from my French employer' which he encloses.[2] As 'it

[1] 33. I. N.L.   [2] 34. I. N.L.

had to be assumed that John Dickens would not rejoin his family for some time', a domestic council was called whereat it was decided that the family must for the time being disperse. The best arrangement Charles could make at the moment was to rent cheap lodgings for his mother, sister and the other children and take Frederick under his own wing in the unfurnished rooms he was renting at Furnival's Inn. Manfully and cheerfully he shouldered these heavy responsibilities, telling Beard that his salary was 'completely mortgaged for weeks to come' and adding, 'I am determined to see everything in as bright a light as possible'.

This was the first step on the long road of family commitments, commitments which in the end were to be his spiritual undoing. Just because he was open-hearted as well as open-handed and seemed able to deal with difficulties of the kind easily, it became the custom in his own family, and later on in his wife's family, to expect him to find money and appointments for as spineless a set of people as ever bread-winner was saddled with. He was too capable, prompt and generous in the beginning not to fall victim to his own ability in the end. To this theme we shall have to recur.

Thus it came about that for the first time since he had taken to earning his living Charles was short of cash and had to camp sans curtains or crockery in the 'three-pair-back' at 13 Furnival's Inn. The 'flare' or house-warming he had meant to give his friends was for the time being postponed. In a letter of January 1835 a bleak statement lets the curtain down on John Dickens: 'I have just returned from accompanying father to Coldbath Fields'.

Shortly after this melancholy outing Charles was ordered to cover the Chelmsford election. It was a joy to get out of London for the time being and his spirits rose as he drove himself to Braintree in a gig,

> tooling in and out of the banners, drums, conservative emblems, horsemen, go-carts, with which every little green was filled as the processions were waiting for Sir John Tyrell and Baring. Every time the horse heard a drum he

bounced into the hedge on the left side of the road and every time I got him out of that he bounded into the hedge on the right side . . . with the trifling exception of breaking my whip, I flatter myself I did the whole thing in something like style.[1]

A wet week-end at the Black Boy Hotel exhausted his good temper and turned Chelmsford into 'the dullest and most stupid spot on the face of the earth'.

> I can't get an *Athenaeum* or *Literary Gazette*—no not even a penny magazine and here I am on a wet Sunday looking out of a d——d large bow window at the rain as it falls into the puddles opposite: wondering when it will be dinner-time and cursing my folly in having put no books into my portmanteau. The only book I have seen here is one that lies upon the sofa. It is entitled 'Field Exercises and Evolution of the Army by Sir Henry Towers'. I have read it through so often that I am sure I could drill a hundred recruits from memory. There is not even anything to look at in the place except two immense prisons, large enough to hold all the inhabitants of the county—whom they can have been built for I can't imagine.[2]

Quotations from letters often cause one to deplore the fact that Dickens never kept a diary and never described the houses he was entertained in nor his meetings with famous people.

Twice during the year 1835 Dickens went reporting into the west country, once in May and once in November, each time to take down the speeches of Lord John Russell. In May, on accepting the office of Home Secretary in Lord Melbourne's government, Lord John had to offer himself for re-election in South Devon. The *Chronicle* men, Dickens and Tom Beard, set out in tearing spirits and worked in rain that lasted through the short campaign. In the castle yard at Exeter Lord John made an open-air speech which Dickens took down at full speed while friends held a pocket-handkerchief over his notebook to keep it dry 'after the manner of a

[1] 39. I. N.L.   [2] 40. I. N.L.

state canopy in an ecclesiastical procession'. By dint of
bribing the post-boys 'tremendously', he got his report to
London in time for the *Chronicle* to print before the *Times*,
and as his account was longer and more accurate than that
of any other London paper it gave great satisfaction. John
Black, clapping him on the shoulder, told him the whole affair
was a complete and signal success. The triumphant reporter
said the rain had made him deaf and had given him rheumatism, that Lord John had been defeated, but that all the
same he had enjoyed the excitement immensely.

Lord John Russell being the Government candidate at a
by-election in Stroud in November 1835, Dickens and Beard
took the road to the west country again and kept their sub-
editor, Thomas Fraser, informed what their scheme for transmission was. They had arranged for 'a Horse Express from
Marlborough to London to go the whole distance at the rate
of thirteen miles an hour for six guineas'. If they are as
fortunate in 'laying chaise horses' from Bristol to Marlborough
the packet should reach town by seven. He and Beard are
'working together sharply' and were expecting to sit up all
night.

> As all papers have arranged to leave Bristol the moment
> Russell is down . . . one of us will go to Marlborough in the
> chaise with one *Herald* man and the other remain at Bristol
> with the other *Herald* man to conclude the account for the
> next day. The *Times* has ordered a chaise and four for the
> whole distance, so there is every prospect of beating them
> hollow.[1]

And the result was that the *Chronicle* could print three and a
half columns of the speech the following morning and this
was noted by the *Spectator* as 'a feat'. The occasion coped
with was a dinner to Lord John Russell on November 10.
In another letter (ante-dated by Forster by six months)
written from the Bush Inn, Bristol, he stated that a full
account of the Bath dinner of November 17 should reach the
office two days later.

[1] 50. I. N.L.

In the last week of May 1836 he was sent to report
O'Connell's speech at Ipswich. There he stayed at the
Suffolk Hotel and the whole episode is said to be incorporated
in Eatanswill, but then the same is said of other political
episodes in which he took part.

The wear and tear of these gallopades caused Dickens
to indent for broken hats, broken luggage, and damage to
clothes from wax candles guttering during transcription *en
route*. He always found his employers 'great gentlemen' in
meeting his claims. Whenever he arrived in London after a
reporting tour he would be welcomed by an admiring editor
in 'the broadest of Scotch accents from the broadest of hearts'.
He would say 'Dear old Black, my first out and out appreci-
ator. . . . It was John Black that flung the slipper after me!'

If Dickens can be said to have had a favourite political hero
it would be Lord John, for by dint of reporting his speeches
both inside and outside the House he had conceived a great
respect for him. For one thing he was a consistent advocate
of educational reform and always struck Dickens as speaking
on this subject with intelligence and conviction. Somewhere
they met and talked and a kind of friendship was engendered
which later on ripened into mutual confidence. One night,
years later, Dickens dined with Lord John and aired his views
about the Lord's Day Observance Act, 'giving them a little
truth about Sunday that was like bringing a Sebastopol
battery among the polite company'. Dickens's views on
Sunday observance had always been continental and by now
he was convinced that the type of religion to which the poor
English had been obliged to sacrifice theatre-going and much
innocent enjoyment must be to say the least of it defective.
Meyerbeer, another guest, burst out, 'Ah mon ami illustre!
que c'est noble de vous entendre parler d'haute voix morale à
la table d'un ministre!'

In December 1835, while watching a by-election at Ketter-
ing, Dickens wrote to John Macrone,[1] 'If you could see the

beastly swine who wallow in the public-houses down here under the denomination of Conservatives, you would renounce your creed for ever'. In their convivial moments the people of the place seemed to him 'perfect savages'.

> If a foreigner were brought here on a first visit to an English town, to form his estimate of the national character, I am quite satisfied he would return forthwith to France, and never set foot in England again. The remark will apply in greater or less degree to all agricultural places during the pendency of an election, but beastly as the electors usually are, these men are superlative blackguards. Would you believe that a large body of horsemen mounted and armed, who galloped on a defenceless crowd yesterday, striking about them in all directions and protecting a man who cocked a loaded pistol, were led by clergymen and magistrates?[1]

Escaping the mob for an hour or two, he walked up the Boughton avenue to inspect the house and pacify his temper. The opening by Lord Melbourne of the Licensed Victuallers' School in Kennington was reported by Dickens about a month before he accepted the *Pickwick* contract which brought the end of journalistic work in its wake. In June 1836 we find him writing to Macrone: 'I am tired to death to-night, though I have been in bed all day. Melbourne *v.* Norton has played the devil with me.' The reporting of this sensational trial was his last job for the *Morning Chronicle*. It took place in the Court of Common Pleas at Westminster on June 22 (now a lawn to the west of Westminster Hall where the statue of Cromwell stands) and was tried before Lord Chief Justice Tindal. Captain Norton, who brought the action for criminal conversation against Lord Melbourne, the Prime Minister, had as counsel Sir William Follett,[2] and Lord Melbourne's defence was conducted by the Attorney-General, Sir John Campbell. Dickens's great friend, Serjeant Talfourd, was in court, having been retained in support of the

---

[1] *Mr. and Mrs. Charles Dickens*, p. 44.
[2] Solicitor-General in the Peel administration of 1835.

defendant's counsel. Mrs. Norton made a tensely observed entry on the arm of Samuel Rogers.

The court was packed with men and women of fashion some of whom had given five or ten guineas for a seat. It was believed that compromising letters would be read and the lives of the great exposed in all their deceit and littleness. It turned out to be a disgusting case based not on Lord Melbourne's correspondence, but on the evidence of servants. Lady Blessington's comment to Countess Guiccioli is to the point: 'Nothing can be more calculated to strike at the root of morals than the vile system in England of bringing forward discharged servants, often of bad character, to give evidence against their mistresses'.[1] Stories were told of Mrs. Norton painting and powdering herself up to receive her lover's visits at the house with two entrances, one in Birdcage Walk and the other in Prince's Court, of Lord Melbourne's afternoon calls lasting from three to six, of his visits to her bedroom, of her disarray, of her visits to him in South Street. No other evidence was brought by the plaintiff, and when in cross-examination the witnesses called were shown to be themselves of low moral character the case crumbled. Sir William Follett asked his client whether he had ever escorted his wife to Lord Melbourne's door, and when Captain Norton admitted that he had done so, Follett told him it was the end of the action. No witnesses were called for the defence, and the jury without leaving the court at 11.50 P.M. declared Lord Melbourne acquitted of the charges brought against him. The verdict was received by the House of Commons that night with acclamation. The nauseous and trivial evidence dragged out by the plaintiff's counsel sickens us as no doubt it sickened Dickens, but Lord Melbourne had to submit to indecent allegations implying proof of sexual intercourse, evidence such as no newspaper ought to have published then and no newspaper would dream of publishing now even were a judge to-day to allow such questions in open court. Lord Melbourne, who had been Home Secretary in 1833, was

[1] *Letters of Marguerite Blessington*, vol. ii. p. 235.

Prime Minister by 1836 and therefore excellent quarry for a blackmailer, and it seems clear that Captain Norton expected to be bought off with hush money.[1]

Just after the trial Dickens wrote to a friend:

> I see a decent prospect of the House being up at last, and I devoutly hope ere next Session I may make some arrangements which will render its sittings a matter of indifference to me—as the story-books say—for ever after.

The 'arrangements' adumbrated in this letter matured, and in July he was in a position to abandon journalism and shake the dust of Westminster off his shoes. In taking to reporting as a means of keeping himself, Dickens had chosen a job that brought him in touch with a great variety of human beings. The legal types he found sympathetic, but the political or parliamentary types were never congenial. He had spent five years in and out of law offices and law courts, and four years in and out of the House of Commons and up and down the country reporting elections. He made no use of this political experience. The octopus-quality so observable where a legal *entourage* was concerned appeared to desert him, negatived, it would seem, by the make-believe atmosphere of politics. To him political life was a sham—to be escaped from as soon as might be. Dickens told Mrs. J. T. Fields, wife of the Boston publisher, that never since he left the House of Commons as a reporter had he entered it again, and that his hatred of the falseness of the talk and his horror of the bombastic eloquence he had been obliged to record made it impossible for him ever to go there to listen to another speech.

The father of one of his colleagues on the *Morning Chronicle*, William Hazlitt, had also served his turn as a reporter in the House of Commons. He too had been repelled by the somnambulism of the proceedings, and has left these words on record:

> It may appear at first sight that here are a number of persons got together, picked out from the whole nation

who can speak at all times upon all subjects . . . but the fact is they only repeat the same things over and over on the same subjects. . . . Read over the old debates, they are *mutatis mutandis* as those of yesterday. . . . You serve an apprenticeship to a want of originality, to a suspension of thought and feeling. You are in a go-cart of prejudices, in a regularly constructed machine of pretexts and precedents . . . there is a House of Commons jargon that must be used by everyone . . . you are hemmed in, stifled, pinioned, pressed to death. . . . Talk of mobs! Is there any body of people that has this character in a more consummate degree than the House of Commons?[1]

Dickens gave expression to what he really felt about the House of Commons in that strange skit *The Thousand and One Humbugs*, written in early life and tinkered at, brought up to date and published when Palmerston became Prime Minister. Modelled on the *Arabian Nights*, this burlesque shows a Sultan, 'Taxedtaurus' (Fleeced Bull), who has been married scores of times and who in so doing has raised to the dignity of 'Howsa Kummauns' (or Peerless Chatterer) a great variety of beautiful women. The result of their promotion was uniformly unfortunate for the Sultan. All proved unfaithful, talkative, idle, extravagant, inefficient and boastful. And so it came about that a 'Howsa Kummauns' very rarely died a natural death, she was generally cut short in some violent manner. The youngest and fairest of all the Peerless Chatterers was the lovely 'Reefawm' (Light of Reason). 'Taxedtaurus' had looked to her to recompense him for all his many disappointments, but she turned out quite as unreliable as her predecessors. The poor Sultan fell into a profound melancholy and wailed, 'Every Howsa Kummauns has deceived me. Every Howsa Kummauns is a Humbug. I must slay the present Howsa Kummauns as I have slain so many others.' His grief so overpowered him that he fainted away. At this juncture the glib vizier, 'Parmarstoon' (or Twirling Weathercock) tried to console him by introducing to the

[1] *Hazlitt's Selected Essays*, p. 551.

harem his lovely daughter 'Hansardadade'. Preceded by 'Mistaspeeka', the black mute, chief of the Seraglio, she entered the presence, and taking a one-stringed lute sang a lengthy song in prose. Its purport was, 'I am the recorder of brilliant eloquence, I am the chronicler of patriotism, I am the pride of sages, and the joy of nations. The continued salvation of the country is owing to what I preserve and without it there would be no business done.

> Sweet are the voices of the crow and chough
> And Persia never, never, never can have words enough.'

At the conclusion of this delightful strain, the Sultan and the whole divan were so faint with rapture that they remained in a comatose state for seven hours.

Dickens in telling *The Story of the Talkative Barber* pokes fun at all the stock performances he had witnessed from the Gallery. The barber dances the dance of 'Mistapit', sings the song of 'Mistafoks' and jokes the joke of 'Jomillah'. He even proceeds to improvise impertinent verse:

> When Britteen first at Heaven's command
> Arose from out the azure main
> This was the charter of the land
> And guardian angels sang this strain:
> Singing, as first Lord was a wallerking the Office-garding around
> No end of born barbers he picked up and found,
> Says he I will load them with silvier and gold,
> For the country's a donkey, and as such is sold.

A significant light is thrown on Dickens by this burlesque, which shows that he deliberately preferred to make war on what he conceived as shams by appealing to the Englishman's sense of humour rather than to his judgment and deliberative faculties. And the shrewd Americans, apprehending this, were the first to hail him as a reformer who had done more in his short life to better the condition of the downtrodden than the whole of the House of Commons put together.

It is evident from his letters as well as from this skit that Dickens was totally unimpressed by the accomplishments of

the Reform Ministry which claimed as its 'chief glory' the
Poor Law, the Poor Law with its simple invention of hiding
up poverty and its magic formula 'No out-door relief'.   How
long, he wondered, would the helpless people of England put
up with the barmecidal feast set before them?   In all the
hundreds of columns transcribed for the *Mirror* and the
Chronicle, on Canada, the West Indies, the Game Laws, Hill
Coolies, the Irish Question, Dogcarts and the rest, was there
any mention of the condition-of-England question?   It was
plain to him that Parliament, so far as England was concerned,
had for decades undertaken the adjustment of one thing and
one alone, itself and its own interests, leaving domestic
interests to rub along as best they could.   It was high time
that the do-nothing-for-the-people routine should be ended,
for to carry the eighteenth century over into the nineteenth
must sooner or later provoke a revolution.

At the time Dickens left the Gallery he had not met Carlyle
who had arrived at similar conclusions by quite different
paths.   Carlyle had welcomed the Reform Bill till he found
it in no way affected the existing form of society with its
extremes of poverty and wealth.   Prosperity only made the
rich richer and the poor poorer.   The 'huge damp putrid
mass' remained rotting and would continue to rot if men had
to depend on an extended suffrage to clean it up.   There was
a right way and a wrong way to do things, and it was absurd
to suppose that the right way of organising a people could be
ascertained by a majority of votes any more than could the
cultivation of the soil, the maintenance of public health or the
promotion of public education.

De Quincey draws a distinction between the literature of
Knowledge and the literature of Power.   The function of the
first is to teach; the function of the second is to move.   The
first appeals to the intellect and the second to the heart and the
emotions, and from this point of view it is not the understanding, but the understanding heart that matters.   It is not
so much the subject in itself that affects us as the treatment of
it, the charging of it with humanly generated electricity.   No

better illustration of this contention can be brought forward than that of Mrs. Trollope's novel on the factory child, *Michael Armstrong*. Informative, didactic, derived from official reports and intended to influence opinion, it neither interested nor moved anyone, whereas the story of the parish boy, Oliver Twist, not only moved every reader, but left on their minds an indelible impression. As Dickens's friend Gilbert à Beckett said, 'There is something feminine about Dickens that leads him to the core of the heart of the situation in hand'.

If it were not for the literature of Power, justice, for example, might remain an ideal whereas in a book it may germinate into vitalising activity. The commonest novel, by moving in alliance with human fears and hopes, with human instincts of right and wrong, sustains and quickens those affections, and working by deep agencies rescues them from torpor. Dim in origin, these emotions welled up like hidden springs in Dickens and influenced his whole being as may the forgotten incidents of childhood.

Chapter 4

THE UNDERTOW

The muffled majesty of authorship.
HENRY JAMES

IN the professions it is always possible to change roles: a soldier may become a company promoter or a lawyer a politician, but in the deeper vocational life that calls for the emission of power duality is abolished, for an artist is inwardly compelled to be true to himself and his purpose whatever it may be. Charles Dickens had chosen by profession to become a shorthand expert and worked so hard in the process that he soon topped the list of political reporters, giving his colleagues the impression that his whole mind was set on excelling them. This is the measure of his tremendous will, a will that seems to have operated in retarding his vocational instincts and forcing his attention to external achievement. For a man whose tendency was to emotionalise all experience it must have been a struggle to turn himself into the perfect, passionless recorder of other men's utterances and to win commendation for accuracy and speed.

After working for over a year in the Gallery, Charles Dickens began to set things down, as they struck him, in a very simple, handy, even ordinary way. Like many of the people who possess in a strong degree the story-telling faculty, his work showed a relish for the commoner stuff of human nature. He called these jottings 'Sketches'. They were to begin with snapshots of actual people and actual occurrences, and then were given the humorous twist which became their leading characteristic. Amusing to write, they made him forget the drudgery of perpetual shorthand. Many young authors have had their first work rejected, so it was without any particular feeling of optimism that he pushed one of his 'Sketches' anonymously into the letter-box of the *Monthly*

Magazine in Johnson's Court, Fleet Street.

The *Monthly Magazine* or *British Register* had just changed owners, having been bought for £300 by a Captain Holland from South America. Only one number had appeared under the new editorship so its files were unlikely to be cluttered up with old manuscripts. On his way to the House late one afternoon Dickens stepped into Chapman and Hall's double-fronted shop, 186 Strand, and spent half a crown on the December number to find that it contained his 'Sketch', *A Dinner in Poplar Walk*. Too excited and upset to feel pleasure in the discovery, he wrote asking for Mrs. Kolle's verdict, 'I am so dreadfully nervous that my hand shakes to such an extent as to prevent my writing a word legibly'. With tears in his eyes he walked into Westminster Hall to master his emotion before going into the Gallery. The undertow had made itself felt powerfully for the first time, the undertow that was to surge up and sweep away his avocational life. Hugging his secret from all but the Kolles, he quickly followed up his first success by pushing six other 'Sketches' into the same letter-box, content to be for the time being unpaid and unrecognised. He soon made acquaintance with Captain Holland and found that it was an understood thing among writers that contributions to his magazine were never at this time paid for. The editor had made it clear to aspirants for fame that as he was fresh from the Bolivar campaigns in South America, and had no financial reserves, he could only serve youthful authors by giving them a chance to see themselves in print. If they liked to avail themselves of the publicity he offered, it might advantage them as well as the public at large. The authors chose to write for him and Captain Holland soon managed to build up a reputation for the magazine and was able in the autumn of 1835 to sell it at a profit.

Dickens soon became confident that he could write what people wanted to read, but it was not till August 1834 that he ventured to set up a second personality and sign himself 'Boz', a nickname derived from his young adenoidal brother,

Augustus, who answered in the family to the name of Moses and called himself 'Boses'. When he let John Black and George Hogarth into his secret, they at once offered to place some 'Sketches' in the *Morning Chronicle*, and on September 26, 1834, the first of four London *Street Sketches* was printed in their paper. These articles were widely read and attracted the notice of editors on the look-out for new writers. Albany Fonblanque of the *Examiner* liked them and so did S. C. Hall of the *New Monthly*. Best of all, William Jerdan of the *Literary Gazette* approved of them and at this time a laudatory notice in the *Literary Gazette* would sell an edition of any book. It stood alone (1820–40) as the arbiter of fame, literary and artistic, till the *Athenaeum* under Dilke rose and killed it.

At last Charles Dickens could savour the kind of approval his whole being craved for, recognition as an author, which was something very different in quality from the kudos attaching to professional reporting. He now undertook any job of work that might help him to get known in the sphere he meant to make his own, writing dramatic critiques for plays at the Adelphi and Olympic Theatres, and correcting the proofs of *Journies through France and Italy*[1] to oblige Macrone. Universally obliging and untiring, he did not at first ask for payment for his *Street Sketches* in the *Morning Chronicle*, but earned merit from his employers by throwing them in for his five-guinea wage as a reporter. Having, however, created a demand for his work he could, when the *Evening Chronicle*[2] was launched under the editorship of George Hogarth, offer as one of its regular features *Sketches of London* and thus extract from the management another two guineas a week. Some twenty *Sketches* dealing with London were published in this way. He also, as a sideline, contributed twelve *Scenes and Characters* to *Bell's Life in London* under the hush-hush name of Tibbs. No one but Robert Smith Surtees was doing quite this sort of work and there can

---

[1] By William Thomson, uncle of Mrs. George Hogarth.
[2] January 31, 1835.

be no doubt that Dickens profited greatly from reading Mr. Jorrocks's adventures at Ramsgate, Herne Bay and other places, which had been coming out in the *New Sporting Magazine* for three years. They were technically far in advance of anything he could at the time accomplish. Surtees, however, though he wrote well within the compass of the un-educated reader, was never a serious competitor with his younger contemporary, partly owing to the fact that his medium of publication circulated exclusively in clubs and country house, partly because his preoccupation with field sports appealed particularly to the richer sections of society, and partly because he left London to live in the north of England in 1834. For these reasons, if for no others, the more vulgar and universal publicity of the *Sketches* was denied to his *Jaunts and Jollities*.

In the Gallery it soon leaked out that the star reporter, Charles Dickens, was really 'Boz' of the *Sketches*, and presently authors began to take notice of this new recruit to their ranks. Harrison Ainsworth, who had read his articles as they came out, was the first professional writer to invite him to his house as a fellow author. Ainsworth was seven years older than Dickens and in a miniature, feline way very handsome; women called him the Antinous of literature. He had come to London from Manchester in 1824 to finish his legal education at the Inner Temple. In London he got to know John Ebers, publisher, and manager of Covent Garden, married Fanny Ebers in 1826 and began business as a publisher himself. Having brought out a book for Mrs. Norton and a cookery manual by Ude, he gave the job up and sat down at The Elms, Kilburn, to write *Rookwood*. By the time Dickens got to know him he was separated from his wife and with his little girls was living with a Mrs. le Touchet and her sister at Kensal Lodge, near the scattered village of Willesden. Mrs. le Touchet, a hunting woman from Cheshire, used to quiz the Cockney horsemen who visited Ainsworth. Dickens, to avoid her critical eye, would mount and dismount out of

sight.   After the sensational success won by *Rookwood* the
Lodge became a literary rallying-point with many writers
flocking to its pleasant Sunday afternoon parties.   Ainsworth's publisher was Macrone, a Manxman, with business
premises at 3 St. James's Square.   He and Dickens met one
day at the Lodge and took a great fancy to each other.   As
they walked towards London together it pleased Dickens to
find that Macrone, too, was bound for Furnival's Inn.
Almost at once we find him volunteering to help Macrone
with proofs and being told in return that his *Sketches* were
'capital value' and ought to be gathered into a volume.   It
was also suggested that George Cruikshank, with whom they
had been talking at Kensal Lodge, should illustrate the
Sketches.   This was a highly complimentary suggestion, for
this fine draughtsman and cartoonist had made a great name
for himself and was twenty years older than Dickens.   Co-
operation with such a distinguished man would certainly
insure the commercial success of the *Sketches*.

John Macrone, whose publishing career was almost as
ephemeral as Captain Holland's, was a sociable young man
of a certain charm who borrowed money from his fiancée,
Sophie Sala, to promote his business, then threw her over and
married somebody else.   At the time Dickens made his
acquaintance he was handling a book by the American author
Nat Willis, an amusing fellow commissioned by the *New
York Mirror* to report on Europe.   Willis, who had reached
England on June 1, 1834, had at once begun to pay court to
the women writers.   Jane Porter liked him and Mary Russell
Mitford said he was 'more like one of the best of our Peers'
sons than a rough republican'.   It is no wonder that he made
this silky impression as in character he was something between a d'Orsay and an Oscar Wilde.   To J. G. Lockhart,
for whom a 'society reporter was little better than a spy', he
was a bugbear.   Lockhart vented his spleen on Willis in the
Quarterly by citing him as 'an example of a man creeping
into your home and before your claret is dry upon his lips
describing table-talk and guests for an American paper'.   In

MR BOZ   MR TINTO   MR MAC.   Mr PROUT.

Dickens, Thackeray, Maclise, and Mahony conferring together at Macrone's publishing office in St. James's Square. A sketch made by Thackeray in 1837

spite of J. G.'s strictures Willis was made welcome by the ladies of the greater country houses of England and Scotland, and petted to such an extent that, though always maintaining his native American shrewdness, he became even more dandified and conceited than when he arrived. Macrone hobnobbed a good deal with him when he was bringing out his 'Letters' and one day offered to take him to see his new friend 'Boz', who was the author of some rather clever pictures of London life published from time to time in the *Morning* or *Evening Chronicle*.

It is from Nat Willis that we get a really unaffected vignette of Charles Dickens at this time. Some Dickensians have tried to demolish the story and to pretend Willis never saw him, because it seems they do not think the account reflects credit on their hero. They are the same critics who deny the validity of Dickens's liaison with Ellen Ternan, being themselves unable to reconcile it with their preconception of his character. Almost as soon as Dickens had settled into his three-pair-back at Furnival's Inn,[1] he received a visit from the American *littérateur*, who described 'the young paragraphist' for the benefit of his fellow countrymen. He told how Macrone had driven him from St. James's Square to Holborn and had pulled up at the entrance of some buildings used for lawyer's chambers, not far from the door of the Bull and Mouth Inn. This area is that now covered by the Prudential insurance offices, a vast pseudo-Gothic structure of red brick wherein, under the vaulting on the left of the gateway, a small bust of Dickens cowers.

In Dickens's day it presented a façade of pale brick broken by stucco pilasters and cornice built round three sides of a courtyard, the whole being known as Furnival's Inn. After following Macrone up a long flight of stairs, Willis found himself ushered into 'an uncarpeted and bleak-looking room with a deal table, two or three chairs and a few books, a small boy and Mr. Dickens for the contents'. This 'three-pair-back' was indeed a contrast to his own luxurious apartment

[1] January 1835.

in New York, which was graced at all seasons by singing birds and hothouse flowers. Quickly this observer glanced around, noting that even the journalist's clothes betrayed his poverty. As they entered he was changing rapidly from a ragged office coat to a blue surtout and stood 'collarless and buttoned up before them', overpowered, as Willis assumed, by the honour of his publisher's visit. It was, as he said afterwards, the strongest instance he had seen of 'English obsequiousness to employers'. This interpretation of Dickens's obvious embarrassment was of course nonsense. Dickens was never socially embarrassed. Macrone, however, had broken in on him at a bad moment, the moment at which he had handed over all the cash he could raise to his father at Sloman's sponging-house, the moment in which he had resolved to adopt his young brother Frederick, postpone his furnishing, and give up all idea of a house-warming.

As Nat Willis seated himself on one of the two chairs in the room he said to himself, 'My good fellow, if your were in America with that fine face and your ready quill you would have no need to be condescended to by a publisher'. Though neither Macrone nor Willis knew just why Dickens's room was so comfortless and his manner so constrained, they would have been even more mystified if they could have had a preview of this same young man in seven years' time installed in a luxury suite in the Tremont Hotel at Boston with all the distinguished folk of America competing to pay him homage.

Presently at Macrone's instigation Dickens began to assemble his *Sketches* and discuss their publication in volume form. He will write as many more as are required to make a good volume, he can describe anything Macrone thinks ought to be described. He has visited the House of Correction at Coldbath Fields and has begged Black 'to get old Alderman Wood' to take him to Newgate. . . . 'I have long projected sketching its interior and I think it would sell extremely well.' He has memoranda by him for 'The Cook's Shop', 'Bedlam', 'The Prisoner's Van', 'The Streets—Noon and Night',

'Banking Houses', 'Covent Garden', 'Hospitals' and 'Lodging Houses'. He thanks Macrone for his belief that he will write a successful book and approves his choice of Cruikshank as illustrator. He is still working hard at reporting, as we may see from a note written November 7, 1835, in which he says that he cannot keep his appointment with Cruikshank as he is off to Bristol. He is shivering with cold and writing by candlelight, the kettle will not boil, it is foggy, there are no cabs on the stand, he must shoulder his portmanteau and be off to catch the coach.

On his return he found that though George Hogarth had completed his proof-correcting for him, Cruikshank had not yet delivered the illustrations. Cruikshank was altogether too dilatory, he told Macrone, and must be prodded: the list of illustrations and frontispieces should be sent to him with all possible dispatch. There seems to have been a scramble in getting the book out, but it was not altogether Cruikshank's fault. Dickens found *The Visit to Newgate* 'a very difficult subject'; he could not work himself up to the requisite pitch about it, and it was not till November 20 that he got it off to the printer. In December we find him going over Coldbath Fields again in order to put vigour into *The House of Correction*. Comparing it with *Newgate* he observed, 'the treadmill will not interest men like the gallows'. Macrone praised his melodramatic sketch *The Black Veil*, so did Ainsworth, and so did another publisher, and this appreciation went to fortify the young author's belief in his creative faculty. Private interests were constantly impinged on by reporting assignments from the *Chronicle*. In December he was sent to Hatfield to cover a fire, and writing thence to Catharine Hogarth from the Salisbury Arms, says, 'Here I am waiting until the remains of the Marchioness of Salisbury are dug from the ruins of her ancestor's castle. I went over the place this morning and shall "flare" briefly in the *Chronicle* to-morrow.'

To Furnival's Inn soon after Christmas 1835 came a partner of the newly-formed publishing firm of Chapman and Hall.

It seemed to 'Boz' like the visit of an angel, for in young Mr. Hall he recognised the man who had two years earlier sold him the copy of the *Monthly Magazine* containing his first printed story. The unforgettable moment in which he knew himself, first, last and all the time, an author, came surging back. Mr. Hall explained that he had come on the recommendation of Charles Whitehead, editor of their Library of Fiction, to ask for more work on the lines already contributed by Mr. Dickens to this series, notably *The Tuggs's at Ramsgate* and *A Little Talk about Spring*. Mr. Dickens's heart bounded in his breast and was only quietened by the nature of the proposals made to him. The new series were to be continuous in character. Mr. Hall's firm could assure this continuity by providing illustrations of a sporting character which it would be Mr. Dickens's task to link together. Sport? Mr. Dickens jibbed at the word, he knew nothing of sport and anyway could only write on subjects chosen by himself. Mr. Hall was persuasive; his firm had already published a little book, the *Squib Annual*, with plates by Seymour, and Seymour would like to do 'something superior on the same line' to illustrate the mishaps and adventures of a band of amateur sportsmen who had formed themselves into a Nimrod Club. It was not an engaging vista to Mr. Dickens, only the money offered, £14 a month plus additional payment on sales, made him so much as consider it, but 'the emolument was too tempting to resist' and we shall presently see the reason for his decision.

About the same time James Grant, newly made editor of the *Monthly Magazine*, wrote to ask the price of contributions by Mr. Dickens. The author replied that he was pledged to Chapman and Hall for a monthly serial, but would write 'Sketches' for him at eight guineas a sheet. This was a moderate charge as Grant knew well, since for similar work he was himself getting ten guineas a sheet from Captain Marryat of the *Metropolitan Magazine*, and twenty guineas a sheet from the *Penny Cyclopaedia*. Moderate as the fee demanded was, the proprietors, rather to Grant's annoyance, refused to sanction the outlay. He thought it extremely short-sighted of them.

As the time for launching his first book drew near Dickens began to worry about publicity. How soon can he count on Macrone for sending first advertisements to the *Chronicle*? 'I can hardly begin to puff it till then.' But when it actually comes to drafting a notice of the *Sketches*, it turned itself into a modest little paragraph, for, like every other artist invited to praise his own work, he shied off doing it, pleading, 'I really *cannot* do tremendous puffing of myself'. Two days later we find him condoling with 'poor Macrone' on the death of his baby, and a week later again trying to get Cruikshank to hand in his last illustration. The book appeared on Dickens's twenty-fourth birthday: its full title was *Sketches by Boz. Illustrative of Every Day Life and Every Day People*.[1]

The reviews caused the author's heart to flutter. George Hogarth, who had corrected the proofs, likened his style to that of Washington Irving 'in his happiest hours', and said that the most remarkable sketch in the volume, *The Visit to Newgate*, was reminiscent of Victor Hugo's *Dernier Jour d'un Condamné*, thus in a skilful way setting Dickens in the gallery of great contemporaries. The *Literary Gazette* praised the book, so did the *Satirist* and the *Athenaeum*. John Forster reviewed it in the *Examiner*, and the *Sun, Sunday Times* and *Sunday Herald* noticed it favourably. It was particularly gratifying to the author that the *Morning Post* should commend it under 'Literature'.

A copy was sent to Lord Stanley, who had been one of the first to recognise how unusual were Dickens's capacity and intelligence. Reminding him of the report he had taken down from his own mouth on the Irish Disturbances Bill, the author humbly placed the *Sketches* at his feet, begging him to accept the volume as a mark of admiration. Thomas Noon Talfourd also received a copy of the book.

Dickens had first met Serjeant Talfourd when he was law reporter for the *Times* and in 1835 had watched him take his

[1] 2 vols. duodecimo at one guinea. February 1836.

seat as member for his native town of Reading. He was extremely lucky to have his friendship, for everyone of the date testifies to Talfourd's charm, sincerity and generosity and to his desire to do right before God and man. He had a special weakness for writers and therefore took Charles Dickens under his wing socially, introducing him both to Lady Blessington and Lady Holland, and engineering his early election to the Athenaeum. Talfourd's clerk used to say that half his time was employed in preventing the Serjeant from giving away the hat off his head or the watch from his pocket. Author of *The Memorials of Lamb*, he made a hobby of play-writing. Miss Mitford, who thought his talk 'dazzling', one day took Byron's friend, William Harness, to listen to it. The clergyman was amused by the talk but even more amused to find that Mr. and Mrs. Talfourd's devotion to cats was such that they sat at dinner each with a cat on their knees.

Everyone with any literary pretentions wrote plays at this time just as in Scott's day everyone wrote ballads, and Talfourd had *Ion* and *The Athenian Captive* (of which he was very vain) to his credit. Bulwer had written *Richelieu*, Browning *Strafford*, Miss Mitford *Rienzi* and *Otto of Wittelsbach*. Macready, to whom most of these dramas were submitted, used to groan at the time he was forced to spend on 'the unprofitable labour' of reading them. An entry in his diary in May 1835 complains of being 'reduced to despair' by three acts of a play by his dear friend, Agnes Strickland. Even when he did light on something actable he had to doctor it into acting shape. This process was not popular with authors. *Ion* was one of the plays made over in this way. Miss Mitford tells that she was staying with the Talfourds for the first night at Drury Lane. It happened to follow a fifty-night run of her own *Rienzi*. To Talfourd's annoyance *Ion* got a bad notice in the *Times*, and when his guest tried to console him by saying that if the same strictures had been made upon *Rienzi* she would not have minded, he exclaimed testily, 'Your *Rienzi* indeed! I daresay not. That is very different.' *Ion* in the end turned out a box office success and Miss Mitford, who could on occasion be as tart as Macready, says that it quite turned Talfourd's head and indeed he gloated over it for the rest of his life. One summer evening at Broadstairs years later Dickens and Rogers were talking together and Dickens remarked, 'We shall have Talfourd here to-night.' Rogers asked, 'Why? Is he here?' to which Dickens replied, '*Ion* is to be acted at Margate and he is never absent from any of its representations.'

We shall meet Talfourd at book dinners and over the copyright bill, but to clinch the impression that he was a good friend to Charles Dickens in early days it may be well here to quote Dickens's words spoken at the time of his death in 1854:

> The hand that lays this poor flower on his grave was a mere boy's when he first clasped it—newly come from the work in which he himself had begun life—and little used to the plough it has followed since—obscure enough with much to correct and learn. Each of its successive tasks through many intervening years has been cheered by his warmest interest and the friendship then begun ripened to maturity in the passage of time.

Another man who turns up in Dickens's life at this time is Edward Marjoribanks, a partner in Coutts's about whose relationship with Dickens little has been recorded except that it was to him that Dickens applied for letters of credit to the United States. Marjoribanks, however, proved a very important factor in Dickens's life, for it was he who invited the young author to dinner late in 1835[1] to meet Miss Angela Burdett, so soon to be known to the world as Miss Burdett Coutts, the great heiress.

Angela was the fifth daughter of Sir Francis Burdett, member for Westminster, a girl who had been brought up in the society of Rogers, Moore and Disraeli at home, and abroad had studied under foreign masters and had met

[1] *Letters of Charles Dickens to Baroness Burdett Coutts*, p. 29.

leaders of advanced opinion on the continent. Eager to learn and eager to meet rising authors and philanthropists, she never till the end of her long life considered her education completed. Of his first meeting with Miss Burdett Dickens wrote, 'It must have been on a Friday, for I was born on a Friday and never began a book or began anything of interest to me or done anything of importance to me, but it was on a Friday'. Angela Burdett, a demure slip of a girl with deep-set eyes, was twenty-one at the time she met Charles Dickens, and he was twenty-three; they took to each other at once. In a flash there was established between them a profound and faithful friendship that manifested itself in a life-long correspondence. Dickens's understanding of her and her at first romantic idealisation of him may have contributed to her decision not to marry till she was an old woman. Though no touch of sentiment has been allowed to seep into the selection of letters published, there is evidence that for many years she relied on him for advice in personal matters and for guidance in the direction of her often original and immense benefactions. With Charles Dickens she planned to reclaim slums, to rescue girls from a life of shame, to educate children, and to humanise the lives of those degraded by grinding poverty. In Angela Burdett Charles Dickens recognised a heart aflame with indignation against existing social conditions. As a natural humanitarian she found in Dickens her complementary self and a genius who, though she had no inkling of it, had in his own soul experienced the searing fate of the social outcast.

CHARLES DICKENS, AGED 25
by Samuel Laurence

CATHARINE HOGARTH BEFORE
HER MARRIAGE
by Daniel Maclise, R.A.

CATHARINE DICKENS SIX
YEARS LATER
by Daniel Maclise, R.A.

Chapter 5

MARRIAGE AND OTHER MATTERS

Life is all a variorum.
ROBERT BURNS

To try and understand how a sensitive human being comes to respond to the promptings of a mercurial and complex nature is in itself intensely interesting. Charles Dickens, almost over-eager to lead a completely adult life, marry, and set up a family, being cast adrift by his first love, fell easily into the company of a circle of sisters, the daughters of George Hogarth, with whom he came in daily contact on the *Chronicle*. Only one of the Miss Hogarths was old enough to be marriageable and to her he paid his court. Three of these young ladies were as alike as chestnuts; they were small, sweet, and pretty in a general rather characterless way. So unindividualised were they that when Dickens came to feel he could love every one of them in turn, one is not at all surprised. On becoming engaged to Catharine Hogarth, or 'Kate' as he called her, he ordered as betrothal gift a miniature of himself by Rose Drummond[1] and, in order to see as much as possible of his future wife's relations, took rooms at Selwood Place close to 18 York Place, Fulham Road, where the Hogarths had their home, and startled them all by appearing, dressed as a sailor, outside their window dancing a hornpipe with immense gusto, an accomplishment acquired at Wellington House. George Hogarth was an Edinburgh man, a Writer to the Signet, who had what, even by Victorian standards, would be called 'a long family' comprising fourteen children. Mrs. Hogarth and the elder girls spoke with a Scotch accent. During a discussion on Eve in the Garden of Eden his daughter Catharine is reported to have said, 'Eh,

[1] Rose Drummond, said to be the original for Miss La Creevy in *Nicholas Nickleby*.

mon, it would be nae temptation to me to gae rinning about a gairden stark naked ating green apples.'

Catharine has been described by a woman friend as pretty, plump and fresh-coloured with 'the large heavy-lidded blue eyes so much admired by men'.   A slightly *retroussé* nose, good forehead, red rosebud mouth and receding chin completed a physiognomy which was animated from time to time by a sweet smile.   Daniel Maclise, who was in love with her as a girl, painted a charming portrait before marriage and made two pictures of her as a married woman at the ages of twenty-six and thirty years.

Quiet, silent and unenterprising, Catharine had dull friends, and as she never developed the social gift of discriminating between one person and another essential to intelligent intercourse, she was incapable later on of playing her part as celebrity's wife.   None of these things seemed to matter at the time she married, though in the long run her inadequacy in these respects became a kind of grievance. Charles was not unduly worried by her persistently low spirits, for the warm welcome extended to him by the entire family more than made up for any coolness on her part at this time.   It seems improbable that she was ever really in love, for there is no sign in her of the *élan* proper to young persons in that state.   Early in the engagement, which lasted for about a year, the lover wrote, after spending an evening in her company:

My dear Catherine,

It is with the greatest pain that I sit down before I go to bed to-night, to say one word which can bear the appearance of unkindness or reproach; But I owe a duty to myself as well as to you, and as I am wild enough to think that an engagement of even three weeks might pass without any such display as you have favoured me with twice already, I am the more strongly induced to discharge it.

The sudden and uncalled for coldness with which you treated me before I left last night surprised and deeply hurt me—surprised because I could not have believed that such sullen and inflexible obstinacy could exist in the breast of any girl in whose heart love had found a place; and hurt me because I feel for you far more than I have ever professed, and feel a slight from you more than I can tell.[1]

Kate must often have suffered from depression for we find him writing, 'I hope you will not get low again' and 'you are in better spirits than yesterday I hope?'   Charles had spirits enough for two, but it was uphill work making this lethargic, unimaginative girl understand just how hard he was working and how anxious he was to make their future secure.   'You know that my composition is peculiar . . . and that I never can write till I have got my steam up or . . . until I have become so excited with my subject that I cannot leave off.'   His 'dearest Mouse' and 'dearest Life' is exacting and seems incapable of understanding the claims of his profession.   One night he writes that he must stay at home, he has not produced sufficient copy to justify him in going out.   'If the representations I have so often made to you, be not sufficient to keep you in good humour . . . why then my dear you must be out of humour, and there is no help for it.'   These words, written three weeks before the marriage day, show that Kate had learnt nothing during their long engagement.

Charles had formed for himself an ideal picture of home, of a fireside presided over by a kind and gentle wife, and he thanks God for the many opportunities he will have in the future of showing Kate how unjustly she had judged him, and of convincing her that his pursuits and labours were not selfish and that her advancement and happiness was the mainspring of them all.   When Kate complained of her health he almost snapped, 'I hope your cold is better and that you have no other complaint bodily or mental'.   Surely it should have been proof of devotion enough that her lover should sit with her daily when she took the scarlet fever though he fully believed he could not escape catching it from her, but it was little to her credit that she should have let him run so grave a risk.   In writing of Dickens some authors have accounted

[1] W. Dexter, *Mr. and Mrs. Charles Dickens*, p. 1.

for the final break in the marriage by saying that he married in haste, but, as his letters show, he did not marry in haste. He married after a most deliberate and long-drawn courtship.

As soon as his earnings warranted it, Charles Dickens applied for a special marriage licence which, as every reader of *Pickwick* knows, was to be obtained from the Vicar-General's office in Doctors' Commons. It consisted of a highly flattering address on parchment from the Archbishop of Canterbury to his 'trusty and well-beloved Charles Huffam Dickens and Catharine Hogarth' enabling them to be married at any time or place without banns. Lord Byron in his day had made use of a similar licence in order to avoid a fashionable wedding. The ceremony was fixed for Easter at the vast new parish church of St. Luke, Chelsea. The bridegroom had asked Macrone to be his best man, but this was disallowed by the ladies as he was not a bachelor. In the end Tom Beard took his place. A faintly literary flavour might have been imparted to the occasion had they been married by the rector, Mr. Kingsley (father of Charles), but it was the curate who made them man and wife.

Two days beforehand Dickens wrote to his uncle Thomas Barrow informing him that 'the great success of his new book' (*Sketches by Boz*) enables him 'to settle at an earlier period' than he had anticipated and that his 'marriage to Miss Hogarth, daughter of the author of the celebrated work on music and intimate friend of Sir Walter Scott', had been fixed 'for midday Saturday the 2nd of April'. We note that the cultural aspect of the connection is stressed as if it must impress his uncle favourably. He would, of course, have liked to introduce his wife to his uncle, but how could he 'married or single visit a relation's house from which his father is excluded'? He continues:

> I should be more happy than I could possibly express if you would place it in my power to know you once again on those terms of intimacy and friendship I so sincerely desire, I hope you will not misunderstand my meaning. I do not ask you—I should conceive that I lowered and

disgraced myself if I did—to alter your determination. I might think that time might have softened the determined animosity. . . . I do not presume to arraign your decision. Nothing that has occurred to me in my life has given me greater pain than thus denying myself the society of yourself and aunt.[1]

This letter serves to show that John Dickens was still on the Barrow black list. It is possible that he had borrowed money from them and had never repaid the loan.

The first number of *Pickwick* was published on March 31 and by the evening of April 2 Charles and Kate had arrived at the little slatted house in Chalk near his dream city of Rochester. The honeymoon lasted a week, and Dickens, who did not care about the country for its own sake and had never had a complete holiday before, was restless. He did his best to amuse Kate by turning a 'Sketch' into a play and devising a burletta, but he was glad to get back to Furnival's Inn, glad to begin work on the second number of *Pickwick* and eager to see how Robert Seymour's illustrations were turning out. Tom Beard showed him some of the reviews of the first number: they were neither flattering nor encouraging, in spite of the fact that the *Pickwick Papers* were in every way an advance on the *Sketches*. Confidence in wielding words and characters now enabled their author to produce effects of extraordinary richness and variety. He is sure of his power of differentiation and is not afraid of handling at the same time several people of a kind and in the shortest time individualising them. Take Mrs. Bardell, for example, and her two cronies sitting down to a cosy evening over 'pettitoes and toasted cheese', or Bob Sawyer entertaining his student friends in Lant Street, scenes that go easily. Dickens has become a master of men and can get their common comfort and their fun down on to paper, portraying the kind of enjoyment and humour that will warm the cockles of all hearts. Not, however, till the introduction of Sam Weller in the fifth number (August 1836) did the circulation leap visibly. With

[1] 68. I. N.L.

Sam Weller, the Sancho Panza to Mr. Pickwick's Quixote, England took these *Papers* to her heart for ever. So far Dickens had not become obviously conscious of a mission. This creeps into the texture of the narrative with the Fleet and the deplorable conditions obtaining there. Indeed the whole book takes on a purposeful character after he had experienced a great personal sorrow. As a presentation of the day-to-day life of his age *Pickwick* is perhaps Dickens's greatest achievement.

Robert Seymour's design for *The Stroller's Tale*, 'The Dying Clown', was not to Dickens's liking, so writing a very polite letter he asked him to make another and to bring it completed to Furnival's Inn the following Sunday. He will invite Chapman and Hall to meet him, and together, over a glass of grog, they can discuss further illustrations. Seymour turned up as requested: the publishers did not. Seymour had not met Dickens previously and now found himself shaking hands with Mrs. Dickens and a young brother of his host. As an established illustrator, with *Figaro in London*, *Humorous Sketches* and the *Book of Christmas* to his credit, he was inclined to stand on his dignity and think that he was being treated in an offhand way by a cocky young fellow who was presuming to teach him his business. Dickens tried to be amiable, but his visitor would insist on pointing out that if there were to be no sporting scenes in *Pickwick* a younger and more adaptable artist would perhaps suit Mr. Dickens better. Seymour was but twelve years the senior of the two but spoke as if the disparity in years was considerable. Vainly did Dickens try to conciliate him; Seymour would have none of it, cut the interview short and left. Two days later Frederick, newspaper in hand, rapped at his brother's door to say that Mr. Seymour had been found shot in his Islington garden. It came out later that Seymour, after working at a new design for *The Stroller's Tale*, had committed suicide. Naturally Dickens was shocked by the occurrence, but it was not the kind of tragedy that moved him deeply and he was too busy finding someone to take Seymour's place to worry over it.

John Jackson, wood engraver working for Chapman and Hall, recommended Robert Buss who had 'never had an etching needle in his hand', but his designs for the third number of *Pickwick* did not please at all. He could neither cope with the philandering of Mr. Tupman nor the cricket-match at Dingley Dell. Cruikshank then recommended John Leech, but he was considered too young, and when Thackeray recommended himself with sample drawings by Mr. Michael Angelo Titmarsh tucked under his arm, he also was turned down as unsuitable. In the end Hablot Browne, aged twenty, was produced by Jackson. Dickens took an immediate fancy to him, he became 'Phiz' of the fourth number and was to prove a most congenial partner for 'Boz'.

Work for the *Morning Chronicle* had still to be coped with. A Bill for the stricter observancé of Sunday (sponsored by Sir Andrew Agnew) was reported at this time by Dickens. Edward Bulwer spoke most strongly against the bill, arguing that there was no warrant for Sabbatarianism in Scripture— and that it was anti-Christian and anti-social. Dickens, very much concerned, and fearful lest the Bill pass into law,[1] wrote a pamphlet, *Sunday under Three Heads*, signing it Timothy Sparks.[2] He dedicated it to the Bishop of London who had expatiated on the vicious addiction of the lower classes of society to Sunday excursions, thus showing himself like all the members of both Houses completely out of touch with common life. 'That your lordship could ever have contemplated Sunday recreations with so much horror if you had been at all acquainted with the wants and necessities of the people who indulge in them I cannot imagine possible.' Sunday, he went on to say, has been for many workers a happy day, a day to look forward to. What was wrong with numerous boats standing at river piers to take people out to excursions? Why should they not go off early with their picnic-baskets to Kent and Greenwich, Shooters Hill and Twickenham? What was wrong with opening a few coffee

---

[1] Rejected on third reading by 32 votes.
[2] Chapman and Hall, June 1836.

and food stalls to enable them to fill those baskets? Junketings of the sort in no way interfered with the Sunday observances indulged in by the well-to-do. He has himself watched
carriages with footmen rattle up before the porticoes of St.
Martin, St. George and St. Marylebone: he has seen 'the
powdered minions glide along the aisles and place the prayer-
books in the right pews'. He has waited for the carriages'
return to pick up their smart owners, has observed the
carriage steps being pushed up, the carriage doors shut, and
above all studied the complacent faces of the worshippers
who drive away congratulating themselves on the excellent
example they have set to the lower orders.

Look at this Bill, he says, and see how far the fanatics are
prepared to go. It proposes penalties for keeping shops
open, for travelling on steamboats, attending public meetings
and hiring carriages. It is an egregious specimen of legislative folly. Dickens had always been in favour of opening
museums and galleries and of playing cricket on Sunday
afternoons, for what point could there be in making the only
holiday of the week miserable?

Now that he had definitely made up his mind to give up the
Gallery and live by his pen Charles Dickens accepted almost
anything offered to him in the way of work, including a June
contract from Macrone for a novel at £200 to be ready in six
months. In August, when the *Carlton Chronicle* requested
him to supply a fortnightly 'Sketch' (mentioning, as befitted
the Carlton Club, liberal terms), he agreed to do so, telling
Macrone that the circulation of the *Carlton Chronicle* though
small was 'all among the nobs' and the nobs were the people
who bought books. At this moment, too, he was negotiating
with Thomas Tegg, the well-known Cheapside publisher, for
a child's Christmas book to be called *Solomon Bell: the Raree
Showman*. For this he was to be paid £100. It never
appeared; possibly he had to cancel it when he signed his
agreement with Bentley to edit a new magazine. On July 25
Dickens in a postscript to a letter to Macrone wrote PICK-

WICK TRIUMPHANT. The triumph was so striking that his publishers raised his monthly pay.

Kate Dickens had been brought up in a musical *milieu* and Dickens, through his sister Fanny, who was now on the stage, already knew a good many singers and actors. We have seen him employing his short honeymoon in working for the theatre to amuse Kate, and the result was *The Strange Gentleman*, a stage version of his story *The Great Winglebury Duel*. This farce was followed up by a burletta, *The Village Coquettes*, for which John Hullah supplied the music. The family collaborated in trying music and libretto out on Saturday evening, July 23, at Furnival's Inn 'before a few confidential friends literary and musical'. Macrone was bidden by Dickens in a civil note:

> I intend reading my opera and trying the music next Saturday evening at 7 o'clock. Mrs. Dickens desires me to say that if you will with Mrs. Macrone join the friends who wish to hear it she will be most happy to see you.[1]

The little audience demonstrated its approval and at the end of the first act Macrone offered to purchase the copyright. Dickens half accepted, but on second thoughts wrote:

> Mr. Hullah and I have come to the determination of publishing the books of the songs ourselves. Being required only for distribution in the theatre, they do not require a bookseller's aid.[2]

Publication of the libretto was left open for the time being: the music, however, was disposed of to Cramers for 'a good round sum'.

Mr. and Mrs. Dickens rented a furnished house, Elm Lodge, Petersham, for August 1836. There they had the happiness of being visited by Braham of the newly-built St. James's play-house, 'the most splendid theatre in Europe'. He brought with him his stage-manager Harley; both were enthusiastic about the operetta. Harley wrote, 'It's a sure card: nothing wrong there. Bet you ten pounds it runs fifty nights'. While at Petersham they were flattered at being approached by Richard Bentley, the Savile Row publisher. Bentley offered 'Boz' £500 for the 'entire copyright' of a novel of undetermined title and subject without any time limit for delivery. The author jumped at this offer and signed a contract[1] promising to supply a second novel on the same terms as the first, just as if his engagement to Macrone of two months earlier had entirely slipped his mind. Richard Bentley was on the alert for new writers, for he had recently dissolved partnership with Henry Colburn, who was setting up a rival establishment in Great Marlborough Street and drawing away some of his authors. Jealousy almost amounting to enmity existed between the two men. When Bentley announced that he was about to produce a comic miscellany, or rather a magazine of which humour was to be the leading characteristic, Colburn immediately countered by scheming to produce a similar monthly with Theodore Hook, editor of *The Joker's Magazine*, in control. Hook, who was always in financial straits, accepted the post and an advance of salary, but when Colburn changed his mind about launching a new magazine, he told Hook he must work out the advance he had received on the *New Monthly*, an arrangement that disgusted S. C. Hall since it relegated him to the position of subeditor. Hall resigned and Hook became editor. Eventually the *New Monthly* was sold to Harrison Ainsworth. Bentley meanwhile was completing his plans for *The Wits' Miscellany*, but who to make editor was the puzzle. George Hogarth put forward the name of his son-in-law, 'young Dickens', and young Dickens was appointed.[2] Owing to the threat of Colburn's competition the name *Wits' Miscellany* was changed to *Bentley's Miscellany*, whereupon Barham of *Ingoldsby Legends* fame exclaimed, 'But why go to the other extreme?'

When Mr. and Mrs. Dickens took up residence again at Furnival's Inn they invited Mary Hogarth, a pretty child of

---

[1] August 22, 1836.
[2] Editorship offered November 4, 1836. First issue January 2, 1837.

sixteen, to live with them in their tiny apartment. Kate stayed at home a good deal for she was expecting a baby at Christmas, so Mary went about everywhere with Charles. One day he took her to Macrone's office in St. James's Square which was furnished with busts of 'distinguished men' (including one of Macrone himself and one of John Sadleir, M.P., reputed to have been the model for Mr. Merdle in *Little Dorrit*). These busts had been presented to him by John Strang, the wine-merchant author, who had cultivated his taste by travel in France and Italy. Angus Fletcher, the maker of some of them, was often in the office. Dickens annexed Fletcher at once as a friend and called him 'Kindheart'. All the people with whom Charles brought Mary in contact took a fancy to the girl whose coy appearance covered a keen sense of fun. At New Year 1837 John Strang wrote to Macrone:

> Our acquaintance 'Boz' seems also not to be sleeping. His name appears to irradiate three publishers lists. How does his pretty little sister-in-law get on? She is a sweet interesting creature. I wonder some two-legged monster does not carry her off. It might save many a yonker losing his night's rest.

In looking back on this halcyon autumn Dickens described the way he sat at home working over the fire 'among merry banterings' and basking in 'a sympathy more precious than the applause of the whole world'. How often he felt like trilling 'Home sweet home' as he walked about the streets!

While *The Strange Gentleman* and later on *The Village Coquettes* were in rehearsal, Dickens had to spend a good deal of time in the theatre wrestling with rather absurd difficulties such as the objection of the two Miss Smiths, who were singing in the operetta, to the immodesty of some of the lines.

> A winter's night has its delight,
> Well-warmed to bed they go:
> A winter's day we're blithe and gay
> Snipe-shooting in the snow

was something they really could not bring themselves to voice.

> If the young ladies are specially horrified at the bare notion of anyone going to bed, I have no objection to substitute for the objectionable line, 'Well-warmed to bed they go', 'Around old stories go' [wrote Dickens to John Hullah]. But you may respectfully signify to Cramers that I will see them d——d before I make any further alterations . . . you will see that we ought not to emasculate the very spirit of the song to suit boarding schools.[1]

Madame Sala made such a success of the part of Julia Dobbs and *The Strange Gentleman* ran for so long that the production of *The Village Coquettes* had to be postponed till December 6. The reviews were none too kind. Forster, who was as yet unacquainted with Dickens, was depreciatory in the *Examiner*, and the *Sunday Times*, *Weekly Dispatch* and *Satirist*, 'all', as Dickens put it, 'blow their little trumpets against unhappy me'. It was suggested that the plays would 'blast his reputations as a periodical writer'. Both plays, however, got good notices in the *Carlton Chronicle*; it is just possible that Dickens wrote them himself. Another burletta by 'Boz' was staged at the St. James's Theatre in March 1837, in which Madame Sala and J. P. Harley played. Its name was *Is She his Wife?* and it may have some bearing on the tastes and bickerings of Mr. and Mrs. Charles Dickens themselves, since Mr. Lovetown hates the country with its blooming hedges, feathered songsters and such like, while adoring area railings, dustman's bells and pavements. Mrs. Lovetown loves flowers, country walks and the song of birds and is distressed that her husband should yawn with ennui if taken out of London. The play had but a short run but its copyright was sold to Braham for £100. Dickens lived to be ashamed of his early dramatic experiments as we learn from Frederick Locker Lampson, who once asked him at Gad's Hill whether he possessed a copy of *The Village Coquettes*. 'No,' he retorted; 'if I knew it was in my house and if I could not get rid of it in any other way, I would burn the wing of the house where it was.'

During the autumn Dickens made a second contract with Bentley. He was getting £20 a month for editing the *Miscellany* and now was to receive an extra £2 for the sixteen pages of original matter he was to provide for each number. The agreement ran for twelve months and was renewable by Bentley for three years. The copyright was to be Bentley's absolutely. To 'Boz' this, for-the-time-being, satisfactory arrangement secured for him nearly £500 a year which, added to some £300 a year for *Pickwick*, gave him a feeling of security. In view of the eventual estrangement of Bentley and Dickens it is not uninteresting to note that at this time Bentley thought so well of his new editor as to insist on putting him up for the Garrick Club. And indeed the publisher had every reason to be pleased with his choice.

Bentley's Miscellany was from the first a success. At the end of six months its editor could announce that he was 'inundated' with orders and that all looked well for the future. The contributors, most of whom were friends of Bentley, were Father Prout, Samuel Lover, Theodore Hook, C. Whitehead, Fenimore Cooper, Dr. Maginn, Captain Medwin, Morier the author of *Hajji Baba*, William Jerdan and George Hogarth. It can have required but slight editing and was in every sense of the word easy money both for promoters and contributors. Except for the Dickens serials and *Handy Andy*, little has been found worth reprinting. In the original opening of *Oliver Twist* the workhouse in which he was born was situated in Mudfog; this was deleted later. Dickens had begun *The Public Life of Tulrumble*, its Mayor, in the second number of the magazine and evidently at one moment meant to link Oliver with Mudfog. He also wrote two stray chapters, one on '*Pantomimes*' in which he guys the opening of parliament and the other on '*Lions*' in which he cuts some heavy jokes about literary celebrities at parties.

At last Dickens with over £65 a month assured income felt

himself justified in giving notice to the *Morning Chronicle*, terminating his engagement as a parliamentary reporter. Mr. Easthope, the proprietor, extremely annoyed to receive it, was disposed to suggest that his employee was behaving unfairly, for had he not been paid in advance to supply weekly *Sketches?* Nettled, Dickens replied, 'I shall return the six guineas with the utmost pleasure', and then went on to say how on many occasions at a sacrifice of health, rest and personal comfort, he has done what was always before considered impossible and what in all probability will never be accomplished again. He had been selected for difficult, harassing duty—travelling at a few hours' notice hundreds of miles in the depth of winter—leaving hot and crowded rooms to write, the night through, in a close, damp chaise—tearing along and copying the most important speeches under every possible circumstance of disadvantage and difficulty. He has eclipsed other papers again and again, other papers with double the means, there is not another newspaper office in London where these services have not been watched and appreciated. 'Instead of an appreciatory farewell letter he gets a reminder that he has been overpaid by six guineas!'[1]

Resentment over the behaviour of an employer he had served with all his might, made Dickens feel he had been treated like a servant, and a dishonest servant at that. It confirmed him in his belief that the rich were heartless and had an inveterate tendency to exploit those in their power. Life certainly taught one lessons. Again he set his teeth and determined to ride on. One day he might be able to pay Easthope back in his own coin.

He had no time to waste on recrimination, for the *Pickwick* instalments had to be produced to time. To Chapman and Hall they seemed of unequal merit, and in reply to their complaint that the papers were getting a little tedious Dickens replied:

> You may rest assured that the disease has reached its height and that it will now take a more favourable turn. I

[1] 88-9. I. N.L.

only entreat you to recollect two things—first that I have many occupations; and secondly that spirits are not to be forced up to *Pickwick* level every day. Although, thank God, I have as few worldly cares as most people, you would scarcely believe how often I sit down to begin a number and feeling unequal to the task, do what is far better than writing under such circumstances—get up and wait till I am. . . . If I were to live one hundred years and wrote three novels in each I should never be so proud of any of them as I am of *Pickwick* feeling as I do that it has made its own way and hoping as I must own I do hope, that long after my hand is withered as the pens it held, *Pickwick* will be found on many a dusty shelf with many a better work.[1]

Charles now had domestic affairs as well as serial instalments to worry over. A Christmas baby was expected, and what a first baby means to a young couple has to be experienced to be believed. In the rather cramped chambers of Furnival's Inn a son was born on Twelfth Night 1837. When the mothers of both parents settled in to preside over the birth, Dickens and Mary were obliged to fend for themselves. The ejectment made Charles realise how necessary it was to find a house to live in where upheavals of the kind would not be a regular feature of family life. After all he and Kate might reasonably expect to have a number of children, and a home ought to be a refuge in all domestic crises whether of joy or sorrow as well as an inviolable workshop for the breadwinner. With his sister-in-law Charles went house-hunting and, before getting rid of the Furnival's Inn chambers, took over the lease of a twelve-roomed house in Doughty Street, just north of Gray's Inn, a no-thoroughfare with gates and a liveried watchman at either end in which Sydney Smith had lived when chaplain at the Foundling Hospital hard by. In great spirits Mr. and Mrs. Dickens, the baby and Mary Hogarth moved into this place in April 1837. Mary helped Kate with the baby, and Charles's brother Frederick, aged sixteen, who was too young to live by himself, was also

[1] 86-7 I. N.L.

included in the household.　Mary seemed to grow more lovable and happy every day and certainly showed no symptom
of delicacy.　The little family was thoroughly satisfied and
rejoiced at the space and convenience of its new home.[1]

Charles settled down seriously to work: he was, as we
know, writing *Pickwick* and *Oliver Twist* fortnight and fortnight about.　The mornings he spent in strict solitude in his
study overlooking the tiny back garden: in the afternoons he
went for long walks or, when money became more plentiful,
hired a horse and rode to Epping Forest, Highgate or Richmond.　Many people came and went, including Macready
who had by this time become a close friend.　It is from
Macready's diary that we see how life went on in Doughty
Street.　One day he went there to meet Cattermole, Browne
('Phiz') and Forster and then they all went on to see the House
of Correction in Coldbath Fields.　What were they planning
in that scene of punishment and why did they go straight
from there to Newgate?　In Newgate they saw a man with
long heavy moustaches reading quietly.　Macready gave a
start and exclaimed, 'Good God! there's Wainewright the
poisoner!'　Another man was pointed out to them who was
just about to be hanged for rape.　These sights did not affect
the high spirits of the party, who returned to Doughty Street
for a jolly dinner at which Harley, Hogarth and Maclise's
brother-in-law, Banks, joined them.

One of the visitors at Doughty Street that summer was
young George Lewes, 'a miniature Mirabeau' to George
Eliot, and 'Ape' Lewes to Carlyle.　Dickens had asked him
to call as he was pleased with what he had written about
Pickwick.　It damped Lewes's enthusiasm a little to be set
down in a small study with bookshelves containing nothing
but three-volume novels and books of travel, all obvious
presentation copies.　There were no treasures from the book-
stall, no pick-ups of any kind.　As he observed later, 'I did
not expect to find a bookworm nor even a student in the
marvellous 'Boz', but nevertheless the collection of books was

[1] Leased for three years April 3, 1837.

a shock.' Presently Dickens burst into the room in great spirits and Lewes confessed himself 'more impressed with Dickens's fulness of life and energy than with any sense of distinction'.

There was nothing Dickens enjoyed more than dispensing hospitality unless it was taking his 'petticoats' to the theatre. One evening some seven or eight weeks after the move to Doughty Street, they all came home in tearing spirits from the play. Mary's laugh rippled as she tripped upstairs. Bedroom doors were closed, candles blown out, when suddenly Dickens heard a strange choking cry from Mary's room. Running in he found her struggling for breath; Kate joined him and Frederick was sent for a doctor. Charles held Mary up in his arms, but neither the doctor nor any one of them could save the precious life. It was unbelievable and unbearable to Charles that this angel should be deprived of breath. In an agony he took the ring from her hand and slipped it on his little finger where it remained till his death. The shock to Kate brought on a miscarriage and a happy united family was reduced to mourn the extinguishment of life and hope. It fell to Charles to arrange the 'last dreadful ceremony' in the new cemetery at Kensal Green and to write for little Mary Scott Hogarth (named for Sir Walter) a gentle epitaph.

Young, beautiful, and good, God in His mercy numbered her among his angels at the early age of seventeen.

After the funeral Charles left a note with Ainsworth begging him to arrange for a rose tree to be planted on that early grave, and then carried Kate off 'to the country', to Collins's Farm, North End. He could write no *Pickwick* that month and no *Oliver Twist*, and *Bentley's Miscellany* carried the following notice:

Since the appearance of the last number of this work the editor has to mourn the sudden death of a very dear young relative to whom he was most affectionately attached and whose society has been for a long time the chief solace of his labours.

Collins's Farm, the home of Linnell and the haunt of Blake, still stands. To Dickens a country bolt-hole, to us a strangely secluded, touching relic of the fifteenth century existing as if by a miracle amidst a garrotting crowd of villa-residences. In form it is substantially the same as it was five hundred years ago and the grey match-boarded walls are well screened from passing eyes. A rickety-looking lean-to (a kind of verandah) runs along the front of the house and a huge cherry tree has become incorporated in the angle of the building. Why one should get the sense of great nearness to Dickens in this place is a mystery; but in walking through the narrow door and up the narrow stair to the slanting rooms above he springs to life, as does the pursuing grief from which he fled to this refuge.[1] Here in the rickety lean-to he sat with Forster and Maclise and talked and talked of Mary.

Never did Charles lose the sense of grief caused by Mary's death. In all the descriptions of all the deaths in his novels we get reminders of his suffering, in Little Nell, in Paul Dombey, in Rose Maylie, whom at the last moment he spared, for how could he let Rose die in May when humbler things were glad and gay? May was no time for death; graves were for the cheerless winter, shrouds for the old and the shrunken. Writing with infinite tenderness he said:

> We need be careful how we deal with those about us, when every death carries to some small circle of survivors thoughts of so much omitted and so little done, of so many things forgotten and so many more which might have been repaired.

Hablot Browne helped them through the sad days and persuaded them to venture on the continent. They were away under a fortnight, but there was time to pilot them to Calais

---

[1] The fact that this remarkable relic has been preserved at all is due to the foresight of a distinguished architect who preserved it and some of its land from development.

and arrange for a post-coach to take them to Ghent, Brussels and Antwerp. In Brussels Browne took them to see his friend, Charles Lever, at that time appointed physician to the British Legation, but with no licence to practise among Belgians. This continental trip was a revelation. Charles now knew that he enjoyed meeting foreigners and the plunge into foreign parts woke in him the longing to repeat the experience, a longing that was to lead him later on to live abroad for months together.

By the time he returned home he had, as it were, assimilated Mary's death into his subconsciousness where it lay germinating and enriching his imaginative life. Superficially he was able to enjoy himself again, as a vist to Broadstairs proves. Broadstairs was a favourite playground for the theatrical profession. The Macready and Sala families went there for summer bathing and Dickens's great friends, the Smithsons, had arranged to move there during the hot weather of 1837. Charles and Kate dined with them in London on returning from abroad, and at the dinner was present a certain 'Eleanor P.' (whom we get to know later as Mrs. Christian), the first of the many young women over whom Dickens cast a spell. She was fascinated by 'the power of his eyes'; they looked to her warm grey in repose, and they seemed to light up with a luminous depth of hue as she watched him. When her eyes were 'released by his eyes', she began to see him as a whole. His get-up she did not like; why should he wear so wide a collar and lapel to his surtout? why should it be thrown back to give effect to a vast expanse of white waistcoat? Then his drab trousers and his drab boots with their black patent toe-caps were dreadful, and the flowing locks that emphasised his poetic air were surely an affectation? Why did he let other guests do the talking and sit apparently abstracted and with a rapt preoccupied look? Why did he make no effort to be amusing? When 'Eleanor P.' got to know this preoccupied look better, she knew it meant that he was taking things in 'most comprehensively'.

Smithson was a partner of Tom Mitton and one of Dickens's earliest friends. Mrs. Smithson was the sister of T. J. Thompson, another early friend whom we shall meet on several interesting occasions. Broadstairs that summer was packed with people. The John Dickens', their married daughters and Frederick, were there. When 'Eleanor P.' arrived to stay with the Smithsons she met them all: John Dickens a cork-like optimist, and jolly Mrs. John Dickens who entered heartily into any amusement going. Charles, like one or two other members of the family, spoke as if their tongues were too large for their mouths; Charles's speech in especial had a certain thickness in it. It intrigued this young woman, though it did not surprise her, to find that both the Dickens parents stood a little in awe of their eldest son, his moods being to them so unaccountable. The weather was fine and everyone basked on the sands and played absurd games like 'Animal, Vegetable and Mineral'. Kate Dickens would perpetrate terrible puns with an expression of innocence and deprecation. Charles would assume disgust, she would pout and he would giggle and altogether they behaved like lovers. But this did not prevent him from flirting hard with 'Eleanor P.'

The Tivoli Gardens at Broadstairs were a kind of miniature Vauxhall where people listened to concerts and danced in the evenings. Eleanor would dance in quadrilles there, but 'Boz' stood out, afraid of being recognised. One evening he was watching 'a young Morleena Kenwigs' capering about, when a man, who had been following him, took his stand beside him. Lifting his hat Charles said, 'Are you a native of this place, sir?' 'No, no sir, I am not,' replied the stranger. 'I beg your pardon, I fancied I could detect broad stares upon your face.' So much for his professed horror of puns!

Sheer high spirits inspired Charles to many pranks. Impulsive, erratic Angus Fletcher had joined the party and played the fool as well as any man. On the pier one evening they railed off a space with long benches in which to dance a private quadrille. They called it 'the family pew'. Dickens oved dancing there in the dusk as he escaped recognition by gaping holiday makers. For music he blew upon the comb to Fletcher's whistling and this was all the melody they had. After dancing they would stroll to the end of the pier to watch the tide flooding in. One evening Charles, seemingly bedevilled, flung his arm round 'Eleanor P.'s' waist and whirled her down the inclined plane of the jetty towards a tall upright pole fixed at the extreme end. To this pole he clung with his disengaged arm, declaiming theatrically that he would hold her till the wild waves drowned them both. Eleanor struggled; he held her fast saying, 'Let your mind dwell on the column in the *Times* wherein will be vividly described the fate of the lovely E. P. drowned by D. in a fit of dementia. Don't struggle, poor little bird! You are powerless in the claw of such a kite as this, child!' The water plashed round their knees. 'My dress! my best dress! my only silk dress!' screamed Eleanor. 'Dress,' shouted her captor, 'talk not to me of dress when we already stand on the brink of the great mystery. Am I not immolating a brand new pair of patent leathers still unpaid for? Perish such low-born thoughts! In this hour of abandonment to the voice of destiny, shall we be held back by the puerilities of silken raiment? Shall leather or prunella (whatever that may be) stop the bolt of Fate?'[1]

At length Eleanor managed to free herself and, leaving a watery track behind her, stumbled up the incline in a dress soaked well above the knees. Mrs. Smithson in a displeased voice told her to run home and change. She was both shocked and surprised at her guest's hysterical behaviour.

To Pegwell Bay the same party drove one day in two landaus. Charles had bought a sheaf of ballads from a pedlar and insisted on shouting them all the way there, to the great amusement of the people they passed on the road. On another sunny day they went sailing in a hired boat, and Dickens kept the crew in fits of laughter by roaring 'A reef in your taff-rail! Sheepshank your mizzen! Brail up your

[1] *Temple Bar*, LXXXII.

capstan bar!' In the evenings they sometimes acted charades. For Pompadour (pompadore) Dickens, in a wide brimmed hat pinned up at the side with a long feather, played Louis XV majestically. At one concert they attended, a gentleman sang 'By the sad sea waves', finishing on a high note with an embellishing turn. 'What does that mean?' asked 'Eleanor P.' Dickens flashed back with, 'That's quite the rule in music, as well as in accordance with proverbial philosophy. When things are at their worst they always take a turn.' One day he was discussing *Childe Harold* and took exception to 'Dazzled and drunk with beauty, The heart reels in its fulness' as too suggestive of the beverage (gin and water) which sometimes inspired the poet's high flights. The friend to whom he spoke defended the verses, whereupon Dickens tossed back his hair shouting, 'Stand back, I am suddenly seized with the divine afflatus! Don't disturb me till I have given birth to my inspired conceptions.' Seizing a pencil, he stalked to the window and wrote on the white paint of the shutter:

Lines to E. P., after Byron

O maiden of the amber-dropping hair
May I Byronically thy praises utter?
Drunk with thy beauty, tell me, may I dare
To sing thy paeans borne upon a shutter?

Dickens had an odd trick of sucking his thumbs when thinking, and of worrying at a lock of hair with his left hand. As the result of her experiences and of watching him when he was staring with lustreless eyes at the sea and recognising no one, 'Eleanor P.' became 'horribly' afraid of him. One day she told him this. 'Why, there is nothing to be afraid of about *me*,' he protested. 'Isn't there?' she retorted. 'You look like a forest lion with a shaggy mane on the prowl,

He roared so loud and looked so wondrous grim
His very shadow dare not follow him.'

Dickens laughed. 'What? do you play shadow to my lion? Nay then, as Bottom the Weaver says,

I will aggravate my voice so that I will roar you as gently as any sucking dove.'

Never again was 'Eleanor P.' to see him in this hilarious, care-free mood. When they met in London a year or two later he had changed and seemed both preoccupied and self-important.

During the autumn of 1837 Dickens worked hard at *Oliver Twist* and edited the *Memoirs of Grimaldi*; at least he wrote the preface and dictated the book to his father from the narrative compiled by Egerton Wilks. It seemed to him great twaddle, but his father enjoyed the work and Cruik-shank's illustrations were satisfactory. The commission brought with it the useful fee of £300.

One of the serious interests of the spring of 1837 had been Serjeant Talfourd's Copyright Bill the provisions of which he had talked over in detail with Dickens. Its aim was to safe-guard the rights of an author in his own work for sixty years. As things stood books could hardly be classed as property in the real sense of the word, as all rights expired at death and during life there was no protection against piracy. The classic example of hardship was Scott, whose bankruptcy might have been averted had the French and American publishers given him a share in the profits they amassed by the sale of his books. But it must be admitted that the firms of Galignani in Paris and Cary in Philadelphia behaved no worse in this respect than the less reputable publishers of London. Even Dickens, when he brought an action against a firm for pirating *A Christmas Carol*, though technically he won his case, had to pay such heavy costs that he determined never to hunt pirates again. Talfourd's Bill was thrown out in October 1837 and in the same month Dickens received a letter from an American publisher[1] offering him a small bonus from the profits derived by them from sales of his works. He refused it, possibly because Talfourd thought it better that he should take his stand with other authors in demanding as a

[1] October 26, 1837.

right what was now being offered as a gratuity. While declining to accept any money present for *Pickwick*, he stated that he would be willing to enter into an arrangement with Messrs. Cary to transmit early proofs of *Oliver Twist* and *Barnaby Rudge* should the firm consider it desirable.

Dickens dedicated *Pickwick* to Serjeant Talfourd in recognition of his services to authors and wrote:

> If I had not long enjoyed the happiness of your private friendship, I should still have dedicated this work to you, as a slight and most inadequate acknowledgment of the inestimable services you are rendering the literature of your country, and of the lasting benefits you will confer upon the authors of this and succeeding generations by securing to them and their descendants a permanent interest in the copyright of their works. . . . Accept the dedication of this book, my dear sir, as a mark of my warmest regard and esteem, as a memorial for the most gratifying friendship I have ever contracted, of some of the pleasantest hours I have ever spent, and as a token of my fervent admiration of every fine quality of your head and heart.

It was a handsome testimonial, but no more than Serjeant Talfourd merited. Copyright was a cause Dickens had very much at heart and we shall see that his outspokenness in America on this subject roused the greatest personal animosity against him and made a comparative failure of what should have been a triumphal tour.

Chapter 6

JOHN FORSTER

What a thing friendship is, world without end!
ROBERT BROWNING

WHEN Charles Dickens first met the man who was to be his close friend and eventual biographer, John Forster, his reputation was already considerable. We may, in reading Forster's *Life of Dickens*, get the impression that the author acted as *compère* to his hero though this was not in fact the relationship, since by the time the two young men of twenty-five met, Dickens had already published the *Sketches*, an operetta, a play, was writing monthly instalments of *Pickwick*, was booked to write two novels for Bentley, and had been appointed editor of a new Miscellany. All of which goes to show that he was not in need of any man's patronage.

Two months younger than Dickens, John Forster had the manner of a mature business man. Son of a northern cattle-dealer, he did brilliantly at Newcastle Grammar School and was fired by a passion for literature as real as Talfourd's. In coming to London in 1830 he had attached himself to S. C. Hall, editor of the *New Monthly Magazine*, with whom he dined weekly. Later on he dropped Hall, who said of him, 'I found him a friend when he needed me, but not a friend when I needed him'.

Forster began his literary career as theatrical critic on the *True Sun* and in this way got to know Sheridan Knowles, Barry Cornwall, W. J. Fox, Edward Bulwer, Maclise and Macready. He then became colleague on the *Examiner* of the brilliant Albany Fonblanque whom he eventually succeeded as editor. It was while working for the *Examiner* that he received a 'My dear Sir' letter from Charles Dickens accompanied by the book of *The Village Coquettes* just published by Bentley. A few days later they met face to face under

Harrison Ainsworth's roof. In a way it is odd that they had not come across each other earlier, as it was Forster's hobby to get to know every scribbler in London. Macready used to say that Forster was sycophantic in his approach to the literary figures of his day, but Macready picked holes in most people and was unfair to a man who did his best to be of service to authors and tirelessly pushed the books he admired. The first critic, except W. J. Fox of the *Monthly Repository*, to appreciate Browning's quality, he, in 1836, was already badgering Ainsworth to get *Sordello* published and Macready to produce *Strafford*. Landor, Carlyle and Tennyson came to hold Forster in high regard and he was to prove a useful friend to all of them. His unadvertised finger was in many a literary pie and it was reward enough for him if his manipulations turned to the advantage of the author concerned. He is best known to posterity as Dickens's Boswell.

It is through John Forster's biography that we get to know Dickens; in fact till the Nonesuch *Letters* were published, it was the only way we could get to know him except by reading his books and some expurgated letters edited by members of the family.

Everyone of the day testifies to Forster's unflagging interest in writers. He was helpful to Lady Blessington over manuscripts and so kind to L. E. L. over her poems that men assumed he must be going to marry her. Bluff in manner, he was rather apt to talk people down even at their own tables, but it was generally agreed that by nature he was 'a block of gold', which possibly means that he was without the alloy of self-interest and was thoroughly dependable. Rosina Bulwer hated him and said his manner was a bad understudy of Macready's. In her novel *Cheveley* she caricatured him as Fuz-Buz, 'a very ugly noseless likeness of a great tragedian whom he tried to imitate even to his handwriting . . . a sort of lick-dust to Mr. Fonnoir (Fonblanque) and to Mr. Anybody and everybody else to whom he could gain access.[1] It was he who did the theatrical plasterings in the "Investigator"

[1] p. 115.

. . he being a perfect Boreas at a puff.' Other less cruel
observers, including Espinasse, confirm Forster's habit of
imitating Macready and tell how he would stride into a room
with his hand on his heart and a stock phrase on his lips such
as 'It is with infinite regret', or 'Believe me I feel it sensibly'.
Sturdily built, with fresh complexion, dark hair and what
was called a 'stentorian' voice, he made a rather bullying
impression on most people. In drawings by Cruikshank,
Browne and others one sees John Forster as a stocky man
tightly buttoned up in a short frock-coat, twiddling a monocle
in one hand and looking as if he were sitting in judgment on
the follies of his friends. Dickens, who was supposed to stand
a little in awe of him, used to call him 'the Lincolnian mam-
moth', and Douglas Jerrold, picking up a pencil stump, said
it was like Forster, 'short, thick and full of lead'. When
Our Mutual Friend came out, some people recognised a
portrait of Forster in Podsnap, 'the Mr. Podsnap who was
well-to-do and stood very high in Mr. Podsnap's opinion'.
Mrs. Lynn Linton, usually uncharitable about authors, said
he was 'pompous, cynical and jealous', and snapped at the
chance when his *Life of Landor* came out of reviewing it
venomously. On the other hand Lady Blessington told
Landor that he was 'a noble-minded man'. Carlyle, though
at first put off by his manner, came to feel affectionately towards him and, copying Rosina Bulwer, nicknamed him
'Fuz'. 'Fuz' was for ever quarrelling with those he most
admired and imperilling their relations. Dickens was no
exception and their friendship was on several occasions on the
edge of rupture. In August 1840 for example Macready
records a dinner at Devonshire Terrace at which 'a most painful' scene occurred. Forster embarked on 'one of his headlong streams of talk (which he thinks argument) and waxed
warm. . . . His sharp observations led to personal retorts with
Dickens.' Forster was so tactless and overbearing that his
host flew into a violent passion and told his guest he would be
glad if he would leave the house. Mrs. Dickens ran out of
the dining-room in tears and for some angry moments it

looked as if an association valuable to them both was about to be destroyed. James Payn tells us that many people, including himself, could not understand Dickens's feeling for Forster. 'I have rarely seen them together without witnessing some sparring between them, sometimes without the gloves.' Forster would pay compliments to the Inimitable in a patronising way which Dickens would acknowledge in the drollest manner. In 1847 the friendship again was on the verge of collapse. Forster dining with Macready spoke as if it were almost at an end, but somehow things righted themselves and intercourse persisted, which may be a tribute to something rare in the quality of Forster. Dickens used to say rather plaintively, 'I don't quarrel with my other friends'.

Forster never cared at all about Ainsworth and mentions his name but five times in his *Life of Dickens* and these are incidental, unavoidable allusions. Possibly Forster was jealous of the part Ainsworth had played in introducing 'Boz' to his first publisher and first illustrator. Ainsworth to him was a very boring third party 'who shared with us incessantly for three years in the companionship begun at his house'. 'Boz', 'Fuz' and Ainsworth used to ride together and sometimes spend week-ends in each other's company, but we are left in no doubt that Forster would far rather have been alone with Dickens.

The possessiveness of Forster manifested itself in rather tiresome ways. He treated Mrs. Dickens as a cypher and took no pains to ingratiate himself with her. Not only did he seem suspicious of all Dickens's friends and anxious to be his one and only confidant, but he tried to exercise proprietary, almost patent, rights over his latest literary discovery. Dickens, who was not at this time very business-like, was tremendously impressed by Forster's competence and at once fell to discussing with him the business side of authorship. In the intoxication of initial success, one can explain it by no rational process, Dickens had signed contracts with three publishers, Macrone, Bentley and Chapman and Hall. He was beginning to be worried by what he had done and was only too thankful to unburden his mind to so sympathetic and experienced a person.   As he talked to Forster in rather an aggrieved way about the boggle he was in, Forster realised that it was all of his own contriving and that the over-eager author wanted rescuing from himself quite as much as from the over-eager publishers!   What was bothering Dickens most was a novel he had promised to Macrone which was already long overdue.   Why had he promised it?   He didn't quite know now, but he had been grateful at the time and only too glad to accept the £200 offered.   He had committed himself in writing, perhaps Forster should see a copy of the letter he had sent to John Macrone.   He had actually signed his name to the following undertaking:

> I shall have great pleasure in accepting from you the sum of £200 for the first edition of a work of Fiction (in three volumes of the usual type) to be written by me and to be entitled *Gabriel Vardon, the Locksmith of London*, of which not more than 1000 copies are to be printed.   I also agree to your printing an extra number of copies, if it should appear desirable; on condition that the profits therefrom, all expenses being first deducted, be divided between us.   I also understand that the before-mentioned £200 are to be paid by you on delivery of the entire manuscript on or before the 30th day of November next, or as soon after as I can possibly complete it by your acceptances at such dates as may be acceptable to both of us.[1]

Was it possible to annul this obligation? he asked earnestly. Forster thought not, contracts were binding in law, but he would first like to hear how he stood with regard to publishers generally, so Dickens proceeded to give an account of commitments which were both numerous and conflicting.   In the first place, he had sold the original series of *Sketches by Boz* to Macrone for £150 and had just handed in another series for which he had received £150 on account.[2]   In the second

[1] 71-2.   I.   N.L.
[2] In a letter to Mitton (1839) he states that he got £400 in all for these books.

place, as he had just explained to Forster, he had agreed to write a novel for the same publisher; this was only partly written and overdue. In the third place, he had contracted to supply Chapman and Hall with a monthly *Sketch* at fourteen pounds a number to be published under the title of the *Pickwick Papers*: this he was in process of fulfilling. In the fourth place, he had signed an agreement with Bentley[1] to supply one novel for £500 and a second on the same terms. In the fifth place, he had accepted the post of editor of *Bentley's Miscellany*[2] which involved supplying sixteen pages of original matter for each issue, and over this Bentley was inclined to be shabby, deducting half-pages and counting up lines. Was it possible for any human being working day and night to fulfil these undertakings? 'Why,' as he protested, 'Sir Walter Scott himself could not have coped with them!' Something would have to be scrapped; what should it be? Forster listened carefully, but did not at once give his opinion. Dickens went on talking. No one could have any idea how worried he was or how it destroyed his pleasure in his success to see in the second series of *Sketches*, published a few days earlier, an announcement of *Gabriel Vardon*, 'a new novel by Boz to be issued in three volumes'. Hurriedly he had stopped further advertisements from appearing in *Bentley's Miscellany* and in the monthly number of *Pickwick*. He was so scared that he had asked Thomas Hansard, the printer of the second series of *Sketches*, whether there was any loophole of escape. Hansard, who was probably at this time financing Macrone, had said 'No', and told him plainly that having agreed to furnish a novel for £200 he must do his best to fulfil his contract. Macready had expressed the same opinion. As a last resort he had then approached Macrone direct and begged him to let him off his bargain. But no move of his could dispel the nightmare.

The case of 'Boz' was decidedly more complicated than anything Forster had hitherto tackled for any protégé. It required a great deal of consideration before he could see his

[1] August 22, 1836.   [2] November 4, 1836.

way to intervene with effect. Meanwhile, he assured his new client that he would take over all his proof-correcting as this would give him more time for writing. Finding Forster too deliberative for his now frantic mood, Dickens fell back on his old friend Tom Mitton. Mitton was shrewd, Mitton knew the legal ropes and Mitton had a real desire to help him. Neither Dickens nor Mitton knew something that we know which may have stiffened the attitude of both Macrone and Hansard, and that is that a trusted friend was behaving in an unfriendly way. At least this is how one may interpret a letter from the legally trained Ainsworth to Macrone which seems to show greater loyalty to his publisher than to a fellow author:

> I write in strictest confidence and I trust to your honour as a gentleman not to quote me, or to shew this letter. I now write I say to advise you to place the matter between Mr. Dickens and yourself immediately in legal hands. Your reply to him ought simply to have been—My dear Dickens, In reply to your note I beg to state that *I shall hold you to your agreement.* Nothing more. . . . I hope you have agreements both for the 'Sketches' and the 'Novel'. I fear the latter does not fix any time for its appearance. But get legal advice at once, and I pray of you to write no more hasty letters in which you commit yourself more than you imagine. Mr. Dickens clearly has no right to destroy his agreement, but this information will be much better conveyed to him by a solicitor.[1]

It may be presumed that Macrone, acting on Ainsworth's advice, informed Dickens that he held him to his agreement. Maddened by the shackles he had wound round himself, Dickens, without consulting anyone, rushed off to Thomas Hansard saying he would waive all claim for ever on the *Sketches* for the return of the *Gabriel Vardon* contract. Mitton then stepped in to regularise matters and regained for Dickens possession of the agreement.

The return of the novel-contract pacified the excited author

[1] January 2, 1837.

for the moment, but he soon worked himself up over a new scare. Friends told him that Macrone was 'making thousands' out of the *Sketches* he had so impatiently surrendered. That was irritating enough, but his binder told him something worse, that Macrone, who had watched the sensational rise in sales of *Pickwick*[1] in its green paper covers, was about to issue all the *Sketches* got up in green covers to look precisely like *Pickwick*. Dickens was so positive that this manœuvre would not only damage his own character with Chapman and Hall, but prejudice the sales of *Pickwick*, that he entreated John Forster to try and dissuade Macrone from carrying out his plan. Forster agreed to do what he could. Macrone, however, flatly refused to meet 'Boz' in the matter, saying that the copyright was his and that he could do what he liked with his own. Forster, at the muzzle of this legal pistol, then asked what he would take for the copyright and he rapped out, 'Not a penny less than £2000'. When reporting to Dickens Forster advised him to let the matter rest, but Dickens in a state bordering on hysteria flew round to Chapman and Hall and urged them to come to terms with Macrone forthwith. The publishers were sympathetic, went into the matter at once and advised Dickens, to his great relief, that 'even at this large price of £2000, we might, besides retaining the copyright, reasonably hope for a good profit on the outlay'. They would buy the copyright for the sum named and themselves issue the *Sketches* in parts. Dickens, of course, would have to stand security for their purchase, but this was easy to arrange; they would just retain the profits from *Pickwick* for five years, and at the end of that period the author might share in them. Furthermore they bound him down to write a similar book in twenty monthly instalments at £150 a month, the copyright of which would belong to Chapman and Hall for five years and then revert to the author. By this arrangement Dickens was assured of a regular income wherewith to support a family and he was not obliged to forfeit the ultimate benefit of the copyright.

[1] 400 copies of first, and 40,000 of fifteenth number sold.

Hardly was the business settled between Macrone and Chapman and Hall than Macrone died suddenly—leaving his wife in very poor circumstances. Dickens, full of regrets, edited *The Pic-Nic Papers* for the benefit of the widow, contributing thereto *The Lamplighter's Story*. As a result £300 were handed to Mrs. Macrone.

The real trouble between Dickens and his publishers was that the market price of his work was rising so fast as to make a contract of a year or even six months earlier appear a swindle. The agreements were certainly not swindles at the time they were made; they were inelastic cash-down contracts, and it drove Dickens nearly mad to think that he was the only person not to profit by the rapidly increasing popularity of his books. In 1835 he was glad to take £200 for a novel. Two months after agreeing with Bentley to let him have the *Barnaby Rudge* copyright for three years for £700, he got paid £3000 by Chapman and Hall for five years' copyright of *Nicholas Nickleby*.

Dickens had no peace of mind or joy in his work because he was so worryingly conscious that his books were 'enriching everyone connected with them' except himself. And this was literally true. The *Sketches* had enriched Macrone, *Pickwick* was enriching Chapman and Hall, and now *Oliver Twist* in the *Miscellany* was enriching Bentley, and all the while the creator of this great body of original work, the maker of their profits, was being paid what he considered a most inadequate share of those profits.[1] Must publishers, he wondered, always drink their wine out of authors' skulls?

Let us look for a moment at Dickens's relations in 1836–7 with Bentley, the publisher he was so soon to refer to as 'the Brigand of Burlington Street'. Bentley was his friend when he published *The Village Coquettes*: Bentley was still his friend when, after reading the first five numbers of the *Pickwick Papers*, he decided to back his opinion of their excellence by offering the young author £500 for a novel with no time fixed for delivering the manuscript. Dickens had been so

[1] See footnote 1 on following page.

pleased at the time that he promised him a second novel on the same terms[2] and Bentley was so pleased with 'Boz' that he put him up for the Garrick Club. Bentley was still a friend when he offered Dickens the editorship of his new *Wits' Miscellany*,[3] and dined him and his contributors, Moore, Lever, Barham, Ainsworth and Marryat, in the cosy 'red room' in New Burlington Street: still a friend when three months later he raised his pay by giving him a direct interest in sales. This concession, though it was almost forced on him by the immense vogue of *Oliver Twist*, was thought at the time to be generous. It would have paid Bentley to be a great deal more generous. If he had not been purblind and mean of soul, the partnership would not have collapsed. As things were, Charles resigned editorship of the *Miscellany* at the ninth number and was only induced to oblige Mr. Bentley further by another rise in salary and an increase of £200 on the second of the contracted novels. The friendship seemed to be warming up again when Bentley asked Dickens to edit the *Memoirs of Grimaldi* for which he offered an advance of £300 and half profits on sales. Though the *Miscellany* prospered exceedingly one is conscious that some disturbing influence

[1] SUMMARY OF INCOME NOVEMBER 1837–JUNE 1841
Extracted from an account book by permission of the late
Mr. Walter Dexter

From	To	Receipts			Expenditure			Balance in Bank		
		£	s.	d.	£	s.	d.	£	s.	d.
Nov. 20, 1837	Dec. 31, 1837	559	10	0	257	18	8	301	11	4
Jan. 1, 1838	June 24, 1838	1297	4	0	1453	8	6	145	6	10
June 25 ,,	Dec. 31, ,,	1271	5	0	1318	13	4	97	18	6
Jan. 1, 1839	June 24, 1839	1915	5	0	1920	9	11	92	13	7
June 25 ,,	Dec. 31, ,,	2244	8	0	1759	14	1	577	7	6
Jan. 1, 1840	June 24, 1840	700	0	0	1304	9	6	27	2	0
June 25 ,,	Dec. 31 ,,	1765	0	0	1510	9	6	227	8	6
Jan. 1, 1841	June 24, 1841	1435	6	7	1626	3	8	36	11	5
June 25 ,,	Oct. 28 ,,	948	1	7	940	11	7	44	1	5

[2] August 22, 1836. [3] November 4, 1836.

was at work, for the more it prospered the more Dickens moped. His suppressed resentment against his employer finally took shape as a real grievance.[1] He had talked to Kate, he had talked to Forster, he had talked to Macready: all sympathised with him and told him he was badly used. Why should he not demand a show-down? Why should he not challenge Bentley to produce the accounts of the *Miscellany*? If it was doing as well as he believed it to be doing, there could be no possible excuse for pinching over half-pages and other irritating economies. It was at this point that Forster took charge of the situation, and we know that in the opinion of Chapman and Hall he was 'a remarkable intermediary' occupying a unique position between patron and literary agent. A letter written to Bentley at this time, which is not in Dickens's style though signed by him, seems proof of his well-timed intervention.

Forster had evidently advised Dickens not to give way to disgust and bad temper, but to go on with the *Miscellany*. If it could be arranged, the serial *Oliver Twist* should be followed by the half-written book *Gabriel Vardon*, now re-named *Barnaby Rudge*. In other words, if Bentley could be persuaded to forgo *Barnaby Rudge* as a novel and allow it to appear as a serial in the *Miscellany*, it would simplify Dickens's problem of production. He would draft a letter for Dickens to send. The author was in a fairly strong position, for the *Memoirs of Grimaldi*, alluded to in this document, had just been completed.

The letter ran as follows:

I have been recently thinking a great deal about *Barnaby Rudge*. Grimaldi has occupied so much of the short interval I had between the completion of *Pickwick* and the commencement of the new work, that I see it will be wholly impossible for me to produce it by the time I had hoped, with justice to myself or profit to you. What I wish you to consider is this: would it not be far more to your interest as well as within the scope of my ability, if *Barnaby Rudge* began in the *Miscellany* immediately on the conclusion of *Oliver Twist* and were continued there for some time, and then published in three volumes? Take these simple facts into consideration. If the *Miscellany* is to keep its ground, it must have some continuous tale from me when *Oliver* stops. If I sat down to *Barnaby Rudge* writing a little of it when I could, it would be clearly impossible for me to begin a new series of papers in the *Miscellany*. The conduct of three different stories at the same time, and the production of a large portion of each every month would have been beyond Scott himself. Whereas having *Barnaby* for the *Miscellany* we could at once supply the gap which the cessation of *Oliver* must create, and you would have all the advantage of that prestige in favour of the work which is certain to enhance the value of *Oliver Twist* considerably. Just think of this at your leisure. I am really anxious to do the best I can for you as well as for myself and in this case the pecuniary advantage must be all on your side.[1]

The answer to this letter is not available, but we do know that John Forster was able to arrange with Bentley that *Barnaby Rudge* should be serialised in the *Miscellany* on the conclusion of *Oliver Twist* in April 1839.

John Forster probably thought he had settled things up in a very satisfactory way, but there was always Dickens's temperament to be reckoned with. Having once begun to dislike and distrust Bentley, Dickens went on disliking and distrusting him. No mere contract could allay his resentment. The relationship was just intolerable to him and no matter at what cost he must end it. Bentley was 'a nefarious rascal who expected to publish serials for his own benefit and authors to acquiesce in toiling to make him rich'. One cannot help suspecting that Ainsworth, of whom Dickens was seeing a great deal, may have been working behind the scenes to promote friction. He had written an odd letter, as we have seen, to Macrone over *Gabriel Vardon*, and is said to have written similar letters to Bentley over *Barnaby Rudge*.

[1] 159. I. N.L.

Although Ainsworth professed sympathy with Dickens in his woes it may have had the effect of aggravating him still further, and we must not forget that in his dealings with Bentley Ainsworth was angling for the reversion of the editorship of the *Miscellany*.

A day came when Dickens had to tell Forster that he simply could not force himself to work for Bentley any longer.

> The immense profits *Oliver* has realised to its publisher and is still realising: the paltry, wretched miserable sum it brought to me . . . the consciousness that I have still the slavery and drudgery of another work on the same journeyman terms;—that I am struggling in old toils and wasting my energies in the very height and freshness of my fame, and the best part of my life, to fill the pockets of others, while for those nearest and dearest to me I can realise but little more than a genteel subsistence . . . I do most solemnly declare that morally before God and man I hold myself released. . . . This net that has been wound about me, so chafes me, so exasperates and irritates my mind, that to break it at whatever cost is my constant impulse.[1]

He took the plunge and relinquished the *Miscellany*. To Talfourd he wrote, 'You will be glad to hear I have burst the Bentleian bonds'.

In the last number he edited, that of February 1839, he inserted a 'farewell to a child two years and two months old'. Everyone, including Dickens, now seemed pacified, but by April, soon after he had handed the editorship of the *Miscellany* over to Ainsworth, 'Boz' had become feverishly anxious to get altogether 'out of the clutches of Bentley'. Appealing once again to Chapman and Hall to rescue him, he, with Forster's help, persuaded them to buy all rights in *Oliver Twist* for £2250 with the annulment of the *Barnaby Rudge* contract thrown in. At last his affairs were being straightened out: he had now eliminated two of his publishers and had Chapman and Hall alone to reckon with.

[1] 196. I. N.L.

Chapter 7

SCHOOLS AND FACTORIES

*To leave one's hand upon the time, with one tender touch for
the mass of the toiling people that nothing could obliterate,
would be to lift oneself above the dust of all the Doges.*

CHARLES DICKENS

A BEING so capable of lightning adjustment to circumstances calling out height or depth of feeling is a puzzling
person to write about, for what is true at one moment becomes untrue the next. As anguish over the death of Mary
alternates with bubbling jubilation over the sweeping success
of *Pickwick*, one stands back astonished at both the depth and
the elasticity of temperament displayed. The same man who
could sit immobile in his study in front of Mary's picture
mourning as if he could not be comforted, would a few hours
later preside over a book-banquet or dance delightedly at a
party. Kate Dickens's friends thought she 'bore sweetly'
with her husband's romantic adoration of Mary, but she, like
ourselves, must have been aware that every experience in turn
was absolute and intoxicated him more or less. His temperament cannot be accounted for; it is only possible to state how
it operated. Kate Dickens, in fact, was not much concerned
by his changes of mood; she was indolent by nature and disposed in any case to let things take their course and not attempt
to control them.

Increasing fame now obliged Dickens to provide portraits
for the press, so during the autumn of 1837 he gave sittings in
Doughty Street to George Cruikshank who was touchy and
would not let him see callers while he was doing his work.
He also sat to his friend and admirer Samuel Laurence and
arranged that he should also paint Kate, insisting on a business
contract 'as if we were strangers. This being so I shall
consign her to you as often as you think proper.' To the
subject of portraits we shall return presently.

Baby Charles, now almost a year old, was christened in December 1837 at 'New Pancridge' church at the east end of Euston Square, a building modelled on the Erechtheum. In its tomb-like, almost windowless interior did Miss Burdett Coutts promise, on the infant's behalf, to renounce the world, the flesh and the devil. At the evening christening party Edward Chapman, the William Halls, the S. C. Halls and the relations drank to the health of the first-born, who went through his ordeal fractiously. Measles supervening two days later, entertaining in Doughty Street ceased for a short while, and Dickens immersed himself in *Oliver Twist*. After Christmas he got down to work on *Sketches of Young Gentlemen*,[1] a windfall contract for £125 that did not oblige him to reveal his identity. Mr. and Mrs. Chirrup, *The Nice Little Couple*, in this series are taken from Mr. and Mrs. William Hall, and their bachelor friend from Hall's partner, Edward Chapman. A letter to Ainsworth of this date shows just how much work had to be got out of the way before Charles could permit himself to go for a short holiday. Inviting his friend to dinner he wrote:

> Little Hall and his wife and big partner are going to dine here on Saturday next at half-past five. . . . The illustrious George [Cruikshank] and his stout lady are coming too so that the anti-Bores will be triumphant and keep the Bores in due subjection. . . . My month's work has been dreadful, *Grimaldi*, the anonymous book for C. and H., *Oliver* and the *Miscellany*. They are all done thank God! and I start on my pilgrimage to the cheap schools of Yorkshire (a mighty secret of course) next Monday morning.[2]

The journey to Yorkshire was being made (in company with the illustrator, Hablot Browne), to gather material for *Nicholas Nickleby*. The 'cheap schools', as Dickens called them, had been on his mind for some time. They advertised regularly in the London papers as teaching Latin, Greek, French, Mathematics and Navigation. Why they clustered

---

[1] Chapman and Hall, 1838. Followed by *Sketches of Young Couples* 1840.   [2] 154. I. N.L.

in Yorkshire is not known, but there were four of these schools in Bowes alone as the burial records show, one at Barnard Castle, and another at Startforth near by. To visit them without awakening suspicion the investigator travelled under an assumed name, taking with him a formal letter from C. Smithson, 'a London attorney', to R. Barnes, 'a Yorkshire attorney', at Barnard Castle. The letter, a plausible one, explained that he was acting for a widowed friend who wanted to place her boys at school in the neighbourhood. In good faith Barnes provided two introductions to local schoolmasters and then, repenting him of his action, walked across to the King's Head to tell the stranger that these schools were sad places for mothers to send orphan boys to. 'It really would be better', he said, 'to let them run errands, hold horses, or fling themselves in any way upon the mercy of the world than consign them to such dens.' The stranger, who had been gazing out on the market-place from the coffee-room window, had noted with interest that a clockmaker's shop with the name 'Master Humphrey' stood across the way. When he had listened to Mr. Barnes's kindly warnings, he stepped over to see Master Humphrey and hear what he had to say about local schools. What a good name for a clockmaker, to be sure: like many other half-conscious observations it sank into his memory to bob up again one day in the title of a book.

Introduction in hand Dickens went to Bowes Academy, kept by a Mr. Shaw who advertised regularly in the *Times* and had a London agent. One of the features of his curriculum was 'no vacations', which in practice meant that it was only boys unwanted by parents and guardians who were put in his charge. This gave the master unlimited power, for no boy could tell during the holidays what life at school was like, nor could he, since letters were read, appeal to any outsider for help. Though Dickens protested that he had no particular school in mind, his readers assumed that Squeers of Dotheboys Hall was taken from Shaw of Bowes Academy, a man who had had a case brought against him six years earlier for gross neglect and starvation of boys entrusted to his care.   The verdict having gone against him, he had been forced to be more circumspect in his ways.

To the atmosphere of Bowes Academy Dickens reacted as if stung, it put him in a fever to get down to work; so hurrying back to London he began on February 6 to write *Nicholas Nickleby*.   By February 9 the first number was complete, and at this book and at *Oliver Twist* he slaved, turn and turn about, for the next eight months.   All Dickens's novels came out serially in 20 parts, and were, with three exceptions, roughly the same length, averaging 350,000 words apiece.   If he had but one book on the stocks, his method of working was to write hard for a fortnight, then knock off and do something different.   In this way he prevented himself from becoming stale and was always eager to get down to the story again.   When he was writing two serials at the same time he played one off against the other and had no leisure at all.

By the end of October 1838 he was so tired from overwork that he did not attend even to private correspondence: letters would lie for a month unopened on his desk.   As soon as *Oliver Twist* was off his hands, he felt he must escape from his study, so taking seats on the Leamington coach he set off again with Hablot Browne to sight-see in Warwickshire. Having just joined the Shakespeare Society run by Payne Collier, he made a point of acquainting himself with Stratford-on-Avon.   He also went to Kenilworth, with which place he was so charmed that he told Kate they really must get lodgings there for their next summer outing.   Warwick Castle, 'an ancient building lately restored and possessing no very great attraction beyond a fine view and some beautiful pictures', did not interest him at all.   Deep down in him, however, something else was being registered that only came to the surface eight years later when Mrs. Skewton, her daughter Edith, Major Bagstock and Mr. Dombey made the same tour. Dickens certainly took no notes at the time; it does not seem that he ever took notes of what he saw at any time, but in this instance we can observe his mind doing its peculiar work of transmuting what seem to be on the surface commonplace impressions into a distillation of an exquisitely humorous character. The subconscious mind had selected its material strictly, taking the party to Kenilworth and Warwick, but not to Stratford. It was on Warwick that it had fixed itself to our great benefit.

'The Castle is charming,' said Mrs. Skewton, 'associations of the Middle Ages and all that—which is so truly exquisite. Don't you dote upon the Middle Ages, Mr. Carker?'

'Very much indeed,' said Mr. Carker.

'Those darling bygone times, Mr. Carker, with their delicious fortresses and their dear old dungeons and their delightful places of torture and their romantic vengeances and their picturesque assaults and sieges and everything that makes life truly charming. How dreadfully we have degenerated.'

'Yes, we have fallen off deplorably,' said Mr. Carker.

. . . .

'We have no faith left positively,' said Mrs. Skewton. . . . 'We have no faith in the dear old Barons, who were the most delightful creatures, or in the dear old priests, who were the most warlike of men—or even in the days of that inestimable Queen Bess, upon the wall there, which were so extremely golden. Dear creature! she was all heart and that charming father of hers; I hope you dote on Harry the eighth?'

'I admire him very much,' said Carker.

'So bluff,' cried Mrs. Skewton, 'wasn't he? so burly. So truly English. Such a picture, too, he makes, with his dear little peepy eyes, and his benevolent chin!'

After this digression we must follow Dickens to north Wales which he reached by way of Birmingham and Shrewsbury, travelling through 'miles of cinder paths and blazing furnaces and steam engines—a mass of dirt and misery'. And these glimpses of an industrial world will, as we shall presently see, reappear in *The Old Curiosity Shop* in a sudden transfer of little Nell and her grandfather to a setting of the kind.

At Manchester Dickens met John Forster who brought with him some letters of introduction from Harrison Ainsworth. One of them was addressed to James Crossley, who was informed that Dickens's object in coming north was to see the interior of a cotton mill. Dining with Mr. Gilbert Winter, Dickens met Mr. Crossley and the brothers Grant who worked in Cheeryble House, Canon Street, and were to be perpetuated as 'the Cheeryble brothers' in *Nicholas Nickleby*. The visitors spent three days in Manchester and found time to go to Cheadle Hall to see Ainsworth's three little girls who were at a boarding school there. Dickens made one of them a present of an inscribed copy of Agnes Strickland's *Juvenile Scrapbook*, while Forster and Browne provided books for the other two.

Rather surprisingly—but then one is constantly surprised by the number and variety of Dickens's contacts—we find him writing to Edward FitzGerald about his visit to the cotton mills:

> I went to Manchester [he writes] and saw the *worst* cotton mill and then I saw the *best*. *Ex uno disce omnes*. There was no great difference between them. I was obliged to come back suddenly on some matters connected with the publication of *Oliver Twist*. . . . On the eleventh of next month I am going down again only for three days, and then into the enemy's camp and the very headquarters of the Factory System advocates. I fear I shall have very little opportunity of looking about me, but I shall be most happy to avail myself of any introduction from Lord Ashley which in the course of an hour or so would enable me to make any fresh observations. . . . So far as seeing goes, I have seen enough for my purpose, and what I have seen has astonished and disgusted me beyond all measure. I mean to strike the heaviest blow in my power for those unfortunate creatures, but whether I shall do so in *Nickleby* or wait some other opportunity I have not yet determined.[1]

This letter reveals what is nowhere else indicated, that Dickens had been turning over in his mind the idea of writing a novel to back Lord Ashley's campaign to alleviate the lot of

[1] *Life of 7th Earl of Shaftesbury*, by E. Hodder, vol. i. p. 227.

children in factories.   Once he had inspected the cotton mills
he found himself so disgusted and so angered at the horrors
he had witnessed that he did not find it possible to sit down
and write about them in the half-sentimental, half-humorous
way that alone got under the skin of his readers.   A third visit
to Manchester in company with Ainsworth (in January 1839
to attend a public dinner to both authors) had no more fruitful
results though he spent two whole days sightseeing.   Perfectly aware that his power did not lie in being either didactic
or minatory, he had to give way to his immediate reactions
of fury and despair at the 'keeping down of thousands and
thousands of God's images', and for the time being had to
leave the subject alone.   When he did recur to the exploitation of human beings under the industrial system he wrote a
different kind of book, *Hard Times*, different because by then
he was strongly under the influence of Carlyle.

From the time of his visits to the cotton mills Dickens
began with increasing seriousness, partly at Miss Coutts's
request and partly on his own account, to study social conditions in London.   He read, for example, Dr. Southwood
Smith's report (drawn up by order of the Poor Law Authorities) on the housing of the poor in Whitechapel and Bethnal
Green.   Nothing more disgusting in the way of human
habitations could be imagined than the houses he described as
responsible for the abnormal death rate from typhus.   Dr.
Southwood Smith's report had so impressed the Home
Secretary, Lord Normanby, that he had decided to make
a personal inspection of the hideous conditions disclosed.
Lord Ashley followed suit and then Charles Dickens, who
reported to Miss Coutts with results observable later on, when
the first model dwellings were erected at her charge in Bethnal
Green.

In many ways Dr. Southwood Smith, whose acquaintance
Dickens now made, was a very important reformer, a reformer,
howbeit, who has never received the credit due to him as the
originator and tireless advocate of the first Public Health Act
of 1848.   Of angelic appearance, he faced horrors with the

courage of a martyr. He was the disciple and friend of Jeremy Bentham and it was to him that Bentham (owing to the difficulty of obtaining corpses for medical students to dissect) had bequeathed his own body with instructions that Smith must himself deliver a lecture on it in the Webb School of Anatomy. Dr. Smith carried out this behest, but it was observed by students present that his face was as blenched as that of the corpse. The clothed skeleton of Bentham with a face made up in wax sat with broad-brimmed hat covering long white hair, in a mahogany case in his house, and everyone who dined with the doctor had to face this *memento mori*. Dickens used to dine with him and learnt to love and respect his selfless host. Presently we shall find him helping Dr. Southwood Smith to establish the first private-patient nursing home in England.

As always in Dickens's life, light interludes succeeded serious experiences and some of these lighter interludes were generated by his growing popularity. Theatrical producers were beginning to see money in dramatising his novels, and one named Sterling seized upon the story of *Nicholas Nickleby* when it was but one-third written, gave it a plot and ending of his own, and produced it with Yates at the Adelphi. Dickens protested vehemently, but, after seeing what they had made of the Mantalinis, he felt obliged to withdraw his objection and say that it was 'beyond all praise and admirably done in every respect'. An unauthorised version of *Oliver Twist* at the Surrey, however, upset him terribly. Forster, who was with him, said that after glancing at the production for a few moments he lay down on the floor of the box and never rose from it till the drop scene fell.

The Old Curiosity Shop was adapted for the Adelphi in 1840, and as Yates was now a friend of Dickens, the author attended rehearsals and 'made a great many improvements'. Even so he could not brace himself to be present on the first night, and Kate, escorted by Frederick, went to the theatre without him. He said to Tom Mitton, 'The thing may be better than I expect, but I have no faith in it at all'.

Chapter 8

LONDON SALONS

*I have heard . . . that the sense of being well-dressed gives
a feeling of inward tranquility which religion is powerless
to bestow.*   R. W. EMERSON

LIKE Mrs. Boffin in *Our Mutual Friend*, Charles Dickens was
'a highflyer at fashion'. He had always been fond of
clothes and by this time was the proud owner of many bright
waistcoats, coloured neckcloths and jewelled pins and rings.
Both he and Ainsworth modelled themselves upon Count
d'Orsay, in so far as two little men could venture to imitate a
man of six feet four, and very natty do they appear in the
sketches of Alfred Croquis. Dickens, however, was lured
from the straight and narrow path of good taste by his admiration for Disraeli's dress and his own love of the stage. It was
irresistible to him to combine the role of personable young
man with that of famous person, indeed in practice one could
be made to set off the other. Before he became a public
figure he had short hair and his Aunt Janet's miniature shows
a severe young face poised on the top of a very high stock.
An engraving adapted from this miniature was used in the
Court Journal to illustrate an article on 'the genius of Boz, the
portrayer of the true and the natural'. It was a little out of
date, but Laman Blanchard, the editor, could find nothing else
to insert, though actually by this time Cruikshank had included several likenesses of 'Boz' in his illustrations for the
Sketches showing a dark-haired youth buying a coach ticket,
or in 'Public Dinners' as an usher leading a procession of
children to a feast,[1] as well as in a drawing labelled 'Sir Lionel
Flamstead and his Friends'[2] in which the likeness of Ainsworth

---

[1] In company with Chapman and Hall.
[2] Etched by Cruikshank for Macrone but not used by him. See *Ainsworth's Magazine*, 1840.

also appears.   Cruikshank introduced himself in an easy-to-be-recognised way into all of these scenes.

In a more serious pencil sketch made of Dickens in his study in Doughty Street, Cruikshank shows us an elegant figure in slim-waisted frock-coat, tightly fitting trousers strapped over pointed boots, voluminous satin cravat and curled locks producing a finnicky dandified effect.   Samuel Laurence drew Dickens about the same time in chalk, and a few months later made a painting of him in water-colour. Laurence, who saw him less effeminate-looking than Cruikshank, depicted his subject with determined jaw, firm countenance and uncurled bobbed hair.   It is probably the best portrait ever done of him and gives, as it were, the eternal qualities resident in the man who could set his teeth and write stories that almost eviscerated him in the telling.   Laurence at least realised that though Dickens had risen very fast, it had been entirely by his own exertions—in other words, by the exercise of terrific will-power.

There must have been something very striking and attractive about Dickens's appearance at this time.   Not only did women fall before him, but Leigh Hunt said, 'What a face to meet in a drawing room!   It has the life and soul in it of fifty human beings!'   And it must have been his personal distinction and adaptability as much as his genius that opened to him the doors of the more particular houses of Mayfair and St. James's, but, however it came about, at twenty-six Mr. Dickens had the to him great satisfaction of being recognisably distinguished, the kind of young man that every artist wanted to paint and every hostess to see in their salons.   Of course he was socially inexperienced, but his aplomb was such that neither the exotic atmosphere generated by Count d'Orsay nor the asperities of Lady Holland could now disturb the assurance of a celebrity most of whose spare time had hitherto been spent in furnished lodgings and a three-pair suite in Holborn.

One should bear in mind that all the people of the world he was now so confidently entering had had natural advantages

that he had never enjoyed. They had come from country
houses well furnished with libraries and 'marbles': they had
travelled in Italy: they knew Paris: they could read French
and Italian: they were well grounded in the classics: they had
a nodding acquaintance with the great pictures, statues and
buildings of Europe. Monckton Milnes had travelled in
Greece and Landor had lived in Italy, but Dickens, except as
a child, had lived nowhere except in London. Nothing he
saw in the way of objects meant anything to him; he would
not at this time have recognised the Apollo Belvedere or the
Venus de Milo. He had done some reading in past years at
the British Museum to post himself in history, law and politics,
but, judged by public school and university standards, he was
still under-educated. He now applied himself with extraordinary success to another kind of self-instruction, that of
contacts with the then leaders of literary and political society.
How unpredictable it was that a few years later he would
be talking Italian easily with Genoese friends and con-
versing in fluent French with Émile de Girardin and George
Sand!

Dickens was very sharp, of course, at picking up hints,
especially in the matter of social behaviour. One can imagine how on the alert he must have been when first admitted
to the house of Mr. Rogers, whose windows looked into
the Green Park at its most pleasant point. With the exception of a few visits to Sir Francis Burdett's house, it was
the first cultivated *milieu* to which he gained access. If he
thought a young guest worth while Mr. Rogers was quick
at the uptake, so as soon as Sir Francis Burdett presented
'Boz', the foundation of a friendship was laid which we see
reflected in the glowing dedication of *The Old Curiosity Shop*,
wherein Mr. Rogers is depicted as 'one of the few men whom
Riches and Honours have not spoiled and who have preserved
in High Places active Sympathy with the Poorest and the
Humblest of their kind'. Mr. Rogers was always extremely
nice to Mrs. Dickens which some of the people who took
Dickens up were not; in fact he was one of the very few

literary people she liked or trusted or to whom she signed
herself 'Yours very affectionately'.

More significant, in a manner of speaking, was 22 St.
James's Place than Gore House or Holland House, because it
was a revelation to Charles Dickens, brought up as he had
been, to see what a member of the elastic middle class could
achieve in the way of distinction of living. Sydney Smith
used to say that Sam 'hived very comfortably' and most
Americans were impressed by the hospitality meted out by
the banker-poet. Washington Irving spoke of his 'classic
little mansion', and Bancroft described it to Emerson as 'a
Pantheon in miniature'.

Though Rogers kept but very few servants, he entertained
everybody of note and said he did it on £2000 a year. Owing
to his purchase of pictures from the Orleans Gallery and to
their being hung against a background of crimson damask,
his rather small rooms made an opulent, half-suffocating impression which the gold frames, silver wall-sconces and red
brocade-upholstered furniture enhanced. The rooms were
far too dark for Sydney Smith's taste as there was no light
except that thrown on to the pictures by candles. But grand
as were his surroundings, Mr. Rogers was very unalarming in
himself, being so small of stature and so small of voice and so
anxious always to bring the best out in people. The pictures
Mr. Dickens was not capable of appreciating, though he soon
learnt to recognise the Raphael Madonna, the two Titians on
which their owner doted, and the little St. George of which he
was so proud because he believed it to be the work of that
rarest of masters, Giorgione. It was easier for an author,
even a not very well-read author, to admire the well-bound
books arranged in bookcases painted by Stothard with scenes
from Boccaccio, Chaucer and Shakespeare, as well as to
appreciate the fine workmanship of the Flaxman mantelpieces
and the claw-footed mahogany tables 'carved by a journeyman
of the name of Chantrey working for 5/- a day'. The rooms
were strikingly characteristic of the taste of a man who had
made the grand tour, written verse and worshipped literature.

Not the least considered of his treasures was a cast of Pope's face taken after death by Roubillac, and Milton's receipt for *Paradise Lost* which hung framed upon a door.

Taking note of habits and manners as well as objects, Dickens especially liked the way Mr. Rogers entertained children and grown-ups on Twelfth Night with his skilful conjuring tricks. He also admired his easy conversational breakfasts of eight people and longed to emulate them. But the breakfasts could not be copied at Doughty Street because he was neither an old bachelor like Mr. Rogers nor a young bachelor like his imitator Richard Monckton Milnes. He could, however, reproduce the delightful Twelfth Night entertainments, and as soon as he had a suitable house of his own we find him doing so with great enjoyment.

Mr. Rogers invited ladies to his breakfasts, but they had to qualify either by intelligence or position for inclusion in this select coterie. Mrs. Charles Dickens never breakfasted with Mr. Rogers. That they were fond of each other is clear from the letters she wrote to him when abroad, but she was just not conversable. Let us look at a guest's account of a breakfast in order to see what kind of conversation was expected of the company round the table. On this occasion Mr. Rogers was entertaining Mrs. Norton, Lady Blessington, Mr. Macaulay and Dr. Mackay, and as host indicated that 'rhyming' was to be the topic for discussion.[1] Mrs. Norton spoke of *Hudibras* and laughed at Butler's 'desperate ingenuity'. Why his lines,

> Pulpit, drum, ecclesiastic,
> Was beat with fist instead of a stick,

were really comparable to those comic lines of Lord Byron,

> But—Oh! ye lords of ladies intellectual,
> Inform us truly, have they not hen-peck'd you all?

'But they are *meant* to be comic lines!' objected Macaulay, adding that he certainly preferred what he called 'real rhyming', whereupon Lady Blessington remarked how poor

[1] Ch. Mackay, *Through the Long Day*.

we were in rhymes. Could anyone tell her whether there were rhymes to music, silver, orange, noble, herald? Much English verse struck her as hurdy-gurdy like. Someone then raised the subject of assonance in ballads. Macaulay said blank verse was not satisfactory to the English ear unless, as was so often the case with Shakespeare and Milton, it was decasyllabic. Mrs. Norton chipped in with, 'Narrative verse palls in any case; why, look at *The Lay of the Last Minstrel* and *The Lady of the Lake*'.

Mr. Macaulay turning to his host asked, 'Can I have a *Piers Plowman*, Mr. Rogers?' When it was handed to him he read,

> In a somer seson whan soft was the sonne
> I shope me in shroudes as I a shepe were,

and then jumped to

> Patriarchs and Prophets and Preachers of God's Wordes,

saying how pleasing to him was the sound of alliteration. 'Tedious to a modern ear like mine', commented Lady Blessington, but Mrs. Norton stopped her by spouting,

> Rushed into the *f*ield and *f*oremost *f*ighting *f*ell.

They then discussed *The Ingoldsby Legends* about which opinion was sharply divided, and then the hexameter for which all expressed dislike, though Macaulay intoned lines from *The Vision of Judgement* to show what an effect Southey got with the metre:

> . . . Toll, toll, through the silence of evening;
> 'Tis a deep dull sound that is heavy and mournful at all times,
> For it tells of mortality always.

Mr. Rogers was so upset by this passage—he was seventy-five and hated to be reminded of death—that Mrs. Norton tried to cheer him by bringing forward *Chevy Chase* and Lady Blessington *The Nut-Brown Maid* as fine *happy* ballads. The ladies managed to put their host in good humour again and they parted in a spirit of enjoyment, for they were all versifiers. It was to this kind of company and conversation that Dickens now chose to adapt himself.

It would seem that Charles Dickens was introduced to Count d'Orsay by Serjeant Talfourd in 1836 and that his first appearance in the Gore House salon of Lady Blessington was at the house-warming in May of the same year. Walter Savage Landor, an old and dear friend from Italian days, had come up to stay for the occasion and she was ransacking the town to secure for him pleasant company nightly, and a sight of the new lions. 'I wish to procure for him as much enjoyment as I can', she wrote when inviting Talfourd to meet him. He must not fail her whatever happened and he must bring a young writer with him. And in Talfourd's company Dickens went to his first great party, drove through the carriage gates and walked through doors flung wide by powdered footmen in green and gold—on through the hall to the library, a long room with a fireplace at either end and columns supporting the ceiling. He was gifted, as Taine was to discover later, with the camera's eye and nothing escaped him. He saw the ivory-coloured bookshelves with their glass inlay, the white-and-gold furniture, the apple-green damask, the green carpet at his feet, and last of all his hostess beaming a welcome on him. As the author of a widely-read book on Lord Byron, Lady Blessington was regarded as a friend by editors and contributors to magazines. She was, as it were, of their confraternity, for she worked steadily producing a book a year from 1833 on. She also edited the *Keepsake* and various *Books of Beauty*. Few women, excepting Miss Landon, Mrs. S. C. Hall, Lady Emmeline Stuart-Wortley, Countess Guiccioli and her own sisters Lady Canterbury and the Countess de Saint Marsault, ever set foot in her house, for her relations with Count d'Orsay, her stepson-in-law, were considered unconventional. Nat Willis got his first glimpse of this most attractive woman sitting reading half-buried in a *fauteuil* of yellow satin

in 'a room of rather crowded sumptuousness'. Hall[1] had
come to know her very well when he was persuading her to
set down her conversations with Lord Byron for the *New
Monthly* which he, at the time, was editing.   Mrs. S. C. Hall
liked her for her good heart and said there was 'nothing
artificial about her, nothing fussy or self-distrustful', and that
though conscious of power she was 'utterly without pre-
tension'.   To her there seemed an admirable fitness in all
Lady Blessington did and a deep-seated good intent in both
her words and actions.   Every man took to her, including
the Duke of Wellington, who was amused to be greeted by
her talking crow with, 'Up, Guards and at 'em!', and Disraeli
paid her the extravagant compliment of saying her pen must
have been plucked from the pinion of the bird of paradise.
Her evenings in Seamore Place had been famous for five years,
and her receptions at Gore House, to which abode she moved
in 1836, were to be even more famous.

Most of the well-known men in London were to be met in
her rooms.   In reading the diaries of the day, in which the
names of Disraeli, the brothers Bulwer, Captain Marryat,
Albany Fonblanque, Barry Cornwall, Sir Martin Shee, Lords
Durham, Abinger, Strangford, Lyndhurst appear, we see how
wide was her circle.   Nat Willis had once spent an exciting
evening watching Disraeli (not at that time in the House),
'lividly pale, eye black as Erebus, ringlets falling over left
cheek', sitting in the window looking out over the Park, 'his
gold-flowered waistcoat reflecting the rays of the setting sun',
a contrast indeed with ill-dressed Lord Durham who 'would
never have passed for a lord at all in America'.   To Nat
Willis Count d'Orsay appeared 'very splendid and very in-
definable'.

The Count was one of the sights of London as he drove
from his little house in Curzon Street to Hyde Park.   To
his smart, hooded cabriolet was harnessed a seventeen-hand
horse, and behind, clinging to the straps, bounced a tiny tiger.
The reins were handled in white kid gloves and Dickens,

[1] *Memories of S. C. Hall*, p. 403.

who watched him carefully from the pavement, noted with admiring approval that his wristbands were turned back over his coat cuffs, a fashion he was not slow to imitate, nor the Bostonians to observe and comment on. The equipage of the Countess of Blessington, glistening with varnish and emblazoned with heraldic devices, was also to be seen daily in the Park. Its green hammercloth edged with white, its silver-wigged coachman, its tall footmen, cane-carrying, powder-headed and silk-stockinged, formed the stately setting to the still beautiful woman who acknowledged the bows of the innumerable men who saluted her.

For young Mr. Dickens the Blessington-d'Orsay parties were most polishing for they acquainted him with the ways of the *beau monde*. They were not alarming as were the parties at Holland House for no one quizzed him under Lady Blessington's roof. The talk was not like the talk at Mr. Rogers's because it was not directed, but allowed to flow freely. Mr. Disraeli, who when worked up talked 'like a racehorse approaching a winning post', one evening described Beckford's *Italy* and went on to tell of its author's fantastical life at Bath where he was said to own two houses joined by a covered bridge, his servants living on one side and he and his companion, a Spanish dwarf, 'who believes himself a duke and is treated as such', on the other. Then he told of a high tower lined with books and of a grave below the pavement in which he was arranging a double sepulchre for himself and the dwarf. Victor Hugo and his newest books also came in for discussion, champagne flowed, and all the while d'Orsay kept the conversation alive by a running fire of witty parentheses in French and English. Usually silent and often aloof, in a corner of the saloon sat Prince Louis Napoleon, the future Emperor of the French.

One never ceases to wish that Dickens had kept a diary in which he recorded his first impressions of well-known people and houses, but his mind did not work like that: it was too busy registering and transforming a different set of impressions and describing a different and irreconcilable set of people. No matter how much he enjoyed his evenings with d'Orsay or Rogers, they did not make him wish to write down anything about them. Whatever the secret processes of absorption that went to the making of his books and the stimulation of his creative powers, they were automatically selective and independent of his conscious will. As to keeping an engagement book methodically he could not do it, as it depressed him too deeply to record the dying days. Therefore we have no description from him of Sydney Smith, no Carlylean vignette of those piercing hazel eyes, that massive Roman nose, the shrewdness and fun that lent life to every gathering he attended. Nor have we any picture from his pen of the Misses Berry or of Lord and Lady Holland.

The Holland House circle differed from that of Gore House in being more political and diplomatic in composition than literary. The discussions that took place there were also more serious in tone, and it was a feather in the cap of a mere writer (without birth to recommend him or make him *salon-fähig*) to be invited there. In another way the company was not different, for it was as masculine in character as that of Gore House. Many ladies of the day refused to know Lady Holland since she had once violated their code and still remained outside the pale of society. This embargo was imposed even in Dickens's day, as we realise only too clearly in reading a letter written by Sydney Smith to Lord Denman in 1841. Sydney Smith was one of Lady Holland's dearest and most intimate friends and yet he could write to a prospective dinner guest as follows:

> Mrs. Sydney and I have made a blunder. . . . Lady Holland dines with us on the 17th. Does Lady Denman know Lady Holland, and if not will that deprive us of the pleasure of Lady Denman's company? Lady Holland sinned early in life, with Methuselah and Enoch, but still she is out of the pale of the regular ladies, and the case ought to have been put.[1]

A letter like this from one *habitué* of Holland House to

[1] *Thomas, First Lord Denman*, by Sir Joseph Arnould, vol. ii. p. 150.

another recreates for us the stuffiness and rigidity of early Victorian society better and more exactly than any description, for it is a slice from life as it was being lived at the moment.

Lady Holland in her turn would not know Lady Blessington, and their two circles, though intersecting frequently, never coalesced. It was two years after his introduction to Gore House that Dickens made his bow at Holland House. Serjeant Talfourd, whom Lady Holland liked very much, had waited for a favourable opportunity to present his young friend. Lady Holland asked 'dear Bulwer' whether Talfourd's protégé was presentable, and on receiving an affirmative reply invited queer little 'Boz' to visit her. For the date she named he had an engagement he could not throw over, so was obliged to wait for another summons. That moment came when she began to read *Nicholas Nickleby*. When finally he could make his bow, Lady Holland found him 'modest and well-behaved', and Lord Holland said he was 'very unobtrusive, yet not shy, intelligent in countenance and altogether prepossessing'.

Carlyle described Lady Holland as 'a proud old dame' in the habit of being obeyed and entertained, and used to say that her face when he caught it in profile had something of the falcon character, if a falcon's bill were straight. Macaulay thought there was a good deal of Queen Elizabeth about her. Till Dickens got used to her ways he could not defend himself against her acute questioning and found himself forced against his will to disclose to her the plot of *Nicholas Nickleby*, of which the first numbers only had appeared. To steel oneself against such persistent and ruthless probings was an art in itself, for, as Talleyrand used to say, 'Lady Holland is all assertion'.

Soon after his first venture into this exclusive circle, Dickens was annoyed to find that Bentley had inserted into the September number of the *Miscellany* a gossipy article on Holland House entertaining. Writing off at once to Lady Holland, he said:

I saw yesterday for the first time that in this month's number there is some impromptu of Sydney Smith's purporting to have been written at your table some years ago which Bentley, I assume, obtained gratis from some well-informed babbler and printed accordingly.

To clear himself of indiscretion, he here reveals that though his name appears as that of editor of *Bentley's Miscellany* he had 'little to do with the business part of the publication', and therefore had no previous knowledge of the list of contents. He wishes her to understand that he entertains so great an abhorrence of printed recollections of private conversations and so great a detestation of the impertinence and vulgarity which makes them public that he must assure her that the production in question has never been authorised by him.[1]

A born dictator, Lady Holland kept control of the guests invited to her table both as to quality and conversation. Lord Holland, incurably good-natured, would, if not checked, have invited almost anybody to dinner, but she always had the general level in view and not the particular kindness, and a bore was to be feared like death. She did not hesitate to stem a monopolistic talker and would squeeze sixteen people into a table laid for nine and not mind that no elbow could be raised. She levied tribute of game, venison and cheeses from guests capable of paying it, as well as foreign delicacies from ambassadorial houses. She could be coldly offensive to those for whom she took a dislike and also so frigidly polite as to paralyse the neophyte. Writers inclined to be vain might be told off like poor Rogers with, 'Your poetry is bad enough so pray be sparing of your prose', and she liked Rogers! Macaulay she would pull up remorselessly. Having cut short one of his discourses and switched the conversation on to the Christian Fathers, Macaulay showed himself too fluent about St. Chrysostom and St. Athanasius, so once more she tried to floor him with, 'Pray, Macaulay, what was the origin of the doll? When were dolls first mentioned in history?' Macaulay, neither floored nor out of temper, at once began to

[1] September 1838. *The Dickensian*, 1936, pp. 33-41.

tell the company about the Roman doll. Guests were sometimes ordered about like servants and few resented it. No
one but Sydney Smith, however, on being told peremptorily
to ring the bell, would obey promptly and then inquire
should he dust the room?[1]

Somehow Dickens managed to get through the preliminary
ordeal of Holland House entertaining with calm and credit,
and when he dined there Lord Holland's sister wrote that she
liked everything about him except the intolerable dandyism of
his dress. 'His countenance' she thought 'beautiful, because
blended with his intelligence there is such an expression of
goodness.' Somehow this nondescript young man managed
to touch the heart of Lady Holland, and we see from his letters
to her after Lord Holland's death that he seemed to understand her and give her the kind of friendship she required.
The letters are cosy, straightforward and confidential.

Almost as soon as Holland House had set the seal of its
approval on Dickens the Misses Berry got on his track.
They really must have the remarkable young author of
Nicholas Nickleby to their parties. From Richmond, where
they were living for the hot months, they called on Mr. and
Mrs. Dickens, who were summering once again at Petersham.
Mrs. Dickens was in no condition to dine out, and Mr.
Dickens excused himself on the plea that he 'had not finished
the month's instalment of his new book'. This did not
satisfy the eager Berrys, who got Sydney Smith to write
again on their behalf. His letter, written from 'The Hole'
(33 Charles Street, Berkeley Square), is so characteristic of the
man that it is irresistible to quote his actual words:

Nobody more, and more justly talked of than yourself.
The Miss Berrys now at Richmond live only to become
acquainted with you and have commissioned me to request
you to dine with them on Friday 29th [June] or Monday
July 1st to meet a Canon of St. Pauls, the Rector of Combe
Florey, and the Vicar of Halberton, all equally well known
to you; to say nothing of other and better people.   The

[1] *The Greville Memoirs*, vol. i. pp. 367-8.

Miss Berrys and Lady Charlotte Lindsay have not the smallest objection to be put into a Number, but on the contrary would be proud of the distinction; and Lady Charlotte, in particular, you may marry to Newman Noggs. Pray come, it is as much as my place is worth to send them a refusal.—SYDNEY SMITH.

And to the Misses Berry Dickens went, though he tells us nothing about it; indeed, had it not been for Sydney Smith we should not even know that these delightful ladies had craved his acquaintanceship.

One of the hall-marks of success in the society in which Dickens now moved, as of right, was election to the Athenaeum Club, for which Serjeant Talfourd had proposed him in May 1838, getting Serjeant Storks to second him. He became a member the following month, being brought in as one of forty persons eminent in literature, art and science. Among the forty were Grote and Charles Darwin, Macready and the grandson of his grandmother's employer, Richard Monckton Milnes. One sees from looking at the dates when Dickens's contemporaries were admitted to membership what a compliment it was to 'Boz' that he should be made free of the Athenaeum at the age of twenty-six. Macready had been turned down three years earlier. Robert Browning with *Paracelsus* and *Strafford* to his credit was not elected till 1862. Thackeray was not admitted till 1851 and John Forster with five volumes of historical biographies to his pen was not chosen till 1852. The Athenaeum not only gave the younger men elected to it a certain cachet, but also the opportunity for meeting almost everyone of note. The Club had been Croker's idea, for by his day the meeting-places of the wits—coffee-houses and taverns—had gone out and it had become desirable to have a common meeting-ground not so much for wits as for men of achievement. Sir Walter Scott, Samuel Rogers, Sir Thomas Lawrence, Sir Francis Chantrey and Lord Spencer were on the original committee and proceeded solemnly to choose the first members from the lists of the Society of Antiquaries, the Royal College of Surgeons, and from the judges' and bishops' benches. It was decided that the Club premises must be noble in themselves and distinguished in decoration, and the result was that a palace was erected in Waterloo Place capped by a classical frieze of Bath stone carved by John Henning. The sum of £500 was allocated to a library, which eventually housed Captain Basil Hall's collection of publications on the United States of America, the Civil War tracts of Gibbon, and, in another century, was to receive the Warren Vernon books on Dante. A certain cachet was given to the note-paper by a Minerva seal cut by Sir Francis Chantrey to the design of Sir Thomas Lawrence. Intended to be a centre of culture, the Club, owing to its non-political character, could open its doors to foreigners of heterodox views. It also threw wide its portals on the occasions of the Coronation and Royal Wedding. Eleven hundred and thirty ladies and children sat there in a stand to see the Queen go by to her marriage, and among them was Mrs. Charles Dickens.

The social success that came so swiftly and easily to Charles Dickens carried with it implications that affected marital adjustments in so far as it tended to create a gulf between his amusements and those of his wife, since in the Holland-Berry-Blessington world Mrs. Dickens never gained a foothold. Rosina Bulwer, who loathed men's clubs, said in *Cheveley* that lexicographers should in future define the word 'home' as 'a pen in which to keep women and children'. Mrs. Dickens would certainly have endorsed this recommendation.

Chapter 9

BOOK-BANQUETS AND FRIENDS

The friendship of some men is quite Briarean.
DOUGLAS JERROLD

CONFIDENCE in himself was one of Charles Dickens's lead-ing characteristics and it never failed him no matter how adverse the circumstances he had to face. Neither worry over social conditions, quarrels with publishers nor fluctua-tions in income deterred him from his decision to live his life on a grand scale. He had no doubt whatever that once his affairs had been put into Forster's competent hands he could make all the money he needed. Feckless relations were still a drain upon his resources and threatened to become a menace to his good name; indeed the ingenious dodges contrived by his father to obtain advances from Chapman and Hall on the strength of his son's success, and the fact that he from time to time parted with autographs or sheets of manuscript for cash, tended to make his presence in London an embarrass-ment. Now Charles, as we know, was not a man to shirk family responsibilities, and in talking over his dilemma with Forster it became clear to him that he must establish his parents and brothers in a home of their own sufficiently far away from London to shield him from new annoyances. As there could be no financial peace while they were on his door-step, he took steps to shift them to the country. Acting swiftly as was his wont, he hurried down to Exeter, pitching on this district because he had known it well in reporting days and carried in his mind pictures of pleasant cottages and gardens on the Plymouth road. At Alphington he rented a six-roomed house and garden for £20 a year, arranged for it to be papered 'snowy-clean' immediately, ordered in coal and wood and bought seventy pounds' worth of carpets, furniture, glass and crockery, all to be delivered within two days. He had left London on a Monday (March 4), had arranged for his mother to join him in an hotel at Exeter on the Thursday, and for his father, brothers, and Dash the dog to arrive on the Saturday so that he himself could be back at work on the Monday. Speed and secrecy were essential to the success of the scheme, as John Dickens was liable to re-arrest by any one of the tradesmen to whom he owed money, and the only chance his son would have of compounding his debts was, as Forster agreed, for the debtor to be *non est inventus*. Forster advanced the pocket-money and Tom Beard played the part assigned to him of buying the coach-tickets and seeing the travellers off. Both parents seemed to fall in amiably with the arrangements made, though John Dickens was heard wondering what on earth he would do with himself in the country. Mrs. Dickens reached Exeter on the appointed day and was taken to see the cottage on the Friday: it was a contrast to the shabby lodgings in which she had camped for so many years. When his father turned up in good spirits with the rest of the family, Charles began to think he had 'settled the governor for life', and went back to London happy in this belief, but at the end of March his troubles began again with an 'unsatisfactory' letter from Mrs. Dickens. By June both parents were writing 'sneering, hateful letters' and Charles groaned to Forster over his mother's behaviour, 'I do swear I am sick at heart with both her and father too.' By July, however, they appeared to him to have settled down into a kind of contentment, and he was able to report after a visit that 'the dolls' house was perfect and beautifully kept'. Seven years later, Charles was to recall his father to London to take up a post on the *Daily News* of which he was editor-designate. In the intervening years it is evident that John Dickens did not stay put at Alphington, for we hear of him at Greenwich, the Isle of Man and other places, and as scheming to take his boys to Paris to complete their education. He was every bit as buoyant as Mr. Micawber.

We shall have reason to remember the Alphington episode

when we come to the parting between Dickens and his wife. The same rather ruthless speed is noticeable in the execution of the later sentence as is observable in the earlier, and with both arrangements Forster had a good deal to do.

Having disposed for the time being of his parents, Dickens resumed his personal life again, attending at the end of March a dinner to Macready on his retirement from management of Covent Garden. One of the guests, Mrs. Cowden Clarke, the compiler of a well-known Shakespeare concordance, was struck by the 'superlatively handsome face' of the young writer as he stood to speak. His 'magnificent lustrous eyes', his rich 'wavy locks of hair', his 'perpetually discursive glances' which seemed to miss nothing. What a picture he made, never had she seen anyone who interested her more! And to crown all he spoke with real feeling and understanding of the stage, with intelligence of the experimental and instructive seasons they had all enjoyed under Macready's management, of the living playwrights whose works he had presented—Bulwer, Mitford, Browning, Talfourd—and of the manner he had produced the dramas of Shakespeare. And it passed through her mind that nothing could have been more impressive than the performance of *Henry V* for which Stanfield had painted the scenery and Bulwer, Forster and Dickens himself had supervised the mounting. The young man's ringing speech brought tears to the eyes of the guest they had assembled to honour.

The Shakespeare Society dinner over which Charles Dickens presided a few months later did not go quite so smoothly. Present were Talfourd, the two Landseers, Forster, Maclise, Macready, Frank Stone, Jerrold, Thackeray, Stanfield, Cattermole, Proctor, Blanchard, Charles Knight and many more. Charles Knight records that Forster addressed the assembled company very pompously in his Macready manner and that some young men sitting at the table began to laugh, crack nuts and jingle glasses loudly. Forster, irritated by the din, spoke sharply to his interrupters. The noises got worse, the chairman tried to restore order, did

not succeed, abandoned the chair, and this was the end not
only of the dinner but of the Society.

At the end of April the Doughty Street household repaired
to Petersham for four months, Charles taking with him quite
a variety of books—translations from French and German
novels, Swift's Works, a volume of English Essays and Leigh
Hunt's *Indicator*. He was playing with the idea of a new
magazine to be written, compiled and edited by himself,
and talked ceaselessly about the project. Experience with
Bentley's Miscellany disposed him to believe that there was
a good deal of money to be made in a threepenny weekly
that would appeal to a poorer class of people than a shilling
monthly could attract. He seems at this time to have been
haunted by visions of lonely people sitting by desolate
hearths all of whom might be comforted if the right word were
said. If he could create an intimate and personal magazine
he might be the man to say that word, for no one understood
better than he that it is the unexpected human touch that
makes the whole world kin and sometimes kind. If *Master
Humphrey's Clock*[1] when it finally took shape did not for long
carry out its mission of 'addressing friends from the chimney-
corner', it was because the public showed no interest in the
sentiments of Master Humphrey and his deaf old friend and
could only be lured to purchase the magazine by the promise
that each number would contain part of a straightforward
serial by 'Boz'.

At Petersham Dickens still worked on *Nicholas Nickleby*
which had been running for a year and had six months to go
before completion. Its sales surpassed those of the *Pickwick*
serial, and *Pickwick* in volume form was selling briskly. As
there was nothing to follow them up with except the partially
written *Barnaby Rudge*, Dickens felt that it was time he made
a move to get his future straightened out. It seemed to him
odd that Chapman and Hall had not approached him with
some 'handsome retaining offer'; could it be that they were

[1] April 4, 1840.

CHARLES DICKENS, AGED 30
by Francis Alexander

" Very like the original " GEORGE PUTNAM

READING TO FRIENDS 1844
by Daniel Maclise, R.A.

"In the grave attention of Carlyle, the eager interest of Stanfield and Maclise, the keen look of poor Laman Blanchard, Fox's rapt solemnity, Jerrold's skyward gaze, the characteristic points of the scene are sufficiently rendered." JOHN FORSTER waiting for him to take the initiative? With Forster to back him he felt in a stronger position vis-à-vis of publishers than ever before; perhaps Forster could find out for him how matters stood. Obligingly Forster interviewed Chapman and Hall and was able to report them ready to consider any scheme put forward by Mr. Dickens. This induced Dickens to set down on paper the ideas he had been turning over in his head.

> I should be willing [he wrote] to commence on the thirty-first of March, 1840, a new publication consisting entirely of original matter, of which one number price threepence, should be published every week. . . . The best general idea of the plan of the work might be given perhaps by reference to *The Tatler, The Spectator* and Goldsmith's *Bee*; but it would be far more popular both in the subjects of which it treats and its mode of treating them.[1]

He went on to expound his plan of contents. It would include amusing essays, stories, satirical papers on the administration of justice, conversations on historic London between Gog and Magog, and a club of originals to carry on in the Pickwickian way. Nebulous as his plans were on the literary side, they were definite enough on the financial side. He demanded to be paid fifty pounds weekly and would undertake no risk of any kind. Profits must be shared on a fifty-fifty basis, and the periodical to be named *Master Humphrey's Clock* must be continued for twelve months certain. To these rather onerous conditions Chapman and Hall agreed.

For September the Dickens family moved from Petersham to Broadstairs, and as it happened 'Eleanor P.', now Mrs. Christian, was spending the end of a long honeymoon there. One night they all met in the Tivoli Gardens where 'Eleanor P.' watched Dickens dancing with Georgina Hogarth. It was extremely pleasant by the sea. Sam Rogers was living at the Albion and Harley and his sister in lodgings close by. 'We enjoy this place amazingly', wrote Dickens to Forster, in spite of the fact that Kate was preoccupied with the thoughts

[1] 218. I. N.L.

F

of an October baby—and Charles himself with the planning of
the *Nicholas Nickleby* banquet. Both baby and book were
to be dedicated to Macready. During this summer they
discussed leaving their home in Doughty Street for a house
nearer to an open space. Macready frequently praised
Clarence Terrace overlooking the Regent's Park which, compared with other districts of London, was in his opinion a
health resort. Why should not Dickens have a look at his
former house in Kent Terrace which was vacant? Dickens
did so and favoured it until he fell in love with a bow-fronted
house, 1 Devonshire Terrace, almost next to the imposing
portico of St. Marylebone. Here indeed was a residence of
'great promise and undeniable situation' with a private garden
shielded by a high wall. He secured a twelve-year lease of it
at once and took John Chapman, 'a genius in houses', over it
to make suggestions about water-closets to be carried out
forthwith. Doughty Street had been rather meagrely fitted
out with chattels from Furnival's Inn and second-hand
furniture picked up piece by piece with Mary. These things
would do no more than furnish the top floor of the new house.
Mr. and Mrs. Dickens now had recourse to the big firms in the
Tottenham Court Road where they placed orders for complete
suites for reception rooms and bedrooms. White window-
blinds and festooned curtains were installed and thick pile
carpets laid. Doors of deal were replaced by doors of
mahogany and wooden mantels by carved marble chimney-
pieces. In all this one sees the taste of Forster who was
sumptuous-minded and always acted in accordance with his
adage 'The best is good enough for me'. Forster himself
lived under painted ceilings in Lincoln's Inn Fields in the
fine rooms described in *Bleak House* as inhabited by Mr.
Tulkinghorn. Later on, after his marriage to the widow of
Henry Colburn, his setting in Palace Gate Gardens became
almost princely.

Baby Kate Macready made her appearance in October and
in the same month the *Nicholas Nickleby* dinner took place.

Nicholas Nickleby was the second of the novels to be honoured in this way, the completion of *Oliver Twist*, six months earlier, having passed without notice of the kind. It is interesting to scrutinise the list of guests at these periodical book-banquets for they are valuable pointers in a biography. Dickens was what would now be called a good mixer and had no desire for solitude as such, since he was neither a thinker nor a reader.

1 Devonshire Terrace, by Daniel Maclise, 1839

Except when engaged in the violently creative effort of planning or writing a book, when he was inaccessible to every-one, he liked to have people about. Convivial, sentimental and easily moved to tears and laughter, his path through life bloomed in a series of happy attachments few of which shrivelled under the touch of time or circumstance. It is evident that his power of attraction was immense. Anthony Trollope confirms this when he says:

> Of the general charm of his manner I despair of giving any idea to those who have not seen or known him. He warmed the social atmosphere, wherever he appeared, with

that summer glow which seemed to attend him. His laugh was brimful of enjoyment.

Dickens's earlier friendships are for the most part enshrined in the lists of guests attending the book-dinners. The first of these, given to celebrate the completion of *Pickwick*, had taken place on November 18, 1837, when the diners were Harrison Ainsworth, William Jerdan, Thomas Hill[1] (book collector), Samuel Lover,[2] Chapman, Hall, Maclise, Macready, John Forster and of course the guest of honour, Serjeant Talfourd. They met at the Prince of Wales's Hotel in Leicester Street and, just as Talfourd was about to give the health of the chairman, Charles Dickens, the head waiter, to everyone's delight, carried in a snowy temple of sugar under which stood a miniature Mr. Pickwick, a complimentary confection made by the landlord himself. When Chapman and Hall presented 'Boz' with a bonus cheque and a set of 'apostle' ladles embodying characters in *Pickwick*, there was great laughter and applause.

At the *Nicholas Nickleby* dinner held at the Albion, Aldgate, the new names are those of Clarkson Stanfield, Hablot Browne, David Wilkie, George Cattermole, Thomas Beard, Bradbury, Evans and J. P. Harley. Again Chapman and Hall proved themselves worthy of the occasion, for, following the fine tradition of Constable in commissioning Raeburn to paint Walter Scott, they had commissioned Maclise to paint Dickens, and this portrait was displayed in the room in which the dinner took place. An engraving from it was used as frontispiece for *Nicholas Nickleby* in volume form. The picture was later presented to Mrs. Dickens. Macready in his speech acknowledged the honour done to him by the dedication, and recently knighted David Wilkie, painter in ordinary to the Queen, lauded 'the reality of Dickens's genius' and said rather breathlessly that 'there had been nothing like him issuing his novels part by part, since Richard-

---

[1] The Hull of Hook's *Gilbert Gurney*.

[2] Miniaturist and composer of songs. Best remembered for *Handy Andy*.

son had issued his novels volume by volume', and how in both cases people talked about the characters as if they were next-door neighbours or friends and how 'as many letters were written to the author of *Nickleby* to implore him not to kill poor Smike as had been sent by young ladies to the author of *Clarissa* to save Lovelace's soul alive'.

Many of the book-guests we get to know well as in company with Dickens we travel along the road of a life marked by prandial milestones. Macready, twenty years older than Dickens, we meet again and again. Their first encounter had taken place at Covent Garden in June 1837. Forster had, as it were casually, thrown open a green-room door saying 'Here is Boz!' *Othello* was in rehearsal at the time and Macready was worrying over the King's health. Was William IV going to die? Would he have to cancel his first night? What an absurdity that the natural ailment of an old and ungifted man should be the cause of such perplexity and annoyance! Macready rambled on, airing his republican views, kings were no use, and lords were blots on humanity. He did not mind bending the knee to Voltaire, for he was a man of taste and virtue and 'in every way superior to the gold-besotted prurient people for whom nonsensical entertainments like *Semiramide* had to be devised'. The visitors had struck Macready on a bad day, but, in spite of his display of petulance, Dickens took to him at once and found in him a very faithful friend. In a sense they had a common background or grievance, for Macready's father too had been committed to prison for debt and his son had had to go straight to the boards from Rugby instead of to the University as planned. Macready's diary shows him to have been very sensitive to opinion and very easily depressed. His temper was difficult and he took for his motto the saying of Seneca, *Inveniat viam aut faciat* (Find a way or make one). In spite of his temperament he never quarrelled with Dickens and remained, in bad days and good, one of his closest confidants.

Another lifelong friendship had come into being when Kate's friend Daniel Maclise entered the family circle.

Dickens describes this young Irish artist as a wayward, delightful fellow 'golden throughout', a man who 'could have been as good a writer as he was a painter'. As Alfred Croquis of *Fraser's Magazine* he was very well known in literary circles, for he had made pen sketches of all the writers from Lady Morgan to L. E. L. and from Sir Walter Scott to Thomas Campbell. He spent a good deal of time with the Dickenses at Twickenham in 1838 and again at Petersham in 1839 when he was making studies for the Nickelby portrait. As a sitter Charles Dickens was difficult to please and insisted that Maclise should scrap all his first sketches, but the morning came when he could write 'Maclise has made another face of me which all people say is astonishing'.

William Jerdan, editor of the *Literary Gazette*, had been one of the first to recognise the merits of Sam Weller when he made his bow in the fifth number of *Pickwick*. Seizing his pen he begged the author 'to develop the character to the uttermost'. A 'genial alliance' ensued and Jerdan, who liked helping young writers, seems to have exercised his good offices in helping to persuade Bentley to relinquish all claims to *Barnaby Rudge*. Jerdan was a standing dish at the 'Boz' banquets.

Not all the early friends, howbeit, were bidden to the book-dinners. Leigh Hunt, for example, was only invited to birthday parties at the Dickenses' home, on which occasions he proved himself a charming converser and a lovable companion. When presenting Leigh Hunt with his novels in 1838 their author wrote:

> You are an old stager in works, but a young one in faith —faith in all beautiful and excellent things. If you can only find it in that green heart of yours to tell me one of these days that you have met, in wading through the accompanying trifles, with anything that felt like a vibration of the old chord you have touched so often and sounded so well you will confer the truest gratification on your faithful friend.[1]

Douglas Jerrold's name does not appear in the first dinner lists though Dickens had got to know him as early as 1835 when he was living at Brompton as a temporary invalid. Seven years older than Dickens, he had been midshipman, actor and playwright and is best remembered to-day for *Black-eyed Susan* (1829) and *Mrs. Caudle's Curtain Lectures* (1846). It was Jerrold who made one of his former shipmates known to Dickens—Clarkson Stanfield. Stanfield, like Macready, was twenty years older than 'Boz', but this proved no barrier and as 'Stanny' he became a dearly loved friend. Stanfield was called by his contemporaries the English Vandervelde, and, when Dickens first knew him, was employed as a scene-painter at Drury Lane. He designed a few illustrations for the 'Boz' novels, but only enters seriously into the pattern of Dickens's life as limner of stage sets for the theatrical performances at Tavistock House,—*The Lighthouse* and *The Frozen Deep*. He turns up both at the *Nickleby* and *Chuzzlewit* dinners and to the latter brought his friend the 'eccentric Turner'. In after years *Little Dorrit* was to be dedicated to him.

Another artist friend was George Cattermole, a relation by marriage living at Clapham, who did many of the illustrations for *Master Humphrey's Clock* and *The Old Curiosity Shop*. Forster did not like him much, but admits he had fun enough for a dozen humorists though lacking in balance and steadiness.

Hablot Browne was also at the *Nickleby* dinner. He had got to know Dickens well while working at the drawings for *Pickwick* and *Sunday Under Three Heads*. A much feebler artist than Cruikshank, his employer found him amenable and willing to accept suggestions and even orders. Of a retiring nature and dreading company, he had refused to appear at the *Pickwick* dinner though he plucked up courage for the *Nickleby* feast and attended all subsequent celebrations until 1859, when *A Tale of Two Cities* was published and he ceased to work for Dickens.

Thackeray was not invited to any of the earlier book-dinners. As we have seen, these young men had met for a moment in 1835 when Mr. Michael Angelo Titmarsh had called at Furnival's Inn to offer to illustrate *Pickwick*, but they did not meet again till both dined with Ainsworth in 1838. Thackeray, unlike Dickens, was a long time finding out what he could do best, and this was chiefly because he had never had to fight for a living. Maybe that his close association with Dickens in the summer of 1838 at Twickenham had an influence on his decision to become a novelist. At the time he was contributing *The Yellowplush Papers* to *Fraser's Magazine* and also working for the *Times*. *Vanity Fair*, which established his fame, was not published till ten years later and his name first appears as a guest at the *Copperfield* dinner of 1849. Was it the success of *Vanity Fair* or admiration for Dickens's work that led to his presence on this occasion? The break in relations which was one of the literary scandals of 1858 inclines one to assume it was the former, since when true sympathy of personality was the foundation, we find Dickens in friendship faithful to the end.

Chapter 10

THE QUEEN, CARLYLE AND POLITICS

*Royalty is a Government in which the attention of the nation
is on one person doing interesting actions. A Republic is a
Government in which that attention is divided between many,
who are all doing uninteresting actions. Accordingly so
long as the human heart is strong and the human reason
weak Royalty will be strong because it appeals to diffused
feelings.*   WALTER BAGEHOT

FOR many simple British citizens the chief event of 1840 was
the girl-Queen's wedding. It appealed to every home-
lover and brought royalty for the first time for many generations within reach of all hearts. Embosomed in the warm
tide of popular sentiment Charles Dickens went about lamenting his hopeless passion for the princess and envying Daniel
Maclise, who was almost as it were inside the idyll, since the
bride, with whom he was so great a favourite, had requested
him to paint secret pictures for her to give to Prince Albert on
his birthday and like occasions. Dickens wrote to T. J.
Thompson:

> Maclise and I are raving with love for the queen . . . we
> sallied down to Windsor, prowled about the Castle, saw
> the corridor, and their private rooms, nay the very bed-
> chamber lighted up with such a ruddy, homely, brilliant
> glow bespeaking so much bliss and happiness that I lay
> down in the mud at the top of the Long Walk and refused
> all comfort. . . . We drove home in a post-chaise and now
> we wear marriage medals next our hearts.[1]

For days and days he could settle to nothing, work went by
the board, and to Kate's annoyance he wandered about the
house singing,

> My heart is at Windsor
> My heart is not here,
> My heart is at Windsor
> A-following my dear.

[1] 248. I. N.L.

Running off to the Athenaeum, he cracked jokes with Monckton Milnes about what he called 'the national anthem of Seven Dials', which ran like this,

> So let 'em say whate'er they may
> Or do whate'er they can,
> Prince Halbert he will always be
> My own dear Fancy Man,

and asked his friend whether he too had not heard it sung in the streets?   To Forster Dickens spoke of razors, of throwing himself into the Serpentine or Regent's Canal, professed to loathe his family, detest his house, and be irritated by his wife. He told T. J. Thompson as executor of his will that there was a little bequest having reference to Her:

> I have heard on the Lord Chamberlain's authority, that she reads my books, and is very fond of them.   I think she will be sorry when I am gone.   I should wish to be embalmed and to be kept (if practicable) on the top of the triumphal arch[1] at Buckingham Palace when she is in town and on the north-east turrets of the Round Tower when she is at Windsor.[2]

To the puzzled Landor he wrote:

> Society is unhinged by her majesty's marriage and I am sorry to add that I have fallen hopelessly in love with the Queen and wander up and down with vague and dismal thoughts of running away to some uninhabited island with a maid of honour to be entrapped by conspiracy for that purpose. . . .[3]

In spite of these theatrical outbursts, when the actual marriage morning dawned Charles went off docilely with Kate to the stand at the Athenaeum from which they obtained a good view of the wedding procession.   Both craned their necks as Miss Coutts drove by wearing the tiara of Marie Antoinette and other historic jewels.   People round them gossiped about the offers of marriage she had refused from

[1] The Marble Arch, then in front of the Palace.
[2] 249. I. N.L.   [3] 247. I. N.L.

every young man of birth in England, as well as from Prince
Louis Napoleon.   And who, they asked, would there be for
her to marry in the end?   It entered no one's head that she
could remain a spinster for another forty years.

To distract Charles and turn his thoughts from the bride to
his own work Forster now arranged that he should pay a visit
to Landor.   He knew Landor would never tolerate mad talk
about the Queen, but would switch the conversation to books
and especially to his favourite *Pickwick*, which he said had
drawn from him 'more tears and more smiles than were
remaining to him for all the rest of the world real or ideal'.
Near the end of the marriage month 'Fuz', 'Boz' and 'Phiz'
set out for 25 St. James's Square, Bath, where lived one of the
most original of English men of letters, an author who displayed apathy, not to say antipathy, to popular success, saying
he would be well content with ten intelligent readers.   His
rooms, including the doors, were plastered with Italian pictures, each of which he thought the finest specimen of the
finest master and each of which had its story.   It became an
annual habit for 'Fuz' and 'Boz' to go to Bath to dine with
Landor on his birthday.   Eliza Lynn (later Mrs. Lynn
Linton) made a fourth on one of these occasions, and with her
usual plain-spokenness recorded that she did not take to
Forster at all; his tiresome manner gave the impression that
he thought he owned both her host and 'Boz'.   Dickens
struck her as bright, gay, 'winsome' and altogether charming,
but Forster remained throughout the evening heavy, pompous
and ungenial.   Dickens seemed to know instinctively how to
treat his host, first with the respect of a young man for an
older man and then allowing his wit to play about him, bright
and harmless as summer lightning.   At this time Eliza Lynn,
in the early twenties, was being treated as a spoilt daughter by
Landor, who, in spite of his sixty-five years, would hire
sedan-chairs to escort her to the Assembly Rooms for balls.
As she adored him, she was watchful of the behaviour of
visitors and reacted sharply to their remarks.   The conversation between Dickens and Landor on the first meeting was so

pleasant and so stimulating as to put Landor into a good temper and make Dickens anxious to begin work again. A story he heard at Bath now inspired him with the vision of a child who for a year and more was to be his constant pre-occupying companion. The story of Little Nell, when it became public, plunged half the world in tears. It is a story that George Lewes in that day and Mr. Aldous Huxley in our own day have condemned for its ineptitude and sentimentality. The behaviour of the Victorian heart is a study in itself, as we shall see in discussing *The Old Curiosity Shop*. For the moment it may be stated that Nell's odyssey impressed most of Dickens's contemporaries as a credible and beautiful achievement. Almost without exception they wept over it as uncritically as did its author.

On arriving home Dickens set to work to get *Master Humphrey's Clock* 'striking by the end of March'. He took a deal of trouble over the illustrations, which were not to be full plate but 'dropped into the text'. In his instructions for the clock-case on which his scheme pivoted, he told Catter-mole to set it in an old quaint room with antique Elizabethan furniture. 'In the chimney-corner must stand an extra-ordinary old clock, the clock belonging to Master H. in fact.'

The drawing supplied to this order presented a clock of rococo outline, Dutch dimensions and great holding capa-city, the artist having been more intent on producing a good manuscript cupboard than a clock-case of the Eliza-bethan period. Dickens, however, was pleased with it and, as soon as he had passed the last proofs of the magazine, rushed off to the country with Kate so as to avoid being in London on the day the new venture was launched. The *Clock* made a fast start, seventy thousand copies of the first number being sold. With the second number, after the public had discovered that there was no serial by 'Boz' but a good deal of sermonising, sales fell sharply. Praise from critics could not vivify the failure. It was to no purpose that Tom Hood lauded its intention and called Dickens 'the champion of the poor and of worth in low places'; the *Clock* had to have its mainspring changed before becoming popular.

In his leisure hours Dickens was at this time reading a thick pamphlet, *Chartism* by Carlyle. He had not met the sage at this time, but like every man of his day was concerned over the Charter campaign that had been launched shortly after the Queen's Coronation and had arisen out of Lord John Russell's formal declaration in Parliament against further measures of Reform. A group of Liberal members of Parliament at a meeting in Birmingham had drawn up a six-points People's Charter comprising manhood suffrage, annual Parliaments, vote by ballot, abolition of property qualification for election of members to Parliament, payments of members, and the division of the country into equal electoral districts.

Dickens heard that Carlyle saw in this movement an expression of justifiable discontent and found himself in agreement with this view. There was no doubt that government by the upper classes on the principle of letting the under classes alone was as sterile in result as the gospel preached to the workless about being at the mercy of the laws of supply and demand. What, Dickens asked himself, did these laws mean in his own profession? Why, Samuel Johnson earning fivepence a day! or Talfourd fighting a losing battle to safeguard the creations of a writer's brain! *Laissez faire* posturing as freedom was certainly the curse of England.

It had always worried Dickens during his reporting tours to note the apathy displayed by electors and the extent to which the people, in spite of the Reform Bill, were still alienated from their own affairs. He welcomed the People's Charter, for he took it to be a sign that the nation was developing political consciousness. As he read the clauses which 'respectfully' called attention to the existing monopolies of the suffrage, of paper money, of machinery, of land, of the public press, of religion, of the means of travelling and transit, he rejoiced to see these grievances formulated. They might alarm the drawing-rooms of Mayfair, but had they not all arisen from class legislation? and was not class legislation the enemy to be held responsible for the 'accursèd gentility' of English life? This gentility appeared to him as a blight pervading society as a whole and emasculating the natural vigour of the people. The so-called middle class, to which he himself belonged, was not really a class, but only 'the poor fringe on the mantle of the upper class'. It could not be counted on to form a buffer between high and low, for its interests were really identical with those of the governing class, into whose ranks it was slowly and continuously being absorbed.

The year 1840 must be reckoned an important year for Dickens in so far as it brought him under the influence of Carlyle. The first time he clapped eyes on him was at a lecture on 'Great Men' given at Willis's Rooms. Maclise, Macready, Browning, Forster and other friends were also listening, but no one of them imbibed a more definite message than Dickens, who began to feel as if the aspirations of his youth were being precipitated by contact with this powerful brain. From now on he went about with a copy of Carlyle's *French Revolution* in his pocket, reading it over and over again. And we see the outcome in *Bleak House, Hard Times* and *A Tale of Two Cities*.

Carlyle seemed to Dickens to have a deeper understanding than anyone of the inadequacy of the reforms undertaken by Parliament. What was the good of improving the talking apparatus if the acting apparatus was not improved too? Political reform unaccompanied by administrative reform must be a mockery. Carlyle, he found, was all for breaking down what he himself dubbed the Buffy-Boodle system, for did he not hold that the able man should be preferred no matter what his birth? and did he not point out that the 'poor old benighted Catholic Church' had set the world an example in this respect, since by 'a thrice glorious arrangement' she had shown how aptitude should rise and rise to the top of the tree? Right through the dim oppressed strata of society ran the institution of the priesthood like a great mine-shaft opening from the lowest depths towards all heights, towards heaven itself, and inviting noble souls whether neatherds' or butchers' sons to tread the noble path. This was the secret of the health and vitality of the old society, now lungless and wheezing itself to death. In these flights Dickens could not follow Carlyle for he knew nothing about the Catholic Church and in theory despised it, but he was conscious in a quite definite way of the decay of Christian feeling in the economic life of the day and knew this decay to be responsible for much oppression and avoidable misery. This was why he set such store on the spirit of Christmas: it was all he knew of Christianity in action and he preached it with all his might.

On his long night walks in mean streets he often felt suffocated by the conditions he encountered. Could education possibly be the key to the conundrum of poverty, and if it were, how could education make its way in a kingdom wherein children were wage slaves? England, he knew, lay under the stigma of being the worst educated country in Northern Europe, and he also knew, from studying Lord John Russell's figures that out of the 14,000 children in Bethnal Green but 2000 attended any school. So much for the appalling indifference of the Buffy-Boodle gang to the future of England! But then what future except servitude everlasting had a people that could neither read nor write? Day after day with Miss Coutts Dickens discussed these problems as together they drew up schemes for Ragged Schools and slum clearance. He was always very silent about his philanthropic activities which for many years remained a secret between himself and the generous lady in Piccadilly whose benefactions he constantly guided into new channels.

The first face-to-face meeting between Dickens and Carlyle took place under Lord Stanley's roof at what the sage called 'a dinner of lords and lions'. Lord and Lady Holland, Lord Normanby and M. Guizot were among the guests. Carlyle, who had been rather bored than otherwise by Dickens's first books, was in process of succumbing to the sentimental

appeal of *The Old Curiosity Shop* and therefore studied the
appearance of its author in an interested way. He struck him
as a quiet, shrewd little fellow who had sized both himself and
others up. A head with 'a loose coil' of hair and a face of
extreme mobility were carried by a small compact figure
dressed *à la* d'Orsay. Darting eyes, arching eyebrows,
mouth—all expressive, went to produce a 'shuttling' effect,
which was Carlyle's way of saying that Dickens was perpetually responding to the stimulus of the conversation that surged
about him. From Dickens's angle we know nothing about
this meeting, for social happenings were never chronicled by
him; he had far too much to do in getting the creatures of his
imagination down on to paper to have any time to spare for
chance encounters even when they proved as significant as did
his introduction to Carlyle.

Dickens was a man of his day in one sense and far ahead of
his day in another. To begin with, he was a pioneer of the
modern classless type to which we are now accustomed, a type
with little respect for tradition and which is inclined to view
the mechanism of parliamentary government as outworn and
obstructionist. Dickens held no second-hand opinions. His
judgments, such as they were, sprang from experience and
observation, and his four years' service in the House of
Commons had made him doubt the seriousness, integrity and
even the good-will of the majority of members. It was clear
that certain men like Grote, who worked for the extension of
the franchise, Lord Ashley, who strove to secure decent conditions of employment for workers, Lord John Russell, who
fought for education, stood out from their kind as upright
reformers, but he resented seeing their energies and enthusiasm
being fretted away in ceaseless and relentless attack by the
opponents of social reform. The failure too of these good
men to support each other seemed to him another weakness of
the parliamentary system. Each man played a lone hand; for
example Lord John Russell, in spite of his advocacy of universal education, would not consider extending the franchise,

and eyed social legislation of Lord Ashley's type as a danger-ous incline leading to the foundering of the existing social fabric.

In view of his distrust of parliamentary methods it is a surprise when in 1841 we find Dickens beginning to consider putting up for Parliament himself. It may be that Miss Burdett Coutts, whose plans for rehousing slum-dwellers and reclaiming children from the streets needed a spokesman, may have advised him in this matter, or it may be that Serjeant Talfourd recommended him to seize the opportunity for for-warding social reform offered by a seat in the House of Commons. It is almost certainly to Talfourd that we must attribute the final push towards politics. On the fall (in 1841) of Lord Melbourne's government and the initiation of the Free Trade agitation, Dickens was approached by certain persons from Reading with the proposal that he should stand at the forthcoming election as their second candidate. As Talfourd, the son of a local brewer, was their sitting member it seems certain that the recommendation must have come from him.

It would have been superfluous for the author of *Oliver Twist* and *Nicholas Nickleby* to state his convictions and views on the Poor Law or on Education. He was well known, for he had been much spoken of by public men. Sir Francis Burdett had alluded to him as 'the advocate of the poor', Lord Ashley had called him 'a public benefactor', to Tom Hood he was 'the champion of the poor'. In the minds of the electors of Reading he would represent a young and better England, the England of the future. In replying to a formal letter asking for his consent to nomination Dickens wrote[1] that, though obliged and flattered by their communication and aspiring to the distinction they invite him to seek, he cannot afford the expense of a contested election. He was at once requested to come to Reading for an interview and there it was revealed to him that though they wanted him as a candi-date they did not want him enough to pay any part of his

[1] May 31, 1841, p. 325. I. N.L.

expenses.   Subsequently he wrote with reference to the interview:

> The sum you mention, although small I am aware in the abstract, is greater than I could afford for such a purpose; as the mere sitting in the House and attending to my duties, if I were a Member, would oblige me to make many pecuniary sacrifices, consequent upon the very nature of my pursuits.[1]

The next paragraph reveals that 'the magnates' had suggested that Dickens should apply to be financed by party funds, but this proposal was repugnant to him.   He had no wish to become a party hack.

> The course you suggest did occur to me when I received your first letter, and I have very little doubt indeed that the Government would support me—perhaps to the whole extent.   But I cannot satisfy myself that to enter Parliament under such circumstances, would enable me to pursue that honourable independence without which I could neither preserve my own self-respect nor that of my constituents.   I confess therefore . . . that I cannot bring myself to propound the subject to any member of the Administration whom I know.   I am truly obliged to you nevertheless.[2]

And so the proposal came to nothing, and it is well for the world that it did.   The approach to politics had been a diversion and 'Boz' returned to his proper sphere to discover that an undreamed-of success awaited him therein.   With Little Nell he had captured the ardent heart of America, and surely that was a better thing by far than capturing the votes of Reading electors.

Some time in 1838 Dickens had made friends with Dr. John Elliotson, a distinguished physician, who was losing the confidence of his colleagues at University College Hospital owing to his deep interest in hypnotism.   He had founded a small mesmeric hospital where he had cured tic douloureux

[1] June 10, 1841, *ibid.*   [2] *Ibid.*

and had carried out various minor operations under the anaesthesia induced by magnetic passes. His patients were many and among them was Thackeray, who dedicated *Pendennis* to him out of gratitude for having saved his life. One August evening in 1840 Dickens dined with him to meet the Reverend Chauncey Hare Townshend, a rich young clergyman who had made a habit of travelling about the continent in search of health and who had spent some time in Antwerp studying mesmerism. He had just brought out an account of what he had witnessed, *Facts in Mesmerism*, which he had dedicated to John Elliotson in a preface penned at 'Inspruck' in November 1839. His approach to the subject, as he was not a medical man, was different from that of Elliotson, but they had, he asserted, arrived at the same results, *i.e.* that somnambulism could be induced: that spirit demonstrably dominated matter: that the mind was the only source of power. Elliotson and Townshend had only known each other a few weeks when this dinner took place. Dickens listened spell-bound to the conversation of the experts and made Elliotson promise to instruct him in the art of animal magnetism. To his surprise and pleasure he found he was apt at it; it was quite easy, it seemed, to send people to sleep and even to make them wake up again. No one could have foreseen the curious dilemma in which the possession of this knowledge was a few years later to place him. Though he seems to have refused to be magnetised himself, he frequently practised on Kate and her sister and on other non-resisters. We find him recommending 'Townshend's magnetic boy' to Lady Blessington for a séance at Gore House and warning her not to invite more than eight people, four being really the better number for getting interesting results.

Spiritualism, on the other hand, never attracted him at all though it was all the rage. Mrs. Trollope, whom he did not much like, and who was never invited to Devonshire Terrace, tried to lure him to table-turnings and séances, and Lady Morgan, too, through her famous homoeopathic doctor, Quin, would urge him to grace her evenings, but he remained deaf

to their appeals.   He did however make certain experiments
with one Bührer, the owner of a psychograph said to write at
the dictation of the foreign count alleged to materialise in
Bührer's rooms.   These diversions from the main purpose of
Dickens's life could only be indulged in fitfully.   As he
became more famous the claims of the world became more
insistent.

In removing from Bloomsbury and placing themselves in a
quarter of London that was fashionable and specialised in
dinner-giving, Mr. and Mrs. Charles Dickens indicated their
willingness to take and to receive hospitality.   Now that they
had a good cook, three other maids and a man servant of their
own they could and did vie with their neighbours and friends.
This still youthful couple, the host of twenty-eight and the
hostess of twenty-four, cast their net wide, including Lord
Jeffrey, Edwin Landseer, the Carlyles, Mr. Rogers, Canon
Sydney Smith, Miss Burdett Coutts, Richard Monckton
Milnes and Edward Bulwer in their gatherings.   Sydney
Smith, whose humour Dickens admired vastly, accepted one
of his invitations in the following words:

> If I am invited by any man of greater genius than yourself
> or by one in whose works I have been more completely
> interested I will repudiate you and dine with the more
> splendid phenomenon of the two.[1]

But not everyone was such a wag as the Canon of St. Paul's
nor did everyone give such agreeable breakfast parties.   The
Canon used to say that breakfast parties were always pleasant
'because no one is conceited before one o'clock'.   Breakfast
in company was with Dickens a very rare indulgence for he
never allowed amusement to eat into his working hours and
usually shut himself away behind baize doors from early
morning till three in the afternoon.   After this spell of
application he was ready for anything, a long walk, a ride, a
potter round auction rooms or any other pastime.

[1] May 14, 1841.

One day on returning from a visit to the Smithsons in Yorkshire Mrs. Christian and T. J. Thompson dropped in for luncheon at Devonshire Terrace. It ruined Dickens's working day to be hauled out of his study to talk to guests and 'Eleanor P.' received rather a rude shock, for her host seemed to have forgotten all their friendly fun at Broadstairs. He was distant in manner and only thawed a little when the raven pecked at her ankles squawking 'Hullo, old gal!' Fred Dickens, who was standing by, announced that he was going to see Courvoisier receive 'a well-deserved hanging'. Charles looked annoyed. 'What!', he said. 'You're never going to be such an idiot! Whence comes this morbid craving to gloat over such a loathsome exhibition?' 'Oh, Thackeray is going,' retorted Fred, 'and I am joining a select circle of reporters.' On this Thompson observed, 'Well, you'll be squeamish for a couple of days afterwards'. 'Have you ever seen a man hanged?' eagerly questioned Fred. 'No, but I've seen a man guillotined', replied Thompson. Then Dickens gave a shudder and exclaimed, 'Ugh! That's a messy business, all gore and sawdust. The inverted rope-dance is cleaner though less impressive. I'd keep away from such a hideous spectacle from principle. I'm not sure that we ought to dispose of even murderers in such barbarous ways.'

'Eleanor P.' was not the only visitor to notice how greatly Dickens had changed in two years. George Lewes too observed that he took himself with new seriousness and was quite the great man.

From some of those who went to Devonshire Terrace we may learn just what it was like to dine with Mr. Dickens. Mrs. Carlyle, often tart in comment and never making allowances, tells us that the dinner she attended was 'served in the new fashion', in other words that the dishes were not placed on the table but were handed round by servants. Though Mrs. Carlyle was not in a position to give dinners herself, she at least knew how Lady Ashburton did things. The poor inexperienced young Dickenses had artificial flowers, *only*, upon the table and such quantities of them! and then 'the profusion of figs, raisins, oranges, och! such overloaded dessert!' At the Ashburton dinner served on the same principle she had noticed 'just four cowslips in china pots, four silver bells containing sweets, and a silver filigree temple', but at the Devonshire Terrace dinner 'the very candles rose out of an artificial rose!'

From Lord Jeffrey we get yet another glimpse. An enthusiastic admirer of the genius of 'Boz', this Scotsman had gone about saying there had been nothing so good as Little Nell since Cordelia and had invited her creator to come and see him. Stepping across from Devonshire Terrace to visit this near neighbour, Dickens found himself charmed exceedingly by the courtesy shown him and by the veteran reader's praise of *The Old Curiosity Shop*. 'Upon my word,' he said to Tom Beard, 'I came out of the house more delighted than if I had been ten thousand pounds richer than when I went in.' The acquaintance grew and we find Lord Jeffrey writing to Lord Cockburn that he was seeing a good deal of Charles Dickens with whom he meant to strike up an eternal and intimate friendship.

> He lives very near to us and I often run over and sit an hour tête-à-tête or take a long walk in the Park with him ... taken in this way I think him very amiable and agreeable. In mixed company where he is now much sought after he is rather reserved. He has dined here and we with him at rather too sumptuous a dinner for a man with a family and only beginning to be rich.

Pressing the young author to come to Edinburgh later on, Lord Jeffrey assured Dickens of a real Scottish welcome. Kate Dickens was particularly pleased with this invitation. Edinburgh was her birthplace and to her the city of all others where a triumph was worth scoring. As soon as Lord Jeffrey got back home he arranged to take the chair at a banquet in honour of 'Boz', fixing the date for June 25, 1841. In refusing a dinner invitation from Lady Holland for June 19 that year Dickens explained that he was due in Edinburgh for a public dinner and was visiting a friend in Yorkshire beforehand. He thanks her for an introduction to Lord Lauderdale.

Mr. and Mrs. Dickens arrived at the Royal Hotel, Edinburgh, on June 22 and there enjoyed their first taste of real celebrity in finding themselves provided with a grand suite of rooms in a hotel besieged by admirers. The terrors of lionisation were to some extent dispelled for Kate by the kind-heartedness of the people who welcomed them. Miss Allan took her off to renew her acquaintance with the sights while Sir William Allan took charge of her husband. The banquet went off brilliantly though Lord Jeffrey was ill and had to be replaced by 'Christopher North' (John Wilson). Looking down on the guests from the high table, Dickens realised that however warm the 'enthoosymoosy' displayed it did not affect him at all. He felt cool as a cucumber and preened himself on the number of greyheads come to honour his brown flowing locks. In his speech he said that in his books he had tried to 'show forth the soul of goodness in men' of every walk in life,

> The rank is but the guinea stamp,
> The man's the gowd for a' that.

He then referred to *The Old Curiosity Shop* and explained why he had had to kill Little Nell. It was done that he might substitute a garland of fresh flowers for the sculptured horrors that usually disgrace a tomb. He had wanted to fill young minds with better thoughts of death, to soften the grief in older hearts, to console old and young in time of trial. Therefore, in spite of all the letters requesting Nell's reprieve, he had kept to his purpose and Little Nell had died. He then went on to say,

> The distinction you have conferred upon me is one I never hoped for and of which I never dared to dream. I thank you again and again with the energy of a thousand thanks in each one.

Later in the evening he proposed the health of the Chairman and then spoke to the memory of Sir David Wilkie (recently dead and buried at sea off Gibraltar). He had seen a good deal of Wilkie, who had made of humble life a noble thing, who had left memories behind him 'as pure as the blue waves that now roll over him', and who had died in the fulness of fame before age or sickness had dimmed his powers.

No occasion could have given greater satisfaction to speaker or listener, but there was no whisper of the great surprise to be sprung on the guest of honour on the day following when Dickens learnt that the Lord Provost, Council and Magistrates of Edinburgh had voted by acclamation that the freedom of the city should be conferred on him 'in testimony of his distinguished abilities as an author'. In mind Dickens reverted to his experience of seven years earlier when he, a mere reporter, had taken down the speeches made at the banquet to Lord Grey. A further surprise arising from this wonderful visit was another offer of a seat in the House of Commons, this time 'for a Scotch county that's going a-begging'. He turned the offer down at once and notified the same to Forster, writing, 'I have declined to be brought in free gratis and for nothing'.

For the first time Charles Dickens knew what it felt like to perch on a pinnacle of the temple of fame. He was not unduly excited by his elevation: it had in a sense been achieved in his heart's blood. Taking the homage as it came, he remained simple, feeling there was no place like home and thanking God for having given him a quiet spirit and 'a heart that won't hold many people'.

Chapter 11

SAMPLING AMERICA

America, half-brother of the world.
P. J. BAILEY

In his draft scheme for *Master Humphrey's Clock* Dickens had broached the idea that its editor should travel, and by the summer of 1841 his desire to cut free from the fetters of serial slavery had become 'an imperative necessity'. He had reviewed Lockhart's *Life of Scott* for *The Examiner*, and this had interested him so much that he had gone on to read Scott's *Diary*, much of which he found poignantly applicable to himself. The pathetic account of Sir Walter Scott's journey to Italy made him realise with sudden intensity how important it was to travel in youth and 'plenitude of power' rather than in weakness and senility. America was now the lure, partly because in America he thought he could see which way the world was going and partly because he believed that in a modern and kingless country he would feel thoroughly at home and escape from the snobbery engendered by class rule. How much more akin he was to old-fashioned Europeans than to the citizens of the New World it did not require six months' experience in the United States to bring home to him.

Biographers have thought up other reasons that may have induced him to cross the ocean. Some said that he wanted to meet Washington Irving, some have supposed that he had invested savings in the 'Cairo City and Canal Company' and wished to see the grand city at the junction of the Mississippi and Ohio rivers advertised by its promoters in London with 'flaming lithographs': some that the ecstatic letters he had received from America about Little Nell had made him eager to contact a new public: some that he was the secret emissary of London publishers in the matter of international copyright. Perhaps an operative clue is to be found in the fourteenth number of *Pickwick* where Tony Weller says to Sam Weller, 'Have a passage taken ready for 'Merrika and then let him come back and write a book about the 'Merrikins as'll pay his expenses and more, if he blows 'em up enough.'

Fanny Trollope's book *Domestic Manners of the Americans* had appeared in 1832. Of course Dickens had read it carefully as he had that of Harriet Martineau, *Society in America*. Both works had been disapproved of in the United States as much for the patronising tone of their praise, when they gave any, as for the depreciatory nature of their blame, and both confirmed Dickens in his resolve that 'in going to the New World one must for the time being utterly forget and push out of sight the Old one and bring none of its customs or observances into the comparison'.[1] A resolution easy to make and hard to carry out, though as a man of the people Dickens in his heart of hearts believed himself more qualified than either of these ladies to understand and appreciate democracy in being. He was careful, therefore, to check feminine statements and conclusions against those of a male crony, Captain Marryat, who had spent two years in the United States and on his return had not only published his *Diary in America*, but was willing to discuss his more private impressions in long-drawn conversations.

In considering the American adventure we must bear in mind that there was a love of experiment in Dickens's nature. From time to time it overpowered him and then he would jump out of his setting and start a new break—a house in Paris maybe, a palace in Genoa or a villa by Leman. Mrs. Dickens did not share these impulses, went unwillingly abroad, pined in strange surroundings and in the end suffered the penalties entailed in unadaptability. It was with something like dismay that she watched her husband making the arrangements, literary and financial, that would enable him to carry out his plan of conveying her to America. The house, carriages and staff were let over her head to Sir John Wilson for a period of six months, and it was arranged that the four

[1] To A. Bell. October 12, 1841.

precious children should be dumped on the Macreadys during her absence. Half hypnotised by her husband's decisions, she still hoped that something, money perhaps, might hold up the proceedings, but even on the subject of money the publishers were amiable and put no obstacles in the way. Rather the reverse, for Chapman and Hall were perfectly willing to wind up *Master Humphrey's Clock* if Mr. Dickens would promise them a new novel in November 1842—a novel on the lines of that best-seller *Nicholas Nickleby*. In the agreement finally come to between author and publisher[1] Dickens was granted a holiday of fourteen months at £150 a month secured against future earnings. Overjoyed at this arrangement, he offered to write a travel-book on America which Chapman and Hall jumped at the idea of publishing.

October 1841 brought a new shock to the little family in that Kate's young brother, aged twenty, died as suddenly as Mary had died four years earlier. All the pain of the old wound revived as Charles, who had always meant to be buried in Mary's grave, now had to abandon the idea though it 'was still strong in him'. Again he cries, 'I don't think there ever was love like that I bear her,' and we are reminded of Léon Bloy's memorable phrase *Plus on est homme de génie, plus on est homme* and of Carlyle's 'Genius gives intensity of spiritual suffering'. It was almost a relief from heart-ache for Dickens to be told at this time by his doctor that he must submit to 'the cutting-out root and branch of a disease caused by working overmuch, which has been gathering for years'. 'I laboured under the complaint called Fistula, the consequence of too much sitting at my desk.'

While recovering from this cruel operation, which of course had to be endured without an anaesthetic, he discussed with John Forster the planning of his journey. Certain preparations would bring certain results. Money was important, clothes were important, letters of introduction were important. Five pounds a day should cover all expenses

[1] Signed September 6, 1841.

while travelling, but a considerable sum must be disbursed on tailors and dressmakers if Mr. and Mrs. Charles Dickens were to make their American bow in a distinguished way. Kate, who never ceased repining at having to put the Atlantic between herself and her children, wept quietly at intervals, though the business of trying on pretty frocks, shawls and bonnets took up all her spare time. Economy was not allowed to hamper her choice; she must have clothes suitable for all occasions, even for Embassy balls and dinners at the White House. We can see in Maclise's charming portraits of her that she could wear dresses elegantly and that Charles was right in insisting that she should make herself as attractive as possible. In order to smooth her path it was arranged that her competent maid, Anne, should travel with them. Charles was as kind as he could be, and Maclise seconded him by making a life-like group of the children which could be set up in any cabin, bedroom or parlour. This picture, as we shall see, was to prove a great solace in unhomelike surroundings.

Before leaving London Dickens called on Lady Holland. As she disliked Americans, she tried to persuade him not to go to the United States at all, saying, 'Why cannot you go down to Bristol and see some of the third and fourth class people there and they'll do just as well?' Lady Blessington, on the contrary, approved of his plans and wished him godspeed.

One of the most constant factors in Dickens's make-up, his confidence in himself, was, as we have seen, partially derived from his theatrical instinct, and it is plain that the stranger the circumstances the more support and comfort he found in the right clothes. As a frequenter of Gore House and a friend of Macready he had learnt from observation how important it was to look the part one was to play. He was visiting America in the role of a distinguished author and therefore must provide himself with fashionably-cut coats, coloured vests, and the brocade dressing-gowns in which gentlemen gave interviews to callers before donning their frock-coats for the street. He must also buy for his adornment new tie-pins, chains and rings. When preparations were complete, the travellers were accompanied to Liverpool and seen on to the steamship 'Britannia' by John Forster, who presented his friend with a pocket Shakespeare that proved 'an unspeakable source of delight'.   The evening before the ship sailed Dickens found time to write to Lord Brougham (to whom he had already recommended Chapman and Hall as a publishing firm of high integrity for the Society for the Diffusion of Useful Knowledge) telling him that his father-in-law, George Hogarth, may submit a book to the Society and that he has written very admirable works of instruction on Music and History: 'You will remember the name by the great painter's,' and then added, 'The ship weighs anchor at two o'clock'.   After a horrible voyage, eclipsing in terror anything that even Kate Dickens had imagined, they reached Halifax and there enjoyed a foretaste of the excitements Dickens's appearance was to evoke in America.

To begin with, the Speaker of the Legislative Assembly came aboard to carry Charles Dickens off to his house, while Mrs. Dickens was driven away in a carriage by the Speaker's wife.   It happened to be a great day in Halifax, for it was the first day of the session, and Dickens, to whom the mechanism of Crown Colony Government was entirely unknown, attended the opening ceremony and was astonished to hear 'a mock speech from the throne'.   But it was not Lord Falkland or his legislators who really interested the visitor, it was himself and the sensation his appearance created.   'I wish you could have seen the crowds cheering the Inimitable in the streets', he wrote exultingly to John Forster, 'I wish you could have seen the judges, law-officers, bishops and law-makers welcoming the Inimitable, I wish you could have seen the Inimitable shown to a great elbow-chair by the Speaker's throne.'   What he called the 'enthoosymoosy' of Nova Scotians was even warmer than that of Scots in Edinburgh, and yet he was pleased to think that he remained cool and self-possessed as ever.

The 'Britannia' steamed into Boston harbour on a Saturday

afternoon in January 1842.   Spectators waiting on the wharf
discerned on the paddle-box beside the captain a little fellow,
a foppish little fellow, in what he afterwards described as
'full-fig'.   The 'full-fig' consisted of a beaver hat, a brown
frock-coat, a vest figured in red, and a voluminous fancy scarf
fastened by two diamond pins linked by a gold chain.   His
looks, though entirely unlike anything to be met with at the
time in Boston, took no one by surprise; people were merely
seeing what they expected to see, for engravings of Maclise's
portrait had been displayed in every shop window.   This
likeness showed an elegant youth seated nonchalantly beside
a writing-table, curled hair over ears, fully puffed cravat-scarf
fastened with the famous diamond pins, frock-coat with deep
collar and revers, and trousers strapped over pointed highly
polished footgear.   It might have been the advertisement for
a mannequin travelling for a firm of fashionable tailors.   The
only surprise to Bostonians was that the renowned 'Boz'
should look so juvenile, that his skin should flush so easily,
that his lustrous eyes should brim with moisture.   Could he
be even more sensitive than his work had suggested?   But if
so, why did he show no shyness in grasping the hands of the
editors who swarmed on to the 'Britannia's' deck as soon as
she docked?

Before leaving London Dickens had agreed to sit for his
portrait to Francis Alexander of Boston.   The painter was
one of the first to welcome the voyagers at the wharf with a
posy for Mrs. Dickens in his hand.   Amiably enough he had
then rushed away to secure rooms at Tremont House (close
to his own studio), to which hotel he conducted them as soon
as Customs formalities were concluded.   Lord Mulgrave, a
young officer in the Coldstream Guards and a fellow passenger, drove with them, and when he saw the letters, invitations and flowers that were awaiting the novelist's arrival, he
urged Dickens to engage a secretary at once to cope with the
offers of hospitality and demands for lectures and interviews.
Alexander, the ever-helpful, produced George Putnam, an
artist, to act in this capacity.   He is discreetly alluded to as

'Mr. Q.' in Forster's biography. Putnam was modest, and obliging, and silent except when he was 'imitating cows and pigs', and began to work at once at the nominal salary of £10 a month and his keep. To his amusement his new employer and Lord Mulgrave reacted from their cramped voyage by running out after dinner. The moon was at the full and the streets snow-covered. They were as exhilarated as school-boys and laughed as they hurried along, with Putnam at their heels to see they did not get lost.

The travellers having landed in Boston on a Saturday were treated to a specially American form of hospitality, an invitation to a pew in church the following morning. Miss Martineau had commented on this charming civility which Mrs. Dickens, like Harriet, was unable to avail herself of, and for the same reason, that her Sunday dress was not yet unpacked. As it was not considered correct that husband and wife should appear separately for the first time in public, Dickens had the fun of wandering about the city incognito with coat collar up while Mrs. Dickens unpacked. He was all unaware that he was enjoying his last moments of care-free leisure.

Francis Alexander (to whom Dickens in four days' time was signing himself yours affectionately) lost no time in making his first sketch of the author and he begged that his friend Henry Dexter should be allowed to model his sitter at the same time as he was painting him. Dickens had no objection; he was well broken in by sitting to Maclise and d'Orsay. Mr. Putnam recounts that at breakfast-time Dexter would be busy working in one corner of the room while Alexander would make sketches in another, though insisting that Dickens must come to his studio, 41 Tremont Road, to pose for the painted portrait. Dexter would watch Dickens with 'the utmost earnestness' and would sometimes dart out with his calipers to measure his nose, forehead or chin. At one time an unsuccessful portrait painter, he had gained fame by executing (1839) a statue for a tomb in Mount Alban's cemetery known as 'The Binney Child'. To make a good bust of Dickens was obviously for him the chance of a lifetime. He succeeded in pleasing Kate, who wrote 'I think it a beautiful likeness'.

On the Monday began the crowds, the cheers, the verses, letters, dinners, assemblies, for a great free people had decided to offer to a young and self-made man a welcome as appreciative as that given to Lafayette twenty years earlier. 'Boz', the Nation's guest, was to be lionised to capacity and handed on from city to city throughout the far-flung states of the Union. At first he was childishly pleased by the enthusiasm, and even at the end of a week was still delighting in the homage offered him—banquets planned in his honour, theatre audiences rising at his entry, and daily levees packed. It was to be roses, roses all the way, or so it seemed at first sight.

If he felt it odd that he should be treated with such grandeur and solemnity he did not show it, for his adaptability enabled him to rise to every occasion. He was waited on by deputations from the Far West, from state authorities, and bodies public and private of every kind. 'It is all heart', wrote Dr. Channing, the great Boston preacher; 'there never was, never will be such a triumph!' To Charles Dickens it was so stimulating as to be almost supernatural. 'I feel in the best aspects of this welcome something of the presence and influence of that spirit which directs my life', he wrote in all sincerity to John Forster before he had found out what long thorns American roses concealed.

It seems to have dawned on him but slowly that it was not so much as a novelist that he was being fêted as a great moral force. He found himself saddled with a reformer's reputation and was expected to live up to it. Daniel Webster made this clear when he announced that Dickens had 'done more to ameliorate the condition of the English poor than all the statesmen that Great Britain had sent into Parliament'. A Boston preacher followed suit and boomed of 'Dickens's tendency to awaken sympathy with our race and change the unfeeling indifference which has prevailed towards the de-

THE DICKENS CHILDREN
by Daniel Maclise, R.A.

In this water-colour the two elder children, Charley and Mamie, are shown drinking the health of their parents. A toy decanter stands on one volume of Strutt's *Antiques of England* while Katie turns the leaves of the other.

" We carry with us a sketch of our darlings by Maclise. It is a great comfort. We unpack it every night, if we be on a journey; and make as much of this little household god as if it were alive."

CHARLES DICKENS TO LADY HOLLAND (22.3.42)

CATHARINE DICKENS, GEORGINA
HOGARTH AND CHARLES DICKENS
by Daniel Maclise, R.A.

SET OF PUNCH LADLES PRESENTED
TO DICKENS BY CHAPMAN AND HALL.
Designed by George Cruikshank

pressed multitude into a sorrowful and indignant sensibility
to their wrongs and woes'. Americans have a knack of
guessing right, and when they welcomed Dickens less as an
imaginative writer than as a moral force they made what at the
time being was a good shot, for it was only later that he
developed to the full his imaginative power. Never had he
been publicly welcomed in this way in England and at first
it seemed like a lift-up, though it soon proved to be a drag on
his spontaneity and enjoyment of life. No one but a missionary bishop or Mary Baker Eddy could have sustained the part
assigned to him by the Americans.

In becoming the Nation's guest Charles Dickens was soon
forced to realise the utterly binding nature of the new fetters
he was expected to assume. Not only must he give up
leisure, freedom of talk and opinion, but he must henceforth
conform to a pattern portrait. As a moral exemplar borne
shoulder-high on public esteem he must at a nod submerge in
the warm tide of popular favour, a tide that threatened to be
asphyxiating.

A certain discrepancy between the appearance of the
missionary and the solemnity of his mission was noted by
some of the curious strangers who crowded the daily Dickens
levees. No slighter or more effeminate-looking knight could
ever have entered the lists on behalf of humanity. In the
Alexander portrait, completed within a few days of his landing, we see the same slender figure depicted by Maclise. He
is writing at a table and his aquiline nose, mild eyes, parted
locks curtaining the ears, all give the effect of girlishness and
ingenuosity. Nevertheless he was presented to the American
public as a great force, as one who sympathised with the very
dregs of the people and touched hearts to ease their condition,
as a self-made man who had himself experienced the degradation of poverty, a man whose will-power was as terrific as his
industry and whose genius enabled him to get under the skin
of all his contemporaries. His genius, his universality had
been recognised by parliamentarians in London, by teachers
in Russia, by burgesses in Germany and Italy, and yet what

G

was there in his appearance to justify these claims? His first public dinner enabled him to demonstrate that outward appearance was not the most important clue to his personality.

It had been arranged that Mr. Dickens should meet the leading men of Boston at a banquet, the quality of which may be measured by the fact that the tickets were sold at $15 each. Most of the guests were already at the tables when Josiah Quincy with Oliver Wendell Holmes and the distinguished guest appeared in the banqueting chamber. 'God save the Queen' was played and the chairman set the key to the proceedings in his speech of welcome. 'What is Dickens's charm?' he asked, and, answering his own question, stated, 'He is a reformer.' Applause greeted this auspicious opening, and Mr. Quincy went on to say,

> He infuses a moral tone into everything. He is not only a portrayer of public wrongs, but he makes men feel that there is no condition so degraded as not to be visited by gleams of a higher nature.

The fatal germ of complacency had somehow insinuated itself into the company present, which settled itself down comfortably to absorb moral uplift.

Presently a girlish figure rose and, speaking with deep feeling, said: 'You give me no chance of playing at company or holding you at a distance, but flock about me like a host of brothers and make this place like home'. He had received many touching letters from Americans about Little Nell: he was glad to be with friends. The speech pleased all present until he raised the question of international copyright and then immediately and as if by magic he conjured up a host of enemies. He alluded to the fact that his own books had all been reprinted in the United States, most of them in monthly parts, just as soon as they could be ferried over from London. Tens of thousands had been sold at six cents against the twenty-five cents charged in England. 'Of all men living', he said, 'I am the greatest loser by it.' And he was not the only sufferer. Sir Walter Scott had also been a great loser in this matter and had made an appeal through Fenimore Cooper 'to the liberality, perhaps in some sort the justice of American feeling'. It had had no effect. In making his attack on piracy Dickens did not mince matters; he stated it to be 'a plain question of right or wrong, justice or injustice. There *must*', he concluded, 'be an international arrangement in this respect.'

No American speaker at the banquet supported his plea or so much as alluded to copyright. It was bad taste to introduce a controversial subject into a gathering of the kind. Ignoring the painful breach in etiquette, they proceeded to platitudinise on morality and genius and then passed on to formal toasts. The historian Prescott's health was drunk in his absence, the historian Bancroft's in his presence. Mr. Bancroft gave the toast, 'The Memory of Byron, Byron who had so often expressed the wish to visit America'. A letter from Washington Irving was read regretting his enforced absence, and the toast 'Geoffrey Crayon' followed. There were numbers of toasts and numbers of speakers, but no one breathed the word copyright. Mr. Dickens had offended all present by his *gaffe* and caused, as he was to learn from newspaper columns next day, 'huge dissonance where all else was triumphant unison'.

Taken aback at the effect he had produced and feeling for the first time qualms as to his capacity for understanding America, Dickens wrote to Macready:[1]

> Loving you . . . I would not condemn you to a year's residence on this side of the Atlantic for any money. Freedom of opinion! Where is it? I see a press more mean and paltry, and silly, and disgraceful than any country I ever knew. If that is its standard, here it is . . . I speak of Bancroft and am advised to be silent . . . he is a black sheep —a Democrat. . . . I speak of Bryant and am entreated to be more careful for the same reason. I speak of inter-

national copyright and am implored not to ruin myself
outright. I speak of Miss Martineau and all parties . . .
shower down upon me a perfect cataract of abuse. . . .
Americans can't bear to be told of their faults. 'Don't
split on that rock, Mr. Dickens, don't write about America,
we are so very suspicious.' Freedom of opinion! Macready, if I had been born here and had written my books in
this country, producing them with no stamp of approval
from any other land, it is my solemn belief that I should
have lived and died poor, unnoticed, and a 'black sheep' to
boot.

In meeting most of the people of note in Boston, among
them Longfellow, Richard Dana, George Bancroft, Dr.
Channing, Jared Sparks and Ticknor, Dickens made at least
two lifelong friends in Cornelius Felton, professor of Greek
at Harvard, and Jonathan Chapman, mayor of the city.
Rather unfortunately he did not meet either Hawthorne or
Margaret Fuller, both of whom had been absorbed into the
Brook Farm circle the previous year. Hawthorne held
strong views about the conceit displayed by English travellers
in their comments on the American way of life. 'Never', he
used to say, 'has an Englishman spared America for courtesy's
sake or kindness.' One of the few American books specially
praised by Dickens is *Mosses from an Old Manse*, and if he
could have met its author he might have been saved disillusionment and at any rate would have been warned that he
must not expect an extension of New England in other states
of the Union. With Longfellow (who secretly thought
Bostonians were making fools of themselves over 'Boz') he
struck up a sudden intimacy born of the fact that the poet was
just sailing for Europe. At once Dickens made plans for
future meetings in London. Longfellow must stay with him,
an invitation the American author was only too pleased to
accept. Reinforcing his invitation in a letter from New
York he said:

Write to me from the continent and tell me when to
expect you. We live quietly,—not uncomfortably—and

among people I am sure you would like to know as much as they would like to know you. Have no home but mine, see nothing in town on your way to Germany and let me be your London host and cicerone. Is that a bargain?

It was a little surprising to Dickens to find that nearly all the cultivated men of Boston were Unitarians and that Harvard, though undenominational in principle, was staffed by professors of this creed just as in England Oxford and Cambridge Universities were staffed by men of the Church of England. This form of non-miraculous Christianity had established a rather dim association in London in 1825, the same year in which the more prosperous Unitarian Association of America had been founded. As a creed it was in keeping with the movement of an age that was to produce Strauss's *Leben Jesu* and Renan's *Vie de Jésus*, and in Boston it was represented by all that was most cultured and elevated in American life. Dickens was very favourably impressed by the people who called themselves Unitarians and especially with their leading pastor, Dr. Channing. It occurred to him that as he adhered to no formal religion he might do worse than join the London Association at the Essex Street Chapel on his return. He would find no difficulty in accepting his friend W. J. Fox's definition of this faith: 'Belief in God the Father and in the humanity and divine mission of Jesus of Nazareth'. To himself he called it 'the religion that has sympathy for men of every creed and ventures to pass judgment on none'. On getting home from America we shall find him attending the Essex Street meetings, and then renting sittings for himself and family at the chapel in Little Portland Street, the minister of which, Mr. Tagart, was to become a trusted friend.

There was for Dickens an extraordinary relish to be derived not only from the discovery of Unitarianism, but also from meetings with people of achievement, just as for Bostonians there was a rare excitement in entertaining the most talked-of writer in the world. In America the emphasis is always on the man, for Americans are liable to be greatly stimulated by viewing people or listening to people who have actually accomplished something.   Dickens, too, was electrified by his first contacts with distinguished Americans, but even in refined Boston the pace was too fast and the demands made on him too exhausting, as we learn from Mrs. John Motley's letter to her husband written the day 'Boz' left the city:[1]

> Dickens goes to-day, but has promised to return in June. I only had a glimpse of him in the street getting in and out of a carriage when he came to breakfast with Dr. Channing the other morning.   I went to Miss Peabody's where he promised to go; instead of which, however, he went to bed and sent an apology, and disappointed the Paiges too, who had prepared a magnificent dinner for him—half an hour after dinner he sent an apology. . . . Poor man, he is literally used up . . . giving himself up as a spectacle.   He says this second edition, this epitome of London will never do; he must see something besides.

It was only a fortnight since Dickens had stepped ashore and yet already he lay in a state of collapse on a sofa in Tremont House quite unable to face the women who mobbed his movements and even pushed their way into Alexander's studio.   Mrs. Dickens also was quite overcome by the furore her husband had excited and could not speak of it without bursting into tears.   This, to the Americans, strange reaction was accounted for by the ladies gossiping at tea-tables by the suggestion that Mrs. Dickens must be going to have another baby.   One lady, who talked with Kate at a dinner-party given by the W. H. Prescotts, said she seemed highly embarrassed by the situation in which she found herself, being unaccustomed to dwell in the 'fierce light that shone upon every deed and word of the popular idol'.   It was a great satisfaction to her to talk about 'the best shops in Oxford Street and other homely and familiar matters'.   To her fellow guest she showed obvious signs of having been born and bred her husband's social superior.

On leaving Boston Dickens and his wife went to Worcester for a week-end, to stay with George Bancroft's sister, who was married to the Governor of Massachusetts. They then proceeded to Hartford, where they held formal levees each morning and shook hands with at least two hundred people a day. Later in their tour the numbers increased to six and seven hundred. The presence of Kate, Charles used to say, afforded him some protection at these impromptu gatherings. 'If I had not a lady with me I should be obliged to leave the country. But for her they would never leave me alone day or night.'

One of the American muses of the moment, Mrs. Sigourney, was among those who called on him at Hartford. Always on the alert for literary lions, she brought with her a poem written in honour of 'Boz', which she declaimed. The opening quatrain struck a genial note:

> Welcome! o'er the ocean blue,
> Welcome to the youthful West,
> Ardent hearts and spirits true
> Greet thee as a favoured guest.

A contrast with Mrs. Sigourney were the carmen of Hartford, who gave Dickens great pleasure by presenting themselves in their blue overalls to bid him welcome. It appeared from their spokesman's speech that they had all read his books and all perfectly understood them. This was the sort of compliment that made Dickens very much happier than did verses like those of Mrs. Sigourney. A boy of twelve who was watching him on this occasion was struck by his peculiar waistcoat. It was of a 'very vivid colour' and from its pockets dangled 'a very prodigious watch-chain'. As Dickens laughed, he tossed the chain up and down in his hands and then, as he got more excited, twiddled it round his fingers.

At the Hartford banquet that evening chairman William
Hammersley, following Mrs. Sigourney's example, broke into
verse:

> I'll sing you a new-made song,
> But from no agéd pate,
> Of a fine young English gentleman
> Whose mind is his estate.

Nothing really ever came amiss to Dickens in the way of
formal homage, and when he got up to address his fellow
guests it seemed as if he had quietly accepted the uplift cue
tendered him by all speakers.   Of the home-like quality of
his reception he said:

> I have faith and I wish to diffuse faith in the existence—
> yes, of beautiful things even in those conditions of society
> which are so degenerate, degraded, and forlorn. . . . I take
> it that we . . . hold our sympathies, hopes, and energies in
> trust for the Many not the Few.   That we cannot hold in
> too strong a light of disgust and contempt all meanness,
> falsehood, cruelty and oppression.   Above all that nothing
> is high because it is in a high place and nothing is low
> because it is in a low one.   [Loud applause].   This is the
> lesson taught by the great Book of Nature.

So far so good, but he spoiled the effect of these meritorious
sentiments on those present by begging leave to whisper the
words—international copyright.

> I use them in no sordid sense. . . . I would rather my
> children coming after me trudged in the mud and knew by
> the general feeling that their father was beloved and of
> some use than I would have them ride in their carriages and
> know by their banker's books he was rich.   But I do not
> see why one should be obliged to make the choice. . . . A
> copyright law would have saved Scott great suffering. . . .

The faces along the banqueting-table registered dis-
approval, but Dickens was not going to spare his auditors.
As he wrote home, 'My blood so boiled as I thought of the
monstrous injustice that I felt as if I were twelve feet high

when I thrust it down their throats'.[1]   No one of the speakers who followed him mentioned the odious theme.   It was as if the words he had spoken had never been uttered at all.

The public and the press did not follow the example of the dinner guests.   Anonymous letters reached him, newspaper reporters battered him as 'no gentleman, but a mercenary scoundrel'.   In a vigorously administered snubbing the *Hartford Times* said:

> It happens that we want no advice on this subject and it will be better for Mr. D. if he refrains from introducing the subject hereafter, but it is not pleasant to pursue the subject further at this time.

There is something peculiarly affronting to English people in not being allowed to express opinions freely.   We do not object to disagreement, even to contradiction so long as it is expressed in argument and not in condemnatory silence and press abuse.   Dickens was now subjected to the same mortifying experience as Harriet Martineau, who had been taken up with warm enthusiasm and then dropped like a stone when her opinions were found to be unacceptable to the *bien pensants* of America.   She only had to say once that she considered slavery inconsistent with the law of God to be condemned and cut.   After receiving universal homage and enjoying great personal popularity it was humiliating in the extreme to be treated thus, and it caused her to 'revise the over-favourable estimates' made in the earlier part of her tour. With Dickens it was a little different, for he put his foot wrong almost at the start and felt obliged to withdraw from the part he had at first seen himself playing in every great city of the Union.   Indeed he was so upset by the effect of his second copyright speech that he had a mind to abandon his tour altogether.   As this might have been difficult to explain, he adopted an alternative course of action, that of withdrawing into his shell and refusing to be booked for any public occasion.   In the role of private person he at least could hold private opinions. Sadly did he write to Macready, 'This is not the Republic I came to see. This is not the Republic of my imagination.'

New Haven was the scene of the next reception and there a *mêlée* instead of a levee took place at the Tontine Hotel. It was midnight before Mr. and Mrs. Dickens could escape to their room, and even then they were serenaded till dawn by choristers from the College. Hardly had they stepped aboard the New York packet next morning than they were again mobbed. Kate, whose face was dreadfully swollen, longed more than ever for the privacy of home and saw with dismay what unfair advantage was being taken by souvenir-hunters pressing up against Charles. Some 'twenty or thirty people were screwing small dabs of fur out of the back of the costly great-coat' bought by her husband in Regent Street just before they left London. Would they also snip pieces from her dress? Was it possible that they might both arrive at their destination in tatters?

Their friend David Colden had begged them to take no steps about getting introductions to people in New York, he himself would see to it that they were 'brought out' properly and not subjected to persecution. When they got to the Carlton Hotel on Broadway, they found that a committee of influential residents had booked accommodation for them and had arranged that they should attend a great ball at the Park Theatre on the following night, Valentine night. This they were told was to be a gala affair with three thousand guests in 'full dress' and a stage transformed into 'a large magnificent chamber of carved and gilded oak with deep gothick windows and lofty fretted ceiling'—an English baronial hall, in short, 'beyond description grand'. Mr. and Mrs. Dickens were conducted to the central box whence a ramp led to the stage. There they were introduced to the Mayor of New York and had to parade round the enormous ballroom to the tune of 'See the conquering hero comes'. Dickens wore a black suit with a gay vest and Mrs. Dickens 'a white-figured Irish tabinet trimmed with mazarine blue flowers to match her eyes'. A wreath, also of mazarine blue, crowned her fair ringlets and a pearl necklace adorned her neck. Both were carefully scrutinised as they danced in the opening cotillon. The paragraphists said that Mrs. Dickens though smartly dressed was not smart in manner: she spoke little and seemed resigned to her position as wife of a lion. As for the lion, he was 'bright-eyed, intelligent-looking, brisk in manner, lively in talk, somewhat of a dandy with rings and things in fine array', and women were particularly interested in the lion's mane. The hair seemed to wave naturally at the parting, but were the corkscrew curls also natural or merely soap-locks 'fixed' with a lotion? No matter how closely they leered, no female could decide. Had they but seen Count d'Orsay's sketch, made just before Dickens left England, its straight and ragged locks would have convinced them that the much-admired curls had been 'induced'.

Pressmen reported that at Park Theatre 'Boz' looked 'thunderstruck', and wondered whether he was used to such high society. He may have felt half dazed with fever and sore throat; anyway he spent the four days following the ball in bed. It was at this rather depressing moment that Washington Irving called at the Carlton Hotel and persuaded the sick lion and his mate to come and take refuge with him at Sunnyside, a gabled, creeper-clad villa on the Hudson. This lovely interlude of understanding, was remarked on by Professor Felton, another guest, who spoke of the 'mutual cordiality' displayed by both authors.

Irving realised, as few Americans did, the importance of the copyright question, for he had suffered under it himself when his books were published in London. Indifferent to popularity, since he was on the point of leaving America for the embassy at Madrid, he seized the opportunity presented by a public dinner at the City Hotel,[1] New York, to give the toast of 'Charles Dickens, the Nation's guest, coupled with

[1] February 19, 1842.

International Copyright'. 'It is but fair', he observed humorously, 'that those who have laurels for their brows should be permitted to browse on their laurels.'

In responding to this toast Dickens spoke of his great admiration for Washington Irving, who had, after reading *The Old Curiosity Shop*, written him 'a letter so generous, so affectionate, and so manly as to strike a sympathetic chord at once'.

> I answered him and he answered me and so we kept shaking autobiographically as if no ocean rolled between us. . . . Washington Irving! Why, gentlemen, I don't go upstairs to bed two nights out of the seven . . . without taking Washington Irving under my arm and when I don't take him I take his own brother, Oliver Goldsmith. Washington Irving, Knickerbocker, Geoffrey Crayon. Why, where can you go that they have not been there before?

Other speakers followed, one of whom, Cornelius Matthews, inquired by what casuistry does that which is property in one latitude cease to be property when transferred within the limits of another? 'I offer', he said, 'an international copyright as the only honest turnpike between the readers of two great nations.'

The *New York Tribune* supported Dickens nobly in an advance editorial:

> We have heard rumours that Mr. Dickens has ventured to allude in his replies to complimentary addresses to the gross injustice and spoliation to which he and foreign authors are exposed in this country from the absence of an International Copyright. We trust he will not be deterred from speaking the frank round truth. Who shall protest against robbery if those who are robbed may not? Here is a man who writes for a living. Do we look well offering him toasts, compliments and other syllabub while we refuse him naked justice? . . . He has a wife and four children whom his death may possibly leave destitute while publishers, grown rich by his writings, roll by in their carriages.

It was not till fifty years after this article was written[1] that a law regulating international copyright came into operation.

From this time on Dickens seems to have lost something of his zest for experience and something of his native buoyancy of temperament. The vista that had bewitched him in Boston 'of dinners and balls at Philadelphia, Baltimore and Washington and I believe everywhere' had faded. Finding he could do nothing in New York without being mobbed, he sometimes took refuge in a church, but when he did so neighbouring pews filled up with staring faces. In trains, in the street and at parties he found himself smothered and exhausted. To escape 'febrile circumstance' he declined in advance all public entertainments and told Putnam to make no future arrangements of any kind, anywhere. Shocked, melancholy and no longer floating on an ocean of approval, he began to fear that 'the heaviest blow ever dealt to liberty will be dealt by this country', and by liberty he meant not only liberty of thought but liberty of action.

Each one of us forms a mental concept of America and goes there expecting to find this concept operative. Emerging from the toils of a social system heavily weighed down by overhead charges, it was at first a delight to Dickens, as it has been to many others, to find himself in a classless land in which every man had access to the same education and could grow to the height for which his energy and intelligence fitted him. The absence of servile standards and social barriers, the fluidity of society and its interchangeability of parts at the first blush appeared to Dickens to be a realisation of equality, but even equality he found had its snags. Equality to some extent must be a matter of the flat-iron —and where the flat-iron makes itself felt most acutely on the few is in the pressing out of ideas and freedom of opinion.

He had been warned that he would find much to dislike in the United States. Fanny Trollope had told him about the tobacco-chewing and the spitting indulged in by American

[1] 1892.

men of that date. He believed he had discounted these things in advance, but as he cowered 'in the shabby omnibuses called railway-cars' he could not help shuddering at the flashes of saliva that streamed past the windows. Odious to him, too, was the charcoal heating of the trains, and as for the anthracite, burnt in the 'beastly furnaces' of hotels and institutions, it made him faint and gave him a headache 'morning, noon and night'. His spirits sank so low that he could see no fun in anything.

Though depression and a general sense of disillusionment had caused him to decline advance invitations from Philadelphia, and even to stay *perdu* in New York for three days after he was supposed to have left for the Quaker stronghold, the *Public Ledger* of that city got even with him as soon as they heard of his arrival by announcing that Mr. Dickens would be gratified to shake hands with his friends between the hours of 10.30 A.M. and 11.30 A.M. at the United States Hotel on Chestnut Street. As soon as he stepped into the lobby of the hotel, Mr. Dickens was requested by the landlord to name the hour for receiving 'a committee' next morning. The committee, to the author's horror, turned out to be a mob! For two hours poor, angry Mr. Dickens toiled away in a large room shaking hands with everyone, for the landlord had informed him that his refusal to do so would cause a riot. George Putnam who thought the whole business a cruel imposition, stood at his side while introductions were effected, many of them prefixed by the words 'one of the most remarkable men in our country'. 'Good God, Mr. Putnam,' he said, 'they are all so!' This scene is vividly described in *Martin Chuzzlewit*.

There were calmer and pleasanter moments in which he was entertained privately by Carey the bookseller, who was married to a sister of his artist friend, Charles Leslie. Then the editor of *Graham's Magazine*, Edgar Allan Poe, three years older than the English author, left his article on *Barnaby Rudge* and his *Tales of the Grotesque and Arabesque* at the hotel where Mr. Dickens was staying. On calling for an interview

he was received by a small, dapper figure in a dressing-gown
with purple facings. At first the American poet, a slovenly
fellow himself, did not feel too much at ease with the foppish
young man who was decked out with cravat pins and chains
preparatory to slipping on a frock-coat for the street. They
talked of international copyright and of contemporary
writers. Poe was anxious to get his stories published in
England and this Dickens promised to inquire about, a
promise he fulfilled by going to Moxon and other publishers
on his return. In the following November he wrote to Poe,
'They have one and all declined the venture'. Dickens did
not appear to have realised that *The Fall of the House of Usher*
had already appeared anonymously in *Bentley's Miscellany*
under Ainsworth's editorship. Even if he had read it and
known the name of the author, the morbidity of the theme
would not at this time have predisposed him in Poe's favour,
though later in his life he might have greatly admired him.
The interview between the two authors at the Philadelphia
hotel proved sterile and closed coldly. Neither seems to
have liked the other much.

Dickens had brought with him from London a letter
to Lucretia Mott, the Quaker anti-slavery advocate. She
wrote:[1]

> Another lion has just arrived in the city—Charles
> Dickens. Our children have a strong desire to see him.
> I, too, have liked the benevolent tendency of his writings,
> though I have read very little in them. I did not expect to
> seek an interview or invite him here, as he was not quite of
> our sort. But just now there was left at our door his and
> his wife's card with a kind letter from our dear friend
> E. J. Reed, of London, introducing them and expressing
> a strong desire that we would make their acquaintance.
> There is not a woman in London whose draft I would more
> gladly honour. So now we shall call on them and our
> daughters are in high glee.

At Baltimore the travellers tried to evade notice by sticking

---

[1] See Oberholtzer, *Literary History of Philadelphia*.

to the train, but people pressed against the windows and peered at them. Very little fuss was made of Dickens in Washington though he was warmly welcomed in private, and after paying his respects to President Tyler at a levee was entertained by him informally at the White House. Tyler expressed surprise that 'Boz', the famous, should look so young. Dickens says he would like to have returned the compliment, but that the poor fellow looked 'so jaded' that it stuck in his throat 'like Macbeth's Amen'. It gave him a homely feeling to see that the President had a trick of curling his legs under him 'just like Talfourd'. Admitted to the floor of House and Senate as a distinguished visitor, he listened to the speaking, which on the whole struck him as less good than in England. The men seemed to him more remarkable than their orations. But then in America the focus of interest is the man rather than his office or the measure for which he stands. J. Q. Adams, Henry Clay, Calhoun and Quincy were among those he most admired. Daniel Webster, on the other hand, struck him as thoroughly unreal—'a sublime caricature of Lord Burleigh feigning abstraction in the dreadful pressure of affairs of state'. Henry Clay he liked immensely, J. Q. Adams reminded him of Sam Rogers, and Charles Sumner, who had been much in Europe, he found most sympathetic. In his dispatch-case he had brought from New York copies of a petition on international copyright signed by Washington Irving and other American authors. One copy he presented to the House of Representatives and the other, placed in Clay's keeping, was destined for the Senate.

From Washington Dickens and his party visited Richmond and Harrisburg, both seats of State Legislatures. At the Virginian capital he was 'informally' entertained at a *petit souper* where he hobnobbed with ninety of the commission merchants and tobacconists of the city at the Exchange Hotel. They were friendly and assured him that, though they had little time for reading themselves, their wives and daughters liked his books. One man beamingly told him how much he had enjoyed his *Last Days of Pompeii*. The chairman of the supper party, Mr. Ritchie, owner of the *Richmond Enquirer*, praised Mr. Dickens in stilted fashion for having 'sought the violet in its lowly bed so as to give its perfume to the light of day', adding that their guest of honour had 'seized upon humble points in the human landscape and had lighted them up with the fire of his genius'. It was true that 'no Washington Irving or William Bryant had appeared in their midst', the forte of the Old Dominion was rather to be found in the masculine productions of her statesmen—her Washington, her Jefferson, her Madison, 'men who had never indulged in imaginative works, in the charms of romance or in the mere beauties of literature'. With phrases like these did the business men of Richmond, while honouring the success and large sales of Mr. Dickens's novels, pay lip service to the pen-driving profession.

Writing to Lady Holland, Dickens says that she will have heard of the public progress imposed on him, he can't bear it, and has refused everything but an invitation to dine at St. Louis, 'quite next door—2000 miles away'. He has spoken much of her with Washington Irving, and then continues: 'We hold a levee for all comers. The Queen and Prince Albert can hardly be more tied, for ours is a perpetual Drawing-room. Our Crown too is not a Golden one except in opinion. We have been . . . to Richmond and were going on to Charleston, but the sight of slavery turned us back.' Everywhere they 'found themselves a week behind Lord Morpeth'.[1]

At the Pennsylvanian capital, Harrisburg, 'Boz' was acclaimed by both Houses. His spirits rose unaccountably; once again he felt himself to be 'the Inimitable', once again he was delighted that members of the legislature should pay him the compliment of following him back to his hotel. Mixed with this feeling was a certain impatience at the insufferably apish character of the legislatures that honoured him and the men who paid him compliments: he called it 'a feeling of bile'.

[1] March 22, 1842.

Next came a canal voyage to Pittsburg, then a voyage down-river to Cincinnati, the city in which gallant Mrs. Trollope had dwelt so long and which she had described in such detail. Here Mr. and Mrs. Dickens were badly mobbed. By dinner-time they were in a fainting condition. A Cincinnati lady after staring at Mrs. Dickens described her as 'a large woman' with a good deal of colour and a good face. As no one in the city had seen the engraving from Maclise's portrait, no one had any idea in advance how very young Mr. Dickens was going to look or how very smart his clothes and his jewelry were going to be. Porter, the Kentucky giant, called his appearance 'flash, like one of our river gamblers'. It was all very well to call Cincinnati a beautiful city, but meeting its inhabitants was not a beautiful experience, and the poor visitor's face acquired an expression of sadness from 'the constant and unmitigated boring' he endured. A letter written from Cincinnati makes Kate out to be a sort of Tilly Slowboy:

> As we made our way on foot over the broken pavement, Anne measured her length on the ground, but didn't hurt herself. I say nothing of Kate's tumbles—but you recollect her propensity? She falls into, or out of, every coach or boat we enter; scrapes the skin off her legs; brings great sores and swellings on her feet; chips large fragments out of her ankle-bones, and makes herself blue with bruises. She really has, however, since we got over the first trial of being among circumstances so new and fatiguing, made a *most admirable* traveller in every respect. She has never screamed . . . never given way to despondency or fatigue . . . has always accommodated herself well . . . has pleased me very much and proved herself perfectly game.[1]

Somehow Dickens did not go down so well in the west and south as in New England. The people of St. Louis, for instance, were frankly critical. The papers objected to his hair, it did not curl sufficiently; to his dress, it was somewhat too foppish and, contrasted with the black suits worn by the gentry of St. Louis, a little vulgar.

Of course Dickens made a point of visiting 'Cairo', the concession in which he is said to have invested some of his first earnings.   It lay at the junction of the Mississippi and Ohio and is described as 'Eden' in *Martin Chuzzlewit*.   It was 'a dismal swamp vaunted in England as a mine of Golden Hope and speculated in on the faith of monstrous representations to many people's ruin'.

Before they left for Canada the travellers went with David Colden to stay with the Ticknors at Lebanon Springs. Ticknor did his best to introduce Dickens to the Quaker Settlement.   The Quakers would have none of him.   It grieved Ticknor to find that they were so insensible to Dickens's widespread merit and so little respecters of persons as to refuse to show him 'any of their mysteries or managements touching men or beasts'.   The *Western Star*,[1] a Lebanon paper commenting on Mr. Dickens's visit, stated that he had been travelling 'very quietly' in the West, and that it was 'gratified to observe the total absence of all that parade and sycophancy which characterised his reception in Eastern cities', adding with that self-consciousness which at the time was characteristic of American journalism, 'It will give us a better opinion of ourselves even if Mr. Dickens should not think the better of us for it'.

They looked forward to having a rest in Canada, a rest from jolting stages, corduroy roads, tobacco-chewing, spitting, uncouth manners, and all the other disadvantages that seemed to be inherent in pioneer company.   Ears alert to catch the thunder of Niagara, Dickens worked himself up into an extreme state of tension as they got near the frontier, and when not only the thunder was audible, but high clouds of spray visible, he leapt from the carriage and ran down to the water's edge to get ferried without further delay up to the Falls.   What transports of joy they both enjoyed at seeing

[1] April 20, 1842.

an English sentinel! Wet through by spray, Charles joined Kate at the hotel facing the Falls on the Canadian side. As soon as he had changed into dry clothes Dickens hurried his wife off to the Horseshoe Falls and helped her clamber down to the basin, for in those days there seems to have been no staging behind the curtain of water. How green, how marvellous it all was! it quite took their breath away. Rather inexplicably it made Charles think of Mary:

> What would I give if the dear girl whose ashes lie in Kensal Green had lived to come so far along with us—but she has been here many times, I doubt not, since her sweet face faded from my earthly sight.

They spent a whole week, to their 'unspeakable delight, without company'. They had the Falls to themselves, rambled about in old clothes, 'played cribbage o' nights' and did just as they pleased. Dickens in high spirits quoted the words of Mr. Brass to express his contentment, 'A still small voice is a-singing comic songs within us and all is happiness and peace'. Documents reached him at Niagara concerning international copyright. 'Organised by Forster, the Greater Writers of England have flung their gauntlets down on top of mine', he said, and at once posted their manifesto to the editor of the *Evening Post* in Boston and, as he did so, all the old indignation once again boiled up within him. It was horrible to think that scoundrelly booksellers should grow rich from publishing books the authors of which did not reap one farthing. Equally horrible was it that blackguardly newspapers, 'not fit for a water-closet mat', should be free to print the work of great writers side by side with obscenities.

It was at the invitation of the Coldstream Guards, tendered by Lord Mulgrave, that the Dickenses went from Niagara to Montreal to play in garrison theatricals. With delight Charles took over the duties of stage manager and started drilling the actors in the manner of Macready. The pieces chosen were *A Roland for an Oliver*, *A Good Night's Rest* and *Deaf as a Post*. Owing to the shortage of young ladies, Kate had to take a part and her husband said she played 'devilish well'. They stayed at Rasco's Hotel and were very kindly treated by their military hosts, who put carriages and boats at their disposal. On the night of the performance, the band of the 23rd Regiment played in the foyer. Dickens was one of the four gentlemen carrying lighted candles deputed to meet the Governor-General, Sir Charles Bagot, on his arrival. The Commander-in-Chief, Sir Richard Jackson, also attended the opening performance which was 'strictly by invitation'. One other performance was given 'to prevent heart-burnings in a heart-burning town'. Among the officers acting were Lord Mulgrave, the Hon. Paul Methuen, Captain Willoughby and Captain Granville.

Most English travellers coming from the United States relapsed with satisfaction into the extremely English atmosphere of Eastern Canada. Dickens alone among English visitors expressed himself 'appalled' by the Toryism of Toronto.

During his travels Dickens had become the owner of a white Havannah spaniel, the gift of Mitchell, the American comedian. First named Mr. Timber Doodle, a name changed later to Mr. Snittle Timbery, this little dog lived to be very old and accompanied the family in all its migrations, including visits to Italy and Switzerland. The society of 'Timber' and the display of Maclise's group-portrait of the Dickens children made hotel rooms less chilling and impersonal. Nat Willis, who had not seen Dickens since his Furnival Inn days, had been specially interested when they met again to see what the children looked like. In vain did Willis beg Mrs. Dickens to give him the portrait-group as a souvenir. 'Imagine!' she wrote to Maclise, 'the impudence and audacity of such a request!' One of Mr. Putnam's jobs, on arriving at any place they were to spend the night in, was to open the rather big box containing the picture (15 inches in diameter) and set it up on a side-table, after which ceremony Dickens would take up his accordion and play 'Home, sweet

Home'.   Nine years later, when the number of children had been doubled, Charles Dickens wrote to Mr. Putnam:

> The picture of the four we had when in America hangs in our dining-room at home.   It is in a gay round frame now and has these many years forgotten the sliding of the box you used to take off before you set it up on a side table at each of the four and twenty thousand inns we stayed in. I wonder whether you recollect the inn at Hartford where the levee would not go away—or at Newhaven where they kicked the staircase to express their impatience—or at Columbus where they came arm in arm at midnight—or at St. Louis where we had a ball—or at Pittsburg, or at Philadelphia where a little hatter with black whiskers did the honours.   I feel as if I should like to see all those places again.[1]

Distance of time had blurred the sharpness of the original impressions and invested them with a mildly humorous effulgence.   Not till Dickens, twenty years later, re-crossed the Atlantic to expose himself to the immense fatigues and excitements of a reading tour was he reminded that constitutionally he was no American.

[1] 332.   II.   N.L.

Chapter 12

HOME AGAIN

It was home. And though home is a name, a word, it is a strong one: stronger than magician ever spoke, or spirit answered to, in strongest conjuration. CHARLES DICKENS

BY the end of June Mr. and Mrs. Dickens were back in London. Both of them had been home-sick for months and the satisfaction of settling down into their own comfortable groove made them glow with happiness. 'How we enjoy our home and everything connected with it!' piped Charles to an American friend. It was good indeed to be in one's own study again, good to arrange one's books, paper, pens, and specially good, after bleak experiences in hotel rooms, to resume friendly contact with the inanimate furnishings of private life.

Against the return of their parents the four children had been fetched from Clarence Terrace by their uncle Frederick and had been tucked up in bed at Devonshire Terrace. 'We quickly had them up,' said their father, 'little Charley was so excited that he fell into convulsions. Except for this mishap the meeting went off merrily. Kate was all smiles as she cooed to the baby, and Charles, as soon as he could disengage himself from the clinging arms of the little girls, ran across into Regent's Park to see Macready, who had had charge of the whole family for six months. He found his friend sitting in a dark room by an open window looking out at the trees. Never, never could Charles thank his dear Macready enough, the children were 'heartily well' and 'delighted beyond all means' to see their parents. Then followed an eager talk about America.

Among the family faces greeting the arrival of the travellers was that of Kate's sister, little Georgina Hogarth, who had been in close touch with the children during their temporary orphanhood. Georgina could tell Kate about her darlings, recount the changes that had taken place during her absence, and the details of growth and behaviour precious to mothers the world over. It was plain that 'aunt Georgy' had won the love of the infant quartet, and it seemed only natural and convenient that she should continue her ministrations and make her home with Charles and Kate. Perhaps it flitted through Kate's slow mind that her presence might put an end to all the dreams and the talk about Mary to which she had listened so patiently these five years past. Georgina was the same age as Mary had been when she became an inmate of Doughty Street, and was sufficiently like Mary in appearance to be mistakable for her at a short distance. What now began to happen might have been predicted by anyone outside the home circle. Always thinking of Mary as as much part of himself as 'the beating of my heart', Charles after a few weeks began to 'see the spirit of Mary shining out in Georgina', and to find old times coming back 'so that the past can hardly be separated from the present'. This new emotional sublimation was to prove a source of vague contentment to Dickens and, after Georgina had matured to womanhood, a source of subconscious irritation to her placid sister. For the time being, however, no family could have appeared more completely happy and pleased each with the other.

Invitations reached Dickens by every post. Lord Lansdowne was early in the field with a dinner of welcome at which Moore, Rogers and Luttrell were fellow guests, and Forster assembled a party at Greenwich at which the Inimitable made a come-back and expanded like an anemone in a sun-warmed pool. With good companions like Talfourd, Maclise, Barham, Stanfield, Cruikshank, Monckton Milnes, Hood and Procter, he could throw discretion to the winds and give vent to his pent-up feelings about America. The comfort of associating with men who could not possibly misunderstand him and whom he could not possibly offend was in itself bliss; indeed to be with such people was to have the self-respect that had been so aggravatingly frayed by transatlantic treatment and criticism, completely restored.

With Lady Holland, too, he spent an evening soon after his arrival. He found that she had fitted up some of the lower rooms at Holland House in which to give dinners 'as of yore'. But there was not much 'yore' about it, for into the first-floor rooms, the scene of all her brilliant entertaining, she never entered. 'I had a strange sense', writes Dickens, 'of their being dark and vacant overhead.' In spite of Sydney Smith being 'in greater force than ever', it was a ghost-haunted evening, and as he watched the gouty hobble of the Canon of St. Paul's, and the sad expression of his hostess when not actually talking, he asked himself who would or could take the place of these rare personalities when they too stepped into the shadow. Life was a sad business, perhaps 'the saddest dream that was ever dreamed'.

One evening Tom Beard was pressed to come to Devonshire Terrace and 'eat breast of venison at half-past five sharp' in order to listen to the first chapter of *American Notes* being read aloud by Forster. Dickens was pining for literary encouragement. The tour had been a great strain; he only realised what a strain as he rapidly revived his experiences in a travel-book for autumn publication. The welcome he had received in London and the company he was keeping made it extremely hard to buckle to work and especially to concentrate on America. Someone must tell him that the book was worth persevering with, otherwise he could not manage to put good work into it, the truth being that the subject made little or no demand on the creative power that all the while was bubbling up within him and demanding its proper outlet. To his intimates he said, 'I feel my power now more than ever I did, I have a greater confidence in myself than ever I had'. He gave the impression in conversation of being bored to death with the United States, and to cross-examiners of his opinions would say, 'I went there expecting greater things than I found'.

In his first days in London he composed a letter to the *Athenaeum*[1] reporting on his efforts to secure international

---

[1] July 7, 1842.

copyright. He had interested certain transatlantic authors sufficiently to persuade them to draw up a petition for signature by the whole body of American writers. Among these authors were Washington Irving, Fenimore Cooper and Prescott, men as well known in England as in their own country. This petition had been presented by Mr. Clay to Congress and by Congress had been referred to a Select Committee, but in order to discount any advantage that might accrue to authors therefrom, the publishers of Boston had hurriedly passed a resolution to the effect that no change in the existing law was needed. And they justified their attitude by stating that if English authors were invested with any control over the republication of their own books, it would no longer be possible for American editors to alter and adapt them to the American taste. Dickens went on in his letter to say that Mr. Prescott, who could be relied on to behave like a gentleman and man of letters, was most indignant over the action of the publishers. It was high time, he urged, that English authors made some combined stand. As for himself, he was resolved never to enter into any negotiation with any American publisher for transmission of early proofs and was willing to forgo all profit derivable from such a source. In America he had come across newspaper editors and proprietors whose journals were almost entirely made up of the republication of popular English works. He had even read papers describing the success of his books which, over the page, contained scurrilous attacks on himself. The situation was intolerably unjust. He would like to stress the fact that so far he had been fighting single-handed, but now looked to all writers to rally to his support. Miss Julia Pardoe, the popular historian, read the letter in the *Athenaeum* and at once wrote to Dickens to ask how she could protect her own books. Little comfort was derivable from the reply:

The existing law allows them [the Americans] to reprint any English book without any communication whatever with the author. . . . My books have all been reprinted on these agreeable terms. . . . Sometimes one firm of pirates will pay a trifle to procure early copies and get so much the start of the rest as they can. . . . Directly it is printed it is common property and may be reprinted a thousand times.[1]

The great financial interests bound up with the pirating of English books were well able to protect themselves against the pen-pricks of even famous writers. Firms like Lea and Carey of Philadelphia and their rivals in New York had not, at the bidding of a Fenimore Cooper, abandoned the advantages gained by pirating the works of Scott, Byron, Leigh Hunt and Moore. The works of Dickens were almost as good a proposition as the Waverley Novels: there was a fortune latent in them.

For an American publisher at this time the only expense connected with the acquisition of a new English book was empowering an agent to dispatch an advance copy by the fastest ship available. Partly owing to the fact that no royalties had to be paid and partly to the large size of the original impression, American booksellers could produce books more cheaply than English publishers. In England a Waverley novel was printed in three volumes for 31s. 6d.; in Philadelphia it appeared in two volumes for 8s. 6d. and a few weeks later in a cheaper edition for 4s. 3d. Scott's *Life of Napoleon* was printed in nine volumes in England at 94s. 6d. In America it was published at 20s. It was never assumed by American book merchants that the sale of any work would go on quietly from year to year or even from month to month as in England. Demand was stimulated by clever advertisement and rose with extraordinary suddenness. Every publisher worth his salt made a speedy turnover and then scrapped remainders ruthlessly. They had no interests to consider but their own.

Fearful of possible reprisals by English firms, booksellers had asked Congress for protection against the competitive dumping of books printed in England, specifying the Bible as a case in point. It was alleged that between seven and eight hundred thousand Bibles had been imported to the States, and a means to keep them out was sought and oddly enough found, not in a direct embargo, but in the adoption for all schools and places of worship of Noah Webster's edition of the James I. Bible.   When this was promulgated as the orthodox American version of Holy Scripture all imported Bibles automatically became worthless.   From this instance and from other records of the day we may deduce that publishing, as practised in America, could be as exciting and cut-throat an enterprise as any that flourished in that prosperous land.   Dickens had little idea of what he was up against in attacking the bookselling trade.   He saw himself as the champion of an unpopular crusade on behalf of justice to authors and did not realise that the dragon of big business was immune from missiles slung by a mere scribbler.   How unbelievable would it have seemed to him that all the great Victorian novelists would be in their graves before justice came into her own.

Dickens's thoughts were now straying towards journalism. We find him writing to Lady Holland[1] to say that he hears that the *Courier*, formerly a Whig and more recently a Tory evening newspaper, is to be incorporated in the *Globe*.   Had he been in England earlier in the year, he would have put himself in touch with the leaders of the Liberal party and made proposals to them for saving the paper, 'nailing the true colours to the mast and fighting the battle staunchly and to the death'.   What does Lady Holland think about it?   Would she be in favour of an evening paper of the kind?   Could she perhaps sound Lords Melbourne and Lansdowne, Mr. Stanley and a few more?   Of course he could do this himself but would rather trust her to find out how the land lies. With an obvious bid for editorship, he says that he feels confident that he could establish an organ that would do good service and command immediate attention.   A few days later[2] he writes again to Lady Holland, who has evidently sounded Mr. Stanley and perhaps others, telling her that she may be right, but that the Liberal party had very seldom erred on the bold side, adding, 'The notion of this newspaper was bred in me by my old teaching'.   He begs to send her a volume of Longfellow's poems and an eagle feather from Niagara.   And there the scheme for editing a daily paper ended until revived a few months later in another form.

August and September were spent at Broadstairs completing *American Notes*.   In Captain Marryat Dickens had a companion with whom he could discuss each chapter as he completed it.   Marryat liked the book and was full of praise for the humorous way in which his friend had treated his subject.   Few writers concurred in this opinion.   Thackeray, who did not like *American Notes*, was asked to review the book for the *Edinburgh*, but he refused, saying, 'I cannot praise it and I will not cut it up. . . . It is like the worst part of *Humphrey's Clock*, what is meant to be easy and sprightly is vulgar and flippant . . . the book is at once frivolous and dull.' Authorship with its implicit surrender to the judgments of others is not by any means a wholly enjoyable profession. Dickens never read reviews of his own books, saying that if he did so it would gouge all the writing heart out of him, for, taking them all in all, reviewers were good natural sadists.

Just as he had finished the *Notes* he learned that he was being attacked in the United States for a letter allegedly written to the *Chronicle* in which he had criticised hospitality tendered to him while in America.   Headlines 'Dickens is a Fool', 'Dickens is a Liar' flared across the columns of the New York papers.   In an effort to counter this slander he wrote a weak defensive foreword to his new book to the effect that he had always been prejudiced in favour of America and that to represent him as viewing America with ill-nature 'was merely to do a very foolish thing'.   To Jonathan Chapman, Mayor of Boston, he wrote more forcibly, explaining the true integrity of his attitude:

Because I claim to have been kindly received in America by reason of something I had done to amuse its people and prepossess them in my favour; and not with reference to something I was not to do; therefore I write about its people and write freely. And as I have never been deterred by hopes of approbation or visions of greatness from pointing out abuses at home, so no amount of popular breath shall blow me from my purpose, if I see fit to point out, what in my judgment are abuses abroad, and if my being an honest man brings down caprice and weather-cock fickleness-and the falsest kind of insult on my head, what matter it to me—or to you—or to any man who is worth the name and being right can look down on the crowds and whistle while they hiss.[1]

American Notes is a dull book and mainly concerned with visits to public institutions which are contrasted with their counterparts in England. For these institutions he expressed measured admiration. The charity of the people themselves seemed to him better than private charity: he had noted that the 'charity children' wore neither badge nor livery and that, contrasted with the regimented infants of England, 'their individuality seemed unimpaired'. Hospitals for the Insane, Houses of Reformation, Prisons, Deaf and Dumb Asylums, those terrors of the ordinary tourist, were dealt with sympathetically, for they were of compelling interest to one who himself had been an underdog. Taking as his text advertisements from a Washington gazette concerning the sale of slaves, he, to conclude with, delivered a broadside against slavery. One notes that Dickens's last transatlantic excursion was to the Academy of West Point; his last vision of America that of the Catskills and the Tappan Zee; his last thoughts, like his first, of Washington Irving.

He was careful to explain to Mr. Tagart, his new Unitarian friend, that when he determined to tell the truth about America, he determined also that he would not from that time read any American paper, pamphlet or book or review in which he had reason to suppose (from the very fact of its being sent him) there might be the least allusion to himself.

[1] 483. I. N.L.

I do not mean to say that it requires a Roman fortitude to exercise this self-denial. But I have beaten by these means every free and independent citizen who has written to annoy me, and judging from the number of packets I return to the Post Office unopened, I should say their name is legion.[1]

On neither side of the Atlantic was *American Notes* much appreciated by the general reader. Much of it was written with deference, surnames were omitted, opinions were watered down, the copyright controversy ignored; nevertheless four large editions sold before the end of the year and put a much-needed thousand pounds in his pocket.

News reached Dickens as he was leaving Broadstairs that Longfellow was on the point of landing in England. He at once dispatched a note to Dover saying, 'Your bed is waiting, the door gapes hospitality', and presently had the pleasure of welcoming the American poet on his own threshold at Devonshire Terrace. In a letter to Charles Sumner Longfellow said, 'I write this from Dickens's study, the focus from which so many luminous things have radiated. The raven croaks from the garden and the ceaseless roar of London fills my ears.' The visitor spoke much of Dickens's vogue in Germany and of German poetry. He gave his host the works of Freiligrath, the translator of 'Lady Clara Vere de Vere' and other Tennysonian poems. He also spoke of Herder's translations of popular verse, Herder who regarded poetry as a kind of Proteus among peoples breaking out in ballads and songs. Dickens listened to his outpourings and then pushed *American Notes* into his hands. Longfellow read it straight away and said, 'It is good-natured and severe'. The chapter on slavery struck him as 'grand'.

Longfellow's days in London were soon filled with engagements. Sam Rogers journeyed from Broadstairs to book him to breakfast on a Tuesday and dine on a Wednesday, and Dickens pinned him for several meetings with writers who included Tennyson, Browning and Bulwer Lytton. One morning 'Boz' and 'Fuz' carried Longfellow off to Rochester, where, defying the prohibition of the janitor, they overleapt gates and barriers and explored the castle ruins. A far less agreeable excursion was arranged to inspect the worst slums of the Borough. Maclise, who made a fourth on this occasion, was so overcome by the odours and the dirt that he vomited and had to remain outside in the street while the others, stronger-stomached, examined the squalid houses.

After a fortnight of crowded experiences Longfellow started for Bristol to catch the steamship *Great Western*. 'Boz' and 'Fuz' escorted him to Landor's house in Bath, where he dined and spent an evening in brisk discussion. They then accompanied him to his port of embarkation. In a letter to Dickens reporting safe arrival he said that as he lay on his back he 'soothed his soul with songs'. 'In *The Slave's Dream* I have borrowed one or two wild animals from your menagerie.' These verses were printed in a thirty-page pamphlet soon after his return.

As soon as Longfellow had sailed, Dickens, Maclise, Forster and Stanfield set out on a Cornish tour. They hired a conveyance in Devonshire, and from Thackeray we have a pen-and-ink sketch of four top-hatted gentlemen in full-skirted overcoats tightly wedged into a landau. During the trip Tintagel, Land's End and St. Michael's Mount were visited as well as old churches, caverns by the sea-shore and tin mines. Maclise made many sketches, and out of one of them, the waterfall at St. Wighton's Keive, near Tintagel, developed an oil painting. It was shown at the Academy of 1843 and in the same exhibition was hung Maclise's portrait of Harrison Ainsworth. Dickens liked the original sketch of the waterfall, and when Georgina posed as model for the Academy picture he determined to acquire it. Before it was completed he wrote to Tom Beard:

I am very anxious for many reasons to possess a little picture which Maclise is at this moment painting: and I know he would either insist on giving it to me or would

set some preposterous price upon it which he can by no
means afford to take.[1]

Beard was instructed to inform the artist that 'a Mr. S. of
such-and-such a place in Sussex' would like to purchase a
small picture, 'The Girl at the Waterfall', for a hundred or
a hundred and fifty guineas.   This subterfuge was made
necessary by the open-handedness of Maclise who insisted on
giving his beloved Bozzes anything of his they admired and
had refused to take payment for the sketch of the four children
or for the portrait of Kate.   Stanfield also sketched busily
during the tour.   One of his drawings is that of the Logan
Stone with Forster perched on top of it and Dickens and
Maclise rocking it from below.   This sketch and the picture
of Georgina at the waterfall are included in the Forster
Collection.[2] Dickens, always highly suggestible, caught
something of landscape technique from his friends and described the antics of autumn-scattering leaves, the piling-up
of clouds and the lighting-up of fields and coast-lines by
sunburst or lightning.   These effects, which as we shall
presently see were made use of in *Martin Chuzzlewit*, caused
Taine to say that Dickens was a landscape painter.   Much as
the author longed to set his new novel by the Cornish shore,
he could not contrive to do so and somehow found himself
accepting an inland village in Wiltshire as substitute.   By
arranging to open his story in the autumn he could, however,
make use of his landscape jottings of the plough-patterning
of the ruddy earth, the browning hedgerows, the berries like
clusters of coral beads, the sun-glints and the vagaries of the
huffy wind.

Once again ensconced in Devonshire Terrace, Dickens
resisted distractions gay or grave with all his might and distractions were not always amusing, for celebrity brought
with it human claims.   For instance, William Hone, a most
indigent writer, sent a message by Cruikshank to say he was

[1] 495. I. N.L.   [2] Victoria and Albert Museum.

dying and that having read no books but those of 'Boz' since he had lain ill, he aspired to shake hands with their author 'before he went'. So to Tottenham Dickens felt bound to go, just as a month later he felt bound to attend the funeral of this fellow craftsman. But claims or no claims, he somehow had to find the seclusion necessary for work, for his publishers, Chapman and Hall, were pressing him for the date of delivery of the first instalment of his new novel. Once he had given an undertaking to hand it in in January 1843, and regularly thereafter monthly, he had to refuse all invitations. Even Miss Coutts had to be notified that her always-tempting dinners must be declined. A note from her found him

in agonies of plotting and contriving a new book; in which stage of the tremendous process, I am accustomed to walk up and down the house, smiting my forehead dejectedly; and to be so horribly cross and surly that the boldest fly at my approach. . . . Seriously, unless I were to shut myself up obstinately and sullenly in my room for a great many days without writing a word, I don't think I should ever make a beginning . . . the lapse of every new day only gives me stronger reasons for being perseveringly uncomfortable, that out of my gloom and solitude something comical, or meant to be, may straightway grow up.[1]

And so Dickens shut himself up in his study to write, only emerging for food and exercise. Just occasionally something came along that pricked his curiosity, such as Maclise's news that a young artist called Frith had done some charming sketches of the girls in *Barnaby Rudge*. It appeared, too, that he had made genre designs for illustrating *Gil Blas*, *Kenilworth* and the *Vicar of Wakefield*. Fired by Maclise's account Dickens seized his pen and wrote:[2]

MY DEAR SIR,—I shall be very glad if you will do me the favour to paint me two little companion pictures; one a Dolly Varden (whom you have so exquisitely done

already), the other a Kate Nickleby.—Faithfully yours
always, CHARLES DICKENS.

P.S.—I take it for granted that the original picture of
Dolly with the bracelet is sold.

Frith, who was very young at the time, was enchanted to
receive the letter. He and his mother cried over it and they
read it so often that it was a wonder that anything was left
of it. He got to work at once making a picture of Dolly
Varden tripping through the woods and looking back saucily
at her lover. For Kate Nickleby he fixed on a scene at
Madame Mantalini's, with Kate figuring as a seamstress, 'the
point being at the moment when her thoughts wander from
her work, as she sits sewing a ball-dress spread upon her
knees'. Directly the pictures were finished Frith invited
Dickens to come and inspect them. A day for this visit was
fixed and the artist awaited in 'very trembling expectation'
the arrival of the man he regarded as superhuman. A knock
sounded on the studio door and there on the step Firth saw a
pale young fellow with long hair surmounted by a tall white
beaver. His right hand was extended in a frankly cordial
way and in his left he clasped a formidable stick. The
portrait sketches were on the easel and the artist waited 'in an
agony of mind' for the verdict. Charles Dickens sat down
and looked at them closely and then a few minutes later said,
'All I can say is that they are exactly what I want. I'm very
much obliged to you for painting them.' Before leaving he
asked Frith whether he would be at home on the following
Sunday afternoon as he would like to bring his wife and his
sister-in-law to see how well the work had been carried out.
Sunday came and it found Frith at the open door of his studio
when a smart curricle driven by Dickens dashed up. 'I was
not accustomed to curricles,' he says naïvely in his diary, 'the
bright steel bar in front gave the turn-out a very striking
appearance.' A groom jumped to the head of the spanking
bays when the two-wheeled carriage halted and the ladies
floated into the studio and gushed over the pictures, which

were entirely to their taste. That Charles and what he called his 'brace of petticoats' made an attractive trio we can see from Maclise's sketch done at this time, which shows three profiles one behind the other giving the effect of a set of triplets. With all the air of a grand seigneur 'Boz' bestowed on Frith the sum of forty pounds and thanking the artist took his deparure in the same flourishing style in which he had arrived. Frith, aged twenty-three, wondered rather wistfully whether he, when he had reached the age of thirty, would be as successful as his patron, but it was to be twelve years before he caught the public eye with 'Ramsgate Sands' and twenty before 'The Railway Station' had to be gated from the pressure of enraptured crowds at the Royal Academy. He lived long enough to see his portraits of Kate Nickleby and Dolly Varden sold at Christie's, after Dickens's death, for thirteen hundred guineas.

Pricked out of concentrating on his book by Lord Londonderry's pamphlet, *A Letter to Lord Ashley* (attacking the Mines and Collieries Bill), Dickens hurriedly reviewed it in an anonymous letter addressed to the assistant editor of the *Morning Chronicle*, Charles Mackay.[1] Lord Londonderry fiercely resented any interference with labour conditions as he was opening up new collieries and constructing a harbour at Seaham. He was indignant that the 'disgusting pictorial woodcuts' accompanying the Report of the Commissioners should have found their way into the boudoirs of refined and delicate ladies who were weak-minded enough to sympathise with these 'victims of industry'. Adopting a gawkily satirical tone, Dickens rejoiced that the noble Marquis has chosen to express his views in pamphlet form, partly because he writes very badly and partly because he has laid himself open to criticism. He was particularly incensed by the noble Lord's attitude to Dr. Southwood Smith, the most high-minded of commissioners. Measures like the Mines and Collieries Bill cost a world of trouble to bring to birth, they must not be strangled by the Herods of the peerage.[2] That Lord London-

[1] 484. I. N.L.   [2] *Morning Chronicle*, October 20, 1842.

derry should take occasion to remind the public that not all men are born to read and write 'carried within it his condemnation'. Dickens did not add that when he himself had read the Report, he had broken down and sobbed.

Except for occasional interruptions Dickens now worked steadily. His new novel was named for the grandfather of the hero and its cumbrous title was:

> The Life and Adventures of Martin Chuzzlewit, His Relatives, Friends and Enemies. Comprising all his Wills and his Ways; with an Historical Record of What he Did and What he Didn't; showing, moreover Who inherited the Family Plate, Who came in for the Silver Spoons and Who for the Wooden Ladles. The Whole forming a Complete Key to the House of Chuzzlewit. Edited by 'Boz'. With Illustrations by 'Phiz'.

It was published in twenty monthly numbers with forty illustrations in all, and was dedicated to Miss Coutts 'with the true and earnest regard of the author'. There are many well-known characters in this book, among them Mr. Pecksniff, as great in his way as Tartuffe, and Mrs. Gamp, one of the most popular figures ever created by a novelist.

The figure of Mrs. Gamp first came to Dickens when he was lodging in 'a sequestered farm house' at Finchley where he 'buried himself' for a whole summer month to get away from interruptions. From the moment he introduced his readers to Mrs. Gamp's little room over the bird-fancier's shop in Holborn the monthly sales rose. When he had got a firm hold of his story, Dickens moved the family to Yorkshire for the rest of the summer months and in 'the leafy lanes' round Castle Howard Mrs. Gamp blossomed as a humorist. Dickens, who exulted in his creation, asked Forster what he thought of the woman and then wrote to Professor Felton asking the same thing and adding:

> Heaven! such green woods as I was rambling among, down in Yorkshire when I was getting that done last July. For days and days we never saw the sky but through green

boughs; and all day long I cantered over such soft moss and turf that the Horses' feet scarcely made a sound upon it. We have some friends in that part of the country who are the jolliest of the jolly, keeping a big old country house with an ale-cellar something larger than a reasonable church.[1]

One would have thought after seeing the tepid reception accorded to *American Notes* that Dickens would have left America and its inhabitants alone. But this was not the case: he selected certain figures to typify some American characteristics just as he had selected certain figures to typify some English characteristics. Mrs. Jellyby, Mr. Pecksniff, Mr. Bumble have their pendants in Mrs. Hominy, Elijah Pogram and Jefferson Brick, though the American figures do not rival the English figures in vitality and stature. The author allowed Martin and Mark great licence in conversation: they said all the things he had felt and could not at the time express about the bad manners, ignorance and conceit of the Americans he had knocked up against in hotels, river-boats and trains. Scoffing at the levee imposed on strangers, Dickens said no single word in palliation of the attacks he made. In fact he made the ordinary Yankee appear a quite odious creature.

It probably was not the character drawing that offended transatlantic taste so much as the obvious seriousness of the charge against America made by the stranger who talks with Martin in the dining-room at Mrs. Pawkins's boarding house in New York:

'I believe [says the stranger] that no satirist could breathe this air. If another Juvenal or Swift could rise up among us to-morrow, he would be hunted down. If you have any knowledge of our literature and can give me the name of any man, American born and bred, who has anatomised our follies as a people and not as this or that party; and who has escaped the foulest and most brutal slander, the most inveterate hatred and intolerant pursuit, it will be a strange

---
[1] 537. I. N.L.

name in my ears. In some cases I could name to you, where a native writer has ventured on the most harmless and good-natured illustrations of our vices or defects, it has been found necessary to announce that in a second edition the passage has been expunged, or altered, or explained away, or patched into praise.'

In a gratuitously offensive mood Dickens chooses to close a chapter with observations of his own on Tom Moore, whose reflections at Washington forty years earlier had been expressed in the lines:

> Rank without ripeness, quickened without sun,
> Crude at the surface, rotten at the core.

Sydney Smith read *Martin Chuzzlewit* with great amusement and wrote twice while the work was in progress: 'I believe you will excuse me for saying how very much pleased I am with the first number of your new work. Pecksniff and his daughters and Pinch are admirable—quite first rate painting such as no one but yourself can execute,' and again, 'Excellent! nothing can be better. You must settle it with the Americans as you can, I have only to certify to the humour and power of description.' [1]

How little Dickens understood America may be gauged by the great surprise he evinced when told that *Martin Chuzzlewit* had been destroyed on the stage in New York, having been cast (to the great delight of the audience) into the witches' cauldron in a burlesque of *Macbeth*. No English people of that day understood America; we have only to read the books of Mrs. Trollope, Miss Martineau and Captain Marryat to find this out. To them the manners and customs of the Americans seemed either very humorous, very provincial or very provoking. Carlyle summed up the feeling generated in America by *Martin Chuzzlewit* when he said it caused 'all Yankee-doodledum to fizz like one universal soda-water bottle'. Somewhat flustered by the commotion he was responsible for, Dickens wrote to Forster:

[1] January and July 1843.

Martin has made them all stark staring raving mad across the water. . . . Don't you think the time has come . . . to state that such public entertainments as I received in the States were either accepted before I went out, or in the first week after my arrival there: and that as soon as I began to have any acquaintance with the country, I set my face against any public recognition whatever but that which was forced upon me to the destruction of my peace and comfort—and made no secret of my real sentiments.[1]

It was too late for explanations. Dickens had to stand by what he had written and learn by experience how foolish it was to hold a nation up to ridicule.

It was Macready's turn now to go to the United States and before his departure a farewell dinner was given to him at the Star and Garter, Richmond. Marryat, Dickens, Stanfield, Forster, Barham, Maclise, Landseer and six others were present. Dickens, who had every intention of going to Liverpool and bringing Mrs. Macready home after her husband had sailed, proposed from the chair the only toast. He spoke so movingly that Macready broke down in tears. Forster had just told the actor that he had written a very strong letter to Dickens endeavouring to dissuade him from accompanying him to Liverpool, and Marryat that evening took occasion to warn Dickens that Macready would suffer from his attention—the *Nickleby* dedication was damaging enough. Dickens, acting upon his friends' advice, wrote to Macready:

I have lately had grave doubts of the propriety of my seeing you on board the steamer. It will be crowded with Americans at this time of the year and believe me they are not the people you suppose them to be. So strongly have I felt that my accompanying you on board would be, after the last *Chuzzlewit*, fatal to your success and certain to bring down on you every species of insult and outrage, that I have all along determined within myself to remain in the hotel and charge the landlord to keep my being there a secret.

[1] John Forster, *Life of Dickens*, vol. i. p. 308.

But this morning I have heard from Marryat to whom Stanfield had chanced to mention our Liverpool design, and he so emphatically and urgently implores me for your sake not even to go to Liverpool, that I instantly renounced the delight of being among the last to say 'God Bless you!' for when a man, who knows the country, confirms me in my fears, I am as morally certain of their foundation in truth and freedom from exaggeration as I am that I live.

If you but knew one-hundredth part of the malignity, the monstrous falsehood, the beastly attacks, even upon Catharine which were published all over America, even while I was there on my mere confession that the country had disappointed me, confessions wrung from me in private society before I had written a word upon the people, you would question all this as little as I do. Soon after you receive this I hope to come across to Clarence Terrace to shake you by the hand.

In a private talk with Macready Dickens begged him never to champion him when he hears him abused, never even to admit the friendship between them, never to contradict, never to take offence, and then added, 'I wish I could *un*-dedicate *Nickleby* until you come home again!'

Chapter 13

PIRATES AND PUBLISHERS

*Novelty, pleasant to most people, is peculiarly delightful
to me.* CHARLES DICKENS

THE working background of Charles Dickens's life
throughout 1843 was *Martin Chuzzlewit*. Though he
toiled at this book from four to six hours a day there are
many indications in the correspondence of this date that his
mind was opening to new impressions, and that America had
in some ways broadened his sympathies and changed his
judgments. In his leisure time he took more interest than
heretofore in books, partly because in his efforts to entertain
Longfellow he had come in contact with poets and prose-
writers and partly because he was reading more. Though
Dickens never strictly speaking became what we call a literary
man, he managed to enjoy the work of some of his contemporaries, Browning and Tennyson for instance, but one does
not find him praising the novels of Bulwer Lytton or
Thackeray. As he walked along the shore at Broadstairs he
repeated cadences from *The Dream of Fair Women* and exclaimed to a friend, 'I have been reading Tennyson again and
again, what a great creature he is!' From reading this poem
there arose in his mind visions of the bottom of the sea, of
'queer creatures, half fish and half fungus, looking down into
all manner of coral caves and seaweed conservatories and
staring in with their great dull eyes at every open nook'. . . .
'Who but Tennyson could conjure up such a close to the
extraordinary series of pictures?'

> Squadrons and squares of men in brazen plates,
> Scaffolds, still sheets of water, divers woes,
> Ranges of glimmering vaults with iron gates,
> And hushed seraglios.

As Landor would say, it was 'most wonderful'. *The Dream,*

The Lady of Shalott and other poems had just been revived and republished by an author who had had all the writing heart taken out of him ten years earlier by Lockhart in a review in the *Quarterly* and was now for the first time being recognised as an important poet.   When sending a set of his own books to Tennyson Dickens wrote:

> For the love I bear you, as a man whose writings enlist my whole heart and nature in admiration of their Truth and Beauty, set these books upon your shelves believing that you have no more earnest and sincere homage than mine.

Sufficiently curious about poetry to experiment with it himself, Dickens now wrote a prologue in verse for *The Patrician's Daughter*, 'a drama in modern dress', by J. Westland Marston due for a production at Drury Lane.   He was sure that a spirited prologue would give the play a send-off. 'Get the curtain up with a dash,' he said to Macready, 'and begin the play with a sledge hammer blow.'   Macready consented to speak the lines which went to show that the present was as worthy as the past to be the theme of tragedy:[1]

> Awake the Present!   Shall no scene display
> The tragic passion of the passing day?
> Is it with man, as with some meaner things,
> That out of death his single purpose springs?
>
> .   .   .   .   .
>
> Awake the Present!   Though the steel-clad age
> Find life alone within its storied page,
> Iron is worn at heart by many still.
>
> .   .   .   .   .
>
> Learn from the lessons, of the present day
> Not light its import and not poor its mien;
> Yourselves the actors, and your homes the scene.

Despite the prologue Marston's first play was a failure. He decided to read his second, *Strathmore*, aloud in a hall before venturing to get it staged.   Dickens and Forster went to the rehearsal, and Forster told Marston straight out that he

[1] Prologue.   *Sunday Times*. December 11, 1842.

was reading 'like a parrot, a confounded old parrot'. 'You *must* let us know,' he said testily, 'what character you are impersonating.' Marston tried again, turning his head from one side to the other when the characters changed, but he mouthed the words in the same dull monotone. When the small audience had drifted away Dickens said, 'Give me the book, I'll show you how you ought to do it!' He read the act through aloud and automatically impersonated each figure to the life. Thus did he, rather to his surprise, discover himself to be a born entertainer who, merely by reading aloud, could vivify characters of any age.

Another play that Dickens concerned himself with at this time was *The Blot in the 'Scutcheon*, which he read in manuscript. He told Forster that he found it 'Lovely, true, and deeply affecting', and charged him with a message to Browning to the effect that there was no man living and not many dead who could produce such a work. Its heroine of fourteen who, by allowing herself to be seduced by the very man proposing formally for her hand, incurs 'punishment inexorable', for having sinned against the honour of her house, made a strong appeal to him despite the artificiality of the plot. He was particularly touched by the youth of the heroine and by the repeated line, 'I had no mother', in which she excuses her foolish surrender. Nothing interested Dickens more at this time than successes honestly won by writers and painters. To novices worried by cruel reviews he said:

When I first began to write I suffered intensely from reading reviews and I made a solemn compact with myself that I would only know them for the future from such general report as might reach me. For five years (1843) I have never broken this rule once, I am unquestionably the happier for it.

He was not always quick in recognising the work of friends. For example, when Bulwer Lytton's *Duchesse de la Vallière* had been hissed off the stage, the mortified author arranged that his next drama, *The Lady of Lyons*, should be produced

anonymously at Drury Lane. Macready of course knew by
whom it was written, but Dickens, who was at the first night,
did not, and in an excited rush to congratulate his friend the
actor-manager on the great success of the performance he
met Bulwer Lytton in a passage and asked him what he
thought of the play. 'Without our friend,' replied Bulwer
Lytton gravely, 'it might have been a hideous failure.' Believing him to be jealous Dickens retorted, 'You should be
the first to acknowledge a young writer's success!'

Mrs. Cowden Clarke, whom we have already met gushing
over Dickens's appearance at the Macready dinner four years
earlier, now was introduced to Dickens by Leigh Hunt at the
house of Mr. Tagart, the Unitarian minister. They took to
each other at once and were soon talking and laughing as if
they were old friends. They looked at illustrations in *Punch*
—Mr. Punch as Caius Movius seated among the ruins of
Carthage, Mr. Punch swimming in the sea near a bathing
machine. The tears ran down Dickens's cheeks and Mrs.
Clarke had the, to her, deeply moving experience of seeing
'those large, dark-blue eyes, fringed with magnificent long
thick lashes, yes—those orbs now swam in limpid, liquid
suffusion'. It was to Mrs. Clarke a memorable occasion as it
opened to her the doors of 1 Devonshire Terrace.

Owing to the constant companionship of Maclise, Stanfield
and Landseer, Dickens could not help hearing what contemporary painters were doing and almost in spite of himself he
was obliged to take a lively interest in art. The Pavilion in
Buckingham Palace gardens was, at this time, being decorated,
by order of Prince Albert, with frescoes by Etty, Stanfield,
Maclise, Landseer, Leslie and Sir William Ross, the miniaturist. One morning in September 1843 Macready summoned Rogers, Forster and Dickens to meet him at the
London Library for the purpose of seeing the frescoes. They
all strolled across the Green Park to the Palace where they
found Mrs. Dickens waiting to accompany them to the
Pavilion. Her dear Daniel Maclise had painted two of the

pictures, a design for Undine and a repetition of his 'Scene from Comus', and there was no painter who appealed to her so much both as an artist and as a friend.

On several occasions this year Dickens was persuaded to speak in public, notably at the Printers' Pension Society dinner at the London Tavern in March 1843. In toasting the Press, 'that wonderful Archimedes lever which *has* moved the world', he apostrophised it as 'the fountain of knowledge and the bulwark of freedom, the founder of free states and their preserver!' an eulogium that he would never have bestowed on the House of Commons.

At the Manchester Athenaeum a few months later he sat on a platform with Disraeli and Cobden and told his audience how glad he was that amid all the clank and roar of machinery the mind was not altogether forgotten. The Athenaeum with its cheerful rooms, instructive lectures and six thousand books gave opportunities for blameless enjoyment. He would not rake up the arguments against its existence or pay heed to 'the wicked axiom' that 'a little learning is a dangerous thing'. That was arrant nonsense, he would like to carry people who thought like this to certain jails and night refuges he knew of and convince them that ignorance was the prolific parent of crime and all misery. Refusing an invitation from Lord Brougham to go on to Cumberland for a visit, he says he cannot possibly spare the time, every minute of which he is devoting to the inspection of jails. How he longs to be a police magistrate so as to get a chance to show all classes the vital importance of education!

In his speech he confessed that his own heart died within him when he thought of all the immortal creatures condemned to tread a path, not of primroses, but of jagged flints and rough stones cemented together by this most wicked axiom. If only 'the dragon ignorance could be chased from every hearth, self-respect and hope would reign in every heart'. He is looking down on bright eyes and beaming faces, he will not forget the scene, and they, for their part, must remember that 'the more intelligent and reflective society becomes in the mass the more confidently will writers throw themselves on the feelings of the people'.

It was at Manchester that the idea came to Dickens of 'throwing himself on the feeling of the people' in a short story, *A Christmas Carol*. The first of his famous Christmas moralities, it is possibly the most read of all his works. The hero, Ebenezer Scrooge, is the type of the frozen-hearted in all lands. This miserly man, whose better nature had withered, is visited on three successive nights, by three spirits, the ghosts of Christmas past, present and future. Christmas past takes him back to his childhood, Christmas present to the home of his clerk Bob Cratchit, and Christmas future to a deserted grave-yard. The Christmas scene at the Cratchits', the good cheer, the affectionate family atmosphere and above all the courage of Tiny Tim, the cripple, appealed to young and old. When Scrooge's health is drunk in the fifteen-shillings-a-week household the very pitch of magnanimity is reached and Tiny Tim's voice piping 'God bless us every one' is felt by the old curmudgeon to be a call to which he must respond. Christmas future shows him a corpse lying under a sheet in an empty room and then a neglected grave headed by a stone bearing his own name. Must this really happen to me? Scrooge asks himself. Is it impossible to redeem the past? As his nature melts with compassion the spirit trembles and dissolves and Scrooge, with heart new-born, learns to become the good master, the good friend, the good man.

The story took him only a month to write and it was brought out by Chapman and Hall with four coloured illustrations by John Leech. It sold well and its author expected to make a good round sum, but to his annoyed surprise, instead of the anticipated thousand pounds, his publisher handed him £500. 'I never was so knocked over in all my life!' he said to a friend. Lord Jeffrey who was very much interested in his earnings wrote, 'I want amazingly to see you rich and independent of all irksome exertions'. In a way it was Dickens's own fault, for he had insisted that Chapman and Hall should publish *A Christmas Carol* on 'commission terms', under which an author was charged with the full cost of the book and received the entire proceeds of the sale, the publisher taking no more than a fixed percentage on the total amount realised by the sales.   The result in this case proved so unsatisfactory to the author that it made him consider breaking with Chapman and Hall.

Another bad knock was the pirating of the story in a twopenny weekly, *Parley's Illuminated Library*, in which it appeared as 'A Christmas Ghost Story re-originated from the original by Charles Dickens, Esq., and analytically condensed expressly for this work'.   Engaging Talfourd as his counsel, Dickens moved for an injunction against Lee and Haddock to stop publication.   The injunction was granted by the Vice-Chancellor, Sir J. Knight Bruce, and in the application, drafted by Talfourd, the words appeared, 'You use my ideas as gipsies do stolen children; disfigure them and then make them pass for their own'.   To Lady Holland Dickens wrote telling of the pirating of the *Carol* and how he had been plunged into six Chancery suits; it has put his work back and he dare not come and see her till things are straightened out.

I took Serjeant Talfourd out of his own Court to lead my Chancery cases.   Knight Bruce understood the matter so perfectly and appreciates the piracy so well, that he did not require to hear Talfourd at all, which I think was a prodigious disappointment to the Serjeant, who had made up his mind for a great speech.

The Vice-Chancellor said the case was one of 'peculiar flagrancy'.   Lee and Haddock moved to dissolve the injunction and filed an affidavit to the effect that when they had abridged and re-originated *The Old Curiosity Shop* and *Barnaby Rudge* the plaintiff had not interfered.   In the *Carol* they contended that they had made great improvements and important additions, for example Tiny Tim had been given a song of sixty lines to sing.   Far from being a colourable imitation of the plaintiff's work, it had been 'unhinged and put together again' while 'incongruities had been tastefully remedied'. Knight Bruce decided the injunction should be proceeded with, but when Dickens claimed £1000 damages the defendants took refuge in bankruptcy, and the rueful author had to pay £700 for his own costs. Later on when urged to proceed against fresh infringements of copyright he refused, saying:

> My feeling is that it is better to suffer a great wrong than to have recourse to the much greater wrong of the Law. I shall not easily forget the expense, and anxiety, and horrible injustice of the 'Carol' case, wherein in asserting the plainest right on earth I was really treated as if I were the robber instead of the robbed.

Other disagreeable experiences connected with publishing occurred in 1843–4. One of them, the meagre sale of the serial *Martin Chuzzlewit*, also involved him in financial difficulties. Monthly publication enabled Chapman and Hall to gauge readers' reactions to the work in progress, and they found that the average sale of the first six numbers was less than half that of *Oliver Twist* and *Nicholas Nickleby*. It so happened that Dickens dropped into their office one afternoon in June when William Hall was indiscreet enough to refer to the disappointing sales of the story. And then, as if that were not enough, to add that he hoped it might not be necessary to put the penalty clause into effect and get Dickens to refund some of the money they had over-advanced. Dickens flung himself out of the office and going to Forster said, 'I am bent on paying Chapman and Hall down and when I have done that, Mr. Hall shall have a piece of my mind.' 'Publishers are bitter bad judges of an author,' observed Forster.

It will be remembered that by the agreement come to between Chapman and Hall and Dickens in September 1841 the publishers were paying him £150 a month until a new novel was produced. Then supposing the author's share in the profits on the new book (in this case *Martin Chuzzlewit*) should not amount to the total of the various sums of £150 paid him monthly during the year 1842, there should be a repayment to the publishers of the amount of the deficit. The repayment clause was to come into force, if necessary, after the publication of five numbers of *Martin Chuzzlewit* when £50 might be deducted from each subsequent monthly payment until their earlier investment was repaid.

Though the sales rose with the introduction of Mrs. Gamp, they did not rise sharply enough to prevent Messrs. Chapman and Hall putting into operation the clause empowering them to lower the monthly stipend. When the blow fell in July Dickens was enraged and poured scorn on the 'scaly-headed vultures', saying he could have nothing further to do with such monsters of shabbiness. 'I am rubbed in the tenderest part of my eye-lids with bay salt . . . and a wrong kind of fire is burning in my head, I don't think I can write.' He was in a fever to find another publisher. John Forster temporised and advised him to do nothing final about breaking with Chapman and Hall, at any rate until he had been away to Broadstairs and had thought the matter over in all its bearings. This counsel may not have been entirely disinterested for John Forster was literary adviser to Chapman and Hall and intended to remain so.

The more Dickens cogitated the more irritated he became. He already had debts to pay off and was incurring more all the time. Devonshire Terrace with its staff of servants, its entertainments, its carriage and horses, its rent, its rates, to say nothing of four children to educate and another baby on the way, and on top of all this the unceasing demands for cash from Alphington, where his parents were also running up debts, made life almost unbearable. Drastic economies must be planned and means of earning more money discovered. Though it might be unwise to break with Chapman and Hall before *Martin Chuzzlewit* was completed, Forster really must sound other firms; it was always possible that Bradbury and Evans the printers might care to act as publishers. Forster temporised once more and persuaded his friend to talk things over in detail with Tom Mitton and anyway to wait till

Christmas was past before making any change. It might then be sensible to let Devonshire Terrace and go abroad to economise.

Putting his personal troubles on one side, Dickens at Christmas 1843 organised a party at Clarence Terrace, the home of his friend Macready. Macready, as we know, was touring America and the object of the entertainment was to give Mrs. Macready and the children as jolly a Christmas as possible. By one of the guests, Mrs. Carlyle, it was called 'the most remarkable party that I ever was at in London'. Dickens, who had been practising legerdemain for weeks, gave a display of conjuring with Forster for accomplice. All in a minute a plum pudding was cooked over a fire in Stanfield's tall hat and, to the astonishment of children and grown-ups alike, handkerchiefs turned into comfits and bran into guinea-pigs. Helen Faucit, who was there (at the moment acting Juliet), tells of one of the games—'Proverbs'. A proverb was selected and the company by question-asking had to guess what it was. 'The devil is never so black as he's painted' was the saying chosen by Helen Faucit. Maclise challenged her for the second word which she had to insert into her reply. She could not think of an answer when Dickens crept behind her and whispered, 'What did you say last night to the Nurse when she was keeping you in that cruel suspense?' Helen Faucit jumped up and said angrily to Maclise, 'What devil art thou that thou dost torment me thus?' When she tried to thank Dickens afterwards for his prompting, he said, 'Oh, the words must have come into your head. How should I have thought of them?'

After a champagne supper crackers were pulled, toasts given and country dances romped through. Everyone, including Thackeray, Maclise and Jerdan, 'capered like maenads'. Dickens failed to induce Mrs. Carlyle to waltz with him, but Forster seized her by the waist and whirled her round the room. 'For the love of heaven let me go!' she cried. 'You are going to dash my brains against the folding doors.' Whereupon Forster bellowed, 'Your brains? Who cares about brains here?' 'The thing', according to Mrs. Carlyle, 'was rising into something not unlike the Rape of the Sabines', when suddenly someone shouted, 'Twelve o'clock!' and all the guests rushed to the cloak-room. 'It was just a little knot of blackguardly literary people who felt themselves above all rules and independent of the universe', she added by way of commentary. One would like to know the verdict of the Macready children on the fun provided for them by the high-spirited grown-ups. There were more junketings of the same guests at Devonshire Terrace on Twelfth Night when Dickens appeared, all in black, as a magician, with Forster, all in 'fiery-red', as another magician. Between them they produced a séance calculated to send at least 'fifty people into fits'.

In February Dickens fulfilled an engagement to speak at a Mechanics' Institute soirée in Liverpool. When he arrived at Radley's Hotel, he found T. J. Thompson waiting for him. Together they dined, wined and sat over the fire talking, and next morning went to inspect the lecture theatre in which the speech was to be made. They ran into Captain Hewett of the 'Britannia', who carried Charles off for a drink to 'the old ship' which lay at the same berth as she had done when they had embarked for America. Charles was sorry Kate was not there too; it certainly seemed very strange to be on board again. He was glad to think on what friendly terms they still were with the captain; they had had him to stay in London, and Kate had taken him to Drury Lane. Captain Hewett was now invited to the soirée.

Dickens took the chair at 7 P.M. and, as he told his wife afterwards, 'spoke up like a man and distinguished himself considerably'. To his delight his clothes had been remarked on; he had heard people saying, 'What is it? Is it a waistcoat? No it's a shirt!' and so on, and this he took to be very gratifying and complimentary. The clapping of hands and stamping of feet had struck him as 'thunderous and awful'. Expressing high admiration for the civic spirit of Liverpool in tackling ignorance and shedding light in dark places,

Dickens complimented the founders of the Institute on their 11,000 books and their roll of 3000 members, soon he believed to be swelled to 6000. It delighted him to know that women and girls were to be given the same chances as men and boys. Once again he struck the new classless note: 'I look forward from this place as from a tower, to the time when high and low, rich and poor, shall mutually assist, improve and educate each other.' Adding that he would give to all the means of taking out a patent of nobility, he ended his speech by quoting lines from a poet 'who uses his great gifts for the general welfare':

> Howe'er it be, it seems to me,
> 'Tis only noble to be good.
> Kind hearts are more than coronets,
> And simple faith than Norman blood.

A programme of music formed part of the evening's entertainment and in his role of chairman Dickens, reading from a paper put into his hand, said:

> I am requested to introduce to you a young lady whom I have some difficulty and tenderness in announcing—Miss Weller—who will play a fantasia on the pianoforte.

The audience exploded with laughter and, as the performer came shyly forward, Dickens looked towards her and saw the 'angel face of a girl standing out alone from the whole crowd'. His heart bounded in his breast. What could he do to make amends for the discomfiture he had caused her? Pulling himself together he tried to reassure her by whispering in her ear that he hoped some day she would change her name and be very, very happy. Next morning he walked off to ask her to bring her father to luncheon and, thinking it would be nice to write something in her album, made up verses as he went along. Miss Weller, unlike most young ladies of his acquaintance, did not produce an album so he posted her the following lines to explain the joke of the evening before:

> I put in a book, once, by hook and by crook
> The whole race (as I thought) of a 'feller',

Who happily pleas'd the town's taste, much diseas'd
And the name of this person was Weller.
I find to my cost that one Weller I lost,
Cruel Destiny so to arrange it!
I love her dear name, which has won me some fame,
But, Great Heaven! how gladly I'd change it.

At luncheon with Thompson as fourth guest, Dickens realised that they both had fallen for the girl's charm. Surprised by the warmth and suddenness of his own reaction—he had felt nothing like it since Beadnell days—Dickens wrote, 'What a madman I should seem if the incredible feeling I have conceived for that girl should be made plain to anyone. Her face will be always in my sight . . . her green fur-trimmed dress must be preserved in lavender.' He watched Thompson enviously, for though he was an older man and a widower, he was 'irretrievably' in love. As for himself 'the angel's message in her face' smote him to the heart. Would that he could step into Thompson's shoes! When Thompson told him how fathoms deep in love with Christiana he was, Dickens wrote, 'my lips turned white' . . . 'the whole current of my blood stopped', but mastering his strange emotion he advised Thompson (who was uncertain whether to propose to so young a girl) not to hesitate, after all he has means and is irresistibly impelled towards her. It is true that he has only known her a few days, but then can he not say to himself 'hours with her are like years of common women'? He urges Thompson to win her, marry her, and 'join us in Italy'. 'Do not crucify yourself lest in so doing you crucify her.' Thompson acts on his advice and Dickens congratulates him on his 'Noble Prize'.

Two nights after the Liverpool meeting Dickens spoke at a conversazione for the Birmingham Polytechnic Institution. The Town Hall was crammed to the roof by some 2000 persons. When he showed himself the whole company rose, 'rustling like the leaves of a wood'. The ladies had hung the walls with artificial flowers and on the front of the great gallery facing him was WELCOME BOZ in letters six feet high, while behind his head 'immense transparencies' were suspended, 'representing several fames in the act of crowning several Dicks'.

In his speech he welcomed the Polytechnic idea as being neither sectarian nor class and as something in which honest men of all degrees and every creed may associate. It was an idea that might even prevent men working at machines from degenerating into machines. The note he sounded was as before, 'all for each and each for all'. In answer to a vote of thanks in which gratitude and admiration for his books was included, he said:

> So long as I can make you laugh and cry I will. . . . To you, ladies of the Institution, I am deeply and especially indebted. I sometimes think (and he pointed to the balcony) there is some small quantity of magic in that very short name and that it must consist in its containing as many letters as the three Graces.

His financial disappointment over *A Christmas Carol* and *Martin Chuzzlewit* combined with Forster's unwillingness to negotiate with Bradbury and Evans or any other new publisher, caused him to give Tom Mitton a free hand to deal with his business affairs, begging his friend especially to familiarise himself with all agreements, contracts and other documents. A tentative approach to Bradbury and Evans revealed that, though a little alarmed, they were not averse to taking over the publication of future works provided Mr. Dickens was able to come to an arrangement with Chapman and Hall that did not involve them in trouble. To understand this we must bear in mind that Bradbury and Evans was a printing firm, printers indeed to Chapman and Hall and in no sense their rivals as publishers. Tom Mitton handled the situation with competence and matters were settled up before Dickens went abroad. Chapman and Hall's balance was paid off and the whole question of the stock-on-hand of the books gone into. In losing Dickens Chapman and Hall lost their best author and the founder of the fortunes of their house, but as he walked out, Thackeray walked in with his *Irish Sketchbook*.

Thackeray, who was just off to the Middle East, promised further sketches which were to appear as *Cornhill to Grand Cairo*. Carlyle soon became one of their authors and was quickly followed by the Brownings and Arthur Clough. John Forster, though he could not control Dickens, certainly managed to serve the firm that employed him well.

When the transfer from one publisher to another was completed Dickens wrote to Bradbury and Evans to explain what he wanted in the way of an advance to enable him to live in Italy:

> I will begin with the statement of the amount in which I must desire to become indebted to you. The balance payable to Chapman and Hall will be £1500. The sum I shall require for my anticipated expenses will be £1500. I owe you already £500 and against this entire sum of £3500 I propose to place to your credit, when the account for the subscription for the completed *Martin Chuzzlewit* is rendered, £500. . . . But in addition to this sum of £3000 which will then be left, I may require for anything I know, in the spring of next year, £500 more. . . .
>
> Now for the repayment of advances we must look of course to the following heads:
>
> (1) First the new Carol and the new next Christmas issue of the old one.
> (2) The Magazine or Journal and the mutual relations we may agree upon respecting it, I would suggest that it should be commenced within six months.
> (3) The best working of the copyrights in existence.[1]

Oliver Twist he states is his own unconditionally and it has not so far been published in a single volume. *A Christmas Carol* is also his own unconditionally. In *Pickwick* his interest is one-third of the copyright. He can only sell his share to Chapman and Hall and they can only sell their share to him. He has no power to appoint other publishers for this work. *Nicholas Nickleby* will become entirely his in November 1844, that is in seven months' time. He then will have the right to buy the stock at cost price. As for *Master Humphrey's Clock*, i.e. *The Old Curiosity Shop* and *Barnaby Rudge*, he owns half the copyright. In *American Notes* he owns three-quarters of the copyright and in *Martin Chuzzlewit* three-quarters of the copyright. The *Sketches* bought from Macrone by Chapman and Hall for £2250 must remain the property of Chapman and Hall till March 1845, and then if the book has paid for itself, half the copyright must be surrendered to him.

To make a long story short, Bradbury and Evans advanced him a lump sum of £2800 in return for a fourth share of any book he should write during the next eight years.

Business affairs, especially negotiations with publishers, always irked Dickens terribly and by the time matters were fixed up with Bradbury and Evans he had fretted and fumed himself into a state of intense irritation which nothing but an escape abroad could now allay. When the final agreement was signed and he was put in possession of a lump sum of money, he heaved a sigh of relief; at last he was free to let his house and make the economies called for by his debts.

Having begun to learn Italian and having played with the idea of going to Italy, he was thrilled at meeting Mazzini with the Carlyles. Dickens at once became disposed to be the friend of the political refugee from Italy. On being told that Mazzini's correspondence was subject to censorship by order of the Home Secretary, Sir James Graham, he by way of protest took (June 1844) to writing on the back of his envelopes, 'It is particularly requested that if Sir James Graham should open this, he will not trouble himself to seal it'. From 1837 on, Mazzini had been teaching boy compatriots in London and since 1839 had been correspondent of revolutionary committees in Malta and Paris. He was subjected to the usual police supervision. Both Carlyle and Dickens, however, protested against 'this turpitude', the first in a letter to the *Times*, and the second in a letter to the Home Secretary. Espionage they hated, it was unenglish, and the idea that the information obtained by the censor might be passed on to the Neapolitan Government was abhorrent to them both. Carlyle championed Mazzini as 'a man of genius and virtue', 'a rare man worthy to be called a martyr soul'. The matter was hotly debated in Parliament and Sir James Graham's authority called in question. In the opinion of Lord Denman and other peers, the subject was a very grave one. They were emphatic that England should not be made the police office of any foreign state whatever.[1]

For the Italian Relief Committee Dickens offered to draw up an appeal, the forerunner of the countless appeals for exiles with which two wars have familiarised us. 'The English people, distinguished for generosity and love of justice among all the nations of the earth', are urged to welcome to England, the land of the free, the fighters for freedom, 'noble spirits who because of their protest against bigotry and despotism are refugees in an alien land'. Some people affected to take no interest in the refugee question. 'And what is Mazzini?' asked Lady Holland (July 1844). 'A revolutionary man and the head of young Italy,' was Carlyle's reply.

Dickens was this year invited to the Royal Academy dinner. Mr. Brookfield, always a little sniffy about him, wrote to his wife:

> Dickens spoke shortly, and well enough, but it had a very cut and dried air and was rather pompous and shapely in its construction and delivered in a rather sonorous deep voice. Not a jot of humour in it. He looks like Milnes, same height and shape, still longer hair, but not his demoniacal good humour of expression.[2]

Just at this time R. H. Horne, author of *Orion*, published *A New Spirit of the Age*. Twenty years had gone by since Hazlitt's *Spirit of the Age* had appeared and a new set of men, he asserted, animated by a new spirit, were impressing themselves on the public mind. Horne led off with seventy-six

---

[1] *Parliamentary Debates*, 2nd series, Hansard, lxxv.
[2] *Mrs. Brookfield and her Circle*, May 13, 1844.

pages on the most representative of the new men, Charles Dickens, and accompanied his essay by so grim a study by Margaret Gillies from the Maclise portrait as to cause the victim to exclaim, 'Why I look like the man in the iron mask!' With some particularity Horne compared Dickens with Hogarth and noted that 'le célèbre Cruikshank' often would illustrate a book without due reference to the original, thereby turning credible human beings into caricatures, which was deplorable as 'the delineation of characters' was so very much the most prominent and valuable portion of Mr. Dickens's works. His tremendous reputation had been achieved in eight years. Life was being lived at high pressure; Mr. Dickens was manifestly the product of his age, a genuine emanation of its aggregate and entire spirit. He was not an imitator of anyone but an author of unexhausted originality.

Chapter 14

ITALY

A man who has not been in Italy is always conscious of an inferiority.   SAMUEL JOHNSON

PLANS for going abroad were now laid to take effect from the concluding number of *Martin Chuzzlewit* due to appear in July.   When consulting Lady Blessington on the merits of foreign localities, Dickens wrote that, having made up his mind 'to decamp, bag and baggage, for a twelvemonth', he purposes establishing his family in some convenient place from which he can 'make personal ravages on the neighbouring country'.

Both Lady Blessington and Count d'Orsay had advised him to go to Italy where living was cheap and the climate good. They thought 'he should set up his nest at Pisa'.   Later advice from Landor recommended Genoa as preferable to Pisa and suggested that an effort should be made to secure Lord Byron's villa, Casa Saluzzi, at Albaro, the seaside suburb of the city.   Inquiry revealed that this house was in a ruinous state and that the ground floor had been converted into a 'third-rate wine-shop'.   Il Paradiso, the Blessingtons' house, was not available, so Angus Fletcher, who was buying marbles at Carrara, was instructed to select another house which, if possible, should be at Albaro.   Mr. Kindheart had little capacity either as a sculptor or as an agent and none at driving a bargain, but he found the Villa Bagnerollo and was empowered to rent it for three months, during which period Dickens counted on him and his marbles being accommodated on the garden floor so as 'to make company' for the family. It was only after arrival that Dickens found he could have had the Doria Palace, set in beautiful woods to the west of the city with grounds running down to the sea, complete with pictures and furniture, all for £40 a year.   The banker to whom he was accredited had advised Fletcher to take it, but Fletcher had been told to rent a house at Albaro, and rent a house at Albaro he did for four times its proper value, with the result that it soon became to Dickens 'the detestable Bagnerollo'. It was an annoying mistake, but Mr. Kindheart was certainly not a business man.

Before plans were completed Devonshire Terrace was let to 'a desirable widow', who insisted on moving in at once. Owing to her importunity the family had to transfer to furnished rooms. Writing to Lady Holland from 9 Osnaburgh Terrace,[1] Dickens tells her that as he is in the throes of *Chuzzlewit*, he has to avoid all dining-out and walk for hours among streets and fields. The book should be finished 'by the end of this week' and he will call on her on Saturday, 12.30 P.M., to say good-bye. It was at 9 Osnaburgh Terrace that Mr. and Mrs. Charles Dickens gave their farewell dinner.

This dinner was a great worry to Dickens and he consulted Forster as to whether he should drop it, transfer it to the Clarendon, or take Kate's advice and give it at the Star and Garter at Richmond? Could it be done, he wondered, for a couple of guineas apiece at the Clarendon? 'In a matter of importance I could make up my mind. But in a matter of this kind I bother and bewilder myself and come to no conclusion whatever. Advise, Advise!' Forster told Charles to throw over the party, but Kate cleverly managed to arrange that it should take place in the hired house, which pleased Charles much better. The list of guests included Lord Normanby, Lord Denman, Sir John Easthope with his wife and daughter, Sydney Smith, the Macreadys, Babbage, Lady Osborne and daughter, Dr. Southwood Smith, Dr. Quin, Thomas Chapman and his wife, and of course Forster. A rather significant list in so far as it shows that Dickens had no intention of quarrelling with those who might be thought to have treated him shabbily, Easthope and Chapman, and how real was his friendship with his fellow philanthropist and novelist, Lord Normanby. A few days later Lord Normanby

[1] June 10 1844.

took the chair at the *Martin Chuzzlewit* dinner at Greenwich, a feast attended by Turner, Stanfield, Forster and others.

Before leaving England 'Boz' reopened his connection with the *Morning Chronicle* by offering to supply letters from abroad as the fancy took him.[1] The price he asked was high and the new editor, Andrew Doyle, who had succeeded his dear old friend John Black, declined the offer on the ground of expense and even seemed to grudge paying for two articles at ten guineas each. Dickens went off greatly offended and never again entered the office of the *Morning Chronicle*. More than this, his self-esteem refused to be placated by anything less than the setting-up of a paper in opposition to the *Chronicle*. With this end in view he initiated a conference between himself, Forster, Bradbury and Evans, and Paxton to discuss the matter and it was tentatively agreed that the situation should be explored, particularly with reference to finance, and that action should be taken, if feasible, after Dickens's return from the continent.[2]

The preparations for transferring a complete family abroad were initiated by the purchase at the Pantechnicon, Belgrave Square, of a travelling carriage, priced £60 and bought for £45 cash down. A heavy vehicle requiring four horses to draw it, it could, at best, never have gone at more than six or seven miles an hour. It was provided with imperials, leathern cellarettes, wells, night lamps, day lamps and receptacles to hold luggage of all shapes. In *Pictures from Italy* we have a description of this *berline* in Paris as it drew out of the courtyard of the Hôtel Meurice early one summer morning to take the dusty road to Marseilles. Its team of horses, controlled by a postilion with a long whip, wore between them on their collars ninety-six bells which jingled shrilly in the ears of the travellers. Occasionally the jingle was interrupted by an adjuration to the 'pigs of horses' or a loud crack of the whip. Charley, aged seven, remembered all his life walking up inter-

---

[1] T. H. S. Escott, *Masters of English Journalism*, pp. 211-13 (1911).
[2] H. R. Fox Bourne, *English Newspapers*, vol. ii. p. 140.

minable hills in the lonely French countryside. When in the
evening the travelling carriage rumbles into the courtyard of
another hotel its well-known courier is rapturously received
by the landlord he has warned to expect his party. As the
party stiffly bundles out of the vehicle they are greeted by
cries of delight: 'The sweet lady! the sister of the sweet lady!
The first little boy, how beautiful, the first little girl how
enchanting!' Feeling warms towards the whole family, the
second little girl is kissed, the second little boy caressed, but
when the sleeping baby, Francis Jeffrey, is revealed, applause
is let loose and the party disappears into the hotel in a babel
of enthusiastic approval.

By the plain of Chalon (sur Saône), where the irregular lines
of poplars are silhouetted in the evening light, Dickens is put
in mind of 'combs with broken teeth' and some, by his words,
may be put in mind of Lamartine when he makes Eloise say,
'Do you see the disk half sunk behind those firs which are like
the eyelashes of the sky?' Analogy is the magician's wand,
but not all hands can wield it.

At Lyons 'Boz' was fascinated by the cathedral clock. It
reminded him in a way of Master Humphrey's clock, for
things emerged from its case, not old papers, however, but
puppets. Little doors flew open, little figures staggered out,
with the hitch in their gait that one associates with clockwork
of the old type. In the centre stood the Virgin Mary, while
close to her from a small pigeon-hole popped out an evil-
looking puppet that lunged towards her and then flopped
back, banging his little door after him. Thinking it to be
symbolic of the victory of good over evil, Dickens murmured
'Ah! ha! Le Diable!' 'Pardon, M'sieu,' said the sacristan,
'l'ange Gabriel!'

Everywhere he went the traveller noted the 'unscavengered
qualities' of the cities. Lyons was drainless and had grafted
upon it all the miseries of a manufacturing town. Always he
made a point of wandering into cathedrals and always found
therein 'divers old women and a few dogs engaged in contemplation'. Catholic ritual struck him as both soporific and

tawdry and as part of an utterly dead past. Mass in the cathedral at Avignon was attended by a few aged crones and a baby in arms while a dog ran up and down the aisle. There was nothing to claim his interest in these junk-like buildings and their ghosts except the ex-votos, which at least must have been offered up by living, overflowing hearts. How different were the packed Protestant churches of the New World with their attentive, intelligent congregations and their well-lit, well-polished interiors!

From Lyons the party travelled by steamer down the Rhone, past Valence where Napoleon studied, past Avignon with its papal palace, prison of Rienzi whose story Bulwer had romanced over and Miss Mitford had dramatised. During a visit to the offices of the Inquisition, Dickens noticed a wall frescoed, as if in irony, with the story of the Good Samaritan. This horrified him into buying a guide-book from the custodian wherewith to make himself acquainted with other aspects of history in Avignon.

A night at Aix-en-Provence proved 'hot, clean and comfortable', and thence the *berline* rolled on through clouds of dust to Marseilles. There it was hoisted aboard a steamer, the 'Marie Antoinette', and the family, freed from its confinement, loitered on deck and watched the coast slide by. Nice, San Remo, Genoa, the sea journey was all too short.

On the quay at Genoa horses were once again harnessed to the vehicle which they dragged to a house among the vineyards at Albaro. There in the courtyard of the Villa Bella Vista the young family unpacked itself, a little disconsolate, for the approaches to the House of the Beautiful View were mournful, the lanes leading to it neglected, and the rusty entrance gates as they swung back into a shabby little garden rank with weeds had creaked ominously in their ears. Was it really possible to settle in such a place, the grown-ups wondered silently. To Dickens's private eye the building looked like a deserted jail, a pink jail. Pink jail! ha ha! that was not too bad a name for it.

Inspection revealed 'a square hall like a cellar' and 'a

cracked marble staircase' leading to the *sala*—an enormous room with a vaulted roof. On the walls were pictures, on the floor a vast immovable sofa and some stiff chairs upholstered like the sofa in crimson brocade. It certainly was not a home from home, and one member of the party, at least, thought with longing of spick and span Devonshire Terrace with its cosy armchairs, pile carpets, neatly draped windows and admirable lavatories. What could the Bella Vista beds be like? Kate asked herself. How dismaying it was to come so far and to have so much to contend with! There could be no point in disparaging the place before the children and the servants, they must all see the *bella vista* at once. United by a common impulse the whole party began to lean from the eleven windows of the *piano nobile*. Fortunately the view was eminently praisable. One could see from the grassed-over terrace, on to which the windows gave, the sea, other villas, other gardens, and mountains in the background. Near at hand three cows were quietly munching vine-leaves and Kate heard a voice, it may have been Mr. Kindheart's, saying that they were yielding plenty of milk. For the rest, —lizards, rats, scorpions, fleas and flies were in occupation of the many empty rooms. By day they were advised the shutters must be shut against the sun and by night the windows against the mosquitoes, by night too they might be troubled by the singing of frogs. 'Timber', being nearest to the floor, fell an immediate victim to the fleas, had to be shaved and was so ashamed of the appearance he then presented that he nearly died of grief, or so his master said. Bella Vista decidedly was not a house after Mrs. Dickens's heart, it would be out of the question to spend the winter there: all one could hope was that the children would take no permanent harm from camping in this alien environment.

I think that even young Mr. Dickens's spirit may have quailed at the prospect before him—but he reminded himself that he was the breadwinner, that he had come there on purpose to write and must shut himself away from domestic worries. It was for Kate to wrestle with callers and tradesmen and vermin, he must go on with his Italian and rescue his books from the Customs. It would never do for the plays of Voltaire or Ruskin's *Seven Lamps of Architecture* to be confiscated. Having worked diligently at Italian in London with one Mariotti, he immediately engaged 'a little patient revolutionary officer, exiled in England during many years' to come three times a week to read and speak Italian with him. He began on *I Promessi Sposi*. 'How charming and what a clever book!' he observed in a letter to Samuel Rogers. In between his studies he bounced off to see the sights of the city, among them the newly painted, regilded Church of the Annunziata, and standing there before the altar, looking up at the three domes, he was turned 'giddy by the flash and glory of the place'. It seemed to him that 'every sort of splendour were the perpetual enactment in these Italian churches. Gorgeous processions pour from them. There is illumination of windows on festal nights.' For a moment he thought the Church more alive than it was in France, but this impression was evanescent. What fun it was to watch the marriage brokers, queer old women and queer old men, operating in out-of-the-way corners of streets. How strange to see sedan chairs 'gilded and otherwise' plying for hire; but then as he was soon to realise they were not part of a dead past, they were a necessity of daily life, for the entrances to many palaces were in *salite* which no wheeled vehicle could reach and ladies were forced to use these means of conveyance. All about him in Genoa Dickens saw walls mouldering, frescoes peeling, a city crumbling to decay. Its 'squalid mazes' were packed with 'filthy people' and every fourth or fifth man he passed was 'a repulsive-featured religious'. To balance these uglinesses there were everywhere delicious green figs, green lemons, green almonds, and with these ingredients added to 'rare Hollands' he found that very good punch could be contrived. He managed with the help of the French consul to dive into local society and so was introduced to Byron's friend, the Marquis di Negri, the owner of a fine house and a heavily grottoed garden, who entertained freely.

Agreeing with Kate and the rest of his suite that the Bella Vista could only be regarded as a summer perch he diligently sought other accommodation, and found it within the walls of Genoa itself. Thus after enduring the pink jail for three months, the family transferred to the Palace of the Fishponds, the Palazzo Peschiere, than which no lovelier residence could be found in all Italy. Dickens described it to Forster as 'something larger than Whitehall multiplied by four'. The Dickens family took possession of the *piano nobile* and a Spanish duke lived below them. All Genoa could be seen from the terraces and the sweet scents from the garden induced in 'Boz' a dream of happiness. One of the great new pleasures he shared with Kate was a box at the opera which cost them almost nothing. The opera-house was so close to the Peschiere that they could go and sit there 'with no more trouble than in their own drawing room'.

After moving into Genoa they got to know some of the foreign residents and with their introduction to the De la Rues was initiated a period of great mental agitation for Kate. Charles's interest in hypnotism was undiminished and such experiments as he had made on his wife and others had given him great confidence in his powers. Mr. De la Rue was a Swiss banker carrying on business in Genoa, who, with his English wife (an 'affectionate, excellent little' woman, according to Dickens), lived elegantly in a charming apartment at the top of the Palazzo Rosso. It soon became plain to Kate that Mrs. De la Rue had taken a marked liking to her Charles and was bestowing on him her confidences. From the first moment of meeting, Dickens was conscious that some magnetic attraction was drawing them towards each other and creating between them a state of deep sympathy. Soon Mrs. De la Rue was telling him that, in spite of all appearances to the contrary, she, being the victim of delusions, was a very unhappy woman. She was haunted, it seems, by a phantom that spoke to her and a crowd of gory entities which pursued her with veiled faces. Charles was moved by her distress and convinced that he could banish the delusions by means of hypnotism. Mr. De la Rue, he was assured, was anxious that he should make the experiment. And so it came about that Kate had to watch a peculiarly intimate relationship establishing itself between her husband and this stranger, a relationship necessitating one, if not two, meetings a day. Kate cogitated over the situation, was it or was it not love at first sight? or was it what it was alleged to be, the merely magnetic attraction that was a prerequisite of treatment of this nature? Charles was always at Mrs. De la Rue's beck and call and kept urging her to have no reticences with him, insisting that it was dangerous and might invalidate the cure if she kept any secret from him. For the hundredth time Kate wished herself back in Devonshire Terrace, where life was plain-sailing and held no disagreeable surprises. Of course she had been told by Charles that 'poor little Mrs. De la Rue' had been haunted by spectral forms whose faces she could never see, and that he was sure that in the end he could help her to control and finally to dispel these phantasms. Listening to such tales with what sympathy she could muster, Kate lived on tenterhooks, and things were not made easier by the fact that somehow Dickens found himself inhibited from writing. When he did settle down to compose a short story, it was full of spirits and goblins.

It was a disappointment to Dickens to find Genoa so impossible a place to write in, what could be the matter with him? was it merely that he felt strange or was it the clanging of the innumerable bells that was driving him mad? The day was to dawn, however, when he suddenly felt inspired by the bells and knew he could make them work for him. Down on paper went the heading of a short story *The Chimes*. His attitude of mind had changed, he welcomed the clangour, 'Let them clash upon me now from all the churches and convents. I see nothing but the old London belfry I have set them in.' And thus amid the faded grandeurs of an Italian palace he focussed his imagination on a London ticket-porter and his sufferings. 'In my mind's eye, Horatio,' he wrote to Forster, 'I like more and more my action of making in this little book a great blow for the poor.' Continuing in the same strain he said, 'I am in regular ferocious excitement with *The Chimes*! get up at 7: have a cold bath before breakfast and blaze away wrathful and red hot until 3 P.M. or so when I usually knock-off for the day.' When working under emotional strain his hair went lank, his head hot, his face pale, his eyes hollow and brimming with tears. 'I have had a good cry,' he wrote, 'I am worn to death. I was obliged to lock myself in when I finished it yesterday for my face was swollen for the time to twice its proper size and was hugely ridiculous.'

Begun on October 10, *The Chimes: A Goblin Story* was finished on November 3, and so much does Dickens think of it as an achievement that he feels compelled to try and realise vividly the effect on others of what he has accomplished. He must go to the Cuttris Hotel in the Piazza, Covent Garden, for a few nights and Forster must assemble his friends at his house in Lincoln's Inn Fields so that he may try the story out on them by reading it aloud. 'I believe', he wrote to Mitton, 'I have written a tremendous book and knocked the *Carol* out of the field.'

Leaving Kate, Georgy and the children at the Peschiere, Dickens set out by slow stages for London. He crammed a lot of sightseeing into his journey, which took him through Stradella where he lay at 'a galleried inn'; then to Piacenza 'a brown, decayed, old town . . . deserted, solitary, grass grown, with ruined ramparts': from thence he posted to Parma noting its bustling streets and, in the Farnese palace, its desolate crumbling theatre. It depressed him to see the boxes sagging, the festoons dangling and blue sky showing through gashes in the roof. In Parma, too, the neglect of the cathedral upset him, the whole building seemed to mourn the rotting of the Correggio frescoes in the cupola. The melancholy induced by painted figures fading away on walls was, he felt, akin to the melancholy induced by the fading of human forms from our lives. Dickens tired his couriers out. Up by candlelight and sightseeing at lightning speed till dark, he barely left himself time to jot down any impressions. At

Modena, a town of 'sombre colonnades and brilliant skies', he pushed through leathern doors into 'a crooning High Mass'. How strange it was to him to find again as he had found in France and in every stagnant Latin town 'the same heart beating with the same monotonous pulsation, the centre of the same torpid, listless system'. At Bologna he came on the tracks of 'Milor Beeron', dead these twenty years past. 'Milor Beeron had approved of the matting' in his room; 'Milor Beeron never touched milk'. The ancient town arcades, the rich churches with their drowsy masses and tinkling bells, and the Great Meridian on the pavement at San Petronio awakened in Dickens a sadness as of withered romance. Life had ebbed from Italy. Ferrara struck him as more solitary, more depopulated, more deserted, than any city of the solemn series. Grim Ferrara, with the grass growing in its silent streets—Ariosto's house and Tasso's prison did not redeem for him a place which, from its appearance, might have been ravaged by pestilence.

Venice transported him. Venice the magnificent, stupendous reality, utterly beyond the scope of pen or pencil, the wonder, the sensation of the world, now part of him for ever. He is frantic in his admiration for Tintoretto's 'Assembly of the Blest' or Paradise: as for Titian's 'Assumption' it is for him the 'culmination of beauty'. Always one notices his bankruptcy in analogy—in order to heighten his praise of a gallery of pictures he will say 'Hampton Court is a fool to 'em'. From Venice he made for Verona and Mantua, then Milan, where his wife and sister-in-law met him, bringing with them his correspondence; they all three spent a couple of days seeing sights together, then Kate and Georgy returned to Genoa and the author went on to sledge over the Simplon and so by way of Fribourg, Strasbourg and Paris to London.

Forster was surprised his friend should think the journey worth while, though he knew better than anyone that Dickens was compelled by inner tension to come and get, if he could, a vivid sense of the effect his work had on his friends—he calls it 'that unspeakable restless something' which made him feel like a full balloon—obliged to go up. Forster also knew that he was expected to provide the audience, to give a dinner for Dickens and then inquire of him casually would he perhaps care to read his new Christmas story aloud to the other guests. Impulse has no prevision and to those who do not share it always seems to be mad, but to exclude it may be to stifle vitality and development. In Forster's well-regulated life there was no room for anything so anarchical as impulse, but he was a good enough friend to Dickens to fall in with demands made upon him. After talking things over in London the idea of dinner gave way before a plan for issuing a summons for a 'special purpose on Monday, December 2 at half-past six'. Dickens made a list of those to be invited: Carlyle of course was indispensable, so was his wife, for *her* judgment would be invaluable. Maclise must come and perhaps his sister. 'Stanny' and Jerrold he would particularly wish for, and Edwin Landseer, Blanchard, Harness, Fonblanque and Fox must also be thought of.

In the end no women came, but a company of ten more or less distinguished men settled themselves down to listen for two hours to the Goblin Story. The audition took place in Forster's rooms at 58 Lincoln's Inn Fields under the 'Verriolike ceiling' described in *Bleak House* as ornamenting Tulkinghorn's chambers. Maclise sketched the scene drawing rays of light over the reader's head, and Forster described the sketch when alluding to the incident, but added no personal impression:

> The reader may be assured (with allowance for a touch of caricature to which I may claim to be considered myself as the chief and very marked victim) that in the grave attention of Carlyle, the eager interest of Stanfield and Maclise, the keen look of poor Laman Blanchard, Fox's rapt solemnity, Jerrold's skyward gaze, and the tears of Harness and Dyce the characteristic points of the scene are sufficiently rendered. All other recollection of it is lapsed and gone; but that at least its principal actor was made glad and grateful sufficient further testimony survives.

Barham of *The Ingoldsby Legends* is not shown in the sketch though he must have been present, for he gave such an enthusiastic account of the first reading to his friends that a repetition had to be arranged for.

In this informal reading we may sense the germ of all the public readings of later years. Dickens always, like a true actor, had the desire to see himself mirrored in the eyes of his audience. So invigorated did he feel by appreciation of his performance that he arranged with Forster to act a play as soon as he returned home from abroad.

The Chimes, a little volume, was brought out by Chapman and Hall as the Christmas Book of 1844. Lady Blessington wept over the story and found herself obliged to defend the author from 'the charge of wishing to degrade the aristocracy'. Brookfield told his wife[1] that '*The Chimes* was as utter trash as was ever trodden under foot'. Twenty thousand copies of the book were sold at once, giving Dickens a profit of £1500 which for the time being satisfied him.

Forster wrote to Dickens, after he left, to express his grief that he had had so tempestuous a journey for such brief enjoyment, to which he replied that the visit had been one of happiness and delight to him.

> I would not [he wrote] recall an inch of the way to you or from you, if it had been twenty times as long and twenty thousand times as wintry. It was worth any travel— anything! With the soil of the road in the very grain of my cheeks, I swear I wouldn't have missed that week, that first night of our meeting, that one evening of the reading in your rooms, aye, and the second reading too, for any easily stated or conceived consideration.[2]

Macready, who had just returned from America, could only attend the first reading in Lincoln's Inn Fields as he had to rush over to Paris for a brief Shakespeare season. Dickens promised to fall on him 'with a swoop of love in Paris'. And so he did, on his way back to Genoa. Macready was playing

---

[1] March 12, 1845.   [2] *Life of Dickens*, vol. i. p. 372.

Hamlet, Macbeth, King Lear, Othello, Virginius by Sheridan Knowles, and the greatest of all his parts—*Werner*. The performance of the twelve-day season took place at the Salle Ventadour, a building usually devoted to Italian Opera. In Paris Dickens plunged headlong into theatrical and literary society, hobnobbing daily with Macready's acquaintances, Théophile Gautier, Louis Blanc, Victor Hugo and Alexandre Dumas. Dumas gave them a box for his play, *Christine*, and they saw a great deal of Régnier of the Théâtre Français and of Louis Bertin, editor of the *Journal des Débats*, and son of its founder. Dickens also made friends with Paul Delaroche, 'court painter to the decapitated sovereigns Lady Jane Grey, Mary Queen of Scots and Charles I in his coffin with Cromwell raising the lid'; with Delacroix too, painter of dramatic battle-scenes and shipwrecks, he fraternised, while from the lips of Michelet and Quinet he heard all the gossip about Guizot. Macready made him known to Comte de Vigny, author of *Cinq Mars*, and to Mr. Bowes, whose memory in England is perpetuated in the Bowes Museum, Barnard Castle. It was a most stimulating experience and crowded with new contacts. He found it hard to tear himself away, but when he did go he went with the determination to return to Paris as soon as an opportunity offered. To get back to his family in time for Christmas he had to set out in snow by *malle-poste* for Marseilles. A thaw supervened and the horses literally 'waded' to the coast. Detained at Marseilles by stress of weather he, after delays impatiently endured, took the steam-packet *Charlemagne*, and ran through heavy seas to Genoa where the chimes once more 'rang sweetly in his ears'.

Writing to Mrs. Macready to tell of his snowy journey, the traveller says:

I was so cold after leaving you and dear Macready in Paris that I was taken out of the coach at Marseilles in a perfectly torpid state and was at first supposed to be luggage, but the porters not being able to find any directions upon me led to a further examination and what newspapers call 'the vital spark' was finally discovered under a remote corner of the travelling shawls which you were pleased to approbate in the Hôtel Brighton. After that I passed three days of waking nightmare at Marseilles. . . . It may have been two, but I crowded into the space the noisome smells of a patriarchal life. After that I was so horribly ill on board a steamboat that I should have made my will if I had had anything to leave, but I had only the basin and I couldn't leave that for the moment. That suffering over I rushed into the arms of my expectant family. Their happiness is more easily conceived than described. . . .

Re-united at the Peschiere, the Dickens family did their best to generate the Christmas spirit. This was made easier by the thoughtfulness of Miss Coutts, who had sent her godson, Charley, a sugared cake weighing ninety pounds. No Twelfth Night confection had ever been seen in Genoa before, and when it was sent to the pastrycook's to have its sugar ornaments repaired after its journey, it stood on exhibition for customers to wonder at, together with its bon-bons, crackers and Twelfth Night figures complete. Twelfth Night festivities over, Mr. and Mrs. Dickens quitted Genoa for Rome.

Mrs. De la Rue, who had missed him terribly during his five weeks' absence, begged him before he started for the Eternal City on no account to go alone to Trinità dei Monti, for she had been through her first sinister adventure there and was solicitous lest Dickens, after treating her, might not attract the same evil phantoms to himself. During the long drive southwards Kate realised that Charles was worrying about his 'patient' and wondering what bad effects separation from him might not entail. It soon transpired that he was giving her absent treatment and concentrating his thoughts upon her. What could Kate with her matter-of-fact Scottish mind think about her husband's absorption in another woman except that he must be in love with her?

Breaking their journey at Spezzia, they made a detour to the marble quarries of Carrara to visit Angus Fletcher who had gone there to lodge with an English marble merchant, Mr. Walton. He took them to the local opera-house to hear *Norma*, and on their return to the Walton villa they were serenaded by a chorus of marble workers. Pisa was the next stop: the moon was shining on the famous tower which looked 'all awry in the uncertain light'. Next morning on visiting the group of buildings of which it formed a part, they found 'a grave, retired place set in a verdant carpet of turf' and Dickens observed that monuments clustering together as if shrinking from the ordinary transactions of the town 'have a singularly venerable and impressive character. It is the architectural essence of a rich old city, with all its common life and common habitations pressed out, and filtered away.'

Of course Dickens climbed the Leaning Tower, and in so doing got the sensation of being on a ship that had heeled over: the view upwards through the slanted tube struck him as most curious. On the walls of the fretted cloisters lingered ancient frescoes looking down on grassy graves filled with soil brought from the Holy Land six centuries earlier. The impression made by the *campo santo* on his mind was one of solemn, unforgettable loveliness.

After visiting Leghorn, 'made illustrious by Smollett's grave', they returned to Pisa and hired a *vetturino* and his four horses to drive them through Tuscany to Siena. Siena with its old palaces dreamy and fantastic seemed 'like a bit of Venice without the water', but Dickens was no whole-hearted admirer of beauty in decay because these cities were identified in his mind with a vague notion of a tyrannous past and, like the Tower of London, evoked visions of rat-infested dungeons, racks, torture chambers and the headman's axe. As Mr. and Mrs. Dickens drove over the desolate, dangerous Campagna, they strained their eyes for Rome and when they saw the great cupola it put them disappointingly in mind of London! 'There it lay, under a thick cloud, with innumerable towers, and steeples, and roofs of houses, rising up into the sky, and high above them all, one Dome!'

On closer acquaintance Rome failed to impress these

tourists: the shops, the people, the equipages were so ordinary, no flicker of grandeur was anywhere to be discerned. Charles wrote unhappily to Forster, 'It is no more my Rome, degraded and fallen and lying asleep in the sun among a heap of ruins, than Lincoln's Inn Fields is'.

The measure of what one gets from sightseeing is governed by the amount one brings to sightseeing. Dickens brought very little. The educational and cultural background necessary to the understanding of the past was almost completely lacking and his reactions are sometimes silly and often shallow. In the paucity of his analogies the paucity of his general mental equipment is only too evident.

Perhaps he could not apprehend great monuments in their majesty or integrity because there was nothing to link them up with human joys and human tears. On first submitting himself to the overwhelming vastness of St. Peter's he missed the *vox humana*. 'I felt no very strong emotion. I have been infinitely more affected in many English cathedrals when the organ has been playing and in many English country churches when the congregation have been singing.'

They stood there, this little couple from England, gaping up at the Dome and half stunned by the size of the building, till Dickens said, 'We've been here an hour, let us go to the Coliseum'. There he found his paralysed imagination begin to work again, peopling the tiered seats with faces and the arena with a whirl of strife and blood and sand. Never could he be more 'moved and overcome by any sight not immediately connected with his own affections and afflictions'.

Walls and arches overgrown with green, corridors open to the day, long grass growing in the porches, trees in the ragged parapets, birds nesting in chinks and crannies, all this he saw as he climbed to the upper walls and looked down on the triumphal arches of Constantine, Severus and Titus, on the Forum and the Palace of the Caesars, ruin, ruin, ruin all about him, here was his Rome at last! In such a mood he wandered out along the Appian way, out on to the open Campagna with its broken aqueducts, its broken temples, its broken tombs, sombre and desolate beyond all expression. Here indeed was the Rome of his imagination, the city he had pictured when, as a boy, he had visited the Roman bath in London.

One of the first diversions indulged in by the Dickenses was to take part in the Carnival. They hired a carriage, and filling it with nosegays and sugar plums, wore their wire masks and started tossing their flowers and volleying their confetti. Charles gives a lively description of the draperies and banners on the Corso, of scaffoldings turned into glittering bowers, of the battle of the tapers which he enjoyed to the utmost, extinguishing other people's lights, keeping his own burning and jeering 'Senza moccolo!' So lively is his description that Germans have compared it with Goethe's account of his experience on a similar occasion.

Presently they decided to leave Rome for the rest of Lent and to return in time for Holy Week. Georgy was due to meet them in Naples, coming direct from Genoa by sea and bringing with her letters from England and news of the family. At Naples Charles excited himself to fever-pitch over his mail and, when the boat came in from Genoa, watched the unloading of the mailbags through a telescope. On having the De la Rue letters put into his hands, he read them avidly, only to learn how adversely his departure had affected his poor little patient. Impetuously he sent an express letter by the return boat urging her husband to bring her to Rome for further treatment. Relieved in mind by this decision, he set to work to see the sights with a will. He and his ladies went to Pompeii, Herculaneum, Monte Cassino and other places. They made the ascent of Vesuvius (Kate and Georgy in litters) and they explored Naples itself very thoroughly. To Dickens it was not nearly so beautiful a city as Genoa. When he had tired his ladies out with orthodox sightseeing, he spent his time investigating lazzaroni and slum life. The slums he walked through were so squalid that 'those of Saffron Hill seemed genteel' by comparison. He visited the burial sites or pits covered by flat stones into which uncoffined paupers were nightly thrown and they made the congested graveyards of London seem almost decent.

Just before Holy Week the sightseers returned to Rome, putting up at the Hotel Meloni where Mrs. Dickens found that the De la Rues had also reserved rooms. As soon as they arrived Dickens began to mesmerise his patient daily. Her worst moment in the twenty-four hours was between one and two in the morning, as Kate soon had reason to know. She and her husband had gone to bed one night as usual, expecting to sleep till dawn, when Kate awoke to find Charles, with all the candles lit, pacing up and down the room in indescribable terror. He continued pacing up and down till he had mastered his emotion and then went back to bed. It was 1 A.M. A night or two later, at the same hour, Mr. De la Rue came knocking on their bedroom door in great distress and insisted that Charles should rise at once and come and treat his poor wife, who had had an extra bad seizure. Dickens went with him and, in his own words, found Mrs. De la Rue 'rolled up into an apparently impossible ball. . . . I only knew where her head was by following her long hair to its source.' [1] Though he had no experience of phenomena of the kind, Dickens boldly treated her by means of strokings and passes and in fifteen minutes had the satisfaction of seeing her relax, unwind herself, and resume her normal posture.

Charles on the whole regretted having been persuaded to attend the long ceremonies of Holy Week and counselled travellers to visit Rome at any other moment of the year than this. He saw the Pope being 'carried about like a Guy Fawkes', the Washing of the Feet, and the slow Good Friday 'knee-shuffle' up the Scala Santa, 'ridiculous and unpleasant in its unmeaning degradation'. For him that was the keynote of it all, the meaninglessness of the Church, and its infamous taste in draping architectural features in 'impertinent frippery'. The Bambino of the Ara Coeli came in for scathing abuse and so did the frescoes representing the tortures of martyrs. Less irritating experiences are recorded of excursions to Albano, the Ville d'Este, the ruins of Tusculum, as well

[1] 752. III. N.L.

as strolls through the Vatican Galleries and the Barberini
Palace, walks in the Catacombs, and to conclude with an
indulgence in the 'vice anglais,' a public execution.   Dickens
and De la Rue set out in good time for the scene of punishment.   Anxious to miss nothing of the spectacle, they got
places in a kind of wash-house looking straight on to the
seven-foot scaffold on the top of which stood the guillotine.
After noting every detail of the religious procession with its
black-draped crucifix, Dickens watched the victim closely.

> The young man kneeled down below the knife.   His
> neck fitting into a hole made for the purpose, in a cross-
> plank, was shut down by another plank above; exactly like
> the pillory.   Immediately below him was a leathern bag.
> And into it his head rolled instantly.
>   The executioner was holding it by the hair, and walking
> with it round the scaffold, showing it to the people, before
> one quite knew that the knife had fallen heavily, and with a
> rattling sound.
>   There was a great deal of blood.   When we left the
> window, and went close up to the scaffold, it was very
> dirty. . . . A strange appearance was the apparent annihila-
> tion of the neck . . . the body looked as if there was nothing
> left above the shoulder.

After writing this strictly objective account of what his eyes
had seen, Dickens commented sadly that no one seemed to
care, there was no manifestation of disgust, pity, indignation
or sorrow; it was nothing but an ugly careless, filthy, sicken-
ing spectacle.

In Rome Dickens saw something of Father Prout (Francis
Mahony) an old friend whom he provisionally engaged as
correspondent for the *Daily News* to take effect in the new
year.   Father Prout says that they ratified this 'solemn
compact at the Milvian bridge, a spot that had witnessed many
occurrences more important to mankind', with a handful of
cigars.   He pressed them on Dickens with the assurance they
had been 'blessed by the Pope', though they really had just
been bought at Torlonia's shop in the Corso.   'I trust', he

wrote later on, 'that you found their efficacy in traversing the pestilent Campagna.'

On all excursions and on some of their more casual sight-seeing the De la Rues now went everywhere with the Dickenses, and when they came to leave Rome travelled with them in the same carriage. Charles gave his patient treatment 'sometimes under olive trees, sometimes in vineyards, sometimes in the travelling carriage, sometimes at wayside inns during the mid-day halt'. By degrees the delusions faded and by the time the party got back to Genoa Mrs. De la Rue was in a better state of health than she had been in for years.

Florence was one of the cities visited by this strangely assorted party. There they found Lord and Lady Holland at their beautiful villa, Careggi de' Medici, at the moment being frescoed by a shy young Englishman, George Watts, who took refuge in a pavilion when visitors appeared. Lord Holland invited the English colony to meet the great 'Boz', and in this way Dickens saw jovial Mrs. Trollope and her son Augustus. In fulfilment of a promise to Landor, Dickens went to Fiesole and inquired for Landor's villa. From the convent wall on the height a peasant girl pointed out 'La Villa Landora', and Dickens, visiting it, plucked an ivy leaf from the wall and posted it to England. Before leaving he had asked Landor what he should bring him from Italy. 'An ivy leaf from Fiesole,' was the reply. He also made acquaintance with Mrs. Landor with whom he had a pleasant conversation.

In April Charles Dickens and his ladies returned to Genoa to spend their last two months abroad. Mrs. Dickens was not on speaking terms with the De la Rues, and Dickens, in order to explain away a very embarrassing situation, told them that she was subject to nervous breakdowns, a fiction that he employed later on to cover other awkward dilemmas.

Notes on the sights he had seen had now to be sorted and written up, but somehow Dickens found his imagination had stopped working, maybe because he had tried to observe too many unfamiliar things. His genius, which in any case nourished itself on past experience and was retrospective in nature, was as it were anaesthetised by his overdose of present experience. The kaleidoscope of the changing Italian scene had been too much for him and he was to discover from experience that environment of the right kind was quite as essential to his genius as freedom from financial worries. It became obvious that he could not afford too much novelty, or too great and prolonged an effort to assimilate foreign matter.

Combining his letters to Forster with his own notes, he soon had *Pictures from Italy* in shape. Arrangements for publishing in book-form were postponed for the time being as his wish was to bring the *Pictures* out serially if he could manage it. Eventually Bradbury and Evans produced them in a neat blue-cloth volume with illustrations by Samuel Palmer. The last page was embellished with a design showing the gathering-in of the grape harvest and the last paragraph, which might have been written by a Victorian bishop, ran as follows:

> Let us not remember Italy the less regardfully, because, in every fragment of her fallen Temples, and every stone of her deserted palaces and prisons she helps to inculcate the lesson that the wheel of time is rolling for an end and that the world in all great essentials gets better, gentler, more forbearing and more hopeful as it rolls.

The author was quite satisfied with the terms given by Bradbury and Evans: they were certainly treating him better than Chapman and Hall had done, especially in the matter of this small, occasional book *Pictures from Italy*. He was no longer worrying about money and wrote orders to Mitton for the doing-up of Devonshire Terrace against his return. These orders give one an idea of the manner in which living in palatial surroundings had affected his taste. He had been taken with the Italian habit of imitating the graining of wood in paint and of ornamenting ceilings. The skirting board of the drawing-room was to be painted to look like satinwood, the ceiling was to blush pink, wreaths of flowers were to be limned round the gas chandeliers and a flock paper of blue and gold or purple and gold was to be hung on the walls. The estimate he received for the redecoration was such 'a staggerer' that, instead of carrying out his original intention of getting the room done as a surprise for Kate, he told her of his plans and she at once modified them into mere cleaning of walls and a repainting of windows and doors.

By June the party at the Peschiere was packing up. To escape the 'miseries of moving' Dickens went to stay with the De la Rues at the Palazzo Rosso, leaving Kate to wrestle with the situation. Soon the whole family set out for Brussels, where Jerrold, Maclise and Forster were due to meet them. Maclise, who had come from Paris, was full of the new French paintings which had enraptured him, and Dickens was full of his travels which enabled him to talk with familiarity of the Farnese Hercules, the Laocoön and the glorious frescoes in Venice. It was a very happy reunion and the week they spent together was devoted to intensive sightseeing. After a year's absence from London Dickens went back to Devonshire Terrace a far more restless man than he started out. He was conscious of an inner drabness caused by unidentified discontent and felt the need of dramatising his life somehow or another. The eleven months that were to elapse before his second flight abroad were months of experiment, but not of novel-writing.

Chapter 15

DAILY NEWS AND ROSEMONT

*Which of us is happy in this world?   Which of us has his
desire? or having it is satisfied?*   W. M. THACKERAY

EVER since *The Chimes* audition, Charles Dickens had been
promising himself the fun of appearing on a London stage,
and so almost as soon as he returned from Italy he mobilised
his friends and arranged that they should, between them, act
Ben Jonson's comedy *Every Man in His Humour*.   Forster,
Cruikshank, Jerrold, Lemon, Leech, Cattermole, Maclise,
Frank Stone, T. J. Thompson and his brothers Frederick
and Augustus Dickens were all roped in, but Maclise fell away
before rehearsals began.   Though more than a little scornful
of amateurs Macready was persuaded to coach them, at the
same time noting in his diary that the whole troupe 'seemed to
be under a perfect delusion as to their degrees of skill and
power in an art of which they do not know what may be
called the very rudiments'.   The actor-manager was rather
exasperated one day on going to a theatrical costumier's to
find Dickens ruffling it in doublet and hose in front of a
mirror.   He confided to his journal: 'It is ludicrous the fuss
the actors make about this play'.   Some of the rehearsals took
place at 90 Fleet Street, where Dickens, Jerrold and Wills
were secretly working at plans for founding the *Daily News*.
Fuss or no fuss, in his capacity of stage-manager, property-
man, prompter and actor, Dickens managed to keep his team
hard at work and happy, with the result that he could present
a well-rehearsed, workmanlike performance on the night.

A man from the *Daily News* office went to the Royalty
(better known as Miss Kelly's theatre) on September 20 to
help Dickens, Lemon and Jerrold with the final arrangements.
Dickens and Lemon took off their coats and set to work to
number the seats in the boxes and dress circle.   'Boz' wore

his puce-coloured velvet waistcoat and into the pockets put
tacks and bradawl, while in his hands he carried a hammer.
Jerrold kept on his coat as he was preparing a fire on the stage
with slacked lime and red tinsel. 'Lemon, will this do?' he
shouted, and Lemon shouted back, 'The smoke's all right,
but a little more tinsel would improve the fire!'

Admission to the performance was by printed card of
invitation and each member of the cast had thirty to thirty-
five tickets. Even Macready was obliged to admit that the
despised amateurs scored a considerable success. 'Captain
Bobadil' played by 'Boz' was outstandingly good, or so the
critics said. Leslie, the American painter, admired him so
much in this part that he asked him to sit for him as Bobadil.
On November 15 the same company, with Maclise (half
fainting from stage fright), repeated its performance for
charity in Prince Albert's presence. This time they acted in
the St. James's Theatre as the Royalty would not hold all the
peers and peeresses who applied for boxes and who found
awaiting them play-bills printed on white satin. It delighted
Dickens that the Duke of Devonshire should travel two
hundred miles from one direction and Alfred Tennyson the
same distance from another direction in order to be present.
Charles Greville reported that the audience was 'cold as ice',
and Lord Melbourne was heard by everyone in the interval
saying, 'I knew this play would be dull, but that it should be
so damnedly dull as this I did not suppose.' Thackeray, it
appears, had offered to help by singing between the acts, and
had received a rebuff which hurt him very much.[1] The
proceeds of the performance were given to Dr. Southwood
Smith's nursing home, The Sanatorium, in Devonshire
Terrace.

For Dickens, play-acting was as near heaven and complete
self-realisation as anything he ever did. We shall see the urge
to act (growing stronger in the next two years) suppressed for
novel construction, and in the end dominating him by making
him act his own stories to vast appreciative audiences. Life

[1] G. Waterfield, *Lucie Duff Gordon*, p. 101.

has a way of going in cycles and we return on ourselves and
our early loves sometimes to find them more attractive than
ever and sometimes to find them utterly distasteful.

In October 1845 another baby was born, a sixth child, and
a fourth son. This event filled Dickens, as every addition to
his family now did, with apprehension about the future.
How could he make more money? How could he hope to
support so large a household? To have a whole family
dependent on the slender thread spun by a master spider was
madness, the mere thought of his responsibilities made him
restless. Would the floating of another weekly periodical
perhaps ease the worries that beset him? Would a three-
halfpenny magazine with some such name as 'The Cricket'
meet the case? Forster threw cold water on the suggestion
and urged him to concentrate on a story: it was a far quicker
way of making money. Why could he not write a tale called
'The Cricket' for the Christmas market? Dickens fell in
with this suggestion at once and sat down to write *The
Cricket on the Hearth: A Fairy Tale of Home*, inscribing it to
Lord Jeffrey 'with the affection and attachment of his friend
the author'. It was garnished with woodcuts from drawings
by Maclise, Doyle, Leech, Stanfield and Landseer, but this did
not save it from being savagely attacked in the *Times*.
Forster warned his friend that this must do him great harm,
but found Dickens so angry and so fixed on his own opinions
and in his admiration for his own work, as to be impossible
to talk to on the subject. Rather exasperated by his attitude,
Forster jotted down the reflection that 'this partial passion
would grow on him till it became an incurable evil'. Dickens,
however, knew his public: they liked the little book as much
as he did, and read it rapturously. Caleb Plummer, who
made the life of his blind daughter beautiful by wielding 'the
only magic art that still remains to us, the magic of devoted,
deathless love', won the hearts of readers, as did Mrs. Peery-
bingle, and her nurse-maid, Tilly Slowboy. The sales of
The Cricket doubled those of his two other Christmas tales.
Dramatised for the Keeleys at the Lyceum for Christmas 1845,

a fortnight later versions of it were being played at twelve London theatres.

During the autumn weeks when Kate was laid up, Georgy inevitably played a more active part in Charles's life: they took long country walks together and he discussed with her his journalistic plans and worries. They talked much of Dan Maclise for whom both Kate and her sister had a great weakness, and they talked of themselves. What is one to make of the cryptic sentence (referring to Georgy) in a letter to Mrs. De la Rue, 'I have left that matter where it was; trusting to its wearing itself out, on her part, in due course'. Who was in love with whom? All that autumn Dickens was immersed in the hitherto hushed-up activities connected with the founding of a new daily newspaper. Though Forster knew all the ins and outs and was at his elbow throughout, he states that it does not come within the plan of his biography to record the episode in detail and that in principle he disapproved of it. For six months Dickens now devoted his best energies to seeking information on how to conduct a paper; how the foreign departments of papers like the *Herald* and *Morning Chronicle* were run; how the mail service from the Far East worked; how information from correspondents in Ceylon, Aden and Malta was transmitted. He was plodding away industriously at plans in September 1845 when he called rehearsals of *Every Man in His Humour* at 90 Fleet Street (in a second-floor room overlooking St. Bride's spire), but exactly how he came to shoulder this work at all has never been clearly explained.

The actual inception of the paper may be said to have lain in the conversation between Dickens, Paxton, and Bradbury and Evans (and probably Forster) in the spring of 1844, referred to in the last chapter. When on his return from Italy Dickens reopened the subject he learnt from his publishers that the firm was agreeable to putting up capital and that Joseph Paxton (who had made money during the railway boom) was willing to stand in with them. Dickens then mentioned two personal friends of his own living in the north of England, Sir William Jackson and Sir Joseph Walmsley, who might both be counted on for financial backing. Sir Joseph, who had hailed Dickens publicly as 'the best friend to progress and reform yet seen in English fiction', was the parliamentary champion of Liberalism in the north, and was regarded by Cobden as the foremost organiser of the party, a man who had managed to bring together middle-class and Chartists without setting them by the ears. This object, we should note, was from the first the policy of the *Daily News*.

For some months after his return from abroad Dickens was absorbed and excited by the scheme, which involved him in many interviews and business meetings, and gave him a feeling of great importance. He rushed down to Derbyshire at a minute's notice (a day or two after the birth of his fourth son) on 'matters of great moment connected with *my* scheme', and discussed with Paxton 'the stunning venture'. Writing to Tom Mitton, he said:

> Paxton has command of every railway influence in England and abroad except the Great Western and he is in it heart and purse. One other large shareholder is to come in; and that is to be a house which has the power of bringing a whole volley of advertisements upon the paper always. The commercial influence that will come down on it with the whole might of its aid and energy; not only in the City of London, but in Liverpool, Manchester, Bristol and Yorkshire, is quite stunning. I am trying to engage the best people right and left.[1]

Fixing his own salary as editor at £2000 instead of the £1000 allotted for the purpose by Bradbury and Evans, Dickens at once took a high-handed line in dealing with his colleagues, announcing that he could not be depended on to be in the office himself: 'When I am not there I shall have a sub-editor to whom I can hand over the management with perfect confidence. . . . On these terms I am willing to become the head and leading principle of the thing',[2] and on these terms,

[1] Unpublished letter (W. Dexter).
[2] 714. I. N.L.

owing to his great drawing power, they accepted him, but how soon they must have regretted it! Some of his letters at this time show lack of nerve, almost panic, when certain City failures take place that he thinks may affect the stability of the backers of the paper, and this nervousness he imparted to his staff, some of whom tried to get back to their original jobs. A week or two later he was in good heart again and boasting of having received a proposal for a second sub-editor 'which will drive Sir John Easthope raving mad'. There was a growing fear in the minds of Bradbury and Evans that he was a very difficult, if not an impossible, man to work with or control.

If we glance at the political situation in England in the summer of 1845, we shall see why it must have appeared to Radicals the moment of all others to float a new paper in which their gospel could be preached. To both Protectionists and Free Traders a great shock had been imparted by the famine in Ireland, and Whigs and Tories alike felt impelled to try and cope with the crisis. Important political leaders were reported to be modifying their views on the Corn Laws, and it was widely rumoured that Sir Robert Peel himself was converted to the idea of Free Trade. When Lord John Russell's letter to his constituents in London, announcing that the time had come 'to put an end to the whole system of Protection', appeared in the *Times*, Peel realised that on this issue the Whigs were prepared to make common cause with the anti-Corn Law League. His Foreign Secretary, Lord Aberdeen, told Delane confidentially that Peel, if he could not secure agreement in the cabinet, would resign. Next day the *Times* carried a statement to the effect that the cabinet would summon Parliament to meet in January to propose the total repeal of the Corn Laws. This broke the Government as no cabinet agreement on the subject had been arrived at. Two days later Peel resigned and Lord John was sent for by the Queen, but as he could not form an alternative Government Peel was sent for again and reconstituted his cabinet, bringing in, as one of the new team, Mr. Gladstone, Secretary for the

Colonies, who had no seat in the House. Parliament was summoned to reassemble on January 22 and on the preceding day the *Daily News* made its well-timed first appearance.

Dickens had collected his staff regardless of expense. 'Critics, leader-writers and reporters were offered terms so favourable that seceders from existing newspapers were numerous. . . . Editors and publishers were angry and disturbed as some of their best writers were being drawn away.' [1] Eyre Crowe, Paris correspondent of the *Morning Chronicle*, and Thomas Hodgkinson of *The Economist* are examples of this. Among the leader-writers was W. J. Fox, M.P., golden-tongued apostle of untaxed bread. Forster was a permanent leader-writer, and with him were working W. H. Wills, F. Knight, Leigh Hunt, Charles Mackay and Father Prout, soon to become 'our Rome correspondent'. Provincial intelligence, military and naval news, the City, sport and commerce were all in charge of the best men Dickens could get hold of. Douglas Jerrold, Albany Fonblanque, Mark Lemon all supported him personally to the utmost of their ability. Perhaps he was unwise to put his father in charge of the reporting staff with Laman Blanchard, William Hazlitt, Jerrold, J. A. Crowe and a dozen others under him, for though energetic and good-tempered he was by this time very bulky and rather old for all-night work. His father-in-law, George Hogarth, was made musical and dramatic critic: his uncle, John Henry Barrow, whom he failed to get sent out to India, became a sub-editor: and Lady Blessington was engaged for six months at £500 to supply 'exclusive intelligence of a social kind'. The price of the *Daily News* was 5d., as against the 7d. charged by the *Times* and most other dailies.

On January 17 the printing machines were 'christened' in the presence of a party of ladies and gentlemen, and the machine against which the wine bottle was dashed was named 'Perseverance'. A dummy paper was then printed with the date January 19. Dickens by this time was installed in an editor's room on the third floor, 'up aloft in Whitefriars'.

[1] Violet Markham, *Paxton and the Bachelor Duke*, p. 169.

He had in the early autumn insisted that this room should be 'properly furnished' as he intended to occupy it 'every day'. The office furniture was installed together with shelves of Hansard, 'Annual Registers', 'Mirrors of Parliament', 'State Trials', Shakespeare's works, the Bible, 'a complete set of the classics' and a fair supply of dictionaries and works of reference.

On the eve of the appearance of the *Daily News* its prospects had been discussed at dinner by Eyre Crowe, Henry Reeve, C. W. Dilke, Forster and Dickens. Dilke and Reeve walked away together. 'I foresee,' said Reeves to his companion, 'your knowledge will some day be invoked to remedy the mischief done by Dickens's genius to this new paper,' a prophecy that was realised in fact three months later. On the day of its appearance W. H. Russell, opening the first copy, was delighted to see it 'ill-printed and badly made up'. The *Times* had nothing to fear from this upstart radical organ.

In the opening number of the paper the editor wrote:

> The principles advocated by the *Daily News* will be principles of progress and improvement, of education, civil and religious liberty and equal legislation—principles such as its conductors believe the advancing spirit of the times requires, the condition of the country demands, and justice, reason, and experience legitimately sanction.

The leading article was by W. J. Fox (who had agreed to write four leaders a week) and the number contained a report of Mr. Cobden's meeting at Norwich of the evening before, a long review of railway affairs, two gossip columns, a critical article on music by George Hogarth, 'Voices from the Crowd' by Charles Mackay and the first of Dickens's 'Travel Letters'. After the paper had been dispatched, the staff, much elated at getting it out ahead of the *Times*, assembled to drink success to the enterprise. Next day, when the Queen made her speech in person, enormous efforts were made by John Dickens to keep his men moving briskly in and out of the Gallery. It was an exciting sitting to all newspaper men, for Peel made it quite clear that he was a convert to Cobden's views, and this gave Disraeli his great opportunity of denouncing him as one who had betrayed his party and his principles.

What happened to Dickens now cannot be explained by any ordinary standards of behaviour. Two days after Peel had made his great speech the editor began to flag in energy. A week later he wrote to Forster, 'I have been revolving plans in my mind this morning for quitting the paper and going abroad again to write a new book in shilling numbers'. Suddenly he lost all interest in the paper and ten days later, without apparent compunction, resigned. For weeks past he had been looking on the *Daily News* as a thing of his own creation to be dealt with exactly as he saw fit. Whether his collapse was due to adverse criticism or whether he had all along meant just to launch the paper and then hand it over to Forster, no one can now say. It would seem that, as in Boston, he had one of those curious nervous and temperamental breakdowns which overtook him whenever things became vexatious or disappointing. The hostility evoked by his copyright speech in Boston had drained him of vitality, and difficulties connected with his wholesale bribing away of men from other journals must have arisen in the *Daily News* office. He hated to realise that he was making enemies. If it is hard to believe that Dickens ever seriously intended to remain editor, it is equally hard to imagine what could have induced him to undertake a job that he had no intention of carrying to its conclusion. He complained of being 'worn out', but no one knew better than he the penalties of office work, and to those collaborating with him during the autumn and winter of 1845 he appeared to enjoy good health and to be putting his whole heart into the venture. It is clear from the Nonesuch *Letters* that there was serious friction between him and Mr. Bradbury, the controller of general expenditure, salaries and staff qualifications. Dickens complained to Mr. Evans of his partner's 'interposition between me and almost every act of mine at the newspaper office', which is 'as disrespectful to me as it is injurious to the enterprise'. He complained, too, that his father had been treated with rudeness and ended by saying that Bradbury was far worse than Easthope to deal with, which was saying a great deal. The net result of all this friction was that Forster found himself in Dickens's shoes and Dickens found himself a free man, except that he was under an engagement to write two articles on capital punishment and some 'Travel Letters' for the newspaper he had abandoned.

Dickens had always taken extreme interest in capital punishment, but though he had considerable experience of executions he had hitherto made no use of his observations except in *Oliver Twist* when he described the scene of Fagin's hanging as follows:

> Day was dawning. . . . A great multitude had already assembled; the windows were filled with people, smoking and playing cards to beguile the time; the crowd were pushing, quarrelling and joking. Everything told of life and animation, but one dark cluster of objects in the very centre of all—the black stage, the cross-beam, the rope, and all the hideous apparatus of death.

For the *Daily News* he now defined his attitude to the death penalty, declaring that nothing human ingenuity could devise worked such ruin as a public execution. Out of 167 persons who, being sentenced to death, had been questioned by a clergyman, only three had not been present at a hanging. Further, Dickens said that some natures feel themselves heroes at a public execution: it almost seems to console them for dying, therefore the glamour and distinction of a public death should be denied them. The crowd attracted on these occasions is always criminal. When standing close to a scaffold in Rome, Dickens was wearing a shooting-jacket and he could feel its many pockets being systematically gone over by thieves, but as the pockets were empty he pretended to notice nothing. An execution must be condemned as an utterly useless, barbarous, brutalising sight, and the sympathy of all beholders, who have any sympathy at all, is certain to be always with the criminal and never with the law. From studying comparative statistics, he is able to state that wherever capital punishments are diminished in number, there crimes diminish in number too. In bringing his three letters to a close, Dickens expressed his general conclusions quite plainly:

> I beg to be understood to advocate the total abolition of the Punishment of Death as a general principle, for the advantage of society, for the prevention of crime. . . . I am the more desirous of being so understood, after reading a speech made by Mr. Macaulay in the House of Commons in which that accomplished gentleman hardly seemed to recognise the possibility of anyone entertaining an honest conviction of the inutility and bad effects of Capital Punishment in the abstract . . . without being the victim of 'a kind of effeminate feeling'. Without staying to enquire what there may be that is specially manly and heroic in the advocacy of the gallows or to express my admiration of Mr. Calcraft, the hangman, as doubtless one of the most manly specimens now in existence, I would simply hint a doubt whether this be the true Macaulay way of meeting a great question.

Victor Hugo, writing at this time in Paris, condemned all executions, public or private. Dickens returned to the charge three years later after attending the hanging of Mr. and Mrs. Manning at Horsemonger Gaol,[1] a spectacle witnessed from a neighbouring house. 'We have taken', he wrote to Leech, 'the whole of the roof (and the back kitchen) for the extremely moderate sum of ten guineas or two guineas each.' Dickens arranged that his party should sup at the Piazza Coffee House, Covent Garden, at 11 P.M. He then wandered about for some hours in the streets among the poor folk to gather impressions. At the site of the gallows there was a dense sea of heads and above them the roof-tops black with people. Men and women were fainting around him. That evening he wrote his famous letter to the *Times* saying

[1] November 13, 1849.

that the wickedness and levity of the immense crowd could be imagined by no man and could be presented in no heathen land under the sun.

Some people like to think that it was owing to Dickens's protests that executions in public were prohibited, and this may be partially true as we are notoriously slow about reforms, but it was not for twenty years (1868) that a law was passed ordaining that the death penalty be carried out behind prison walls.

The Dickenses' fourth son was nearly six months old when they decided to have him christened at St. Marylebone and give a party afterwards. For some reason or other, possibly because of the choice of godfathers, the tongues and pens of the literary folk of the day got busy on the event. To Father Prout it was a rhyming occasion:

> What eye but glistens
> And what ear but listens
> When the clergy christens
> A babe of 'Boz'.

Edward FitzGerald wrote to his friend Edward Barton[1] that Tennyson had been standing godfather to one of Dickens's children, Count d'Orsay being the other godfather, and that the poor child had been named 'Alfred d'Orsay Tennyson', which to his mind proved clearly enough that 'Dickens was a snob'. 'For what', he went on to say, 'is Snobbishness and Cockneyism, but all such pretensions and parade? It is one thing to worship heroes and another to lick their spittle.' And kindly Robert Browning, writing to Elizabeth, who was so soon to marry him in the very church in which Master Dickens was baptized, wonders if she knows why it is that Alfred Tennyson has been dining with Dickens to meet celebrities.

What do you suppose caused all the dining and repining? He has been sponsor to Dickens's child *in company with Count d'Orsay* and accordingly the *novus homo* glories in

---

[1] *New Letters of E. FitzGerald*, p. 122.

the praenomina Alfred d'Orsay Tennyson Dickens . . .
You observe: Alfred is common to both the godfather and
the devil-father. . . . When you remember what the form
of sponsorship is, to what it pledges you in the Church of
England—and then remember that Mr. Dickens is an
enlightened Unitarian,—you will get a curious notion of
the man, I fancy.

Monckton Milnes also joined in the ribaldry and made jokes
appropriate to the occasion.   'The baby', he said, 'is in good
truth not *the* Alfred of either personage, but of Mr. Alfred
Bunn', Alfred Bunn being the manager of Drury Lane and
the butt of the wits who nicknamed him 'Laureate Bunn'.
Contemporary opinion, especially if it is of a humorous
nature, is often stifled by the blare of praise that goes up on
the death of a great writer, and it is only in the by-paths of
private correspondence that we savour the actual verdict of
the hour. Until one has actually read with one's own eyes
Alfred d'Orsay Tennyson Dickens, the entry in the baptismal
register at St. Marylebone, one can hardly believe that any
parent could saddle a child with such names.

Alfred Tennyson had been much in the public eye this year
over a sparring match he had been engaged in with Bulwer
Lytton.   At Christmas 1845 Bulwer Lytton had published
The New Timon anonymously.   It was a novel in verse
dealing with life in London.   Certain lines in it have sur-
vived, as, for example, 'Stanley, the Rupert of Debate' and
'Languid Johnny, grown to Glorious John'.   'School-miss
Alfred', however, was treated with contumely.   Bulwer
Lytton wrote of his verse as

> Out-babying Wordsworth and out-glittering Keats
> Where all the airs of patchwork pastoral chime
> To drowsy ears in Tennysonian rhyme.

He also animadverted on the pension Tennyson had recently
been given (on the recommendation of Hallam) by the
Government[1] and spoke of him as 'belonging to a wealthy

[1] He had been given a Civil List allowance of £200 a year which enabled
him to travel abroad.

family'. Tennyson, of course, soon heard from Forster and
others who the author of this attack was, and at once riposted
with *The New Timon and the Poets*, which Forster insisted
must appear in *Punch*. After a reference to 'Old Timon and
his noble heart', Tennyson let fly at *The New Timon*:

> So died the Old; here comes the New!
> Regard him—a familiar face;
> I *thought* we knew him!—What, it's you—
> The padded man that wears the stays!
>
> Who killed the girls and thrilled the boys
> With dandy pathos when you wrote!
> O Lion, you that made a noise
> And shook a mane *en papillottes*!

Before deciding to transfer the household abroad Charles
Dickens made one more effort to secure a regular stipend by
applying to a leading member of the Government to be
appointed a police magistrate for London. He was decidedly
rueful when his application was turned down, for what
excellent copy such experience would have provided! Life
now took on for him the semblance of a waking nightmare in
which his heavy commitments, his inability to write, his bills,
his health all oppressed him by turns. Was the very ground
under his feet giving way beneath him? had he really no foothold on present or future in spite of all his work and all his
celebrity? Harassed by the possibility of 'failing health or
fading popularity', he would from time to time tell Forster
that he felt giddy and could scarcely see. It soon became
obvious that there was only one sensible course to pursue, and
that was to let his London house and once more take the
family abroad. He tried to get Kate to agree to his renting
the Peschiere again, but she refused, as the following characteristic letter written to his 'dearest' Mrs. De la Rue shows:

> I need not tell *you* that *I* want to go to Genoa? But
> Mrs. Dickens, who was never very well there, cannot be
> got to contemplate the Peschiere though I have beset her
> in all kinds of ways. Therefore I think I should take a
> middle course for the present, and coming as near you as I

THE HOSTESS OF DEVONSHIRE TERRACE
by Daniel Maclise, R.A.

A MUSICAL EVENING AT ROSEMONT
"The Duet," by Frank Stone, A.R.A.

could, pitch my tent somewhere on the Lake of Geneva, say at Lausanne, whence I could run over to Genoa immediately.

My Diary of March the 19th 1845 is lying open on my desk, and looking at it I see this entry—*Madame D. L. R. very ill in the night. Up till four* . . . what a miserable Devil I seem to be cooped up here, bothered by printers and stock-jobbers, when there are bright Genoas (with bright patients in them) and ruined coliseums in the world!

I talk to all the nice Italian boys who go about the streets with organs and white mice and give them mints of money *per l'amore della Bell' Italia.*[1]

Once the decision had been made to settle at Lausanne, Charles was miraculously relieved of all untoward symptoms and, as soon as Sir James Duke applied to rent Devonshire Terrace for twelve months, his spirits rose enough to enable him to take the chair at the first banquet of the General Theatrical Fund Association and thoroughly to enjoy himself.

This Association had been founded seven years earlier for granting permanent pensions to poor, retired or invalid actresses and actors, singers and dancers. Dickens, in his speech, explained that the promoters of the fund had worked hard and without advertisement, and that in his opinion the Association should now be placed on a sound financial footing. Covent Garden and Drury Lane each had their pension funds, both richly endowed and of long standing. To qualify for help under these funds it was necessary, in the case of Drury Lane, to have played there for three consecutive seasons. As for Covent Garden, it was but a vision of the past. 'The human voice is rarely heard within its walls save in connexion with corn or the ambidextrous prestidigitation of the Wizard of the North.' In like manner Drury Lane was being conducted with a sole view to the opera and ballet, 'in so much that the statue of Shakespeare over the doors served as emphatically to point out his grave as his bust did in the

[1] 744. I. N.L.

church of Stratford-upon-Avon'. It was really impossible
for the profession generally to hope to qualify for the Drury
Lane and Covent Garden benefits, for its oldest and most
distinguished members had been driven from the boards, on
which they had earned their reputation, to theatres to which
the General Fund alone extended. Those to whom he spoke
must not let them pass from the footlights into gloom and
darkness. Speaking for himself, he could truthfully say that
he had never been in any theatre 'without carrying away some
pleasant association, some favourable impression'.

A week or two before leaving England Dickens had a long
talk with Miss Coutts on the desirability of establishing a
rescue home for girls. He thought that if such a home were
run in conjunction with an emigration scheme financed by
Government, the girls, after re-education, would make excellent wives for colonists. Clarifying his recommendations
by putting them down on paper, he said that the training
must aim at making the girls useful and happy and be mainly
domestic in character. It would be advisable to link up with
the governors of prisons as no machinery was in existence to
help females serving short sentences. Almost invariably they
were forced back into bad ways. For his own part he would
very much like to be entrusted with some share in the supervision and direction of the institution proposed. To this end
he will make it his business to examine every scheme of the
kind operating in Paris where he feels much valuable knowledge may be acquired. He will tabulate the information he
collects so that Miss Coutts may grasp it at once. A year
later when Dickens was once more settled in London we shall
find him helping Miss Coutts to organise and administer a
rescue home known as Urania Cottage, Shepherd's Bush.
Made doubly impatient to escape from London and the claims
of friends by the sense that a new story was rapidly forming
itself in his mind, he left England with Switzerland as his goal.

With the circumspection to be expected from the father of
a large family, Charles Dickens piloted his party to Ostend,

and then shepherded them to a river steamer on the Rhine. There was something patriarchal about the movement of two ladies, six children, four servants and a dog, and the patriarch in question was just thirty-four and still looked very young. At Mainz a German came aboard and addressing Mrs. Dickens in good English said: 'Your countryman Mr. Dickens is travelling this way just now our papers say. Do you know him or have you passed him anywhere?' Explanations followed and the stranger, Josef Valckenburg, soon found himself talking to the great 'Boz' whose books had made such a furore in Germany, books which, as he pointed out, were at that moment being read by many people on the steamer. Charmed by the stranger's civility, Dickens apologised for not being able to understand or speak German. He was politely told by Mr. Valckenburg that he need not regret it, for 'even in a small town like ours where we are mostly primitive people and have few travellers I could make a party of at least forty people who understand and speak English as well as I do'. Mr. Valckenburg, a wine merchant, came from Worms, a city Dickens was to visit and to describe as 'a fine old place, greatly shrunken and decayed in spite of its population, with a picturesque old cathedral standing on the bank of the Rhine and some brave old churches shut up and so hemmed in and overgrown with vineyards that they look as if they were turning into leaves and grapes'.

It was no news to Dickens that his books were widely known in Germany and in steady demand, for the first instalment of *Pickwick*[1] issued in five small volumes had had a great sale, and before the last volume appeared a German version of the *Sketches* was printing as *Londoner Skizzen*.[2] In the same year *Nicholas Nickleby* was published[3] and *Oliver Twist* advertised. Even the *Memoirs of Grimaldi* had been trans-

---

[1] 1837–8. [2] 1838.

[3] 1838–9. *Leben u. Abenteuer des Nicolaus Nickleby*, von Boz mit Feder-bezeichnungen nach Phiz, 1838–9 (Braunschweig, Georg Westermann), green covers on English model, slightly reduced in size. In the last of the twenty numbers appears an advertisement of *Oliver Twist, oder die Laufbahn eines Waisen Knaben.*

lated twice in 1839.   R. H. Horne[1] did not think the German
translations as accurate as they might have been and specially
commended the Italian translations *Oliviere Twist* of Gian-
battista Basaggio published in Milan, and the *Nicolas Nickleby*
of E. de la Bedollière.   By 1843 some of Dickens's books had
appeared in Dutch and Russian.

The chief ground for the popularity of *Pickwick* in Germany was what the Germans call its *Behaglichkeit* for which
we have no word, a radiating kindliness arising out of solid
comfort and the enjoyment of things in common.   Georg
Freytag in *Ein Dank für Charles Dickens* said that *Pickwick*
was like a ray of sunshine in Germany at a time when conditions of life were dreary in the extreme and characterised by
complete absence of warmth and good nature in literature as
well as in private and public life.   'The joyful conception of
life,' he writes, 'the unending cosiness, the brave good sense
that shines through the comic treatment was as moving to
Germans of that day as a melody from home that strikes unexpectedly on a wanderer's ear.'   No similar, happy, national
life was observable anywhere among his compatriots; in fact
Germany, like Italy, was in his time little more than a geographical expression.

German readers sensed in Dickens's pages the outcropping
of a tender vein of sympathy, and the glowing of a heart that
brought him much closer to the ordinary man and woman
than the elegance and learning displayed by their own classical
and romantic writers.   High-born ladies and gentlemen were
at a discount in the newly crystallising strata of society that
were in process of becoming self-conscious.   The mere fact
that Dickens's books are formless, unconventional and styleless must have recommended them to the reader of few books,
who only understood life as an ordinary day-to-day business
in which kindness counts as the chief good.   There is
another point which may account for the immediate welcome
accorded to the works of 'Boz', and that is that there is something distinctively German about his excursions into the

[1] *Spirit of the Age*, p. 76.

world of phantasy.   He had certainly read Hoffman's *Tales*, *The Golden Pot* in particular, for we may notice that the knocker in *A Christmas Carol* which changes into Marly's dead-alive face, and yet remains a knocker, has its counterpart in this tale.   His friend Carlyle had translated some of the *Tales* and was for ever talking, to anyone who would listen, of Germany and German books.   George Eliot, George Lewes and William Thackeray all learnt German well, but as a language it was not much better known among the generality of Englishmen than it had been at the turn of the century when Sir Walter Scott, Matt Lewis, Taylor of Norwich, Wordsworth and Coleridge were among the few studying the language.

For nearly ten years Dickens had been in correspondence with Germans about the translations of his books and during that time had become very well known in German literary circles by name and reputation.   Dr. Flügel had presented him with a copy of his German-English dictionary, and Dr. Künzel in 1838 had asked him for biographical particulars to be included in the Brockhaus *Conversations-Lexikon*.   In 1841 he had even invited his co-operation in an Anglo-German magazine to be called *Britannia*.   In wishing success to this magazine Dickens avowed that 'next to his own people he respects and treasures the Germans'.   He goes so far as to say that he honours and admires them more than he is able to express and that he realises that, because of their great mental gifts and their culture, Germans are the chosen people of the earth.   Never was he prouder than when he learned for the first time that his writings had been warmly taken up in Germany.   'God bless you and your work', he concluded. 'By heaven, I wish I could speak German even badly.   If I could I should be with you in six months.'[1]

Bernhard Tauchnitz had commenced his famous series of English books in 1841 with *Pelham*, which was followed by *Pickwick* the same year and by *American Notes* the next.   In

[1] Ellis N. Gummer, *German Romance and Specimens of its Chief Authors*: C. D. to K., September 13, 1841.

1843 this enlightened publisher visited authors in England and generously arranged to pay them a fee though no international copyright existed to oblige him to do so. In return Dickens offered to supply him with early corrected proofs of future works which would enable him to publish in Germany at the same time as the book came out in England. Ten works by 'Boz' were issued in a Tauchnitz edition between 1843 and 1846. Tauchnitz had no monopoly, for several Germans firms specialised in translations while others again went in for imitations such as Stolle's *Deutsche Pickwickier* and Hesslein's *Berliner Pickwickier*.

The novels of Dickens and the friendly, get-together spirit he engendered were even welcomed by the editor of the *Rheinische Zeitung*,[1] Karl Marx. The mere fact that 'Boz' never attempted to conceal or palliate the unpleasant truth that conditions in England were bad, quite as bad as Lord Ashley's reports testified and as Friederich Engels reported, lifted the novelist, in Marx's esteem, into the category of social reformers, despite the fact that the methods of betterment he indicated were extremely vague and hopelessly sentimental. Engels thought of Dickens as 'a member of a great spiritual family united in all lands in spite of the hindrance of language'.

Taking the train at Strasbourg, the Dickens family journeyed to Basle and thence by road to Lausanne. On the way they stopped for a few hours at Schloss Riedenburg near Bregenz, a four-square fortress commanding wonderful views. Here they were entertained by Charles Lever who was renting it from Baron von Pöllnitz and was busy writing *The Knight of Gwynne* and corresponding with Hayman. At Lausanne the Dickenses all lodged at the Hôtel Gibbon (which they were amused to hear pronounced 'Jibbone') till they found in 'Rosemont' a villa to suit them. It was 'a doll's house' with enough bedrooms for the whole party and a colonnade supporting a balcony, all to be rented at £10 a month. It had the advantage of seclusion without loneliness,

[1] 1841–2.

and the riot of roses in the garden was enough, Dickens said, 'to smother the whole establishment of the *Daily News*'. The bowers and pavilions in the grounds put him in mind of the Chalk Farm tea-gardens of his childhood, except that these were far more beautiful. The branchy places, bright flowers and singing birds, the walks, the views, the people delighted him and, best of all, 'there was not a monk or priest to be seen in the streets crammed with bookshops'; in fact there was but one Catholic church, all the others were used as 'packing warehouses'. There is no mention in his letters of any of his literary predecessors at Lausanne, Gibbon, Rousseau, Shelley or Byron, though one apprehends that, as at Albaro, Charles Dickens liked to consider himself the heir of those English writers who had the love of Europe in their blood.

Deciding to make a room with a view over Leman his study, he set his table at the balcony window to await the arrival of the fighting frogs and the writing equipment which were as 'indispensable to his work as blue ink and quill pens'. When the box containing his particular treasures was de-livered at the villa he took out a book and said to the watching family, 'Now whatever passage my thumb rests on, I shall take as having reference to my work.' The book was *Tristram Shandy* and opened at these words, 'What a work it is likely to turn out! Let us begin it!'

Next morning he took the plunge and wrote the first slip of *Dombey and Son*, 'the study in pride' he had discussed with Forster in London. It was two years since he had finished *Martin Chuzzlewit*; he was out of practice and to begin with the new book progressed but slowly. In a letter to Forster he said:

> You can hardly imagine what infinite pains I take or what extraordinary difficulty I find in getting on FAST . . . the difficulty of going at what I call a rapid pace is pro-digious. I suppose this is partly the effect of two years' ease and partly of the absence of streets and numbers of figures. I can't express how much I want these. It

seems as if it supplied something to my brain, which it cannot bear, when busy, to lose. For a week or a fortnight I can write prodigiously in a retired place (as at Broadstairs) and a day in London sets me up again and starts me. But the toil and labour of writing, day after day, without that magic lantern is IMMENSE. . . . I wrote very little in Genoa (only *The Chimes*) and fancied myself conscious of some such influence there—but Lord, I had two miles of streets at least, lighted at night, to walk about in; and a great theatre to repair to every night![1]

Dickens, as Forster points out, never thought lightly of his work, but he was not self-important about it, though it was his paramount interest and essential life. Even now it is not generally recognised on what difficult terms, physical as well as mental, Dickens held the tenure of his imaginative life, or the high price he had to pay for his triumphs and successes. 'I hold my inventive faculty', he said, 'on the stern condition that it must master my whole life, often have complete possession of me, make its own demands upon me and sometimes for months together put everything else away from me.' In being delicately balanced, easily cast down and equally easily elated, Dickens was sharing the lot of most imaginative writers, and, however steadily he might be working, he was liable at any time to be overcome by 'an extraordinary nervousness almost impossible to describe'.

His system of work was always the same. Just before 10 A.M. he sat at his writing-table; sometimes he wrote much and sometimes nothing, but whether he wrote much or nothing he did not leave his table before 2 P.M. The quietude of Rosemont was in one way favourable to industry, but after a day at the desk it would become almost unbearable to the author, who would tear over to Geneva for a night or two to wander about the streets.

In Geneva he had the strange experience of meeting two American ladies at dinner, a mother and daughter, who habitually smoked cigars, cigarettes and hookahs. Dickens confessed himself 'ridiculously taken aback' when the daughter smoked six to eight cigars on end, for he had never seen any woman, not even a gipsy, smoke before, and it opened up vistas of what he 'might be in for when his own daughters were full grown'.

English people came and went at Lausanne. The Talfourds appeared and so did Mrs. Charles Brookfield; Harrison Ainsworth and his daughters turned up at an hotel, as did the T. J. Thompsons. The hub of English life was the house of Henry Hallam, a summer resident. 'Good Heavens, how Hallam did talk!' said Dickens after an evening spent in his company, 'I don't think I ever saw him so tremendous.' Then Lord Vernon, the Dante scholar, arrived and the Ladies Taylor, 'fair and charming daughters of Lord Headfort'. All English people, whether they were travelling to economise or travelling to educate their families, expected to be received at Rosemont. Among the English living in Lausanne were the former member of Parliament for Ipswich, William Haldimand, and his sister Mrs. Marcet, the educationalist, who was very lively and a dear friend of Sydney Smith and Sam Rogers. Apropos of Sydney Smith's jokes, Mrs. Marcet told Dickens that when she had stayed with him at his parsonage at Combe Florey she had complimented him on the excellence of his ham. 'Ah yes,' he said, 'ours are the only true hams, all the rest are shems and japhets.' And Dickens in return told her that the Canon had said he was 'the richest author that had ever browsed on the commons of literature'.

Haldimand was a great benefactor to the blind asylum at Lausanne and took Dickens there several times. At Haldimand's house Dickens also met M. de Cerjat, a Swiss citizen with an English wife, who became a lifelong friend and regular correspondent. Here, too, he first met the Watsons of Rockingham Castle, Northamptonshire, who were spending the summer in a villa by the Lake. With both the Watsons Dickens also formed a lasting friendship. As Richard Watson was a Liberal and had represented his county during the Reform debates, there were reminiscences to be gone over and public figures to be discussed. Both men wondered why Lord Grey (whom Dickens had always disliked) and unassuming, friendly Lord Lansdowne had proved equally incapable of attaching a single young man to their party, and then they passed on to discuss the demerits of Disraeli. With some of these companionable people the Dickenses made excursions to the Great St. Bernard, Chamonix, Chillon and other places later to be worked into the texture of *Little Dorrit*. We never hear of visits to the Villa Diodati in search of Milton or Byron, or of Madame de Staël's Coppet, Voltaire's Ferney or even Rousseau's Bosquet de Julie—all so accessible by land and water; but then Dickens's interests were never consistently literary though they were consistently human and nearly always contemporary.

When in London Dickens had tried to persuade Alfred Tennyson to share a house at Lausanne with him for the summer, but the poet had declined to do so, and had explained his refusal to his confidante, Elizabeth Barrett, by saying that he found Dickens's sentimentality highly irritating, and that if he had been foolish enough to accept, 'it was a sure thing they would quarrel and part and never see one another any more'. That summer, however, in company with his publisher Moxon, Tennyson set out for Switzerland, making a bee-line for Leman quite as much to see his uncle Henry Hallam as his friend Dickens, and thus found himself at Lausanne.

Sprightly Mrs. Brookfield has something mocking to say about this tour with Moxon. One day while they were walking together Alfred said, 'Moxon, you have made me very unhappy by something you said at Lucerne'. It was the unfortunate remark, 'Why, Tennyson, you will be as bald as Spedding before long!' Poor Alfred brooded over it and 'put himself under a Mrs. Parker, who rubs and pulls out dead hairs at 10/- an hour. Fancy the Queen's pension being spent like this! but really his hair is such an integral part of his appearance it would be a great pity if he should lose it.'[1]

---

[1] See *Mrs. Brookfield and her Circle.*

Wandering up the Rosemont road one golden evening, Tennyson was surprised to hear a girl's voice singing 'The Queen of the May' to a piano accompaniment. Open stood the French window of the villa from which the sound came, and he stood listening till the song ended. Charley Dickens well remembered that evening of fading twilight when his sister Mamie sat at the piano and tall Alfred Tennyson 'strolled in among them through the window that opened on to the lawn, as if the odd coincidence were quite a matter of course'.

In turning over the pages of *Early Victorian England*[1] I came on an illustration, evidently chosen as of typically period interest, showing a group of persons in evening dress listening to a piano duet. The original, from which the reproduction was taken, was a painting by Frank Stone that had been exhibited at the Royal Academy of 1847 under the title of 'The Duet'. As I looked closely at this elegant Victorian gathering I realised that, though the bevy of ladies, gentlemen and children were unmistakably English, the room in which they were sitting was foreign. Their setting was a neat French salon. The cornice-moulding, the curtains, the bookcase with its bust, the *guéridon*, the portraits, the furniture were French. Why, I wondered, should these English people be living in a foreign house, and why should children be included in an evening party unless they formed part of a family picture? The small child on the tabouret was playing with a white dog, the sort of dog given to Dickens in America. Could it possibly be Mr. Timber Doodle? was my first query and then tumbling after came other queries: Could the child be Francis Jeffrey Dickens? Could the tall man with the steeple head leaning chin-in-hand on the piano possibly be Alfred Tennyson? Could the whole group, instead of being anonymous assistants at a *soirée musicale*, be identified as the Dickens family at Rosemont?

Reference to the Dickens letters quickly established the fact that Frank Stone had visited Rosemont. On inquiry at the Rischgitz Institute a portfolio of Dickensiana was pro-

[1] Edited by G. M. Young.

duced in which was the photograph of an engraving with a note supplied by Marcus Stone, son of Frank Stone:

'The Duet' by Frank Stone

(introducing Tennyson, Dickens, and the latter's dog and Miss Hogarth one of the figures seated at the piano).

Though no locality was indicated in this note, the furnishing of the room made it obvious that it was a contemporary snap-shot of an actual Victorian family abroad and that it was in this cultivated, prosperous, happy *milieu* one could establish Dickens! Stone had evidently made a sketch of the incident on the spot and had built it up into an oil painting later, just as later on he did studies of the Dickens children in the verandah at Bonchurch.

Dombey and Son was by now developing steadily and Dickens read the first numbers aloud to Mrs. Marcet and a few chosen friends. 'The old lady', observed the author, 'was so devilish cute' that she realised at once that he intended to kill Paul. As he sensed his auditors gripped by interest so tense as to flower into apprehension, Dickens began to enjoy himself vastly and read better and better. The sensation he derived from their sympathy was so delightful that it occurred to the author that, 'if it were not *infra dig.*', it would be most pleasurable to read to larger audiences 'from one's own books', and incidentally that a great deal of money might be made that way. He mentioned his idea to Forster and then pushed it to the back of his mind whence it emerged again when his need for money became more acute.

In September Dickens began to apply himself intently to his new Christmas tale *The Battle of Life*, 'cordially inscribed to my English friends in Switzerland'. It is the story of a girl who gives up her sweetheart to her sister, and some people have read significance into the theme. *Dombey* of course had to be laid aside, though it put him out to have to interrupt a story that was now going well and in sales was outstripping *Chuzzlewit* by more than twelve thousand copies a number. In forcing himself to work at *The Battle of Life*

Dickens found his writing going 'all awry', and his health too, but somehow with the help of a visit to an hotel in Geneva he managed to finish it. The *Times* repeated its *Cricket* performance and gave it a very bad notice which he foolishly read. 'I see the good old *Times* is again at issue with the inimitable B. Another touch of a blunt razor on B.'s nervous system. . . . Dreamed of "Timeses" all night. Disposed to go to New Zealand and start a magazine.'

By mid-November the Dickens household had been established at Rosemont for six months: it was long enough for one to whom city streets were an inspiration. If *Dombey* was ever to be finished he must get to a big city, not necessarily London; Paris would serve his purpose, so to Paris the family journeyed in three carriages, a *fourgon* and a cabriolet, taking five days to cover the distance. To begin with they put up at the Hôtel Brighton. On the evening after their arrival Dickens took 'a colossal walk' and found the brilliance and brightness of the streets frightening. He then set about looking for a house to rent for the winter. That of the Marquis de Castellane was bizarre enough to attract Dickens's fancy. It was 48 rue de Courcelles in the Faubourg St. Honoré, and Sir Henry Bulwer while at the British Embassy had occupied it and had had the walls of one room painted to look like a grove of trees brightened by bits of glass stuck in among the leaves. Dickens described it as 'a Paris mansion in miniature with courtyard, garden and Concierge's lodge complete with a cordon to open the door'. The bedrooms were so small as to be comparable to opera boxes and their partitions were almost as frail. Charley remembered his father saying, 'It was something between a baby house, a shades, a haunted castle, and a mad kind of clock, and not to be imagined by the mind of man. One room is a tent, another room is a scene at the Victoria. The upstairs rooms are like fanlights over street doors. The inventor got frightened at what he had done and went away.'

The month of December was intensely cold and the water in the jugs froze at night, but the house had the merit of providing Dickens with something new in the way of experience. He soon was to find out that it was not a place in which he could write. Taking a dislike to the upstairs room he had chosen as a study, he would come down disconsolate to the drawing-room and, finding no corner that suited him, would sit there stubbornly for hours getting perhaps half a dozen lines on to paper. Dejectedly he took to wandering about the streets and to looking in frequently at the Morgue, for he never knew in advance what would set him working again and had to take his chance and often waste time waiting for the moment of kindling. The French people with whom Dickens came in contact impressed him at first unfavourably; they could not hold a candle to the Swiss for reliability. He came to change his views when he knew them better, but to begin with he found them indifferent, careless, procrastinating and their semi-sentimental devotion to Liberty seemed to have nothing in it of American vigour or purpose. Possibly they were fit for nothing but soldiering, but what, he asked himself, could he expected from a people bled white by the great Revolution and the Napoleonic wars?

So dull did he find himself in Paris that he went over to London for a week before Christmas to arrange for a cheap double-column edition of his books with new prefaces, a series to be dedicated to 'the English People'. Part of his time was spent at rehearsals of *The Battle of Life* which had been rapidly dramatised for the Keeleys by Albert Smith. He found that in the copying of the parts the whole play had been reduced to 'insufferable nonsense'. He put this right and could not resist waiting for the first night at the Lyceum. It went very well and the house accorded him an ovation.

During this short visit he had to wrestle with his brother Frederick who was anxious to marry Christiana Weller's sister. In spite of stiff opposition by the families on both sides the wedding took place two years later and turned out disastrously. He also found time to swoop on Gore House for 'a heart-to-heart talk' with Lady Blessington. Charley was a spectator at this dinner, and in his Reminiscences says:

As we sat down to dinner there was a vacant chair next to mine. 'It is only the Prince,' explained Lady Blessington to my father, 'he is always late,' and indeed some minutes passed before a sallow, rather sullen, heavy-looking man came in and after kissing Lady Blessington's hand and taking very little notice of the rest of the company, who, for their part, seemed to be content to take very little notice of him, sat down by my side. The newcomer took very little part in the general conversation, but talked to me pleasantly enough about my school life and recent stay in Paris, and then very soon after dinner after an interval of moody silence took himself off.

Charley's father also watched the man he had so often seen there 'biding his time', the man who through circumstance had assumed a new significance, the self-contained, reticent person nicknamed Prince Taciturn, soon to be the ruler of France.

Returning to the family for Christmas he resolved to shut himself up in order to write, but found it extremely difficult to refuse the invitations of Mrs. Norton's brother, Charles Sheridan, and, of course, he could not shirk entertaining the Watsons who arrived in Paris for the New Year. With Lord Normanby, the British ambassador, he also dined; their friendship was of old standing and they had a constant link in Lord Mulgrave with whom Dickens had crossed the Atlantic five years earlier. Though the ambassador was informal and friendly in private intercourse, he seemed harassed by the political situation and weighed down by responsibility and apprehension about the future. Louis Philippe's reign was tottering to an inglorious close and it was his duty to report to his government every fluctuation in the political barometer. Was monarchy doomed in France, and if so what president would or could take over supreme authority? Those of us who have read Lord Normanby's memoirs and official reports may see expressed in them an intelligent observer's reactions to events. Our policy at the moment was far from rigid. Palmerston as Foreign Secretary (in Lord John Russell's government) in writing to Lord Normanby had laid down,

'Our principles of action are to acknowledge whatever rule may be established with apparent prospect of permanency, but none other'.

Dickens at this time was going to the opera so frequently and dining out so constantly that he began to wonder whether he had ever had anything to do with a book called *Dombey* or ever sat over a chapter of it day after day until he began to think it the only reality in life and to mistake all the realities for short-lived shadows. Sometime he jerked himself into refusing an invitation. For instance, when Lord Albert Conyngham invited him to a masked ball he declined the invitation as it 'would play the very devil with my to-morrow's occupation'. Paul Dombey was about to die and Dickens was miserable, his head ached; he says he took 'prodigious pains' over the child's end. When it was over he wrote to Miss Coutts: 'Between ourselves, Paul is dead. He died on Friday night about ten o'clock and as I had no hope of getting to sleep afterwards I went out and walked about Paris until breakfast next morning.' How could any-one combine moods of this kind, moods necessary to creation, with the routine of dining out? As it was, the printers found he had underwritten *Dombey* by two pages, and he had to hurry over to London to make good the deficiency.

We shall see when we come to examine the novel in detail how differently it was received by different readers. Henry Hallam, writing to Mrs. Brookfield, said: 'Everybody is pre-tending that the death of Paul Dombey is the most beautiful thing ever written. Milnes, Thackeray, and your uncle own to tears. I am so hardened as to be unable to look on it in any light but pure business.' Thackeray strode into the *Punch* office, and, flinging down his number on Mark Lemon's desk, said, 'There's no writing against this, one hasn't an atom of a chance; it's stupendous'. The Dickens family felt out in the cold. 'I am certain', Charley was in the habit of saying, 'that the children of my father's brain were much more real to him at times than we were.'

Forster joined his friend in Paris on the day of Paul's death. The climax reached, Dickens was only too thankful to put work aside to entertain 'Fuz'. The two friends spent an exciting fortnight together, going to a play each night and consorting with authors, actors and such celebrities as were accessible to visitors. The aged Chateaubriand was one of the great figures to whom they paid homage, but the author of *Les Mémoires d'outre-tombe* was an ailing man, and Dickens, having but little in common with him, was hard put to it to find subjects of conversation. It was easier to get on with Alphonse de Lamartine whom he had learned to like at Albaro. Madame de Lamartine's salon was a meeting-ground for foreigners, she herself being English. With Alexandre Dumas, Eugène Sue, Théophile Gautier, Alphonse Karr and Amédée Pichot Dickens conversed, for he now spoke, as Lamartine tells us, fluent French though with a heavy English accent. Macready's friend Régnier gave him the freedom of the green room at the Français where on Molière's birthday he saw his *Don Juan* revived.

The Frenchman who made the greatest impression on Dickens was Victor Hugo. Not only was he the most influential literary figure of the day, but also, as Louis Philippe had recently made him a peer of France, the political man of the moment. Dickens describes him as under middle height with pale face and an intense sweetness of expression combined with keen intellectuality. He spoke warmly of the English and their literature and showed a flattering appreciation of the works of 'Boz'. Writing to Lady Blessington[1] in the afterglow of his wonderful visit Dickens says that the home of Hugo was crowded with armour, tapestries, coffers; it was not an ordinary apartment, it was more like 'an old palace wherein old golden lions played at skittles with ponderous old golden balls'. The romantic setting seemed more like a chapter from one of his books than the furnishings of real life. It interested Dickens very much to hear that Madame Hugo was loved by Sainte-Beuve and Julie Drouet,

[1] January 24, 1847.

the actress, by Victor Hugo, and that no one of their friends took these arrangements amiss.

The author of *Hernani*, *Ruy Blas*, *Lucrezia Borgia*, those operas without music, at this time a man of forty-five, was living on the first floor of 37 rue de la Tour d'Auvergne, a big solitary house backing on to the Palais-Royal with windows looking out over a panorama of Paris. By way of a deserted courtyard one approached the flight of steps that led to the door of an apartment crammed with antique treasures. So great a variety of objects could not be grasped all in a moment. Cordova leather adorned the walls of the *salle d'attente*, Gothic tapestry, and folios standing on lecterns, an anteroom. The salon with its blue damask walls, its Venetian negroes, its white satin upholstery, its bust by David, its glass pictures, made a sumptuous impression. So did the dining-room with its carved oak, gleaming lustre-ware, tapestry and glass 'all assembled', as Théophile Gautier says, 'by the patient fantasy of the poet'. To Dickens the scene resembled 'some gloomy vast old theatre' or some equally gloomy vast curiosity shop. 'I was much struck', he told Lady Blessington, 'by Hugo himself, who looks like a genius as he is every inch of him, and very interesting and satisfactory from head to foot.' The antique setting Victor Hugo had chosen for himself was in no way indicative of a conservative temper. He was already at work on *Les Misérables*, that epic novel on the sufferings of the poor, and he had already declared for a League of Nations and a Republican United States of Europe.

Most of the contacts made by Dickens in Paris during this visit were with men of letters and of the theatre. He did not meet their wives or go to their houses. It was not till nine years later, after two French-talking summers at Boulogne, that he was able to take his place as *grand écrivain* at the parties of George Sand, Madame Viardot, Madame Scribe and Madame Scheffer. By then his novels had been serialised in *Le Moniteur* and were so widely read that compliments were showered on him by shopkeepers and hotel clerks.

At this time Kate was unable to accompany him on excursions to the environs and Georgy was his constant companion. As the new baby was expected in April Dickens, though his own house was still in the possession of Sir James Duke, transported his family to London in March. This necessitated his renting a furnished house, 3 Chester Place, where a fifth son, Sydney Smith Haldimand, was born.

Just at this time (1847) Lord Jeffrey bobbed up again with inquiries about Dickens's earnings and on receiving a full statement wrote, 'I am rather disappointed I must own, to find your *embankment* still so small'. He really cannot make out why this should be, as the public had paid at least £100,000 for his books. Is it due to mismanagement? improvident arrangement with publishers? or careless control of their proceedings? His young friend must secure *independence* though he is far from 'grudging him the elegancies and indulgences suitable to his tasteful liberal nature'. He feels paternal anxiety on Dickens's behalf—or will his young friend call it the caution of senility? He is not in any way a father confessor, but he would dearly like to know whether Dickens has ever felt the promptings of prudent avarice, pride of purse or the like? Dickens answered the questions for a while, but as Jeffrey continued to importune him with a kind of cross-examination he stopped replying to his letters. A year later we find Jeffrey writing that as he is the godfather of a Dickens child he does not wish to 'grow quite out of acquaintance'. 'You really must take a little notice of me now and then.' In the month of his death, January 1850, he informed Dickens, 'Living or dying, I retain for you, unbated and unimpaired, the same cordial feelings of love, gratitude and admiration as for these many years past'.[1]

Just at the time *Dombey and Son* was coming out in its green covers *Vanity Fair* was being issued in yellow covers and there was a kind of rivalry between the books, though *Vanity Fair* only sold 7000 as against *Dombey's* 25,000. Carlyle spoke of the relief he found it to turn from Thackeray's 'terrible cynicism' to the cheerful geniality of Dickens. He

[1] *The Dickens Circle*, p. 432.

preferred Charles Dickens to Thackeray as a man, for
Dickens always treated him with deference whereas Thackeray
would oppose his opinions or even 'practise persiflage on
him'.　The name of Thackeray was really unknown to the
British public as he had chosen hitherto to write as 'Michael-
Angelo Titmarsh'.　*Catherine*, *Barry Lyndon* and the *Snob
Papers* for *Punch* were published under this name.

Abraham Hayward, writing to Thackeray about *Vanity
Fair*, said:[1] 'Don't get nervous or think about criticism or
trouble yourself about the opinion of friends; you have
completely beaten Dickens out of the inner circle already'.
Mrs. Carlyle wrote in the same strain: 'Very good indeed.
Beats Dickens out of the world.'　Thackeray laughed and
forwarded the letters to Mrs. Brookfield.

Early in 1847 Thackeray wrote some parodies on contemporary writers entitled *Punch's Prize Novelists*.　In April
appeared 'George de Barnewell' (Bulwer Lytton), then 'Cod-
linsby' (Disraeli).　These were to be followed by some kind
of a 'Boz' skit, but the proprietors of *Punch* (Bradbury and
Evans) would not permit such an outrage.　It is certain that
Dickens intervened on his own behalf.[2]　In a way he was easy
game for a parodist, as Anthony Trollope, in *The Warden*,
was to show.

[1] November 1847.　　　　　　　[2] 80. 35. D.

Chapter 16

THEATRICALS

Man is an embodied paradox, a bundle of contradictions.
C. C. COLTON

DURING the three months now spent at Chester Place
Dickens worked steadily at *Dombey and Son* and dined
out more than he had ever done. Sometimes he went out as
a bachelor and sometimes with Georgina, who, as a companion, suited him better and better. By this time she was
twenty-one and had become more sure of her power to charm
and amuse: the tears literally ran down Charles's cheeks when
she started mimicking the people they met. Entries in
diaries show that during the weeks after the birth of Sydney
Smith, Charles and Georgy were always about together.
One night it would be a dinner with Forster to meet the
Macreadys, Régniers, Stanfield and Maclise, and another
night it would be a dinner-party at Chester Place for a play.
Lord Ellesmere's rhymed translation of *Hernani* was being
presented with Fanny Kemble in the principal part (a part in
which she had played sixteen years earlier at Bridgewater
House). In Dickens's box at the St. James's Theatre sat the
Régniers, Harrison Ainsworth, Maclise, Jerrold and Stanfield.
Two evenings later Charles and Georgy, Forster, Maclise and
the Régniers dined together again in the company of Landor.
As soon as Mrs. Dickens was about again, her husband took
her to a large party at the Macreadys' to meet the Lord
Advocate and Mrs. Rutherford, Mr. and Mrs. Carlyle, Eastlake, Panizzi, Rogers, Miss Jewsbury, Edwin Landseer and
Jenny Lind. These dinners now formed the natural conclusion of Dickens's writing day, a day that often lasted from
six to eight hours. Before transporting his family to Broadstairs at the end of June, Charles and Kate dined with the
Douglas Jerrolds at Putney Heath where once again the

Macreadys and Maclise turned up; this time they foregathered to meet the perennially penniless Leigh Hunt for whom they were devising a benefit performance. Hardly had their plans been perfected than Lord John Russell to some extent forestalled them by giving Leigh Hunt a Civil List pension of £200 a year. This caused the would-be helpers to abandon all idea of playing *The Merry Wives of Windsor* in London, but to implement their scheme for paying off Leigh Hunt's debts by giving performances of another play in Manchester and Liverpool only. For this purpose *Every Man in His Humour* was revived and most of Dickens's original cast rallied to his support, the only new names being those of Augustus Egg and George Henry Lewes, at that time living with his wife, later to become Mrs. Thornton Hunt. Rehearsals were carried on at Miss Kelly's Theatre with 'Boz' in supreme control.

The company played at Manchester on July 26, where Dickens delivered a prologue written by Talfourd, and at Liverpool on July 28, when Forster spoke another prologue composed by Bulwer Lytton. The tour was very good fun, and the amateur company did themselves so handsomely that though takings were good, clear profits amounted to but £400. The meagreness of this sum set off against the energy and time expended rather disappointed Dickens, who now planned to add to it by writing a narrative of the tour. The theme was suggested to him by the condition of Mrs. Leech, who, touring with her husband, nearly had her baby in the train and only just succeeded in reaching the Victoria Hotel, Euston Square, before it was born. 'What a tremendous chance', wrote Dickens to Mark Lemon, 'that Leech's little girl was not born on the railway!' In 'Piljian's Projiss,[1] or Mrs. Gamp and the Strollers' the humour and the characterisation are alike heavy. Mr. Wilson the wigmaker and Mrs. Gamp meet on the departure platform as the players assemble and Mr. Wilson points out the celebrities. 'George the Crookshank who draws for *Punch*' is one of them, and Mrs.

---

[1] Written August 1847, and preserved in Forster's *Life*.

Gamp says with a sniff 'which I never touches on account of the lemon!' a joke involving another member of the cast, Mark Lemon.   Frank Stone and Augustus Egg are explained as 'well-beknow'd at the Academy as sure as stones is stones and eggs is eggs'.   John Forster figures as 'a resolute gent, apperrently going to take the railway by storm, his weskit very much buttoned up, his mouth very much shut, his coat a-flying open and his heels a-giving it to the platform'.   He is quickly followed by Mrs. Gamp's 'beeograffer . . . a wild gent that's been tearing up and down with a great box of papers under his arm a-talking to everybody very indistinct and exciting himself something dreadful'.   'That's the Manager!' cries Mr. Wilson the wigmaker.

This is an aspect of Dickens's humour that appeals as little to present-day readers as his Victorian treatment of birth and death generally.   Perhaps it is just as well that 'Mrs. Gamp and the Strollers' remained a rough sketch, as the dragging in of characters from earlier books or rather their resuscitation— of which Mr. Pickwick and Sam Weller in *Master Humphrey's Clock* are examples—is not satisfactory.

Dickens seldom read the work of foreign writers, but oɪ Hans Andersen's *Fairy Tales* he made an exception and they were relegated at once into the class of 'special favourites' that included the works of Washington Irving and Oliver Goldsmith.   The first man to introduce this Danish author to English readers had been William Jerdan who, in his capacity of editor of the *Literary Gazette*, was able to advertise his merits.   In response to a complimentary letter sent to the author he had received an effusion from Andersen expressing love of English books and English authors, naming 'Scott, Bulwer and Dickens' as among those he most cherished.

How much I should like to shake the hand of Boz [he wrote].   When I read his books I often think I have seen such things and feel I could write like that.   Do not mis-understand me. . . . I do not know how better to express myself than to say that what completely captivates me seems to become part of myself.   As the wind whistles round his bell-rope, I have often heard it whistle on a cold, wet autumn evening, and the chirp of the cricket I remember well in the cosy corner of my parents' humble room.

And so with Jerdan's encouragement, the fairy-tale teller began planning a visit to England.   The welcome prepared for him ensured that, as soon as he reached his hotel in Leicester Square, he should find himself an honorary member of the Athenaeum Club.   Calling on Count Reventlow, the Danish Minister, next morning, he was told he must present himself at Lord Palmerston's party that evening in order to be introduced to his English admirers.   Eagerly Hans Andersen asked whether he would meet Jenny Lind at the reception, but the Count could hold out no hopes that 'the Lind' would be there; she lived in retreat at Brompton, refusing all invitations, so if he really wanted to see her he must go to Brompton.   To Brompton he hied, and was greatly comforted to be received 'like a dear brother' and promised easy access to the opera house whenever he wished to go there.

At Lord Palmerston's house Andersen was overcome to find himself the centre of attraction, smiled on and compli-mented by ladies in sparkling tiaras and billowing satin gowns. Each looked to him a queen and each had something ravishing to say about his tales.   When his English gave out, he took refuge with his revered patron, the Duke of Saxe-Weimar, and talked to him in German.   Andersen thought the English women around him 'flower-like and lovely', and at Lady Paulet's ball, given to celebrate Queen Victoria's birth-day, he described them 'standing like rose-petals in the press'. Vainly at these parties did he crane his neck looking for 'Boz': there was no 'Boz' to be seen.   William Jerdan told him that Dickens was with his family at Broadstairs, and that Lady Blessington was contriving a meeting for the two authors at Gore House.   No less anxious to meet Andersen than Andersen was to meet 'Boz', Dickens had written to Lady Blessington 'I *must* see Andersen', and she at once made it her business to see that he did so.   To the Duke of Saxe-Weimar Andersen wrote of this happy meeting:

> At Lady Blessington's I made the acquaintance of Dickens. . . . He is just what I thought he would be.   We understood each other at once, clasped each other's hands and talked English—I unfortunately not well, but as I said before we understood each other.[1]

The Dane, who was accustomed to very simple surroundings at home, found the Gore House hospitality overwhelmingly palatial.   His host, Count d'Orsay, tried to put him at his ease by rallying him in a 'very jolly' way, and he was allowed to admire in silence all the 'very fine' flowers, pictures and statues.   A second meeting grew out of the first, and this time Dickens brought with him to Gore House a set of his books, each volume inscribed 'To Hans Christian Andersen from his friend and admirer Charles Dickens'.   He also warmly invited him to come and share 'the crowded family life' at Broadstairs.

Andersen spoke in enthusiastic but limited terms to Dickens and Jerdan of the English literature that had 'enriched his fancy and filled his heart'.   Those who have read his biographical sketch, *The Improvisatore*, will remember how as a little boy he made his dolls perform Shakespeare's tragedies in a toy theatre, and how on first arriving in Copenhagen he would spend his few pennies in getting a Scott novel and, while reading it, would forget hunger and cold.   Stories of this kind show that Hans Andersen was in the true tradition of those who lead the inner life of imaginative authors, for whom the world is the shadow show and the life of the mind the only reality.   Dickens, too, understood this life very well, for, when he was clothing his imperishable figures in flesh, the world in which his own body moved became remote and insubstantial.

Just before recrossing the channel Hans Andersen dined

---

[1] For this and other excerpts see F. Crawford, *Correspondence with Grand Duke of Saxe-Weimar*, *Dickens*, etc., 1891.

with Dickens at Broadstairs and next morning his host walked over to Ramsgate to see his boat leave. Andersen recorded the farewell:

> We pressed each other's hands and he looked at me so kindly with his shrewd sympathetic eyes, and, as the ship went off, there he stood waving his hat and looking so gallant, so youthful and so handsome. Dickens was the last who sent me a greeting from dear England's shore.

No one could say that gawky, easily confused Hans Andersen had ever looked young, though equally no one could say he had ever grown up. From the financial angle his visit was a success, for Bentley, with whom he had stayed in Kent, arranged to publish seven of his fairy tales as *A Christmas Greeting to my English Friends*, and fourteen of his new stories under the title *A Poet's Day Dreams*. The latter volume was dedicated to Dickens.

> I feel a desire, a longing to transplant in England the first produce of my poetic garden as a Christmas greeting and I send it to you, my dear noble Charles Dickens, who by your works have been previously dear to me and since our meeting have taken root in my heart.

During the ten years that went by before Hans Andersen revisited England, he kept up a desultory correspondence with Dickens. None of these letters have survived, save a note in which Dickens assures him that he lives fresh in his remembrance and that everyone is asking when he is going to make everyone happier and better by writing a new book. 'We feel jealous of Stockholm and jealous of Finland and we say that you ought to be at home and nowhere else with a quill in your hand and a goodly pile of paper before you.'

The Dickens family remained at Broadstairs till early in September 1847 and then reinstalled themselves in Devonshire Terrace, of which they had but two years further lease. Dickens had waited with some impatience to regain possession of his own house, for in Broadstairs, unless it was pouring with rain, he could not get half an hour's peace to work on *Dombey*. The place had become an inferno of excruciating organs, fiddles, bells and glee-singers. He now had no worries about money, for *Dombey* was selling far in excess of what he had anticipated. 'The profits of the half-year are brilliant. Deducting the hundred pounds a month paid six times, I have still to receive two thousand two hundred and twenty pounds, which I think tidy.'

The autumn simply flew by at Devonshire Terrace. *Dombey* absorbed most of Dickens's waking hours and on account of *Dombey* he postponed for a twelvemonth the writing of a Christmas story, *The Haunted Man*. He spoke at Leeds on December 1 at the Mechanics' Institute, and was rather surprised at the giant advertisements of his lecture that met his eyes in the streets. Speaking with a heavy cold on him, he said he looked to Institutions such as this to refine and improve the social edifice. He rejoiced to see in the report that French and German were being taught as well as drawing and chemistry. 'The Creator having breathed a mind into men must have intended them to be educated.' These words evoked a warm response.

A domestic Christmas was followed by a journey to Scotland with Kate to open the new Athenaeum in Glasgow. He had promised to speak on 'the friendships we make with books'. As they were travelling to Glasgow by rail from Edinburgh Kate was taken suddenly ill with a miscarriage and could not attend the meeting, at which Charles praised Athenaeums in general, partly because they were initiated by working men and partly because they aimed high in teaching Spanish, Italian, French and German as well as music, mathematics and logic. He ended his speech by hoping that money for more books would soon be raised. Mr. Alison proposed an enthusiastically supported vote of thanks. In writing an account of this occasion to Georgy, Charles casually mentioned Kate's mishap and then described the packed meeting at which 'the Inimitable did wonders. His grace, elegance, and eloquence enchanted all beholders.' Whenever he uses

the word 'Inimitable' we know that he is in the highest
spirits, and it is no surprise to find him telling Georgy, 'I have
never enjoyed myself more completely'.   They were staying
with the Alisons who, Dickens tells us, lived 'in style' in a
handsome country house outside Glasgow with everything
very pleasant about them. Kate was kept in bed and
Dickens, 'treated as a person of great distinction', ate a
'gorgeous state lunch with the Lord Provost and City
Council' and was entertained at a banquet in the evening.
After two nights Kate was supposed to be well enough to
travel, but she collapsed in Edinburgh and had to take to her
bed again.   This gave Dickens the opportunity of sightseeing
and of a good gossip with Lord Jeffrey.   Macaulay had just
lost his seat in the House of Commons and people said no one
else could possibly have lost it, and that he had gone out of
his way to be disagreeable and get himself disliked. He also
heard from Lord Jeffrey that Sheridan Knowles, the author
of two highly successful plays, *Virginius* and *The Hunchback*,
had just made a declaration of bankruptcy before him.
Easily moved to compassion by the troubles of authors,
Dickens at once cast about him for ways and means of helping the poor fellow.   There was a scheme afoot for buying
Shakespeare's house at Stratford-on-Avon in order to preserve it as a national monument. He had attended the
committee called by Payne Collier in August at the Thatched
House Tavern in St. James's Street, and now discussed with
Lord Jeffrey the possibility of installing Knowles at Stratford
as curator, but, as his friend drily observed, Sheridan Knowles
quite recently had rather compromised his position as a literary
figure by having become a Baptist minister.   This might well
prove an obstacle to his appointment as custodian of a literary
shrine.

Dickens's sightseeing centred on Sir Walter Scott. Lord
Jeffrey showed him the memorial, which seemed to him 'like
the spire of a Gothic church taken off and stuck in the
ground'; Abbotsford was also inspected, and there he was
shocked by 'the vile glass case' containing the clothes last

worn by Sir Walter. It depressed him deeply to be shown
an old white hat 'tumbled and bent and broken by the uneasy,
purposeless wandering hither and thither of his heavy head.
It so embodied Lockhart's pathetic description of him, when
he tried to write and laid down his pen and cried, that it
associated itself in my mind with broken powers and mental
weakness.' Clothes, both his own and other people's,
always meant a great deal to Dickens, and one calls to mind
his insistence to Cattermole on the pathos to be conveyed to
readers by Nell's bonnet and shawl. Clothes affect some
people in a very peculiar way and Dickens was particularly
sensitive in his reactions to their appeal.

On returning to London he found that the Borough
Council of Stratford-on-Avon had made themselves responsible for the purchase and conservation of the Shakespeare House, so he concentrated on collecting money to
endow a curatorship. Even if Knowles did not directly
benefit, some other writer might be chosen for the post.
Jumping at once to the idea of a theatrical production, he
summoned his cast together to choose a play. He was very
bright and lively on his return from Scotland, but the prospect
of acting was not the only cause of exhilaration, for the end
of *Dombey* was in sight and he had time to let his mind play
on other matters. The abdication of Louis Philippe, King
of the French, threw him into the wildest spirits. What
had happened to Lamartine? and what would d'Orsay do?
Forster (to whom he talked) said that now, of course, d'Orsay
would rush back to Paris. 'But not at all,' retorted Dickens,
'Monsieur le Comte is still giving dinners at Gore House!'
The explosion of democracy in France went so completely to
his head that he declared he would renounce his native tongue
for 'the language of gods and of angels'. Vive la France!
Vive le Peuple! Plus de Royauté! Plus de Bourbons!
Plus de Guizot! Voilà les sentiments du citoyen Charles
Dickens! Historian friends of his were also convulsed by
the news. Henry Hallam ate no breakfast and paced up and
down his dining-room, an empty plate pressed against his

heart, and Carlyle wrote in his journal, 'Louis Philippe is flung out; he and his entire pack with a kind of exquisite irony driving off in a street cab!' What Dickens thought of the London repercussions we do not know; he does not allude to them in any letter of the date. But, absorbed as he was in concerns theatrical, he cannot have ignored the fact that when the Chartist petition was presented in April no private carriages were to be seen on the streets, or that the gates of Green Park and Constitution Hill were closed and the iron shutters of Apsley House bolted. Emerson, who was in London at the time, took notice of everything and made a point of attending the meeting convened by the Chartists in London to receive the report of the deputation they had sent to Paris to congratulate the French Republican Government. At this gathering the 'Marseillaise' was as lustily sung as at Abolition demonstrations in the United States. Like other intelligent Americans Emerson was horrified by the depths of tragic poverty revealed in the streets of Liverpool and London and, in view of the general smugness of the propertied classes, it was hardly possible to believe such miseries could be terminated without a revolution. Emerson, on Carlyle's advice, went on to Paris to see how things were for himself and found all the enthusiasts for the new regime 'bearded like goats and lions'. Having satisfied his curiosity, he returned to London to deliver six lectures at the Portman Square Literary and Scientific Institution on the Laws of Thought, Politics and Socialism, Poetry and Eloquence, and kindred subjects.

Though Emerson had come to London in October 1847, Dickens did not play any part in welcoming him. He was the house-guest of the Carlyles and the particular charge of Mrs. George Bancroft, who took him to see Rogers and other men of letters before he set out for the north to deliver the lectures that were the reason for his coming to England. In this connection one may mention that George Bancroft, the Harvard historian, had been appointed minister to the Court of St. James in 1846. He had, as we know, been a kind friend to Dickens during the American tour, but now he saw nothing of him and there is no allusion to him in the many available letters of this date. It is doubtful whether any Bostonian wished to see much of the writer of *Martin Chuzzlewit*. It was not till Bancroft was on the point of leaving for America a year later that an entry appears in his diary for April 19, 1849, 'Dine at Mr. Charles Dickens'. On May 8 he returned the civility by asking Dickens to breakfast in company with the Duke of Argyll, Hallam, Macaulay, Milman, Bunsen and Frothingham. There was no resumption at any time of the friendliness generated in Boston in 1842.

On May 4, 1848, Forster, at Dickens's request, invited him to meet Emerson at his rooms in Lincoln's Inn Fields. Carlyle was also of the party of four and was greeted by his host in a stentorian voice as 'My Prophet!' which surprised the American guest. The conversation turned on the shameful lewdness of the London streets and Carlyle had a good deal to say about whoredom generally and the wickedness of our so-called civilisation. Carlyle said that chastity in the male sex was as good as gone and Dickens endorsed this opinion. Emerson protested that it was quite otherwise in America and that men of good understanding and education went to their nuptial bed as virgin as did their brides.[1] Dickens replied that incontinence was so much the rule in England that if his own son were particularly chaste, he should be alarmed on his account as if he could not be in good health. Emerson's heart did not go out to garrulous Dickens as it had done to the sensible, quiet-mannered Alfred Tennyson with whom he had had such charming talks.

The play chosen for the Shakespeare Curatorship Fund was *The Merry Wives of Windsor* and it was to be followed by *Animal Magnetism*, *Love, Law and Physic*, *A Good Night's Rest* or some other farce. Most of the old cast took parts and there was one important newcomer, Mrs. Cowden Clarke, who asked to be allowed to play Dame Quickly to Dickens's

[1] R. W. Emerson, *Journals*, vol. vii. p. 441.

Master Shallow. She found Dickens a very businesslike stage manager. He usually sat at a small table to one side of the stage and sometimes would stand with back to the footlights to watch entries and exits. The amateurs opened their series of nine performances at the Haymarket on April 15 and, after visiting Manchester, Liverpool, Birmingham and Edinburgh, ended it in Glasgow on July 20. The announcement for the first night ran as follows:

THEATRE ROYAL, HAYMARKET

AMATEUR PERFORMANCE

in aid of

THE FUND FOR THE ENDOWMENT OF A PERPETUAL CURATORSHIP OF SHAKESPEARE'S HOUSE

> To be always held by some one distinguished in Literature and more especially in Dramatic Literature, the profits of which it is the intention of the Shakespeare House Committee to keep entirely separate from the Fund now being raised for the purchase of the House.

Directors of Arrangements: John Payne Collier, Charles Knight, Peter Cunningham, and the London Shakespeare House Committee.

Stage Manager: Mr. Charles Dickens.

Evening dress in all parts of the House.

The Carlyles took seats for this performance and Mr. Carlyle watched Dame Quickly's performance with great interest. When the curtain went down Carlyle was heard to say, 'A poor play, but *plaudite, plaudite!*' In Mrs. Cowden Clarke we have a better chronicler[1] than Mrs. Gamp, for her recollections are natural and charmingly expressed. She and her sister, Emma Novello, accompanied the troupe on tour and always travelled in the same compartment as Mr. and Mrs. Dickens and Mark Lemon. Dickens made a habit of getting to the station early and greeting his 'strollers' as they turned

[1] C. and M. Cowden Clarke, *Recollections of Writers*.

GEORGINA HOGARTH (circa 1850)
by Augustus Egg, R.A.

" My little housekeeper Miss Hogarth "

CHARLES DICKENS, AGED 46
by W. P. Frith, R.A.

up with 'a beaming look', which affected the railway officials so benignly that they took every possible care of his whole company. Mrs. Clarke goes on to tell of

> the delightful gaiety and sprightliness of our manager's talk, the endless stories he told us, the games he mentioned and how they were played. The bright amenity of his name at various stations when he showed to persons in authority the free pass-ticket which had been previously given in homage to Charles Dickens and his party. The courteous alacrity with which he jumped out at one refreshment room to procure food for somebody who complained of hunger. . . . His indefatigable vivacity, cheeriness and good humour from morning to night, all were delightful.

The way in which he acted amused her very much:

> In *Love, Law and Physic* he used to tuck me under his arm with the free and easy familiarity of a lawyer patronising an actress whom he chances to find his fellow traveller in a stage coach. . . . It is something to remember having been tucked under the arm by Charles Dickens and had one's hand hugged against the side! one thinks better of one's hand ever after.

And it was not only on tour that she found the company of Dickens delightful; she also loved going informally to the house in Devonshire Terrace and being treated as one of the family. Altogether she outlines one of the most attractive pictures of Dickens that has survived. Charles, to her thinking, showed up well in his own family, especially with the smallest children, and she looked on it as a much enjoyed privilege to be allowed to share the intimate life of his home.

> On one of the quiet occasions [she writes] when Mr. and Mrs. Dickens, their children and their few guests were sitting out of doors in the small garden in front of their Devonshire Terrace house enjoying the first warm summer evening I recollect seeing one of the little sons draw Dickens apart and stand in eager talk with him. [Dickens a few minutes later told her what the child wanted.] 'The

L

little fellow gave me so many excellent reasons why he should not go to bed so soon that I yielded the point and let him stay up half an hour later.'

All this to her was far more delightful than being bidden to one of the 'brilliant dinners' at Devonshire Terrace, dinners at which large companies assembled and everything was done in 'superb style with a bouquet of flowers beside the plate of each lady present'. Sometimes she dined alone with them before the opera, for which Miss Burdett Coutts often lent them her box. It was a great treat to be taken to hear Jenny Lind in *La Sonnambula* by Mrs. Dickens, to whom she became very much attached. Kate at this time was in great good looks and made an elegant figure in clothes of the latest fashion. Maclise's third portrait of her conveys a distinctly *mondaine* impression.

Just before Dickens moved to Broadstairs in the late summer he made an excursion down the Thames evidently in high spirits and in holiday mood. He had several reasons for being pleased: the sales of *Dombey* for one, and the success of the theatrical tour for another. The total realised, when all expenses had been deducted, was £2551, of which Sheridan Knowles received a share and John Poole, author of *Paul Pry*, a lesser share. As we have learnt, Knowles had already been assisted with a Civil List pension, and now Poole was also allocated an income by the ever sympathetic Lord John Russell. With the money provided by Dickens they could now pay their debts and make a fresh start. It was a very satisfying reflection to the contriver of the theatrical scheme.

Dickens was always fond of down-river and up-hill excursions as his many journeys to Greenwich and Hampstead testify. This summer he went to look for a Chinese ship reported to be moored in the Thames near Blackwall Tunnel. In a casual letter to Forster (afterwards expanded into an article for the *Examiner*) he described what he had seen and what he advised his readers to do. They should drive down to the Blackwall railway, where, for a matter of eighteenpence, any one of them can reach the heart of the Chinese Empire in no time. 'In half a score of minutes the tiles and chimney pots, backs of squalid houses, frowsy pieces of waste ground, narrow courts and streets, swamps, ditches, masts of ships, gardens of duckweed and unwholesome little bowers of scarlet beans, whirl away in a flying dream and nothing is left but China.'

Gingerly he climbed aboard, wondering at the frailty of the craft that was so unlike a ship of any kind.

> So narrow, so long, so grotesque; so low—in the middle; so high at each end, like a Chinese pen-tray; with no rigging, with nowhere to go aloft; with mats for sails, great warped cigars for masts, gaudy dragons and sea-monsters disporting themselves from stem to stern and in the stern a gigantic cock of impossible aspect defying the world. . . .

And then the Chinese figures lounging on deck, who on earth could guess them to be mariners?

> Imagine a ship's crew, without a profile among them, in gauze pinafores and plaited hair; wearing stiff clogs a quarter of a foot thick in the sole; and lying at night in little scented boxes like backgammon men or chess-pieces, or mother of pearl counters.

More surprising was the cabin with its swinging lanterns, its figure of Chin Tee of the eighteen arms curtained in a celestial Punch's show; the threads of smoke from joss-sticks, the tissue umbrella. Dickens wondered what would happen in a storm at sea. Would all the cool and shiny little chairs and tables continually slide and break each other, and if not why not? And the Mandarin passenger, what was he thinking about as he lay sick on a bamboo couch in a private china closet of his own signing autographs for curious visitors? Would he or anybody else on the voyage ever read those two books printed in characters like bird-cages and fly-traps? There was matter enough for reflection in this vision of a static civilisation. 'Finality in perfection', he called it, and commented, 'no blade of experience grown in centuries, what a contrast was the perfect junk with all its exquisiteness to the river it floated in'. And yet to English minds the river-banks were mighty in their signs of life, enterprise and progress. One might look at it that way or one might take it in another way, and Dickens was most struck, not by the signs of progress, but by the mimic eyes painted on the prow of the junk to help it find its course across the seas, and could not but ask himself whether we ourselves do not grope along relying on conventional eyes that have no sight in them. The cameo-like quality of this sketch is an example of that singleness of sight which enabled him on occasions to achieve effects with a true economy of words. Parallel effects are to be found scattered through all his books: an exemplary paragraph from *David Copperfield* reads thus:

> The water was out over the flat country, and every sheet and puddle lashed its banks, and had its stress of little breakers. When we came within sight of the sea, the waves on the horizon, caught at intervals above the boiling abyss, were like glimpses of another shore. . . . The people came to their doors all aslant and with streaming hair.

'If thine eye be single, thy whole body shall be full of light' is a text of special application to writers. Dickens's eye was not always single. It was, as Taine discovered, sometimes multiple, which may be why, in spite of felicitous examples of perfect prose, we have to admit that in the main the body of his work is styleless. His extraordinary fertility of invention often got in his way. Pullulating with power and variety, he was constrained to surrender himself to life as it poured through his brain. For a serial worker there was no time to do otherwise.

Chapter 17

HOUSEHOLD WORDS

Nullum magnum ingenium sine melancolia.

IN the desultory frame of mind induced by holiday-making with the family at Broadstairs, Dickens could not apply himself to serious novel-writing. Instead, he snatched at the opening given him by Cruikshank's shilling sets of plates, 'The Bottle' and 'The Drunkard's Children', to preach on temperance.[1] Drunkenness to him had always been 'the great national horror', but Cruikshank's plates would do no good at all; why, even Hogarth had not ventured to depict the progress of a drunkard because he knew that the causes of drunkenness lay so 'far down in sorrowfulness and human misery' that he could never bring them 'fairly and justly into the light'. The real origin of the vice was to be found in the desire to forget 'disgusting habitations, bad workshops, scarcity of light, air and water'. In fact 'the disastrous condition of England' was at fault, and it was folly to preach against the gin-shop when the conditions of existence made the gin-shop irresistible. His deep desire to change English life and to get rid of complacency and shams made Dickens long for a pulpit from which to expound his ideas of reform. This pulpit he was eventually to construct for himself in *Household Words*, a magazine intended to find its way into all the poorer houses in the land.

Before planning to carry out this scheme, he had to fulfil his pledge to produce another Christmas book and another full-size novel. To write the Christmas book, which had been simmering in his head for a long time, he went to Brighton and there conjured up another Scrooge in Mr. Redlaw and another Cratchit family in the Swidgers, with the Tetterby's and their Moloch of a baby thrown in, as it were,

[1] *Examiner*, July 8, 1848.

for luck. Redlaw, a studious man, is haunted by painful memories of a great wrong done him in early life. Interviewed by a spectre, the presentment of his gloomy past, a kind of second self, he is offered the power to forget with the penalty attached that he will make everyone he meets oblivious not only of past unhappiness, but of kindnesses and benefits received. This gift turns out to be destructive of all human relationships, and the moral of this story, *The Haunted Man, or the Ghost's Bargain*, is that it is better not to seek forgetfulness. In less than a fortnight Bradbury and Evans got a letter from Brighton saying, 'I finished last night, I've been crying my eyes out over it, not painfully but pleasantly—these last three days'. Tenniel, Leech, Stanfield and Stone were at once called in to illustrate the little book, while Mark Lemon, to steal a march on the pirates, hurriedly dramatised it for the Keeleys to present at the Adelphi. Eighteen thousand copies were sold in the first week of publication, and the success was celebrated by a book-dinner at Devonshire Terrace.

The Haunted Man may be taken as a pointer to the way Dickens's mind had been working. He had sought by some stratagem to induce forgetfulness of his own past which held incidents he had never breathed a word of even to Kate. Having at the time of his engagement emerged victorious from a hard struggle to become independent, he had seen no reason to expose the details of his squalid upbringing to anyone. Respectability being the master-key to Victorian society, he must have thought his past connection with jails shaming and have believed that if people knew his story it would prejudice his chances of success, and cause him to sink in the esteem of the Hogarths. To the world he was just a successful journalist blossoming into a super-successful novelist and, as far as the people he entertained or associated with were concerned, had no past. This was not at all the way he felt about himself; he was desperately conscious of his past; it was for ever pushing itself forward in one way or another, and he was for ever pushing it back into what he hoped might be oblivion, but after wrestling with the problem in *The Haunted Man* he could promise himself no comfort in a ghost's bargain. It was quite a while before the idea of coaxing the past to display itself in all its hatefulness and humiliation and pinning it down on paper, as one pins butter-flies to a setting board, occurred to him. Forster says that it was a chance question that put the notion into his mind. Dickens's belief that the secrets of his boyhood were unknown was shattered by a man called Dilke, a fellow clerk of his father's at Somerset House. Dilke one day inquired of Forster whether the little boy, Dickens, he had seen at Thomas Barrow's lodging in Gerard Street was not the famous 'Boz'. He then went on to say that he had once walked with John Dickens to a warehouse near the Strand, and had tipped a small boy, working there, half-a-crown and had received in return a very low bow. Forster at once asked Dickens whether he remembered Mr. Dilke. As no reply of any kind was forthcoming, his questioner judged that he must have put his finger on a sore spot. Weeks later, Dickens told Forster that he had unwittingly touched on a matter so painful that 'even to the present hour' he 'could never lose the remembrance of it while he remembered anything'. Soon after this talk he began to write down the account of that part of his childhood which hurt him most. The notion of writing a complete autobiography flitted across his mind, but he soon abandoned it in favour of using such parts of his manuscript as suited him in a new novel, the novel we know as *David Copperfield*. With Forster he now talked over many things he did not care to write about, and from time to time said, 'How much I suffered it is utterly beyond my power to tell'. The actual autobiographical material was only seen by Forster after his friend's death.

The fact that his parents, at the time of his worst humilia-tion, were living happily in the Marshalsea with 'every bodily comfort to hand' had made his own circumstances appear all the more forlorn. He had seen that they had money enough to live in the best prison style, but that they gave him no help until he insisted on getting himself lodged near enough to the prison to take meals with them. This callousness was for him an unforgivable offence. And even when they were released these same parents had made no immediate move to free him from servitude. But one happy day his father had given him a note to hand to James Lamert which, when read, made Lamert turn on him sharply saying it would now be impossible to keep him in the factory. 'With a relief so strange that it was like oppression, I went home', wrote Dickens in his confession; but from that hour till the hour of writing a quarter of a century later no word of his experience was ever breathed by him, and his parents remained as dumb as himself.

What exactly was it that made this facing up to the past so painful? Why did those six weeks spent in the blacking factory hurt so much in retrospect? Why did he mind the fact that his parents lived in the Marshalsea when he was able to make such good use of the Marshalsea in his books? Was he unusually sensitive? Was he peculiarly proud? Was he deeply ashamed of the discreditable hand-to-mouth existence in which his mother had involved him and in which she would have liked to keep him? Was he always measuring himself and his defective education against the more fortunately born friends he made? Was he consumed with self-pity? Was he in fact compartmented from the rest of the world?

The answer to those questions is to be found to some degree in all of us. There are certain things in our lives that, if we are sensitive, we never get used to, which, in other words, never become retrospective but are eternally present. I will give one instance from personal life. As a child of ten I was cleaning a box in which a dormouse lived, and in throwing the hay and food crumbs into the fire I emptied out the sleeping dormouse and heard its one squeak as it fell into the red heart of the coals. It is as vivid and horrifying to me now as it was decades ago, and it enables one to understand why Dickens's childhood never became retrospective, but remained an ever-present reality. The Beadnell romance and the death of Mary Hogarth fell into the same category of experience, for Dickens had in an extreme degree a faculty that we only have in a lesser degree. Because of it he never, in spite of all his warm friendships, his high spirits, his acting, his huge successes, was a truly happy man.

When beginning *David Copperfield*, Dickens had the usual difficulties in hitting on a good title. This time he began with 'Mag's Diversions' and ran through a gamut of 'Copperfield Disclosures', 'Copperfield Survey', 'Copperfield's Confessions', 'Copperfield's Entire', till he finally decided on the title we know.

The Devonshire Terrace household being keyed up over the imminent arrival of a new baby, Dickens ran down to Norwich on New Year's Eve 1848 to get his story started. Leech and Lemon accompanied him and they visited Stanfield Hall, scene of the murder of Isaac Jermy, Recorder of Norwich. To Dickens 'the place seemed to invite such a crime: it had a murderous look about it'. Before going on to Yarmouth he saw the jail in which the murderer Rush was imprisoned and the place of execution which 'we found fit for a gigantic scoundrel's exit'. At Yarmouth he bought a shawl of local make to take home to his wife. After an enjoyable walk to Lowestoft and back he returned to London on January 10. Having got himself into a writing mood he did not lose it even in the commotion caused by the birth of a sixth son, Henry Fielding, on January 13. Immersed in work, he accepted the event calmly, and carried on with his social life with Georgy at his side. At the end of January (1849) Forster and Dickens went as usual to Bath to dine with Landor on his birthday. In thanking them for this visit their host wrote, in his huge sprawling hand:

My thanks were not spoken to you and Dickens for your journey of two hundred miles upon my birthday. Here they are not visible upon the surface of the paper, nor on any surface whatever, but in the heart that is dictating this letter. On the night you left me I wrote the following:

DYING SPEECH OF AN OLD PHILOSOPHER

I strove with none for none were worth my strife.
Nature I loved, and next to Nature, Art;
I warmed both hands before the fire of Life;
It sinks and I am ready to depart.

On his return from Bath, Charles took Kate to Brighton as he always found it possible to work there and the bracing air was good for both of them. The first instalments of *David Copperfield* appeared in May 1849, and at a dinner the following month, at which Mrs. Gaskell, Thackeray, 'Phiz', Mr. and Mrs. Tagart and Mr. and Mrs. Carlyle were his guests in Devonshire Terrace, it delighted their host, when asking after Carlyle's health, to get the reply, 'I am a lone lorn creatur and everythink goes contrairy with me'. Mrs. Gummidge, like her forerunner Mrs. Gamp, was in a fair way to becoming a national figure.

In June he was working at top speed most of the day and in the evening walking about fields in the neighbourhood of London. One evening was spent with Professor Owen at Richmond. A rather faddy young man, Mountstuart Grant Duff, records meeting him there. Dickens struck him as 'singularly unprepossessing' and a little vulgar. This may have been because he was in an 'inimitable' mood and chattered away about Gore House, d'Orsay, and the 'squabbles' that went on at Holland House. There was, of course, every reason at the moment to talk about Gore House, for everyone had been to the auction there and it was estimated that 20,000 people had come to gape. Lady Blessington's friends had been observed as they walked round the rooms by d'Orsay's French valet, who wrote an account of the people he recognised. 'M. Thackeray est venu aussi; et avait les larmes aux yeux en parlant. C'est peut-être la seule personne que j'ai vue réellement affectée à votre départ.' It was one of the last letters Lady Blessington received before her death.

Dickens somehow managed to combine great social

activity with heavy work. Forster chronicles dinner-party after dinner-party at Devonshire Terrace this year. Besides the old stagers like the Macreadys, Sam Rogers, Edwin Landseer, Stanfield, Talfourd and Fonblanque, we find the names of Julius Benedict, Lord Strangford, the Procters, Sir James and Lady Graham, Mrs. Norton, Lady Dufferin, Lord and Lady Lovelace, the Milner Gibsons, Mowbray Morris and Horace Twiss and their wives, Lady Molesworth, Charles Babbage, the John Delanes, Isambard Brunels, Thomas Longmans, Lord Mulgrave, Lord Carlisle and others listed as guests. He also went about a great deal and everywhere his infectious high spirits made a success of almost any party. He was not above giving hosts the humblest assistance. John Millais, asked by a friend to describe 'the dance at Mrs. Collins's', says, 'It was a delightful evening . . . there were many lions, amongst others the famous Dickens, who came for about half an hour and officiated as principal carver'. At this time, whenever Dickens was held up over a chapter, he would run down to the sea for recreation. Near-by beaches having become noisy and crowded, he had to seek some more secluded place to which to migrate with the family in the summer. Rather opportunely, a clergyman friend, James White, who had retired from his profession to write Scottish historical tragedies in the Isle of Wight, offered to let him a house next his own at Bonchurch. At first sight Dickens fell in love with the place, the 'prettiest he had seen at home or abroad'. Conveying the family to this paradise, he rollicked through picnics at Shanklin, dinners at Blackgang Chine, and tea-parties in Lady Jane Swinburne's garden where his own youngsters played with a red-headed boy called Algernon. Till two o'clock each day he remained shut away writing, but in the afternoon laid himself out to amuse the children with excursions, games and conjuring tricks. Charley remembered continual outings and picnics. John Leech commemorated one of them in *Punch*, 'Awful appearance of wops at a picnic party'. Old friends like Talfourd, Leech or Browne, were bidden to share his enjoyment, but

suddenly the rose-tinted glasses turned black; the life became
'hateful', and the place 'a mortal mistake'. Depressed and
tearful, he found himself succumbing to a desire to sleep by
day or waste precious hours in languor. He blamed the
climate. Bonchurch was 'a smashing place', far more disagreeable than 'hot and dirty Naples', 'feverish New York',
'raving Paris' or 'exciting Genoa'. 'A year here and I should
die of prostration', he gasped. To pacify himself he began
to plan his magazine pulpit, now called 'the Dim Design',
then, in a new state of intense irritation, suddenly whisked the
entire family to the Albion Hotel, Broadstairs. There he recovered his spirits and finished the seventh number of *David
Copperfield*.

In *Mr. Brown's Letters to a Young Man about Town*
appearing in *Punch*, *David Copperfield* was highly commended: 'How beautiful it is . . . there are little words and
phrases in his books that are like personal benefits to his
readers'. The writer of *Mr. Brown's Letters* was Thackeray
who was generous-spirited enough to tell a friend that 'the
green chap had beaten the yellow chap of this month hollow'.
And the yellow chap was *Pendennis*, his own autobiographical
novel!

In November 1849 Charles went with Kate to Rockingham
Castle to stay for the first time with the Watsons. He was
very much impressed by its situation and 'its bastion-like
entrance, dating from the days of King Stephen', but even
more impressed by the great honour and consideration paid
him by his host and hostess. He was in 'inimitable' form,
got up theatricals, conjured and danced till three in the
morning. With Mrs. Watson's cousin, Mary Boyle, he
struck up a great friendship. Mary Boyle was two years
older than Dickens, fair, blue-eyed, and only five feet high.
The tradition in the Boyle family to this day is that Dickens
was a naughty man to make love to great-aunt Mary. Like
Dickens, Mary Boyle loved acting, and together they staged
scenes from *The School for Scandal* and concocted a duologue
from *Nicholas Nickleby*. Soon to become 'my dearest

Meery', this young woman was to prove a faithful friend and loving worshipper. To express her constancy to him, she arranged that buttonholes should be provided for him at every public reading and was clever enough to keep this up even during the second American tour. As she herself puts it, 'I now took the hand that for twenty successive years was ever ready to grasp mine in tender friendship and whose pressure still thrills my memory'.[1] It is always said that Dickens took his descriptions of Chesney Wold, the ancestral home of the Dedlocks, from 'green-hearted Rockingham', but *Bleak House* had yet to be written.

Meanwhile at the back of his mind 'the Dim Design' was taking shape. It had begun to define itself as a weekly magazine in which contributors, however distinguished, would be nameless. It would include a serial novel, good poetry, and essays on subjects 'such as knight-errantry, piracy, savages or the sangraal'. Associated with the publication would be 'a Shadow', who would know everything and would comment on everything. The 'Shadow' would haunt the London streets, the churches, the theatres, the prisons, the House of Commons itself: it would talk about what it saw and, when anything new or startling happened, it was hoped that people would wonder what the 'Shadow' would have to say about it. To Dickens it was 'an odd, unsubstantial whimsical new thing, a sort of previously unthought-of power going about . . . the "Thing" at everybody's shoulder'. He wondered whether the paper itself might not be called *The Shadow*. Forster thought this a silly idea and insisted that the word 'Household' should be incorporated in the title. *Household Words* was at last decided on and an office rented in Wellington Street, Strand. There, as his chief helper, was installed his former employee on the *Daily News*, W. H. Wills, an experienced man who had been assistant-editor of *Chambers's Journal* for three years (1842–5), and there, as editor, or as he preferred to call it, conductor, Dickens him-

[1] *Mary Boyle: Her Book*, p. 231.

self settled in to work. We have it from one of the staff, Garett Dumas, that the editor would arrive about 8 A.M. and dictate while pacing up and down the room. One of his tricks was to comb his hair on arrival, a process he repeated again and again, sometimes a hundred times in a morning. By 11 A.M. he had tired himself out and usually went off to the Garrick Club. The office book for *Household Words* shows that R. H. Horne was engaged at five guineas a week, but left after three months, and that both Charles Knight and G. A. Sala were contributors, as well as young George Meredith. It is clear that John Dickens and George Hogarth were also included on the permanent staff.[1] Half the magazine was the property of Dickens (who paid himself £500 a year as conductor); one-quarter was allocated to Bradbury and Evans; one-eighth to Forster; and one-eighth to Wills, who drew a salary of £8 a week. In time *Household Words* became a valuable property soon to be known as the training-ground for the rising generation of writers. On no one was Dickens's influence more stamped than on young Sala, the creator of the miscellaneous leader, the pen-and-ink impressionist doing sketches of Paris and later of Petersburg.

The first number, dated March 30, 1850, exuded in its fore-word a matey, get-together spirit. The editors aspired to be the good comrade of persons of both sexes and all ages, a cherished member of every household in the land. The magazine announced itself as 'the gentle mouthpiece of reform'. Among its more immediate and practical objectives were the removal both of the paper tax and the light tax. It was hoped that through its agency greater and lesser folk would be brought to better acquaintance and kindlier understanding. All countries and nations were to be dealt with, 'for nothing can be a source of real interest to one that does not concern all the rest'. The editor thinks he can hear voices, 'encouraging voices', that say 'Go on!' and he responds, 'We go on cheerily!'

The editorial 'Word' is followed by the first chapter of

[1] March 6, 1850: letter to Wills.

Lizzie Lee by Mrs. Gaskell, a short and dismal serial opening with a Christmas corpse and this an Easter number! In
true miscellany style, 'Valentine's Day at the Post Office',
'Abraham and the Fire Worshippers', 'The Amusements of
the People', 'Incident in the Life of Mademoiselle Clairon'
and a bundle of 'Emigrants' Letters' are included in the
number. These items and others were printed in twenty-
four pages of double-column small type. The presentation
was poor and the material makes dull reading, but if we refer
to contemporary opinion we shall find nothing but praise.
To Edmund Yates the first numbers of *Household Words*
appeared to be 'perfect models of what a magazine intended
for general reading should be'. Dickens's own work was
considered 'admirable', the dawning Sala 'excellent', the
antiquarian lore of Peter Cunningham and Charles Knight
'interesting'. Forster was praised for 'trenchant criticism',
Wilkie Collins for 'first fruits', Horne for his descriptive
powers, Adelaide Procter for her poetic pathos, Henry Spicer
for his odd humour and the 'Roving Englishman' for the
value of his observations.

Not altogether satisfied with his first number, Dickens tried
to infuse more sentiment into the second, for taking all in all
'the lay-out lacked heart'. To make good this deficiency he
wrote *A Child's Dream of a Star* which he could make tender
because it concerned his newly dead sister, Fanny, with whom
as a child he had often wandered in a churchyard under the
stars. One of the functions assumed by the editor was to
clip and improve all contributions so as to give a strictly
family atmosphere to the whole. Mrs. Gaskell found the
editor's blue pencil very trying and protested, only to be told
that he had made the cuts in perfect good faith and would not
willingly do anything to cause her a minute's vexation; but he
continued to use his pencil. Miss Jewsbury, Miss Berwick
(A. Procter) and Mrs. Linton also objected, and George
Eliot would never write for him at all. Elizabeth Lynn (Mrs.
Linton) was inclined, Dickens thought, to imitate Balzac
and her story *Sentiment and Action*, though paid for, was held

up as 'not quite wholesome'. So adversely was the conductor affected by Holm Lee's tale about an unhappy marriage, *Gilbert Massenger*, that he returned it for fear of 'waking too painful emotions'. Emily Jolly, author of *The Wife's Story*, was encouraged to persevere as in her he thought 'a great writer was coming up'. The complaints Dickens received from the ladies he edited only seem to have made him more artful in his emendations, for we find remarks in his letters to the effect that he has cut Miss Martineau in such a way that she will never see the changes. Dickens by degrees evolved a pattern of his own for serial publication. He explained it from time to time in letters to contributors. Movement and action were essential in a first instalment and the early introduction of plot was important. Writing to Bulwer Lytton over his *Strange Story*, the conductor explained his method:

> For the purpose of weekly publication the divisions of the story will often have to be greatly changed. . . . I think I have become by dint of necessity and practice rather cunning in this regard; and perhaps you would not mind my looking to such points from week to week.

It has been calculated that in the weekly serials Dickens tried to arrange for an episode every ten pages and in the monthly serials every eighteen pages. Mrs. Gaskell never learnt to accept his rulings and was infuriated when *North and South* was cut. When it came out in volume form, she explained how she had been obliged to hurry on events. In those days authors had no second copy to refer to and it is doubtful whether Dickens ever let them see the proofs. By the third number the conductor had devised a threepenny monthly supplement called a *Narrative of Events*. This was a valuable publication, edited by John Dickens, giving excellent condensed reports of proceedings in Parliament as well as chronicling the principal law-suits and the important books. There was no editorial or other comment. Opening with a Narrative of Parliament and Politics, it went on to Law and Crime, Accident and Disaster, Social, Sanitary and Municipal

Progress, Obituaries, Colonies and Dependencies, Foreign Events, Literature and Art, Commercial Record, Stocks and Shares and Emigration Figures. Dickens defined the purpose of the *Narrative* as 'another humble means of enabling those who accept us for their friend to bear the world's roughcast events to the anvil of courageous duty and then beat them in shape', a rigmarole of a typically Dickensian type.

Household Words showed signs in the fourth number of becoming even more 'matey' in spirit: it was suggested that with a little goodwill and a little good-humour society might be reformed. 'Supposing', wrote the editor, 'we were all of us to come off our pedestals and mix a little more with those below us, would it do any harm or would it be productive of great and lasting good?' . . . 'Supposing a Watt, a Jenner, a Brunell, a Stevenson or a Hogarth were to sit in the House of Lords, would any one of them really disgrace our Old Nobility?' These 'Supposings', which cover many subjects, are often surprisingly modern and always full of good sense. Dickens is revealed in them as a typical nineteenth-century reformer, and the ideas that he put forward half humorously, half seriously, but always with deep conviction, are ideas that subsequent generations of men have adopted and made applicable to daily life. Thinking it rank folly to exclude whole classes from the management of public affairs when there was such a wealth of ability to draw on, Dickens, with a fraternal instinct rare if not unique in his day, urged those in power to say to the powerless, 'Come, brothers, let us take counsel together and see how we can best manage. . . . Let us all improve ourselves and all abandon something of our extreme opinions for the general harmony.' Having mocked at stock politicians in *Nicholas Nickleby*, he now tried a more direct form of pressure. The people had been fooled long enough. If the country was to be properly run, everyone must henceforth put their shoulders to the wheel. 'Supposing', he asked, 'that governments were to consider public questions less with reference to their own time and more with reference to all time?'

Secret diplomacy was one of the questions tilted at in
'Supposings'. The editor wondered whether the world
would not get on a great deal better if the Foreign Office were
shut up for three days a week. Diplomacy, after all, was a
form of conspiracy and half the time of the Foreign Secretary
was taken up with bringing about situations that must result
in wars, an idea pushed to its cynical conclusion by Adolf
Hitler when he wrote, 'An alliance that does not comprise the
intention of war is senseless and worthless'.

Household Words had a good deal to say about education
and illiteracy. 'The Schoolmaster at Home and Abroad'
must have been written either by Thomas Hughes, the author
of *Tom Brown's Schooldays*, or by someone who had read his
reports on continental education. It is filled with comparative statistics: 'Taking the whole of northern Europe including Scotland, France and Belgium, there is one child to
every two and a quarter of the population acquiring the rudiments of knowledge, while in England there is only one such
pupil to fourteen inhabitants'. This meant that a quarter of
the population could neither read nor write and that half the
children of England attended no place of instruction. These
shameful facts were viewed callously by the Government of
the richest nation in the world, and it was left to private
philanthropy to run schools, 'ragged' schools at that, to save
children from the perils of the streets. In all the German
states as well as in the Scandinavian countries all children from
six upwards were being educated, and taught cleanly ways,
with the result that their appearance equalled that of middle-
class children in England. Abroad, people usually read and
spoke correctly, and had good manners.

Dickens commented on so many important subjects and
advocated so many reforms that it would take more space
than can be spared in a biography of moderate length to deal
with them adequately. It is necessary to compress, even
suppress, much of the material available.

In 'Pet Prisoners' the editor drew attention to the contrast
in diet between the new model prison of Pentonville and the

nearest workhouse, St. Pancras. Why, he asked, should paupers be treated less well than criminals? Why should a man in prison receive 28 ounces of meat weekly and a man in the workhouse 18? The same discrepancy was noticeable in other rations: 140 ounces of bread against 96, 112 ounces of potatoes against 36, and so on. About the man who is neither pauper nor prisoner—the free labourer—he has something even more serious to say. Wages at 12s. a week worked out at £31 : 4s. a year. A prisoner cost £34 to maintain, therefore a free labourer with young children to support, rent to pay, and clothes to buy, had, for the maintenance of himself and family, between £4 and £5 a year *less* than the sum spent on keeping one man in a model prison. Dickens wrote in 1850 and half a century later agricultural workers were still earning a pittance of 12s. a week. It has taken two wars to raise their standard of life. Whirlwinds of Westminster dust were being scattered in men's eyes, 'but it cannot blind us to the real state of things'.

The 'Happy Family' articles or 'Comments by the Raven', are for the most part Dickens's own. His study gave on to the garden in which Grip, the raven, lived. As he watched it cocking its head in a knowing way he made it pass remarks on current events. For example, Grip attacked the conventional practices at funerals by describing a typical *cortège*.

What a scene it was. First of all two dressed-up fellows came, then a hearse and four, then two carriages and four, then horses with plumes and feathers on their heads and black velvet on their backs, and then there was a fellow in the procession carrying a board of them like Italian images, and then there were about five and twenty or thirty men often red in the face with eating and drinking, dressed up in scarves and hat bands and carrying fishing rods, I believe.

The raven's master was careful to leave instructions in his will that his own burial ceremony should be as plain as possible and include but two mourning coaches.

English railways were not immune from censure. Their discomfort was contrasted with the high degree of comfort achieved on the continent, but then, as the editor wryly observed, 'foreign trains were not run in the interests of shareholders'. In an article called 'Lungs for London' (which may be by Wills) attention was drawn to the jerry-building of the moment:

> Bricklayers spread webs and meshes of houses with powerful rapidity in every direction, suburban open spaces being entombed in brick and mortar mausoleums, the Lungs of London are undergoing congestion. Finsbury and Islington have suffered most. Within my recollection Clerkenwell Green was the right colour. Moorfields, Spafields and the East India Company's fields were adorned with grass, and he must be young indeed who cannot remember cricket playing in White Conduit, Canonbury, Shepherd and Shepherdess, Rhodes and Laycock. Thanks to the window tax and the bricklayer fresh air will be thoroughly bricked out. A bath for Finsbury is too urgent a demand for dense population to allow of much time being wasted in knocking at the door of the Treasury. The public must bestir *themselves*.

Many of the wrongs attacked by Dickens remained wrongs for generations, some of them still endure. The spirit of *Household Words* is the spirit of reform: its slogan is to inspire people to become alert and active in bringing about their own salvation.

Henry Morley, founder of Morley College, was a contributor and wrote articles accusing employers of not providing adequate protection for operatives against machines. Miss Martineau, on behalf of the National Association of Manufacturers, was put up to reply. Morley then attacked the editor for printing her 'misstatements'. It seemed that the editor had not read her disclaimer before it went to press. Put into a very bad temper by the incident, he wrote, 'I do not suppose there was ever such a wrong-headed woman born—such a vain one or such a humbug'.

For the next twenty years Dickens was to be a magazine editor. Later on his controllership loosened into a general overseership and the spade-work was all carried out by Wills, who was continually exhorted to keep *Household Words* imaginative.

One would have thought that work on *Household Words* and the writing of *David Copperfield* provided employment enough for one spring, but almost as soon as the magazine was launched Dickens took Kate and Georgy to Knebworth for a week to discuss a new scheme propounded by Bulwer Lytton for improving the lot of writers and artists. The scheme took Dickens's fancy and he hurled himself into plans for producing money to finance the undertaking, and as a consequence we shall presently see how much of his priceless time was squandered on theatrical productions.

In June Dickens went to Paris with Maclise to see pictures and plays. They stayed at the Hôtel Windsor, but the weather was far too hot for them to enjoy being cooped up in theatres. 'I am half dead', he wrote, 'and have nothing on but a shirt and a pair of white trousers.' Ostensibly he had timed his visit to see Rachel in her last performance of 'Lucretia' before she came over to London for the season, but his sense of anxiety about *Household Words* made him feel after two days that he had been absent for a year. On his return he commissioned Augustus Egg to paint him a portrait of Georgina. It is a small circular picture of considerable charm and shows a girl in profile bending over needlework.

As Kate was expecting a baby in August, Dickens arranged for his sister-in-law and the rest of the family to go to Broadstairs for the hot months while Kate remained in London. As soon as the new baby was born, Dickens joined the Broadstairs party, and it is now for the first time that we find him talking of 'my little housekeeper Miss Hogarth'. It was the first occasion they had kept house together. Who could have foreseen that in seven years' time Kate would have been eliminated from her position as wife and mother and that her sister would be installed as permanent housekeeper in her stead?

The year ended with the 'extra' Christmas number of

Household Words for which Dickens wrote *The Christmas Tree*. It is a kaleidoscope of burning tapers, sparkling ornaments and changing pictures of angels talking to shepherds, travellers following a star, a baby in a manger, and scene after scene in the life of Jesus. A whispered message may be heard coming from the branches of the Tree, 'This in commemoration of the law of love and kindness, mercy and compassion. This in remembrance of ME.' For Christmas 1851 Dickens in like mood wrote *What Christmas is as we grow older*. At Christmas we should shut out from our firesides—Nothing. We must welcome the dead, the living, all whom we love. 'Lost parent, dear child, dear husband, wife, brother, sister, we will not discard you. You shall hold your cherished place in our Christmas hearts and by our Christmas fires, and in the season of immortal hope and on the birthday of immortal mercy we will shut out Nothing.'

Chapter 18

THE GUILD OF LITERATURE AND ART

Every reform was once a private opinion.
R. W. EMERSON

THE Guild of Literature and Art, planned at Knebworth in the spring of 1850, was in essence a scheme for persuading authors and painters to band themselves together in their own interests.[1] It was proposed that each member should take out a life-policy at some recognised insurance office, and that those who through ill-health or age were uninsurable should be elected as associates of the Guild and share, if indigent, in the benefactions of the Fund to be accumulated by the founders. Certain land in the vicinity of Stevenage was by the generosity of Bulwer Lytton to be made over to the Guild, and moneys to be derived from certain theatrical performances as well as the copyright in certain plays were to be ear-marked for building houses and endowing the Guild. The scheme, as at first outlined, resembled the prospectus of a provident society and, as such, was not smiled on by the people it was designed to benefit. The promoters, however, were so convinced that the Guild was wanted and that they could by forging ahead with their plans make certain of eventual popularity among writers and artists, that coldness and indifference on the part of writers and artists did not discourage them.

In considering the lot of authors of the past and the means of benefiting authors of his own day, Dickens was haunted by these lines of Goldsmith:

> The men who to mankind most good have brought
> Have had the world's worst evils to endure;
> Nor till the world, for which its fools have thought,
> Thinks for itself, can wisdom bring the cure.

[1] See *Household Words*, May 12, 1851.

Nothing seems to have touched him more than the acute poverty in which many writers lived and the want of appreciation accorded to them by their contemporaries. Every time he went into Sam Rogers's house he used to glance at Milton's receipt for *Paradise Lost*, and remind himself that great Dr. Johnson sold his rights in *Rasselas* to pay for his mother's funeral. It was a bad tradition that must at all costs be broken with.

When staying with Bulwer Lytton in the spring, Dickens had suggested that it might be well to advertise the nascent Guild to their friends by playing *Every Man in His Humour* in the banqueting hall at Knebworth. It would not take long to rehearse, he could get his old cast together, and the clothes were still in good condition. Would it not be a good plan to prepare to give three representations in the autumn as soon as he had got *David Copperfield* off his hands? Bulwer Lytton welcomed the idea and was more than ready to put his house at the disposal of the actors. So in November the troupe arrived with all their properties. *Animal Magnetism*, a farce by Mrs. Inchbald, was to be included in the programme and in this Kate Dickens was to act, but, as she sprained her ankle at the last moment, Georgy took her part. Fired by the theatrical atmosphere, Bulwer Lytton set to work to write a play for Guild production in London, while Dickens and Mark Lemon concocted another.

It was a good moment to launch a scheme of the kind, for the Great Exhibition (to be opened by the Queen on May 1, 1851) would draw crowds of visitors to London many of whom would have money to spend. In February, Dickens, a shivering figure in furs, was piloted over the vast glass building which was only partially roofed. He observed that it did not look as if it could possibly be finished in time and Paxton replied, 'I think it will, but mind I don't say it will'. When the structure was completed and filled with exhibits, Dickens found it even more unattractive and uninteresting than when it was half finished and empty, and this despite the fact that homage had been paid to his genius in statues of Oliver Twist and Little Nell, both of which were conspicuously displayed.[1] In deference to the demands of his family he visited the Exhibition twice, wandered miserably through its avenues for a short time, then left saying that his 'eyes refused to focus' and that he felt 'used-up' and bewildered. To Mrs. Watson he wrote, 'It is to me terrible duffery'.

> I have a natural horror of sights and the fusion of so many sights in one has not decreased it. I am not sure that I have seen anything but the fountain and perhaps the Amazon. It is a dreadful thing to be obliged to be false, but when anyone says, 'Have you seen?' I say 'Yes,' because if I don't I know he'll explain it.

The Guild committee, agreed that in spite of the spending capacity of holiday crowds they should aim at economy in their London productions, hired the Hanover Square Rooms so as to avoid the expenses of a regular theatre. In the provinces they hoped to secure concert halls for their purpose. Someone suggested that it would be well to begin their campaign in a private house and try to get the Queen to patronise the scheme in person. This idea was warmly taken up and discussed, with the result that Dickens was deputed to approach the Duke of Devonshire and ask him whether he would lend Devonshire House for the first performance of *Not So Bad as We Seem*, a new play by Bulwer Lytton. In a carefully composed letter he threw himself on the Duke's 'generous attachment to Art and Letters', explaining that no trouble would be incurred by him should he accede to the request, and that no damage would be done since, by means of a transportable stage, light scenery and new mechanism, any room could be made to serve as a theatre at a few hours' notice. The opening of Devonshire House for this purpose would render the success of the scheme certain.

---

[1] By Hughes Ball of Boston (English born). He is said to have executed an Oliver Twist in marble for Chatsworth, but no trace of it exists. His Little Nell was removed in 1852 to the Athenaeum, Boston.

Within a couple of hours of dispatching this appeal Dickens received from the Duke a charming letter placing his services, his subscription and his house at the disposal of the Fund. He added that he had long wished to know Dickens better, having so far only met him in crowded rooms. With all the enormous energy that on occasion he could put forth, Dickens now set himself to make the performance perfect of its kind. His old cast rallied gladly round him and attracted to its ranks new members. The newcomer who concerns us most is young Wilkie Collins who had been sounded by Augustus Egg as to whether he would take the part of Smart, valet to Sir Robert Wilmot (played by Dickens), in *Not So Bad as We Seem*. Egg then invited Dickens and Collins to meet at his home, Ivy Cottage in Black Lion Lane (Queen's Road), and this initiated the friendship that was to squeeze Forster out of his position as Dickens's unique confidant. Collins, generally portrayed with a bushy beard, at this time was a clean-shaven man in spectacles, with hands and feet so small that he took women's sizes in gloves and shoes. This quiet rather smug-looking young person, with his taste for coloured ties and waistcoats, charmed Dickens as no young man had charmed him for years. Soon he became the indispensable companion of his more frivolous hours.

Dickens, as we know, was autocratic as a stage manager and he now urgently exhorted all players to put their backs into rehearsals. Macready was permitting them to use Covent Garden for this purpose and was even going to watch them at work. The later rehearsals would be taken at Devonshire House when the stage had been erected and the scenes assembled. These scenes were in course of painting in the studios of Stanfield, David Roberts and Landseer. The manager's desire was that the production should reach perfection in every detail.

The cast, when the first rehearsal was called at Devonshire House, were delighted with the 'condescension' of the Duke in permitting them, in their 'common cabs', to drive through his wooden gates in Piccadilly, and in giving them 'splendid

luncheons' which he himself attended and at which his 'footmen waited equally on all'.[1]   Some of the players made an
unfortunate mistake on the first day they set foot in the house,
for on seeing a tall elderly gentleman in black examining the
stage, they had ordered him out of the way.   It turned out to
be the Duke.

Paxton, with great efficiency, put the theatre up, arranged
for the seating of the audience, and for the masking of the
pictures by hoardings covered with crimson velvet.   A
special box was built for the Queen, and her chair, raised above
the floor, was set in a bower of magnolias, jasmine and roses
while the sides and arches were hung with tendrils dotted
with stephanotis on which shimmered dew-drops of crystal
and opal.   There was a profusion of candles, and scented oil
was provided for the lamps.[2]   Dickens as a stage manager
was consulted about every detail and Thackeray compared
him to Goethe in the theatre at Weimar.   Helpers worked
with a will and soon Dickens could write to the Queen's
equerry to inquire what date would suit her Majesty for the
first night.   He also asked the Duke of Devonshire whether
it would be in order to charge three guineas for each seat.
The answer he got encouraged him to ask more, and every
seat was sold at the £5 printed on the ticket of admission.   A
second performance took place ten days later to console
would-be ticket-buyers for the first, and on this occasion two
guineas was charged.

Just when Dickens had completed all his arrangements,
he was overtaken by a run of great misfortunes.   Kate, who
had been very poorly, was recuperating at Malvern with
Georgy for company.   Charles, who had taken her there,
was paying her another visit from which he was recalled
almost at once to London by the news of his father's serious
illness.   He was just in time to see him alive, and then had
to postpone all rehearsals till the funeral was over.   A few
days after they had been resumed, Charles, under very great

pressure, consented to fulfil an old standing engagement, that of taking the chair at the annual dinner of the General Theatrical Fund which they said would be a financial failure without him. Just before leaving Devonshire Terrace for the dinner he ran up to the nursery to say good-night to baby Dora who had always been a rather ailing child. Before he had concluded his appeal for the Theatrical Fund little Dora had fallen into convulsions and by the time he got home she was dead. It was a terrible shock.

Forster at once offered to go down and break the sad news to Kate at Malvern, taking with him a letter from Charles, who had to arrange for the child's funeral. Next morning the harassed producer wrote to the Queen's equerry begging that the first performance be postponed till some date between May 13 and May 20. May 16 was chosen. This was the occasion when Rosina Bulwer, always apt to be spiteful about her husband's friends, especially where Forster and Dickens were concerned, made the malicious comment, 'Oh, Mr. Dickens makes a habit of acting with a dead father in one pocket and a dead baby in the other'.

Meanwhile the Duke had studied *Not So Bad as We Seem* carefully and told the author that he liked it, but that in rehearsal Forster was liable to be rather loud-voiced and vulgar. Frank Stone, on the other hand, made a grave, dignified Duke of Middlesex, and Dickens, though hearty enough to be a sea captain, played the fop about town with credit. In the production he found much to praise; the clothes were gay and correct; the snuff-boxes the better for being real; on the whole the picture of high-life in the reign of George I was exact. The Duke cautioned Dickens about possible gate-crashing, and Bulwer Lytton, nervous lest his wife should force her way in as an orange-girl or get someone to transfer a ticket to her, arranged for personal passes to be issued even for dress rehearsals. On the first night every window on the stage or in the property room had to be left wide open by the Queen's wish, and no farce followed the play as 'the Queen got very restless about midnight'.   Orders were given that everyone must be seated by 8.45 P.M. and must sit quiet while the Duke's private band (composed for the occasion of students from the R.A.M.) entertained the company with a specially composed overture by Mr. Coote.

Dickens had been under considerable strain, and at the first performance felt terribly unwell.   He was alarmed, as he played his part, to see his legs and ankles swelling up rapidly. Somehow he got through the evening and was rewarded for his immense pains by immense applause led by the Queen herself.   At the second performance at Devonshire House ten days later he was himself again, and played in *Mr. Nightingale's Diary*, the farce concocted by himself and Lemon.   It is worth noting that in this farce Dickens took several parts, throwing himself whole-heartedly into each. The play was set in Malvern Wells and he impersonated an old woman in trouble over a missing child, a sexton with a quavering voice and a complacent smile, a *malade imaginaire*, a waiter and so on, six characters in all.   Arthur Helps, who knew him well, said, 'When he read or spoke, the whole man read or spoke'.   *Mr. Nightingale's Diary* was the forerunner of all the later 'Readings'; it gave him the conviction that he could impersonate as many people as he chose.

Macaulay, after attending the first performance of Bulwer Lytton's play, wrote at once to the author asking whether he had no misgivings about the Guild it was proposed to found. Would he not be wise to form a list of the thirty best writers, strike off all who required no assistance, all who required assistance and were receiving state pensions, and then see who was left?   Twenty-five out of the thirty were bound to fall into one or the other class and the Guild would then be left to support second-rate writers or even failures.   No letters could at this time damp Bulwer Lytton's ardour for the scheme, though Macaulay was in the long run to be justified in his apprehensions.

The two performances at Devonshire House were followed by three at the Hanover Rooms, all of which were well attended. The short London season was, however, but the prelude to a campaign organised for the following year, a tour in which Derby, Sheffield, Nottingham, Sunderland, New-castle, Manchester and Liverpool were included. The Duke of Devonshire continued to support them and at Derby sat among the audience while scene-shifters peeped through cracks to get a look at him. The Duke also graced the Sheffield performance and asked Dickens to come and stay at Chatsworth, but the author had to rush home 'lest there should be no *Bleak House* for October'. The enthusiasm displayed by the audience in the Free Trade Hall in Liverpool put 'Boz' in mind of the nights he had spent at the opera in Genoa and Milan. He wrote to Bulwer Lytton about it:[1]

> I left Liverpool at 4 o'clock this morning and am so blinded by excitement, gas, waving hats and handkerchiefs, that I can hardly see to write; but I cannot go to bed without telling you what a triumph we have had. . . . I sincerely believe that we have the ball at out feet and may throw it up to the very Heaven of Heavens.

Manchester was equally rapturous. Four thousand people stood and cheered and most delightful of all a stage-carpenter told him, 'It's a universal observation in the profession, sir, that it was a great loss to the public when you took to writing books'. Bristol showed 'prodigious enthusiasm'. Birming-ham gave them the warmest of welcomes. 'We have won a position for the idea,' trumpeted Dickens. 'We carry the fiery cross! I have been so happy I could have cried.' Kate and Georgy, who toured with the company, shared in the excitements of the experience. The tour closed with a Manchester banquet at which Dickens and Bulwer Lytton explained the aims of the Guild. They were glad to announce that a sum of £4000 had been made by means of plays, and Bulwer Lytton (just returned as a Tory for the county of Hertford) told his audience of his intention of introducing a bill into Parliament to incorporate the Guild which relied for

[1] February 15, 1852.

its support on the adherence of all writers and artists. In 1854 he carried this bill through Parliament and the Guild was incorporated.[1] Its objects were as follows:

1. To aid those of its members who follow Literature or the Fine Arts as a profession, and obtain the insurances upon their lives;
2. To establish a provident sickness fund for its members;
3. To provide dwellings for its members and to grant annuities to them or their widows.

One of the several weak features of the bill was that it could not become operative for seven years, which gave more than enough time for the enthusiasm that generated the scheme to evaporate. We shall assist later on in this book at the opening of the first Guild houses.

Having followed the fortunes of the Guild in 1852, we must now revert to the year 1851 in order to record the evacuation of Devonshire Terrace by the Dickens family and the hunt for another London home. For most of the summer of this year Dickens made a point of sleeping in the country whenever he got the chance, partly because the lease of his house had come to an end and partly because of the crowded condition of London. Fort House, Broadstairs, was rented by him and the family moved there in May. It was from Fort House that he came up for the *Copperfield* banquet in June. Given at the Star and Garter at Richmond and remarkable in so far as women writers were for the first time bidden to the feast, it is said to have been 'the pleasantest of all the book-dinners'. Thackeray and Alfred Tennyson were among the guests.

Now that Dickens was a world figure many of the foreign visitors to the Exhibition brought with them letters of introduction to 'Boz'. 'Boz', however, was not able to do much for them as he could not occupy Tavistock House till October. Tavistock House, Bloomsbury, belonged to his friend Frank

[1] In 1897 another Act was passed dissolving the Guild and bestowing its funds on the Royal Literary Society. The houses were sold for £2000.

Stone and he was only lured to live so far from a park by
the idea that the big studio or some other room would be
easily convertible into a small theatre. As with Devonshire
Terrace, he saw to all the furnishing himself, ordering
curtains and carpets, arranging for glass mirrors and console
tables on the landing and planning bookcases between study
and dining-room, complete with dummy book-backs bearing
titles that it had amused him to invent. Here are some of
them:

> *Five Minutes in China* (3 vols.)
> *Forty Winks at the Pyramids* (2 vols.)
> *Abernethy on the Constitution* (2 vols.)
> *History of the Middling Ages* (6 vols.)
> *The Quarrelly Review* (4 vols.)
> *Lady Godiva on the Horse*
> *Hansard's Guide to Refreshing Sleep*
> (as many vols. as possible).

He enjoyed getting in to the new home and was observed
while doing so by a German author, Theodor Fontane, who
sauntered in the garden in front of Dickens's house, fervently
wishing that the air that blew there would communicate to
him the secret spirit of London. 'Dickens', he wrote, 'lives
in a charming garden-surrounded building standing between
St. Pancras and our house. I have not yet had the courage to
look him up, and I probably never shall have it, as he is
so overrun by Germans.'[1] He was also overrun by other
foreigners. A Frenchman made the excuse of admiration
in calling on him. 'Your fame and the universal sympathy
you inspire doubtless expose you to innumerable intrusions.
Your door is always besieged, you must be visited every day
by princes, statesmen, scholars, writers, artists and even madmen.' 'Yes, madmen! madmen! Madmen! they alone
amuse me,' shouted Dickens, and pushed his visitor out by
the shoulders.[2]

---

[1] *Ein Sommer in London in 1852.*
[2] *The Dickensian,* vol. ix, p. 156.

The use made by Dickens of the material to hand in the city of London had, as we have already seen, been a cause of envy and admiration to all literary Germans. More than ever did they seem to feel themselves provincials. Auerbach said, 'Dickens had the luck to be born an Englishman. What are we? Always, always provincials. What has Freytag done? what have I done? We have dealt with provincial life.' Time and again the complaint went up that Germany had no national existence, no centre of national culture, no focus of modern life.

Household Words seems to have had an immediate influence in Germany, for Gutzkow produced a publication with the same kind of title—'Conversations by the Household Hearth', but then everything Dickens wrote now had its repercussions abroad. *Soll und Haben* by Freytag is under his influence, and Gustav Frenssen says of *Pickwick* in his diary: '*Pickwick* is a wonderful work produced with dynamic power'. Comparing Dickens with Balzac, Frenssen found the Frenchman's work 'rather hollow'.

So much for Dickens's German admirers. His own belief in German education was such as to cause him to send his eldest boy, Charley, straight from school to Leipzig and a younger boy to Hamburg. The results were not what he had hoped for.

When the Duke of Wellington died, Charley, at the moment a wet bob at Eton, entreated his father to take him to St. Paul's for the funeral. By the good offices of the Duke of Devonshire six permits for the Cathedral were secured for 'Mr. Dickens and family'.

Reporting on the ceremony to Miss Coutts, Dickens said:

The whole public has gone mad about the funeral of the Duke. I think it a grievous thing, a lapse into barbarous practices and a most ludicrous contrast to the calm good sense and example of responsibility set by the Queen Dowager . . . a pernicious corruption of the popular mind just beginning to awaken from the long dream of inconsistencies, monstrosities, horrors and ruinous expenses

M

that has beset all classes of society in connexion with death. I shall try and present the case in *Household Words*; at present I might as well whistle into the sea.

Trading in Death appeared in *Household Words* in November.[1]

A panegyric on the dead Duke was delivered in the House of Commons by the leader of the Conservative Party, Disraeli. His speech reminded some reporters of something they already knew and the *Morning Chronicle* made a scoop by hunting up Thiers's oration on Marshal Mortier and printing it in parallel columns with Disraeli's speech: they were identical. Pleased with their astuteness, they went on to extract from *Venetia* the character of Lord Cadurcis and printed it side by side with the character of Lord Byron drawn by Mr. Macaulay in the *Edinburgh Review*, in which all contributors were anonymous. The explanation offered by Disraeli was that he copied anything that struck him and did not know afterwards whether he had written the extracts or not. Macaulay ignored the incident.

In reading through Dickens's letters it is a continual surprise to see how much time and consideration he gave to Miss Coutts's many projects of social reform. Whether it is the furnishing of the little house of rescue at Shepherd's Bush or the uniform to be worn by its inmates or the leaflet to be handed by the police to women on the streets, he was always at her service, and all the time he was helping with the Urania Cottage scheme, he was writing *David Copperfield*. He explained in his leaflet that Miss Coutts, as she watched the girls on the pavements by her house, had been troubled and moved and was now resolved to make a home for them, a place where they can be taught household work. She wishes to give them a chance to begin life afresh and hopes to restore them to society in a place where no one will know of their past and where they will be able to find husbands. 'Leave prison, leave your present life!' urged Dickens. 'Resolve to begin anew, but don't, if you are not resolved and

[1] November 27, 1852.

not serious, take up the space another girl might occupy. Whether you accept or reject the offer think it over' [1]—signed, Your Friend.

Miss Coutts, as eager to abolish slums as to save girls, decided (since no government would take action in the matter) to rehouse ten thousand slum dwellers of Bethnal Green. With Dickens she discussed what form the building should assume. Dickens was of opinion that tenement houses offered the best chance of good air and green open spaces.

I have no doubt [he wrote] that the large houses are the best. You never can, for the same money, offer anything like the same advantage in small houses. It is not desirable to encourage small carpenters or builders to run up small dwelling houses. If they had been discouraged long ago London would be an immeasurably healthier place than it can be made in scores of years to come. If you go into any common outskirts of the town now and see the advancing army of brick and mortar laying waste the country fields and shutting out the air, you cannot fail to be struck by the consideration that if large buildings had been erected for the working people instead of the absurd and expensive walnut shells in which they live, London would have been about a third of its present size and every family would have had a country walk miles nearer to their own door. Besides this, men would have been nearer to their work . . . there would have been thicker walls of separation and better means of separation than you can ever give (except at preposterous cost in small tenements) and they would have had gas, water, drainage, and a variety of other humanizing things which you can't give them so well in little houses. Further, in little houses you must keep them near the ground and you cannot possibly afford such sound and wholesome foundations (remedying this objection) in little houses. [2]

As a result of Dickens's advice Miss Coutts paid for the erection of tenement buildings in Bethnal Green.

The problems raised by rehousing and sanitary reform had

interested Dickens passionately ever since he had got to know Dr. Southwood Smith. At a dinner of the Metropolitan Sanitary Association presided over by Lord Carlisle at Soyer's Symposium[1] (Gore House) Dickens proposed a toast to the Board of Health coupled with the name of Lord Ashley and expatiated on the sufferings of the suburbs without water, pleading earnestly for the poor man for whom 'cleanliness must be legislated for before godliness'.

> Give him and his a glimpse of heaven [he pleaded]. Give them water, help them to be clean. Take the body of the dead relative from the room where the living live with it, and where such loathsome familiarity deprives death itself of awe. Then, but not before, will they be brought willingly to hear of Him whose thoughts were so much with the wretched and who had compassion for all human sorrow.

On the same theme Dickens at this time also wrote an article for *Punch*, 'Dreadful Hardships'. It never appeared in *Punch* as it was considered better to refer to the matter in a cartoon. To say that Dickens was always working for social reform is almost to understate his constant attitude to human suffering and human degradation. He did more than work, he put his whole being into it, and where the poor and helpless were concerned his tenderness of heart was unsurpassed.

[1] May 10, 1851. See Spielman's *History of Punch*.

Chapter 19

COOKERY AND BOULOGNE

*His genius was his fellow-feeling with his race; his mere
personality was never the bound or limit to his perceptions.*
                                                    JOHN FORSTER

As soon as he was comfortably established in Tavistock
House, Dickens began work on a new novel. The book
was some time settling into its permanent name as he wanted
the title to indicate that it was the story of 'a house that got
into Chancery and could not get out': eventually it became
Bleak House. Written primarily to draw attention to the
abuses of Chancery practice, he based the case of Jarndyce
and Jarndyce on the notorious Jennings case which had been,
at intervals, before the Court for ninety years. He also made
use of a case supplied him by a correspondent which figures
in the fifteenth chapter as the Gridley case. In the preface he
is careful to state that the facts set out in the book are substantially true and even within the truth.

The success of *David Copperfield*, so largely due to self-
portraiture, encouraged Dickens, in *Bleak House*, to be a
little bolder and to incorporate among its characters two well-
known literary men, who recognised themselves in its pages,
and one, if not two, literary women who did not see themselves as others saw them. These experiments were really an
extension of that method of romanticising familiar things in
which Dickens used to say his art consisted. Some readers
professed to be shocked that he should make use of friends in
this manner, but they must have been people unacquainted
with the fact that the imagination does not work in a vacuum
and that most novelists, and certainly all great novelists,
create capital from the material of their own experience.
Dickens's masters, Smollett, Fielding and Goldsmith, had
modelled their characters on themselves, their womenkind

or their friends; even Scott had been no exception to this practice. There is, however, an unwritten code which novelists must not ignore: the likeness must never be photographic, for in that case, as Forster points out, it becomes mere reporting and may result in 'a radical wrong to the victim'. The line of demarcation being really an aesthetic one, it is in practice hard to define. According to contemporary opinion, it was not overreached in the case of Landor and considerably overreached in the case of Leigh Hunt.

Landor at this time was still living at Bath, worshipping Dickens, and in process of dedicating his latest book to him, but Leigh Hunt was in London and the conductor was constantly dealing with him as the contributor of dull articles [1] to *Household Words*. Admittedly the portrait of Skimpole is a far less agreeable one than that of Boythorn, but then Dickens liked Leigh Hunt less than he liked Landor and preferences will out. Lawrence Boythorn is described by Jarndyce, who had been at school with him, as

> The most impetuous boy in the world, and he is now the most impetuous man. He was then the loudest boy in the world, and he is now the loudest man. He was then the heartiest and sturdiest boy in the world and he is now the heartiest and sturdiest man. He is a tremendous fellow . . . there's no simile for his lungs. Talking, laughing, or snoring they make the beams of the house shake . . . but it's the inside of the man, the warm heart of the man, the passion of the man, the fresh blood of the man . . . that I speak of.

There is nothing unattractive about this description; one is drawn to Boythorn rather than repelled, and when he comes into the room he is even more likeable:

> He was not only a very handsome old gentleman—upright and stalwart as he had been described to us—with a massive grey head, a fine composure of face when silent . . . he was such a true gentleman in his manner, so chivalrously polite his face lighted by a smile of so much sweet-

<hr>

[1] See 'Lounging in Kensington', 'Gore House', etc. etc.

ness and tenderness, and it seemed so plain that he had nothing to hide but showed himself exactly as he was . . . that really I could not help looking at him with equal pleasure as . . . he smilingly conversed with Ada and me, or was led by Mr. Jarndyce into some great volley of superlatives, or threw up his head like a bloodhound, and gave out that tremendous Ha, ha, ha!

And here is the description of Harold Skimpole, in other words, the portrait of Leigh Hunt, that gave so much offence:

> He was a bright little creature, with rather a large head; but a delicate face, and a sweet voice, and there was a perfect charm in him. All he said was so free from effort and spontaneous, and was said with such a captivating gaiety, that it was fascinating to hear him talk. . . . He had more the appearance of a damaged young man, than a well-preserved elderly one. There was an easy negligence in his manner and even in his dress (his hair carelessly disposed, and his neckerchief loose and flowing, as I have seen artists paint their own portraits) which I could not separate from the idea of a romantic youth who had undergone some unique process of depreciation.

Stressing as it does the eternal wish to be youthful that led Hunt to such posing at sixty-five, this presentation was cruel, but it may have been the character study in irresponsibility that hurt him most:

> I am constantly being bailed out, like a boat; or paid off like a ship's company. Somebody always does it for me. *I* can't do it, you know, for I never have any money; but Somebody does it. I get out by Somebody's means, I'm not like the starling: I get out. If you were to ask me who Somebody is, upon my word, I couldn't tell you. Let us drink to Somebody. God bless him!

Though Leigh Hunt was considerably offended by these passages and by the description of Skimpole's life in the Polygon, he did not quarrel with his bread and butter, but went on inviting his 'dear Dickens' to his house in Hammersmith. Several letters of refusal are printed in the Nonesuch *Letters*, but no acceptances.

The organising, pamphleteering Mrs. Jellyby was said by some contemporaries to be a caricature of Harriet Martineau, who had written twenty-five tales illustrating aspects of Political Economy. Mrs. Jellyby is breathlessly described in *Bleak House* as

> a lady of remarkable strength of character, who has devoted herself to an extensive variety of public subjects, at various times, and especially to the subject of Africa with a view to the general cultivation of the coffee berry *and* the natives, and the happy settlement of our superabundant home population in Borrioboola-Gha on the left bank of the Niger.

Possibly Dickens as 'conductor' of *Household Words* had his contributor, Harriet Martineau, as much on his mind as Leigh Hunt at the time he wrote this book, for there is a hint of her in Mrs. Pardiggle, 'a School lady, a Visiting lady, a Reading lady, a Distributing lady, and on the Social Linen Box Committee and many general committees', but then Harriet Martineau's activities were so multiple that she might well be split up into several persons. Neither Mrs. Jellyby nor Mrs. Pardiggle gave offence to anyone, for Harriet Martineau did not recognise herself in either character. But Mrs. Hill, the original of Miss Mowcher in *David Copperfield*, protested against being guyed.

Forster was fussed by the likenesses when he went over the *Bleak House* manuscript, and made Dickens change the Christian name of Skimpole from Leonard to Harold, and modify certain sentences in which the portrait was, in his opinion, too particular. The practice of drawing from life, as we shall see in *Little Dorrit*, was henceforth persevered in by Dickens. As a prolific author writing to schedule he was driven to employ a realistic technique based on experience.

The fly-wheel of the story of *Bleak House* is the Court of Chancery: all cogs move in connection with it. Principal and lesser persons alike are all drawn insensibly into the machinery and are one by one lethalised by the monster operating as Justice and Equity. The villain of the piece is the Law, protector of the Vested Interest. The Lord Chancellor and his Court represent the apparatus of evil. And not only were real institutions and real people depicted in this book, but real places like Chancery Court, Belgrave Square and Forster's chambers, and real scenery from Rockingham, observations on trees, and the behaviour of light, clouds and shadows. *Bleak House*, though it demanded great concentration, did not give its author so much trouble to construct as *Dombey and Son* had done. It was dedicated to his colleagues in the Guild of Literature and Art, and illustrated with forty plates by 'Phiz'. 'Browne has done Skimpole and helped to make him singularly unlike the great original', wrote Dickens to Forster.

That it was not favourably reviewed is no matter for surprise. Few of Dickens's novels ever were, and this time he was told that as a writer he had every fault and as a reformer tilted against windmills. In this connection it is well to remind ourselves of the words written by Landor to Edith Southey on the subject of reviewing in general: 'In my father's library was the *Critical Review* from its commencement; and it would have taught me, if I could not even at a very early age teach myself better, that Fielding, Sterne, and Goldsmith were really worth nothing'.

Lord Denman, Chief Justice of England, who disapproved of *Bleak House* on account of its central theme, attacked it as it came out on the minor issue of Mrs. Jellyby, saying that it would discourage efforts to put down slavery, and Miss Harriet Martineau followed suit. These attacks had no effect on general readers, who showed their appreciation by buying nearly twice as many copies of *Bleak House* as they had done of *David Copperfield*.

During the summer of 1851, Kate Dickens, who was as usual expecting a baby, had taken to her pen and beguiled the months of comparative inactivity by putting together a

cookery book entitled *What shall we have for Dinner?*[1]
Writing as Lady Maria Clutterbuck, Kate, in a foreword,
explained that the late Sir Jonas Clutterbuck had, in addition
to a host of other virtues, enjoyed a good appetite and excellent digestion and that he had been kept in a state of connubial
bliss by a wife who studied his food:

> Sir Jonas was not a gourmand, although a man of great
> gastronomical experience.   Richmond never saw him more
> than once a month and he was a rare visitor to Black-
> wall and Greenwich.   Of course he attended most of the
> Corporation dinners as a matter of duty and now and then
> partook of a turtle feast at some celebrated place in the
> City; but these dinners were only exceptions, his general
> practice being to dine at home.

His relict believed that by her study of his appetite she had
been enabled to 'secure possession of his esteem unto the last'.
Female confidantes had told her that their daily life had been
embittered by 'that surplusage of mutton or redundancy of
chops that drives men to the club'.   To rescue her friends
from such domestic suffering she has consented to give to
the world her bills of fare.   And the really awful secret of
this little book was that the bills of fare it contained were all
taken from dinners given by Mr. and Mrs. Dickens!   Charley
in his 'Reminiscences' says: 'My mother published under the
name of Lady Clutterbuck a book of our daily bills of fare at
Tavistock House'.

In reading it one learns odd things about Victorian dishing-
up and about the sequence of viands.   Dressed crab was
served at the end of a meal: cod's head went with soles, smelts
with turbot.   It was advised that a leg of mutton be stuffed
with oysters, eggs and minced onions.   Most menus conclude with toasted cheese or bloaters.   Calling to mind the
atmosphere of his home, Charley Dickens later exclaimed,
'How many meals began with milk punch and ended with

---

[1] *What shall we have for Dinner?* Satisfactorily answered by numerous
Bills of Fare for from two to eighteen persons by Lady Maria Clutterbuck.
Bradbury and Evans, 1851.

toasted cheese I cannot tell you!' Reviewers, though they praised the book, wondered how long any man could survive the consumption of so much toasted cheese.

Some of the recipes were à *la Soyer* after the famous cook who at the time of the Great Exhibition had set up a restaurant, Soyer's Symposium, in Gore House. There is not much difference in fare between small dinners and large. A dinner for six to ten persons would consist of

Carrot Soup
Turbot with Shrimp Sauce
Lobster Patties
Stewed Kidneys
Roast Saddle of Lamb
Boiled Turkey
Knuckle of Ham
Mashed and Brown Potatoes
Stewed Onions
Cabinet Pudding
Blancmange and Cream
Macaroni

A dinner for eighteen would have two of all courses. Two soups, two fishes, followed by many *entrées* such as Mushroom Patties, Pork Cutlets, Oyster Curry, Lamb's Fry or Grenadine of Veal. These were succeeded by Forequarter of Lamb, Boiled Chicken and Tongue, New Potatoes, Spinach, Salad Larded Capon and Roast Pigeons. Then came Asparagus, Italian Macaroni, Ice Pudding, Brunswick Sausage, Anchovies and Cheese.

The sweets in all the menus are dull and limited and it is obvious that Sir Jonas, alias Mr. Dickens, could not have been a sweet-tooth and that Lady Maria, alias Mrs. Dickens, took more trouble to provide savouries than sweets.

To supplement this account of Victorian feeding we will look at what Nathaniel Sharswell Dodge had to say about Dickens at this time:[1]

[1] See an American scrap-book presented to the Boston branch of the Dickens Fellowship in May 1939.

The personal habits of Dickens were those of the average English gentleman. He was abstinent from breakfast to about half an hour before dinner. This was his working time. He told me that four hours at his desk and four hours afield—on foot or on horseback—rarely in a carriage —was the rule of his working life. He took brandy and seltzer before dinner, drank, as everybody drinks in England, sherry with his meals and port with dessert, sat long at table; enjoyed his cigar; spent an hour perhaps in the drawing room at the conclusion of the evening and then retiring to his study, read, smoked, and sipped brandy-and-water till his bed time at midnight.

Perhaps the cookery book and the American vignette are not really so side-tracking to our narrative as they may at first sight have seemed to be, for they bring home to us the normal habits of the well-to-do people of the time and show us what it might otherwise be difficult to understand, why so many of the early Victorians aged so young. By forty, Mrs. Dickens had become fat and lethargic and her husband's arteries were hardening fast. Lady Maria Clutterbuck's book makes it clear that every well-to-do household expected to be regaled daily as at a City banquet and spend what to us would be an inordinate time at table.

The advent of a seventh boy gave no joy to either parent. To a lady asking to be godmother to one of his children Dickens at this time replied with sardonic humour, 'May I never have the opportunity to give you one'. To another he wrote: 'My wife has presented me with No. 10. I think I could have dispensed with the compliment.'[1] Again he says, 'I have some idea of interceding with the Bishop of London to have a little service in Saint Paul's beseeching that I may be considered to have done enough towards my country's population'.[2] Frankly he writes to Mark Lemon: 'I don't congratulate you on the Baby, because I can't bear to be congratulated on my own Babies'. Kate penned a note her-

[1] 394. II. N.L.   [2] 416. II. N.L.

self to Bulwer Lytton asking him to stand godfather to the
newcomer and attend the christening dinner.[1]   Charles asked
Forster to be the other godfather.   Mrs. Brookfield tells that
'Fuz' came in late to dinner begging ten thousand pardons and
explaining that he had had to act as godfather 'to one of
Dickens's children'.   Whereupon Douglas Jerrold observed,
'I hope that if you gave the child a mug it was *not* your own'.

We do not know what Mrs. Dickens's thoughts on child-
bearing were, but her husband was desperately tired of the
babies he seemed to think she alone was responsible for.   He
was wearied, too, by the eight children who swarmed over
the house, of whom only Charley was at school, but this did
not prevent him from doting on the little boys so long as they
were little.   Like Queen Victoria, he ceased to be quite so
fond when the children grew to years of discretion.

The year 1852 saw the passing of old friends, for Watson,
d'Orsay and Mrs. Macready all died during its course.   'The
tremendous sickle', as Dickens put it, was 'cutting deep into
the corn around him' and he realised that his own blade had
ripened.   Rather out of heart and intensely occupied with the
Guild tour in the north of England, he, almost absentmindedly,
rented a house at Dover for the children from July to September.   Kate and Georgy went on tour with him and as
soon as the children could be sent back to their home in
London Dickens took a trip with his wife and sister-in-law to
Boulogne.   Of course he fell in love with the ramparts, as
Isabel Arundell had done that same summer when she first
set eyes on Richard Burton.   He was also greatly taken by
the fisherfolk and indeed by everything about the place.
Why was it that these foreigners were so much more alive and
interesting than the dull inhabitants of Dover?   Why were
they able to display such individual fancy in their gardens and
their houses?   Why could they express life as they did?
'Please God', he wrote to Forster, 'I shall be writing on these
ramparts next July.'[2]

Kate and Georgy agreed with him that it would be a great

[1] Letter seen at Knebworth.   [2] 418.   II.   N.L.

deal more amusing to spend a summer in France than among
their own compatriots, so they decided to rent a house
recommended to them by a Swiss friend, the Château des
Moulineaux. Facing the ramparts and unfinished cathedral
of the Haute Ville, it stood clear of the town on a terraced
hillside of fir-woods. It was an amusing place with five
summer-houses and fifteen fountains—a veritable children's
paradise. The mere idea of spending a summer in these
delightful surroundings put Dickens into tearing spirits and
he became at once 'the Sparkler of Albion', which was the
equivalent of the Inimitable in England and America.

The family got back to Tavistock House at the end of
October and the autumn was devoted to work on *Bleak House*
and *Household Words* and to the society of his old cronies,
Leech, Lemon and Maclise. Christmas was spent by the
family together, but for Twelfth Night (1853) Dickens went
to Birmingham with Kate, where a dinner was given in his
honour. Beforehand in the rooms of the Society of Art in
Temple Row a presentation took place of a silver-gilt salver
and a diamond ring. In accepting them Dickens solemnly
promised to remove his own old diamond ring from his left
hand and in future wear the Birmingham ring on his right
where its grasp will keep him in mind of his very good friends
in Birmingham. The gathering adjourned to Dee's Hotel
for the banquet of two hundred and twenty guests, among
them 'many distinguished Royal Academicians'. Dickens,
speaking in reply to a toast, rejoiced that the age of patronage
and venality was over. It is the people of England, he stated,
who have set writers free from the shame of the purchased
dedication, the dependence at my Lord Duke's table one day
and at the sponging-house the next, and from all the scurrilous
and dirty work of Grub Street. Who now may be said most
to encourage the dissemination of the writings of Macaulay,
Wellington, Layard or Tennyson? Why, the working men
of England!

And my creed in the exercise of my profession is that
Literature cannot be too faithful to the people—cannot too

ardently advocate the cause of their advancements, happiness and prosperity. I have heard it sometimes said that Literature has suffered by this change, that it has degenerated by being made cheaper. I have not found that to be the case: nor do I believe that you have made the discovery either.

He went on to deride 'the coxcombical idea of writing down to the people', a remark that elicited warm applause: his whole speech was punctuated with quick approval. Delighted with the appreciation of this Midland audience and the generosity of their gifts, he offered to return at Christmas to read two of his stories aloud.

All through February and March he worked steadily. Something of a sensation was caused by an anonymous article in *Household Words* describing life in a workhouse in which it was alleged that the youths in these institutions were 'positively kept like wolves'. It was said to be by the conductor.

At the Royal Academy banquet on April 30 Dickens was bracketed with Dean Milman to reply to the toast of 'Literature'. He did so quite shortly. Addressing the President, Sir Charles Eastlake, whose crimson-velvet chair had been placed in front of the picture of the year, 'The Victory' by Stanfield, he congratulated him and his better half (not visible on this occasion) for their tasteful writings. On the following night Mr. and Mrs. Dickens dined with the Lord Mayor. Mr. Justice Talfourd proposed 'Anglo-Saxon Literature' with allusion to Charles Dickens as having employed fiction to awaken attention to the condition of the oppressed and suffering classes. 'Mr. Dickens replied playfully', says Mrs. Beecher Stowe who faced him at the table. Earlier in the proceedings Vice-Chancellor Wood, who spoke in the absence of the Lord Chancellor, had made a sort of defence of the Court of Chancery, not distinctly mentioning *Bleak House*, but evidently not without reference thereto. The explanation of the Law's delays was the inadequate number of judges. More had now been appointed and unnecessary delays would be done with. This item of intelligence was quizzically treated by 'Boz' as he rejoiced in the good news. The incident showed that the Chancery Bar was not insensible to his representations. In this respect Mrs. Stowe thought the English remarkable; everything met with the freest handling, but nobody took offence. Dickens had gone on unmercifully exposing all sorts of weak places in the English fabric, public and private, yet nobody cried out upon him as the slanderer of his country. 'He could go on serving up Lord Dedlocks to his heart's content.' In this respect Americans, she thought, had much to learn from English people. Mrs. Stowe, moving off with the ladies after dinner to the reception-room, was introduced to Mrs. Dickens, who, to her eyes, appeared 'large, tall, well-developed and high-coloured with an air of frankness, cheerfulness and reliability'. Other distinguished Americans were visiting England at this time, including Dickens's dear friend Professor Felton for whom he gave a dinner at the Trafalgar, Greenwich, after which Stanfield displayed to the guests the glories of the Hospital.

Cranford was appearing in *Household Words*. Dickens was extremely pleased with it and told Mrs. Gaskell she could write as much as she liked for his magazine. Miss Lynn was still sending in stories such as *Marie's Fever* which seemed to him (and probably were) 'imitations from the French', she having worked for some time in Paris. In such time as he could spare from his own work Dickens now took on himself the arranging of a benefit for Miss Kelly and served, in company with the Dukes of Devonshire, Beaufort and Leinster, on a committee got together for the purpose. Writing to Régnier, he said the audience would be of the *élite* and that if he could arrange to come over with his company and play *Le Bonhomme de Jadis* it would be a very great help. Régnier consented and the play was fixed for June 15, by which time Dickens, having fallen ill, had escaped from London to Boulogne.

Dickens was doing work for Miss Coutts by day and diverting himself in the evening with table-turning when he was suddenly taken ill.   The weak kidney that had given him trouble as a boy and the sharp pain in his side from which he had suffered in the blacking factory once more laid him low.   With a head feeling as if it would split, he cut free from all engagements and dashed off to Boulogne with Kate and Georgy, leaving the family to follow three weeks later with the London carriage, horse and groom.   For relaxation he read a manuscript, 'Anne Rodway', on the journey, a new story by his dear young friend Wilkie Collins, and it made him shed those half-pleasurable tears that were never far from the surface.   It was delightful to think that Collins was going to join him for the summer and live in the Tom Pouce pavilion in the garden of the Château des Moulineaux, and that 'Pumpion' (Frank Stone) too would come over with his family.   How he revelled in his French 'doll's house'; Rosemont too had been a 'doll's house'.   It was charmingly situated and 'the best place I have ever lived in abroad'.   He got on capitally with the owner, portly M. Beaucourt, who displayed the improvements he had thought out with the intense pride of a property owner.

The château was approachable by thirty-six stone steps set tribune-wise from the road.   Its hall was almost all of glass, the dining-room looked like a conservatory, and every room had a mirror over the mantelpiece.   Dickens being particularly partial to mirrors, it was a house after his own heart.   A map of the property hung on the wall, giving the impression that it was about the size of Ireland: on it were marked the bridges of Austerlitz and Jena, the cottage of Tom Pouce, the Hermitage, and the Bower of the Old Guard.   The many clocks in the house ticked away busily, keeping what Dickens said must be 'correct Australian time which sometimes would vary nine or ten hours from the French norm'.

The Dickens children were enraptured by their setting, but in a different way from the grown-ups: they liked the goldfish in the pond and the rose-alleys running in all directions.   It was a wonderful playground.   Old and young alike were pleased, and the oldest person there was Charles Dickens aged forty-one and feeling very much the Sparkler.

Mary Boyle came with Peter Cunningham to this abode of bliss. She describes the approach to the steps as 'an avenue of hollyhocks'. How greatly privileged she felt at being taken for long walks alone by Charles, walks which would have been far more enjoyable if Georgy had not occasionally insisted on coming too.

Bleak House allowed itself to be written easily in this happy place. 'We had a little reading of the final double number here the night before last and it created a great impression', wrote the author to Forster. The book was finished by August 27 and the dinner in honour of its completion was given at Boulogne and attended by John Leech, Mark Lemon, Frank Stone and Wilkie Collins.

After working steadily for the best part of a year, the author's heart leapt to think that he could soon go for a care-free holiday and cut loose from the family. Before doing so he dictated to Georgy the last instalments of his *Child's History of England* (originally undertaken for the instruction of his own children), which since January had been appearing in *Household Words*. Like Macaulay's *History*, it concluded with the Revolution of 1688. Forster gives no account of this rather deplorable production. Dickens had far better have left the teaching of history to tutors than disfigure his narrative with phrases like these: Henry VIII was 'a corpulent brute, grunting and growling in his own fat way like a royal pig. A disgrace to human nature. A blot of blood and grease on the history of England.' And again: 'There was a bad fever raging in England and I am glad to write the Queen took it and the hour of her death came. . . . As Bloody Mary this woman has become famous and as bloody Queen Mary she will ever be justly remembered with horror and detestation' in Great Britain. James I 'who wrote of witches' was alluded to as 'His Sowship'. The book comprises some 150,000 words and must have been an adaptation of some other history intertwined with the expression of personal opinions. In its shallow, vituperative judgments it is a little reminiscent of Hawthorne's contribution to English history for schools (1836). A few words about the accession and marriage of Queen Victoria are tacked on at the end of the book.

All work for the moment polished off, Dickens summoned his two young friends, Augustus Egg and Wilkie Collins, inseparables since the Devonshire House rehearsals, to go with him on holiday. He was in 'Sparkler' form and prepared to enjoy himself enormously. The party had rooms at the Falcon Hotel, Lausanne, but Chauncey Hare Townshend insisted on putting them all up at his villa, Mon Loisir, just above Rosemont. Dickens renewed acquaintance with the Haldimand and Cerjat circles and then went on by way of Chamounix to Milan, where he started talking Italian volubly and rushed excitedly to the Scala only to find the performance 'execrable'. 'It is so strange and like a dream to me to hear the delicate Italian once again—so beautiful to see the delightful sky and all the picturesque wonders of the country, and yet I am so restless to be—half desperate to begin some new story.'

The railroad from Turin took Dickens within twenty miles of Genoa, where he lost no time in getting in touch with the De la Rues, T. J. Thompsons and Yeats Browns. Mrs. De la Rue, though still suffering from delusions, refused his offer of further treatment. Old friends hardly recognised the soberly clad figure with black vest and black cravat who presented himself at their doors. Dickens found the Thompsons living in a ruinous Albaro-like palace at Nervi on the road to Portofino. Christiana had lost her glamour and now showed herself too engrossed in oil painting to be able to spare much time for two untidy little slips of girls,[1] crop-headed and stockingless, who were being taught arithmetic by their father, in 'a billiard-room with all manner of messes in it'. Mrs. Yeats Brown said Mrs. Thompson had far better have stuck to her music than work at painting which she was no good at. Visiting the Peschiere, he found it had been

---

[1] Lady Butler and Mrs. Alice Meynell.

turned into a school for girls and that all the painted gods and
goddesses had been covered up.   A tour of the gardens revealed their state of complete neglect.

On the ship that transported the Dickens party to Naples he
found handsome, courteous Sir Emerson Tennent, M.P. for
Belfast, his family, and a number of tourists.   All complained
of the P. & O. service.   It was bad and overcrowded (forty
per cent more first-class tickets sold than there were berths)
and all hoped that it might soon be superseded by an Italian
or French service.   'It would serve the exploiters right to be
pinched out,' said one passenger.   At Naples, which he had
always thought one of the most detestable places on earth,
Dickens met Henry Layard, who was travelling with Lord
and Lady Somers.   With Layard he climbed Vesuvius again
and explored Pompeii.   Long political discussions with this
new friend caused him to write, 'I am more than ever confirmed in my conviction that one of the great excuses for
travelling is to encourage a man to think for himself and be
bold enough to declare it'.

Henry Layard was Dickens's great discovery on this trip.
Layard had made a name for himself over his excavations at
Nineveh and his book describing them sold very well.   He
was at this time busy revising Kugler's *Italian Painters* and
making tracings in outline of Italian pictures.   He spoke
Italian, for his youth had been spent in Italy.   The two men
took to each other at once.   There was but a difference of
five years between them and each confided to the other that
his principal preoccupation was hunting for solutions to the
problems that riddled the social life of their country.   Dickens
was planning *Hard Times* and Layard, newly elected Liberal
M.P. for Aylesbury, was hoping to cut a figure in the House
of Commons as a serious reformer.   They discussed the
writings of Carlyle and agreed as to the hopelessness of
solving political, much less economic problems by Downing
Street methods.   More and more did Dickens feel it laid
upon him to strike a great blow for the poor and Layard

thought that in Dickens he had found a man whom he could trust to advise him and whom he could look up to in the perilous days to come.

On arriving in Rome Dickens sought out J. G. Lockhart, who was, as he told Kate, 'very weak and broken':[1]

> One bright day [in Rome] I walked about with him for some hours when he was dying fast, and all the old faults had faded out of him and the now ghost of the handsome man I had first known when Scott's daughter was at the head of his house, had little more to do with this world than she in her grave, or Scott in his, or small Hugh Littlejohn in his. Lockhart had been anxious to see me all the previous day (when I was away on the Campagna) and as we walked about I knew very well that *he* knew very well why. He talked of getting better, but I never saw him again.

In St. Peter's Dickens found David Roberts and Louis Haghe painting. He knew them well, for they had both helped him over scenery for *Not So Bad as We Seem*. Sending Egg and Collins out sightseeing by themselves, he took long walks alone cogitating on a story for the Christmas extra-number of *Household Words*, to which he always gave his most careful personal supervision, even if he did not actually write the entire number.

When the party left Rome for Siena, a two days' drive, they did so with some trepidation, as to expose oneself at night to the malarial air of the Campagna was a serious risk. Dickens writes in a half-scared way of marshlands and deserted plains where shepherds shut themselves up in stuffy huts at night with families languishing from fever. He hired a light carriage, the sooner to get out of the danger zone, but had to pass a night at Bolsena on the fringe of the Campagna. There in great mouldering rooms the party snatched a little fitful sleep. By Bologna and Ferrara they at last reached Venice, where the Inimitable appeared at the Opera in perfect evening dress while spindle-legged Collins, with his spec-

[1] 514. II. N.L.

tacles, moustache and dirty gloves, cut no better a figure than scrubby Egg with his little black beard and his undistinguished air. From Venice Dickens posted his contribution to the Christmas number.

During this tour Charles's letters to Kate are particularly affectionate, solicitous and intimate, and as his travels have evoked old memories, he, on reaching Turin, wrote at some length suggesting that nine years having gone by, she ought to patch up the differences that had arisen when they were living at the Peschiere, when by her strange behaviour she had constrained him to make a painful declaration of her state of mind to the De la Rues which De la Rue had had too much delicacy and gratitude ever to allude to.

> Whatever made you unhappy in the Genoa time had no other root beginning, middle or end than whatever has made you proud and honoured in your married life, and gives you station better than rank, and surrounded you with many enviable things. . . . Your position beside these people is not a good one, is not an amiable one, or a generous one—is not worthy of you at all. . . . You have it in your power to set it right. . . .
>
> Nine years have gone away since we were in Genoa. Whatever looked large in that little place may be supposed in such a time to have shrunk to its reasonable and natural proportions. You know my life and character, and what has had its part in making them successful; and the more you see of me, the better perhaps you may understand that the intense pursuit of any idea that takes complete possession of me is one of the qualities that makes me different, sometimes for good; sometimes, I dare say, for evil, from other men.[1]

This letter plainly refers to the hypnotic treatment of Mrs. De la Rue. Kate now acted on his suggestion and wrote in a friendly way to the woman of whom she had been so jealous and whose interest in her husband she was now persuaded she had misunderstood during the miserable months at Genoa.

---

[1] W. Dexter, *Mr. and Mrs. Dickens*, p. 227.

The holiday-makers reached London in mid-December just in time for Dickens to keep Christmas with his family and make good his offer to read his Christmas stories aloud in Birmingham. Mr. and Mrs. Dickens were entertained before the readings at the Hen and Chickens Hotel and Mrs. Dickens was presented with a silver flower-stand. A red pulpit, like a Punch and Judy stand without the top, was provided for Mr. Dickens's convenience in the Town Hall and from it he read *A Christmas Carol* on December 27 and *The Cricket on the Hearth* on December 29. Next day he read the *Carol* again to a specially summoned audience of working men and their wives. In a few introductory words he said how important he thought it that the working man should take his share in management; indeed it seemed to him essential to the healthy life of the community that he should do so. As, in his opinion, no class could of itself do much for the good of the community as a whole, the fusion of all classes must be aimed at, co-operation between employers and employed stressed, and common interests defined. In this way only could the stamping out of exploitation be achieved. In the Mechanics' Institute set up in their midst he sees a temple of concord, a model edifice for the whole of England. In conclusion he read three verses from a favourite poem.

And should my youth, as youth is apt, I know,
    Some harshness show,
All vain asperities I day by day
    Would wear away
Till the smooth temper of my age should be
Like the high leaves upon the Holly Tree.

And as when all the summer trees are seen
    So bright and green,
The holly leaves a sober hue display
    Less bright than they,
But when the bare and winter woods we see
What then so cheerful as the Holly Tree?

So serious should my youth appear among
    The thoughtless throng,

So would I seem among the young and gay
　　More grave than they
That in my age as cheerful I might be
As the green winter of the Holly Tree.[1]

These Birmingham readings brought home to Dickens
that whenever he pleased he could with his sympathy and his
mimetic power not only draw large audiences but could hold
them spell-bound. This was a consoling reflection, for
should his writing faculty fail him, as sometimes he feared it
might, he would have another means of livelihood at his
command.

[1] R. Southey, 1798.

Chapter 20

THE CONDITION OF ENGLAND

*All things considered, there never was a people so abused as
the English at this time.*   CHARLES DICKENS

THE year 1854 opened with rehearsals of Fielding's burlesque *Tom Thumb*, played by the Dickens and Lemon
children on Twelfth Night at the 'Theatre Royal', Tavistock
House. Mark Lemon took the part of the giantess Glum-
dalca, and Dickens that of Gaffer Thumb. The acting of the
children, especially of Henry Fielding aged four, was amus-
ingly grave, so much so that one of the spectators, Thackeray,
rolled off his chair with laughter.

Dickens began writing *Hard Times* this month, and as he
was finding it uphill work fixing the setting to his fancy, he
went off to Preston to get first-hand impressions of a strike.
It was annoying that Peter Cunningham should paragraph
him in the *Illustrated London News* and give the public to
understand that the book was to be written on the spur of the
moment and deal specifically with Preston. This in no way
corresponded with facts, for he had been turning the subject
over in his mind for months and making notes for the book.
Only now that he saw his way to printing the first instalment
in *Household Words* (in April) was he going to Preston just
to see what a strike looked like. It was a Saturday, and he
was disappointed to find the scene neither tragic, dramatic nor
even pathetic, though the lock-out had been in operation for
twenty-three weeks. Owing to the cold furnaces, skies were
clear, streets empty and people moping indoors. As there
was nothing to do and nothing to see, he went to *Hamlet* at
the local theatre, and sat through the performance feeling he
would have done quite as well to 'sit within doors and mope'
as the workmen were doing. On the Sunday morning he
attended the meeting of delegates in the Cock-pit and was

impressed by their fortitude, good sense and restraint in speaking. On the Monday he went to see the strike pay distributed and then to an open-air meeting at which the whole assembly sang

> Awake, ye sons of toil! nor sleep
> While millions strave, while millions weep
> Demand your rights; let tyrants see
> You are resolved that you'll be free.

Preston was reputed to be a model town, but Dickens found it a place so 'nasty' that he became more than ever set on lifting the working people out of the dreary districts into which industrialism had forced them. It was all very well for Lord Derby and Mr. Bright to call such places 'centres of manufacturing industry'; he would follow Cobbett and Carlyle in calling them 'hell-holes'. It was quite certain that capitalists could make their own fortunes in these places, and it was equally certain that they did not make the fortunes of their employees. The writing of *Hard Times* drove him 'three-parts mad', for being no economist he found it uncongenial work trying to animate his narrative by expounding the falseness of certain accepted economic doctrines such as that of the law of supply and demand: it obliged him to try and rival the pedagogic efforts of Miss Martineau. To Macaulay, Dickens in this book seemed to be heading for 'sullen socialism'.

Coketown, the scene of his story, and the country round were described graphically and formed the background for a satirical picture of the employers Bounderby and Gradgrind. Ruskin, who read each number eagerly, said that its value was impaired by displaying Bounderby as a monster instead of a worldly employer and Stephen Blackpool as a saint instead of an honest employee.[1] He thought, however, that the author had succeeded in proving that the principle of buying in the cheapest and selling in the dearest market was a vile practice conducive to the suppression of all that was best in man. Intent on keeping humanity human, Dickens said that his

[1] *Unto this Last*, pp. 14-15.

satire was directed against those who think in figures and averages. They seemed to him 'representatives of the wickedest and most enormous vice of our time'. In writing a book so contrary to his own instinctive genius, Dickens was taking his stand alongside Carlyle, Kingsley, Hood, Mrs. Gaskell, Charlotte Brontë, George Eliot and other writers who resented the exploitation of the powerless. Persevering in this uncongenial work 'for righteousness' sake' made Dickens more than usually short-tempered and restless. Virtue is always a disagreeable task-mistress, and in order to complete his weekly instalments he had rigidly to deny himself to all visitors and to refuse all invitations.

Edmund Yates was one of these visitors. Ringing at the doorbell of Tavistock House, he was ushered by a footman into the drawing-room, a large room at the back of the house. Presently Miss Hogarth came in and greeted him pleasantly, saying that Mr. Dickens was too busy to see him but that if he was the son of Frederick Yates (the actor) he would receive him on Sunday at 2 P.M. On the Sunday he found Dickens in a room on the first floor. Yates saw no trace of the 'Maclise view' of him, indeed he was already looking like the Frith portrait painted years later. His bearing was hearty, almost aggressive. 'God! how like your father!' he exclaimed and then began to talk about the old Adelphi. Yates sent him a copy of *My Haunts* and marked him down as godfather for the child he was expecting in the autumn. Dickens dined with him in November 1854 for the christening of his son. We see from the account of this interview that Georgy was playing the part of receptionist to a great author. There is no doubt that she had great charm of manner and nothing very much to do.

As Dickens worried away at *Hard Times* he felt overwhelmed by the number of things that were wrong with England. One of the principal wrongs he held to be the landed system of the country at large. To his mind it was responsible for many 'locked-up social evils', evils that remained unexposed because the land was its own legislator.

If only the people could grasp this plain truth they would
'make themselves heard like the sea all round this island'.
Often he talked with Layard in this strain.   Layard, he said,
was 'the most useful man in England, and his speeches should
be broadcast at every market cross, in every town hall . . . up
in the very balloons, and down in the very diving bells'.   He
can help support him in the press, for Lemon of *Punch* is
ready to back him, so is Shirley Brooks of the *Illustrated
London News* and *Weekly Chronicle*, and as for his own
Household Words, Layard may count on him as being
'Damascus steel to the core'.   In carrying out this pledge he
told his readers baldly that unless they seriously set about
improving the houses of the poor they would be guilty before
God and man of wholesale murder.   He cautioned working
men not to be tricked by speakers calling themselves reformers who are merely angling for parliamentary votes, but
to go on organising trade unions.   Working men should
never lose sight of the basic fact that but for them the world
would not go round.   They must see to it that their exertions
shall not in the future be devoted to the maintenance of a
workless, extravagant upper class whose interest it was to
focus public attention on foreign rather than domestic affairs.
The House of Commons was still, for Dickens, the ash-heap
of his youth, and its members sifters and resifters of cinders.
'It appears to me,' he said, 'that Parliament is become just the
dreariest failure and nuisance that ever bothered this much
bothered world.'

The English and French declaration of war on Russia at the
end of March 1854 filled Dickens and his friends with despair,
put an end to social planning, and forced Lord John Russell
to withdraw in April the new Reform Bill he had introduced
in February.   So the people were to be made fools of again,
'made to sing their own death-song in "Rule Britannia" and
allow their own wrongs and sufferings to be obscured by
cannon-smoke and blood-mists!'   Everyone Dickens knew
was already contributing to the Patriotic Fund 'without
giving a thought to the wretchedness engendered by cholera,

of which in London alone an infinitely larger number of English people than are likely to be slain in the whole Russian war have miserably and needlessly died'. 'I feel', he sighed, 'as if the world had been pushed back five hundred years.' Layard, who had been attaché to our embassy in Turkey under Stratford Canning, made ready to go to Constantinople, thence to take his chance of getting on to the Crimea. When British and French troops landed near Sevastopol in September he managed to get aboard the *Agamemnon*, and from her main-top witnessed the battle of the river Alma.[1] To his experiences and the effect of his reports on Dickens we shall return later.

Before doing so we must see how Dickens tried at Boulogne, during the summer months of 1854, to fight against ever increasing restlessness and depression. He had rented another of M. Beaucourt's houses (the Villa du Camp de Droite), for the family and in these congenial surroundings quickly polished off *Hard Times*. At Boulogne, however, he seemed closer to the war than at home. Buglers sounded calls at all hours, his favourite walks were ploughed up by baggage waggons, and sixty thousand soldiers were in camp near Wimereux. When the Prince Consort came over to inspect the troops, Dickens ran up a Union Jack with a tri-colour atop of it. On the day of the review he went for his usual walk and, returning by the Calais road, found himself face to face with the Prince and Louis Napoleon. He snatched off his wideawake, whereupon the Emperor swept off his cocked hat, and Prince Albert did the same. The Emperor appeared more solid than in the old days at Gore House, but this may have been the effect of uniform. He looked tired and 'stooped in the manner of Albany Fonblanque'. That night an *entente cordiale* was celebrated in Boulogne, English sailors and guardsmen could be seen everywhere dancing, drinking and embracing French soldiers in the streets. Dickens contributed to the gala effect by lighting

[1] September 20, 1854.

one hundred and twenty wax candles in his seventeen front windows, thereby earning the applause of M. Beaucourt. Prince Albert's September review was followed in October by the Emperor's review at which the storming of the Malakoff redoubt was announced, as it happened prematurely, but the men were not to know that! The cheering of the troops on parade sounded very feeble to Dickens, who said, 'fifty English throats could have made more noise than those French divisions'. The Empress sat her grey horse 'capitally', looked charming, and when the Emperor handed her the dispatch, 'kissed it with as natural an impulse as one could wish to see'

In England Nathaniel Hawthorne, from his consular post at Liverpool, noted the rejoicing over the same news of victory. When it turned out to be incorrect, he wrote, 'I am glad of it . . . it is impossible for an American to be otherwise than glad. Success makes an Englishman intolerable . . . an Englishman in adversity is a very respectable character.'[1] Hawthorne's reflections on the Englishmen he came in contact with during his residence in our country are worthy of note, as they are representative of educated American opinion of the day.

> An Englishman [he says] likes to feel the weight of all the past upon his back; and moreover the antiquity that overburdens him has taken root in his being and has grown to be rather a hump than a pack . . . he appears to be sufficiently comfortable under this mouldy accretion.

When Dickens returned to London, he found the clubs buzzing with Crimean stories. William Russell, the *Times* correspondent, was sending home highly disquieting and damaging reports. The shameful organisation of supplies, it appeared, was causing great hardship on troops in the field, and the condition of the lazar-house at Sevastopol was described by Cobden as 'unutterably shocking'; but Layard said, what could be expected of a government so conscience-

[1] Henry James, *Life of Hawthorne*, p. 153.

less as to 'go on vacation for eight weeks without once summoning a cabinet meeting'? Why, ministers had paid less attention to the affairs of the country than a merchant did to his business! Dickens of course was in full sympathy with Layard's strictures and reflected ruefully on the Boodle-Buffyism that made such a state of affairs possible. His friend Sir Joseph Walmsley told him he never would forget the gloom of these weeks 'when each man asked the other with whom did the fault lay, was it with the commanders abroad or with the government at home?' Cobden had told him that the French had covered themselves with great glory, adding, 'I am sorry to say nothing but discredit and shame attaches to us . . . crowds of officers, including the Duke of Cambridge and Lord Cardigan, have slunk home, boys had been left in charge of boys, for there were few grown men out there.'

After Christmas Roebuck in the House of Commons moved that a committee be appointed to inquire into the conduct of the war. His voice faltered when he told how an army of 54,000 men had left England a few months earlier, how only 14,000 of these were still alive of whom but 5000 were fit for duty. In face of an overwhelming vote of censure the ministry resigned on February 1, and by February 16 a new government had been formed with Palmerston as prime minister in place of Aberdeen. Dickens at once took his political skit, *The Thousand and One Humbugs*, out of a drawer and brought it up to date. 'Parmastoon has newly succeeded Abbadeen (or the Addled) who has for his misdeeds been strangled with a garter.' It amused him to read through his old satire; it should now see daylight in *Household Words*. Dickens had a particular distrust of Palmerston, the statesman he called 'the glib vizier'. Palmerston, who had been in office before he was born and who had been joining governments in some capacity or other as long as he could remember. Palmerston with his traditional policy of suspicion of Russia, encouragement of Poland, support for Turkey, backing of Italian Liberals, and the whole balance of power box-of-tricks that he was such an adept at conjuring with. Reluctantly did the new prime minister grant an inquiry into the conduct of the war and on assuming the premiership fuse the offices of Secretary for War and Secretary at War, giving the post to Lord Panmure over whom he could exercise the tightest control. Palmerston's hatred and distrust of Russia, which set the course of opinion in England for generations, was so strong that Dickens felt he might carry on the war for years. As Cobden said:

> If our ignorant clamourers for the 'humiliation of Russia' are allowed to have their own way, look out for serious disasters to the Allies! No power ever yet persisted in the attempt to subjugate Russia that did not break in pieces against that impassive empire . . . the Russians can beat all the world at endurance . . . we exaggerate the power of a naval blockade . . . Russia has resources we cannot touch.

It is extremely strange in reading patriotic war speeches to see how the idiom of one war always fits another war. At a dinner of the London Commercial Travellers Schools,[1] Dickens was asked to propose the health of the army in the Crimea. He said, 'It does not require any extraordinary sagacity in a commercial assembly to appreciate the dire evils of war'. War paralysed enterprise, enfeebled trade, beat down the peaceful arts, but 'there are seasons when the evils of peace are immeasurably greater and when a powerful nation by admitting the right of any autocrat to do wrong, sows by such complicity the seeds of its own ruin and over-shadows itself in time to come with that fatal influence which great and ambitious powers are sure to exercise over their weaker neighbours'. Even Dickens placed the guilt on 'one man who had plotted against mankind. One man having effaced peace and justice, forces us to fight in the cause of human freedom.' All wars seem somehow to be the same war.

At Christmas-time Dickens gave readings of the *Carol* at Bradford, Reading and Sherborne, at which place Macready

[1] December 30, 1854.

was living in unhappy retirement. For his own children he
arranged some theatricals, *Fortunio and his Seven Gifted
Servants*, by Planché. This performance, over which he took
infinite trouble, gave him the desire to produce a play for
grown-ups during the summer. Play production was the
most satisfying recreation of all. Still the prey of restlessness, he made plans for going to Paris, warning Régnier that
he was about to hurl himself in company with his young
friend Wilkie Collins into all the 'diableries of that delightful
city'.

Just as he was packing for Paris Maria Beadnell made an
unexpected come-back. Going through the pile of letters
he found waiting for him one evening at Tavistock House,
he recognised her handwriting on an envelope. 'Three or
four and twenty years vanished like a dream. I opened it
with the touch of my young friend David Copperfield when
he was in love.'[1] What a relief to turn from war and hell-
holes to personal romance again. Eagerly he told Maria in a
hastily written note:

> You cannot remember more tenderly than I do. I
> hardly ever go to the city, but I walk up an odd little court
> at the back of the Mansion House and come out by the
> corner of Lombard Street. . . . I forget nothing of those
> times. . . . I shall be charmed to have a long talk with
> you.[2]

Explaining that he was on the point of starting for Paris, he
was tripped up by the word 'Paris'. The very word evoked
memories of a day 'when my existence was entirely uprooted
and my whole being blighted by the Angel of my soul being
sent there to finish her education'.

This reply gave intense pleasure to Maria, who obviously
took it as evidence that he still secretly adored her above all
others. Another letter, written from the Hôtel Meurice, also
seemed to be under the spell of the old enchantment. The
little blue gloves he once matched for her, does she remember?
Has she not read in one of his books a faithful reflection of his

passion for her?   Perhaps on laying down the book she may
have thought, 'How dearly that boy must have loved me!' or
perhaps, 'How vividly this man remembers it!'

Yet another note reached her a week later written from
Tavistock House.   It seemed to show a wish for intimate
friendship.   She had 're-opened the way to a confidence
which . . . may be between ourselves alone'.   Mrs. Winter's
dull heart glowed at the language used by her old lover:

> My entire devotion to you and the wasted tenderness of
> those hard years which I have ever since half-loved, half-
> dreaded to recall made so deep an impression on me, that I
> refer to it a habit of suppression, which now belongs to me,
> which I know is no part of my original nature, but which
> makes me chary of showing my affections even to my
> children except when they are very young.[1]

Maria Winter could not handle such correspondence at all and
made the fatal mistake of accusing her ex-adorer of having
'exaggerated' his feeling for her.   This hurt Dickens, who
retorted:

> I don't quite apprehend what you mean by my over-
> stating the strength of the feeling of five-and-twenty years
> ago.   If you mean of my own feeling, and will only think
> what the desperate intensity of my nature is, and that this
> began when I was Charley's age; that it excluded every
> other idea from my mind for four years, at a time of life
> when four years are equal to four times four; and that I
> went at it with a determination to overcome all the diffi-
> culties which fairly lifted me up into the newspaper life,
> and floated me away over a hundred men's heads, then
> you are wrong, for nothing can exaggerate that.   I have
> positively stood amazed at myself ever since!   And so I
> suffered, and so worked, and so beat and hammered away
> at the maddest romances that ever got into a boy's head and
> stayed there, that to see the mere cause of it at all, now,
> loosens my hold upon myself. . . . No one can imagine in
> the most distant degree what pain the recollection gave me
> in *Copperfield*.   And, just as I can never open that book as

I open any other book, I cannot see the face (even at four-and-forty) or hear the voice without going wandering over the ashes of all that youth and hope in the wildest manner.[1]

There can be no doubt that in the Maria Beadnell romance lay the clue to much that we do not understand in Dickens's behaviour.

A few days later Kate Dickens, who knew nothing of these letters, called on Mrs. Winter at Charles's request and asked her to dinner, arranging that their carriage should fetch her and her husband to Tavistock House. The disillusionment of this meeting, even if we had not Georgy's confirmatory comments to rely on, was obviously complete. Dickens, however, chose to pull himself together and visit Mrs. Winter as if to make quite sure that the Maria Beadnell he once knew had no physical existence. The glass eyes of little 'Jip' stared at him in the hall and he watched his hostess adding brandy to her tea. There was nothing more to say and no action to be taken. A month later Dickens, in reply to Maria's suspicion that he never wants to see her again, fends her off with, 'Whoever is devoted to an art must be content to deliver himself wholly up to it. I can't help it, I must go my own way whether or no.'[2]

He talked to her of Spain, Greenland, the North Pole, Constantinople, saying he was driven by a demon of restlessness. 'You say that once upon a time I was not like this—now it has become myself, and my life.' Unwilling to abandon hope, Maria offered, somewhat obtusely, to come and see him on a Sunday and he replied that he would be out of town for many Sundays. And from henceforth fatuous, foolish Maria was transferred to the crucible of Dickens's imagination, whence she was to re-emerge in the guise of Flora Finching in *Little Dorrit* and he to figure as Arthur Clennam.

On his way to Paris Dickens got out of the train at Chatham to look at the house which in boyhood he had dreamed of possessing—Gad's Hill. He had heard through Wills that it would shortly be in the market, as his contributor, Eliza Lynn, had been left the property by her father, but could not afford to live there. Comprising a medium-sized house and one hundred and twenty acres of land, it was altogether a place after his own heart and he at once made up his mind to buy it as soon as the oppotrunity offered, for to make one of his dreams come true would be to achieve the height of happiness. In Paris Dickens and Collins went to two and three theatres a night and dined at all the best restaurants. Dickens was pretending to be quite as young and sportive as his companion and able to enjoy everything quite as much, but in reality he was for the first time feeling his age. He toyed with the idea of settling permanently in *la ville lumière* and in long walks by the Seine cogitated how to make his new book an attack on the bureaucracy of England. One day there flashed into his mind the word 'circumlocution'. In a moment he knew he had *le mot de l'énigme*. This was the book in embryo. The organisers of circumlocution followed automatically—giving themselves the wonderful name of Barnacles, Tite (undislodgeable) Barnacles. He could now get on swimmingly with the story.

Neither editorial duties nor work on his new novel were enough to fill the empty spaces of a life which somehow, in spite of its success, was beginning to seem a failure. With infinite trouble he began arranging plays for Tavistock House. The theatre at least never lost its attraction. Wilkie Collins had written *The Lighthouse*, 'a Domestic Melodrama in two acts', and he would produce that. It contained an excellent part for him, that of the lighthouse keeper, Aaron Gurnock. He would get 'Stanny' to paint a drop scene of the Eddystone as the action took place inside the lighthouse. Three performances[1] were given and delighted guests crowded into 'the smallest theatre in the world'. The plays were followed by excellent suppers at which speeches were

[1] Saturday June 16, Monday 18, Tuesday 19: *The Lighthouse* and *Mr. Nightingale's Diary*.

made.   On one of the nights Lord Campbell pleased his host
and the company generally by declaring he would rather have
written *Pickwick* than be Lord Chief Justice of England or a
peer of Parliament.

The play was repeated on Tuesday July 10 at Campden
House for the Bournemouth Sanatorium for Consumption.
In this house, which was owned by a Colonel Waugh, there
was a miniature theatre, complete with pit, boxes, stage and
footlights which delighted Dickens, but Kensington knows it
no more.

And all the time he was organising these entertainments
he kept in touch with the member for Aylesbury who was
as active as ever in attacking bureaucracy and demanding
administrative reform.   Dickens stuck closer and closer to
Layard.   Whatever it cost him, he would support him in his
campaign.   When a meeting was organised at Drury Lane[1]
at which Layard was to denounce maladministration in
Government offices, Dickens promised to be on the platform
at his side, but could not manage to get there.   Quoting from
blue-books issued by the Sevastopol commissioners, Layard
referred to 'records of inefficiency, records of indifference to
suffering, records of ignorance, records of obstinacy', all
casting shame on us and our system of government.   The
Civil Service was grossly over-staffed, every member of the
Service was busy making work for another member and passing things on.   He accused Lord Palmerston personally of an
attitude of levity towards the sufferings of the people of
England.

Greatly offended by the attack, the Prime Minister con-
temptuously alluded in the House to 'the private theatricals
staged at Drury Lane' by Layard.   Dickens, who had
pledged himself to speak at another meeting at the same
theatre, under the chairmanship of Samuel Morley, took this
reference up in his speech:[2]

The noble Lord at the head of the Government [he said]
wonders why Mr. Layard accuses him of habitually joking

[1] June 20, 1855.   [2] June 27, 1855.

when the country is plunged in deep disgrace and distress. He turned his period with a reference to 'private theatricals' at Drury Lane. . . . I will try and give the noble Lord the reason for these 'private theatricals'.

The public theatricals which the noble Lord is so condescending as to manage are so intolerably bad, the machinery so cumbrous, the parts so ill-distributed, the company so full of 'walking gentlemen', the managers have such large families and are so bent on putting those families into what is theatrically called 'first business'—not because of their aptitude for it, but because they *are* their families— that we find ourselves obliged to organise an opposition.

Explaining his own position on the platform, Dickens said:

This is the first political meeting I have ever attended. . . . By literature I have lived and through literature I have been content to serve my country. . . . In my sphere of action I have tried to understand the heavier social grievances and to help to set them right. The country is silent, gloomy, England has never found an enemy one-twentieth part so potent to effect the misery and ruin of her noble defenders as she has been herself. . . . Discord is piled on the heaving basis of ignorance, poverty, crime. There is no understanding of the general mind in Parliament . . . the machinery of government goes round and round and the people stand aloof.

He has joined the Society for promoting Administrative Reform because men must get together over good citizenship. It is hoped to influence the House through the constituencies, but he has not the least hesitation in saying that he has scant faith in the House of Commons as at present existing.

As he looked back to the years when he served his apprenticeship in the gallery he saw little change in the House itself; certain things indeed were exactly the same. Now as then, personal altercation, *i.e.* the retort courteous, the quip modest, the reply churlish, the reproof valiant, the countercheck quarrelsome, the lie circumstantial and the lie direct were of immeasurably greater interest to the House of Commons than the health and education of a whole people.

The Society for Administrative Reform had come into existence because the well-being of the country was of more importance for the future of England than the maintenance of
unmeaning routine and worn-out conventions. The association does not seek, as its enemies say, to set class against class,
but to bridge the gulf between governed and governors.

After this plunge into political controversy Dickens
retired to his desk again. If direct attack did not make
'Twirling Weathercock' see the error of his ways, maybe the
indirect attack he was planning in *Little Dorrit* might be of
service.

Folkestone this summer proved almost intolerable owing
to the vulgarity of trippers. Determined to absent himself
from England in the autumn, he crossed with Georgy to
France in order to find winter quarters for the family in Paris.
Writing to 'dearest Catharine', he reported that he had had
an 'awful job to find anything at all to suit them, for Paris is
perfectly full'. He had managed, however, to secure 'two
apartments—an *entresol* and a first floor with a kitchen and
servants' room' at seven hundred francs a month. 'You
must be prepared for a regular continental abode', he wrote;
'the front apartments all look on to the Champs Elysées . . .
the situation almost the finest in Paris and the children will
have a window from which to look on the busy life outside.'
A more comfortable apartment in the rue du Faubourg St.
Honoré had been rejected because the children's rooms would
have looked on to a dull courtyard, and that would never have
done. He and Georgy will try and get the apartment into
running order at once so that they may be ready to receive
the family as soon as may be. The servants must join him at
once and Kate must cross to Boulogne and stay there with the
children till the rooms are ready. Charles and Georgy and
the servants moved in to 49 Avenue des Champs Elysées.
During the first night Charles heard Georgy moving about,
got up, and asked what was the matter.[1] 'Oh, it's so dread-

[1] 697. II. N.L.

fully dirty. I can't sleep for the smell in my room,' replied Georgy. Next morning he exerted all his energy and persuasiveness to get the apartment 'purified'. It was like summoning a cast and assuming the role of stage-manager again. The porter, the porter's wife, the porter's wife's sister, a feeble upholsterer of enormous age and all his work-men—four boys. To these were added the co-proprietors of the apartment, an old lady, and a martial little man with a François Ier beard. 'It's not the custom,' objected the proprietor, but somehow Dickens got round them and they agreed to scrub and cleanse and even to provide new carpets. At last he could report that the place was exquisitely cheerful and 'as clean as anything human can be'. On receiving this encouraging intelligence Kate and the children joined him.

Chapter 21

LIFE ABROAD

The fuming vanities of Paris.
CHARLES DICKENS

THE plunge into Parisian life turned Dickens into a
'Sparkler' again.   Blue as in Italy was the sky above the
Elysian Fields, bright were the tossing fountains, the very
heavens seemed to shine and, when the strains of martial
music made themselves audible, 'all bloused Paris, led by the
Inimitable', tripped along in a kind of hilarious dance.   The
younger members of the family took their pleasures more
sedately and through the winter months spent many hours
watching from their windows the moving panorama which to
them was Paris.   The apartment, over a carriage repository,
had six windows facing the Avenue, each of them a vantage-
point for sightseeing.   One day they would see the Emperor
and Empress driving to St. Cloud; another day the Emperor
riding alone on horseback, looking so mortally ill that they
would wish him in bed; yet another day a battalion of red-
trousered Zouaves marching to the Barrière, stock on shoulder,
preceded by their mascot, a black dog.   Thoroughbreds
ridden by dashing young men would prance along and
elegant equipages roll by with white-harnessed black horses
curvetting under their tight bearing-reins.   In this wise did
the wives of men who had made fortunes on the Bourse
advertise their husband's success and display their own fine
feathers and furs.   Not less entertaining were the ladies of
ton who, when the sun shone, floated by in their orange-
coloured or russet shawls, the points of which spread over
silky crinolines that, swaying, revealed glimpses of white
stockings and glinting bronzed bootlets.   It was the vogue
that year to wear autumn tints, and Mamey and Katey were of
an age to dote on the new fashions and, in so far as their

mother and father would permit, to dress themselves in the same sort of clothes.

The impression the family received from watching at these windows was of a gay world of almost fantastic wealth and luxury, and this impression was intensified when their father, returning from some bachelor dinner, gave them an account of the entertainment he had enjoyed. Charles Dickens, who always took colour easily abroad, became at this time floridly Parisian in gesture, and was given to talking voluble French at home. It was good practice for him and the children and qualified him for compliments from *convives*, who told him that he spoke 'the celestial language in a most angelic way'. Paris to him was a climate to bask in, almost a terrestrial paradise.

One evening he dined with the press magnate, Emile de Girardin, who lived 'in an opulence worthy of an eastern potentate', and was ushered through gorgeous drawing-rooms, lit with 'ten thousand candles in gold sconces', to a 'magnificent' dining-room whence, through plate-glass doors, one looked straight into the kitchen at cooks, in high white caps, stirring pans and basting viands. On the dinner-table, laid for eight, stood mounds of truffles and jugs of the best champagne. In reading the menu Dickens was puzzled by an item entitled *Homage à l'illustre écrivain de l'Angleterre*. This turned out to be a plum pudding far larger than any ever seen in England, served with a 'heavenly white sauce'. To watch the courses being carried through the glass doors fascinated him. The food was certainly 'the best ever tasted by mortal', but the wine was even more astonishing. With the third course was served a port 'costing at least two guineas a bottle', and after dinner a brandy 'buried these hundred years and more'. Exquisite coffee 'brought from the remote east in exchange for a quantity of gold dust' concluded the repast. Replete, the company returned to the drawing-room, where tables, moved by an unseen agency, arrived laden with cigarettes. Cool drinks 'flavoured by lemons fresh from Algeria and delicate oranges from Lisbon' next made their appearance and presently the guests, reposing on divans, ended a Luculline evening sipping 'caravan tea of finest quality from China. The lavishness, as Dickens explained to his family, was almost embarrassing to an Englishman, and the most amusing thing of all was that, in reply to the compliments he had paid to M. de Girardin on his marvellous entertainment, his host had replied, 'This is just nothing, Mr. Dickens, nothing at all. You must really come and *dine* another day.' And of course Mr. Dickens did so, accepting with alacrity an invitation to meet his friend Régnier, Jules Sandeau and other writers. This time it was not the wine that struck him most, for he was expecting that, but the cigars, 'five thousand inestimable cigars in prodigious bundles'. Such a display of riches was really stunning!

The difference in the wealth and standing of newspaper proprietors in England and France struck Dickens very much. M. de Girardin was the first press baron he had met. Not only was he the owner and editor of a powerful political organ, *La Presse*, but he was a pioneer in what we should call magazine journalism and made a bid in his weeklies to serve a large and varied public. They included the *Musée des Familles*, *Panthéon Littéraire*, *Journal des Connaissances Utiles*, *Journal des Institutions Primaires* and, most successful venture of all, the *Journal du Bien-être Universel*. It interested the French editor to compare notes with his colleague, the conductor and part owner of *Household Words*, whose notion of catering for the people was rather like his own. From his newspapers M. de Girardin had built up a fortune which he had been lucky enough to amplify on the Bourse. Even this magnate, it seemed, had had his political ups and downs. From 1834 to 1848 he had sat as deputy, but in the latter years he had resigned and had advised the King to resign too. At the moment of the revolution of 1848 *La Presse* was suspended and Girardin found himself consigned to prison by General Cavaignac. After spending eleven days in the Conciergerie, he was released, and got back on his incarcerators with a wildly popular pamphlet, *Le Journal d'un*

Journaliste au secret. From this successful man Dickens was able to pick up a good many ideas.

One of the many charms of Paris was that literary men were made much of by everyone connected with books and the theatre, and, unlike London, where nearly all writers were poor, writers in Paris were often very rich and always highly considered. Eugène Sue, for example, had a luxurious apartment crammed with pictures, statues, antiques and painted glass, hothouses full of flowers and fountains playing on gold and silver fish. And the joke in Paris was that Eugène Sue was believed to be the coiner of the famous mot, 'No one has the right to superfluities while anyone is in want of necessities'. A great fillip had been given to journalistic enterprise and trade generally by the war in the Crimea and authors in France did not seem to lead so parochial an existence as in England: they were sufficiently in touch with the world of affairs to improve the occasion and gamble on the Bourse.

It was rather head-turning to Dickens to be made so much of in Paris and to be entertained on a scale that even in America he had never experienced. The contagious cordiality of his reception by French people everywhere, and the fact that no explanatory introductions were ever required in any company, struck him most agreeably. A porter delivering a parcel would say pleasantly, 'Cette Madame Tojair. Ah! qu'elle est drôle, et précisément comme une dame que je connais à Calais.' As 'l'écrivain célèbre' Dickens had already burst into all homes, strangers would say, 'On connaît bien que Monsieur Dickin prend sa position sur la dignité de la littérature'. At long last he was recognised for what he was, the greatest novelist in the world. Why was it that his compatriots had never treated him in this way? And can we wonder that he took to Parisian life as a duck to water and felt himself the good comrade of all French authors?

The Dickens family were not allowed to waste too much time looking out of the window, for their father insisted on regular study hours and intensive cultivation of the French and Italian languages. Through Ary Scheffer, he secured for them as tutor Daniele Manin, ex-president of the Venetian Republic, 'best and noblest of unhappy gentlemen'. Dickens could not but reflect, as he looked on his seven sons in 'the banquet-hall' at No. 49 at Christmas 1855, that if he himself in youth had had half the advantages he was now bestowing on his children his life might have been entirely different!

The best and oldest friends Dickens now had in Paris were the Régniers whom he had so often entertained in London. Régnier, as on a previous occasion, made 'Boz' free of the green room at the Théâtre Français and it was through Régnier that he got to know Scribe, Auber and Alexandre Dumas. Kate Dickens managed to get on, after a fashion, with Madame Régnier and Madame Scribe too, but, unlike her husband, she was not electrified by contacts, nor did she in Paris acquire any vivacity of manner. Kate just remained what she had always been, amiable, placid and slow at the uptake, and she was at the great disadvantage of not daring to try and talk French. Great hospitality was shown to both of them by Sir Joseph Olliffe, physician to the British Embassy and the English colony in Paris. At Olliffe's house all birds of passage naturally perched and the doctor's parties were known for their pleasantness and informality.

With M. and Mme. Scribe, Mr. and Mrs. Dickens dined 'frequently', and at these dinners M. Auber was often present. By December Dickens spoke of Scribe as 'my particular friend'. Scribe not only had the charming apartment in Paris already alluded to but a château in the country as well, and his 'sumptuous carriage and magnificent span of horses' were admired by the Dickens family when they drew up at No. 49. Rather naïvely pleased with his possessions, Scribe would say to Dickens, 'All this I have earned with my pen, for, as you see, my dear Dickens, I began as a little law clerk'. And 'Boz's' heart went out to him, for had not he too begun as a little law clerk?

M. Auber could not have been more friendly. Dickens

describes him as 'a solid elderly little man having agreeable recollections of England' where he had once lived at 'Stock Noonton'. The first time they talked together he told of his meeting with the Queen of England, to whom he had been presented by King Louis Philippe, and of how the Queen had smiled and said, 'We are such old acquaintances through M. Auber's works that an introduction is quite unnecessary'. One evening the Dickenses were dining at a party that included both the Scribes and Aubers. It was the first night of the new opera *Manon Lescaut*, and though he had attended four hundred of his own first nights Scribe showed great fidgetiness towards the end of the meal, pulling out his watch from time to time and at last bouncing up and bolting from the table. Madame Scribe at once rose from her chair next to Dickens and, 'looking twenty-five though she had a son of thirty', laughed, curtsied to the company and ran after her husband. How wonderfully alert and alive these French women were; middle age and child-bearing seemed to have no effect on their vitality.

With rapidly increasing experience we find Dickens becoming a very bold critic of plays and developing a horror of the Comédie Française. He hated its dreary conventions, which, he said, were calculated to freeze the marrow. To him it was like 'a vast tomb such as you see in eastern legends where one goes to think of unsuccessful loves and dead relations'.

He saw *Le Paradis Perdu* at the Ambigu, a compound of Milton's epic and Byron's *Cain*. The wildest rumours had been flying about before the first night as to the nudity of 'our first parents', for all Paris had been ransacked in a hunt for a woman with brown hair falling to the calves of her legs. 'At last', says Dickens, 'she was found at the Odéon!' Going to a performance of *Comme il vous plaira*, he was much amused to watch the company sitting down as often as possible on as many trunks as possible: ' "gammon" was no word for it!' Macready, who attended a rehearsal, said the speech of the seven ages was delivered as a light comedy joke. Jacques married Celia and 'everything was as wide of Shakespeare as possible'. He counted Jacques sitting down seventeen times on roots of trees and twenty-five times on grey stones, and at the end of the second act he left saying, 'It must have been got up by patients in an asylum for idiots'. It was George Sand who had adapted it, though she told him privately that to adapt Shakespeare was to murder Shakespeare—adding with a shrug, 'As Paris would not accept him *au naturel*, something had to be done about it'.

It was the custom at the moment to suspend performances in theatres to admit of the reading of a bulletin on the war in the Crimea. To an Englishman it was surprising to note the complete apathy with which the French heard these announcements; the audience was 'stagnant as ditch-water'; even the claqueurs remained silent, the war seemed to be nobody's business.

At the Odéon Dickens sat out a play in verse, *Michel Cervantes*, which he pronounced to be 'an infernal dose of ditch-water': and at the Porte Saint Martin saw *Orestes* versified by Dumas. It was so bad as to be almost good. 'If I had not already learnt to tremble at the sight of classic drapery on the human form, I should have plumbed the utmost depths of terrified boredom.' Often he left before the end of a play. He would turn to Kate or Georgy saying, 'It is really unbearable. I shall go and walk two or three miles. You must tell me the end to-night.'

Making friends quickly was, as we know, a Dickens characteristic, and he found he could make delightful women friends in Paris without drawing down on himself the jealousy of anyone. He was greatly attracted to the famous contralto Madame Viardot, sister of La Malibran. 'Elle est parfaite,' he would say with his hand on his heart. 'Je suis son esclave.' Together they talked eagerly of writers and it was she who had been quick to arrange for Dickens the meeting with George Sand. Madame Viardot lived in the new quarter of Paris in a house so impersonal and bare that it looked as if she had moved in the week before and was to leave again the following week. The piano was shut, there was no music about and no books: it was the very last house one could associate with an opera singer, and when she told M. Boz that she had lived there for eight years he was more surprised than he could say. The dinner-party included the Ary Scheffers, the Sartorises, George Sand and 'a typical English lady' fresh from the Crimea, dressed *en paletot*, who smoked incessantly and monologued on her adventures. Dickens describes George Sand, who sat next him, as 'chubby, matronly, swarthy and black-eyed'. 'Chubby' does not seem a very happy adjective for that heavy, sleepy-lidded face with its strong Jewish features, but he further says, 'The human mind cannot conceive anyone more astonishingly opposed to all my preconceptions. If I had been shown her in a state of repose, I should have said the Queen's monthly nurse. *Au reste* she has nothing of the *bas bleu* about her and is very quiet and agreeable.'[1] At a disadvantage in not having read any of her books, whereas she had read all his, Dickens found that in conversation she took the initiative and had a little final way of settling his opinions for him which he took to have been acquired in the province where she lived and where he heard she dominated local society.

At the house of the great anglophile Amédée Pichot, director of the *Revue Britannique* and translator of *David Copperfield*, the Dickenses were also entertained. There, one evening, they renewed acquaintance with Alphonse de Lamartine, who always alluded to the English novelist as 'un des grands amis de mon imagination'. Lighter in hand than George Sand, he made a very unaffected and simple impression as he discussed the writings of Defoe and Richardson and their genius for minute detail in narrative. It was a tribute to Dickens when Lamartine said to Pichot that he had rarely met a foreigner who talked French so easily as 'ce cher Boz'.

Almost more gratifying than any social success was an article in the *Revue des Deux Mondes* which appeared in

February 1856 entitled 'Charles Dickens, son talent et ses œuvres'. It was by Henri Taine and of high importance in placing Dickens for ever among the immortals. The French critic had found it difficult, he confided to a friend, 'de disséquer Boz', but after infinite pains he had done so.

At the time Taine wrote, literally nothing was known of Dickens's life-story, but that he was the son of a stenographer and himself trained to the same profession. Men spoke vaguely of an unhappy youth and of the great wealth and reputation that had come to him through the writing of serial novels. To know more they supposed they must wait till the day when 'M. Boz' published his memoirs. Forty volumes represented the inner history of genius, and as far as anyone knew they in no way depended on the circumstances of his outer life. As Taine sagely observed, 'On a beau être illustre, on ne devient pas pour cela la propriété du public.'

The author of the article had been reading *Martin Chuzzle-wit* in the *Moniteur*. He notes the tendency to depict and the power of seeing in the manner of the camera's eye. With the description of a storm, taken by lightning, he illustrates his contention:

> The eye, partaking of the quickness of the flashing light saw in its every gleam a multitude of objects which it could not see at steady noon in fifty times that period. Bells in steeples with the rope and wheel that moved them; ragged nests of birds in cornices and nooks; faces full of consternation in the tilted waggons that came tearing past: their frightened teams ringing out a warning which the thunder drowned; harrows and ploughs left out in fields; miles upon miles of hedge-divided country, with the distant fringe of trees as obvious as the scarecrow in the beanfield close at hand; in a trembling, vivid, flickering instant, everything was clear and plain: then came a flush of red into the yellow light; a change to blue; a brightness so intense that there was nothing else but light: and then the deepest and profoundest darkness.

There was something definitely new about Dickens, and Taine thought that nothing comparable to this daguerrotype view had been either attempted or achieved by a novelist before. It struck him as astonishing, he felt the need to cover his eyes to shield them against this brilliant and extraordinary perception. To Dickens, Taine's dissection was a revelation. For the first time he had been taken seriously as a literary man by the leading critic of literature in France instead of being torn to pieces by anonymous reviewers.

Work on *Household Words*, which incidentally at this time carried many articles on Paris and France generally, obliged its conductor to make at least one journey a month to London. Sometimes he combined it with readings of *A Christmas Carol*. To please Mrs. Watson, he read it at Peterborough on December 18 from a 'tall pulpit of red baize', so tall that only his head and shoulders were visible. It was this experience that caused him to design and carry about his own reading-desk. The reading was a tribute to Mr. Watson's memory and a great occasion in Northamptonshire. A vote of thanks proposed by Mr. George Fitzwilliam was seconded by Lord Huntley. On December 22 Dickens read the *Carol* again at the Mechanics' Hall, Sheffield, and was presented with a service of table cutlery, a pair of razors and a pair of fish carvers, which he gratefully accepted as indicative of the skill of Sheffield hands and the warmth of Sheffield hearts.

Returning from London to Paris in February, he halted at Chatham in order to make final arrangements for the purchase of Gad's Hill. Though the Reverend James Lynn, who had lived there for thirty years, had died in 1855, his daughter Eliza was unwilling to give him possession before Lady Day 1857. An agreement to this effect having been reached, Dickens paid her the sum of £1790 and then put his dream castle out of his mind till he could live in it. Paris had certainly spoiled him for London, but thank God he would never have to look on London as his only home again.

In March he attended the annual general meeting of the Royal Literary Fund, really to indict the management, which was absorbing 40 per cent of the income. The house in Bloomsbury seemed to him inhabited by gliding ghosts engaged on mysterious occupations. What are these shapes about? To what end are their inquiries and confabulations directed? Do they seek to know whether an applicant deserves relief? It was plain to Dickens that the Fund was being pompously and badly administered at great expense instead of being simply administered at small expense. The secrecy to which it laid claim as its essential attribute was not preserved, for, through the 'two respectable householders' to whom reference must be made, the names of deserving applicants became perfectly well known to numbers of people. He begged the committee to decide what the Literary Fund was for and what it was not for. Was it a public corporation for the relief of men of genius and learning, or a smug, tradition-ridden, conventional society 'bent upon maintaining its own usages with a vast amount of pride, upon its own puffing at costly dinner tables and upon a course of expensive toadying to a number of distinguished individuals'. 'These are the questions', he told his audience, 'that you cannot this day escape from.' This speech was but one of the many efforts made by Dickens during his lifetime to raise the position of authors to a dignity accorded to them in France, but denied to them in England.

From this March outing he returned to Paris with an account of the burning down of Covent Garden, and with some 'pulverising', 'scarifying' *secret* news about Forster that excited Kate and Georgy to frenzy. Imagine old 'Fuz' getting himself engaged to Henry Colburn's widow and never telling them a word about it! Charles said you could have knocked him down with a feather when he first heard of it, and Kate and Georgy simply could not believe the news was true.

Once more Dickens settled down happily in Paris, where the delightful parties, the sympathetic conversation, the kindness and appreciation shown by the Parisians he most wished to be on good terms with made it difficult to concentrate even on *Little Dorrit*, the earliest issues of which had already surpassed those of *Bleak House*, for forty thousand copies of each number were being disposed of. 'It is a tremendous start', he wrote, 'and I am overjoyed at it.' In order to get his monthly fascicule completed within the prescribed fortnight he would walk round the walls of Paris, leaving it by the Barrière de l'Etoile and turning right one day and left the next. On the road he would often meet French regiments with bands playing airs from *Il Trovatore* and *Il Barbière di Siviglia* to which his thoughts jigged along in pursuit of the Tite Barnacle family and their antics at the Circumlocution Office.

In April Dickens dined with M. Hachette the publisher, in order to make acquaintance with his translators. It was, he commented, an 'odd sticky dinner' with salmon coming late on the menu and lobster following sweet. M. Hachette offered to pay him for French rights at the rate of £40 a month for a year, and Dickens was glad to acknowledge in a printed address to French readers of his books that M. Hachette had behaved throughout the negotiations in a 'spirited, liberal and generous manner'.

Almost as soon as he had settled in the Champs Elysées Dickens had been pounced on to pose for his portrait by Ary Scheffer, who on first seeing him said, 'You are not at all like what I expected to see; you are like a Dutch skipper.' Every day in November Dickens had to sit to this artist and the inaction drove him half distracted because the time wasted might have been given to writing. Ary Scheffer was a nice enough man and the people who frequented his house were delightful, but, as Dickens wrote to a friend, 'I can hardly express how uneasy and unsettled it makes me to have to sit, sit, sit with *Little Dorrit* on my mind and the Christmas business too . . . and the crowning feature is that I do not discern the slightest resemblance either in his portrait or his brother's! They both peg away at me at the same time.'

The sittings dragged on into the new year and made the sitter long to escape to the St. Bernard Hospice or somewhere equally remote. After a while the likeness became 'a nightmare portrait'; Dickens said it was very well painted with 'a fine spirited head that does not look at all like the original'. Wilkie Collins praised the picture and said Scheffer had been 'particularly successful with the eyes', which is untrue as they droop and lack vitality. One looks in vain for the confident alert expression of a man who has the world at his feet.

It was with fresh interest that Dickens attended the Royal Academy dinner in May, for he was able to tell Panizzi, whom he sat next, many details about French artists in Paris and the interesting work they were doing. London at the moment was celebrating the end of the Crimean War with illuminations and Dickens asked permission of Dean Milman to describe the scene from the top of St. Paul's for *Household Words*.

By the time the International Exhibition of art opened in Paris Dickens was very dissatisfied with the way English artists were painting. Frith, Egg and Ward seemed to him to come out best, but on the whole the work of his compatriots appeared to him lifeless, niggling and conventional. 'There is a horrid respectability about most of the best of them—a little, finite, systematic routine in them, strangely symptomatic to me of the state of England itself.' Of course there were bad French pictures, but the goodness of the good ones, their fearlessness, action, passion, left him lamenting that 'mere form and conventionalities usurp in English art, as in English government and social relations, the place of living force and truth'. And when we call to mind that Dickens had seen the work of Degas, Puvis, Manet, Courbet, Corot, Ingres, Millet and others, we are not surprised at his strictures. The exhibition attracted crowds of English visitors, including the Brownings, Thackeray, Owen Meredith, and many artists, among whom Dickens makes special mention of his friends Edwin Landseer and Charles Leslie. Several times he went to the English section and each time tried to praise and admire with 'great diligence', but it was of no use; his 'convictions as to their want of interest' remained unchanged.

More and more did Dickens seem to be drifting away from the insular point of view both of England and the continent.

The very thought of London now filled him with apprehension. 'I have never taken to it kindly since I lived abroad. Whenever I come back from the country now and see that great heavy canopy lowering over the housetops, I wonder what on earth I do there except of obligation.' He simply could not face the idea of returning to England for the summer: they must all go back to M. Beaucourt's château at Boulogne. There he felt more free than at Broadstairs, for he could don a workman's blouse, complete with leathern belt and cap, dawdle among the terraces and fountains, loaf on the pier and with regret observe the little seaport being vulgarised by 'insolent' English day trippers. And when the call came to him to work he could count on writing the next number of *Little Dorrit* without much trouble.

Although the Wimereux camp was by this time evacuated, an act was staged at the local fair showing the capture of the Malakoff redoubt—the key to Sevastopol—a triumph for French arms. Most French soldiers wore an English medal which they called 'The Salvage Medal', meaning that they got it for saving the English army. 'I don't suppose there are a thousand people in all France who believe that we did anything except get rescued by the French. . . . Nobody at home has yet any adequate idea of what the Barnacles and the Circumlocution Office have done for us.'

Cattermole and his family had also become tenants of M. Beaucourt for the summer—unsatisfactory tenants, as they could not pay their bills or their servants. In the end one of their sons had to act as cook to the whole family, who between them in the washing-up managed to break all the glass and china. In spite of this loss the good-hearted Beaucourts insisted that the poor little cook, Walter, should dine with them every day.

The outbreak of an epidemic known as 'Boulogne sore-throat' (really diphtheria) in late August sent the Dickenses hurrying back on Dr. Olliffe's orders to London. Gilbert à Beckett and his child had died after a few days' illness, and the *plage* had suddenly become desolate. The George

Hogarths, who were in possession at Tavistock House, were told to find other quarters at once and Dickens remained at Dover till he was certain they had cleared out, as 'he really could not bear the contemplation of their imbecility any longer'.

Both in Paris and Boulogne Wilkie Collins had danced in constant attendance on Dickens. Though he had not actually slept at 49 Champs Elysées, he had engaged a room at No. 63 so as to dine every day with the family, and when the transfer to Boulogne took place he occupied a cottage in the grounds. So indispensable had he become to the conductor of *Household Words* that in September 1856 he was appointed assistant editor at five guineas a week. Dickens admired Collins's stories at this time extremely and found him always ready to work for him. As the friendship grew ever closer we cannot but notice a falling-off in Forster's biography, and Forster as a married man was almost entirely superseded in intimacy and influence by the younger friend. It may be for this reason that the biography becomes a less reliable and almost a different kind of book, just as Dickens himself, under Collins's influence, became almost a different kind of man.

Chapter 22

ARCTIC CONCERNS

*Here, then, you have a tragedy, by its very origin, in mere
virtue of the accidents out of which it arose.*

DE QUINCEY

THREADING through the letters written by Dickens during
the spring and summer of 1856 are allusions to a play that
is being written by Wilkie Collins for Christmas production.
Miss Coutts and others were told it was 'a very special sort of
drama', and the family, who were to help act it, were kept on
the tiptoe of excitement as to its subject.   Ever since reading
Dr. Rae's Report on Sir John Franklin's last Arctic expedition, published by the Admiralty, Dickens had been haunted
by the tortures its members had endured before dying of
starvation.   He was particularly shocked by the paragraph in
which Dr. Rae said of the encampment in which they
perished:

> From the mutilated state of the corpses and the contents
> of the kettles, it is evident that our wretched countrymen
> had been driven to the last resource—cannibalism—as a
> means of prolonging existence.

Dickens maintained that Franklin's manly record of his own
sufferings and those of his men, all picked for character, gave
the lie to this monstrous inference, and he set himself to dis-
prove the paragraph and so remove from the minds of these
brave men's relations a most painful impression.   The task
he undertook was to write an article testing the story by the
most trying and famous cases of hunger and exposure on
record.   For a time he immersed himself in the stories of the
wrecks of the *Bounty*, *Peggy*, *Pandora*, *Juno*, *Medusa*, just as
Byron had done before writing canto II of *Don Juan*.
Dickens studied the records of those and other unfortunate
ships until he had familiarised himself with every possible

aspect of the horrors of shipwreck. These he talked over with Wilkie Collins, who in his turn wondered whether they could not be dramatised. With Dickens's help *The Frozen Deep* came to be written.

Still in holiday mood, Dickens, on his return from Boulogne in the first days of September, began to turn Tavistock House once again into a theatre. A meeting was summoned for October 20 of Stanfield, Lemon, Egg, Forster and other potential helpers at which the new play, *The Frozen Deep*, was read aloud. Dickens seemed delighted with the effect it produced and at once ordered a fair copy to be made for his own use. Then, after allocating the parts between friends and family, he told the members of the caste that each was responsible for copying out his or her lines. Rehearsals would take place every Friday in November, and later there might be more frequent repetitions. It was to be the most perfect amateur production imaginable.

At a cost of £50 and a clangour like that of 'shipbuilding in Chatham Dockyard', the schoolroom was converted into a neat theatre. Everything to do with the stage, even the hammering, put Dickens into the highest spirits, and when 'dear old Stanny' arrived with seventy pots of paint, a ball of string and an umbrella for measuring boards, backcloth and curtain, his mood became hilarious. At intervals he disappeared from view to get on with his *Little Dorrit* quota. In one of these retired moments he wrote to Macready:

> Calm amidst the wreck, your aged friend glides away on the Dorrit stream, forgetting the uproar for a stretch of hours, refreshing himself with a ten or twelve miles' walk, pitches headforemost into foaming rehearsals, placidly emerges for editorial purposes, smokes over buckets of distemper with Mr. Stanfield aforesaid, again calmly floats upon the Dorrit waters.[1]

The autumn, as Charley, aged nineteen, recollected it, was 'one long rehearsal', during which hospitality was dispensed on the most lavish scale. Such abnormal quantities of meat were ordered in that the butcher thought he was but doing his duty to Mrs. Dickens (when she returned from a short rest-cure in the country) by calling to inquire if everything was in order. Kate had gone away to escape the worst of the noise, but now she and Charles put their heads together over the invitations to the play. There would be in all nearly four hundred guests to accommodate, which meant that the performance would have to be repeated four times. Just over ninety chairs could be placed in the auditorium each night, but the problem of seating 'was intensified by crino-lines'. It was obviously necessary to put up an extra room outside the house for cloaks and if necessary use it as an extension for standing at the back of the seated audience. January 6, 8, 12 and 14 were decided on for the nights, and the Duke of Devonshire was requested to name his own evening as Lord Lansdowne, Lord Houghton, Miss Coutts and Bulwer Lytton were to be invited to supper to meet him. Mrs. Dickens had a great deal of work to do in arranging for the grand refections that were to follow the acting as well as for the endless hospitality enforced on her by ever more frequent and prolonged rehearsals.

The better to imagine himself an arctic explorer, Dickens grew a beard instead of the neat moustache and tiny chin-tuft depicted by Ary Scheffer. Forster found this a very tiresome innovation since he had commissioned Frith to paint him a portrait of his friend for £50.[1] The artist was now told to hold his hand until such time as Dickens shaved again, but, after two years of waiting, he had to go ahead with the paint-ing, as the beard was evidently there for life. Wilkie Collins, who up to that time had been clean-shaven, also grew a beard for the part of Frank Aldersley which he never again removed. To get word-perfect in his Wardour lines Dickens used to walk of an evening along the Finchley Road to Willesden 'shouting his part to the great terror' of the localities he

---

[1] In 1859 he paid 300 guineas to Frith, 150 for the portrait and 150 for the copyright.

passed through. Clara Burnham was played by Mamey Dickens and two other female characters were taken by Katey Dickens and Georgy Hogarth. Francesco Berger, a Leipzig friend of Charley Dickens, wrote the overture and incidental music for the play.

The play was to be preceded by a prologue written by Dickens. Forster was to speak it and could be heard mouthing his words as he prowled about the house. It seemed to Kate, when taken off her guard, that dear Macready must have come to help them as of old.

The action of *The Frozen Deep* is set in the arctic regions which, owing to the Franklin voyages, were now everyone's concern. The two principal male characters in the play, Richard Wardour and Frank Aldersley, are officers on two ships of an arctic expedition seeking the North-West Passage. Both are in love with the same girl, Clara Burnham, who favours Aldersley. After two years of adventure and privation both men find themselves adrift on the same ice-floe. Wardour, the stronger of the two, has Aldersley in his power and could leave him to freeze to death. He saves him by sacrificing his own meagre comforts and food, thus preserving him for Clara, who, having been given a passage on the Government relief ship, is awaiting them in Newfoundland.

On the first night Forster was ordered to recite the Prologue behind the scene and could be heard inviting an audience keyed to the highest pitch of expectancy to

> Pause on the footprints of heroic men,
> Making a garden of the desert wide
> Where PARRY conquer'd death and FRANKLIN died.

> To that white region where the Lost lie low,
> Wrapp'd in their mantles of eternal snow;
> Unvisited by change, nothing to mock
> Those statues sculptured in the icy rock,
> We pray your company; that hearts as true
> (Though nothings of the air) may live for you;
> Nor only yet that on our little glass
> A faint reflection of those wilds may pass.

> But, that the secrets of the vast Profound
> Within us, an exploring hand may sound,
> Testing the region of the ice-bound soul,
> Seeking the passage at its northern pole,
> Soft'ning the horrors of its wintry sleep,
> Melting the surface of that 'Frozen Deep'.

The lighting effects were of a very special kind and denoted the passage of time. Day faded into evening, and evening into night. The audience was entranced by these unexpected novelties.

The first act makes us acquainted with four young ladies living in Devon, each of whom has a lover serving with a Polar expedition. Clara Burnham not only has her betrothed out in the icy regions, but the rejected lover who has sworn to kill him wherever and whenever they meet, though he does not even know the name of his rival. Clara, haunted by the fear that some mysterious influence may reveal them to each other, tells her story to Lucy Crayford. As she does so, a crimson sunset dies away to grey and Nurse Esther goes about the house murmuring of scenes that come to her from 'the land o' ice and snaw'. She stands, as night falls, by the misty blue of the window, describing to the young ladies her bloody vision from the Northern seas. Lucy Crayford shudders and calls for lights: Clara Burnham swoons.

The second act is set in the arctic regions. The stranded men are in a hut deciding who is to go and seek relief. Frank Aldersley is chosen by lot, and when somebody else falls out Richard Wardour has to accompany him. Just before they start Wardour discovers that Aldersley is his hated rival.

The third act takes place in a cavern in Newfoundland. The girls, smartly dressed in crinolines, their Scotch nurse, and some members of the expedition are present, but neither Wardour nor Aldersley. Presently a ragged maniac rushes in and is given food and drink. He has escaped from an ice-floe but is not too demented to recognise and be recognised by Clara Burnham, who suspects him of having

murdered her Frank   As soon as he understands this he
goes off, returning a few minutes later with Aldersley in his
arms to lay at Clara's feet.   'Often', he gasps, 'in supporting
Aldersley through snow-drifts and on ice-floes have I been
tempted to leave him sleeping.'   He has not done so and is
now exhausted to death.   Wardour's distraught looks, his
hysterical burst of joy at being able to prove himself no
murderer, the melting tenderness with which he kisses his
only love and then his 'fearfully fine' death under the Union
Jack, reduced his audience to tears.   Everyone said it was a
most touching and beautiful performance.

Dickens enjoyed the sacrificial role of Richard Wardour
immensely.   No eye was dry when he bestowed upon the
happily reunited lovers his dying benediction.   A hush
followed the fall of the curtain and was maintained while the
little orchestra, led by Francesco Berger at the piano, played
the music specially written for the occasion.   Recomposed,
the audience was led into a more cheerful mood by Buck-
stone's farce *Uncle John*, which prepared them for the
champagne, oysters and other delicacies they were presently
to enjoy.

'I am perfectly happy with the success', wrote Dickens
next morning, and when all four performances were over
and the stage in process of being dismantled he was pleased
to be told, 'The play has been the talk of London these three
weeks'.   How sore he was to think that two of his dearest
friends, Mrs. Watson and 'Dan' Maclise, had missed it!

It is important at this point to note that during all the
months of 1856 relations, according to the private correspondence, remained obviously normal between Charles
Dickens and his wife.   There is no thought of separation in
his mind or in hers.   Letters to 'My dearest Catharine' were
written, when they were apart, about family affairs, all showing the ordinary confidence of a man in his partner.   She will
be interested in the weather, in the Channel passage, in the
Academy dinner, in what he said to Panizzi and what Webster

said to him.   A large lilac tree has been blown down in their
Tavistock garden.   He will see about a new passport.   The
house has had a thorough cleaning, every room has been
scrubbed, aired, purified from roof to hall.   Maclise has
given him a funny description of Mrs. Henry Colburn which
he proceeds to quote.   It is safe for the boys to return to
school at Boulogne, for the epidemic has ended.   He fears
she will have a rough passage taking them across the Channel
and encloses a cheque.   Writing after the first rehearsal of
The Frozen Deep he tells her that the new cook 'is no good'.
'All love, and Forster's new house is excellently done up.'
Again he says that 'the rehearsals are most satisfactory considering Mark Lemon has a rheumatic jaw and Berger a
frightful cold'.   This is the tone of all the letters of 1856.

Dearest 'Meery' Boyle danced the old year out at Tavistock
House.   With Charles as partner she romped through
'avenues' of guests in a country dance.   It was but one of
'the innumerable evenings' spent at the house of enchantment
'where all that was eminent in Literature and Art or endowed
with social and intellectual gifts was sure to find a welcome'.
She was also present on Twelfth Night when *The Frozen
Deep* was produced and a smiling, handsomely-gowned Mrs.
Dickens received the guests while an excited Mr. Dickens was
putting the last touches to Richard Wardour's expressive
countenance.   On three subsequent nights Mrs. Dickens
beamed a welcome to her many guests.

In February 1857 Charles obtained possession of Gad's
Hill and took Kate to Waite's Hotel at Gravesend, a house
known for its comfort and good cooking.   From there he
intended they should both superintend the alterations needed
in their new house, the changes in the garden, and the boring
for water.   While at Gravesend he went on working at
Little Dorrit who was creating for herself a circle of warm
admirers.   Among the letters that reached her creator was
one from Hans Andersen to say he was spell-bound by the
book and found little Dorrit quite as lovable as little Nell.

I would and must admire you for the sake of this one book alone even if you had not previously bestowed upon the world those splendid compositions, 'David Copperfield,' 'Little Nelly' and the rest. When I last spoke with you . . . in England you presented me with your published works. . . . I possess the latest books, but you must give me a copy of *Little Dorrit* when we greet each other again. God's blessing and delight be yours as you delight us all.

In this letter Andersen was obviously fishing for an invitation to stay. He was thinking of coming over to London, but not for London's sake; no, it would be for Dickens's sake and for Dickens's sake alone. Charles and Kate agreed there was nothing for it but to press him to come to them, tell him to make Gad's Hill his home and assure him that he may live as quietly there as in Copenhagen. The fairy-tale author took his dear 'Boz' at his word, arriving on June 8 and (as we see from his letter to the Queen-Dowager in Denmark) he made a long stay. 'I have now been in England five weeks and have spent the whole time with Charles Dickens at his charming villa at Gad's Hill.'

Mrs. Dickens liked him and his childish dependent ways and took complete charge of him. He thought her a 'charming chatelaine', and her 'womanly repose, china blue eyes and smile' made him associate her with the character of Agnes in *David Copperfield*. Hans was very simple and Kate was simple too, there were no barriers between them and they talked much of the children. How delightful it was to learn that the little boys were all called after poets and writers! What talents their names conjured up, and what fun it was to play in the hay with Edward Bulwer Lytton and Henry Fielding, Sydney Smith and Alfred Tennyson, and then to discuss their aptitudes with their mother! The large field of clover close to the house made a good playground. 'The sons and I are often lying there', wrote Hans naïvely, 'there is a fragrance of clover, the elder tree is in blossom and the wild roses have an odour of apples so fresh and strong.' He basked in the family life and saw no sign of any rift between his host and hostess: both personified for him 'the spirit of true amiability'.

One evening they strolled to the top of Gad's Hill and lay on the grass in a circle to watch the sun go down. The windings of the river turned into a ribbon of gold: ships stood out like black silhouettes: blue smoke curled over cottages: bells in the distance pealed, while near by the grasshoppers chirped. A great bowl of claret-cup, complete with its bunch of borage, circulated from hand to hand, and presently the moon came up round, red and large, mounting the heavens till it shone in clear purity and made the fairy-tale teller feel as if he were living in a midsummer night's dream. That evening his host was full of joy, very fresh, very impulsive. What a memory to take home to Denmark!

His first trip to London was made for the funeral of Douglas Jerrold whom he had got to know well during his former visit and who had died about the time he landed in England. Only a week before his collapse Jerrold had dined at a party given at Greenwich by William Howard Russell to meet Dickens, Delane and other old friends. When Jerrold died so unexpectedly Russell begged for an assurance from Dickens that he was not the cause of his demise. This Dickens readily gave him, telling him at the same time that he was planning help for Jerrold's widow. One gathers from the Jerrold side that this was not altogether a welcome intervention. But there was no gainsaying Dickens when he had made up his mind to theatricals. The proposed benefit offered a wonderful chance of reviving *The Frozen Deep*; he had other ideas, too, in his head such as reading the *Carol*, persuading Thackeray to give a lecture, and coaxing Wilkie Collins to co-operate in some way. Intentions seethed in his head; he would announce his decisions after the funeral. On the morning of the funeral Edmund Yates received a note from Dickens inviting him to dine that evening at the Garrick. Albert and Arthur Smith were to be of the party. They had all been to the ceremony at Norwood earlier in the day and Dickens spoke very strongly against the extravagant

way it had been conducted.   Mourners had worn bands of
crape round their arms with the initials D. J., and the car for
the coffin was like that provided for the Duke of Wellington.
After dinner he unfolded his plan for helping Mrs. Jerrold,
for whom he hoped to collect £2000.   Andersen was much
touched by his host's spontaneity and eagerness to help a
friend's widow and much impressed, too, to see the business-
like way Dickens assembled his cast, organised rehearsals,
and set up a committee office at the Gallery of Illustration in
Regent Street.   Notices headed 'In Remembrance of the late
Mr. Douglas Jerrold' appeared in no time announcing that on
Saturday, July 4, *The Frozen Deep* by Wilkie Collins would be
staged at the Gallery of Illustration privately for the Queen
and that other performances for the public would follow.

While this philanthropic activity was absorbing the time of
Dickens and his daughters, Andersen was taken about by
Mrs. Dickens, who, after driving her guest to the cemetery at
Norwood for the Jerrold interment, took him on to the
Crystal Palace for the first of the Handel festivals when *The
Messiah* was given before an audience of 12,000 persons.
The vast glass building seemed to Hans Andersen like an
Aladdin's palace, and when the music began to swirl round
him he told Kate he wanted to cry and ended by doing so.
From the concert hall they moved to the terrace and watched
the water 'from a thousand fountains blown in a sweepy veil
over gardens all sparkling in the sunshine'.   It amused him to
watch 'many little crinolined monsters reeling before the
spray'.   Another outing with Mrs. Dickens was to the
theatre to see the great Italian actress Ristori in the part of
Lady Macbeth.   He felt rather forlorn next day when Mr.
and Mrs. Dickens returned to 'dear' Gad's Hill leaving him
to the hospitality of his great admirer, Miss Coutts.   Miss
Coutts was not nearly so scaring to the nervous Dane as
were her 'proud servants' who understood nothing he said.
His hostess talked German and he could explain to her what
they failed to understand, that his bed in her house in Stratton
Street was not to his liking as he was accustomed to sleeping

o

high on a mound of pillows. Miss Coutts smiled comprehension and, going up with him to his room, helped him
to remake the bed. He then confided to her that he could
not exist without soda-water, which she at once ran off to
fetch 'with her own hands'. His bedroom, 'the like of which
I have never seen before', had 'a bright fire, costly carpets and
windows giving on to a garden and Piccadilly'. That
evening in Miss Coutts's drawing-room he met the whole
fashionable world and next day his hostess drove him out to
her Highgate estate, Holly Lodge, to walk in the garden there.
This was all very gracious and very pleasant, but the fairy-tale
writer had not come to England to go to parties, shake hands
with smart people and receive compliments. It was Dickens
he wanted to be with all the time, just walking 'arm-in-arm'
with this greatest of living authors through the streets and
squares so remarkably described by him.

To the private performance of *The Frozen Deep* Andersen
was taken by Mrs. Dickens and it gratified him to see what a
select affair it was, only fifty persons present, and among them
the Queen, Prince Albert and the King of the Belgians.
Georgy Hogarth, who had by this time taken up a very
amicable confidential pose with Mrs. Winter, wrote to her new
friend, 'The Queen and Her party made a *most excellent*
audience'. Andersen expressed particular satisfaction with
the lovely hothouse flowers, provided by the Duke of
Somerset, but it seemed to him very odd indeed that his host
should excuse himself from presentation to the Queen.
Neither in Denmark nor in Germany could one brush Royal
personages aside in this way. The English were certainly a
very odd race and how they could endure the London air in
summer-time he could not think. To him it seemed 'very
coaly' and the June heat difficult to bear. How preferable it
would really have been to stay at Gad's Hill all the time, but,
if he had insisted on doing that, he would have missed those
wonderful walks through the streets with 'Boz'. One day
he had to submit to being taken to the house of Dickens's

lawyer, Mr. Ouvry, North End Lodge. Another day he was conveyed to Albert Smith's party at Walham Green, when the 'Glaciers of Mont Blanc' found great amusement in entertaining the 'Icebergs of the Frozen Deep'. Albert Smith was the author of *Christopher Tadpole*, who combined work for *Punch* with entertaining at the Egyptian Hall: Mark Lemon, editor of *Punch*, and other members of the staff were among the guests dining on the lawn and quaffing 'great goblets of champagne'. It was all very different from the frugality Andersen was used to at home.

To Andersen's first English friend, William Jerdan, Dickens confided that his guest got into embarrassing entanglements if left to himself in London and to fits of chagrin if left to himself in the country. One day they brought him up from Gad's Hill and had lost him at the London Bridge terminus whence he had driven away in a cab by himself. When he turned up he told them that as he passed through the new unfinished streets of Clerkenwell he made sure his driver was carrying him off 'to a remote fastness' to be robbed and murdered, and he had stuffed his watch, his pocket-book and all his money in his boots! Another day at Gad's Hill, Mrs. Dickens had found him, weeping bitterly, face down in the clover. Seeing that he clutched a newspaper she asked, 'Are any of your friends dead?' 'No, no,' faltered Andersen. He had, it appeared, been reading an adverse review, 'a perfectly nasty criticism', of his latest story. It was easy in a way to cheer him up for his sense of humour was that of a child. He could be made quite happy again by being asked to cut fairies and elves out of paper or mats with intricate lacy patterns. He also delighted in being dragged off by the Dickens children to gather flowers in the woods, of which he would make 'the strangest little nosegays'. Wilkie Collins had only to appear in a wide-awake for Andersen to manage, unobserved, to slip a daisy-chain over its crown. He then took Collins and the children to the village, where the wearer of the wide-awake was surprised to see everyone laughing at his appearance.

It was with a feeling akin to relief that Dickens one July day drove his friend to Maidstone and after embracing him affectionately put him in the train. Hans Andersen was tearful, and recorded, 'I travelled alone in the steam serpent to Folkestone. Dickens was like a dear brother to me to the last moment.'

The visit had been an outstanding success from the Dane's point of view; he had on the whole been happy, for the entire family had laid themselves out to amuse him, and Dickens had even invited his old enemy Bentley for a couple of nights to Gad's Hill for his benefit. When the great man was safely gone Dickens stuck a card up on the dressing-table mirror in the room he had used and on it was written, 'Hans Andersen slept in this room for five weeks which seemed to the family ages'.

One might have hoped for interesting impressions of Charles Dickens from so practised a writer, but there is nothing more than he set down at the time in his letters to the Queen-Dowager of Denmark and Henrietta Wulff, except for a short article of reminiscences published in *Temple Bar* after Dickens's death. Paris seemed terribly dreary to him after London; he said it seemed to him like 'a beehive without honey'. As time went on Andersen tended to become even to Dickens what he had long since become to his girls Mamey and Katey, 'a bony bore'. Many were the strangers who arrived on the Dickens doorstep with letters of introduction signed by Hans Christian Andersen. Eventually the friendship languished and died, maybe because Dickens got to know that Andersen gossiped by letter with his friend the Grand Duke about the Jerrold benefit, saying that Jerrold's son had protested against 'the hat being carried round' as his mother had not been left in 'straitened circumstances'.

Four days after Andersen left England Walter Landor Dickens sailed for India. With a good deal of forethought Charles Dickens was mapping out lives for his seven sons. Charley, after returning from Leipzig, had been, through the interest of Miss Coutts, entered to Baring's and through the same interest an East Indian cadetship had been secured for Walter Landor. Walter had at one time shown signs of following in his father's footsteps, but his tutor was instructed *not* to press him to write, 'the less he is encouraged to write the better . . . and the happier he will be'. Though the actual leave-taking shattered Dickens for a day or two, he soon got over it and was able to preen himself on having provided a career for a second son, even though the boy had no inclination for the life he had been assigned to. A very small figure in a uniform made to allow for development appears pathetically in a faded photograph. The face that looks out beneath the military shako is that of an unhappy child. But it was part of the Victorian tradition to ship boys to India. So fitted out with flannel, quinine, essence of ginger and Jeremy's opium, Walter Landor was conveyed to his ship by father and eldest brother. 'A sad trial', wrote Dickens, 'thank God it is over. The dear boy bore it a great deal better than we could have hoped.'

Walter Landor never set foot on English earth again. The climate of India affected him adversely during his attachment to the East India Company and, after his exchange into the Black Watch and his posting to a hill station, his health broke down completely. Many rosy-faced English lads have died in the far corners of the world and Walter joined their company. Invalided home too late, death snatched him as he was passing through Calcutta. He died there of a haemorrhage on the last day of 1863.

Chapter 23

SEPARATION

Unless we hoped and feared, life would have no meaning for us. Apart from such commotions of our inner selves there could be no living.
BENEDETTO CROCE

TEN days after Walter Landor had sailed for the Indies his father was reading *A Christmas Carol* to enraptured audiences at Manchester and deriving immense pleasure therefrom. He was receiving overtures, too, from 'Manchester Magnates' begging him to produce a play again in their city. Most willingly did he agree to do so, and writing to Wilkie Collins said that he had arranged for *The Frozen Deep* to be acted in the Free Trade Hall on August 21 and 22. 'It is an *immense* place and we shall be obliged to have actresses; I am already trying to get the best who *have been* on the stage.' Two days earlier he had written to Mrs. Compton asking her co-operation. 'The place is out of the question for my girls. Their action could not be seen, their voices could not be heard'; but Mrs. Compton could not oblige, and so he applied to Wigan, manager of the Olympic Theatre, for names of substitutes and on his recommendation engaged Mrs. Ternan and her two daughters, Maria and Ellen, for the parts. One member at least of this theatrical family was already known to Dickens, for some months earlier he, who rarely missed seeing a new play, had watched Ellen Ternan act the part of Hippomenes in *Atalanta*,[1] a play by Talfourd. Going to Ellen Ternan's dressing-room before she went on the stage, he found her in tears at having 'to show so much leg'. Charmed by her modesty, Dickens thought her 'most attractive and a sweet little thing'. After 'Boz' had engaged the professional ladies to replace 'the Tavistock girls', he bustled up from Gad's Hill to give them 'a three-days drill in

[1] Haymarket, April 1857.

their parts' and now for the first time we become aware that a serious emotional disturbance may be brewing. Little, fair-haired Ellen Ternan, with her sympathetic blue eyes, took up such a worshipping attitude and seemed so pathetically anxious to interpret every line and gesture according to Dickens's wishes that she completely captivated him. The rehearsals took place at Tavistock House and the more its owner coached his team, the more his infatuation for Ellen grew. Both the Miss Ternans were charming and both ran in and out of the study, but only one sat on the arm of the manager's chair, sang duets with him at the schoolroom piano and seemed, to the family, to take possession of the house. *The Frozen Deep* had always to be followed by a farce so that the audience should not be sent away in tears. The farce chosen on this occasion was *Uncle John*. 'Uncle John' was an old gentleman who had educated a young girl and in the process had fallen in love with her. When she was eighteen he asked her to marry him, and the piece opens on their wedding morning with the arrival of Uncle John's niece and her husband. This couple somehow contrive to persuade the bride that she is really in love with her drawing-master and each to believe the other the prey of unrequited passion. After a few rehearsals Dickens's emotional equilibrium was upset. In the play Uncle John had to load his bride with 'wonderful presents—a pearl necklace and diamond earrings', and his impersonator found it irresistible to give his sweet little friend some real jewelry. Kate Dickens, who knew the plot and the words only too well, realised what must be going on when a bracelet ordered for Ellen was delivered to her by mistake. It annoyed her extremely, for her husband was not a boy and after twenty years of married life it was an insult to her to make love under her very roof to a girl of eighteen. At once she flared into a scene with Charles, who told her that it was within her power to show her confidence in him and her belief in the girl's innocence by calling on her mother. He did not at all want his daughters to think he was not behaving correctly, the daughters of course being of an age to notice

things and draw their own conclusions. The second girl,
Katey, was quite alive to the situation and tells[1] us that at the
very commencement of this affair, as she passed her parents'
bedroom, the door of which was ajar, she heard sobs, and on
going in found her mother seated at the dressing-table
putting on her bonnet. When she asked what the tears were
about a stifled voice replied, 'Your father has asked me to go
and see Ellen Ternan'. 'You shall not go,' said Katey,
stamping her foot; but Mrs. Dickens did as she was asked,
for her complyingness, where Charles was concerned, was
boundless.

On August 20 Dickens, in 'inimitable' form, went up to
Manchester with his troupe, where *The Frozen Deep* was
played on August 21 and 22, followed as usual by *Uncle John*.
Never had Dickens acted so well, never had he enjoyed himself so much. Wilkie Collins says 'he electrified the audiences', and well he might, for he had fallen violently in love
and was a passionate youth again.

The part of the heroine, Clara Burnham, was not played by
Ellen Ternan but by her sister Maria. And Dickens in a
letter to Miss Coutts appears to be making an effort to put her
off the scent of any scandal for he focusses all interest on
Maria and does not so much as mention her sister. If his
sub-editor, Wills, now Miss Coutts's secretary, has been
gossiping to her, this letter should disarm criticism:

Perhaps Mr. Wills has not told you how much impressed
I was at Manchester by the womanly tenderness of a very
gentle and good little girl who acted Clara's part. She
came to see the play beforehand at the Gallery of Illustration, and when we rehearsed it, she said, 'I am afraid, Mr.
Dickens, I shall never be able to bear it: it affected me so
much when I saw it, that I hope you will excuse my trembling this morning, for I am afraid of myself.' At night
when she came out of the cave and Wardour recognised
her I never saw anything like the distress and agitation of
her face—a very good little pale face, with large black eyes:

[1] G. Storey, *Dickens and Daughter*, p. 96.

—it has a natural emotion in it which was quite a study of expression. But when she had to kneel over Wardour dying, and be taken leave of, the tears streamed out of her eyes into his mouth, down his beard, all over his rags——down his arms as he held her by the hair. At the same time she sobbed as if she were breaking her heart, and was quite convulsed with grief. It was of no use for the compassionate Wardour to whisper, 'My dear child, it will be over in two minutes—there is nothing the matter—don't be so distressed!' She could only sob out, 'O! it's so sad, O! it's so sad,' and set Mr. Lemon (the softest-hearted of men) crying too. By the time the curtain fell we were all crying together, and then her mother and sister used to come and put her in a chair and comfort her, before taking her away to be dressed for the Farce. I told her on the last night that I was sure that she had one of the most genuine and feeling hearts in the world; and I don't think I ever saw anything more prettily simple and unaffected. Yet I remember her on the stage, a little child, and I daresay she was born in a country theatre. . . . Miss Maria Ternan, that is the young lady.[1]

It might be possible to put Miss Coutts off the scent, but it was less easy to delude Forster to whom on the same day he wrote:

You are not so tolerant as perhaps you might be of the wayward and unsettled feeling which is part (I suppose) of the tenure on which one holds an imaginative life, and which I have, as you ought to know well, often kept down by riding over it like a dragoon—but let that go by, I make no maudlin complaint. I am always deeply sensible of the wonderful exercise I have of life and its highest sensations and have said to myself for years, and have honestly and truly felt, this is the drawback to such a career and is not to be complained of. . . . I claim no immunity from blame—there is plenty of fault on my side in the way of a thousand uncertainties, caprices, and difficulties of disposition. The gist is that it is a mistake to marry too young and that the years are not making things easier . . . reasons have been growing which make it all but hopeless that we should even try to struggle on. . . . It is too late to say put the curb on.[1]

The elation at Manchester was followed by a very bad slump in spirits. 'Partly from grim despair and subsidence from excitement and partly for the sake of *Household Words*', he invited Wilkie Collins to take a tour with him *anywhere*. 'I want to escape from myself, my misery is amazing.' To Stone he spoke of 'low pulse, low voice, low spirits, intense reaction'. Early in September the two friends went off to Carlisle, and climbing Carrock Fell, Collins sprained his foot and had to be transported 'Wardour-wise' to the hotel whence they moved to Allonby, 'a deserted, clean little place with fifty houses, five bathing machines, five young men and five young women'. The landlady of the Ship hotel recognised her illustrious guest at once; she had seen him years earlier at Greta Bridge, when, as a girl, she had been slipped into the coffee-room to have a look at him. This, on the whole, dull outing was chronicled for *Household Words* as *The Lazy Tour of Two Idle Apprentices*.[2] Doncaster was included in the schedule as 'the St. Leger with all its saturnalia' was being run. In spite of his annual trip to see the Derby run, racing was not at all in Dickens's line: every moment spent on the Doncaster course was hateful to him in spite of the fact that on being handed a card of the race he ticked off three successive winners. He came away certain that if a boy had a taste for betting nothing would cure him sooner than a visit to Doncaster 'to see the misery caused by losses on the turf'.

During the whole tour Dickens was restless and could concentrate on nothing. Why did he feel so desperately low? Had he perhaps missed something very important in life, a great friendship, a great romance, a great tragedy? What could it be that spurred him into such dissatisfaction with his lot? Was there some part of him undeveloped or was it merely that some men never find rest in this life?

Could it be entirely Kate's fault that he felt like that? After all they had never really been in step. He had developed, but she had remained more or less what she had been in the beginning, amiable, complacent, and now, according to his ideas, subsiding into a kind of fatuity. Viewed objectively, she was a mediocre, kindly woman who did not fill the bill of celebrity's wife. How badly she contrasted with the women he had met in Paris! Could one want a more intelligent and sympathetic wife than Madame Scribe, who was older than Kate, or Madame Viardot, who was the same age? His thoughts then strayed on to masterful George Sand and muse-like Madame de Girardin. What a mistake it had been to marry a woman so limited in knowledge and sympathy as Kate, a woman who could contribute nothing to any dis-cussion and viewed every subject with apathetic want of interest or a meaningless smile. As he reviewed the past he began to wonder whether she had ever suited him at all. It was the American tour that had first revealed to him her springlessness and lack of resource. Only the efforts of an extremely competent maid had dragged her through those months of travel. He had given her chances of education and experience of the world, but she had never even responded to the stimulus of housekeeping in a foreign country. What tears there had been at Genoa, what repinings in France! Her main interest was the nursery; it was natural enough that she should be absorbed in that way, but babies as the one bond and topic of conversation were liable to be boring. He had nothing to reproach himself with. He had been a good father and had done all that was possible for his earthly children, but he could not pretend to idealise them as he did his spiritual children, Oliver, Nell, Paul and the rest. Kate had sometimes complained of his friends and their off-hand manners, of John Forster in particular, who hardly noticed her at all. 'Fuz' had never thought her adequate or interest-ing, and how right he had been! 'She is amiable and comply-ing but nothing on earth would make her understand me.' It was something to be able to write frankly to Forster, though the situation as he saw it was an irremediable one. Here was the world-famous Charles Dickens with his genius, his compelling imagination, his very peculiar disposition, his caprices, his impatience, his tempers, driven nearly demented by one woman's fatuity, a fatuity that was magnified for him by those relations of hers who were always in the house, whose faces now appeared to him idiotic, and whose manners now struck him as exasperating. But in condemning them he did not condemn his dear Georgy, who never lost her charm or interest and now shone as the paragon of an entirely worthless family.

In making these reflections he generated in himself a fund of self-pity and refrained from dealing with the core of the situation, his infatuation for Ellen Ternan. The terror as well as the beauty of love lies in the fact that it alters all values. Men talk of a world well lost for love when it is love itself that has caused their world to perish and appear as worthless as a worn-out shoe. Dickens's attitude to his own life changed from the fatal moment at Manchester when he believed himself capable of loving a young girl in the same idealistic whole-souled way that he had once adored Maria Beadnell.

The close companionship of Wilkie Collins and his levity on sex-relationships combined with his own passion for Ellen made Dickens feel as if he had renewed his youth, almost as if he belonged to another generation. Kate might look her part of materfamilias; it was hard for him to believe himself the father of ten children, when he felt more like their elder brother than their parent. What must he now do to readjust his life? Readjust it he simply must.

A letter[1] written to his wife's maid at this time shows how his mind was working. It embodied what in Victorian days was a momentous decision—self-banishment from the large double bed in which he had lain beside his wife for all the years of their marriage. Anne is instructed to have the recessed communicating door between the dressing-room and the bedroom closed by a carpenter who must fill the space

[1] 890.   II.   N.L.

with white deal shelves and enclose it with 'a light deal door, painted white'. He has ordered for his own use a small iron bedstead and the bedding to go with it. Anne is specially warned not to talk about these arrangements and is told 'the sooner it is done the better'.

Forster says that at this time he found Dickens impossible to deal with and 'inaccessible' to friendly advice, but he says nothing in his *Life* about the Ternan family and nothing about the Manchester performances. It is obvious that he wished to have the episode expunged, for it did 'Boz' no credit after twenty years of respectability to go off the rails with an actress. As far as Forster was concerned, Ellen Ternan did not exist and therefore could have had nothing to do with the separation. Thus, leaving out of his account the principal factor in the situation, he was obliged to own that there was nothing in the actual circumstances in which Mr. and Mrs. Dickens found themselves that would not have admitted of reasonable rearrangement. A middle course, to his regret, was not taken. Even so he consoled himself by assuring those principally concerned that no decent person could regard the separation contemplated save as 'a purely private family matter' which it would be most ungentlemanly to allude to. This opinion put heart into Dickens as it removed his fear that his position with the public would be 'aspersed' if scandal were permitted to attach to his name.

Despite spiritual, psychical and physical upheavals appearances were still kept up during the autumn of 1857 at Tavistock House. Dickens took the chair in November at the fourth Anniversary Dinner of the Warehousemen and Clerks Schools at the London Tavern. He spoke of schools he did not like, of his own school and master, 'by far the most ignorant man I have ever had the pleasure to know, one of the worst tempered men that ever lived. . . . I did not like the ladies' school with which my school danced on Wednesdays.' The Schools for which he is appealing are designed to educate 'Orphans and Necessitous Children'. A beginning had been made four years earlier with a rented house at New Cross.

Dickens urged his hearers to enlarge the scope of their activity. In toasting the president, Lord John Russell, he said of him that as with 'the seal of Solomon there was enclosed in a not very large casket the soul of a giant'.

Miss Coutts was invited to attend the party given by Mr. and Mrs. Dickens on December 1, 1857, to listen to the new Christmas story for *Household Words*, about the behaviour of white women during a pirate's raid at Silverstore, Belize, 'off the Mosquito shore'. It was said to have been suggested by accounts of the Indian Mutiny. Entitled *The Perils of Certain English Prisoners*, the second of its three dull chapters was written by Wilkie Collins. There was nothing of the old Christmas spirit about any of it and the party dispersed feeling that a light had gone out.

Under the blight of impending change Christmas and Twelfth Night were lived through by a diminished and rather dejected family. Henry Fielding, aged eight, had been packed off to join his brothers at school at Boulogne, which left Charley, the two girls and Edward Bulwer Lytton, aged six, at home. Charles Dickens continued to function normally in the world's eye as editor, serial writer and chairman of charity banquets. In February he spoke for the Hospital for Sick Children. Addressing 150 guests, he made amusing allusions to the spoilt children of the well-to-do, children who come down to dessert, children who won't go to bed, children who kick and say they hate us. It is not for these he speaks, but for the children he has seen languishing in damp, bare rooms, for the babies pining to death in egg-boxes. Why in the name of GOD must such things be? The old courtly house in Great Ormonde Street now converted into a child's hospital already deals with 10,000 of such out-patients a year. The in-patients in their doll-like beds can only number thirty and even these cannot be maintained without further support. It was exactly the kind of appeal Dickens could drive home with his plea to those present to think 'of the dear child you love, the dear child you have lost, the dream-child you might have had'. He melted the hearts

of his hearers and by so doing added £3000 to the funds of
the hospital.

The letters written by Dickens this spring are concerned
chiefly with plans and projects for 'readings'.   It had become
to him the most reassuring of exercises to play upon an
audience in this way.   Each reading not only gave him fresh
zest, but endowed him with the power of riding, as in a life-
boat, over the troubled waters of private life.

Under the placid round of family existence at Tavistock
House a silent conflict was seething.   There was Charles set
on readjustment without publicity; Georgina willing to co-
operate in securing this solution; and Kate the sport of she
did not know what kind of forces.   In the background the
watching eyes of Mrs. Hogarth, her daughter Helen, and her
sister Helen Thomson missed nothing of the changes and
turns of the situation: their sympathies were all with Kate.
How was it that Georgy did not seem to share them?

By degrees their suspicions of Georgy grew.   Could she
be acting the part of confidante to Charles?   Was it she who
was responsible for the proposals for readjustment in domestic
affairs at Tavistock House?   Was it she who, after the
significant blocking of doors between bedroom and dressing-
room, suggested further segregation?   A letter written by
Helen Thomson to her friend Mrs. Stark in Glasgow[1] makes
it clear how disappointed the Hogarth contingent were with
Georgina: 'We had thought her disinterested'.   Someone had
proposed to Kate that she should have her own suite of rooms
quite apart from his, that she should act hostess at parties
and make *actes de présence*, if necessary, at public functions.
Another suggestion was that they might play Box and Cox
between Tavistock House and Gad's Hill, yet another that
she should settle abroad.   These mortifying proposals involving her, as they would have done, in much pretence were
all declined by Kate.   If Charles felt like that about her, it
would be better to be gone altogether or to die.   The idea of
separation from her children upset her terribly: her spirits

[1] Unpublished MS. (W. Dexter).

had never been high and now she spent hours together in tears.

Resenting these attempts at compromise, the Hogarth family intervened; rather than have poor Kate subjected to insulting offers they would prefer that she should be provided with a separate establishment. It was pitiful to see her in so low a condition. And so a legal separation was put through by Forster, who saw that the situation was intolerable to Dickens. Mark Lemon chose a solicitor for Kate and during the actual negotiations Mrs. Hogarth carried her daughter off to Brighton. On her return Kate became party to a settlement securing her £600 a year, and was installed in a small house in Gloucester Crescent on the edge of Camden Town. While this arrangement was being put through Charles suddenly became aware that certain 'scandalous rumours' anent Georgina were circulating within the family. These rumours maddened him, as well they might. He took prompt measures to scotch them, presenting the hostile Hogarths with a document and threatening, if they refused to sign, that Kate would be turned out of the house without a penny. The Hogarths stood out against his ultimatum for 'a fortnight of sleepless nights' and then put their names to the following declaration:

It having been stated to us that in reference to the difficulties which have resulted in the separation of Mr. and Mrs. Charles Dickens, certain statements have been circulated that such differences are occasioned by circumstances deeply affecting the moral character of Mr. Dickens and compromising the reputation and good name of others, we solemnly declare that we now disbelieve such statements. We know that they are not believed by Mrs. Dickens and we pledge ourselves on all occasions to contradict them as entirely destitute of foundation.

[Here follow the signatures of
Mrs. Hogarth and Helen Hogarth.]

So far few people were in the secret, just the family, near friends and kind Miss Coutts, who tried in writing to effect a reconciliation and then offered a temporary home to Kate whom she knew well and liked. Charles wrote a long, rather hysterical letter to Miss Coutts and stated that things had gone too far to admit of compromise.

Georgy was at this crisis intensely useful to Dickens. She kept his house together. She had Mamey and Katey under her thumb and managed to persuade them by her own cheerfulness that there was nothing to be regretted in the banishment or, as she called it, the 'voluntary departure' of their mother. A more natural and happy arrangement could not be thought of. They must all be very loving together and take care of Papa. In a way Georgina covered the scandal of Ellen, for people soon began to talk about the invidious position of a sister-in-law being content to supplant her own sister at the head of Charles Dickens's house.

With the exception of Miss Coutts, Charles now treated any sympathiser with Kate as a 'disloyal' friend. Mark Lemon and his family came into this category and so did F. M. Evans of Bradbury and Evans. W. M. Rossetti, dining with a friend of Kate's, Rintoul, founder and editor of *The Spectator*, heard the separation canvassed and the verdict go dead against Dickens, but this was all in strict privacy. It may be said that the separation, owing to Kate's determination 'to resign herself to God's will', passed off well and so secretly that except to the family and a few intimate friends it might have remained a nine days' wonder. The Dickens façade remained unchanged: Charles moved on in his majestic way, responding with Thackeray for Literature at the Academy banquet (May 2) and speaking for the Artists' Benevolent Fund. Then, seized by a fit of terrifying exhibitionism, he decided to take the world into his confidence in a personal statement in *Household Words*. He was anxious that Mark Lemon should also print it in *Punch*. When Mark Lemon very sensibly refused, Charles cut him dead. He also drafted a second statement for the discretionary use of Arthur Smith, his sub-editor.

The first statement was printed on June 12, 1858, in

Household Words, on the front page, headed 'Personal'. In it he explained that owing to his long friendship with the public he feels he must take them into his confidence over a personal matter of a domestic and sacredly private character of which they are almost certain to have heard reports. He solemnly declares that all the lately whispered rumours 'are abominably false, and that whosoever repeats one of them after this denial, will lie as wilfully and as foully as it is possible for any false witness to lie before Heaven and earth.'

This statement, as Forster plainly told him, served but to draw attention to what, if treated with silence, might have slipped by almost without notice. To his friend's horror, Dickens consulted Delane about printing the 'personal statement' in the *Times* before publishing it in *Household Words*, but, to Forster's relief, this came to nothing. Worse, however, was to follow, for the second statement, drafted for Arthur Smith's confidential use, also found its way into print. In this document Dickens dwelt on the incompatibility of temperament that had always existed between himself and his wife, and stated that had it not been for Georgina the separation would have taken place earlier. Georgina has sacrificed her youth and life to his family. For some years Mrs. Dickens has been asking to go away and live apart. He has prevented her doing so. It is at Forster's suggestion that he has finally consented to reconstruct and rearrange his home. Mrs. Dickens has thankfully agreed to his terms. He hopes no one will put any misconstruction on the separation, which the children thoroughly understand and accept. He goes on to say that 'two wicked persons' (by whom he means Mrs. Hogarth and her daughter) have coupled with the separation the name of a young lady for whom he has a great attachment and regard. 'Upon my soul and honour, there is not on this earth a more virtuous and spotless creature. I know her to be innocent and pure and as good as my own dear daughters. Further, I am quite sure that Mrs. Dickens, having received this assurance from me, must now believe it, in the respect I know her to have for me, and in the perfect confidence I know her in her better moments to repose in my truthfulness.'

Handed to Arthur Smith for 'discretionary use', this letter somehow found its way into the *New York Tribune* and from that source was copied into several English newspapers.

If we examine the statements we find that they are a smoke-screen put up not only to cover Kate's disappearance but to defend Georgina's continued presence at Tavistock House. There is something about them that creates suspicion: it is almost as if an alibi had been faked. And, oddly enough, as we shall presently see, Dickens's statements were backed up by letters from Georgina to Maria Winter. Both Charles and Georgina felt the need of justifying themselves. Dickens desired to absolve himself from the accusation of ingratitude and cruelty, Georgina wished to set herself right with Charles's friends, and both of them followed Forster in hiding up the explosive charge, Ellen Ternan. Between them they invented a new set of circumstances, a new chronicle of married life, all of which falls to shreds when the letters written by Charles to Kate on his Italian tour of 1853 are considered. These intimate, warm-hearted letters, as we have already seen, show Dickens as a normal affectionate family man. They allude to common experiences in Italy nine years earlier, revive old jests, poke fun at his companions Egg and Collins, and towards the end of the eight weeks' tour reveal the most simple and unfeigned pleasure at getting home. To 'my dearest Catharine' he wrote, 'I shall be very happy to be at home myself and to embrace you, for of course I miss you very much'. The letters are far from perfunctory. He sends love to the children and 'last but not least to yourself, whom I hope so soon to see in a blooming state'. 'Looking forward to meeting you so soon, ever, my dearest, most affectionately C. D.'

There is nothing here to support the contention that the marriage had been acutely unhappy for years and years, and evidently Dickens felt this aspect of his case to be weak, for to strengthen it he made mysterious allusions to a 'mental disorder' which caused his wife to think 'she would be better away'. In fact she, who took the initiative in nothing, was credited with initiating the separation. It would have been better for Dickens's reputation as an honest man if he had admitted that he had fallen violently in love with a girl of eighteen and that the sensation of youth released in him made him regard his own children as 'brothers and sisters' and his own wife with physical disgust. After all, the senses know no constancy. Kate was certainly dull and she may have been a bore, but her husband with his mercurial temperament had really been lucky to be linked with anyone who asserted herself so little and was on the whole so amenable. Their marriage, like many Victorian marriages, had been of the kind indicated in the Church of England wedding service as 'for the procreation of children', of whom they had ten in fifteen years, to say nothing of four miscarriages. There is no record that Kate ever complained of her fate though she must often have had reason to do so, for her lively husband's attitude to pregnancy and childbirth was outwardly unsympathetic and often that of a low comedian. It is remarkable that she betrayed no jealousy of her sister Georgina, who usurped many of her privileges and replaced her as diner-out and hostess during many weeks of every year. In all but parenthood Georgina played the part of an unofficial wife. 'Do you believe in a sister-in-law living in the house?' someone asked Kate Perugini in her old age. 'No, no, it is the greatest mistake!' she exclaimed. We must remind ourselves that Charles Dickens had never even at Furnival's Inn lived in a *solitude à deux*. There were but three rooms in their suite; but somehow they had squeezed Mary in. At Doughty Street they had made a home both for Mary Hogarth and Frederick Dickens, and after their return from America had adopted Georgina as a permanent member of the household; and so it went on till Tavistock House days when the Hogarth parents were often put up for months together. There is no question but that Charles had been a very good family man and had shouldered one responsibility after the other. Parents, brothers and his wife's relations, all had been helped, and all had proved unsatisfactory and all ungrateful. When he began to suspect that Kate was siding with her parents against Georgina, he lost his sense of propriety and in a blind rage threatened to drive her from the house.

At the time of the separation Kate was forty-three years old and Charles forty-six. They had been married for twenty-two years. When pressed out of her home Kate left behind her Edward Bulwer Lytton aged six, Henry Fielding aged eight, Sydney Smith aged ten, Alfred Tennyson aged twelve, Francis Jeffrey aged thirteen, two girls of eighteen and nineteen, and the oldest child of all, Charley, aged twenty. Walter Landor, aged seventeen had, as we have seen, been banished to India. It would have been an extraordinary step for any woman in Kate's position and of her indolent disposition to take voluntarily and that is why one must use the word 'pressed'. For some time an influence had been prising her slowly out of control till the tendrils that bound her to family life had relaxed so much that by a determined effort she could be easily dislodged. The family were, taking them all in all, rather characterless as well as very young, and made no stand against their father's decision. The predicament was puzzling to young minds, but it was drummed into them that 'their father's name was their best asset'. Though the little boys felt twinges of terrible loneliness, the family, as a whole, swallowed the fairy-tale they were told by kind Aunt Georgy and accepted their situation as inevitable, just as a little later on the Dickens sons were hypnotised into looking upon their early exile to India or the Antipodes as 'inevitable'. Georgina Hogarth could on occasion act with resolution and finality.

What are we to think of this survivor of the cataclysm that drove father, mother, aunt and sister from Dickens's house for ever, and to whom Kate, till dying of cancer twenty-one years later, never spoke again? Who but Georgina could have contrived the circumstances that levered the mother of her nephews and nieces out of the house of which she remained the permanent and apparently satisfied inmate? The part played by this attractive young woman appears equivocal. Was she pursuing some scheme of her own when making up to Maria Winter? Why did she write so affectionately to explain to her how the separation between her sister and her brother-in-law had come about? 'My dearest Maria' was told that no one was in any way to blame, that it was all quite natural, that Kate and Charles had agreed to live apart and would be happier like that. Poor Kate's incapacity for looking after children was no secret to anyone: they had always been thrown on others. 'My sister has often expressed a wish to go and live away', but Charles would never agree to it. Now by mutual consent and for *no other* reasons they have come to an arrangement to live apart. Georgina need hardly tell her 'dearest Maria' that where such a public man as Charles is concerned 'wonderful rumours and wicked slanders have been flying about'. Charles's friends must show their friendship by 'quietly silencing with the real solemn truth any foolish or wicked person who may repeat such lies and slanders'.

One asks oneself for what reason except that of pleasing Charles or of entering into sole possession of the home did Georgina become demonstratively affectionate to a woman whom she had a short while previously dismissed as almost a comic figure, 'a kind of good-natured woman, but fearfully silly'. How she and Charles had laughed together over Flora Finching when he was writing *Little Dorrit*! We should note the fact that once Georgina was firmly in control at Tavistock House, Mrs. Winter dropped as if through an oubliette out of her affections and correspondence.

For a long time Georgina had off and on acted as amanuensis to Charles. Nearly all *The Child's History of England* is in her handwriting, and she had always encouraged him in his self-absorption by saying, 'a man of genius ought not to be judged by the common herd of men'. For a long while she had made things difficult for Kate by always siding with Charles in any minor dispute. Georgina, it is evident, had a love of power and liked to control so celebrated a person as her brother-in-law and to make herself indispensable in his eyes. He praised her a great deal and thought that she took immense trouble over the children, who otherwise would have been neglected. According to Mrs. Hogarth, all that Georgina ever did for the children was to teach the little boys to read before they went to school: she had nothing to do with the girls; they had a competent governess. The curious method she adopted when editing a selection of Dickens's letters—that of cutting out sentences in praise of her sister— may indicate the jealousy that is part and parcel of possessive love.

By midsummer Kate was settled in Gloucester Crescent. Charley, by his father's wish, went to live with her, but Dickens was afraid lest Leech or anyone else should suppose he 'sided' with his mother. 'Between the children and me there is absolute confidence', he wrote, when forwarding him a copy of a note received from Charley in which he told his father, 'Don't suppose that I am actuated by any feeling of preference for my mother to you. God knows I love you dearly and it will be a hard day for me when I have to part from you and the girls.' Charley may have had a kindly nature, but he was determined to persevere with his courtship of Bessie Evans, the daughter of the man his father now looked on as his mortal enemy. It was perhaps as well that in future they would not be called on to live under the same roof. 'Dear Charley', wrote Kate, 'is so kind and gentle. I hope to resign myself to God's will and to lead a contented, if not a happy life . . . my position is a sad one. Time only can blunt the keen pain I feel at my heart.'

Chapter 24

READING FOR A LIVING

And if I laugh at any mortal thing
'Tis that I may not weep.

BYRON

DURING the negotiations recorded in the last chapter
Dickens worked to organise a series of entertainments
calculated to absorb his leisure for the rest of the year.   Beginning with an advertisement in *Household Words* on April 2
of sixteen readings to be given at the St. Martin's Hall, he
went on to plan a comprehensive tour in the provinces to
include both Scotland and Ireland.   Forster objected strongly
to this rather cheap-jack way of earning a livelihood, but when
remonstrated with, Dickens countered his objections by saying that everyone believed he took a fee, even when he was
reading for charity.   'Let me read where I will,' he said impetuously, 'an effect is produced which seems to belong to
nothing else.'

The condensation of excerpts from his own novels and
stories so as to get the maximum dramatic effect took up a
good deal of time.   He contrived sixteen of these arrangements in all.[1]

A Christmas Carol	Mr. Chops the Dwarf
The Trial from Pickwick	The Poor Traveller
David Copperfield	Mrs. Gamp
The Cricket on the Hearth	Boots at the Holly Tree Inn
Nicholas Nickleby	The Barbox Brothers
Bob Sawyer's Party	The Boy at Mugby
The Chimes	Dr. Marigold
The Story of Little Dombey	Sikes and Nancy

The favourite among these for seventeen years was 'A
Christmas Carol'.   In these readings so certain were his
impersonations that he could cut out much of the descriptive

[1] See *Charles Dickens as a Reader*.   C. Kent, 1872.

matter in his books.   For example, Scrooge, who is carefully delineated in the 'Carol', came to life in one sentence, 'Ah! but he was a tight-fisted hand at the grindstone was Scrooge', delivered in a grating, shrewd voice.   The elision in the pathetic parts was ruthless, though a few of the poignant points were left in the life and death of Tiny Tim.   The visit of Bob to the death-bed was cut out, but Dickens got all the greater effect from the mother's words over her mourning needlework, and over the father's promise to visit the grave. 'He broke down all at once.   He couldn't help it.   If he could have helped it, he and his child would have been further apart perhaps than they were.'

'Bob Sawyer's Party' is just another chapter from *Pickwick*. 'The Trial from Pickwick' has not been corrected or cut. Except for the compression at the opening of chapter thirty-four, Bardell *v.* Pickwick was read as originally written. 'David Copperfield', on the other hand, has been rearranged and greatly cut.   It opens on the beach at Yarmouth and closes with the death of Steerforth.   'Nicholas Nickleby' is entirely concerned with the Yorkshire school, the meeting with Mr. Squeers, the journey north, life at Dotheboys Hall and the final departure.

The Cricket on the Hearth was too short and slight to be cut at all.   In 'The Chimes' the introduction was omitted and the reading opened with the words, 'High up in the steeple of an old church, far above the town and far below the clouds dwelt the Chimes I tell of'.   The whole of Will Fern's speech is omitted.

'The Poor Traveller' is the only Dickens story of which an army officer is the hero.   Richard Doubledick, who has made a mess of life, walks to Chatham to enlist and get himself killed.   Captain Taunton reforms him and turns him into a good sergeant-major.   At Badajos, Taunton, supported by Ensign Doubledick, performs acts of great valour and receives a mortal wound.   Doubledick registers the face of the Frenchman who kills Taunton and swears to have his revenge. Doubledick fights again at Quatre-Bras and Ligny and falls

half dead on the field of Waterloo. He is adopted by
Taunton's mother and stays with her at a house near Aix.
There, looking down from a gallery, he recognises the French
officer. The spirit of Taunton takes possession of him, the
man had merely done his duty as he had tried to do his.
That evening Doubledick touches the Frenchman's glass with
his own and secretly 'forgave him in the name of the Divine
Forgiver'.

Some of the readings are very poor indeed, for instance
'The Boy at Mugby' about a juvenile 'refreshmenter', 'The
Barbox Brothers' and 'Mr. Chops the Dwarf'. One of the
most popular readings was about the elopement of a boy of
eight with a girl of seven, 'Boots at the Holly Tree Inn'.
Provincial audiences found it very sweet and touching.
'Little Dombey' moved every listener to tears and so did
'Dr. Marigold', which at the time was considered 'one of the
most humorous revelations of imaginative literature'. Dr.
Marigold was a cheap-jack with a clever dog 'who had taught
himself to growl if anyone bid as low as sixpence'. In impersonating Pickleson, 'the giant with the little head and less
in it', Dickens spoke in a high falsetto. Tears gushed when
Dr. Marigold went through his accustomed patter on the
footboard with his poor little Sophy slowly dying on his
shoulder.

Something more than histrionic skill must have gone to the
fascination of audiences. The reader himself must have
radiated the magnetism that hypnotised these seated crowds
of people. His capacity for suggestion seems to have been
unlimited. Moncure Conway (who as a boy had run to see
him alight from a coach at Fredericksburg) said that it was
quite impossible to convey the idea of the readings, Dickens
being in himself a whole stock company with endless voices
and power of putting shapes across.

The texts of the readings were revised and re-revised; they
were scored, interwoven and cobwebbed with lines, often of
different colours. The script of 'Little Dombey', for
instance, was corrected and emended in red ink and in blue.

In 'Sikes and Nancy' there were a mass of stage directions to himself: 'action', 'cupboard action', 'murder coming' and so on.

The readings were a quicker way of making money than novel-writing, but they involved him in careful work and numberless rehearsals. For the actual performances Dickens put himself entirely into the hands of his manager, Arthur Smith, who relieved him of all worry; he merely had to turn up at the right time in the right place. After his London season had ended on July 22, he opened his provincial tour on August 2 at Clifton and closed it on Saturday, November 13, at Brighton. His programme included 'The Story of Little Dombey', 'The Poor Traveller', 'Boots at the Holly Tree Inn' and 'Mrs. Gamp'. There were eighty-seven readings given at forty-four different places. It was a great strain on the nerves, though he came back home every few days to rest and to keep an eye on *Household Words*. Cuthbert Bede went to hear him read the 'Carol' at Wolverhampton. He was introduced by his friend Arthur Smith to the reader, who told him what a contrast there was between the quiet, sympathetic audience of the Midland town and the frigidly genteel audiences of London who sometimes had almost stopped him from reading at all.

From one cause and another Dickens found himself more variable in mood and self-control than ever. There are few happy pictures of him at this time. One of them, a dinner at Forster's with Lord Chief Justice Cockburn as a guest, was broken in on by Landor 'who was fleeing from justice', in other words a law-suit at Bath. Dickens went out to console Landor who had been shown into a bedroom. It was thought that he might talk over with him the unpleasant crisis in which he was at the moment involved and which made it improper that he should meet the Chief Justice. Dickens came back into the room laughing; he said he had found Landor 'sitting on a bed, very jovial, and that the whole conversation was upon the characters of Catullus, Tibullus and other Latin poets'.

Among Dickens's younger cronies was Edmund Yates, the

bright but tactless journalist who at this time was contributing regular articles, at £3 a week, to *Town Talk*. His pen-sketches of celebrities, unsigned, had already featured Dickens. To use Yates's own words, 'it had given satisfaction and I felt I could not do better than follow on with a pen-portrait of his great rival'.[1]

> Mr. Thackeray [he wrote] is forty-six years old, though from the silvery whiteness of his hair, he appears somewhat older. He is very tall, standing upwards of six feet two inches, and, as he walks erect, his height makes him a conspicuous figure in every assembly. . . . No one meeting him could fail to recognise in him a gentleman; his bearing is cold and uninviting, his style of conversation either openly cynical or affectedly goodnatured and benevolent; his bonhomie is forced, his wit biting, his pride easily touched. . . . His success with *Vanity Fair* culminated with his *Lectures on the Humourists of the Eighteenth Century*, which were attended by all the court and fashion of London. The pieces were extravagant, the lecturer's adulation for birth and position was extravagant, the success was extravagant. No one succeeds better than Mr. Thackeray in cutting his coat according to his cloth. Here he flattered the aristocracy, but when he crossed the Atlantic George Washington became the object of his worship, the 'Four Georges' the object of his bitterest attacks. . . . Our own opinion is that his success is on the wane. . . . There is a want of heart in all he writes. . . . It was with the publication of the third and fourth numbers of *Vanity Fair* that Mr. Thackeray began to dawn upon the reading public as a great genius. This great work which—perhaps with the exception of *The Newcomes*—is the most perfect dissection of the human heart, done with the cleverest and most unsparing hand, had been offered to and rejected by several of the first publishers of London. But the public saw and recognised its value; the great guns of literature, the *Quarterly* and the *Edinburgh*, boomed forth their praises.

Yates went on to speak of other novels and was so pleased with his article that he told Trollope all about it, and it seems

---

[1] Edmund Yates, *Recollections*.

that Trollope told Thackeray and so the mischief began. Thackeray naturally resented what he regarded as a personal attack by a young member of his club. He wrote an angry letter to Yates.

> We meet at a club where, before you were born I believe, I and other gentlemen have been in the habit of talking without any idea that our conversation would supply paragraphs for professional vendors of 'Literary Talk', and I don't remember that out of that club I have ever exchanged six words with you. Allow me to inform you that the talk which you have heard there is not intended for newspaper remark and to beg—as I have the right to do —that you will refrain from printing comments on my private conversations; and that you will forgo discussions, however blundering, upon my private affairs; and that you will consider any question of my personal truth and sincerity as quite out of the province of your criticism.

Instead of apologising, Yates drafted a truculent reply which Dickens persuaded him not to send, it was 'too flippant and too violent'. He said that Thackeray in *The Yellowplush Papers* had held up Lardner and Lytton ('lisping Bulwig') to ridicule and that in *The Book of Snobs* he had given 'sketches of three at least of the members of the club and illustrated them with recognisable caricature drawings'. It was no better than a fresh attack. With Dickens's help he composed another letter, but even so did not apologise.

Thackeray on receiving it decided to report the incident to the committee of the Garrick, and by them Yates was called on to make ample apology or retire from membership. He declined to do either and appealed to put his case before a general meeting. At this meeting Dickens, Wilkie Collins and Samuel Lover spoke in his favour, but the decision went against him. He then started an action at law, and Dickens, who throughout had been his adviser, wrote to Thackeray asking whether he could appoint some third person to meet him and find an accommodation of 'this deplorable matter'. Thackeray forwarded this letter also to the committee. The

committee did not accept the offer. When the legal proceedings owing to a technicality fell through, Yates left the
Garrick Club, and Dickens, who walked out with him,
resigned his place on the committee. Not very long after, in
high dudgeon at the blackballing of a friend, Dickens resigned
from the club himself.

The way Dickens championed Yates in this matter shows
how much he was under the Collins influence and how in a
way he liked to flout public opinion. He went out of his
way to insult Evans for sympathising with Kate, writing to
him that he could have no truck with anyone who had been
false to him under the greatest wrong he has ever known.
He also made secret plans to dissolve partnership with
Bradbury and Evans in *Household Words*. Katey is a witness
to his strange irascibility, part of which we must attribute to
his uneasy conscience and all of which she put down to his
infatuation for Ellen Ternan. His balance she thought had
been completely upset. From a psychological point of view,
1858 was a thoroughly unsatisfactory year, for though 'Boz'
felt young and free again and could make more money than
ever before, he had lost his self-esteem and moral standing,
requisites which neither wealth nor success could redeem. In
Katey Perugini's words,

> More tragic and far-reaching in its effect was the associa-
> tion of Charles Dickens and Ellen Ternan and their
> resultant son than that of Nelson and Lady Hamilton and
> their daughter. My father was like a madman. He did
> not seem to care a damn what happened to any of us.
> Nothing could surpass the misery and unhappiness of our
> life.[1]

At some time in 1858 Ellen Ternan was living (possibly
with her mother) at 2 Houghton Place, Ampthill Square, on
the confines of Camden Town, and later on we find her set
up in what Katey terms 'an establishment of her own at
Peckham'. This establishment was Windsor Lodge, a house
standing in a garden and facing country fields. Peckham,

[1] *Dickens and Daughter*, p. 94.

then a rural locality, was on the south side of the Thames and therefore almost equally accessible from Gad's Hill and from Wellington Street, Strand. Like the piano legs and mantelpieces of the Victorian era the tenancy of this house was well covered up. The Camberwell rate-book reveals that it was rented in 1867 by 'Frances Turnham' (Dickens was at the time in the United States) and from 1868 to 1870 by 'Charles Tringham'. Local gossip purveyed by a char-woman and a job-master spoke of Charles Tringham as an author engaged in writing a mystery story. Visited by Mr. and Mrs. Thomas Wright in 1935,[1] the then occupants of Holme Dene (alias Windsor Lodge) pointed out the sumach tree and the quince tree under the shadow of which Mr. Tringham had liked to sit. The brackets of the Venetian shutters were also shown, though the shutters had gone. They were said to be of the sliding pattern exactly like those installed at Gad's Hill Place.

Thomas Wright, who made a specialty of discoveries in the private lives of the eminent, wrote an article[2] concerning an interview he had sought with a friend of Mrs. Ternan and her girls—Canon Benham. The article was written on the assumption that the liaison was a short and temporary one, an opinion that he endorsed the following year. By 1938, however, he had nosed out the Peckham establishment which, if it proved nothing new, demonstrated that the liaison, far from being ephemeral, lasted twelve years. *Dickens and Daughter*, giving Katey Perugini's account of Ellen Ternan, had not appeared when Mr. Wright's autobiography was published. It is not to be supposed that with Ellen Ternan Charles Dickens entered into the ideal relationship he had all his life hankered for; nevertheless the association must have

---

[1] *Thomas Wright of Olney*, 1938.

[2] Thomas Wright, in the *Daily Express* of April 3, 1934, stated that Canon Benham had conversed with him about Ellen Ternan and said that she had 'disburdened her mind' to him. He repeats this in his *Life of Charles Dickens* (p. 356). Canon Benham was a friend of Mrs. Ternan and her family. In telling the story I have relied not on Mr. Wright but on the information supplied by Dickens's own daughter, Mrs. Perugini.

given him some pleasure as it was kept going till his death, and letters prove that the adaptable Georgina made a friend of the girl and welcomed her to Gad's Hill. There are notes in print from Dickens to his manservant, John, ordering him to convey delicacies to 'Miss Ellen' when poorly. 'Take Miss Ellen a little basket of fresh fruit, a jar of clotted cream from Tucker's and a chicken, a pair of pigeons or some nice little bird. Also on Wednesday and Friday morning, a little variety each day.' Such notes convince us of his solicitude and kindly affection for the girl who had thrown in her lot with his. Probably his letters to her would reveal his passion and warmth, but these are either lost or destroyed.

So much for the existence of 'the explosive charge' un-acknowledged by Forster, but for which some less drastic and painful solution of the domestic dilemma might have been arrived at. The terms of the settlement made with Kate allowed her to have access to the children, but on the condition that they were not to be brought in contact with the Hogarths or Helen Thomson or the Evans family. How this worked out in practice it is hard to say, for the girls Mamey and Katey were so intimidated by their father's state of mind that they did not dare, during the first months of separation, to show any sympathy with their mother. Later on when things had settled down in their new groove it seems certain that the boys were allowed to go to Gloucester Crescent, always provided that there were no Hogarths or Evanses about.

Mamey, the eldest Dickens daughter, was entirely under Georgina's influence and never went to see her mother. Katey went occasionally; Charley, at the time a clerk in Baring's bank, lived, as we know, with her until by some arrangement of his father he was sent to China the following year. Kate Dickens was then alone except for the visits of the boys during their holidays.

For some time, indeed ever since the Manchester perform-ance of *The Frozen Deep*, Dickens had been wondering

The Last Reading
March 15, 1870.

whether he could so steep himself in the French Revolution as to convey to his public what it actually felt like to be living through its terrors. All that he had gone through over the separation had unsteadied him and had made it almost impossible to settle down to work of the usual kind. It was imperative that he should get out of his own *milieu*. Making the resolution not to look at books dealing with any other subject, he began a course of reading, but from every book he waded through he turned with ever increasing admiration and amazement to Carlyle's *French Revolution*, 'which was aflame with the very essence of the conflagration'. He, too, would become an actor in these scenes and allow them to possess him utterly. Of his completed book he says, 'I have so far verified what is done and suffered in these pages, as that I have certainly done and suffered it all myself'. One of his projected titles for the book was 'Memory Carton' which gives the clue to the state of mind which he had induced in himself. His decision to write an historical novel was wise since it enabled him to regain an emotional balance that for some time had appeared highly precarious and which the recurrent excitement of readings did nothing to stabilise.

On the other hand, the direct appeal of the readings gave him immediate confidence in his public; there was no waiting for proofs, nor delay of publication, but the effort always involved a great outpouring of sensibility which was hurled back at him by displays of personal affection from his auditors. Till he had found the knack of managing his voice he would lose it before the end of the evening and altogether exhaust himself by impersonating character after character. He read to halls crammed to capacity, and always the hordes turned away insisted on their right to hear him on another occasion. Fresh readings had constantly to be planned to meet the immense demand. For these public appearances Dickens chose his clothes very carefully, always took a dresser to fix him up advantageously and always wore a buttonhole. In Ireland, ladies, sitting with their chins against the platform, would gather up the petals falling from his red geranium and

even beg the denuded stalk as souvenir. This was all gratifying enough to an actor's self-esteem, but occasionally a tactless
representative of 'the Emerald press' would administer a cold
douche by observing that 'though Mr. Dickens was only
forty-six, he already looked like an old man'.

In Belfast and Dublin he scored great successes and even in
Cork more than a thousand stalls were reserved in advance for
three readings. Exultant, he wrote to Wills, 'I made last
week a clear profit of £340 and have made in the month of
August a profit of one thousand guineas'. In England it was
the same story. 'Little Darlington covered itself with glory'
and at Durham he 'had a capital audience'. Walking from
Durham to Sunderland he felt as if he were making fancy
photographs of the Pit country. 'I couldn't help looking on
my mind, as I was doing it, as a sort of capitally prepared and
highly sensitised plate'. It was a great pleasure, he said, to
work with this mind, it 'took the impression so easily'.
Readings on the whole were a fatiguing enterprise, for he had
often to travel by night, especially at week-ends, when the
restrictions on Sunday travelling were severe. At York he
was pleased when a lady begged to touch 'the hand that
had filled her house with many friends'. Mamey and Katey
joined him at Newcastle and went the rounds, just as their
mother had done on all his theatrical tours except the last.
Their presence on a platform effectively disarmed criticism;
'the dear girls', said their father to Georgy, 'have really been
a great success'. Four readings at Edinburgh went off
brilliantly, although Dickens had been warned that there was
a certain coldness about the audiences there. He told Wills
that the triumph there was 'the greatest he had ever made.
The city was taken by storm and carried. "The Chimes"
shook it; "Little Dombey" blew it up. On the last two
nights the crowd was immense and the turn-away enormous.
Everywhere nothing was heard but praises, nowhere more
than at Blackwood's shop, where there certainly was no disposition to praise.' The girls, made much of, were enraptured
with Edinburgh. James Payn (later editor of *Chambers's*

Journal) went on an excursion to Hawthornden in company with the whole family. A more delightful talker than Dickens it had never been his lot to meet, for he eschewed all commonplaces and never uttered a platitude. Hawthornden was not open to the public the day they went there so it was difficult to get access to the glen or to see the house. Payn, expostulating with the custodian, explained how distinguished was the visitor and how short his stay in Edinburgh, but the man seemed never to have heard the name of Dickens. In the end Payn had his way and they saw what they had come to see. 'We laughed all the time', recorded Dickens. The custodian's face, Payn tells us, registered extreme surprise when the great man handed him one of his usual lavish tips.

After further triumphs at Manchester and Birmingham the tour concluded at Brighton on November 13, and two days later the conductor was back in his office getting to work on the Christmas number of *Household Words*.

The Christmas number, however, was not his only concern since his plans for eliminating Bradbury and Evans from partnership in the magazine had by this time taken shape. He would teach his 'enemies' a lesson they would not soon forget. Before Christmas a writ was served, on his behalf by Forster, on Bradbury and Evans which eventuated in the filing of a bill in Chancery dissolving the partnership. By order of the Court the right to use the name of the periodical *Household Words* together with 'the printed stock and stereotyped plates of the same' was put up to auction at Hodgson's on May 16, 1859. Dickens was the purchaser at £3350.[1] To Georgy he wrote that he only had to pay down £500 in cash.[2] It was a very severe blow to Bradbury and Evans as the author also refused them any further novel contracts and returned to Chapman and Hall, now a prosperous firm with premises in Piccadilly. Acting throughout in a very disagreeable, peremptory way, Dickens somehow managed to float a new magazine, *All the Year Round*, of exactly the same format and

[1] E. Yates, *Recollections*. [2] May 16, 1859.

make-up as *Household Words*, five weeks before the old contract expired. Strong objection to his procedure was raised by Bradbury and Evans and Dickens dealt with this in the last number of the expiring magazine. Like a cock flapping his wings, the conductor indulged in a good crow:

> The first page of these Nineteen Volumes was devoted to a Preliminary Word from the writer by whom they were projected, under whose constant supervision they have been produced, and whose name has been (as his pen and himself have been) inseparable from the Publication ever since. The last page of the last of these Nineteen Volumes is closed by the same hand. He knew perfectly well, knowing his own rights and his means of attaining them, that it *could not be* but that this work must stop if he chose to stop it. He therefore announced many weeks ago that it would be discontinued on the day on which this final Number bears date. The Public have read a great deal to the contrary, and will have observed that it has not in the least affected the result.

It was war to the knife between Dickens and Bradbury and Evans, who now as a counterblast to *All the Year Round* launched a new magazine, *Once a Week*. 'What fools they are', commented Dickens, 'to try to make it look like *Household Words* and *All the Year Round*!'

The office of *Household Words* had been at 16 Wellington Street, Strand; the new office was at number 11 in the same street. Dickens carried Wills on with him and Wilkie Collins too, whose artist brother Charles now became a regular contributor and incidentally a person of some interest to Katey.

Determined to invigorate the new magazine, Wills was instructed by his employer to approach 'both the Trollopes', to secure a story from Mrs. Gaskell, and poems from young George Meredith, who had just taken Forster's place as literary adviser to Chapman and Hall. The said employer would write to George Eliot himself, and would get Mrs. Carlyle to speak to Ruffini about articles on the fighting in Italy (describing the battlefield of Magenta and the sack of Perugia) to be entitled 'A Track of War'. His blood being up, Dickens could spur himself as well as his contributors to action, managing to get the first instalment of *A Tale of Two Cities* ready for the first number of the new magazine. It was much shorter than most of Dickens's novels and was to be followed by *The Woman in White*. 'The Roving Englishman' would offer a new and, it was to be hoped, popular feature. It was written by Grenville Murray, vice-consul at Mytilene, who in one number presented so merciless a caricature of Sir Stratford Canning (as Sir Hector Stubble) that Canning's friends, fearful lest he might miss it, all sent him copies; the Foreign Office bag to Constantinople bulged with them. Charles Lever and Charles Reade also wrote for Dickens. Reade is described by Katey as 'perching his person upon a small circular-topped piano stool and singing comic songs in a tiny voice'. Charles Collins, so soon to become her husband, was 'Eye-witness'. Enough has been said about the inauguration of the new magazine to show that Dickens expended a great deal of energy upon it and made of it an immediate success. He could never afford to let up on his own writing, and Frith tells us that, when putting the finishing touches to his portrait of Dickens in Tavistock House, he noted his sitter pulling at his imperial and muttering to himself as he pored over a small portion of *A Tale of Two Cities*. A parcel of books lay on the table. Tapping one of them, Dickens said, 'That's a very good book by George Eliot, but unless I am mistaken George Eliot is a woman'. It was *Adam Bede*.

Meanwhile offers from New York for readings became more and more tempting, and by July 1859 Dickens thought he was far enough advanced with his new novel to venture on an American tour in September. He could perhaps, if he worked hard enough, finish the book before he sailed. His friend J. T. Fields was very insistent that he should start at once, but he delayed deciding to do so and the opportunity vanished with the looming up of the Civil War six months later.

In the autumn of 1859 Dickens began to wish to get rid of Tavistock House. The conventional Forster told him it would be very damaging to his reputation if he did not maintain an establishment in London for the benefit of the girls, but after considering the arguments for and against, he decided to complete the sale. Most of the furniture was transferred to Gad's Hill, but some was reserved to furnish a sitting-room and two bedrooms at the office of *All the Year Round* so that he or any of the family could stay in London when they wanted to. At Gad's Hill he could house plenty of furniture, for he had built additional bedrooms and turned the coach-house into living-rooms for sons and servants. The book-backs were carefully transferred to his country library, where they gave him the same pleasure as they had done when he first designed them for Tavistock House.

Dickens now took great pride in his Kentish freehold, for he felt it rounded off his career in a very satisfactory way. Cobham Woods and Park lay behind the house, the distant Thames in front, the Medway with Rochester and its old castle and cathedral to one side, 'the whole stupendous property' lying on the Dover Road. One of the first occasions on which he entertained there was on his daughter Katey's wedding day. Katey had become engaged to his new contributor, Charles Collins, a very tall young man with 'orange-coloured' hair framing a white face, who had belonged to the pre-Raphaelite brotherhood though never as a full member. His best painting, 'May in the Regent's Park', was exhibited at the Academy of 1852 when, in response to a suggestion by Ruskin, the walls blossomed with hawthorn and flowering shrubs. During the engagement he took Katey to sit to his friend John Millais for the girl in 'The Black Brunswicker'. Dickens viewed him leniently though he could not, knowing the strange nervous nature of the man, have thought him really a suitable husband for Katey; but Katey was proving less amenable to Georgy's management than Mamey and showed signs (to which she owned later) of wishing to escape control. Family life might run more smoothly without her. The wedding took place at Gad's Hill with Holman Hunt as best man. After the guests had gone

Mamey went up to her sister's bedroom, and on opening the door found her father on his knees with his face buried in Katey's wedding gown. She stood there quietly for a minute or two and then he, becoming aware of her presence, said in a broken voice, 'But for me Katey would not have left home'.[1]

For the Christmas number of *All the Year Round* (1859) Dickens produced the first of nine yearly stories, *The Haunted House*, written partly by himself and partly by Wilkie Collins. The idea of collaboration, which in itself was a very poor one since it appeared to stultify Dickens's genius, was originated by Collins at the time he became the adored young friend of the editor of *Household Words* and wanted to make himself indispensable to his patron. From time to time we find Dickens regretting that material good enough to go into a novel was being frittered away in these anonymous Christmas numbers, but he could never resist giving pleasure to his dear Wilkie, who was amiable enough to make himself responsible for the greater part of each story. For *The Haunted House* he wrote six out of the eight chapters. It must not be overlooked in discussing these Christmas numbers that they were very enriching, as they sold in large quantities, sometimes as many as 250,000 to 300,000 copies being printed.

As soon as Dickens had cut adrift from London he began to express his dislike of the place, a dislike that had been growing on him for years. He found the Thames 'most horribly stinky', it made him sick to cross Waterloo Bridge or London Bridge. Nobody seemed to know how to tackle the river and the 'cartloads of chloride of lime that are shot into the filthy stream' have no effect upon it.

> London is a vile place. . . . I have never taken kindly to it since I lived abroad. Whenever I come back from the country now and see that great heavy canopy lowering over the house-tops I wonder what on earth I do there except of obligation.

It was not till nine years later that a good road was built from Westminster Bridge to Waterloo Bridge. Trees were then

[1] G. Storey, *Dickens and Daughter*.

planted and a footway opened to the Temple. Because of
these improvements the scour of the river deepened and
quickened and soon a neat embankment rose from Westminster to Blackfriars. Dickens said it was the finest public
work ever executed.

Great play is always made with Dickens's love of London
but there is little evidence of that love in his books. London
was, in boyhood and youth, his medium—the place in which
he grew up, learnt about life and made a position for himself.
It was the only medium he really knew and it was perfectly
natural that he should make it the setting of his first work and
that it should figure preponderatingly in his novels. Great
as was his interest and his curiosity, love is not the word that
expresses his attitude towards London. He sketched, however, incomparable vignettes of its streets and their denizens
as well as of the spirit of its differing localities. But in considering Dickens's feelings about London we must never lose
sight of the fact that as soon as he could possibly afford it
(and that was at the age of twenty-seven) Charles Dickens
moved his domicile out of authentic London into Regents-
land, thus showing his personal preference for modern drainage, clean surroundings and green open spaces.

Dickens may now be considered as settled for life. It is to
be hoped that he derived some happiness from his Ternan
connection, but it seems plain that Ellen was an ornament or
addition to an existence that would have been quite wretched
without the support and companionship of Georgy. The
girl, however, taught him something real about women and
his later heroines benefited from her example. The characters of Lucie Manette, Estella and Bella Wilfer are supposed
to be modelled on her, but probably it is the very charming
Rosa Bud who best embodies her qualities. Anyway, the
day of the long-suffering angel is done. She is now replaced
by someone more complicated, more sensitive and more
human. We might expect to find Georgy in one or other of
the female characters in the novels, for she was her brother-in-
law's constant mainstay. Little sentences in his letters show

on what comfortable, confidential terms they were. She pays the house-bills with the money he provides; she finds papers in his private drawers; if he is unwell she goes to London to be with him, leaving Mamey in charge of the boys. They dine out together; 'Laura (Lady Olliffe) wants us to dine at the Mansion House. Shall we go? Perhaps it would be as well to take the opportunity . . . bring my dress suit and black trousers.' One could go on quoting indefinitely, but these few sentences suffice o show what an important part Georgy played in Dickens's life and how dependent he was on her.

Let us stand back for a moment and look at Charles Dickens in 1860. He is a world figure (aged forty-eight), financially prosperous and immensely successful. He has Britain at his feet: obviously he has gained the world: but has he somehow managed to abdicate the overlordship of his soul? To those who knew him intimately his life appeared to have changed in quality. The old equal friendships were a thing of the past, they had been replaced by intimacies with younger men, like Wilkie Collins, George Sala, Percy Fitzgerald, Edmund Yates. To some extent their relations to him were sycophantic, for they were all definitely inferior in character and ability to the older men who had dropped away, and they all derived their livelihood from him. Dickens's very amusements tended to be those of a younger man, though he was so conscious of being an older one in looks that he darkened his grizzling locks and beard with dye, as we may see in the photographs of 1858. Even if the stories of a French mistress are not true and the frequent journeys to Paris were undertaken for some other reason, it is clear that in slipping his marital moorings he had lost balance and sense of direction. With the new way of life went a passion for novelty. Illustrations by 'Phiz', for instance, no longer appeared suitable for his stories; modern designs by very young Marcus Stone or Luke Fildes were preferred and took their place. He had fallen out of love with his old setting and he did not find it too easy to create a new one.

Prosperity enveloped him as with a garment. *All the Year Round* attracted to itself an ever vaster public. Dickens could get £1000 for a short story any day of the week. His family responsibilities have lessened. Charley is in the Far East, Sydney is at sea, Walter in India, Alfred in Australia, whither he is planning to send another boy to join him. Impetuous, warm-hearted Katey has left the shelter of his roof and has a house of her own. Mamey and Georgy cosset him and produce the comfortable home-like atmosphere on which he is so dependent. Mamey and Georgy never criticise his ways, they understand him perfectly. Georgy indeed complaisantly enough calls her sister's supplanter 'dearest Ellen', and invites her to Gad's Hill.[1] Easy-going as his circumstances were, he found himself plunged from time to time in profitless retrospection and a passionate wish to kill the past. How would it be to destroy the letters he had received during a lifetime? To biographers who might write asking to see his letters from Maclise or Leech he could then reply, 'Shocked by the misuse of the private letters of public men, which I constantly observed, I destroyed a very large and very rare mass of correspondence'. And this is what he really did. Old letters from Catharine, from 'Fuz', from Talfourd, from Ainsworth, from Miss Coutts, from Maclise, from all the people he had known and loved in his passage through life, were assembled in their packets. He would not untie them, he would not re-read them for he did not want to remember anything of the old days; these reminders of past joys must go. As the last packet was thrown on to the bonfire he exclaimed, 'Would to God every letter I had ever written was on that pile!' Henry Fielding and his brother Edward Bulwer Lytton, who had watched the proceedings, then roasted onions on the ashes. The ghosts of old friendships could no longer haunt Dickens, for had he not buried the dead past as his friend Longfellow said it ought to be buried? Nothing must exist for him henceforth but the living present, genius within and God o'erhead. Even the pet names he had given

[1] *Dickens and Daughter*, p. 128.

to his boys no longer reminded him of the grand figures after whom they had been called, those gods of his youth to whom he had paid domestic homage. 'Wally' did not bring Landor to mind nor 'Syd' Sydney Smith. As for 'Harry' and 'Ally', who could guess that they were called after Henry Fielding and Alfred Tennyson? And 'Frank', once the baby Francis Jeffrey, he had almost forgotten after whom he was named; and as for 'Plorn' he had long ceased to be Edward Bulwer Lytton. Blurred and smudged associations at best, and the irony of it all was that they none of them could write and that none of them cared about books! Must everything as in dreams fade phantom-like in time's desert? Was life really like that? Was the flame of human endeavour and human aspiration always extinguished, leaving behind no vestige of its heat or brilliance? Melancholy questions leading to melancholy conclusions.

Luckily Dickens had his routine work at the office to attend to and the obligation to grind out a series of papers, *The Uncommercial Traveller*, as stop-gaps for the magazine. He was worried at the effect Charles Lever's novel *A Day's Ride* was having on the circulation. It was obviously a dismal failure, must be cut short and immediately followed by a novel of his own. Luckily he knew what he wanted to write about. At last, with forty-eight years of life behind him, he was free to settle down to tell the story of Cooling and the marshes by the river. Wandering there he can recapture the mood of boyhood and weave the story he knows to have been waiting for him ever since the day he first saw the coffin-shaped stones covering the bodies of the thirteen little Comport children. The story was no trouble to invent, it was all lying there in his mind. He was 'Pip' every bit as much as he was Oliver, Paul and David. Recoiling sharply to the imaginations of childhood and the half-fearful dreams of hulks, gibbets and escaped criminals made him in a way happy; he had returned to the empyrean of reality, to creation; he could still know himself for the angelic lad, sweet and sensitive, who had lured the hearts of countless readers from their breasts. He could once again see the prison ships at Egypt Bay, 'the old battery at Cliffe', the old sexton who knew him as a boy. How wonderful to shake himself free of facts, of reference books and all the grim reading he had done for *Hard Times* and *The Tale of Two Cities* and let himself go with the kind of people he loved and understood, the Gargerys who were so like the Peggottys and the Toodles and the rest of the pure in heart. He knew that people liked crime entanglements in novels nowadays; the new novel must have its melodramatic framework. He had used the device in *Bleak House*, he would use it again. All 1860 and part of 1861 was devoted to this book, *Great Expectations*, and he felt as he had felt in writing *David Copperfield*. Sensible of this identity of mood, he re-read his earlier book, for he must make sure the new novel was not too like the old. Some people have called *Great Expectations* the better novel of the two and in certain respects of even rarer limpidity. It appeared in *All the Year Round* from December 1860 to August 1861 and while writing it he gave no public readings.

In November 1860, feeling the need of change and motion, he went with his dear Wilkie to Bideford and posted to Liskeard. It was not as productive as the old tour he had made when beginning to write *Martin Chuzzlewit*, but it restored his elasticity and eagerness to write. Clovelly delighted him enough to make him open his Christmas story, *A Message from the Sea*, with the description of a village 'built sheer up the face of a steep and lofty cliff'. Collins at this time was still working on *The Woman in White* which, like Bulwer Lytton's *Strange Story*, was nearing completion. Both were booked for *All the Year Round*. The circulation of the Christmas number for 1860 reached a quarter of a million copies. At last Dickens had found out how to give the public exactly what it wanted. He had been experimenting in magazine editorship for over twenty years and now he knew the measure that must be meted out to eager readers.

Chapter 25

LONDON AND GAD'S HILL

The contagion of sympathy runs electrically through society, searches high and low for congenial powers, and suffers none to lurk unknown to the professor.

During the spring of 1861 Dickens rented 3 Hanover Terrace so that his girls might enjoy a London 'season' while he gave six readings at the St. James's Hall to what he termed 'model audiences'. The series enabled him to clear £500. If money could satisfy him he was getting plenty of it, for *Great Expectations* was 'doing gloriously'. He had a mind at this time to introduce his third son, Francis Jeffrey (a stammerer to whom all professions were closed), into the office of *All the Year Round*, as he seemed to be 'the only one of the family with natural literary taste and capacity'. Two years later Francis Jeffrey, tried and found wanting, was packed off to join the Bengal Mounted Police. Letters show that, like some of the older generations of his family, he spent more money than he received. Writing to Georgy, who it appears paid her nephew the allowance of £3 a month allotted to him by his father, Dickens says, 'Perhaps it would be a damaging thing, suddenly to withhold from him money that he expects. Therefore I would give him his month's three pounds—with a caution. . . .'

The lesson taught him by salvaging his impecunious brothers made Dickens fear a like disappointment in his own children, especially if they remained in London. Members of the estranged Hogarth family were inclined to attribute the exodus of Charles's sons to the influence of their aunt Georgina, whose affection for their father seemed to take a more and more possessive turn. Dickens would sometimes joke about the helplessness of his sons and say he thought he ought to be presented 'with a smock frock, a pair of leathern breeches, and a pewter watch for having brought up the largest family ever known with the smallest disposition to do anything for themselves'.

Charley, who had returned from China as much in love with Bessie Evans as ever, now decided to get married. His attachment had been for some time past a source of mortification and annoyance to his father, who had rather hoped that the journey to the Far East might cause him to change his mind, but when he saw that Charley's heart was fixed, he showed himself paternal and kind to the young couple though he refused ever to darken their doors. 'I will never go to Mrs. Charley's house', he wrote to Georgy and of course he did not attend the wedding, the vendetta between himself and Evans being still operative.

When *Great Expectations* was completed, that is to say in the late summer 1861, Dickens, with Georgy and Mamey in attendance, went to stay at Knebworth for a week, ostensibly to discuss the future of the Guild of Literature and Art and to see how the houses at Stevenage were progressing. During this visit he walked with Mr. Arthur Helps, Lord Orford and 'the girls' to inspect the buildings. After doing so they all crossed the road to pay a visit of curiosity to the so-called 'Hertfordshire Hermit', James Lucas, who appears as Mr. Mopes in *Tom Tiddler's Ground*.[1] Lucas, though he had abjured washing and slept on cinders, was an educated man and the son of a West India merchant. He was intensely annoyed with Dickens for singling him out as subject of a story and gave vent to his feelings in the press. Rather unexpectedly he has a place in the *Dictionary of National Biography*.

The rest of the summer was spent at Gad's Hill preparing for an extended reading tour which was to include Norwich,

[1] See *The Queen*, December 21, 1861, showing the Committee of Con-coction (Sala, Collins, Hollingshead and the editor): 'It was decided that the next number of *All the Year Round* should consist of seven chapters entitled *Tom Tiddler's Ground*'.

Ipswich, Colchester, Canterbury, Hastings, Brighton, New-castle, Edinburgh, Liverpool, Chester, Plymouth and Tor-quay. For this tour Dickens set himself to prepare new effects. Writing to Forster, he says:

> With great pains I have made a continuous narrative out of *Copperfield* that I think will reward the exertion it is likely to cost me. I have also done Nicholas Nickleby at the Yorkshire school, also the Bastille prisoner from *A Tale of Two Cities*.

By now he was treating each reading as if it were to be a play in which he was not only to act every part himself, but to learn every word by heart. It was a great blow to Dickens when his excellent manager, Arthur Smith, fell ill and had to give up working for him. His place was taken by one Head-land, who muddled the tour, the tickets and the bills in the most incompetent way, though even so he failed in choking off the audiences.

The series of readings had to be broken at Liverpool because of the death of the Prince Consort, and Dickens promised disappointed audiences to return later to compensate them for what they were missing. 'What Jackasses people are making of themselves over this death!' he exclaimed, unconsciously echoing the impatient sentiments of Macready on hearing of the mortal sickness of William IV. He was to some degree consoled for the interruption of his tour by the phenomenal popularity of his new Christmas story, *Tom Tiddler's Ground*, of which 300,000 copies were sold.

Soon after New Year it was considered correct for him to resume reading and in a hectic tour he visited Birmingham, Leamington, Cheltenham, Plymouth, Torquay, Exeter and Liverpool. In March and April he addressed himself to 'perfectly astonishing audiences' at the St. James's Hall. For the London series he established himself in a friend's house, 16 Hyde Park Gate, which he had exchanged for three months against Gad's Hill. He found it 'the nastiest little house in London'. 'I have hit upon nothing for a story', he wrote, 'again and again I have tried, but this odious little house has stifled and darkened my invention.' To celebrate John Forster's birthday (April 2) a dinner was given at the Star and Garter. After it Dickens, who was feeling wonderfully well, walked back to London with Lehmann.

During the spring he spoke at two public banquets, one of them in aid of the Artists' General Benevolent Institution[1] and the other the annual feast of the Newsvendors' Benevolent and Provident Institution.[2] At the first of these dinners he reminded those present that an artist is not a man who can make his livelihood out of buying and selling, that he is compelled to strike out of himself every spark of the fire which lighted, burned and, perhaps, consumed him. He must 'win the battle of life with his own hand, and with his own eyes . . . by his own unaided self'. It was a plain duty to help the artist, it was really part payment of the great debt which all sensible and civilised creatures owe to art, a way of expressing appreciation and a mark of respect. He added that artists of the highest rank were not slow or cold in supporting the Institution for which he was appealing.

Dickens told the Newsvendors (after giving a bird's-eye survey of the function of the modern newsman and the paper he is responsible for) that the newsman's profits were small, that he was subject to anxiety and much personal wear and tear. Indispensable to civilisation and freedom, he is looked for every day with pleasurable excitement. Society owes much to the newsman and it is only just that it should afford him assistance in times of sickness and indigence. No organisation could be more worthy of support.

In the summer he rested at Gad's Hill. F. D. Finlay, editor of the *Northern Whig*, stayed with him there in June. He was met by his host driving a jaunting car and found a pleasant little family party consisting of the Charles Collins, Mamey and Georgina. The food was excellent and elegantly served. Everyone seemed gay and they played croquet by day and vingt-et-un by night. Finlay was particularly taken with Georgina Hogarth, 'a really delightful person', easy in manner

[1] March 29, 1862.   [2] May 20, 1862.

and conversation and quite unassuming.

In July Georgy, to her brother-in-law's great distress, fell seriously ill and when she became better he decided to arrange for her to recuperate in Paris. Leaving strict injunctions with Mamey to bring her over as soon as he had found a suitable lodging, he crossed to France, visiting Hazebrouck and Dunkirk on his way to *la ville lumière*. In Paris Dickens rented 24 rue du Faubourg St. Honoré, and there they all three lived till close on Christmas. Wills came over from time to time to the Hôtel St. Honoré opposite, in order to put through the forthcoming issue of *All the Year Round*. On his November visit he brought with him a 'boxful' of flowers from Miss Burdett Coutts to be delivered by Dickens's hand to the Empress Eugénie. Dickens unscrewed the box, as 'if exhuming a dead body from a coffin'.

He reported 'Flowers a little crushed but corpses in very good preservation', screwed the box down again and started for Compiègne. At the station he hired the only omnibus and went 'to titivate', dressed in a delightful little bedroom trellised and creepered, then drove off again in the omnibus to the Palace. When the driver asked him whether he should go to the *cours d'honneur* Dickens replied '*Décidément*'! Arrived, he sent in a letter and card for the Duke of Atholl, and was shown to his rooms. His Grace in a dressing-gown poured tea for him, a servant brought in the box, the flowers were exhumed, and pronounced 'in wonderful preservation considering'. The Duke would deliver Miss Coutts's letter to the Duchesse de Bassano and get the Imperial gardener to touch up the bouquets. Presently the simple, elegant Duchess came in, had a chat about the flowers, then said good-bye. It was a fiasco from the undertaker's angle, for he would have liked to meet the Empress—but she was not even told that Mr. Dickens had called.

Somehow even his beloved Paris induced no cheerful mood. Wherever he went in the streets, the theatres, the restaurants, Dickens was haunted by the great figures of the past. Some of them were dead, one of the noblest was an exile.   Sadly he wrote:

> Last time I was here, I went to the theatre with Scribe, and the last time but one, Victor Hugo had the most fantastic of apartments, and stood in the midst of it, a fine-featured, fiery-eyed, gallant fellow.   Now Scribe is in Père la Chaise, the fantastic apartment in the Channel Islands, and Victor Hugo is an old photograph in the shops with a quenched eye and a stubbly beard and no likeness to anyone I ever saw.

Though there was no inspiration or exhilaration to be drawn from the life of Paris, Dickens at any rate could make arrangements with Sir Joseph Olliffe to read at the Embassy in aid of a British charity.   Readings from old works were considered by some of his admirers an unsatisfacotry substitute for a fresh book, but it was essential for him to keep his name before the public somehow and he had no fresh book on the stocks.   The title of a possible novel was hovering in his mind, *Our Mutual Friend*, but so far no story had gushed up from the hidden springs of creative life to give the words any meaning.   Perhaps having to take 'the girls' about was preventing him from settling to work; when he returned to Paris in the New Year he would return alone and see whether solitude would not serve his turn better than company.

Christmas was spent at Gad's Hill with the boys, and Mamey, whose amiability sometimes makes the impression of imbecility, says, 'These "tides" were the happiest of all'. Her father, on the other hand, writes as if he were rather oppressed.   'The house is pervaded by boys.'   'Every boy has an incalculable power of reproducing himself in every part of the house at every moment.'   'They boil over the house. . . .'   These are constantly recurring phrases.   He hears their boots trampling about, their whistling, their shouts; he cannot write at all.   He managed to see the holidays through without betraying irritability or displeasure, and it cheered him to know how well his Christmas story, *Somebody's Luggage*, was selling.   Though not quite as popular as its predecessors, it had put a good deal of money into his pocket. *All the Year Round* might be said to be going better than ever. At the end of January he escaped to Paris. There he stayed at the Hôtel du Helder, and for some reason connected with his interest in the Revolution spent his birthday at Arras thinking on the 'amiable sea-green Robespierre'.

The readings presided over by Lord Cowley at the British Embassy were 'a brilliant success'. Two were given in January and 'never, never, never was anything like the enthusiasm'. Dickens was positively chased out of Paris by his admirers, but not before he had promised to return for two more readings. These also went off incredibly well.

Going a good deal to the play, Dickens lost his heart to Fechter as the lover both in the *Maître de Ravenswood* and in the *Dame aux Camélias*. He had already met Fechter in London when he was playing *Hamlet* and *Ruy Blas* and had tried to persuade him to engage Maria Ternan for his cast. Now for the first time he was swept off his feet by what he called this actor's 'unmistakeable genius'. The critics had done their best to crush him, but the critics, he thought, were entirely wrong-headed. 'By Heavens!' he exclaimed after watching him in the *Maître de Ravenswood*, 'the man who can do that can do anything.' The very manner in which, as lover, he pressed the hem of the lady's dress was 'something wonderful'. Then, too, Fechter's interpretation of *Ruy Blas*, *Hamlet* and *Othello* were to his English admirer simply perfection. Knowledgeable people thought Dickens mistaken in his estimate, as the man was really but a moderately good actor, and this general opinion was to be confirmed when he became lessee of the Lyceum Theatre in London in the summer of 1863 with Dickens as his financial backer. Dickens, however, for the time being was infatuated by him.

His dear Madame Viardot proved as fascinating as ever. In *Orphée*, indeed, Dickens found her 'unapproachably fine'. After being much moved by her performance, he ran into M. Viardot in the corridor, who took him, 'disfigured as he **was** by crying', to her dressing-room. Could she have been

paid a more touching compliment? He managed to turn the
tables on the great contralto a few days later when he read
The Cricket on the Hearth aloud at the Ary Scheffers. It is
Mr. Arthur Russell who tells how 'when the reading was over
Madame Viardot was asked to sing, but could not do so as she
was still choked by tears'.

Forster deals very shortly with the years between 1862 and
1867 and says that he relied much on the papers known as
The Uncommercial Traveller to write on them at all.   He was
no longer in close touch with Dickens, and did not find his
activities so interesting as of old.   We know that he continued to disapprove of the readings.

'The girls' always looked forward to a 'season' in London,
and the 'season' of 1863 was to some extent rendered romantic
by the arrival of the sea-king's daughter, Princess Alexandra
of Denmark, who made her first public appearance as Princess
of Wales at the unveiling of the Memorial to Prince Albert in
June.   From Alfred Tennyson with his poem of welcome to
the humblest citizen all were out to give their hearts to the
lovely bride.   As Bulwer Lytton said, 'The Princess seems
to have bewitched the English world'.

The year 1863 was a year of deaths.   Augustus Egg died
in Algiers, Mrs. John Dickens in London, Mrs. George
Hogarth also in London.   Thackeray died suddenly, at the
age of fifty-two, on Christmas Eve, and Walter Landor
Dickens in India on the last day of the year, though the news
of his death did not reach his father till February, by which
time Francis Jeffrey was more than half-way to Bengal.

For the *Cornhill Magazine*, of which Thackeray was editor,
Dickens was requested to write a valedictory article.   A few
weeks earlier Thackeray had come up suddenly to Dickens in
the Athenaeum and had shaken him warmly by the hand, thus
putting an end to the Yates feud which had kept them apart
for five years.   It was considered appropriate by contemporaries that one great novelist should write about another even
though he might be no admirer of his work.   Dickens said

he had known Thackeray for twenty-eight years, ever since he had proposed to illustrate *Pickwick*, and that he had last seen him just before Christmas at the Athenaeum Club. He went on to tell how when Thackeray had stood for Oxford he had made a droll appeal to the speaker to come down and tell his constituents who he was, 'for he doubted whether more than two of the electors had ever heard of him and he thought there might be as many as six or eight who had heard of me'. He and Thackeray had of course had their differences of opinion. 'I thought that he too much feigned a want of earnestness and that he made a pretence of undervaluing his art, which was not good for the art that he held in trust.'

Dickens would not take on himself to discourse on Thackeray's works, but he had on the table before him all that he had written of his latest story. This was *Dennis Duval* 'which might have rivalled *Esmond*'. The condition of the little pages of manuscript where Death stopped his hand shows that he had carried them about, and often taken them out of his pocket here or there, for patient revision and interlineation. The last words he had corrected in print were, 'And my heart throbbed with an exquisite bliss'. Dickens reminded his readers that Thackeray was in his fifty-third year and that the mother who had blessed him in his first sleep also blessed him in his last. Great things were known of him in the way of warm affection, quiet endurance, unselfish thoughtfulness for others and generosity. These things may not be told. No one more genial, natural, cordial, fresh and honestly impulsive has been seen in these times. 'No one can be surer than I of the greatness and goodness of his heart.'

A great concourse of mourners stood round a grave at Kensal Green on December 30 of the year 1863. An observer says of Dickens on this occasion 'he had a look of bereavement on his face which was indescribable'. When all others had turned aside from the grave, he still stood there, as if rooted to the spot, watching with almost haggard eyes every spadeful of dust that was thrown upon it. Walking away with some friends, he began to talk, but presently his voice quavered a

little, and shaking hands all round rapidly, he went off alone.[1]
Even more 'woefully upsetting' to him was the death of his
crony John Leech which took place shortly afterwards.

For Christmas 1863 Dickens wrote part of *Mrs. Lirriper's
Lodgings* and cogitated over the novel for which he had the
name but not the story. Two years had gone by without a
long book, but at last he found himself able to get the first
three numbers down on to paper. He then went off with
Browning and Wilkie Collins 'to keep Shakespeare's birthday
in peace and quiet' at Stratford. The first instalment of *Our
Mutual Friend* was issued on May 1 and thirty thousand copies
of it were at once sold. On May 11 Dickens presided at the
Adelphi Theatre over a meeting called to found Shakespeare
schools in connection with the Royal Dramatic Academy.
He was anxious that a start should be made with forty foundation scholars, all to be children of actors, actresses or dramatic
writers. The Provost of Eton was supporting the scheme
and he took occasion to say that he believed 'there is not in
England any institution so socially liberal as a public school'.

From February to June 1864 he rented 57 Gloucester Place
and indulged in a perfect orgy of dining out. 'The most
severe dinner-eating season I have ever known in London.
Every week I had sworn to go out no more and every week
I have perjured myself seven times.' Various diaries of the
moment record some of these outings, one a dinner with
Fechter in St. John's Wood to meet Bulwer Lytton, and
another with Chorley in Westbourne Terrace. To many of
them he was accompanied by Georgina. Browning and
others were at Chorley's party and Sir George Grove noted
'Dickens was very amusing, but not in the least forced. He
was full of a ship of Mormon emigrants which he had been
seeing, 1200 of the cleanest, best conducted, most excellent
people he ever saw.' This excursion may be seen reflected
in an article entitled 'Bound for the Great Salt Lake' in *The
Uncommercial Traveller*.

In June Dickens fled to Belgium to recuperate from all the

<hr>

[1] *Dickensian*, 1937, p. 131.

port, champagne and rich food. He complained of severe pain in the left foot and leg but did not call it gout though at times it almost incapacitated him. Ten days abroad worked wonders and on his return Dickens settled down at Gad's Hill to his novel, swearing he would 'stick to his last', and 'dine out never again till next year'. No readings were arranged while he applied himself to his creative work and, with the exception of visits to the office of *All the Year Round*, he remained absorbed in *Our Mutual Friend*.

During the summer Charles Collins's health gave cause for great anxiety; it had broken down in the spring and Katey had taken him to Wiesbaden, but the German doctors could not do much for him and she had now settled with him at Nice. His illness had been diagnosed as cancer and Dickens began to think that Katey would soon be left 'a young widow'; but Charles Collins survived his father-in-law.

In November we find Dickens writing to his manager, Wills, alluding to his generous present of a brougham, a 'token of your ever generous friendship and appreciation'. The carriage will be to him 'a memorial of happy intercourse and perfect confidence that have never had a break and that surely never can have any break now but one'. In return he proposed Wills for the Garrick Club, getting Wilkie Collins to second him. It was very mortifying to them both that their candidate should be blackballed and because of it both resigned membership.

Dickens liked receiving large presents and was delighted when the ninety-two sections of Fechter's gift of a Swiss chalet began to arrive at Higham station. There was a discussion where it should be erected; the garden was too small to hold it, and as it was intended for quiet work it had to be sited at some distance from the house. Finally it was put up on the other side of the Dover Road to be approached by a flight of steps leading to a tunnel, like the Pope passage at Twickenham.

In the early part of 1865 Dickens was in Paris again for a brief holiday, after which he worked 'like a dragon' on *Our*

Mutual Friend. His swollen feet, treated with 'poppy fomentations', prevented him from taking exercise so he allowed his thoughts to dwell on the American war, and told Fanny Kemble that he 'was a southern sympathiser to the extent of not believing in the northern love of the black man nor that the northern horror of slavery had much to do with the war'.

For May and June the Dickens party was in London, this time at 16 Somers Place. The usual round of public engagements was fulfilled, the usual mill of private dinners. There were family concerns, too, to occupy his mind, for Alfred Tennyson d'Orsay was to be sent out of the country. For two years the boy had been working in a 'China house in the city', no doubt the house to which his brother Charley had gone to work after his return from the East and which now had failed. Writing to Henry Layard, Dickens informed him that his young son was sailing for Melbourne on May 29. 'At his own desire Alfred Tennyson,' he said, 'will seek his fortune.' He had obtained a few introductions for him, and possibly Layard may furnish others, perhaps one to the Governor?

Again Dickens crossed to France, this time with Ellen Ternan, and on their way back both were involved in the Staplehurst accident, when eight coaches toppled into the river and a number of people were killed and injured. Ellen was not hurt, neither was Dickens, who set to work with the flask strapped like field-glasses to his person to pour brandy down the throats of persons suffering from shock, concussion and broken limbs. Some of them died immediately. Dickens did not understand it at all and noted with sad surprise that 'Mr. Dickenson was the first person the brandy saved'. He worked hard in extricating the victims and later was presented with plate by the railway company for his services on the occasion. In a postscript to *Our Mutual Friend* Dickens says that Mr. and Mrs. Boffin were also involved in the accident but suffered no permanent injury.

In July he went to Knebworth for the formal inauguration

of the houses built by the Guild of Literature and Art. Owing to the provisions of the Act constituting the Guild it had not been possible to implement any of its intentions for seven years. Only now, in the year 1865, were the three Guild houses, built on land given by Lord Lytton, ready for occupation. It had always been part of the scheme to provide artists and authors with quarters where they could confederate themselves into a society for the diffusion of light and culture; at least this was Dickens's idea, but it worked out quite differently. The houses were located on the road near Stevenage and a party was given to celebrate the founding of a new Arcadia. Every artist and author of eminence was bidden to the feast and 'the county' was invited to meet them. They did not mix, and Charles Collins heard 'the county' commenting on the party and saying that they had been asked to meet 'a dem'd funny set of people'. At the luncheon that followed the throwing open of the houses, both Dickens and Bulwer Lytton, as co-founders of the Guild, were announced to speak.

During the morning Percy Fitzgerald had a talk with John Forster, who made the unpleasant impression on him of 'being impregnably mailed in self-complacency'. He was also carried off by Dickens to be introduced to the master of Knebworth. They found him lying on a divan smoking a chibouk. He mumbled a few words of greeting, seemed but dimly conscious of their presence, and had a far-away look in his eyes. By luncheon-time he had revived enough to make an eloquent speech, and, when all but the house guests had left, became brilliant, talkative and droll, discussing with Dickens his own novel, *Strange Story*, with great animation.

In thanking Bulwer Lytton at the luncheon for the toast he had proposed in his honour, Dickens explained that 'the three houses built in the Gothic style' had been erected out of Guild funds on land donated by the master of Knebworth. They had surveyed these satisfactory buildings and were now enjoying the hospitality of their originator. He would like to make it clear that the ladies and gentlemen, whom we shall invite to occupy the houses we have built will never be placed under any social disadvantage. They will be invited to occupy them as artists, receiving them as a mark of the high respect in which they are held by their fellow workers. As artists I hope they will often exercise their calling within those walls for the general advantage; and they will always claim on equal terms, the hospitality of their generous neighbour. . . . Health, long life, and prosperity to our distinguished host. Ladies and gentlemen, you know very well that when the health, life and beauty now overflowing these halls shall have fled, crowds of people will come to see the house where he lived and wrote. . . . This is the home of a very great man whose connection with Hertfordshire every other county in England will envy for many long years to come.

It is sad to have to record that the well-intentioned efforts of the promoters of the Guild failed completely in persuading authors or artists to come and live rent free in the houses at Stevenage designed for their comfort. No one of them would consent to do so on any terms. Those approached pointed out that the times of the trains would make it impossible for them to reach their proposed residences after the theatre. Others went so far as to ask what they were to be paid for 'being buried alive' at Stevenage. To the unprejudiced person visiting them to-day the houses seem entirely without point. Three miles from Knebworth, its hospitality could not be frequently enjoyed: facing a dusty high road, they were just too far from the station to be convenient to anyone. R. H. Horne called them 'those doleful cottages standing in a field'. To authors and artists the whole scheme was tainted with the idea of patronage, and, though paved with blameless intention, the road to Stevenage appeared to them the road to extinction.

Chapter 26

AMERICA AGAIN

An educated American is one of the most endearing and generous of friends.   CHARLES DICKENS

ON finishing *Our Mutual Friend* in September 1865, Dickens light-heartedly polished off a Christmas story, *Dr. Marigold's Prescriptions*, and then devoted his attention exclusively to preparing new readings, making no attempt to write another novel until his return from America in April 1868. Among the scenes dramatised at this time was the murder of Nancy by Bill Sikes from *Oliver Twist*. Dickens experimented with this presentation until he could say, 'I have got something so horrible out of it that I am afraid to try it in public.' It curdled the blood of his family to hear 'the awful noises' he made in rehearsing his effects in the garden at Gad's Hill, and it awed them to see his exhaustion afterwards, 'as if it took all the breath out of his body'. The murder reading was not brought into his repertory for three years.

On St. Valentine's Day 1866 Dickens took the chair at the annual dinner of the Dramatic, Equestrian and Musical Fund at Willis's Rooms. To his delight ladies were present at the table, and he laid 'the utmost devotion sanctioned by St. Valentine at their feet'. He spoke of the professional brotherhood that honoured the claims of kindred 'in the dingiest and dirtiest concert room, in the least lucid theatre, in the raggedest circus-tent ever stained by weather'. He could say from experience that there is no class or profession that so well helps the other. In toasting the ladies he gave the name of the distinguished actress Mrs. Stirling, who responded on behalf of her sex. Soon after this date Dickens felt himself to be very unwell. The doctor said he was suffering from 'irritability of the heart', but the observable symptoms were great pain and lameness of one leg and the word 'erysipelas' was whispered. It appears that his heart was not contracting properly and he was dosed with iron, quinine and digitalis. To take his mind off his fast-ageing body, he chose this moment to accept a contract offered by Chappell to read for thirty nights in England, Ireland, Scotland or Paris. Chappell guaranteed all expenses incurred by the reader, his servant and his 'gasman', and proposed to pay him £500 at the start, £500 half-way through and £500 at the finish. The organisation of the tour was to be Chappell's business and no responsibility of any kind was to be thrown on Dickens. He merely had to decide the composition and order of his programmes and to turn up at the time and place arranged for.

As *Dr. Marigold's Prescriptions* had sold over a quarter of a million copies, its author decided to introduce it into his repertory. Unable to judge of its effects without an audience, he summoned friends to the furnished house he was at the moment renting in Southwick Place (6), to hear him read the sketch aloud. He was practically word-perfect for he had rehearsed it to himself 'considerably over two hundred times'. Robert Browning received a note inviting him for '6.30 sharp' on Monday March 18 to listen to 'Dr. Marigold'. John Forster had suggested that the poet might be interested. Collins, Fechter, Chappell and Dolby were also invited and were so warm in their praises that 'Dr. Marigold' was adopted forthwith as a reading.

Dickens chose Wills to companion him on his tour and Chappell's business manager, Dolby, joined them in the railway carriage. To begin with Dickens seemed a little suspicious of Dolby, perhaps not without reason, for in the end he turned out to be 'the chiel amang them taking notes'. At the opening reading at St. James's Hall on April 10 the cheapjack 'Dr. Marigold' was welcomed by an enthusiastic audience. To Carlyle, who was present, the reader appeared to act better than Macready and 'to make a whole tragic, comic, heroic *theatre* visible, performing under one hat, and keeping us laughing—in a sorry way some of us thought—the whole night'. 'Dr. Marigold' was next repeated in the St. George's

Hall, Liverpool, where the listeners were noticeably slower at the uptake than in London. Something of a scrimmage over seats was going on when the reader, at the advertised hour, took his place on the platform. In so doing he lost the effect of a majestic, spot-lighted entry. It was a lesson to him never again to enter a hall until told by his manager that all was ready for his appearance.

The setting contrived by Dickens for his readings is described by Dolby, whose business it was to convey the properties about. At the back of the platform was a large screen or framework covered with canvas, over which a maroon-coloured cloth was tightly stretched: in the centre stood the reading-desk, rather spindly in effect, with a projecting ledge on the left for gloves and handkerchief, and on the right for water-bottle and glass. Further forward were two upright rods (secured by copper-wire guys) supporting the gas apparatus. Reflectors were arranged so that 'the reader's face and figure were fully and equally distinct to the vision of the audience'. After the readings Dickens would often say that he felt as if he had been slowly cooked.

The first strangeness with Dolby soon wore off and Dickens became quite friendly and affectionate with him. Beside 'Dr. Marigold', the readings included 'David Copperfield', the 'Trial from Pickwick' and 'Little Dombey'. Shuttling about from place to place proved very tiring and more than a little tiresome, but all inconveniences were forgotten the moment Dickens found himself standing at his desk facing an audience. He then felt fresh, confident and master of the scene. He would read in Liverpool one night, Manchester the next, then Liverpool again, followed by Edinburgh, Glasgow, London, Aberdeen, then Glasgow and Edinburgh again, and once more fulfil an assignment in Manchester. When not in bed wrestling with acute catarrh or on a platform, Dickens spent his time wholly in a railway carriage. Dolby noticed that whenever an express gathered speed his companion would writhe with the nervousness induced by the Staplehurst smash. The tour ended as it had begun, with

'Dr. Marigold' at the St. James's Hall.

Though, in a sense, it had been a triumph and had once more demonstrated how great was his power of attracting audiences, Dickens ended the round 'tired and depressed'. Chappell, having made a handsome profit, begged him to carry out a second tour of fifty nights. The reader raised his price to seventy pounds a reading instead of fifty, and after some bargaining agreed to perform for forty-two nights for £2500, beginning on January 15, 1867.

This contract at least gave him the chance of a six months' rest which was really essential, for during the tour he had had to tonic himself up with oysters and champagne and had slept badly after readings. In May he had suffered from streaming colds and even fainting attacks, all indicative of the strain he was putting on his nervous system, his liver and his heart, but he still had great resistance and as usual the resumption of routine life at home helped him back to health.

In the odd evenings between readings he spoke during the spring of 1866 at three public dinners. He also dined out privately, though not so frequently as of old. One evening at the Forsters he met Mrs. Carlyle. It was the day after her husband had delivered his inaugural address as Lord Rector of Edinburgh University. She came into the room flourishing a telegram from Professor Tyndall announcing the great success of the speech. Her good spirits made her unusually expansive, and 'the radiance of her enjoyment was upon her all night'. She gave Dickens the subject for a novel taken from her own observation in her own street: it was to be about the house opposite. She was positive that from the blinds, the curtains, the callers, the vehicles that drew up at the door, the life within might be deduced and a romance constructed. As the party broke up before she had finished her story she laughingly promised Dickens to continue it at their next meeting. But there never was to be another meeting, for, three weeks later, Mrs. Carlyle died suddenly after picking up a pet dog which had been run over in Hyde Park. Taking the injured dog in her arms she got back into her brougham to drive home. The coachman presently sensed that something was wrong and looked into the carriage. Mrs. Carlyle sat there dead with the dog on her knees. No one who knew Mrs. Carlyle could fail to miss her desperately when she died. There was a richness and solidity about her intellectual gifts, her knowledge of books and her capacity for friendship, a 'beyond and beyond quality which is so rare and so irreplaceable'. She occupied a most special niche in Dickens's pantheon, and when he heard of her death he said, 'None of the writing women came near her at all'.

In the early autumn of 1866 Dickens busied himself as usual with his Christmas story for *All the Year Round*. It was entitled 'Mugby Junction'. He read one of the chapters, 'The Boy at Mugby', to Mary Boyle, Mamey, Katey and Georgy, and they all shook with laughter till the tears flowed. Encouraged by this demonstration, he combined this sketch and another chapter, 'The Barbox Brothers', into a reading for his Christmas party at Gad's Hill in 1866, a party which included Henry Layard and was so large as to overflow into the Falstaff Inn. Local M.P.s and officers from Chatham were invited to be present and Dickens even had his desk sent down from London for the occasion. The reading was not a success; at least it did not seem to amuse the audience as much as he had hoped it might. The girls' facile laughter had misled him sadly over his effects. He repeated the reading at his opening meeting on January 15 at the St. James's Hall, but there also it had no success. When Liverpool and Birmingham condemned it, it was thrown out of repertory. The grind of the readings, even though they were mapped out in every detail, was intense. 'Nearly every week we were in London for a reading at the St. James's Hall and on the following morning set off for some provincial town.'

Dickens took every chance that offered of air and exercise. He walked, for example, from Preston to Blackburn, passing on his way Hoghton Tower, a curious old ruin with a farmhouse attached. This place went to the making of *George Silverman's Explanation*, a £1000 tale written for American publication. 'I feel as if I had read something (by somebody else) which I shall never get out of my head', wrote Dickens to Wills when composing it. This story has been examined in the light of Freudian psychology. The clergyman hero has been interpreted as being the victim of an abnormal rift between idealistic love and physical desire, he can only mate with a woman he does not idealise. This want of harmonisation is put down to his upbringing. He has been reared in a slum, longed to be loved, always disapproved of, but always his childish ego has found itself adorable, important and beyond criticism. Viewed objectively, it is a tiresome story, though viewed subjectively it may be, as its elucidator supposes, a clue to Dickens's own psychology.

The matter that preoccupied Dickens most during 1866 was the prospect of the American tour he had been urged to undertake by J. T. Fields. There was not much time in which to think about it, for the presidential election was due in 1868, and the very latest date for which he could get a good contract was November 1867. As Dolby was going to America on business, he instructed him to spy out the land and report whether it was really worth while to undertake so exhausting an enterprise. Dolby must certainly try to have a heart-to-heart talk with Fields. He would give him an introduction and he could also deliver into his own hand a Christmas story, *Holiday Romance*, written for Fields's *Children's Magazine*.

Dolby sailed on August 3 and was back by September 29 with promises of rewards so large that Dickens was persuaded that it would be well worth his while to make the American tour. Forster put all the pressure he could on his friend to hold him back, but something about the glittering returns dangled in front of his eyes fascinated Dickens and made him determined to set out, though he knew perfectly well that he was going to hate every moment of exile and feel ill all the time. He at once commissioned Dolby to return to America by an October boat to organise details of the tour.

Q

It was J. T. Fields who was really responsible for tempting him in this way by offering to guarantee £10,000 and bank the money in England in advance. Talking it over with Wills at the office, Dickens said, 'My worldly circumstances are very good. I don't want money. . . . Still, at the age of fifty-five or fifty-six, the idea of making a very great addition to one's capital in half a year is immense.' Wills, like Forster, did his best to prevent his accepting any American offer, but he brushed his objections aside and despite all persuasion booked passages for himself and his two men in the 'Cuba' for November 9.

Dolby meanwhile, as Dickens's forerunner, was being made a great fuss of in Boston. He had been met at the wharf by Fields, Ticknor and James Osgood, who introduced him to Oliver Wendell Holmes. Emerson took him round the halls and public rooms in which readings might take place. Dolby finally decided on Tremont Temple which held 2000 people, had a sloping floor and excellent acoustics. He then visited Longfellow at Nantucket and went on, escorted by Osgood, to New York. There he saw Horace Greeley of the *New York Tribune*, William Cullen Bryant, editor and proprietor of the *Evening Post*, and J. Gordon Bennett of the *New York Herald*, a very powerful trio of press magnates. All showed great eagerness over the Dickens readings and all guaranteed that no echoes of past unpopularity should mar the warmness of a universal welcome. After booking the Steinway Hall, New York, Dolby took rooms for Dickens at the quiet Westminster Hotel. Forster continued to object very strongly to the whole enterprise but his friend put on an adamantine expression and would listen to nothing.

People who knew Dickens best were most apprehensive about the second American tour, for not only was his health undependable, but no one really knew what attitude the ordinary American was going to take up towards him. Twenty-five years had passed since the burning of *Martin Chuzzlewit* in New York; there really had been time to forget, for a new generation had grown up on the novels. Even so Dickens, in spite of Dolby's assurances, was a little nervous about American public opinion. The press had been pretty plain-spoken in old days and maybe still cherished a grudge against him. When a New York paper stated that 'even in England he is less well known than here', it reassured him somewhat, as did the words that followed, 'millions treasure every word he has written and tens of thousands would make a large sacrifice to see and hear the man who has made so many hours happy'.

Many friends wrote him letters of farewell and arranged send-off dinners for him. Frith, dining with Wilkie Collins (November 1) to meet him, says, 'We were none of us in evening dress and Dickens wore one of the large black cravats not yet gone out of fashion and a wonderful pin large in size, strange in form'. A touch of the old Inimitable flashed up as everyone fixed their eyes on his scarf-pin. Smiling, he said, 'I hope you all like my pin; it is uncommon, I think. I hope there is no such pin as this in America. I have invested in it for the whole and sole purpose of pleasing my friends over the water.' Next evening he attended a banquet at the Freemasons' Tavern with Lord Lytton in the chair.

> Happy is the man [said Lord Lytton] who makes clear his title deeds to the royalty of genius while he yet lives to enjoy the gratitude and reverence of those he has subjected to his sway. . . . Seldom has that kind of royalty been quietly conceded to any man of genius until his tomb becomes his throne and yet there is not one of us now present who thinks it strange that it is granted without a murmur to the guest whom we receive to-night.

Such vials of eulogy were poured on Dickens's head on this occasion that he almost collapsed with emotion. He took the opportunity when rising to reply to affirm his faith in the American people. 'I know full well, whatever little motes my beamy eyes may have descried in theirs, that they are a kind, large-hearted, generous and great people. In that faith I am going to see them again: in that faith I shall, please

God, return from them in the spring; in that same faith to live and die.' Quoting in lieu of further thanks a short sentence of his own, he ended on Tiny Tim's note, 'God bless us every one'.

On Friday November 8 a royal saloon conveyed Charles Dickens to Liverpool. Equipped with his high reading-desk, his books, his 'sun-pictures' of himself and Gad's Hill (inside and out) and attended by his faithful John and his gasman, he embarked on the 'Cuba' on November 9. Ten days later he stepped ashore at Boston and drove to reserved rooms in the Parker House which had been filled with flowers and books by Mrs. J. T. Fields. There he held a colloquy with Dolby who told him that the first reading had been fixed for December 2. This meant that he would have to kick his heels for ten days, a rather annoying proceeding when one wanted to spend as little time in America as possible. There were to be eighty-four readings in all, but for various reasons, the impending presidential election being one of them, they were in the end cut to seventy-six. The chief difficulty Dolby had to contend with was the unprecedented demand for tickets. For thirteen hours he had sat at his desk in Ticknor and Fields's book-store selling tickets and taking $12,000. He had thought to defeat speculators by refusing to sell more than six tickets to any applicant, but was euchred when they sent fifty buyers at a time to join the queue. The result was that the undergraduates of Harvard could not buy a single ticket and private people who by queuing up for hours had secured seats were immediately approached to sell them at an enhanced price. Dolby was dubbed 'pudding-headed' by the press and abused for the way he was muddling the readings, but he stuck to his job and in the end things went smoothly.

While tickets were being sold Dickens was greatly in demand as a guest. He dined with Longfellow at 'the awful hour of 2.30 P.M.' and sat on till 8 P.M. thinking 'of nothing but the beautiful Mrs. Longfellow burning to death'. He renewed acquaintance with Emerson and Oliver Wendell Holmes and met Agassiz. His old friends Felton, Washington Irving and Prescott were dead, but Henry Dexter, the sculptor, visited him, and Putnam, his secretary of twenty-five years earlier, was delighted to welcome him and talk of former adventures. Putnam was now grey-haired and without front teeth, but he did not look so venerable as Longfellow whose hair was as snowy as his beard. People had changed, Boston itself had altered and grown. Hot and cold baths had come in, and the comfort of the hotel was great.

Dickens was billed to read for four nights in succession, that is Monday to Thursday inclusive, for three weeks, first in Boston and then in New York and later in other cities. To open with, he read the 'Carol' and the 'Trial from Pickwick' and on the following night 'Copperfield' and 'Bob Sawyer'. Writing home, the reader said, 'The success here COULD NOT be greater . . . I was as cool as though I were reading at Chatham'; and to Mamey he betrays a spark of his old inimitability in 'your respected parent is immensely popular in Boston society'. His 'dear Meery's' buttonhole turns up on his dressing-table every evening which gives him the homely feeling of being loved for his own sake. The money takings were really exciting. He was able to remit £3000 in gold at $7 to the pound on December 15 and a month later consigned another £10,000 to London.

In New York he read four times in the week of December 9 and four in the week of December 16. The city was plastered with orange bills, a colour he was said to favour. Two tons of paper had been ordered to advertise readings that did not require advertising at all, for every meeting was sold out as soon as announced. In order to cosset himself and rehearse his effects Dickens henceforth refused all social engagements. To take the air and to convey him to his appointments he hired a brougham and, when the snow fell, a sleigh. In this he drove 'furred up to the moustache, with furs on the coach-boy and on the driver, with an immense white, red and yellow striped rug for a covering, you would suppose me to be of Hungarian or Polish nationality'. Suffering a good deal from what he called 'American catarrh', brought on chiefly in heated

trains, he spent his days on a sofa and his evenings on a platform.   Some people thought he resembled the Emperor Louis
Napoleon, others were reminded of the Emperor of China
and others again thought that he looked the typical American
gentleman.

In New York he lodged at the quiet hotel discovered for
him by Dolby: it really was as quiet as Mivart's in Brook
Street and he could get in and out unobserved by a private
door.   The waiters were French and this gave him the pleasant
illusion of living in Páris.   The Westminster was to his thinking 'a faultless hotel'.   In New York his success was greater
even than in Boston; the people seemed quicker at the uptake
and certainly were more demonstrative.

When the eight readings at New York were over Dickens
returned to Boston for two or more readings and, as he had
parted with Dolby, who had gone on to Philadelphia, he
accepted the hospitality of Mrs. Fields.   His rooms in her
house were festooned with holly and moss, looking glasses
and picture frames included.   It all produced such a homely
impression that he was deeply affected, and when a sea-captain
arrived to present him with a sprig of English mistletoe he
could not restrain his tears.   After reading in Boston on
December 23 and 24, though suffering from a heavy cold, he
took the train for New York on Christmas Day.   As the cold
became worse he felt less and less inclined to face an audience,
but somehow forced himself to do so.   It surprised him to
see that at almost every theatre a version of one or other of
his novels was being played.   'I can't get down Broadway
for my own portrait.'   It seems that Dolby had not organised
the tour with any foresight, for he again had to trek back to
Boston for readings on January 3, 4, 6 and 7.   On January 8
he was back in New York, but four days later went to Philadelphia where George W. Childs, owner of the *Public Ledger*,
met him at the station and showed him every civility.   The
treatment he now received was in strong contrast to his former
visit.   After reading twice at Philadelphia he was told he really
must go to Chicago and that if he didn't the people there

would have fits. 'Well, I had rather they had fits than I did,' was his retort. From Philadelphia he went back again to New York. On January 17, 18, 19, 20 he was advertised to read in Brooklyn at the church of Mrs. Stowe's brother Mr. Beecher. This unnecessary double crossing caused him immense fatigue and occurred over and over again during the tour.

Dickens had a very good reason for not wanting to go to Chicago. His brother Augustus ('Moses') had already been there and the newspapers blazoned the news that he had gone away leaving a wife behind him 'in deep poverty'. Having made this discovery, the reporters featured her as 'starving' and inquired why a man who was taking tens of thousands of dollars out of the country could not spare a dime for his own kith and kin. Once again Dickens felt obliged to defend himself by making a personal statement. He explained that the only legal Mrs. Augustus Dickens was living in England and that for many years he had helped to support her.

At Baltimore there was feasting on canvas-back duck, terra-pin and blue oysters, a reading in 'a charming little theatre', and then a move to Washington where he put up at a quiet German establishment kept by one Wheleker, who owned the best restaurant in the city and had a reputation equal to Vérey in London. He provided Mr. Dickens with a suite of rooms, a French waiter and perfect cooking. At Washington, however, Dickens did not feel at all well and found it difficult to adapt himself to what he called 'its congress of climates'. Breaking his rule never to accept hospitality, he dined with his old friend Charles Sumner to meet the Secretary for War, Mr. Stanton. Mr. Stanton had served with Abraham Lincoln in the same capacity during the Civil War and at that time had never gone to bed without reading something from *Pickwick*, with the result that he could repeat, if he were started with the first lines, whole chapters from memory. Mr. Dickens capped this anecdote by saying that he had been sent Russian copies of his books from the Crimea. They had been found, some-times stained with blood, in the enemy's camp.

They went on to talk of President Lincoln and the manner

of his death, and Mr. Stanton told the story of the last cabinet meeting over which the President had presided. He himself was late, and, as he appeared, Lincoln broke off what he was saying with, 'Let us proceed to business, gentlemen'. Instead of lolling in his chair, as his custom was, the President sat upright and still. As he left the meeting Stanton said to the Attorney-General, 'What an extraordinary change in Mr. Lincoln!' And the Attorney-General replied, 'We all saw it before you came in. While we were waiting for you, the President, with his chin well down, said, "Gentlemen, something very extraordinary is going to happen, and that very soon". "Something good, sir, I hope," interposed the Attorney-General, whereupon the President said very gravely, "I don't know; I don't know. But it will happen, and shortly, too!" All present were impressed by his manner and the Attorney-General asked him straight, "Have you received any information, sir, not yet disclosed to us?" "No," answered the President, "but I have had a dream. And I have now had the same dream three times. Once on the night preceding the Battle of Bull Run. Once on the night preceding" such another (naming a battle also not favourable to the North). His chin sank to his breast again and he seemed to be reflecting deeply. "Might one ask the nature of this dream, sir?" said the Attorney-General. "Well," replied the President without lifting his head or changing his attitude, "I am on a great broad rolling river— and I am in a boat—and I drift—and I drift——!—but this is not business!" ' Suddenly raising his face and looking round the table as Mr. Stanton entered he said, 'Let us proceed to business, gentlemen'. Mr. Stanton and the Attorney-General agreed, as they walked away together, that it would be curious to notice whether anything untoward ensued; they would both watch coming events. Mr. Lincoln was shot that night.

On his birthday, February 7, Dickens had an interview with President Andrew Johnson. He was due to read that evening and in the afternoon Sumner found him lying poulticed and voiceless in his bedroom. It did not seem possible that he could face an audience, much less use his throat. And yet that very evening he looked debonair as he entered the hall and, though he had been croaking harshly all day, his voice rang strong and clear. At his command was always a reservoir of nervous force that could be drawn on in an emergency. It had got about that it was his birthday and 'exquisite flowers in baskets and bouquets' arrived at his rooms as well as presents of gold and silver pins, studs and links. The platform was like a bower; the audience, however, being official, was cold in the extreme. The President, chief members of the Cabinet, Judges of the Supreme Court and the members of the Diplomatic Corps, as well as naval and military authorities in full uniform, were all there, but there was practically no applause, only some 'feeble clapping'.

When we know what Dickens's regimen was during this tour, it is almost a miracle that he survived the experience. He took a tumbler of new cream with two tablespoonfuls of rum before rising: at twelve he had a sherry-cobbler and a biscuit: at three a pint of champagne. Just before the reading he slipped down an egg beaten up in sherry, and in the interval between items on the programme sipped strong beef tea. For supper he was given soup, wine, and often, before turning in, a dose of laudanum. Between stimulants and sedatives he managed to fulfil his obligations, but it was at a considerable cost, and even he must have realised that he was shortening his life.

From Wheleker's hotel window Dickens could see the Treasury buildings and was intrigued by the bevy of ladies who issued from them daily. It was a very great surprise to him to learn that all the clerks in the Treasury were ladies (for copying and official work) and that this innovation had come in during the war and had been found most satisfactory.

Dickens left Washington on February 9 for Baltimore while Dolby went on ahead to arrange further readings at Hartford, Providence, Worcester and other cities. By

February 22 they were both at Parker House once more. A new threat imperilled the readings, for when the rumour got about that President Johnson was to be impeached, the sale of tickets at once began to drop. Visits to Albany, Buffalo, Syracuse, Rochester and Springfield convinced Dolby that the tour should be wound up without delay. Dickens insisted on a short holiday at Niagara Falls and then returned to Boston, giving a farewell reading on April 8.

At this leave-taking the reading-stand was wreathed with flowers and palm leaves. Delighted as always by attentions of this sort, Dickens said, 'Before allowing Dr. Marigold to tell his story in his own peculiar way, I kiss the fair hands unknown which have so beautifully decorated my table this evening'. Responding with a sob in his voice to the applause that roared up at the conclusion of this reading from a standing audience, he addressed himself 'to the great public heart' laid bare before him, bidding it a loving good-bye. After going through all this he made 'burnt brandy punch' at Mrs. Fields's house, 'sang songs and made everyone laugh tremendously'.

The press of America gave him a dinner on April 18 at Delmonico's in New York at which he kept everyone waiting for an hour. Rumours flew round the room. Some said he had erysipelas in the foot and could not get a boot on; others that Dolby had been to every shop in New York to get a gout stocking, but that as New Yorkers never had gout he had failed to do so; others that an English gentleman had at last been found ready to surrender his gout stocking for the evening, so as to enable Dickens to meet the pressmen. At last he entered on the arm of Horace Greeley. Once again the strains of 'God save the Queen' sounded in his ears as he hobbled in, and his thoughts went back to the scene of twenty-five years earlier when an alert, agile young man had stepped lightly to the same tune into a Boston banquet. The tours had had few points of resemblance but this certainly was one.

There were two hundred guests at this dinner and the

speakers included Charles Eliot Norton. Dickens, taking his cue from Greeley, reminded those present of the link between himself and them. He too had worked for the press and attributed his success in authorship to the severe training of newspaper work. After complimenting America on the growth and changes evident in her cities and on the remarkable increase in the graces and amenities of life, he went on to stress the essential unity, in spite of points of difference, of the two great nations, America and England, and declared that the notion that an American should be regarded as a foreigner in England was to his thinking incongruous and absurd. He concluded with these words:

> Finally, gentlemen, and I say this subject to your correction, I do believe that from the great majority of honest minds on both sides, there cannot be absent the conviction that it would be better for this globe to be riven by an earthquake, fired by a comet, overrun by an iceberg, and abandoned to the arctic fox and bear, than that it should present the spectacle of these two great nations, each of which has, in its own way and hour, striven so hard and so successfully for freedom, ever again being arrayed one against the other. Gentlemen, I cannot thank your president enough or you enough for your kind reception of my health, and of my poor remarks, but believe me, I do thank you with the utmost fervour of which my soul is capable.

At the final New York reading he took his leave saying:

> I shall never recall you as a mere public audience, but rather as a host of personal friends, and ever with the greatest gratitude, tenderness and consideration. God bless you and God bless the land in which I leave you.

Then using Peggotty's words, as if in eternal farewell, he said, 'My future life lies over the seas'. Two days later he boarded the 'Russia'. Among the friends who waved him farewell from the tender was bearded and benevolent-looking Anthony Trollope.

Chapter 27

THE LAST YEARS

If we judge from history, of what is the book of glory composed? Are not its leaves dead men's skins: its letters stamped in human blood: its illuminations tears and broken hearts?

On seeing Dickens fresh from his voyage, his doctor exclaimed, 'Good Lord! seven years younger!' But then his patient was tanned by sea air, and in such good spirits at getting safely home that he gave a carefree impression to everyone. He seemed to take new delight in Gad's Hill, in the singing of the birds, the welcome of the dogs and the ringing of the church bells. Having the true Victorian predilection for glass and gilding, he brightened up the chalet by installing in it five mirrors. These gave him great pleasure 'as they reflected and refracted in all kinds of ways the leaves quivering at the windows, the fields of waving corn, and the sail-dotted river'. High up among the trees he sat at his writing-table, birds and butterflies flying in and out, green branches swaying all about him and shadows of clouds passing across his manuscript.

Another source of pleasure was the success of Wilkie Collins's drama *No Thoroughfare*, adapted from his last Christmas story. It had a complicated plot based on a confusion of identity between foundlings and culminated in a fight in an Alpine pass. It was drawing full houses at the Adelphi with 'Fechter playing the part of Obenreizer to perfection'. The play certainly had good things in it, though to Dickens's thinking it dragged a bit in places. However, it was considered good enough to be produced in Paris, and as Fechter was going over to see how it went in French, he decided to accompany him. The friends crossed the Channel (May 30) in time for the first night, from which in the end they stayed away. Nervous and depressed, Dickens sat at an adjacent café with Fechter (whose face was the colour of lead) and waited till Didier, the translator, came over between the acts to report that all was going well. Next night they felt bold enough to attend the performance and then returned to London to give a first-hand account of their experience to the company at the Adelphi.

Owing to Wills having had an accident, Dickens found himself at this time entirely responsible for the production of *All the Year Round*. Wilkie Collins's story, *The Moonstone*, had been accepted as a serial, but its construction Dickens found was really very wearisome, and running through it was a 'vein of obstinate self-conceit that makes enemies of all readers'. In June he was already beginning to worry about the Christmas number: 'I cannot raise the ghost of an idea for it,' he wrote to his manager. 'I am in a positive state of despair. I have invented so many of these Christmas numbers and they are so profoundly unsatisfactory after all. . . . I can see nothing with my mind's eye which could do otherwise than reproduce the old string of stories in the old inappropriate bungling way.' In the end he gave up the idea of producing a Christmas number at all. His example had been too widely imitated and he was 'tired of being swamped by other people'. There had been nine of these Christmas stories all written in collaboration with Wilkie Collins. In most of them Dickens was responsible for less than half the script. For instance in *Somebody's Luggage* he wrote four out of ten chapters; in *Mrs. Lirriper's Lodgings*, two out of seven chapters; in *Dr. Marigold's Prescriptions*, three out of eight chapters; in *No Thoroughfare*, which is divided into an overture and four acts, only the overture and the fourth act are by Dickens. No one at the time of publication knew who had written what as contributions to *All the Year Round* were anonymous.

Gad's Hill was the scene of much hospitality this summer. Longfellow and his daughter came for a week-end and so did the Charles Eliot Nortons. Very special arrangements were made to drive them about in a chaise with four horses and two red-jacketed postilions in accordance with the tradition of the old Dover Road. Sir James Emerson Tennent, the admired friend to whom he had dedicated *Our Mutual Friend*, was also favoured by this attention. Gone were the days when Dickens drove his own guests about the country. Ever since the Staplehurst accident he had not dared to drive himself on the roads nor did he get on a horse 'for fear of a momentary seizure'. This he confided to de Cerjat.

Plans were maturing in his brain at this time for shipping Edward Bulwer Lytton overseas to join Alfred Tennyson in Australia. In a way it is the most peculiar of the evictions, and the most cold-blooded, for Plorn had been Dickens's idol as a child. The allusions to him in letters are more numerous and tender than the allusions to any of the other children, and yet, when the time came, his expatriation was planned and carried out as 'all for the best' despite the protest of the victim. As the day drew near for Plorn's departure Dickens wrote, 'He seemed to me to become once more my youngest and favourite little child'.

Mrs. Dickens appeared momentarily out of the shadows in which her life was then lived with a few words of sadness: 'I miss you most sadly, my darling Plorn. Please God you and dearest Alfred will be happy.' These words suggest that the relations between the boys and their mother had been maintained and it is possible that they were the secret cause of their Aunt Georgina's resolve to get the young nephews out of the country, for, as far as she was concerned, her sister no longer existed. Handing him a New Testament, Dickens impressed on Edward Bulwer Lytton the truth and beauty of the Christian religion and 'the wholesome practice of private prayer' which he himself 'had never abandoned', and in a letter written to be studied on board ship, Dickens enjoined on his young son that

this life is half-made up of partings and these pains must be borne. It is my comfort and my sincere conviction that

you are going to try the life for which you are best fitted.
. . . What you have always wanted until now has been a
steady, constant purpose. I therefore exhort you to persevere in a thorough determination to do whatever you have
to do as well as you can do it. I was not so old as you
are now when I first had to win my food, and I have never
slackened at it since.

Plorn cried in the railway carriage and was supposed to
have brightened visibly when Aunt Georgina's farewell gift
of cigars was handed to him. Six months later Dickens
received a report from the Mr. Rusden to whom Plorn had
been consigned. It was evidently not too satisfactory, for
Dickens wrote in reply: 'Plorn is a queer wayward fellow.
I am heartily sorry he should have disappointed you. . . . I
still hope he may take to colonial life.'

In September the most independent and successful member
of the family, Henry Fielding, went up to Cambridge, where
his father allowed him £250 a year, supplied him with wine
and warned him he must contract no single debt. Dickens
had had enough of family debts to sicken him. There were
his parents, his brothers, his brother-in-law and now his own
Charley who had just been declared a bankrupt. It was
more than enough for one lifetime.

> You know [he wrote to Henry Fielding] how hard I
> work for what I get, and I think you know that I never
> had money help from any human creature after I was a
> child. You know that you are one of many heavy charges
> on me, and that I trust to your so exercising your abilities
> and improving the advantages of your past expensive
> education, as soon to diminish this charge. . . .

The third tour of readings (arranged for before the journey
to America) opened at the St. James's Hall on October 5, 1868.
Visits to Manchester and Liverpool followed. The arrangement with Chappell had been for a hundred readings at £8000,
but the prospect of a general election caused some modifica-
tion in the original programme as it was considered wiser to
suspend all readings in November. This gave Dickens a

breathing-space in which to try out his murder scene from *Oliver Twist*. He thought it would produce a 'petrifying' effect and he must leave it to Chappell to decide whether to sanction it as part of the regular programme or not. It was arranged that a private rehearsal of the reading should be given before fifty critics, artists and literary men at the St. James's Hall on Saturday evening, November 14. They assembled in response to an invitation to a 'Private Trial of the Murder in *Oliver Twist*'.

Before going on the stage, Dickens said to Charles Kent, 'I want you to watch this particularly, for I am very doubtful about it myself'. He then flung himself into impersonating Fagin, Morris Bolter, Bill Sikes and Nancy. Fagin, the Jew, was complete with high shoulders, contracted chest, bird-like claws, and penthouse eyebrows working almost like antennae. Morris Bolter appeared as a long-limbed, clownish, sneaking varlet, and then Sikes was before them, a burly ruffian with a voice of Stentor delivering appalling blows with passion. Lastly, Nancy exquisitely pathetic from the scene of suppressed emotion on London Bridge to her last gasping shrieks of 'Bill!—dear Bill!' There was more in this reading than histrionic skill: there was the growing power to hypnotise a number of people simultaneously.

Forster was dead against the proposal; the subject seemed to him altogether outside the province of a reading. Mrs. Keeley, the famous actress, who was present at the experiment, was eagerly asked by Dickens, 'What do you say? Do it or not?' whereupon she replied, 'Why, of course do it. Having got such an effect as that, of course it must be done. But', looking straight at him with her black eyes and speaking in her famous deep voice, she added, 'the public have been looking for a sensation these last fifty years or so, and by heaven they have got it!' On the night of the reading the ladies' doctor, Priestley, buttonholed Dickens and said, 'You may rely upon it that if only one woman cries out when you murder the girl, there will be a contagion of hysteria all over the place'. These comments made Dickens very apprehensive of the result of a public performance. For the trial reading fifty persons were assembled all of whom could be relied on not to scream, or so he believed.

Dickens had arranged new effects and a surprise for this occasion. Beside the usual back-screen, he had two side-screens of the same maroon colour and beyond them were curtains to shut in the stage. The setting gave more value to desk and reader. When the reading was over, the bright gas reflectors were turned by Dickens's order away from himself on to the guests. Though the ladies in their coloured dresses looked like 'a great bed of flowers and diamonds', their faces were pale and horror-stricken. No one could question the success of the experiment in mass-hypnotism. Next moment curtains and screens were whisked away and a supper-table, beautifully lighted, was revealed with a staff of men ready to open oysters and bottles of champagne. How fortunate it was that smiles could be so rapidly restored by a glass of wine! How fortunate that he, Charles Dickens, had thought to order it!

Next morning came a note from his old friend, the Reverend William Harness, telling him that the reading was 'a most amazing and terrific thing'. He added, 'I am bound to tell you that I had an almost irresistible impulse upon me to *scream* and that if anyone had cried out I should have followed'. The murder of Nancy by Sikes was now put into repertory and its first public performance advertised for January 5, 1869.

Just before Christmas he gave a reading at the St. James's Hall of *A Christmas Carol*. Mamey and Georgy were commissioned to give the desk a festive look by entwining holly round its front legs and in and out of the fringe that ran along its top. A little bunch of holly should also be affixed to each corner.

Christmas was spent quietly at Gad's Hill, and a few days after the first public reading of the Sikes murder had proved its drawing power Dickens set out for Ireland. 'Miss Hogarth', he wrote to Dolby, 'so clearly wants a change that I think I will take her to Ireland along with the caravan as she is a good sailor.   She is highly delighted.'

The Irish readings were to take place at Dublin and Belfast.
Police had to control the crowds round the Rotunda, which
were specially large on the 'murder' night.   Two hundred
extra seats had to be squeezed in, and the performance was
described in the press as 'a masterpiece of reading by the
greatest reader and greatest writer of his age'.   The Ulster
Hall, Belfast, was rather sparsely filled by a not very demonstrative audience, an audience Dickens found it difficult to
get in tune with.

After a short stay in London came a tour of the west country.
For Macready's sake a reading was given at Cheltenham.
Macready was old and ill, and, when fetched from his stall
by Dolby to come and see Dickens in his dressing-room,
could only gasp a vague compliment, 'It comes to two
Macbeths!'   His speech then trailed off into irrelevancies; he
was but a wraith of his former self.   From Cheltenham
Dickens went for a week-end to Dolby's house at Ross and
actually walked from Ross to Monmouth, eleven miles at the
smart pace of four miles an hour.   Dolby then took him on
to Clifton where the Sikes and Nancy scene caused a 'contagion of fainting'.   Bath and Torquay followed.   Bath
Dickens described as 'a mouldy old roosting place that comes
out mouldily as a let. . . .'   'I hate the sight,' he added,
'of the bygone old Assembly Rooms and the Bath chairs
trundling the dowagers about the streets.'   It made him think
of his first visit to St. James's Square eighteen years earlier,
when he had gone laughing down the street with 'Fuz' after
a merry dinner with Landor.   'Landor's ghost goes along
the silent streets before me. . . . The whole place looks like
a cemetery which the dead have succeeded in rising and taking.
Having built streets of their old gravestones they wander
about scantily trying to look alive—a dead failure.'

It was a relief to get to Torquay with its signs of spring
and its plate-glass windows through which he commanded
both sea and sunshine.   Sea and sunshine were no longer of
much avail to him for he had tired himself to death and his

feet were badly swollen. Sir Henry Thompson suddenly
forbade all further readings. Engagements in London and
Scotland had to be cancelled; but after one week's rest Dickens
jumped up from his bed and insisted on taking to the road
again. All the time his 'atrocious novelty' was getting more
and more of a hold on him. Out of four readings he would
repeat the murder three times, pleading in excuse to Dolby,
who saw how deleterious were its effects, that it had become
'a kind of hobby'.

At Glasgow there was an enormous cram for 'the novelty',
and at Edinburgh Ballantyne, having a seat behind the screen,
was nearly frightened off it by the screeches. Dickens was
pleased as he came off the platform to see that every vestige
of colour had left Ballantyne's face and that 'he sat staring
over a glass of champagne in the wildest way'. And so the
tour de force was repeated until April 10, when a banquet was
given in Dickens's honour in the St. George's Hall, Liverpool.
It was presided over by Lord Dufferin, and Lord Houghton,
Anthony Trollope, G. A. Sala and Mark Lemon (reconciled
over Thackeray's grave) were among those present. The
toast of Her Majesty's Ministers was proposed by Mr. Philip
Rathbone and replied to by Lord Dufferin, who gave the
health of Charles Dickens whom Lord Houghton, in a speech
on the Houses of Parliament, accused of not properly appreciating the House of Lords. Dickens met this charge by speaking handsomely of Lords Brougham, Lytton, Russell and
Cockburn, none of them hereditary peers, and then went on
to show his horror of patronage by saying:

> When I first took literature as my profession in England
> I entirely resolved . . . that whether I succeeded or
> whether I failed literature should be my sole profession.
> It appeared to me that it was not so well understood in
> England as it was in other countries that literature was a
> dignified profession by which a man might stand or fall.
> I made a compact with myself that in my person literature
> should stand by itself, of itself, and for itself.

A turn of giddiness overtook him at Blackpool, and at

Chester he felt deadness of the left side. It was obviously impossible to go on with the tour so Dolby took him back to Gad's Hill with twenty-five readings undelivered. To compensate Chappell for their loss, he promised, if any way possible, to make good the deficiency at some future date.

Dickens ever since Mary Hogarth's death had been deeply interested in dreams. Over a quiet cigar he would from time to time talk over his experiences with George Lewes.[1] Sometimes one could dispel a recurring dream by recounting it, sometimes the same dream would return in moments of crisis, but there were other stranger dreams that seemed to embody a kind of prevision. For instance after a particularly stimulating reading he dreamt that he was in a room in which everybody was dressed in scarlet, and that he stumbled up against a lady standing with her back to him. As he apologised she turned her head saying, 'My name is Napier'. The face was unknown to him. Two days later he read again and before he went on the stage a friend came into his waiting-room accompanied by an unknown lady in a scarlet opera-cloak—'This lady', said his friend, 'is very desirous of being introduced to you.' 'Not Miss Napier?' jokingly inquired Dickens. 'Yes, Miss Napier,' replied his friend.

In May Dickens entertained Mr. and Mrs. James T. Fields of Boston, both in London and at Gad's Hill. American tradition has it that Mrs. Fields had lost her heart to him and doted on every word that fell from his lips as well as every word that fell from his pen, and he certainly was very fond of her. The Fields were shown Windsor and Richmond and then were taken to the east end of London to see the beer taverns of the German sugar bakers in the Ratcliffe Highway, and the less agreeable opium dens in the same locality. This was a favourite excursion to which De la Rue, Yates and other friends were treated. Dolby, who used to make the rounds with him, said that Dickens on these outings looked

[1] *Fraser's Magazine*, XXI.

the picture of health and was in very high spirits.

In June he was well enough to enjoy spending a night with Lord and Lady Russell at Pembroke Lodge in Richmond Park. He found his host in 'wonderful preservation, brighter and more completely armed at all points than I have seen him these twenty years'. How they agreed, having both read Mrs. Beecher Stowe's book on Lady Byron, that the whole edition should be made a bonfire of! Young Lord Ribblesdale, who was staying with his stepfather, committed his impression of Charles Dickens to paper. Dickens, he says,

> was extremely smartly dressed—over-dressed I should say. In the day-time he wore a pair of striped trousers—stripes were the vogue—of broad black and blue, a frock-coat open to a low double-breasted waistcoat, with a general effect of gold chains, charms and eye-glasses; a splendid black satin scarf of amplitude and lustre secured by a fine pin. . . . His evening clothes were extremely well-cut, the shirt frilled with bright, perhaps diamond studs.
>
> At dinner he ate and drank very little. Champagne did not circulate at Pembroke Lodge, nor was it the fashion of those days to have whisky and sodas, but there was port and madeira and we sat for some time over the wine. Mr. Dickens drank madeira sparingly. I remember noticing that with the warmth of the room and food a vein in the centre of his forehead became very prominent.

A few weeks later Dickens attended a dinner (at the Crystal Palace) of Oxford and Harvard boat-racing crews and complimented a young Harvard man, Richard Dana, as having written the best sea book in the English language. In September he went to Birmingham (the city to which, ever since the doge-like giving of the ring sixteen years earlier, he had felt himself indefinably wedded) to address the Birmingham and Midland Institution at the opening of its winter session. No man, he told his hearers, can improve himself without in some degree improving other men. In Birmingham at least it was realised that the more cultivated the employee the better for the employer, and the more culti-

vated the employer the better for the employee. Of the two
thousand five hundred members of the Institute he was glad
to know that half were weekly wage-earners, and that many
of them were women. The penny evening classes (on
arithmetic, chemistry, music) and the library, lecture hall,
laboratory and art department would all encourage the artisan
to think, and to rise superior to

> Those twin gaolers of the daring heart,
> Low birth and iron fortune.

Dickens expressed the hope that the Institution would conceive of its place of assemblage as high ground from which
the human soul may aspire to be wiser and better. Above all
things its members must never patronise or be patronised,
'for the bestowal and receipt of patronage has been a curse to
England'. Warning his hearers against what Sydney Smith
had called 'the foppery of universality', he urged them to
have the courage to be ignorant of a number of things so as
to avoid the calamity of being ignorant of everything.

> The one safe, serviceable, certain, remunerative, attain-
> able quality in every study and in every pursuit is the
> quality of attention. My own invention or imagination
> such as it is . . . would never have served me as it has,
> but for the habit of commonplace, humble, patient, daily,
> toiling, drudging attention. . . . Like certain plants which
> the poorest peasant may grow in the poorest soil, it can be
> cultivated by anyone and it is certain in its own good season
> to bring forth flowers and fruit.

Shortly after Christmas Dickens had to return once more
to Birmingham to deliver prizes at the Institute. Feeling
very ill he made a short speech, and only struggled through
the occasion with difficulty. It was with intense relief that
he resumed his seat at his writing-table in the chalet at Gad's
Hill.

On two and sometimes three nights a week Dickens transferred himself to Windsor Lodge to enjoy the company of
Ellen Ternan. In a facsimile letter reproduced by Thomas

Wright in his autobiography Canon Benham writes of Dickens: 'I have one curious relic, the pen with which he wrote part of the last number of *Edwin Drood*. It was given me by the lady concerning whom he quarrelled with his wife.' This pen was treasured by the Canon and shown by him to Wright at 32 Finsbury Square.

He was careful to arrange that the new book he was engaged on should come out in the old way in illustrated monthly numbers. Charles Collins was to design the cover and Luke Fildes, by John Millais' advice, the plates. The terms offered satisfied the writer: he was to get £7500 for the copyright, and half profits after 25,000 copies had been sold. He was also to receive, from an American firm, £1000 for advance sheets. Writing he now found 'a severe labour' and we may note that the manuscript of this book is very carefully written, revised, corrected and remodelled. As usual, the title presented difficulties, but these were solved round the dinner-table at which, after much discussion, a toast was drunk to *The Mystery of Edwin Drood*.

The first number appeared on April 1. It was to Forster's surprise as good as, if not better than, anything his friend had ever written. The opening chapter delighted him and he pronounced the story 'a clincher!' Only twenty-three chapters in all were written, but these chapters have given rise to more discussion than all the other novels put together. The first scene is laid in the opium den in the east end of London to which the author had taken Mrs. J. T. Fields and other friends. In this squalid place, John Jasper, the choir-master of Cloisterham (black-haired, pale-faced, and so un-English in type as to suggest the Eurasian), in waking from a narcotised vision, rites to reconcile white elephants, nautch girls, dark faces and flashing scimitars with the emerging walls of a cathedral tower. In a remarkable paragraph Dickens dislocates humdrum life and presently introduces us to a Cloisterham (Rochester) outwardly staid, yet vibrating to the impact of mysterious evil. Against the pious background of cathedral routine are thrown, as by some magic lantern, shapes and omens of sinister significance. The very rooks that wheel about the tower are omen-ful, so is the tapping of the stone-mason Durdles in the crypt. The actions and words of Jasper suggest abnormality, the Landless link with Ceylon conveys a sense of far horizons. It is all as different as it can be from the Pickwick-Wardle Rochester with which Dickens's writing life opened. Cloisterham is now a dead and mouldering place fostering human corruption. And, strangest of all for Dickens, the family festival of Christmas is denatured by crime. The taste for horrifying an audience had projected itself into the plot of *Edwin Drood*.

Edwin Drood is a student-engineer working in London who frequently comes to stay with his uncle, John Jasper, at Cloisterham. Since childhood in the East, he has been betrothed to another orphan, Rosa Bud, their dead parents having arranged the match. Rosa is being educated at Miss Twinkleton's Academy at Cloisterham and Jasper, who gives her music lessons, is violently in love with her. It riles him to hear Edwin say casually:

> My dead and gone father and Pussy's dead and gone father must needs marry us by anticipation. Why—the Devil, I was going to say—if it had been respectful to their memory—couldn't they leave us alone! . . . *Your* life is not laid down to scale, and lined and dotted out for you like a surveyor's plan. *You* have no uncomfortable suspicion that you are forced upon anybody. . . . *You* can choose for yourself. Life for *you* is a plum with the bloom on.

On hearing these words Jasper is strangely affected, sweat-drops appear on his forehead as he grips the arms of his chair, and a film comes over his eyes. Murmuring that he has taken opium for a pain, he presently adds banteringly, 'There is said to be a skeleton in every house; but you thought there was none in mine, dear Ned'. It transpires that he hates his post, and that the musical services considered so beautiful by the cathedral congregation seem to him 'quite devilish'. Edwin, when he leaves, remarks cheerfully that in less than a year he and Pussy will be married and go off to the East. Jasper looks at him quizzically and says:

'You won't be warned then?'
'No, Jack.'
'You can't be warned then?'
'No, Jack, not by you. Besides I don't really consider myself in danger.'

Thus is the mystery set. But what has Jasper in his mind?

Attached to the cathedral is the stone-mason, Durdles, a firmly established, grim character who pokes his way about the earthy damps of the crypt, sometimes opening with his pick an abbot's coffin and seeing for a fleeting moment the phantasm of a church dignitary that on the instant dissolves into powder. Scooting through the close, never far from Durdles, is a hideous small boy shrieking, whistling and shying stones who answers to the name of 'Deputy'. In pompous Mr. Sapsea, the auctioneer of Cloisterham, we have a figure of the Chadband type who consults Durdles about his wife's tomb. Jasper, present at this consultation, watches Mr. Sapsea hand over the key of a vault to Durdles. Jasper makes up to Durdles for his own mysterious purposes so that he may familiarise himself with the interior of the cathedral by moonlight.

Next on the scene are Neville Landless and his sister Helena hailing from Ceylon. They are dark, gipsy-looking, and half shy, half defiant in manner. Twin-like understanding exists between them. By the arrangement of their guardian, Mr. Honeythunder, they become resident in Cloisterham, Neville reading with minor-canon Crisparkle and Helena boarding with Miss Twinkleton. Neville shocks the minor-canon by alluding to his stepfather as a cruel brute whom he would 'like to have killed', adding that his sister had run away from him several times 'dressed as a boy and showing the daring of a man'.

Neville Landless and Edwin Drood do not hit it off, latent jealousy over Rosa being the cause. One evening as they walk and argue, Jasper intervenes and asks them in for a drink. After one glass their speech becomes thick and indistinct and they quarrel openly. Drood sneers at Neville, 'You are no judge of white men!'—an allusion to his dark skin. Neville dashes the dregs of his drink over him, but is prevented by Jasper from throwing the glass too. He then flings out of the house, whereupon Jasper goes round to Crisparkle's gasping, 'We have had an awful scene with him . . . murderous! he might have laid my dear boy dead at my feet'.

A more soothing note is sounded by Mr. Grewgious of Staple Inn, guardian to Rosa Bud, who comes to Cloisterham to discuss the girl's future. He impresses on her that two young people cannot be bound by the will of others, but must act according to their own free will and conviction. On his way home he calls in at the cathedral to tell Jasper that he has informed Miss Bud that a betrothal by deceased parents cannot be considered binding on the parties concerned. Jasper's lips go white and he asks, 'Why?' 'My duty,' replies Mr. Grewgious, adding, 'God bless them both!' as he leaves. 'God save them both!' cries Jasper. 'I said bless them,' repeats Mr. Grewgious. 'I said save them,' returns Jasper. 'Is there any difference?' Again we ask ourselves, What is in Jasper's mind?

Meanwhile minor-canon Crisparkle (living with his china-shepherdess mother in the close) is deeply puzzled by Landless who tells him that he is in love with Rosa Bud and hates and despises Edwin Drood. He tells the strange young man that his love is 'outrageously misplaced'; as Miss Bud is to be married shortly, Neville really must compose his differences with Drood. He then goes to talk things over with the choirmaster whom he finds lying down. Jasper calls out, 'What is the matter? who did it?' and then mumbles something about 'dreaming at a great rate'. The clergyman explains that he wants to effect a reconciliation between Neville and Edwin, whereupon Jasper reads him a passage from a diary of his own about the 'demoniacal passion of this Neville

Landless, his strength in his fury and his savage rage for the destruction of his object'. Can the canon answer for the young man's behaviour which bodes no good to his dear Ned. The canon says 'Yes,' so a dinner of reconciliation is arranged for Christmas Eve.

While this has been going on at Cloisterham Edwin is being interviewed in London by Mr. Grewgious who impresses on him too that two young people cannot be bound by the will of others. He hands him a family ring wherewith to plight his troth. If there is no marriage he must return the ring. Edwin puts it into his pocket and goes to Cloisterham to see Rosa. They mutually agree to break their engagement, but how announce this decision to Jack? Rosa thinks they may leave it to Mr. Grewgious. Edwin concurs, and confesses to Rosa that he is secretly afraid of Jasper. He does not tell her of the ring in his pocket and the author warns the reader that because of this 'a chain was forged and riveted to the foundations of heaven and earth and gifted with invincible force to hold and to drag'.

On the first day of the week in which Christmas Eve is the last Jasper visits the crypt by moonlight calling for Durdles on his way. Durdles warns him not to stumble into a mound near the gate. It is quicklime, 'quick enough to eat your boots . . . quick enough to eat your bones'. Jasper plies Durdles with drink and after they have explored the tower the stone-mason falls in a stupor on the floor of the crypt, leaving Jasper free to make any use he pleases of the great keys he carries.

Neville Landless prepares to take a walking tour at Christmas and buys a knapsack and a heavy walking-stick. He takes the stick with him when he goes to say good-bye to his sister before dining with Jasper. It is Christmas Eve. Jasper sings divinely at vespers and is congratulated by Crisparkle, but maybe his throat is delicate, for it is wrapped with a black scarf. Quite unexpectedly Opium Sal turns up in Cloisterham and, accosting Edwin, asks him for money. Noticing a funny look in her eyes he asks, 'Do you eat opium?' 'I smokes it,' she replies. He gives her money and she asks, 'What's your Christian name?' 'Edwin,' he answers. 'You may be thankful your name ain't Ned . . . it's a bad name . . . a threatened name,' murmurs Opium Sal as she moves off.

We hear nothing of the dinner of reconciliation, but early Christmas morning Jasper hurries round half dressed and half demented to Crisparkle's house to inquire where his nephew is. Crisparkle has no idea and Jasper says, 'He went down to the river last night with Mr. Neville. . . .' 'Where is Mr. Neville?' Mr. Neville has already started on his walking tour. The young man is pursued, overtaken and brought back to Cloisterham under suspicion of having murdered Edwin Drood. He declares that he walked with Edwin from the river to Jasper's house where he had left him. Next day the river is dragged. Crisparkle in diving recovers a shirt-pin and finds a gold watch caught in the weir. As there is no proof that Drood is dead Neville goes to work in London, where Helena joins him. Rosa Bud takes refuge with her guardian, for Jasper has told her he loves her and will pursue her to death. A stranger appears in Cloisterham whose business it seems is to watch Jasper. His thick white hair, large head, feminine hands and black eyebrows are suggestive of disguise.

Jasper re-visits the opium den in London. Opium Sal hears him mumbling of something he has done over and over again. She suspects him of having murdered Drood and goes ahead of him to Cloisterham to watch him on his return. Next morning after matins Opium Sal tells Datchery that she knows Jasper 'better far than all the Reverend Parsons put together know him'. It is at this point that death stopped the writer's hand.

If this were an ordinary murder story we should think the number of clues offered absurd. There is almost nothing for us to find out. We are aware that Jasper wraps a scarf round neck or arm, aware that Mrs. Sapsea's tomb is accessible and that quicklime can be had for the shovelling. We know that Crisparkle goes diving in the coldest weather and it is only natural that if a gold watch has been thrown into the weir he should retrieve it. Every clue indicates Jasper as the murderer. Furthermore we know from Luke Fildes, the illustrator, that Drood was to be strangled by Jasper's black scarf, and we have it from Forster that the victim was to be identified by a gold ring which the quicklime could not destroy. We know that Drood had a gold ring in his pocket. If Dickens had lived to complete the story we should probably find that the root of the antagonisms between the characters lay in their Eastern past, and it is fairly clear that Jasper will be convicted on the evidence of the only creature who could have watched his actions on Christmas night— the ragamuffin Deputy. Some of the people who have contrived endings for *The Mystery of Edwin Drood* have puzzled out who Datchery could be. William Archer and Andrew Lang thought he was Drood himself; Mr. Cumings Walter suggests that as Helena Landless and Datchery are never on the scene together Datchery must be Helena in disguise. We see into the minds of all the characters in this book except Jasper's. No inkling as to what he thinks or why he reacts in the strange way he does is given, and just because of this we are tempted to construct theories as to his motives. One theory gathers importance as the mystery is discussed: it is that Jasper was secretly a Thug striving to commit a ritual murder. Dickens, who had published *The Moonstone* in *All the Year Round*, found Wilkie Collins's method of telling this story extremely tiresome. He was sure he could do something better in the way of a murder mystery himself. He had read his contributor, Meadows Taylor's book, *The Confessions of a Thug*, and he had read *Le Juif errant* by his friend Sue in which a Thug figured. It might be possible to create a character so far from normal that he acted in certain stages of consciousness as if he were a Thug, while at other times he practised a kind of animal magnetism by means of which he could suggest thoughts and actions to persons in his *entourage*. According to Meadows Taylor the essence of Thug practice was to sacrifice a human life to Kali, Goddess of Destruction. The sacrifice, however, was unacceptable to the goddess unless carried out in a prescribed way. The victim must be a traveller and a guest. The Thug, after entertaining his victim and speaking fair with him, slings a white silver-weighted scarf round his neck from behind and squeezes the life out of him. The body must be stripped and buried in a secret place prepared for its reception. In this novel we find broad hints of thuggery in Jasper's scarf, in his blandishment and entertaining of Edwin and in his interest in Mrs. Sapsea's vault, but the body though divested of watch and tie-pin is not stripped. The murder has not, it seems, been carried out by an initiated Thug but by a man dreaming of becoming a Thug. On the whole it is not a very satisfactory solution of the mystery to say that Jasper on one plane of consciousness is a Eurasian organist who because of his passion for Rosa Bud kills one rival and hunts down the other, and on another plane of consciousness is an amateur Thug endeavouring to carry out a ritual sacrifice to Kali. What then was Dickens up to in constructing this story, every sentence of which is loaded with meaning, every word of which is significant? He has never written in this precise, intensely careful way before. What does it all mean? The mystery cannot lie in the identity of the killer, but in the character and mentality of Jasper himself. The book leaves an earthy taste in the mouth, the earthy damp of a mouldering, silent city so abounding in monastic graves that its children 'grow small salads in the dust of abbots and abbesses'. All its life is of the past. Even the pawnbroker has taken in no pledges this long while and offers, vainly, an unredeemed stock for sale.

Laying aside the problems raised by the story, we find that the book is distinguished by writing of a superb kind that rivets the attention and must embody the last impressions of Rochester Dickens ever received:

Not only is the day waning, but the year. The low sun is fiery and yet cold behind the monastery ruin, and the

Virginian creeper on the Cathedral wall has showered half its deep red leaves down on the pavement. There has been rain this afternoon, and a wintry shudder goes among the little pools on the cracked uneven flag-stones and through the giant elm-trees as they shed a gust of tears.

The disintegrating quality of the minster is steadily imposed on us:

> . . . a city of another and bygone time is Cloisterham, with its hoarse Cathedral-bell, its hoarse rooks hovering about the Cathedral tower, its hoarser and less distinct rooks in the stalls far beneath. Fragments of old wall, saint's chapel, chapter-house, convent and monastery, have got incongruously or obstructively built into many of its houses and gardens, much as kindred jumbled notions have become incorporated in many of its citizens' minds.

In those last months of his life, when Dickens was wandering in and out of the precincts and down by the tidal river, he was obsessed by the death-diffusing character of the minster, and contrasted it with the ever-renewed life of the waters by which he walked. Listen to the reflections of Mr. Grewgious as he enters the cathedral, saying, 'It's like looking down the throat of Old Time!'

> Old Time heaved a mouldy sigh from tomb and arch and vault; and gloomy shadows began to deepen in corners; and damps began to rise from green patches of stone; and jewels, cast upon the pavement of the nave from stained glass by the declining sun began to perish. Within the grill-gate of the chancel, up the steps surmounted loomingly by the fast-darkening organ, white robes could be dimly seen, and one feeble voice, rising and falling in a cracked monotonous mutter, could at intervals be faintly heard. In the free outer air, the river, the green pastures and the brown arable lands, the teeming hills and dales, were reddened by the sunset: while the distant little windows in windmills and farm homesteads, shone, patches of bright beaten gold. In the Cathedral, all became gray, murky and sepulchral, and the cracked monotonous mutter went on like a dying voice, until the organ and the choir burst

forth, and drowned it in a sea of music. Then, the sea fell, and the dying voice made another feeble effort, and then the sea rose high, and beat its life out, and lashed the roof, and surged among the arches, and pierced the heights of the great tower; and then the sea was dry and all was still.

Can one doubt from this masterly, sensitive presentation that it is Dickens himself who wanders at evensong among the columns and the tombs and Dickens himself who walks beside the river with its seaweed fringe of which

an unusual quantity had come in with the last tide, and this, and the confusion of the water, and the restless dipping and flapping of the noisy gulls, and an angry light out sea- ward beyond the brown-sailed barges that were turning black, foreshadowed a stormy night. In his mind he was contrasting the wild and noisy sea with the quiet harbour of Minor Canon Corner. . . .

Is it any wonder that Longfellow thought *Edwin Drood* was 'a most beautiful work, if not the most beautiful of all'?

They are so intense, so personal, so vivid, the impressions made by these last walks whether they be taken in winter or on a summer day 'in silent streets with the sunblinds barely flapping in the south wind'. The dead hand was on Cloister- ham as it was on other survivals from the past—the Law Courts and the Houses of Parliament. It was 'a city with all changes behind it and no more to come'. What was to happen to a country that sacrificed so universally to outworn tradition? It was easy to see what Progress thought of it all as the express trains tore screaming through Cloisterham.

We do not know what Forster thought, for his one remark on *The Mystery of Edwin Drood* is that it seemed to him 'quite free from the social criticism which grew more biting as Dickens had grown older'. Did not Forster perceive that the book contained the most biting criticism of all, of a civilisation rotting with worship of a dead past?

For the first time in January 1870 Dickens tried to combine readings with writing. Perhaps he knew how short a time he had in which to do either. Twelve readings had been promised to Chappell, the first of which was due to take place on January 11 and the last on March 15. For this series he rented 5 Hyde Park Place, the house of Mr. Milner Gibson. By special request of his theatrical friends he gave a morning reading (3 P.M.) of 'Sikes and Nancy'. His performance astonished the actors and actresses present and made his own pulse jump from 72 to 112: it took ten minutes on a sofa for him to get his breathing normal again. The audiences at the St. James's Hall were immense and sometimes they rose and cheered in a body as he entered as well as when he left. It was on March 15, 1870, that he read for the last time. Radiant pendants glittered over the heads of the two thousand persons who had assembled to listen. His last words were, 'From these garish lights I vanish now for evermore with a heartfelt, grateful, respectful and affectionate farewell'. Tears rolled down his cheeks as he left the platform with the dragging step of a mourner. The prolonged thunder of applause penetrated to the green-room and lured him back for an instant to kiss his hand to the audience. On this occasion Mamey said 'he had never looked handsomer', but Charley noticed that he had mispronounced some of his words, saying Pickswick or Pickwicks for Pickwick.

But ten days before this farewell reading Dickens had written to the Clerk of the Privy Council to accept the Queen's gracious offer of a baronetcy. On account of 'the divine William and Falstaff', he wished to be styled Sir Charles Dickens of Gad's Hill.[1]

Owing to the impending honour or to Mamey's social ambitions, fashionable, rather unsuitable things began to happen to her poor father; for instance, he was presented to the Prince of Wales at a levee by Lord de Grey and, a few days later, Mamey was in her turn presented to the Queen by Countess Russell. These formalities over, both father

[1] 765. III. N.L.

and daughter were eligible to be summoned to a Court ball, an empty compliment except to Mamey, who had taken to hunting in the home counties and canvassing in the Conservative interest.

One day Dickens showed some photographs of the American Civil War to Arthur Helps, who was much interested. Helps described the sun-pictures of battle-scenes to the Queen, who at once expressed an impatient desire to see them too. Dickens, on being approached by Helps, said he would be proud and happy to wait on her as might suit her pleasure and so at long last these two great Victorians met face to face. The talk went on for one and a half hours and Her Majesty kept Dickens standing the whole time. It was not permissible for any man to sit in the presence of his sovereign, and the Queen, wishing to honour her guest, remained standing too, but unlike Dickens she was not suffering from painful, swollen feet. She asked Mr. Dickens's opinion on 'the servant question', and wondered whether he could account for the fact 'that we have no good servants in England as in the olden times'. She also touched on the cost of living. At the close of the interview Dickens was handed an inscribed copy of her *Journal of Life in the Highlands* in return for which she hoped to receive a complete set of Mr. Dickens's works if possible that very afternoon. Mr. Dickens pleaded to be allowed to have a special set bound for her in red and gold. To this request the Queen graciously gave her assent.

The Academy dinner in May was presided over by Sir Francis Grant. Dickens had to reply for Literature and in his speech was careful to include women, 'who even in their present oppressed condition can attain to quite as great distinction as men'. Paying a tribute to his dear Daniel Maclise, now dead, he looked at his picture, 'The Earls of Desmond and Ormond', hanging on the wall behind the President's chair and spoke of this artist's 'prodigious fertility of mind'. Gentle, modest, frank, large-hearted, he could say that 'no one ever went to his rest leaving a golden memory more pure from dross or having devoted himself with a truer chivalry to the art-goddess whom he worshipped'. These were the last words Dickens ever spoke in public.

Life still interested him acutely even though friends were falling by the wayside. He had new friends, but none like the old. Dickens missed Maclise and Lemon terribly. Of course it was interesting to breakfast with Mr. Gladstone and dine with Lord Stanhope, interesting too to meet Mr. Disraeli again, whom he had not seen since Gore House days, and whom he still regretted had given up literature for politics, but the old convivial gatherings with equals were gone for ever. He now had to make do with celebrities.

The last London dinner-party attended by Dickens was given by Lord Houghton in honour of the Prince of Wales and the King of the Belgians. To Mary Boyle, who saw him just before he left his house, Dickens said he would dearly like to send an excuse but that he had promised not to fail his host. When he got to Lord Houghton's he could not mount the stairs so awaited the royal guests till they came down to the dining-room. Even at Hyde Park Place he was subjected to a whirl of entertainments. Both Mamey and Georgy loved parties and it amused them immensely to arrange receptions and concerts to which people of distinction flocked. One evening Santley sang and Joachim and Hallé played, and afterwards supper on a lavish scale was partaken of. Lady Freake, a new friend, asked the help of her host in producing three little plays in which his 'girls' had promised to act. The scenery was at that very moment being painted by Millais. Dickens was reminded by this request of happier days at Tavistock House and, as the theatre still excited him as nothing else did, he agreed to help. On the morning of the day of production, Dickens was seen at the office by Dolby, who thought he looked noticeably ill. He said he was about to sign his will, but mortally stricken as he knew himself to be, he kept his engagement with Lady Freake. It was not so long since he had confessed to Charles Kent, editor of the *Sun*, that his most cherished day-dream all through life had been to run a great theatre, a noble company

—all absolutely under his command, even to the editing and altering of every play produced.

The day after the theatricals he travelled to Gad's Hill and before taking up his pen in the chalet had a prowl round the house. The newly built conservatory blazed with geraniums: the windows of both drawing-room and dining-room looked into it; the mirrors hung on their walls reflected splashes of colour. What an eminently successful 'improvement' it was and how pleasantly it contrasted with 'the green mansions' across the road!

Dickens worked on *Edwin Drood* all the day of his seizure, sitting up at his desk in the chalet. At dinner that night, Georgy, his only companion, suddenly realised that he was looking desperately ill. A few minutes later he had a stroke from which he never regained consciousness. Mamey and Katey were summoned from London, and next day Katey was sent back there to break the news to her mother. She returned in company with Ellen Ternan. Millais, who had seen so much of Dickens over the Freake plays, came down too and made a pencilled sketch of the bandaged head in which Katey saw 'a likeness to Tennyson'. Mary Boyle also came and sat outside in a hired fly till Charley came into the porch and led her to the syringa-scented study in which lay the body of her adored friend. She was enfolded by Georgina in a warm embrace and then went sadly back to London.

Dickens had expressed a wish to be buried near Gad's Hill in great simplicity, but the Archdeacon of Rochester offered to furnish a grave inside the cathedral. Local arrangements of every kind, however, were upset by an article in the *Times* (inspired, it is believed, by Lord Houghton) demanding burial at Westminster Abbey. John Forster called on Dean Stanley to explain that there could be no question of a public funeral, for his friend had left instructions that he was to be buried in a strictly private way, and that no public announcement as to the time or place of interment should be made. The mourning coaches must be limited to three, and the horses must be plainly harnessed, without trappings or plumes; moreover, 'no scarf, cloak, black bow, long hatband, or any other revolting absurdity' was to be displayed on the occasion.

At 9 A.M. on the Tuesday after his death three carriages drove into Dean's Yard behind a hearse. Twelve mourners dismounted and walked into the Abbey to stand beside a grave in the Poets' Corner while the committal sentences were spoken. No choristers were present, but when the short service ended, the organ played a Dead March. By order of the Dean the grave was not to be filled in for two days. When reporters came to inquire the hour of the funeral cere- mony, they were told it was over. As soon as it became generally known that the coffin could still be seen, an ever- swelling stream of mourners flowed through the transept. At dusk on Waterloo day the Abbey was closed to the public, but Lord Houghton received word from Dean Stanley that the grave of Charles Dickens would not be closed till near midnight. With a lantern to light his steps, Lord Houghton walked to the Poets' Corner to look at the plain oak coffin that cased the body of the genius he had known from boy- hood up. Bagehot was certainly right, 'no other Englishman had attained such a hold on the vast populace'.

Lord Shaftesbury's reflections were more romantic. As he looked back over the years, he saw as in a vision a young champion of the disinherited slashing at the same social evils he had spent his own life in combating. 'He was set, I doubt not, to rouse attention to many evils and many woes. God gave him a general retainer against all suffering and oppression.'

INDEX

PENGUIN BOOKS — GREAT FOOD

Exciting Food for Southern Types

PELLEGRINO ARTUSI (1820–1911) was an Italian businessman and gastronome. His working life as a silk merchant allowed him to acquire considerable wealth, which was used to fund his passions: literature and food. He self-published the famous Italian cook-book *La scienza in cucina e l'arte di mangiare bene* (*The Science of Cooking and the Art of Eating Well*) in 1891, and by the time of his death over 200,000 copies had been sold. Writing only two decades after the unification of Italy, Artusi was the first to include recipes from all regions of Italy in a single cookbook and helped establish a national Italian identity.

Exciting Food for Southern Types

PELLEGRINO ARTUSI

PENGUIN BOOKS

PENGUIN BOOKS

Published by the Penguin Group
Penguin Books Ltd, 80 Strand, London WC2R 0RL, England
Penguin Group (USA) Inc., 375 Hudson Street, New York, New York 10014, USA
Penguin Group (Canada), 90 Eglinton Avenue East, Suite 700, Toronto, Ontario,
Canada M4P 2Y3 (a division of Pearson Penguin Canada Inc.)
Penguin Ireland, 25 St Stephen's Green, Dublin 2, Ireland
(a division of Penguin Books Ltd)
Penguin Group (Australia), 250 Camberwell Road,
Camberwell, Victoria 3124, Australia
(a division of Pearson Australia Group Pty Ltd)
Penguin Books India Pvt Ltd, 11 Community Centre,
Panchsheel Park, New Delhi – 110 017, India
Penguin Group (NZ), 67 Apollo Drive, Rosedale, Auckland 0632, New Zealand
(a division of Pearson New Zealand Ltd)
Penguin Books (South Africa) (Pty) Ltd, 24 Sturdee Avenue,
Rosebank, Johannesburg 2196, South Africa

Penguin Books Ltd, Registered Offices: 80 Strand, London WC2R 0RL, England

www.penguin.com

La scienza in cucina e l'arte di mangiare bene first published in Italy 1891
This translation, *Science in the Kitchen and the Art of Eating Well*, first published in the
USA by Marsilio Publishers 1997
This extract published in Penguin Books 2011
This edition published for The Book People Ltd, 2011
Hall Wood Avenue, Haydock, St Helens, WA11 9UL

1

All rights reserved

Set in 10.75/13pt Berkeley Oldstyle Book
Typeset by Jouve (UK), Milton Keynes
Printed in Great Britain by Clays Ltd, St Ives plc

Cover design based on a pattern from a bowl by Ulisse Cantagalli, Florence, 1892.
Tin-glazed earthenware. (Photograph copyright © Victoria & Albert Museum.)
Picture research by Samantha Johnson. Lettering by Stephen Raw

ISBN 978–0–241–96078–3

www.greenpenguin.co.uk

MIX
Paper from
responsible sources
FSC® C018179
www.fsc.org

Penguin Books is committed to a sustainable
future for our business, our readers and our
planet. This book is made from paper certified
by the Forest Stewardship Council.

Contents

A Note

Cooking is a troublesome sprite. Often it may drive you to despair. Yet it also very rewarding, for when you do succeed, or overcome a difficulty in doing so, you feel the satisfaction of a great triumph.

Beware of books that deal with this art: most of them are inaccurate or incomprehensible, especially the Italian ones. The French are a little better. But from either, the very most you will glean are a few notions, useful only if you already know the art.

If you do not aspire to become a premier cook, you need not have been born with a pan on your head to become a good one. Passion, care, and precision of method will certainly suffice; then, of course, you must choose the finest ingredients as your raw materials, for these will make you shine.

The best teacher is experience, under an adept's watchful eye. Yet even lacking this, with a guide such as mine, and devotion to your labors, you should be able, I hope, to put something decent together.

If at first you do not succeed, do not despair; with good will and persistence, you shall manage to make these dishes one day, I guarantee it, and perhaps even to improve them. For I, after all, cannot presume to have reached the acme of perfection.

Yet I may discreetly assume that my dishes have been

generally well received, and that to my great fortune few people, thus far, have cursed me for stomach aches or other phenomena that decency forbids me to mention.

Finally, I should not like my interest in gastronomy to give me the reputation of a gourmand or glutton. I object to any such dishonorable imputation, for I am neither. I love the good and the beautiful wherever I find them, and hate to see anyone squander, as they say, God's bounty. Amen.

From the Author to the Reader

Life has two principal functions: nourishment and the propagation of the species. Those who turn their minds to these two needs of existence, who study them and suggest practices whereby they might best be satisfied, make life less gloomy and benefit humanity. They may therefore be allowed to hope that, while humanity may not appreciate their efforts, it will at least show them generous and benevolent indulgence.

The meaning contained in these few lines, which preface the third edition of this book, was better expressed in a letter to me by the celebrated poet, Lorenzo Stecchetti. It is my pleasure to transcribe them here:

The human race survives only because man possesses the instincts of self-preservation and reproduction, and keenly feels the need to satisfy both. The satisfaction of a need is always accompanied by pleasure. The pleasure of self-preservation lies in the sense of taste, and that of reproduction in the sense of touch. If man did not find food appetizing, or experience sexual desire, the human race would quickly come to an end.

Taste and touch are therefore the senses most necessary, indeed indispensable to the life of the individual and the species. The other senses are only there to help, and one can, after all, live life blind and deaf, but not without the functional activity of the organs of taste.

How is it, then, that on the scale of the senses, the two most necessary to life and its continuance are considered the basest? Why are those things that satisfy the other senses – painting, music, etc. – called art and deemed noble, while those that satisfy the sense of taste are considered ignoble? Why is a person who enjoys gazing at a lovely painting or listening to a beautiful symphony held in higher esteem than one who enjoys eating an excellent dish? Is the equality among the senses perhaps comparable to that among humans, whereby those who work may be well off, but those who do not are even better off?

The blame, no doubt, must lie with the tyrannical sway the brain now holds over all the organs of the body. In the time of Menenius Agrippa, the stomach ruled; nowadays it no longer even serves, or, if so, serves badly. Of all those who over-work their brains, is there a single one who can boast of good digestion? They are all nerves, neuroses, and neurasthenia. The height, chest-size, strength and reproductive powers of this ingenious, rachitic breed of sages and artists, all refine-ment and glands, are in daily decline. Indeed they do not even eat, but rather overstimulate themselves and keep going by dint of coffee, alcohol and morphine. Thus are the senses that direct the brain's functions deemed nobler than those that pre-side over self-preservation – and the time has come to right this unjust verdict.

God bless the bicycle, which lets us know the joys of a hearty appetite, notwithstanding all the decadent and decayed who dream of chlorosis, consumption and boils in the name of the ideal art! Let us go out, out into the open air, into the free-flowing, healthy air! It reddens the blood and strengthens the muscles! Let us not be ashamed, therefore, to eat the best we can and return gastronomy to its rightful place. In the end, even the tyrannical brain will be the better for it, and this nerve-wracked society will finally understand that, even in art, a discussion on how to cook eel is every bit as worthy as a disquisition on the smile of Beatrice.

It is true that man does not live by bread alone; he must eat something with it. And the art of making this something as economical, savory and healthy as possible is, I insist, a true art. Let us rehabilitate the sense of taste and not be ashamed to satisfy it honestly, and as best we can, according to its own dictates.

I beg the kind Ladies and good Housewives, for whom this work of great effort and expense is intended, to study it with love, for they will derive great advantage from it. May they continue to bestow their much-desired favor on me, and I shall be a happy man.

First Courses

It used to be said that pasta was the forage of man. Today doctors advise us to eat it sparingly, lest it overly dilate the stomach and reduce our consumption of meat. Meat strengthens the body's fibers, while starches, which pastas are usually made of, create fatty tissue, which cause flabbiness. To this theory I raise no objection; but if I may be permitted, I would like to make the following suggestions. Small amounts of pasta are for anyone who, not being in his prime or in perfect health, must be treated with special care. Small amounts of pasta are also for those who tend to put on weight and would like to keep such gains in check. Finally, small portions of pasta with a light sauce should be served at banquets, if the guests are to do justice to the various dishes that follow. But aside from these cases, a good and generous helping of pasta will always be welcome at humbler dinners, so go ahead and enjoy it. Governed by this principle, I shall make a point of listing every kind of pasta and soup that experience suggests to me.

Peas with bacon (see page 54) can give flavor and charm, as we all know, to soups made with rice, pastina and malfattini. But if you have no broth, they are better used in risotto (see page 15).

CAPPELLETTI ALL'USO DI ROMAGNA
(*Cappelletti Romagna Style*)

They are called cappelletti (or 'little hats') because of their hat-like shape. This is the easiest way to make them so that they are less heavy on the stomach.

180 grams (about 6⅓ ounces) of ricotta, or half ricotta and half 'raviggiolo' (a soft cheese made from goat or sheep milk)

½ capon breast cooked in butter, seasoned with salt and pepper and finely chopped with a 'mezzaluna'

30 grams (about 1 ounce) of grated Parmesan cheese

1 whole egg

1 egg yolk

a dash of nutmeg, a few spices, some lemon zest (if desired), and a pinch of salt

Mix all the ingredients and then taste, checking for seasonings and flavor. If you do not have a breast of capon, use 100 grams (about 3½ ounces) of lean pork loin instead, cooked and seasoned as above.

If the ricotta or raviggiolo is too soft, leave out an egg white, or if the mixture comes out too firm, add another yolk. Enclose this stuffing in a soft dough made with flour and eggs only, using some of the leftover whites. Roll out the dough in a thin sheet and then cut it into disks.

Place the stuffing in the center of the disk and fold, so as to form half-moon shapes. Then take the two ends, press them together and you will have a 'cappelletto.'

If the dough dries out as you are working with it, then

dip a finger in water and wet the disks along the edges. For best results, this pasta calls for a broth made with capon, that silly animal that every year out of the goodness of its heart offers itself to be sacrificed to mankind during the solemnities of Christmas. Cook the cappelletti in the capon broth, as they do in Romagna, where, on Christmas day, you will find braggarts claiming to have eaten a hundred of them. This can also suffice to kill you, however, as happened to a friend of mine. For a moderate eater, a couple of dozen cappelletti will be quite enough.

Apropos of this pasta, I will tell you a little story, which, though it may be of little importance, may yet give pause to reflect.

You should know that the gentlemen of Romagna are not in the least interested in racking their brains over some tome, perhaps because from infancy children are accustomed to seeing their parents doing anything but turning the pages of books. Another factor may be that, being in a place where one can lead a happy and pleasurable life with little, the Romagnoli do not believe much instruction in life is necessary. For this reason, after they finish grammar school, a good ninety per cent of them takes up a life of leisure, and then no matter how hard you prod or pull, they will not budge. This was the situation a husband and wife living in a village of lower Romagna found themselves in with their teenage son Carlino. The father, however, believed in progress and, though he had the means to leave his son well provided for, would have liked the boy to become a lawyer, or possibly even a member of Parliament, since it is but a short step from one to the other. After many conversations, deliberations, and squabbles within the family over the great separation, the decision was made to send Carlino to continue his studies in a big city. Ferrara was chosen, being the nearest. Carlino's father accompanied him there, but did so with a heavy heart, having had to tear him from the arms of his loving mother, who had drenched him with tears.

Less than a week had passed. The parents were sitting down at table for a dish of cappelletti. After a long silence and several sighs, the mother exclaimed:

'Oh, if only Carlino were here! He so loves cappelletti!' No sooner were these words spoken than they heard a knock at the front door, and into the room sprang a cheerful Carlino.

'Oh, you are back!' exclaimed the father. 'What happened?'

'What happened,' replied Carlino, 'is that wasting away over books is not for me. I would rather be drawn and quartered than return to that jail.' Overjoyed, the mother ran to embrace her son, and turned to her husband.

'Let him do as he wishes,' she said. 'Better a healthy fool than a sickly scholar. He will be busy enough looking after his interests here.' Indeed, from that moment on, Carlino's interests revolved around a rifle, a hunting dog, a frisky horse hitched to a fine little racing gig, and continual assaults on the young country girls.

PANATA (*Bread Soup*)

The people of Romagna solemnly celebrate Easter with this soup and call it 'tridura,' a word whose meaning has been lost in the Tuscan dialect, but which was in use in the early 14th century. We know this because the word appears in an ancient manuscript, which mentions a ceremonial gift to the friars of Settimo at Cafaggiolo (Florence) which involved sending every year to the monastery a newly made wooden bowl full of tridura and covered by sticks that supported ten pounds of pork decked with laurel. Everything in the world grows old and changes, even languages and words, but not the ingredients of which dishes are made. For this soup, they are:

130 grams (about 4½ ounces) of day-old bread, grated, not crushed
4 eggs
50 grams (about 1⅔ ounces) of grated Parmesan cheese
a dash of nutmeg
a pinch of salt

Place the ingredients in a large saucepan and mix them together, but do not let the mixture thicken too much. However, if the mixture is too loose, add more bread crumbs. Dilute with hot but not boiling broth, setting some aside to add later. Cook with embers around the pot, but with little or no heat directly under it. When it begins to boil, try to gather it gently with a wooden spoon in the center of the saucepan by pushing it inwards from the sides of the pan, but without breaking it apart. When it has thickened and set, pour it into the soup tureen and send it to the table. These amounts are enough for six people.

   If the panata has turned out well, you will see it gathered in small bunches, with the clear broth around it. If you like it with herbs and peas, cook these separately, and stir them into the mixture before you pour broth over it.

MINESTRA DI DUE COLORI
(Two-Color Soup)

This is a light and delicate soup which in Tuscany is most likely to be appreciated by the ladies. However, it should not be served in Romagna, that homeland of tagliatelle, where softness to the bite is not to the locals' taste. Even less would they appreciate the pasty texture of tapioca, the very sight of which would, with few exceptions, turn their stomachs.

180 grams (about 6⅓ ounces) of flour
60 grams (about 2 ounces) of butter
40 grams (about 1⅓ ounces) of Parmesan cheese
4 deciliters (about 1⅔ cups) of milk
2 whole eggs
2 egg yolks
salt to taste
a handful of spinach
a dash of nutmeg

Boil the spinach, squeeze it dry and pass it through a sieve. Heat the butter and when it has melted, add the flour, stirring well. Then add the milk, a little at a time. Salt it and, while it is cooking, work the mixture with a wooden spoon, turning it into a smooth paste.

Remove it from the heat, and when it is lukewarm add the eggs, grated Parmesan and nutmeg. Then divide the mixture into two equal parts. Use one part to blend in just enough spinach to make the mixture turn green.

Place the mixture in a pastry-tube using the attachment that has rather wide round holes. Squeeze the dough into boiling broth. This procedure must be repeated twice, once with the yellow mixture and once with the green one.

These amounts serve eight to ten people.

MALFATTINI
(*Easy Egg Noodle Soup*)

In those parts of the country where homemade egg pasta is eaten almost daily, every housemaid has mastered the art of making it, and especially this dish, which is the essence of simplicity. Thus I speak about it not for them, but for the inhabitants of those provinces who know of no other soups than those made with bread, rice or store-bought pasta.

The most simple malfattini are made with flour. Fold the eggs into the flour and knead the mixture on the pastry board until you obtain a firm loaf. Cut this into large slices a half finger thick, and leave them a while to dry in the air. Then chop them with the mezzaluna into tiny bits about half the size of a grain of rice. You can achieve consistency of size by passing them through a strainer, or by grating them from the whole loaf. But do not do as those who leave them large as sparrow's beaks, for this will make them difficult to digest. Indeed, for even easier digestion, rather than with flour, you can make them with bread crumbs, either plain or with a pinch of grated Parmesan cheese and a dash of spices.

However you make them, you can serve them with peas with bacon (see page 54) when peas are in season, or use finely diced beet, or both. *A propos* of beet, I have noticed that in Florence, where they make a great use of aromatic herbs in cooking, dill is unknown. Mixed with beet, as is done in other towns, dill graces the palate. Indeed, I have tried to introduce this fragrant herb to Florence, but with little success. Perhaps this is because in that city beets are sold in bunches, whereas in Romagna they are carried loose to the market or already mixed with dill.

MINESTRONE
(*Mixed Vegetable and Rice Soup*)

Minestrone brings back memories of a year marked by collective anxiety and a singular personal experience.

In the year of Our Lord 1855, I found myself at Livorno during the bathing season. Cholera was then making its way through several provinces of Italy, gripping everyone with the fear of a major epidemic, which, in fact, was not long in coming. One Saturday evening I entered a trattoria, and asked: 'What's today's soup?'

'Minestrone,' was the answer.

'Fine, bring the minestrone,' I replied. I ate, took a stroll, and then went to bed. I had taken lodgings in the Piazza del Voltone, in a whitewashed new villa run by a certain Mr. Domenici. That night, I felt the onset of a frightening disturbance in my body that had me running regularly back and forth to the rest rooms – which in Italy should rather be called an *unrest* room. 'Damned minestrone! You will never fool me again,' I cried out, raging against something which was perhaps quite innocent.

Morning came, and feeling myself totally drained, I caught the first train and escaped to Florence, where I immediately felt much better. Monday the sad news reached me that cholera had broken out in Livorno, and the first to be struck dead was none other than Domenici himself.

And to think I had blamed the minestrone!

After three attempts, improving upon the dish each time, this is how I like to make it. Feel free to modify it to suit the tastes of your part of the world, and the vegetables locally available.

Start by making the usual meat broth, and cooking in it a handful of shelled fresh beans. If the beans are dry, then simmer them in water until they soften. Then cut some Savoy cabbage, spinach and a little chard into thin slices, and soak them in cold water. Then, to get the water out of the vegetables, place them on the fire in a dry saucepan. Drain the contents well, pressing them firmly with a wooden spoon to get rid of excess water. For a minestrone that serves four to five people, finely chop 40 grams (about 1⅓ ounces) of fatty prosciutto, a clove of garlic, and a sprig of parsley, and sauté them together. Add this to the saucepan, along with some celery and carrots, one potato, one zucchini, and very little onion, all cut into short, thin slices. Add the beans, and if you wish, some pork rind (as some people like to do), and a bit of tomato sauce (see page 21) or tomato paste. Season with salt and pepper and cook in the broth. As a last ingredient add enough rice to absorb most of the liquid, and before removing the minestrone from the fire throw in a good pinch of Parmesan cheese.

I should warn you that this is not a soup for weak stomachs.

ZUPPA ALLA STEFANI
(*Stefani Soup*)

The distinguished poet Olindo Guerrini, librarian of the University of Bologna, has a taste for learning so developed that he enjoys digging up the bones of the culinary paladins of old, and drawing astonishing inferences from them that make modern cooks laugh out loud. He was good enough to favor me with the following recipe, taken from a little book, *The Art of Cooking Well*, by Signor Bartolomeo Stefani of Bologna, who was the cook of His Serene Highness the Duke of Mantua in the mid-1600s. At that time, much use and abuse was made of all manner of seasonings and spices, and sugar and cinnamon were used in broth, as well as in making boiled or roasted meat. Omitting some of his instructions for this soup, I shall limit myself, aromatically speaking, to a bit of parsley and basil. And if the ancient Bolognese cook, meeting me in the afterworld, scolds me for it, I shall defend myself by explaining that tastes have changed for the better. As with all things, however, we go from one extreme to the other, and we are now beginning to exaggerate in the opposite direction, going as far as to exclude herbs and spices from dishes that require them. And I shall tell him as well of the ladies who, at my table, have made gruesome faces when confronted with a bit of nutmeg. Here is the recipe for the soup (serves six):

120 grams (about 4¼ ounces) of veal or lamb brains
    (or brains of a similar animal)
3 chicken livers
3 eggs
1 sprig of basil and 1 of parsley, chopped
the juice of ¼ lemon

Scald the brain so as to be able to skin it, and then sauté with the chicken livers in butter. Finish cooking them in brown stock, adding salt and pepper for seasoning.

Put the eggs in a pot and beat them with the basil and parsley, as well as the lemon juice and a bit of salt and pepper. Add cold broth a little at a time, to dilute the mixture. Then dice the brain and the livers and add to the pot. Put this on a low flame to thicken, stirring constantly with a wooden spoon. Take care not to bring it to a boil. After it has thickened, pour into a soup tureen over some diced bread sautéed in butter or oil and sprinkled with a handful of grated Parmesan cheese.

This is a delicate, substantial soup. However, if you, like me, are not particularly fond of foods with such a soft texture, then you may want to substitute sweetbreads for brains. And this reminds me to mention – and I know whereof I speak – that in some regions where,

11

because of the climate, one must be careful about what one eats, the inhabitants have so enfeebled their stomachs by eating light and preferably soft, liquid dishes, that they can no longer withstand food of any weight.

ZUPPA ALLA CERTOSINA
(*Soup Carthusian Style*)

With 500 grams (about 1 pound) of fillets from a variety of fish you should be able to make enough soup for four to five people.

Finely chop ¼ of an onion, some parsley and celery. Put on the fire in a pan with oil and, when it has browned, add the fish, which you will keep moist with water, tomato sauce (see page 21) or tomato paste. Season with salt and pepper. Allow it to cook well and then add the water for the soup – 1 liter (about 1 quart) of water in total should suffice for this recipe. Pass the mixture through a sieve, pressing well against the mesh. Then put it back on the fire and bring it to a boil again. Break three eggs in a tureen and mix them with three spoonfuls of Parmesan cheese. Pour in the broth slowly, and before serving toss in small cubes of bread which you have toasted or fried in the condiment you prefer: butter, oil, or lard. If you like to see the eggs and Parmesan cheese making little lumps in the soup, you can beat them separately and pour them in the pot when the broth is boiling.

It is said that the Granduke of Tuscany first tasted this soup in a convent of friars and, having found it excellent, sent his cook there to learn how to make it. But no matter how hard he tried, the excellent cook could not make the soup as well as the friars, who did not want to tell the Granduke that the soup was made with broth of capon rather than water!

TAGLIATELLE ALL'USO DI ROMAGNA
(*Tagliatelle Romagna Style*)

'Bills should be short and tagliatelle long,' the people of Bologna say, and they are right, because long bills terrify poor husbands and short tagliatelle look like leftovers, attesting to the incompetence of their maker. For this reason I do not approve of the widespread custom adopted simply to satisfy the palate of foreigners of chopping capellini, taglierini and similar types of pasta into the minutest bits and serving them in broth. Since they are unique to Italy, they ought to preserve their original characteristics.

Prepare the pasta dough and cut it. Boil for a short while, drain well, put in a saucepan and heat for a moment to help it absorb the sauce, which is the one for country-style spaghetti (see page 16). Also add enough butter to season the amount of pasta you are making. Toss gently, then send to the table.

To my way of thinking, this is a very tasty dish, but to digest it well, you need air like the kind that you can breathe in Romagna.

I remember traveling once with some Florentines (a toothless old codger, a middle-aged man and a young lawyer) who were on their way to claim an inheritance in Modigliana. We stopped at an inn, and you can well imagine the sort of place it was in that part of the country, this being forty or more years ago. The innkeeper gave us only tagliatelle as the pasta course and cured pork neck as an appetizer, and while this was very tough and displeasing to the taste, the effort the old fellow made to gnaw it was a sight to behold. Such was the appetite he and the other two possessed, that they found this and everything else to be very good, indeed delicious; I even heard them exclaim several times: 'Oh, if only we could take this air with us to Florence!'

Speaking of that fair city, let me tell you about a certain Count from Romagna who was living in Florence when 'francesconi' were still in circulation. This gentleman, a fine match for Goldoni's *Marquis of Forlimpopoli*, had plenty of arrogance, only a few pennies to his name, and a cast-iron stomach. In those days you could live inexpensively in Florence, which was famous for its low prices in comparison to other capital cities. There were many small restaurants that offered a *prix-fixe* meal of pasta, three main courses to choose from, fruit or pastry, bread and wine for a single Tuscan lira. The servings, though small, satisfied everyone who was not as hungry as a wolf. Even the nobility frequented these restaurants, although the Count in question did not deign to do so. What trick do you suppose he had found to maintain such a façade while spending little? On alternate days he would go to the buffet table at one of the best hotels, where for half a francescone (2.80 lire), the fare offered was most sumptuous. Gobbling up everything in sight,

14

he would stuff his stomach enough to last him two days. Then he would go home to diet, on the off day, on bread, cheese and cold cuts. Now you have his example and the recipe.

RISOTTO COI PISELLI
(*Rice with Peas*)

Rice! Behold the fattening food that the Turks feed to their women, so that they will develop, as a celebrated and well-known professor would say, sumptuous adipose cushions.

500 grams (about 1 pound) of rice
100 grams (about 3½ ounces) of butter
Parmesan cheese, as needed
1 medium-sized onion

Rice, as I have indicated earlier, should not be washed; it is enough to clean it and rub it in a kitchen towel.

Mince the onion very finely with a mezzaluna and put it on the fire with half the butter. When it has turned golden brown, add the rice, stirring constantly with a large spoon until it has absorbed all the butter. Then start adding hot water ladleful at a time. Make sure the rice does not boil too fast, otherwise it will remain hard in the center while becoming too soft on the outside. Salt and cook until dry, then add the rest of the butter. Before removing from the fire, stir in a suitable amount of peas with bacon (see page 54), and flavor with a good handful of Parmesan cheese.

This recipe serves five people.

SPAGHETTI ALLA RUSTICA
(*Country-Style Spaghetti*)

The ancient Romans left the consumption of garlic to
the lower classes, while Alfonso King of Castile hated it
so much he would punish anyone who appeared in his
court with even a hint of it on his breath. The ancient
Egyptians were much wiser – they worshipped garlic as
a divinity, perhaps because they had experienced its
medicinal properties. Indeed, it is claimed that garlic
provides some benefit to those suffering from hysteria,
promotes the secretion of urine, strengthens the stomach, aids digestion and, being also a vermifuge, protects
the organism against epidemic and pestilential diseases.
When sautéing it, however, you must be careful not to
cook it too much, as then it acquires an unpleasant taste.
There are many people who, ignorant of the ways of food
preparation, have a horror of garlic merely because they
can smell it on the breath of those who have eaten it raw
or poorly cooked. As a result, they absolutely ban this
plebeian condiment from their kitchens. This fixation,
however, deprives them of healthy and tasty dishes, such
as the one I present below, which has often comforted my
stomach when upset.

> Finely chop two garlic cloves and a few sprigs of parsley,
> as well as some basil leaves, if you like the taste. Sauté
> in a good measure of olive oil. As soon as the garlic
> starts to turn golden brown, toss in 6 or 7 chopped
> tomatoes, seasoning with salt and pepper. When every-
> thing is well cooked, purée the sauce, which will serve

four to five people. Pour the sauce over spaghetti or vermicelli, adding grated Parmesan cheese. Remember to cook the pasta only for a short time in plenty of water. Send to the table immediately, so that the pasta does not have time to absorb all the moisture, and thus remains of the right consistency.

Tagliatelle are also delicious when served in this sauce.

Appetizers

Appetizers or antipasti are, properly speaking, those delicious trifles that are made to be eaten either after the pasta course, as is practiced in Tuscany, which seems preferable to me, or before, as is done elsewhere in Italy. Oysters, cured meats such as prosciutto, salami, mortadella, and tongue, or seafood such as anchovies, sardines, caviar, 'mosciame' (which is the salted back of the tuna fish), etc., may be served as appetizers, either alone or with butter. In addition, the fried breads I describe below make excellent appetizers.

CROSTINI DI CAPPERI
(Canapés with Capers)

50 grams (about 1⅔ ounces) of pickled capers
50 grams (about 1⅔ ounces) of powdered sugar
30 grams (about 1 ounce) of raisins
20 grams (about ⅔ of an ounce) of pine nuts
20 grams (about ⅔ of an ounce) of untrimmed prosciutto
20 grams (about ⅔ of an ounce) of candied fruit

Coarsely chop the capers. Remove all the stems from the raisins and wash them well. Slice the pine nuts crosswise into three sections, finely dice the prosciutto, and chop the candied fruit into little chunks.

In a small saucepan heat a heaping teaspoon of flour and the two tablespoons of sugar. When the mixture begins to brown, pour in a half glass of water with a few drops of vinegar in it. Let it boil until smooth, then toss all the other ingredients into the saucepan and let simmer for 10 minutes. Test for flavor from time to time to make sure the sweet, strong taste is just right (I have not specified how much vinegar is needed, because not all vinegars are of equal strength). While the mixture is still hot, spread it over small slices of bread fried in good olive oil or lightly toasted.

You can serve these canapés cold even midway through dinner, to whet the appetites of your table companions. The best bread to use is the kind baked in a mold, as in England.

CROSTINI DI FEGATINI DI POLLO
(*Canapés with Chicken Livers*)

As you know the gall bladder must be removed unbroken from a chicken liver, a procedure you can best perform in a small basin of water.

Put the chicken livers on the fire together with a battuto made with a shallot or, if you do not have any, a section of a small white onion, a small piece of fat trimmed from prosciutto, a few sprigs of parsley, celery and carrot, seasoned with a little olive oil and butter, as well as salt and pepper. Be sparing with the amounts, so that the resulting mixture will not turn out too spicy or heavy. When half done, remove the chicken livers from the saucepan and chop finely with a mezzaluna along with two or three chunks of dried mushrooms soaked in water. Put them back in the saucepan, and finish cooking, adding some broth. Before serving, however, sprinkle the mixture with a pinch of bread crumbs to bind it and add a little lemon juice.

Sauces

The best sauce you can offer your guests is a happy expression on your face and heartfelt hospitality. Brillat-Savarin used to say, 'Inviting someone is the same as taking responsibility for their happiness and well-being for as long as they stay under your roof.'

The pleasure you would like to give to the friends you have invited during these few hours is nowadays imperiled even before it starts by certain unfortunate customs that are being introduced and threaten to become widespread. I am referring to the so-called 'digestion visit,' to be made within eight days of the meal, and to the tips distributed to the domestics for the meal served. When you have to pay for dinner, it seems best to pay a restaurateur since that way you incur no obligation to anyone. And that bothersome second visit, which is made within a set period of time, like an obligatory rhyme, and does not issue unbidden from a sincere heart, is downright silly.

SUGO DI POMODORO
(Tomato Sauce)

Later I shall speak about another kind of tomato sauce that we call 'salsa,' as opposed to 'sugo.' Sugo must be simple and therefore composed only of cooked, puréed tomatoes. At the most you can add a few chunks of celery or some parsley or basil leaves, when you think these flavors will suit your needs.

SALSA DI MAGRO PER CONDIRE LE PASTE ASCIUTTE
(Meatless Sauce for Pasta)

If I may be allowed to make a comparison between the senses of sight and taste, this sauce is like a young woman whose face is not particularly striking or attractive at first glance, but whose delicate and discreet features you might indeed find attractive upon closer observation.

500 grams (about 1 pound) of spaghetti
100 grams (about 3⅓ ounces) of fresh mushrooms
70 grams (about 2½ ounces) of butter
60 grams (about 2 ounces) of pine nuts
6 salted anchovies
7 or 8 tomatoes
¼ of a large onion
1 teaspoon of flour

Place half the butter in a saucepan on the fire and brown the pine nuts in it. Then remove them from the pan, and grind them in a mortar, adding the flour. Finely mince the onion, place it in the butter in which you sautéed the pine nuts, and, when it begins to brown, add the tomatoes, chopped up. Season with salt and pepper. When the tomatoes are done, purée them. Put the sauce back on the fire adding the fresh mushrooms, cut into thin slices no larger than pumpkin seeds, the pine nut paste diluted in a little water, and the rest of the butter. Allow to simmer for half an hour, adding water to make the sauce rather liquid. Lastly, dissolve the anchovies by heating them with a little of this sauce, but do not let them come to a boil, and then combine with everything else.

Drain the spaghetti and toss with the sauce. If you wish to improve this dish further, add some grated Parmesan cheese.

These amounts serve five people.

SALSA DI POMODORO
(*Tomato Sauce*)

There once was a priest from Romagna who stuck his nose into everything, and busy-bodied his way into families, trying to interfere in every domestic matter. Still, he was an honest fellow, and since more good than ill came of his zeal, people let him carry on in his usual style. But popular wit dubbed him Don Pomodoro (Father Tomato), since tomatoes are also ubiquitous. And therefore it is very helpful to know how to make a good tomato sauce.

Prepare a battuto with a quarter of an onion, a clove of garlic, a finger-length stalk of celery, a few basil leaves and a sufficient amount of parsley. Season with a little olive oil, salt and pepper. Mash 7 or 8 tomatoes and put everything on the fire, stirring occasionally. Once you see the sauce thickening to the consistency of a runny cream, pass it through a sieve and it is ready to use.

This sauce lends itself to innumerable uses, as I shall indicate in due course. It is good with boiled meat, and excellent when served with cheese and butter on pasta, as well as when used to make risotto.

SALSA DEL PAPA (*Pope Sauce*)

Do not get the idea that this sauce takes its name from the Pope in the Vatican, and is therefore some sort of extravagant delight. All the same it is rather good on fried cutlets.

Take a small handful of capers, squeezing out the brine, and an equal amount of sweetened olives, from which you have removed the pits. Mince both with a mezzaluna. Finely chop a bit of onion and put it on the fire with some butter. When the onion begins to brown, moisten it a little at a time with water until it dissolves. Then add the mixture of capers and olives and allow to simmer for a while, eventually adding a droplet of vinegar, a pinch of flour and a little more butter. Finally, add a minced anchovy, and send to the table without letting the sauce simmer any further.

SALSA TARTUFATA (*Truffle Sauce*)

Prepare a well-minced battuto with a small, nut-size chunk of onion, a half clove of garlic and a little parsley. Put on the fire with 20 grams (about ⅔ of an ounce) of butter and, when the onion begins to brown, add two fingers of Marsala or white wine in which you have first dissolved a heaping teaspoon of flour. Season the sauce with a pinch of salt, pepper and the usual spices, stirring constantly with a wooden spoon.

When the flour has thickened the sauce, add a little broth and then add some truffle shavings. Allow to stand for a moment longer on the fire, and serve as a garnish for fried cutlets of milk-fed veal, steaks or roasted meats.

I warn you that wine as a condiment is hard on some stomachs.

Fried Foods

CRESCENTE (*Half Moons*)

What a strange language they speak in learned Bologna!

They call carpets rags; wine flasks gourds; sweet-breads milks. They say 'sigàre' for 'piangere' (to weep), and they call an unsavory, ugly, annoying woman, who would normally be termed a 'calia' or a 'scamonea' a 'sagoma' (Italian for silhouette and, figuratively speaking, a funny person). In their restaurants you find 'trefoils' (instead of truffles), Florentine style 'chops' (instead of 'steaks'), and other similar expressions that would drive anybody mad. It was there that, I think, the term 'batteries' was devised to describe harness races, and where 'zone' is used to mean a tram route. When I first heard the Bolognese mention a crescent, I thought they were talking about the moon. Instead they were discussing the schiacciata or focaccia, the ordinary fried dough cake that everybody recognizes and all know how to make. The only difference is that the Bolognese, to make theirs more tender and digestible, add a little lard when mixing the flour with cool water and salt.

It seems the schiacciata will puff up better if you drop it in a skillet where the fat is sizzling, but which you have removed from the fire.

The Bolognese are, in any case, an active, industrious,

friendly and hospitable people, and one speaks freely with the men, as well as the women, because their candid manner of conversation is quite engaging. If I had to judge in these matters, I would hold that this is the hallmark of a people's general civility and good manners, and not at all like what one encounters in certain other cities whose inhabitants are of an altogether different character.

In one of his tales, Boccaccio, speaking of the Bolognese, exclaims: 'Ah, how singularly sweet is the blood of Bologna! How admirably you rise to the occasion in such moments as these (moments of love)! Sighs and tears were never to your liking: entreaties have always moved you, and you were ever susceptible to a lover's yearnings. If only I could find words with which to commend you as you deserve, I should never grow tired of singing your praises!'

FRITTO ALLA GARISENDA
(*Garisenda Fry*)

You ladies who take pleasure in fine cuisine, do not consign this dish to oblivion, for it will delight your husbands, and due to the ingredients it contains, may well move them to reward you.

Take some stale bread, not too spongy, remove the crust and cut into diamond shapes or squares about 4 centimeters (about 1½ inches) on each side. On each piece place a slice of untrimmed prosciutto, then little shavings of truffle, and over them a slice of Gruyère cheese. Cover the filling with a second slice of bread and press tightly together so that they remain joined. Remember to slice everything very fine so that the pieces do not turn out inelegantly large.

Now that you have prepared the morsels, lightly soak them in cold milk, and when that has been absorbed, dip each piece in beaten egg and then roll in bread crumbs. Repeat the procedure twice so that even the edges remain covered and tightly closed.

Fry in lard or olive oil and serve alone or with another fried food.

Entrements

GNOCCHI ALLA ROMANA
(Roman-Style Dumplings)

These gnocchi, for which I have modified the amounts as follows, I hope will please you as much as they have delighted those for whom I have prepared them. Should that happen, toast to my health if I am still alive or say a *requiescat* in my name, if I have gone on to feed the cabbages.

> *150 grams (about 5¼ ounces) of flour*
> *50 grams (about 1⅔ ounces) of butter*
> *40 grams (about 1⅓ ounces) of Gruyère cheese*
> *20 grams (about ⅔ of an ounce) of grated Parmesan cheese*
> *½ a liter (about ½ a quart) of milk*
> *2 eggs*

It is commonly said that one should not sit down to table in lesser number than the Graces or in greater number than the Muses. If you are approaching the number of the Muses, double the amounts.

In a saucepan, mix the flour and the eggs, then pour the milk in a little at a time. Add the Gruyère cheese chopped into little pieces, and put the mixture on the fire, stirring constantly. When the flour makes it thicken, salt and add half the butter. Allow to cool, and then, in

29

the same way as you would prepare cornmeal gnocchi, place the mixture in little tidbits onto an ovenproof platter. Season them with the rest of the butter, cut into little pats, and with the Parmesan cheese, but do not cover the top layer, because Parmesan on top turns bitter when heated. Brown under an iron lid or in a Dutch oven, and serve hot.

MACCHERONI COL PANGRATTATO
(*Macaroni with Bread Crumbs*)

If it is true, as Alexandre Dumas *père* remarks, that the English live on roast beef and pudding; the Dutch on oven-cooked meat, potatoes and cheese; the Germans on sauerkraut and bacon; the Spanish on chickpeas, chocolate and rancid bacon; and the Italians on macaroni, do not be too surprised if I keep coming back to this topic, since I have, after all, always loved this pasta. Indeed, I once very nearly acquired the distinguished name of Macaroni-Eater, and I will tell you why.

One day in 1850, I found myself in the 'Tre Re' (Three Kings) restaurant in Bologna in the company of several students and Felice Orsini, who was a friend of one of them. It was the season for politics and conspiracy in Romagna, and Orsini, who seemed practically born for that purpose, spoke enthusiastically about these subjects. In his passion he tirelessly strove to show us that an uprising was imminent, that he and another leader he mentioned would lead it, overrunning Bologna with an armed band of followers. Listening to him so imprudently discuss in a public place such dangerous subjects and an enterprise that seemed to me utter madness, I remained indifferent to his harangues and calmly continued to eat the plate of macaroni set before me. My demeanor stung Orsini's *amour propre*, and thereafter, having felt humiliated at the time, whenever he remembered me he would ask his friends, 'How's the Macaroni-Eater doing?'

In my mind's eye I still see that congenial young man, of middling height, lean build, pale round face, refined features, the blackest eyes, crinkly locks, who lisped slightly when he spoke. Another time, many years later, I ran into him in a coffeehouse at Medola just as he was bristling with anger against someone who had abused his trust and offended his honor. He was asking a young fellow to follow him to Florence, to help him, he said, execute an exemplary vendetta. A series of circumstances and events, each stranger than the last, later led him to his tragic end, which we all know and deplore, but which also perhaps prodded Napoleon III to intervene in Italy. Now let's get back to our subject.

300 grams (about 10½ ounces) of long macaroni that hold
   up well when cooked
15 grams (about ½ an ounce) of flour
60 grams (about 2 ounces) of butter
60 grams (about 2 ounces) of Gruyère cheese
40 grams (about 1⅓ ounces) of Parmesan cheese
6 deciliters (about 2½ cups) of milk
bread crumbs, as needed

If you want to add more flavor, increase the amounts of the condiments.

31

Cook the macaroni halfway, salt, and drain in a colander. Put the flour on the fire in a saucepan with half the butter, stirring constantly. When the flour begins to change color, pour in the milk a little at a time and allow to boil for about 10 minutes. To this béchamel, add the macaroni and the Gruyère cheese, either grated or in little chunks. Move the saucepan to the edge of the hearth, so that the macaroni will absorb all the milk while bubbling slowly. Now add the rest of the butter and the grated Parmesan cheese. Then transfer to an ovenproof platter, fill the platter to the rim and cover with bread crumbs.

Put the macaroni prepared in this fashion into a Dutch oven or under an iron hood heated from above. When browned, serve hot as an *entremets*, or preferably, as a side dish for meat.

MIGLIACCIO DI FARINA DOLCE VOLGARMENTE CASTAGNACCIO
(*Chestnut Flour Cake, Popularly Called Castagnaccio*)

Here too, I can hardly refrain from railing against the disinclination we Italians have for commerce and industry. In some Italian provinces, chestnut flour is completely unknown and I think no one has ever even tried to introduce it. And yet for common folk, and for those unafraid of wind, it is a cheap, healthy and nutritious food.

I questioned a street vendor in Romagna on the subject. I described this chestnut cake to her, and asked why she did not try to earn a few pennies selling it. 'What can I tell you?' she replied. 'It's too sweet; nobody would eat it.' 'But those "cottarone" you are selling, aren't they sweet? Still, they are selling,' I said. 'Why don't you at least try the chestnut cake,' I added. 'At first, distribute them free to the children, give them a piece as a gift to see if they start liking the taste. And then the grown-ups are very likely to come after the children.' It was no use; I might as well have been talking to a stone wall.

'Cottarone,' for those who do not know them, are apples and pears, mostly overripe, that are stewed in the oven in a small pan with a little water in it, while the top of the pan is covered with a moist kitchen towel. But let us turn to the very simple way to make this chestnut cake.

Take 500 grams (about 1 pound) of chestnut flour, and because it easily clumps up, sift before using it to make it soft and fluffy. Then put it into a bowl and season with a small pinch of salt. This done, add 8 deciliters (about 3⅓ cups) of cool water, pouring it in a little at a time, until the mixture has the consistency of a runny porridge into which you will throw a handful of pine nuts. Some people supplement the pine nuts with chopped walnuts; others add raisins and a few rosemary leaves.

Now take a baking pan where the chestnut cake can rise to a thickness of one and half fingers. Cover the bottom with a thin layer of olive oil, pour in the chestnut porridge, and sprinkle another two tablespoons of olive oil on top. Take it to the baker to cook in the oven or bake it at home in a Dutch oven with fire above and below. Remove and serve hot.

You can also make fritters with this batter.

PIZZA A LIBRETTI
(*Accordion Cake*)

A woman wrote to me: 'I want to teach you, as I had promised myself to do, how to make a tasty and elegant fried pastry. But heaven help you if you call it flat, because it should turn out quite otherwise. Call it "accordion cake," which would be a fair description.'

Obediently carrying out the lady's orders, I tried out this accordion cake twice, and both times it turned out well. Now I will describe it to you.

Roll out a sheet of dough that is not too firm and as thin as possible by mixing together some flour, two eggs, a pinch of salt, three tablespoons of cognac or spirits, or better yet fumetto. Grease the dough with 20 grams (about ⅔ of an ounce) of melted butter and roll it up, that is fold it upon itself so that it is 10 to 11 centimeters (about 4 to 4¼ inches) wide. Make sure that the inner side is the greased side. Now cut the roll in half lengthwise and then slice crosswise at regular intervals to obtain a number of rectangles. Now press firmly with your fingers on the outer edge of each rectangle, that is, the uncut spine of the rolls. Fry in a skillet with a lot of oil, and before serving, sprinkle confectioners' sugar on top. If they have turned out well, you will see the accordions pop open and stay open.

These amounts serve four people.

Stews

POLLO ALLA MARENGO
(Chicken Marengo)

The evening of the Battle of Marengo, after the turmoil of the day, the cook to the First Consul and to the Generals was unable to find the kitchen wagons; and so he had some chickens stolen and improvised a dish that, prepared more or less as I will describe it to you, was called 'Chicken Marengo.' They say it was always a favorite of Napoleon, not so much for its intrinsic merit, but because it reminded him of that glorious victory.

> Take a young chicken, remove the neck and legs and cut into large pieces at the joints. Sauté in 30 grams (about 1 ounce) of butter and one tablespoon of olive oil, seasoning with salt, pepper, and a dash of nutmeg. When the pieces have browned on both sides, skim the fat and add a level tablespoon of flour and a deciliter (about 7 fluid ounces) of wine. Add broth and cover, cooking over low heat until done. Before removing from the fire, garnish with a pinch of chopped parsley; arrange on a serving dish and squeeze half a lemon over it. The result is an appetizing dish.

FOLAGHE IN UMIDO
(*Stewed Coot*)

The coot (*Fulica atra*) could be called a fish-bird, since the Church permits it to be eaten on fasting days without infringing on Catholic precepts. The coot comes from the warm, temperate countries of Europe and North Africa. As a migratory bird, it travels by night. An inhabitant of swamps and lakes, the coot is a good swimmer, feeding on aquatic plants, insects, and small mollusks. Only two species of coot are found in Europe.

Except during the time when they lay their eggs, coots live in huge flocks, which makes for very entertaining hunting, with huge kills. Quite famous is the coot hunt called 'la tela,' which takes place several times in late autumn and winter and is conducted in small boats on Lake Massaciuccoli near Pisa, on the estate of the Marquis Ginori-Lisci. During the hunt of November 1903, in which hunters in a hundred boats from every part of Italy took part, about six thousand coots were brought down, or so the newspapers reported.

Coot meat is dark and not very flavorful, and being game it should be prepared in the following manner.

Taking, for example, four coots (as I did), skin them and singe them on the fire to remove all their down, then clean and wash them well. Thread them lengthwise on a red-hot skewer, then cut the birds into four parts, discarding the head, feet, and wing tips. Marinate for an hour in vinegar and then wash repeatedly with cool water. I did not use the livers; but I did use the gizzards, which are large and chewy like those of a chicken. Cleaned, washed and cut into four pieces, they went into the marinade.

Now, finely chop a large onion, and the appropriate amount of the usual flavorings, that is, celery, carrot, and parsley. Put this battuto on the fire with 80 grams (about 2⅔ ounces) of butter, the coots, and the gizzards. Season with salt, pepper, and a dash of spices. When the meat starts to dry out, pour in tomato sauce (see page 21) or tomato paste diluted in a generous amount of water to finish cooking and so that there will be plenty of sauce left at the end. When the birds are done, strain the sauce and add to it half a coot breast, finely minced, and another 40 grams (about 1⅓ ounces) of butter, along with some Parmesan cheese. You can use this sauce to flavor three eggs' worth of pappardelle or 500 grams (about 1 pound) of large flat noodles, which will be highly praised for their unique flavor. Serve the coots, with some of the sauce, as the main course, and they will not be sneered at. All of this should serve five or six people.

I have also heard that you can get quite a nice stock by boiling coots with two sausages inside.

PICCIONI IN UMIDO
(*Stewed Squabs*)

Here is a story about squabs that, as unbelievable as it may seem, is indeed true. Let it stand as proof of what I was telling you about the caprices of the stomach.

One day a lady asked a man who happened to be around to kill a couple of squabs for her. Well, he drowned them in a basin of water, right there in front of her. The lady was so shocked by the sight that from that day on she could never eat the flesh of that bird again.

Garnish the birds with whole sage leaves, and put them in a pot or saucepan on top of some slices of untrimmed prosciutto. Season with olive oil, salt, and pepper. When they have browned, add a bit of butter and some broth, and then simmer until done. Before removing from the fire, squeeze a lemon on them and serve in their sauce over toasted bread. Salt them very little, on account of the prosciutto and the broth. During the season when verjuice is made, you can use that instead of lemon juice. As the old saying goes:

> *Quando sol est in leone,*
> *Bonum vinum cum popone,*
> *et agrestum cum pipione.*

> (When the sun is in Leo,
> Wine goes well with melon,
> And verjuice with pigeon.)

TORDI FINTI
(*Mock Thrushes*)

This dish is called mock thrushes because of the flavor that juniper berries and the combination of ingredients lend to it. It is a dish that many people like, and you would do well to try it.

To make six 'thrushes' you need:

300 grams (about 10½ ounces) of lean, boneless milk-fed veal
6 juniper berries

38

3 chicken livers
3 salted anchovies
3 tablespoons of olive oil
lardoon, as needed

These mock thrushes should look like small, stuffed cutlets; therefore cut the veal into six thin slices, flatten them out, give them a nice shape, and put the scraps aside. The scraps, along with the chicken livers, a bit of lardoon, the juniper berries, the anchovies (cleaned and boned), and a sage leaf, make up the mixture you will use to stuff the veal. So mince everything very fine and season with a little salt and pepper. After filling the veal slices with this mixture and rolling them up, wrap them in a thin slice of lardoon with half a sage leaf between the veal and the salt pork, and then tie them crosswise. I think that 60 grams (about 2 ounces) of lardoon in all should be enough.

Now that you have prepared the cutlets, put them over a high flame in a skillet or an uncovered saucepan with the three tablespoons of olive oil and season again lightly with salt and pepper. When they have browned all over, pour out the fat, but leave the burnt bits on the bottom of the pan; finish cooking, adding broth a little at a time, because when they are done the cutlets should be almost dry.

Untie and serve over six slices of lightly toasted bread, pouring over them the concentrated sauce that remains in the pan.

These mock thrushes are even good when served cold.

POLPETTONE
(*Meat Loaf*)

Dear Mr. Meat Loaf, please come forward, do not be shy. I want to introduce you to my readers.

I know that you are modest and humble, because, given your background, you feel inferior to many others. But take heart and do not doubt that with a few words in your favor you shall find someone who wants to taste you and who might even reward you with a smile.

This meat loaf is made with leftover boiled meat, and, though simple, it is an agreeable dish. Remove the fat from the meat and chop the rest with a mezzaluna. Season with an appropriate amount of salt, pepper, grated Parmesan cheese, one or two eggs, and two or three tablespoons of a mash made with crustless bread cooked in milk, broth, or simply in water, and flavored with a little butter. Mix everything together, shape into an oblong loaf, and sprinkle with flour. Then fry it in lard or oil, and you will see that soft as it was before, it will become firm and will acquire a delicate crust on the surface. Remove from the pan, and sauté on both sides in a skillet with butter. When you are about to serve it, coat it with two beaten eggs, a pinch of salt, and the juice of half a lemon. Make this sauce separately in a small saucepan, treating it as you would a cream sauce, and pour it over the meat loaf, which you have placed on a platter.

If the meat loaf is large, turn it over in the pan using a plate or a copper lid, as you would for a frittata; this ensures that you will not spoil it.

COTEGHINO FASCIATO
(*Spiced Pork Sausage or Cotechino Boiled in a Wrap*)

I will not pretend that this is an elegant dish, but rather one for the family, and as such it does the job perfectly well, and indeed you could even serve it to close friends. Speaking of close friends, Giusti says that people who are in a position to do so, should occasionally invite their close friends to get their mustaches greasy at their table. I am of the same opinion, even if the guests will probably proceed to speak ill of you, and of how they were treated.

Skin an uncooked cotechino weighing about 300 grams (about 10½ ounces). Take a large, thin cutlet of lean veal or beef weighing between 200 and 300 grams (about 7 and 10½ ounces), and pound well. Wrap the cutlet around the cotechino, tie it all up with twine and put on the fire in a saucepan with a bit of butter, some celery, carrot, and a quarter of an onion, all coarsely chopped. Salt and pepper are not necessary, because the cotechino contains plenty of these ingredients. If you plan to use the sauce on a first course of macaroni, add some slices of untrimmed prosciutto or some bacon. When the piece of meat has browned all over, pour in enough water to cover it halfway, and throw in some little pieces of dried mushrooms; simmer slowly until completely cooked. Strain the sauce, but add back the mushrooms, then use the sauce, along with cheese and butter, to season macaroni. Serve the cotechino as the main course, keeping it wrapped in the cutlet, but removing the twine, and garnishing it with a good amount of its own sauce.

It is a good idea to thicken the sauce for the pasta a bit with a pinch of flour. Put the flour in a saucepan with a bit of butter, and when it starts to brown pour in the sauce and boil for a while.

A side dish of carrots goes very well with this dish. First boil the carrots until two-thirds done and then finish cooking in the meat sauce.

Cold Dishes

LINGUA ALLA SCARLATTA
(Corned Tongue)

We call this 'alla scarlatta' (scarlet style) because it turns a nice red color. And it is a very fine dish, both in its appearance and its taste.

This talk of tongues brings to mind the following lines by Leopardi:

> *Il cor di tutte*
> *Cose alfin sente sazietà, del sonno,*
> *Della danza, del canto e dell'amore,*
> *Piacer più cari che il parlar di lingua,*
> *Ma sazietà di lingua il cor non sente.*

(Of all things the heart grows sated – of sleep, of love, of sweet song, and merry dance – things which give more pleasure than the tongue does in speech, and yet of the tongue the heart is never sated.)

It is true that the itch of loquacity is not satisfied as one ages; indeed, it grows in proportion as we grow older, as does the desire for good food, sole comfort of the aged who, however, ruled as they are by the inexorable dictates of nature, cannot abuse the comforts of the table, under penalty of grave discomforts. In old age, man consumes less; his organs become less and less active, his secretions imperfect, thus generating in the human body superfluous, harmful humors that cause rheumatism, gout, apoplectic fits, and similar offspring of Lady Pandora's box.

> To return to the subject of tongue, take one from a large animal (veal or beef), and rub it all over with between 20 and 30 grams (about ⅔ and 1 ounce) of saltpeter, depending on the size of the tongue, until it is thoroughly absorbed. After 24 hours, wash the tongue several times with cold water, and while still wet rub it with a great deal of salt; then leave it for eight days. Be sure to turn it every morning in its brine, which is produced as the salt draws the water out of the tongue. Since the best way to cook it is to boil it, put the tongue on the fire in cold water, with its natural brine, a *bouquet garni*, and half an onion studded with two cloves; boil for three to four hours. Skin the tongue while it is still steaming hot, let it cool, and then send to the table. It makes an excellent, elegant cold dish if you accompany it with aspic.
>
> Tongue can also be served hot, either by itself, or accompanied by potatoes or spinach.
>
> Do not try this dish during the hot summer months, because the salt might not be sufficient to preserve it.

ÀRISTA (*Roast Saddle of Pork*)

In Tuscany, spit- or oven-roasted saddle of pork is called 'àrista.' It is usually eaten cold, since it is much better cold than hot. In this case, pork 'saddle' means the piece of the loin with the ribs still attached, which can weigh between 3 and 4 kilograms (between about 6 and 8 pounds).

Stud it with garlic, sprigs of rosemary, and a few cloves, but be parsimonious, because these herbs can come back to haunt you; season with salt and pepper.

Roast it on a spit – the best way – or in the oven without anything else, and use the drippings to brown potatoes or re-heat vegetables.

This is a convenient dish for families, because it keeps for a long time during the winter.

During the Council of 1430, convened in Florence to resolve some differences between the Roman and Greek Churches, this dish, which was known by another name at the time, was served up to the bishops and their entourage. When they found it to their liking, they began to cry '*arista, arista*' (good, good!), and that Greek word continues, four and a half centuries later, to denote saddle of pork cooked in this manner.

Vegetables and Legumes

When they are not misused, vegetables are a healthy part of cooking. They thin the blood, and when served with meat, they make it easier on the stomach. But the amount of vegetables used anywhere depends to a great extent on the climate of the place.

ZUCCHINI COL REGAMO
(*Zucchini with Oregano*)

Oregano (*Origanum vulgare*) is the fragrant seed of a small wild plant of the mint family or *Labiatae*.

Take some long zucchini – a goodly amount, since they shrink a great deal – and cut into round slices as thick as a large coin. Put a frying pan or copper skillet on the fire with a generous amount of olive oil. When the oil starts to sizzle, toss in the sliced zucchini just as they are, and cook over a high flame, stirring often. When they are half-way done, season with salt and pepper. When they look like they are beginning to brown, sprinkle a good pinch of oregano over them, and remove them immediately from the fire with a slotted spoon. They can be served by themselves or as a side dish, and they are sure to please.

Oregano is good for seasoning other foods as well, such as stewed mushrooms, fried eggs, anchovies, etc.

FAGIUOLINI E ZUCCHINI
ALLA *SAUTÉ*
(Sautéed Green Beans and Zucchini)

Cooked this way, these vegetables are served mainly as a side dish. Now, so-called 'refined cooking' has reduced and simplified the use of condiments and seasonings. This might be healthier, and lighter on the stomach, but flavor suffers considerably as a result, and that little something that some people need to stimulate their digestion is lacking. This is a case in point. If you are using green beans, parboil them; if zucchini, keep them raw and cut them into wedges or rounds, then sauté in browned butter. Season with only small amounts of salt and pepper.

If you then add a little brown stock or some tomato sauce (see page 23), you will have gone beyond the rules of foreign or modern cooking. But in my opinion, they will taste better, and your stomach will feel more satisfied. If you do not have brown stock or tomato sauce, at least sprinkle the vegetables with Parmesan cheese when you remove them from the fire.

FAGIUOLINI CON L'ODORE DI
VANIGLIA, O DI NEPITELLA
(Green Beans with Vanilla or Calamint)

Soak the green beans in cold water. If they are tender, use them whole and raw, and when you put them in the pot do not shake off too much of the water.

Finely chop a shallot, parsley, carrot, and celery, and sauté in oil. You can also use a pearl onion or an ordinary onion instead of a shallot. Season with salt and pepper, and when this has browned, add broth and strain, pressing hard against the mesh. Add some tomato sauce to the strained sauce, and then cook the green beans in it. Before removing the beans from the fire, season with two teaspoons of vanilla sugar. If you do not like this spice, use calamint instead.

FUNGHI MANGIERECCI
(*Edible Mushrooms*)

Because of their nitrogenous properties, mushrooms are the most nutritious of vegetables. Their unique aroma makes mushrooms delicious food, and it is a great shame that among its many varieties there are some poisonous ones, which only an expert, practiced eye can distinguish from the harmless varieties. Some guarantee can be provided when they are gathered in a place known by long experience to be free from danger.

In Florence, for example, they use a great many mushrooms that come from the woods in the surrounding mountains. If the season is rainy, they begin to appear in June; but the height of production is in September. In truth, it must be said that Florence has never been afflicted by misfortunes from these vegetables, perhaps because the two species that are almost exclusively consumed there are the bronze-colored 'porcini,' or *boletus* mushroom, and the 'ovoli' or Caesar's mushrooms. So great is the faith in their harmlessness that no precautions are taken with regard to their consumption, not even the one suggested by some people of boiling them in water acidulated with vinegar – a precaution which, for that matter, would come at the cost of their flavor.

Of the two varieties mentioned above, porcini are best fried or stewed; ovoli are best prepared like tripe, or grilled.

FUNGHI TRIPPATI
(*Mushrooms Tripe Style*)

Ovoli are best for this dish, which probably gets its name because the mushrooms are prepared like tripe. Ovoli or Caesar's mushrooms, as you know, are orange-yellow in color. The youngest ones are closed, and shaped like an egg, while the riper ones are open and flat. For this recipe, select young mushrooms, and after you have cleaned and washed them cut them into thin slices. Cook in butter and season with salt, pepper, and grated Parmesan cheese. They will turn out even better if you add some brown stock.

PETONCIANI (*Eggplant*)

The aubergine or eggplant is not a vegetable to be scorned, for it causes neither flatulence nor indigestion. It is very good in side dishes; even eaten by itself as a vegetable main dish, it is anything but unpleasant, especially the less bitter varieties grown in certain regions.

Small and medium-sized eggplants are preferable to the larger ones, which may be overripe and bitter.

Forty years ago, one hardly saw eggplant or fennel in the markets of Florence; they were considered to be vile because they were foods eaten by Jews. As in other matters of greater moment, here again the Jews show how they have always had a better nose than the Christians.

Fried eggplant can be served as an accompaniment to fried fish dishes; stewed eggplant goes with boiled meats; grilled eggplant goes with steak, milk-fed veal chops, or any roasted meat.

TORTINO DI PETONCIANI
(*Eggplant Casserole*)

Peel 7 or 8 eggplants, cut into thin round slices, and salt them to draw out some of their water. After letting them sit for a few hours, dredge them in flour and fry in oil.

Take an ovenproof platter and layer the slices of eggplant with grated Parmesan cheese and the tomato sauce from the recipe on p. 23, arranging them so that they form a nice mound. Beat an egg with a pinch of salt, one tablespoon of the same tomato sauce, one teaspoon of grated Parmesan, and two teaspoons of bread crumbs, and cover the surface of the mound with this mixture. Place the platter under the lid of a Dutch oven, with fire above, and when the egg mixture has hardened, serve. This dish can be served by itself, as an *entremets*, or accompanied by a meat dish.

The purpose of the egg covering is to give the dish a nicer appearance.

TARTUFI ALLA BOLOGNESE,
CRUDI, ECC.
(*Truffles Bolognese Style, Raw, Etc.*)

The great quarrel between the Blacks and the Whites that prolonged strife in Italy after the devastating struggles between Guelphs and Ghibellines is threatening to erupt again with regard to truffles. But fear not, dear readers, for this time no blood will be shed – the present-day partisans of the black and the white are much more benevolent than the fierce adversaries of yesteryear.

I am a supporter of the whites, and in fact I openly declare and maintain that the black truffle is the worst there is. Other people do not share my opinion; they believe that the black truffle is more fragrant, while the white truffle has a subtler taste. But they are not taking into account the fact that black truffles quickly lose their aroma. The white truffles from Piedmont are universally prized, and the white truffles from Romagna, which grow in sandy soil, are very fragrant, although they taste of garlic. In any case, let us leave the great issue unresolved so that I can tell you how they cook truffles in Bologna, 'Bologna la grassa per chi vi sta, ma non per chi vi passa' (Bologna whose bounty is for those who live there, but not for those just passing through).

After washing the truffles and cleaning them with a little brush dipped in cold water, as is usually done, the Bolognese cut them into very thin slices and arrange them on a tin-lined copper platter in alternating layers with very thin slices of Parmesan cheese; the first layer

51

should be of truffles. They season them with salt, pepper, and a generous amount of their best olive oil. As soon as the truffles start to sizzle, they squeeze a lemon over them and then remove them immediately from the fire. Some people add a few little pieces of butter; but if you do add butter, use only very little, otherwise the dish will turn out too heavy. Truffles are also eaten raw, very thinly sliced and seasoned with salt, pepper, and lemon juice.

They also go well with eggs. Beat the eggs and season them with salt and pepper. Put an appropriate amount of butter on the fire, and when it has melted, pour in the eggs and shortly thereafter the thinly sliced truffles, stirring until cooked.

Everyone knows about the aphrodisiacal properties of this food, so I will refrain from speaking about it, though I could tell some very amusing stories. It seems that truffles were discovered for the first time in the Périgord region of France, under Charles V.

I have preserved truffles for quite a long time, but not always successfully, in this way: sliced very thin, dried over the fire, seasoned with salt and pepper, covered with olive oil and then put on the fire just until the oil is heated through. Raw truffles are sometimes stored in rice to impart their fragrance to the rice.

CIPOLLINE AGRO-DOLCI
(*Sweet-and-Sour Pearl Onions*)

This dish does not require much thinking about, but only good taste, to get the amounts right. When prepared properly, it is an excellent accompaniment for boiled meats.

By pearl onions I mean the white ones that are a little larger than a walnut. Peel them, remove any superfluous parts, and scald in salted water. For about 300 grams (about 10½ ounces) of onions, put 40 grams (about 1⅓ ounces) of sugar in a saucepan on the fire without any water. When the sugar has melted, add 15 grams (about ½ an ounce) of flour. Stir constantly with a wooden spoon, and when the mixture has turned reddish-brown add ⅔ of a glass of vinegar water a little at a time. Let the liquid boil until any lumps that may have formed have dissolved. Then toss in the onions and shake the pan frequently; do not stir them with the spoon, because they will break apart. Taste before serving, because if they need more sugar or vinegar you are still in time to add some.

PISELLI COL PROSCIUTTO
(*Peas with Ham*)

Let's leave to the English the taste for eating boiled vegetables without any seasoning, or at the most with a little butter; we southern types need our food to be a little more exciting.

I have never found peas anywhere as good as the ones they serve in the restaurants of Rome, not so much on account of the excellent quality of the vegetables from that part of the country, but because in Rome they flavor peas with smoked ham. Having experimented a bit trying to discover how they prepare them, I might not have yet fully succeeded in reproducing their delicious flavor, but I am pretty close. Here is how to do it.

Cut in half lengthwise one or two spring onions (depending on the amount of peas), and put them on the fire with oil and a generous amount of untrimmed smoked ham diced into small cubes. Fry lightly until the ham shrinks, then toss in the peas, seasoning them with little or no salt and a pinch of pepper; stir, and finish cooking with broth, adding a little butter.

Serve either alone as a vegetable course, or as a side dish; but first discard all the onion.

PISELLI COLLA CARNESECCA
(*Peas with Bacon*)

Peas are also good prepared in the following way, but, unlike the preceding recipes, this one cannot be said to belong to fine cuisine.

Put on the fire some finely chopped bacon, garlic, parsley, and oil; season with a little salt and pepper, and when the garlic is golden brown, toss in the peas. When they have absorbed all the oil, finish cooking them in broth, or lacking that, in water.

If the pea pods are tender and fresh, they can be cooked in water and passed through a sieve. You thus obtain a purée which, when dissolved in broth, adds a delicate flavor to a vegetable soup or a soup of rice and cabbage. It can also be mixed with the water for risotto with peas (see page 15).

CAVOLFIORE COLLA BALSAMELLA
(*Cauliflower with Béchamel Sauce*)

All members of the cabbage family, be they white, red, yellow, or green, are children or stepchildren of Aeolus, god of the winds. Therefore people who cannot tolerate wind should have no difficulty remembering that these plants are called *crucifers*, since for such people these vegetables are truly a cross to bear. The real reason for the name, however, is that the flowers of these plants have four petals arranged in the shape of a cross.

Remove the leaves and the green stems from a large head of cauliflower, make a deep crosslike cut in the stalk, and cook in salted water. Then cut into small sections and season with butter, salt, and pepper. Place in an ovenproof dish, sprinkling with a little grated Parmesan cheese and covering with béchamel sauce. Cook until the surface is golden brown.

Serve hot as an *entremets*, or better yet accompanied by a stewed meat or boiled chicken.

SPARAGI (*Asparagus*)

To make asparagus look better, before cooking scrape the white part with a knife and cut off the end of the stem; then tie the stalks in bunches – not too large – with a string. To keep them green, drop them into salted water when it is boiling hard, and fan the fire so that the water boils up again immediately. When the spears start to bend, they are cooked just right; still you should check from time to time, testing them with your fingers to see if they give a little when you exert some pressure – it is better to undercook them a little than to overcook them. After you have strained the asparagus spears, drop them in cold water, and then strain them again immediately so that you can serve them warm, the way most people like them.

This vegetable, which is prized not only for its diuretic and digestive qualities, but also for the high price it commands, can be prepared in various ways once it is blanched. The simplest and best is the most common way, which is to season with the very finest olive oil and vinegar or lemon juice. Nevertheless, for variety, here are some other ways to prepare asparagus after it has been parboiled. Place the stalks whole in a pan and sauté lightly in butter. After seasoning with salt, pepper, and a tiny pinch of Parmesan cheese, remove the stalks from the pan and pour the browned butter over them. Or, separate the green part from the white part and, taking an ovenproof dish, arrange them like this: sprinkle the bottom of the dish with grated Parmesan cheese and arrange the asparagus spears next to one another, season with salt, pepper, grated Parmesan, and dabs of butter; make another layer of asparagus and season in the same way, continuing until you have used them all. Be spare with the other ingredients, however, so that the dish does not turn out excessively rich. Crisscross the layers of asparagus like a tight lattice, place under the lid of a

Dutch oven to melt the butter, and serve hot. If you have some brown stock, parboil the asparagus and finish cooking in the stock, adding a little butter and a light sprinkling of Parmesan cheese.

The bad smell that results from eating asparagus can be turned into the pleasant fragrance of violets by pouring a few drops of turpentine into the chamber pot.

Seafood

Of the common types of fish, the finest are: sturgeon, dentex, sea bass, weever, sole, turbot, John Dory, gilt-head sea bream, rock mullet, and fresh-water trout; these are excellent year round, but sole and turbot are especially good in the winter.

The seasons for the other best-known fish are: for hake, eel, and flying squid, year round, while eel is better in winter and flying squid in the summer.

For large gray salt-water mullet, July and August; for small mullet, October and November, and all winter. For gudgeon, whitebait, and cuttlefish, March, April, and May. For octopus, October. For sardines and anchovies, all winter, until April. For red mullet, September and October. For tuna, from March to October. For mackerel, springtime, especially May; this fish, on account of its tough and fibrous flesh, is usually used in stews – if you want to grill it, it is a good idea to put it on the fire on a large sheet of greased cooking paper and season it with oil, salt, pepper, and a few sprigs of rosemary.

Of the crustaceans, one of the most prized is lobster, which is good year round, but better in springtime, and of the shellfish, oysters, which are harvested from October to April in oyster beds.

When a fish is fresh, its eyes are bright and clear; if it is not fresh, the eyes are pale and cloudy. Another indication of freshness is the red color of the gills; but since these can be artificially colored with blood, touch them and then smell your finger; your nose will tell you whether it is fresh or not. Another characteristic of fresh fish is the firmness of the flesh, because if it is kept on ice too long it begins to decay and becomes soft to the touch.

Sailors say that crustaceans and sea urchins are meatier when gathered during a full moon.

CACCIUCCO
(Fish Stew)

Cacciucco! Let me say just a little bit about this word, which is understood perhaps only in Tuscany and on the shores of the Mediterranean, since on the shores of the Adriatic it is called 'brodetto' (literally, 'little broth'). In Florence, 'brodetto' means a soup with bread and broth, bound with beaten eggs and lemon juice. In Italy the confusion between these and other names from province to province is such that it is almost a second Tower of Babel.

After the unification of Italy, it seemed logical to me that we should think about unifying the spoken language, and yet few can be bothered with such an undertaking and many are outright hostile to it, perhaps because of false pride and the ingrained habit that Italians have of speaking their own regional dialect.

To return to cacciucco, let me say that, naturally enough, this is a dish prepared in seaside towns more than anywhere else, because it is there that you can find fresh fish of the kind needed to make it. Any fishmonger can tell you the varieties of fish that are best suited to a good cacciucco.

Good as it may be, however, it is still quite a heavy dish, so one needs to be careful not to gorge oneself on it.

For 700 grams (about 1½ pounds) of fish, finely chop an onion and sauté it with oil, parsley, and two whole cloves of garlic. The moment the onion starts to brown, add 300 grams (about 10½ ounces) of chopped fresh tomatoes or tomato paste, and season with salt and pepper. When the tomatoes are cooked, pour in one finger of strong vinegar or two fingers of weak vinegar, diluted in a large glass of water. Let boil for a few more minutes, then discard the garlic and strain the rest of the ingredients, pressing hard against the mesh. Put the strained sauce back on the fire along with whatever fish you may have on hand, including sole, red mullet, gurnard, dogfish, gudgeon, mantis shrimp, and other types of fish in season, leaving the small fish whole and cutting the big ones into large pieces. Taste for seasoning; but in any case it is not a bad idea to add a little olive oil, since the amount of soffritto was quite small. When the fish is cooked, the cacciucco is usually brought to the table on two separate platters: on one you place the fish, strained from the broth, and on the other you arrange enough finger-thick slices of bread to soak up all the broth. The bread slices should be warmed over the fire but not toasted.

SOGLIOLE IN GRATELLA
(Grilled Sole)

When sole (*Solea vulgaris*) are large, it is better to grill them and season with lard instead of olive oil; they take on a more pleasing flavor this way.

Clean the fish, scrape off the scales, rinse, and dry well. Then dab them lightly with cold virgin lard (making sure that it does not taste rancid); season with salt and pepper and coat with bread crumbs. Melt a little more lard in a frying pan and brush this on the fish; brush again with melted lard when you turn them on the grill.

When you prepare sole for frying, you can skin them on both sides or just on the dark side, then dredge in flour, keeping in beaten egg for several hours before tossing them in the pan.

A singular thing about this fish that merits mentioning is the fact that, like all well-constructed animals, it is born with one eye on its right side and the other on the left. But at a certain period in its life the eye that was on the white (or left) side migrates over to the right side and settles, like the other eye, on the dark side. Sole and turbot swim on their blind sides. Because of the quality and delicacy of its flesh, the French call sole the 'partridge of the sea.' It is a fish that is easy to digest, it resists decomposition better than many other fish, and it does not go out of season. It is found in abundance in the Adriatic, where it is caught at night with huge sack-like nets weighted down heavily at the mouth; when these nets scrape the bottom of the sea, they lift up the fish along with the sand and mud in which they lie.

Turbot, the flesh of which is not very different from that of sole, and is even more delicate, is called the 'pheasant of the sea.'

TRIGLIE COL PROSCIUTTO
(*Red Mullet with Prosciutto*)

The saying 'mute as a fish' is not always true, because red mullet, umber, and some other fish emit odd sounds caused by the vibration of special muscles; these vibrations are increased by the movement of the air in their swimming bladder.

The largest, most flavorful red mullet are rock mullet or striped surf mullet. However, this recipe can also be used for cooking medium-sized red mullet, which are called 'rossioli' or 'barboni' in the regions bordering the Adriatic. After gutting and rinsing the fish, dry them well with a kitchen towel, and then place them in a bowl and season with salt, pepper, oil, and lemon juice. Leave them like this for several hours, and when you are about to cook them, cut thin slices of untrimmed prosciutto. The slices should be as wide as and equal in number to the pieces of fish. Take a metal dish or pan and scatter a few whole sage leaves on the bottom. Coat the fish well in bread crumbs, and arrange them upright side by side with the slices of prosciutto between them, scattering more sage leaves on top.

Finally, pour the remaining liquid over the fish and bake with fire above and below. If you want this dish to turn out more refined, remove the spine from the raw mullet by cutting open the belly side, and then close the fish.

STORIONE (*Sturgeon*)

I hope my readers will allow me to give a little of the history of this very interesting fish.

The sturgeon belongs to the order of the *Ganoidei*, from the Latin *Ganus*, which means shiny, owing to the shine of its scales, and to the sub-order of the *Chondrostei*, since it has a cartilaginous skeleton. It constitutes the family of the *Acipenser*, which is defined by those two characteristic qualities, as well as by a skin made up of five longitudinal series of shiny scales. The mouth of this fish is located on the underside of the head; it has no teeth and is shaped like a protractile suction device, with nasal barbels or tentacles for searching in the mud for its food, which apparently consists of tiny creatures.

Sturgeon are highly prized for their flesh, as well as for their eggs, which are used for caviar, and for their enormous air bladder, which is used to make isinglass or fish glue. In the springtime, they swim upstream in rivers to deposit their eggs in calm waters along the banks.

Italy is home to several species of sturgeon, of which the most highly prized for its food is the *Acipenser sturio* (common sturgeon). It can be recognized by its sharp snout and thick lower lip split in the middle, as well as by its simple nasal tentacles, which are all the same size. It prefers the mouths of the Ticino and Po rivers, where not long ago one weighing 215 kilograms (about 475 pounds) was caught. But the sturgeon that grows largest is the *Acipenser buso*, which can reach up to two meters or more in length, with egg sacs one third the size of the entire fish. It is this fish in particular that provides caviar and gelatin. Caviar is made from the raw eggs of the sturgeon, which are carefully strained through a sieve to remove the filaments that envelop them; they are then salted and tightly packed. Isinglass is made on the beaches of the Caspian Sea and along the banks of the rivers that run into it, but more than anywhere else in Astrakhan. It is hardly surprising that there is such an extraordinary amount of it on the market (since isinglass has many uses), if one considers that sometimes in the Volga from fifteen to twenty thousand sturgeon are caught daily; for it is from there – that is, the southern regions of Russia – that we get caviar. It was announced not long ago that some fishermen on the Danube caught a sturgeon weighing 800 kilograms (about 1,950 pounds). The skeleton of this enormous fish, 3.3 meters (about 11 feet) long, is now on display at the Museum of Vienna.

The extinct species of sturgeon include the *Magadictis*, which reached a length of 10 to 20 meters (about 33 to 34 feet).

PASTICCIO DI MAGRO
(Seafood Pie)

I would be failing to give credit where it is due if I didn't tell you that I owe quite a few recipes in this book to the kindness of several ladies, who also favored me with this one. Although it looks like a true pasticcio, when I tried it, it came out worthy to be served at a dinner party, if prepared properly.

a fish weighing between 300 and 350 grams (between
    about 10½ and 12¼ ounces)
200 grams (about 7 ounces) of rice
150 grams (about 5¼ ounces) of fresh mushrooms
300 grams (about 10½ ounces) of green peas
50 grams (about 1⅔ ounces) of toasted pine nuts
butter, as needed
Parmesan cheese
6 artichokes
2 eggs

Cook the rice in 40 grams (about 1⅓ ounces) of butter
with a quarter of a chopped onion and salt it. When it
has cooked in the necessary amount of water, bind it
with the two eggs and 30 grams (about 1 ounce) of Parmesan cheese.

Make a soffritto of onion, butter, celery, carrot, and
parsley, and cook the sliced mushrooms, peas, and parboiled quartered artichokes in it. Finish cooking these
ingredients with a few tablespoons of hot water and season with salt, pepper, and 50 grams (about 1⅔ ounces) of
grated Parmesan cheese after you remove it from the fire.

Cook the fish, which can be mullet, weever, or some
other large fish, in a mixture of oil, garlic, parsley, and
tomato sauce or tomato paste; season with salt and pepper. Remove the fish from the fire, strain the sauce, and
stir in the pine nuts, which you have toasted and
crushed. Remove the head, spine, and bones from the
fish, cut it into small pieces, put it back in the broth,
and add all the other ingredients except the rice.

Now that all the ingredients for the filling are ready,

make the dough for the pie to contain it. Here are the proportions:

400 grams (about 14 ounces) of flour
80 grams (about 2⅔ ounces) of butter
2 eggs
2 tablespoons of white wine or Marsala
a pinch of salt

Roll out the dough and use it to line a mold greased with butter. Pour in first half of the rice, then all the filling, and finally the remaining rice over the filling; cover the top with more of the same dough. Bake in the oven, remove from the mold, and serve lukewarm or cold.

Made with the amounts indicated, this recipe serves twelve people.

ARINGA INGENTILITA
(*'Civilized' Herring*)

All you drinkers out there can put your forks down; this herring (*Clupea harengus*) is not for your jaded palates.

Ordinarily, people want the female herring because it is showier on account of the large amount of eggs; but the male, with its milky sperm sac, is more delicate and therefore preferable. Whether male or female, open the herring along the back, discard the head, and flatten it; then place it in scalded milk and let it sit for eight to ten hours. It would be well to change the milk once during this time. After drying it with a kitchen towel, cook on the grill like ordinary herring and season with oil and a very small amount of vinegar, or with oil and lemon juice if you prefer.

There is also another way to remove the salty flavor from herring. Place it on the fire in cold water, bring to a boil and simmer for three minutes, and then soak in cool water for a moment. Dry, discard the head, open along the back, and season as above.

Clupea harengus is the most common variety of the very important family of the *Clupeidae*, which also includes allice shad, pilchards, anchovies, sardines, and the *Alosa vulgaris*, or *Clupea comune*, which is called 'cheppia' ('shad') in Tuscany. In the spring, they swim upriver to deposit their eggs; at this time they are caught even in the Arno River in Florence.

Herring live in huge numbers at the bottom of the seas at the outer reaches of Europe, and are seen on the surface only at mating time – that is, during the months of April, May, and June. After they deposit their eggs they disappear into the depths of their usual abode. Sometimes the sea appears shimmering and translucent for several miles around because of the frenzy of the spawn and the scales that come loose during it. In England the herring run from July to September; the catch, done with round nets, is at times so abundant that on the shores of Yarmouth they have filled as many as five hundred thousand barrels with herrings.

BACCALÀ ALLA FIORENTINA
(*Salt Cod Florentine Style*)

'Baccalà' belong to the family of *Gadidae*, the most typical variety being cod. The most common species in our seas are the *Gadus minutus* and the *Merlucius esculentus* or hake, quite a bland fish but one that is easy to digest on account of its light flesh. It is good for convalescents, especially when poached and seasoned with oil and lemon juice.

The genus *Gadus morrhua* is the cod from the Arctic and Antarctic regions which, depending upon how it is prepared, is called either 'baccalà' (salt cod) or 'stocca-fisso' (stockfish). As everyone knows, an oil used for medicinal purposes is extracted from the liver of this fish. It is fished with a hook; a single man can catch up to 500 in one day. It is perhaps the most fecund of all fish – nine million eggs have been counted in a single individual.

There are two well-known types of cod on the market, Gaspé and Labrador. The former comes from the Gaspé Peninsula, that is the Banks of Newfoundland (where every year more than 100 million kilograms of cod are caught); it is dry, tough, and difficult to soften. The latter, which is caught along the coast of Labrador, is fat and tender, perhaps on account of a more copious food supply; it softens easily and is much better tasting.

Salt cod enjoys a good reputation in Florence, and deservedly so, because the Florentines know how to soften it well, cleaning it frequently with a little hard brush. Moreover, the cod consumed in Florence is usually the best Labrador cod, which is fatty by nature and relatively tender, considering the tough, fibrous flesh of this type of fish, which is not suited to weak stomachs. For this reason, I have never been able to digest it. On days of fasting, this salted fish competes on the market to great advantage with fresh fish, which is limited in quantity, high in price, and often not particularly fresh.

Cut the salt cod into pieces as wide as the palm of your hand and coat thoroughly with flour. Then put a large pan on the fire with a generous amount of oil and two or three whole garlic cloves, slightly crushed. When the garlic begins to brown, toss in the pieces of cod and brown on both sides, moving the fish around constantly to keep it from sticking. It is not necessary to add salt, or if you do, very little and only after tasting; but a pinch of pepper will not do any harm. At the end, pour in a few tablespoons of tomato sauce (see page 21), or tomato paste diluted in water. Boil a little longer and serve.

BACCALÀ FRITTO
(*Fried Salt Cod*)

The frying pan is an implement used for many lovely things in the kitchen; but, in my opinion, salt cod comes to a most deplorable end in it. This is because, since it has to be boiled first and then coated with batter, there is no seasoning that can give it a proper flavor. And yet some people, perhaps not knowing a better recipe, make the concoction that I am about to describe. To boil it, put it on the fire in cold water, and the moment it starts to boil, take it off the hearth, for it is already cooked. Without doing anything else, it can be eaten like this, seasoned with oil and vinegar.

But let's return to the concoction I mentioned. Feel free to try it, or to send both the recipe and whoever wrote it to the devil. After you have boiled the cod, marinate it whole in red wine for several hours; then

69

dry it with a kitchen towel and cut it into small pieces, removing the spine and bones. Coat lightly with flour and dip in a simple batter made with water, flour, and a drop of oil, with no salt. Fry in oil and sprinkle with sugar after it has stopped sizzling. If eaten hot, the aroma of the wine is barely noticeable. If, however, you still find this to be an inferior dish, it is your fault for wanting to try it.

Roasted Meats

With the exception of birds and squabs, with which whole sage leaves go well, it is no longer customary to lard or baste spit-roasted meats, or to stud them with garlic, rosemary, or other aromatic herbs that tend to leave an aftertaste. If you have some good olive oil, baste them with that; otherwise, use lard or butter, depending on local preference.

People generally prefer roasted meats savory, so be generous with salt when you prepare milk-fed veal, lamb, kid, poultry, and pork. Be more sparing with meat from larger or older animals and with birds, because these meats are already quite flavorful in themselves. But always salt meat halfway or even two-thirds of the way through the cooking. People who salt any kind of meat before putting it on the spit are making a serious mistake, because the fire will dry it out and make it tough.

Pork and the meat of nursing animals such as veal, lamb, kid, and the like, should be cooked well in order to dry out their excessive moisture. Cook beef and mutton much less; being dry meats, you want them to remain juicy. Cook birds over a flame, but be careful not to overdo them, for they would lose a great deal of their fragrance. But take care that birds are not undercooked when you want to remove them from the fire; you can test for this by pricking them under the wing to check whether any blood still runs out. You can tell whether chickens are done by pricking them in the same way.

Poultry will come out more tender and with a better color if you roast it wrapped in paper that has been buttered on the side touching the meat; to prevent the paper from burning, baste it frequently on the outside. Halfway through the cooking, remove the paper and finish cooking the chicken, turkey, or what have you, salting and basting it. If you use this method, it is also a good idea to put a little salt inside the bird before putting it on the spit, and to stud the breast of turkeys and guinea fowl with lardoons. I should point out here that squab and fattened capon, whether roasted or boiled, are better eaten cold than hot; they also have less of an aftertaste when eaten cold.

More than any other way of preparing meats, roasting preserves their nourishing properties, and makes them easier to digest.

ROAST BEEF

This English word has come into Italian as 'rosbiffe' and it means exactly what it says. A good roast beef is a very satisfying dish at a meal where the male gender predominates, since men are not satisfied with trifles the way women are. They want to sink their teeth into something solid and substantial.

The best cut for roast beef is the loin. In order to turn out tender, it should be from a young animal. It should weigh more than 1 kilogram (about 2 pounds) so that the fire will not dry it out, for the beauty and succulence of this dish depend on it being cooked just right, as is shown by a pink color on the inside and the copious juice that runs out when you slice it. Cook over a very hot fire from the start, so that the outer surface cooks quickly; baste with oil, which you will later drain from the dripping pan, and at the end pour a ladleful of broth over it; this, along with the fat that has dripped from the meat, will provide the sauce that you serve with the roast. At the halfway point, salt sparingly, because this type of meat is savory by itself, as I have already said. Always remember that salt, which is good in itself, is the worst enemy of good cooking when used to excess.

Put the meat on the spit half an hour before you serve the first course; this should be sufficient if the piece is not too large. To test for doneness, prick it at the thickest part with a thin larding needle, but do not make too many holes in it, or it will dry out. The juice that runs out should not be blood colored, nor too dark. Pan fry some raw, peeled potatoes in oil to serve as a side dish. If they are small, leave them whole; if large, cut into quarters.

Roast beef can also be made in the oven, but it doesn't come out as well as when cooked on a spit. If you make it in the oven, season with salt, oil, and a bit of butter, surround it with raw, peeled potatoes, and pour a glassful of water into the roasting pan.

If you do not like leftover roast beef cold, slice it and sauté in butter and brown stock or tomato sauce (see page 21).

POLLO AL DIAVOLO
(*Chicken Devil Style*)

It is called this because it is supposed to be seasoned with strong cayenne pepper and served with a very spicy sauce, so that whoever eats it feels his mouth on fire and is tempted to send both the chicken and whoever cooked it to the devil. I shall give a simpler, more civilized way to prepare it.

Take a cockerel or young chicken, remove the head, neck and feet, and, after cutting it open all the way down the front, flatten it out as much as you can. Wash and dry it well with a kitchen towel, then place it on the grill. When it begins to brown, turn it over, brush with melted butter or olive oil and season with salt and pepper. When the other side begins to brown, turn the chicken over again and repeat the procedure. Continue to baste and season as necessary until done.

Cayenne pepper is sold as a red powder, which comes from England in little glass bottles.

GALLINA DI FARAONE
(*Guinea Hen*)

This fowl, originally from Numidia and therefore erroneously called Indian hen, was a symbol of brotherly love in ancient times. When Meleager, king of Calydon, died, his sisters mourned him so deeply that Diana transformed them into guinea hens. The *Numida meleagris*, which is the domestic guinea hen, is still half wild, unfriendly and restless; it resembles the partridge both in its habits and in the flavor of its delicate flesh. Poor creatures, they are so pretty! They are usually killed by cutting their throats, although some people prefer to drown them, keeping them under water by force – a cruel practice, like so many others invented by the gluttony of man. The meat of this bird needs to ripen for quite some time; during the winter, it will keep ungutted for at least five or six days.

> The best way to cook guinea hens is to roast them on a spit. Place a ball of butter rolled in salt inside the bird, stud the breast with lardoons, and wrap in a sheet of paper greased with cold butter and sprinkled with salt. Remove the paper when the bird is two-thirds cooked; then brown it over the flame until done, basting with oil and salting it again.
>
> A young turkey can be cooked in the same way.

Pastries, Cakes, and Sweets

STRUDEL

Do not be alarmed if this dessert seems to you to be a strange concoction, or if it looks like some ugly creature such as a giant leech or a shapeless snake after you cook it; you will like the way it tastes.

500 grams (about 1 pound) of reinette apples, or tender,
*   good quality apples*
250 grams (about 8⅘ ounces) of flour
100 grams (about 3½ ounces) butter
85 grams (about 3 ounces) of dried currants
85 grams (about 3 ounces) of powdered sugar
grated rind of one lemon
2 or 3 pinches of ground cinnamon

Make a fairly firm dough with the flour, warm milk, a piece of butter about the size of a walnut, an egg, and a pinch of salt. Allow the dough to rest a little before using it, then roll it out in a sheet as thin as the one for taglierini noodles. Cover the sheet of dough with a layer of apples (peeled, cored and thinly sliced), leaving the edges free. Scatter the currants, lemon peel, cinnamon, sugar, and finally the 100 grams (about 3½ ounces) of melted butter over the layer of apple slices. Reserve a little of the butter to use later. This done, roll the sheet of dough up so that if forms a nice cylinder of dough and filling, which you will fit into a round copper pan greased with butter. Pour the leftover melted butter all over the outside of the roll, and place it in the oven. Remember that dried currants or sultanas are different from raisins, which are small and dark. Currants and sultanas are twice as large, light brown in color, and seedless. Scrape the lemon peel with a piece of glass.

BISCOTTI DELLA SALUTE
(Health Cookies)

Cheer up, for if you eat these cookies you will never die, or you will live as long as Methuselah. I eat them often, in fact, and when some indiscreet person sees me more sprightly than is becoming to my venerable age and asks me how old I am, I answer that I am as old as Methuselah, son of Enoch.

350 grams (about 12⅓ ounces) of flour
100 grams (about 3½ ounces) of brown sugar
50 grams (about 1⅔ ounces) of butter
10 grams (about ⅓ of an ounce) of cream of tartar
5 grams (about ⅕ of an ounce) of baking soda
2 eggs
a dash of vanilla sugar
milk, as needed

Mix the flour with the sugar and make a mound with a hole in the middle where you will drop the rest of the ingredients, adding a little milk to obtain a rather soft dough. Shape the dough in a slightly flattened cylinder about half a meter long. Grease a baking pan with butter, and divide the loaf into two parts so that it will fit in the pan. Make sure that the two parts are well separated, because they swell a great deal when baked. Bake in an oven or a Dutch oven. The next day, cut the loaves into cookies, which should number about thirty or so, and toast in the oven.

PASTA MARGHERITA
(Sponge Cake)

One day my dear departed friend Antonio Mattei from the town of Prato (of whom I will have occasion to speak again) tasted this pastry at my house and asked for the recipe. Being an industrious man, it didn't take him long to refine and perfect the recipe and begin to sell it in his shop. Later he told me that the success of this sweet was so great that hardly a dinner was given in Prato without it being ordered. People wishing to make their way in the world are quick to grasp any opportunity to seduce Lady Fortune, who – though capricious in how she dispenses her favors – is never a friend to the idle and lazy.

120 grams (about 4¼ ounces) of potato flour
120 grams (about 4¼ ounces) of powdered sugar
4 eggs
the juice of one lemon

First, thoroughly beat the egg yolks and the sugar. Add the flour and lemon juice and work for more than half an hour. Lastly, beat the egg whites and fold them into the rest of the ingredients; but do so gently, so that they don't go flat. Pour the mixture into a smooth round mold or an appropriately sized baking pan, greased with butter and dusted with confectioners' sugar mixed with flour, and place immediately in the oven. Let cool, then remove from the mold and sprinkle with vanilla confectioners' sugar.

STIACCIATA UNTA
(*Greased Flat Cake*)

The portions for this cake and for the Mantuan cake were recommended to me by that good man, the late Antonio Mattei of Prato, whom I've already mentioned earlier. I say 'good' because he was a genius in his art and was an honest, very industrious man. But this dear friend of mine, who always reminded me of Boccaccio's character Cisti the baker, died in the year 1885, leaving me deeply grieved. Letters and science aren't always necessary to win public esteem; even a very humble art, accompanied by a kind heart and practiced with skill and decorum, can make us worthy of the respect and love of our fellow men.

> *Beneath rough manners and humble exteriors*
> *often lie noble hearts and pure souls;*
> *we should be wary of men who are too genteel,*
> *for they are like marble: shiny, smooth, and hard.*

But let's get to the point:

700 grams (about 1½ pounds) of leaven dough
120 grams (about 4¼ ounces) of lard

100 grams (about 3½ ounces) of sugar
60 grams (about 2 ounces) of cracklings
4 egg yolks
a pinch of salt
orange or lemon zest

Knead the dough gently so that it doesn't lose its elasticity. If you make it in the evening and set it aside in a warm place, it will rise by itself; if you make it in the morning, it will need three hours in an earthenware warming oven.

If you want to make it without cracklings, add two more egg yolks and 30 more grams of lard.

Half of this recipe will serve five or six people.

PANETTONE MARIETTA
(Marietta's Panettone)

My Marietta is a good cook, and such a good-hearted, honest woman that she deserves to have this cake named after her, especially since she taught me how to make it.

300 grams (about 10½ ounces) of extra-fine flour
100 grams (about 3½ ounces) of butter
80 grams (about 2⅔ ounces) of sugar
80 grams (about 2⅔ ounces) of sultanas
one whole egg and two yolks
a pinch of salt
10 grams (about ⅓ of an ounce) of cream of tartar
a teaspoon or 5 scant grams (about ⅕ of an ounce) of baking soda

20 grams (about ⅔ of an ounce) of candied fruit, in tiny pieces
lemon zest
about 2 deciliters (about ⅘ of a cup) of milk

In wintertime, soften the butter in *bain-marie* and then blend it with the eggs. Add the flour and milk a little at a time, then the rest of the ingredients except the sultanas, cream of tartar, and baking soda, which you should keep for the last. But before adding them, work the mixture for at least half an hour and dilute it with the milk until it's the right consistency – not too liquid, and not too firm. Pour into a mold twice as large as the amount of batter, deeper than it is wide, so that when it rises it doesn't overflow, and it will come out in the shape of a round loaf. Grease the sides of the mold with butter, dust with powdered sugar mixed with flour, and bake in the oven. If it turns out right, it should rise a great deal, and have a puffed-up, dome-shaped top with cracks in it. This panettone is worth trying, because it's much better than the Milanese-style panettone that's sold commercially, and isn't much trouble to make.

OFFELLE DI MARMELLATA
(*Scalloped Sweet Pastries with Fruit Filling*)

The word 'offella,' in this context, comes from the dialect of Romagna, and, if I'm not mistaken, it is used in the Lombard dialect as well. It probably derives from the ancient word *offa*, which means a flat cake or bread made with spelt and various other ingredients.

Dar l'offa al cerbero, 'to give Cerberus a sop,' is a rather timely expression, since there are so many people these days who seek out public office so that they can gorge themselves on public funds. But we'd better get back to offelle.

500 grams (about 1 pound) of red apples
125 grams (about 4½ ounces) of powdered sugar
30 grams (about 1 ounce) of candied fruit
two teaspoons cinnamon powder

Cut the apples into four sections, peel, and core. Slice the sections as thin as possible and put in a saucepan on the fire with two glasses of water; break apart with a wooden spoon. Since these apples have firm flesh, they need to be cooked in water; if they start to dry out while you're cooking them, just add some more water. Wait until the apples have become mushy before adding the sugar, and then taste to see if they're sweet enough, since fruit in general can be more or less acid, depending upon how ripe it is. Lastly, add the candied fruit, chopped into small pieces, and the cinnamon.

Use shortcrust pastry dough. Spread it out with a rolling pin until it's the thickness of a coin. Then cut it with a round pastry cutter with a scalloped edge. With one disk of dough underneath and one on top (the latter rolled with a ridged rolling pin), put the cooked apple mixture in the middle and moisten the edges so that the two disks of dough stick together. Gild with egg yolk, and bake. Afterward, sprinkle with confectioners' sugar.

CAVALLUCCI DI SIENA
(*Sienese 'Little Horses'*)

The specialty sweets of Siena are panforte, ricciarelli, cavallucci, and cupate. Cavallucci are little pastries shaped liked mostaccioli. You can see that they have nothing to do with horses, and I don't think that they even know why they're called that in Siena, a city, as the saying goes, *where three things abound: towers, bells, and quintains.*

In this recipe I want to give you a close, but not exact imitation of Sienese cavallucci – we've got the flavor just about right, but the consistency leaves something to be desired, which is only natural. When something is made in large quantities and with methods that are kept secret from the uninitiated, any imitation is bound to falter.

> *300 grams (about 10½ ounces) of flour*
> *300 grams (about 10½ ounces) of blond sugar*
> *100 grams (about 3½ ounces) of shelled walnuts*
> *50 grams (about 1⅔ ounces) of candied orange*
> *15 grams (about ½ of an ounce) of aniseed*
> *5 grams (about ⅕ of an ounce) of spices and cinnamon powder*

Chop the walnuts into pieces about the size of beans. Dice the candied orange. Put the sugar on the fire with a third of its weight in water, and when it has reached the point where it threads from the spoon, add all of the other ingredients and blend. Pour the hot mixture over the flour on a pastry board – but to do this, you'll see that you'll need more flour to give the dough the right consistency. Then form the cavallucci, of which, with these amounts, you should get more than 40. Since the dough is quite sticky on account of the sugar, dust the cookies all over with flour. Place in a baking pan and bake them plain, at moderate heat. Be very careful when you cook the sugar, because it will turn dark if it cooks too much. Pick up a drop between your thumb and index finger, and if it starts to form a thread, it's cooked enough for this recipe.

FAVE ALLA ROMANA O DEI MORTI
(*Roman-Style Sweet Fava Beans, or Dead Men's Beans*)

These sweets are usually made for the Day of the Dead, and they take the place of the *baggiana*, the garden-variety fava bean, which is typically cooked in water with a ham bone for this occasion. This custom must have originated in antiquity, since the fava bean was used as an offering to the Fates, Pluto, and Persephone, and was famous for the superstitious ceremonies in which it was used. The ancient Egyptians abstained from eating the fava; they didn't plant it, nor did they touch it with their hands. Their priests wouldn't even dare to look upon it, deeming it a vile thing. Fava beans, especially black favas, were used as a funeral offering because it was believed that they contained the souls of the dead, and were similar to the gates of Hell.

During the feasts of the *Lemures*, people would spit out black fava beans while beating a copper pot, to chase out of their homes the spirits of their ancestors, the souls of the departed, and the infernal deities.

Festus claimed that there was a funereal sign on the flowers of this legume; and they say that the custom of offering fava beans to the dead was one of the reasons that Pythagoras ordered his students to abstain from eating them; another reason was to prevent them from getting involved in government affairs, since fava beans were used for balloting in elections.

There are several ways to make sweet favas. Here are three different recipes: the first two are family style; the third is more refined.

First recipe

200 grams (about 7 ounces) of flour
100 grams (about 3½ ounces) of sugar
100 grams (about 3½ ounces) of sweet almonds
30 grams (about 1 ounce) of butter
1 egg
a dash of lemon zest, or cinnamon, or orange-flower water

Second recipe

200 grams (about 7 ounces) of sweet almonds
100 grams (about 3½ ounces) of flour
100 grams (about 3½ ounces) of sugar
30 grams (about 1 ounce) of butter
1 egg
flavoring, as above

Third recipe

200 grams (about 7 ounces) of sweet almonds
200 grams (about 7 ounces) of confectioners' sugar
2 egg whites
lemon zest or other flavoring

For the first two recipes, blanch the almonds and crush them with the sugar until they are half as big as a grain of rice. Put them in the middle of the flour along with the other ingredients, and make a soft dough using as much rosolio or brandy as necessary. Then make the dough into small pastries shaped like large fava beans; you should get 60 or 70 for each recipe. Arrange in a baking pan greased with lard or butter and dusted with flour; gild with egg yolk. Bake in the oven or Dutch oven. Remember that since they are so small, they bake very quickly. For the third recipe, dry the almonds in the sun or on the fire and crush them very fine in a mortar, adding the egg whites a little at a time. Lastly, add the sugar and, using your hand, mix together. Pour the dough onto a pastry board over a thin layer of flour. Shape into a long roll and cut it into forty or more pieces. Shape like fava beans and bake as in the preceding recipes.

BRIGIDINI (*Brigettine Cookies*)

This is a sweet, or rather an amusing treat local to Tuscany, where it can be found at all the country fairs and festivals. You can see it being cooked in the open air in waffle irons.

2 eggs
120 grams (about 4¼ ounces) of sugar
10 grams (about ⅓ of an ounce) of aniseed
a pinch of salt
flour, as much as needed

Prepare a rather firm dough, kneading it on a pastry board, and shape into nut-sized nuggets which you will place in a waffle iron at an appropriate distance from one another. Turn the iron this way and that over a wood fire, and remove when brown.

Cakes and Spoon Desserts

Not to boast unduly, but to amuse the reader and satisfy the wish of an anonymous admirer, I here publish the following letter, which reached me on July 14, 1906 from Portoferraio, as I was correcting the galley proofs of *Science in the Kitchen and the Art of Eating Well.*

Esteemed Mr. Artusi,

A poet gave me as a gift your lovely book *La scienza in cucina*, adding a few lines of verse, which I transcribe below. Perhaps they may be of use if you print another edition, which I hope you will do in the very near future.

Della salute è questo il breviario,
L'apoteosi è qui della papilla:
L'uom mercé sua può viver centenario
Centellando la vita a stilla a stilla.
Il solo gaudio uman (gli altri son giuochi)
Dio lo commmise alla virtù de' cuochi;
Onde sè stesso ogni infelice accusi
Che non ha in casa il libro dell'Artusi;
E dieci volte un asino si chiami
Se a mente non ne sa tutti i dettami.

Un ammiratore

(This little manual is about health and well-being,
a true apotheosis of the taste buds,

Thanks to which a man can live a hundred years
Sipping life to the fullest drop by drop.
The only joy people have (the rest are a mockery)
God entrusted to the talent of cooks;
So that you have only yourself to blame
If you do not have *Artusi* on your shelves;
And you should call yourself an ass ten times over
If you have not learnt his precepts by heart.

                                                    An Admirer)

TORTA DI PATATE (*Potato Cake*)

Although we are dealing with the humble potato here, do not scoff at this cake, which is worth making. And if your dinner guests cannot detect the plebeian origins of this cake when they taste it, conceal it from them, for they would only scoff.

Many people eat more with their imagination than with their palate. Accordingly, never mention, at least until your guests have finished eating and digesting what you have served them, foods that are considered inferior for the sole reason that they are inexpensive or because they evoke associations that some people might find distasteful. Yet these very foods, when used well and handled correctly, make for good, tasty dishes. Let me now tell you a story on the subject. Once I found myself invited to dine with some close friends. Our host, to impress us, made a little joke about the roast he was serving, for he remarked: 'None of you can complain about the way I am treating you today: we have three different varieties of roast meat: milk-fed veal, chicken and rabbit.' At the word 'rabbit' some of the guests turned up their noses, others seemed dumbfounded, and someone, a close friend of the family, said: 'What on earth did you decide to feed us! At least you could have kept quiet. You've made me lose my appetite.'

At another dinner party, when by chance the conversation turned to 'porchetta' – a suckling pig of 50 to 60 kilograms (about 110 to 132 pounds), stuffed with spices and roasted whole on a spit – one lady cried out, 'If I were offered such filth to eat, I could not possibly do it!' The host, stung by the aspersion she had cast on a dish that was held in high esteem in his part of the country, invited the woman a second time to his house, when he prepared a lovely cut of lean porchetta. She not only ate it but, believing it was milk-fed veal, thought that the roast tasted delicious. I could tell you many similar tales; but I cannot pass over in silence the case of a certain gentleman who, finding a particular pie quite delicious, ate enough for two days. But when he discovered that the pie was made of pumpkin, not only did he never eat it again, but he would also give it such a sinister look you would have thought the pie had seriously offended him.

Now here is the recipe for potato cake.

700 grams (about 1½ pounds) of big starchy potatoes
150 grams (about 5¼ ounces) of sugar
70 grams (about 2⅓ ounces) of sweet almonds and 3 bitter
    almonds
5 eggs
30 grams (about 1 ounce) of butter

a pinch of salt
a dash of lemon peel

Boil the potatoes (or better yet, steam them). Peel and purée, passing them through a strainer while they are still hot. Blanch the almonds and crush in a mortar together with the sugar, until you have a very fine paste. Then add this mixture and all the other ingredients to the potatoes, stirring everything with a wooden spoon for a whole hour, breaking in the eggs one at a time, and then pouring in the melted butter. Place the mixture in a baking pan greased with butter or lard and dusted with bread crumbs. Bake in the oven and serve cold.

* * *

If I were not afraid of annoying the reader, here would be an opportune moment for another digression on German cooking.

As long as I live, I will never forget the array of foods spread out on a big hotel's buffet at the spa town of Levico. From the fried foods and the boiled dishes, all the way to the roasts, all swam in gallons of the same sauce, that always tasted and smelled alike, with what delight to the stomach you can just imagine. And just to add to the torture, very often these dishes were served accompanied by a timbale of angel hair pasta – angel hair, you understand, the thinnest pasta on the planet! – which when prepared in this way must suffer a doubly long cooking time: a bloody mess.

How utterly at odds with our Italian way of doing things! My cook has standing orders to remove angel hair from the water when it has barely begun to boil, and I am already waiting at the table.

Italian cuisine can rival the French, and in some respects actually surpasses it. However, due to the hordes of invading foreigners who bring us, apparently, about 300 million lire annually and, according to rough calculations, an extra 200 million lire in gold during the Jubilee Year of 1900, our cuisine is slowly beginning to lose its special character in the swirl of wandering nations. These unfortunate changes to our diet have already begun to appear, particularly in the large cities and in those areas heavily frequented by foreigners. I recently became convinced of this on a trip to Pompeii, where my traveling companion and I were preceded into a restaurant by a group of German tourists, both male and female, and were served in the same fashion as they were. When the proprietor later came up and courteously asked how we liked our dinners, I took the liberty of commenting on the nauseating slop of seasonings we had just been served. He replied, 'Our cooking has to please these foreigners, since this is how we make our living.' Perhaps this is the same reason Bolognese cuisine has begun to change, as I have heard, and no longer deserves the reputation it once had.

TORTA TEDESCA (*German Cake*)

Our grandfathers used to tell how toward the end of the 1700s, when the Germans invaded our country, there was still something uncivilized in their customs. For example, they used to provoke everyone's horror by preparing broth with tallow candles that they plunged in a pot of boiling water, then squeezing out the wicks. But when, unfortunately, they descended on us again in 1849, they appeared much more civilized. Then tallow could only be seen on Croat militiamen's long mustachios, which were smeared with it so that they could be twisted and their tips rolled to finger-length points that stood up straight and stiff. Nonetheless, from what visitors to that country tell me, tallow has kept a place in German cooking, a cuisine which Italians find in the worst possible taste and positively nauseating, as it uses all manner of fat and makes slop-like soups utterly lacking in flavor.

On the other hand, however, everybody agrees Germans can make delicious desserts. You personally, dear reader, may judge for yourself the truth of this assertion, both from the cake I am about to describe, as well as from some of the other desserts born in Germany that I have offered you in this treatise of mine.

250 grams (about 8⅘ ounces) of sugar
125 grams (about 4½ ounces) of flour
125 grams (about 4½ ounces) of sweet almonds
100 grams (about 3½ ounces) of butter
15 grams (about ½ an ounce) of cream of tartar
5 grams (about ⅕ of an ounce) of baking soda
8 egg yolks
5 egg whites
a dash of vanilla

Blanch the almonds, dry them well in the sun or on the fire, and then crush in a mortar until very fine, adding one of the egg whites. Beat the butter alone with a wooden spoon; in wintertime soften it a little first in *bain-marie*. Add the egg yolks one at a time, then the sugar and blend everything well for at least half an hour. Then add the almonds to the mixture and stir some more. Then fold in the four egg whites (beaten until stiff) and the flour, which you will sift on top of the mixture, stirring gently. Add the cream of tartar and the baking soda at the last, as they will make the cake lighter and softer. Bake in a baking pan well greased with cold butter and lightly dusted with confectioners' sugar and flour. The pan should not be too full.

The only way to blend the almonds satisfactorily into the mixture is to pour a portion of the mixture into the mortar over the almonds and then crush with the pestle.

Now that you have made the cloak, it is time to fashion the hood, which is a light icing that you spread on top of the cake. Here is what you will need:

100 grams (about 3½ ounces) of butter
100 grams (about 3½ ounces) of confectioners' sugar
30 grams (about 1 ounce) of finely ground coffee

Bring the ground coffee to a boil in very little water until you get just two or three tablespoons of clear but very strong coffee. Beat the butter for half an hour (in wintertime softening it first in *bain-marie*), turning the spoon always in the same direction. Add the sugar and stir some more. Finally mix in the coffee a little at a time, in half teaspoons. Stop when you can clearly taste the coffee flavor. Pour this mixture over the cake after it has cooled, and spread it out evenly with a table knife. To make it uniform and smooth, pass a hot spatula just above the icing.

Normally, this very delicately flavored icing should have the color of *café-au-lait*. If you like, instead of coffee you can use melted chocolate.

DOLCE ROMA (*Rome Cake*)

A gentleman whom I do not have the pleasure of knowing personally kindly sent me this recipe from Rome, and I am very grateful to him for it for two reasons: first because this is a dessert of very elegant appearance and flavor, and second because he described it in such a way that I had no difficulty at all testing the recipe. One thing was missing, however, and that was a name for it, since it had none. Thus, considering the nobility of its provenance, I felt it my duty to associate this dessert with Turin Cake and Florence Cake, naming it after the city that one day will be as famous in the world as it once was in Antiquity.

Select quality apples, not too ripe and of average size. Weigh out 600 grams (about 1⅓ of a pound), which should amount to no more than five or six apples. Remove the cores with a hollow tin corer, and peel. Then cook in 2 deciliters (about ⅘ of a cup) of white wine and 130 grams (about 4½ ounces) of sugar, taking care not to break the apples when you turn them as they cook, and not to overcook them. When done, remove them from the pot and arrange them upright in a platter nice enough to use for serving but ovenproof as well. Pour over them a custard made of the following ingredients:

4 deciliters (about 1⅔ cups) of milk
3 egg yolks
70 grams (about 2⅓ ounces) of sugar
20 grams (about ⅔ of an ounce) of flour
a dash of vanilla sugar

Now whisk the three remaining egg whites. When they are quite stiff, add 20 grams (about ⅔ of an ounce) of confectioners' sugar and cover the custard with it. Then place the cake in a Dutch oven or on the stove under the lid of the Dutch oven, with fire above and a low fire below, to brown the surface of the cake. Before serving, dab the cake with the thick syrup left over from cooking the apples, using a baker's brush.

This recipe serves seven to eight people.

BUDINO DI FARINA DI RISO
(Rice Flour Pudding)

This very simple dessert possesses, in my opinion, a very delicate flavor, and although almost everyone has tried it at one time or another, it would not hurt to learn the exact ingredients and quantities, which I think should not be increased or decreased.

1 liter (about 1 quart) of milk
200 grams (about 7 ounces) of rice flour

120 grams (about 4¼ ounces) of sugar
20 grams (about ⅔ of an ounce) of butter
6 eggs
a pinch of salt
a dash of vanilla

First, dissolve the rice flour in a fourth of the cold milk; then put on the fire. When the mixture starts to boil, add a little more warm milk, and finally pour in the rest of the milk when it is at a full boil. This is to prevent lumps from forming. When cooked, add the sugar, the butter and the salt. Remove from the fire and wait until lukewarm before folding in the eggs and the vanilla. Now bake the pudding and serve hot.

This recipe, which in all likelihood is not very old, makes me think that dishes, too, are subject to fashions, and that tastes change in accordance with progress and civilization. Now we prize light cuisine and dishes that are pleasing to the eye, and perhaps there will come a time when many of the dishes I consider good will be replaced by others even better. The sweet, heavy wines of an earlier era have given way to the dry, full-bodied vintages of today; the baked goose stuffed with garlic and quinces, regarded as a delicacy in 1300, has been replaced by turkey fattened domestically and stuffed with truffles, and by capon in galantine. In the olden days, on great occasions they used to serve boiled or roasted peacock, still arrayed in all its plumage, which was removed before preparing the bird and replaced after the bird was cooked. Then the peacock was served surrounded by aspics of various shapes, colored with mineral powders injurious to the health, and flavored with such spices as cumin and scented red clay ('bucchero') – about which I will tell you shortly.

In Florence, sweet pastries and baked goods remained rather primitive and simple until the late 16th century, when a company of Lombards arrived and set about baking pies, little cakes, puffy turnovers and other pastries made with eggs, butter, milk, sugar, and honey. But before that, ancient records mention only the donkey-meat pies Malatesta gave as gifts to his friends during the siege of Florence, when shortages of every kind of food, particularly meats, were acute.

As for bucchero, there was a time when Spain was the fashion trendsetter, just as France is today, and all nations tried to imitate its style of cuisine and flavoring. Thus, at the end of the 17th century and the beginning of the 18th, Spanish-style fragrances and aromas became extremely popular. Above all fragrances, however, bucchero turned everyone's head, and so widespread was its use that ultimately spice merchants and stewards started putting it in tablets and foodstuffs, just as is done with vanilla today. From what fabulous substance was bucchero extracted and what did it taste like? You will be stunned when you hear. Now judge for yourself the extravagant folly of tastes and people! Bucchero consisted of powdered shards of pottery, and its odor resembled that which the earth scorched by the summer sun exhales when rains fall. It is the same smell of earth that is given off by those dark-red, thin and brittle vases called buccheri, which perhaps gave their name to a dark red color, although the most prized were a glossy black. Vases of this material were first imported into Europe from South America by the Portuguese, who used them as drinking vessels and to boil perfumes and colognes; later, the fragments were used in the manner I just described.

In Homer's *Odyssey* (XVIII, 43–49), Antinous says:

> Gentlemen, quiet! One more thing:
> here are goat stomachs ready on the fire
> to stuff with blood and fat, good supper pudding.
> The man who wins this gallant bout
> may step up here and take the one he likes.
> And let him feast with us from this day on:
> no other beggar will be admitted here
> when we are at our wine.
>
> (trans. Robert Fitzgerald)

In volume 6 of the *Florentine Observer*, we find the following description of a unique dinner that deserves to be quoted in part:

'Among the most sumptuous dishes there was also peacock, stewed with its feathers, and colored gelatin, molded in various shapes. A man in Siena, who was preparing a supper for a courtier of Pope Pius II named Goro (around 1450), was given such bad advice regarding these two items, that he became the butt of jokes all over Siena. Particularly amusing was the fact that, unable to find peacocks, he substituted wild geese, removing their feet and bills.

'When the beakless peacocks were served, the

command was given to begin carving them up. But the person in charge did not know how to do it, and though he struggled with the birds for a long time he only succeeded in filling with feathers the banquet hall and the table, as well as the eyes, mouth, nose and ears of Messer Goro and everyone else . . .

'When that accursed bird was removed from the table, many other roasts prepared with a great deal of cumin were served. Nonetheless, everything still might have been forgiven, had not the master of the house and his misguided advisers decided to further honor their guests with a platter of aspic which they ordered custom made for the occasion. Inside the aspic they had the cooks place, as is sometimes done in Florence and elsewhere, replicas of the papal coat of arms, as well as of Messer Goro's crest and additional heraldic figures. So they used orpiment, white lead, cinnabar, verdigris and other absurdities to make these fantastic patterns inside the aspic. Then they set it before Messer Goro as a festive dish and something new and wonderful. He and all his company ate it happily enough, as a way to get rid of all the bitter flavors left in their mouths by the excessive cumin and the other strange dishes.

'And it was a miracle that some of the guests did not die during the night, and first among them Messer Goro, who had a horrible headache and stomachache, and very likely vomited a small bouquet of wild feathers. After these infernal and deadly courses, a great many sweets were served, and the dinner came to an end.'

PUDDING CESARINO

I consider this Cesarino a good boy, and I shall sell his pudding to you under the same strange name it bore when I bought it from a young and rather lovely woman, upright and religious, the sort who, without intending to, can by her flirtatious nature compromise anyone in her immediate vicinity.

200 grams (about 7 ounces) of extra fine crustless bread
250 grams (about 8⅘ ounces) of sugar
approximately 100 grams (about 3½ ounces) of additional sugar, for use in the mold
125 grams (about 4½ ounces) of Malaga raisins
125 grams (about 4½ ounces) of sultanas
½ liter (about ½ a quart) of milk
3 tablespoons in total of Marsala wine and rum
5 eggs

Cut the crustless bread into thin slices, and soak it in the milk. Meanwhile, clean the sultanas, remove the seeds from the Malaga raisins and prepare the mold for cooking. Use a copper mold intended for puddings. Put about 100 grams (about 3½ ounces) of the sugar into a saucepan and, once it has turned nut brown, pour it into the mold, coating it thoroughly. After the mold has cooled, grease the sugar glaze with cold butter.

Combine the milk-soaked bread with the other 250 grams (about 8⅘ ounces) of sugar, the egg yolks and the liquors. Blend everything thoroughly. Finally, add the raisins and fold in the egg whites, beaten until stiff. Place the mixture in the mold prepared as described above, then put the mold in *bain-marie*, and cook for three whole hours; but heat from above only for the last hour. Serve hot as a flambé, sprinkling rum generously over the pudding and setting it ablaze with a table-spoonful of lit spirits.

These amounts should be enough for ten to twelve people.

MIGLIACCIO DI ROMAGNA
(*Romagna Blood Pudding*)

Se il maiale volasse
Non ci saria danar che lo pagasse.

(If pigs had wings to fly on,
you couldn't afford to buy one.)

This is what someone once said; and someone else replied: 'A pig, with all the cuts of meat it provides, and all the various manipulations these cuts can be subjected to, lets you taste as many flavors as there are days in a year.' I let the reader decide which of these two silly say-ings comes closer to the mark. As for myself, I will be happy to evoke the so-called 'pig's wedding,' for even this filthy animal can be amusing, but, just like the miser, only on the day of his death.

In Romagna, well-to-do families and peasants slaugh-ter pigs at home, which is an occasion to make merry and for the children to romp. This is also a great oppor-tunity to remember friends, relatives and other people towards whom you may have some obligation by making a gift of three or four loin chops to one, a slab of liver to another, while sending to yet a third a good plate of blood pudding. The families receiving these things will of course do the same in return. 'One gives bread in exchange for flour,' one might say. But regardless, these are customs that help maintain goodwill and friendships among families.

Coming at last to the point, after this preamble, here is the recipe for Romagna blood pudding. On account of its nobility this blood pudding would not even deign to recognize as kin the sweet-flour blood pudding you can find on any street corner in Florence:

7 deciliters (2⅘ cups) of milk
330 grams (about 11⅔ ounces) of pig's blood
200 grams (about 7 ounces) of concentrated must, or
*   refined honey*
100 grams (about 3½ ounces) of shelled sweet almonds
100 grams (about 3½ ounces) of sugar
80 grams (about 2⅔ ounces) of very fine bread crumbs
50 grams (about 1⅔ ounces) of minced candied fruit
50 grams (about 1⅔ ounces) of butter
2 teaspoons allspice
100 grams (about 3½ ounces) of chocolate
1 teaspoon nutmeg
a strip of lemon peel

Crush the almonds in a mortar together with the candied fruit, which you have first diced, moistening the mixture now and then with a few teaspoons of milk. Then pass through a sieve. Boil the milk with the lemon peel for ten minutes, then remove the lemon peel, add the grated chocolate and stir until melted. Remove the milk from the fire and let it cool a little. Then pour into the same bowl the blood, which you have already passed through a sieve, and all the other ingredients, adding the bread crumbs last, so that if you have too much you can leave some of it aside.

Cook the mixture in *bain-marie*, stirring often so as not let it stick to the bowl. You will know that the mixture has achieved the right consistency and is done when the mixing spoon remains upright, if you stand it in the center of the mixture. If this does not happen eventually, add the rest of the bread crumbs, if you have not already used all of them. Pour the mixture into a baking pan lined with crazy dough and when it has cooled completely, cut it into almond shaped pieces. Cook the dough as little as possible, so that it is easier to slice, and do not let the pudding dry out over the fire, but rather remove it from the hearth as soon as the broom-twig with which you are pricking it to test for doneness comes out clean.

If you are using honey instead of the concentrated must, taste it before adding the sugar to avoid making it too sweet, and keep in mind that one of the beauties of this dish lies in a creamy consistency.

My fear of not being understood by everyone often leads me to provide too many details, which I would gladly spare the reader. Still, some people never seem to be satisfied. For instance, a cook from a town in Romagna wrote to me: 'I prepared the blood pudding described in your highly esteemed cookbook for my employers. It was very well liked, except that I didn't quite understand how to pass the almonds and the candied fruit through the sieve. Would you be good enough to tell me how to do this?'

Delighted by the question, I answered her: 'I am not sure if you know that you can find sieves made especially for this purpose. One type is strong and widely spaced, and is made with horsehair. Another is made of very fine wire. With these, a good mortar and *elbow-grease*, you can purée even the most difficult things.'

Ice Creams

I read in an Italian newspaper that the art of making ice cream belongs preeminently to Italy, that the origin of ice cream is ancient, and that the first ice creams in Paris were served to Catherine de' Medici in 1533. This article added that the Florentine pastry makers, chefs, and icers of the royal palace would not share knowledge of their art. As a result the secret recipe for making ice cream remained within the confines of the Louvre, and Parisians had to wait another century to taste ice cream.

All my research to verify this story has been in vain. One thing that is sure on the subject of ice cream is this: the use of snow and stored ice to produce iced drinks is of oriental origin and goes all the way back to remote antiquity. Ice creams came into fashion in France around 1660, when a certain Procopio Coltelli from Palermo opened a shop in Paris under his own name: *Café Procope*. The establishment was across from the *Comédie Française*, which was then the meeting place of all the Parisian *beaux esprits*. The immediate success of this place, which was the first to serve ice cream in the shape of an egg in stemmed cups, drove the vendors of lemonade and other drinks to imitate it. Among these should be remembered Tortoni, whose delicious ice creams were so in vogue that his café acquired a European reputation, and made him his fortune.

According to Atheneus and Seneca, the ancients built ice boxes to store snow and ice using a technique not so different from ours today, namely: digging deep into the earth and, after compacting the ice and snow, covering them with oak branches and straw. But the ancients did not yet know the properties of salt, which when added to ice accelerates the freezing process, making it much easier to make sherbet with liqueurs of every kind.

You will almost surely please all your dinner guests, especially in the summer, if at the end of the meal you offer them sherbet or ice cream. These desserts, in addition to satisfying one's palate, also aid digestion by recalling heat to the stomach. And today, thanks to the American ice cream makers, which have triple action and need no spatula, making ice cream has become so much easier and faster that it would be a shame not to enjoy much more frequently the sensual pleasure of this delicious food.

To save money you can re-use the salt by drying it out on the fire, thus evaporating the water that had resulted from the freezing process.

PONCE ALLA ROMANA
(*Roman Punch*)

This recipe serves six people.

Lately, this kind of ice cream has become popular at fancy dinner parties. It is usually served before the roasted meat course, because it aids digestion and prepares the stomach to receive the remaining courses.

450 grams (about 1 pound) of sugar
5 deciliters (about 2 cups) of water
2 oranges
2 lemons
2 egg whites
1 small glass of rum
a dash of vanilla

Boil 250 grams (about 8⅘ ounces) of the sugar in 4 deciliters (about 1⅔ cups) of water with a little lemon and orange peel. Remove from the fire and squeeze the juice of the oranges and lemons into the syrup. Strain the mixture through a cloth, and pour it into the ice cream maker to freeze.

Put the remaining 200 grams (about 7 ounces) of sugar in the remaining 1 deciliter (about ⅖ of a cup) of water, add the vanilla, and boil until a drop does not run when poured onto a plate or makes a thread when tested between two fingers. By now you will have beaten the egg whites quite stiff, and you are ready to pour the syrup over them while it is still very hot. Then beat well to obtain a smooth consistency. After this mixture has cooled, combine it with the ice cream and blend well. Add the rum just before sending to the table in stemmed glasses.

MACEDONIA (*Mixed Fruit Ice Cream*)

And now we bid welcome to Madam Macedonia, to whom I would rather give the simpler name of 'Mixed Fruit Ice Cream,' a dessert that will be especially welcome in the scorching months of July and August.

For this dessert, if you do not have an ice cream mold, you can use a tin-plated metal container (shaped like a mess tin or a small saucepan) with a lid that can be hermetically sealed.

Take many varieties of fruit in season, ripe and of good quality, for example: red currants, strawberries, raspberries, cherries, plums, apricots, a peach and a pear. Starting with the cherries, peel all the fruit and chop to the size of pumpkin seeds, discarding the cores and stones. Use only a very small amount of red currants because their seeds are too big and too hard. Some fragrant melon would make a nice addition.

Weigh the fruit once you have prepared it in this manner; let's say you have 500 grams (about 1 pound) of fruit, then sprinkle 100 grams (about 3½ ounces) of confectioners' sugar on top, and add the juice of 1 garden lemon. Blend well and let sit for half an hour.

Use a piece of paper to line the bottom of the metal container, then pour in the fruit, packing it well. Cover the container and place it in a tub filled with ice and salt. Leave it to freeze for several hours. If it will not unmold easily, wet the sides of the container with warm water. It will make an attractive display as a frozen, marbled block of ice cream.

These amounts serve four to five people.

GELATO DI LATTE DI MANDORLE
(*Almond Milk Ice Cream*)

I describe the following dish especially for you, ladies of delicate, refined taste, for I am sure that you will find it delightful; and since I often think of you when I create these dishes, which, I hope, take into account and satisfy your taste, I must take advantage of this opportunity to say that I hope you long preserve the enviable qualities of blooming health and beauty.

200 grams (about 7 ounces) of sugar
150 grams (about 5¼ ounces) of sweet almonds, and 4 or
    5 bitter almonds
8 deciliters (about 3⅓ cups) of water
2 deciliters (about ⅘ of a cup) of heavy cream
a dash of orange-flower water or coriander seeds

Boil the sugar in the water for ten minutes together with the coriander seeds, if you are using the coriander or comfits for flavor. Blanch the almonds and crush them very fine in a mortar along with a few tablespoons of the syrup, then stir them into the syrup. Strain the mixture through a loosely woven cloth, squeezing well to extract as much of the flavor as possible; crush the almonds in the mortar with some syrup a few more times if necessary. Add the cream to the extracted liquid and then freeze in the ice cream maker. Once it has hardened, serve it in stemmed glasses.

This recipe serves nine to ten people.

GREAT  FOOD

A TASTE OF THE SUN

Elizabeth David

LEGENDARY COOK AND WRITER Elizabeth David changed the way Britain ate, introducing a postwar nation to the sun-drenched delights of the Mediterranean, and bringing new flavours and aromas such as garlic, wine and olive oil into its kitchens.

This mouthwatering selection of her writings and recipes embraces the richness of French and Italian cuisine, from earthy cassoulets to the simplest spaghetti, as well as evoking the smell of buttered toast, the colours of foreign markets and the pleasures of picnics. Rich with anecdote, David's writing is defined by a passion for good, authentic, well-balanced food that still inspires chefs today.

'Above all, Elizabeth David's books make you want to cook'
TERENCE CONRAN

····· GREAT FOOD ·····

A MIDDLE EASTERN FEAST

Claudia Roden

AWARD-WINNING FOOD WRITER Claudia Roden
revolutionized Western attitudes to the cuisines of the
Middle East with her bestselling *Book of Middle Eastern
Food*. Introducing millions to enticing new scents and
flavours, her intensely personal, passionate writings
conveyed an age-old tradition of family eating and shared
memory. This selection includes recipes for tagines from
Morocco, rice from Iran, peasant soup from ancient
Egypt and kofta from Armenia, as well as discussions of
spices, market bargaining, childhood memories of Cairo
and the etiquette of tea drinking; evoking not only a
cuisine but an entire way of life.

*'Roden's great gift is to conjure up not just a cuisine
but the culture from which it springs'*
NIGELLA LAWSON

GREAT FOOD

RECIPES AND LESSONS FROM A DELICIOUS COOKING REVOLUTION
Alice Waters

A CHAMPION OF ORGANIC, locally produced and seasonal food and founder of acclaimed Californian restaurant Chez Panisse, Alice Waters has recently been awarded the *Légion d'honneur* in France for her contributions to food culture. In this book, she explores the simplest of dishes in the most delicious of ways, with fresh, sustainable ingredients a must, even encouraging cooks to plant their own garden.

From orange and olive salad to lemon curd and ginger snaps, Waters constantly emphasizes the joys and ease of cooking with local, fresh food, whether in soups, salads or sensual, classic desserts.

'Waters is a legend'
JAY RAYNER

GREATE  FOOD

THROUGHOUT the history of civilization, food has been livelihood, status symbol, entertainment – and passion. The twenty fine food writers here, reflecting on different cuisines from across the centuries and around the globe, have influenced each other and continue to influence us today, opening the door to the wonders of every kitchen.

He stood there in the moonlight, a perfectly formed warrior. And he was staring at her.

Lycans always shifted naked. Trinity had seen others, and others had seen her. But for the first time, she was vitally aware of her body, as well as another's.

She stood tall, her shoulders back. The cool wind played with her hair, the tendrils caressing her bare shoulders. His gaze skittered over her, from the top of her head, halting briefly at her lips before continuing its journey downward. When he raised his gaze, she sucked in her breath at the clear and visible hunger in his eyes.

Trinity couldn't ever remember anyone staring at her so openly, so intently, so freely displaying his desire.

She stared back at Matthias for a moment. Powerful. Strong. The ring on the chain glinted in the moonlight.

And he bore the brand of another woman.

LYCAN
UNLEASHED

SHANNON CURTIS

First Published in Great Britain 2016
By Mills & Boon, an imprint of HarperCollins*Publishers*
1 London Bridge Street, London, SE1 9GF

© 2016 Shannon Curtis

ISBN: 978-0-263-92181-6

89-0816

Our policy is to use papers that are natural, renewable and recyclable products and made from wood grown in sustainable forests. The logging and manufacturing processes conform to the legal environmental regulations of the country of origin.

Printed and bound in Spain
by CPI, Barcelona

Shannon Curtis grew up picnicking in graveyards (long story) and reading by torchlight, and has worked in various roles, such as office admin manager, logistics supervisor and betting agent, to mention a few. Her first love—after reading, and her husband—is writing, and she writes romantic suspense, paranormal and contemporary romance. From faeries to cowboys, military men to business tycoons, she loves crafting stories of thrills, chills, kills and kisses. She divides her time between being an office administrator for the Romance Writers of Australia and creating spellbinding tales of mischief, mayhem and the occasional murder. She lives in Sydney, Australia, with her best-friend husband, three children, a woolly dog and a very disdainful cat. Shannon can be found lurking on Twitter, @2BShannonCurtis, and Facebook or you can email her at contactme@shannoncurtis.com—she loves hearing from readers. Like. . .LOVES it. Disturbingly so.

This one is for Eugenia. For all the giggles, the junk-food comas, the heartthrob crushes and the enduring good times. So many years, and yet we haven't aged a bit.

No, wait, that should be "we haven't matured a bit."

Matthias and Trinity are for you. Okay, so mainly Matthias.

Chapter 1

"What the hell are they doing?" Zane Wilder whispered.

"They're training," Matthias murmured. He tucked his ring and the chain it hung on around his neck under his T-shirt, not wanting a glint of sunlight on metal to give away their position. Both he and Zane lay prone on the ground as they peered over the edge of the ridge. A group of juveniles were clustered below in a clearing, and all listened avidly to the woman instructing them.

He and Zane were on a scouting mission, gathering as much information as possible on the Woodland Pack. Four months earlier his alpha prime, Jared Gray, had been poisoned in a dentist's chair. The dentist, Ryder Galen, had ultimately proved his innocence and uncovered the conspiracy between Rafe Woodland, alpha prime of Woodland Pack, and Arthur Armstrong, the head of one of the oldest families in the capital city,

Irondell. Arthur was currently remanded to a Reform prison, awaiting his trial.

Arthur Armstrong was a human, not a werewolf, so his crime—being a crossbreed crime—fell under the control of Reform Authority. Getting justice from that individual was out of his hands. Rafe Woodland, though, was a different matter entirely.

As neighboring werewolf packs, his own pack, Alpine, had requested to transfer the matter out of the Reform justice system, to deal with it under tribal jurisdiction. The Reform justice system governed all of the tribes, be they shadow breed or human, and had to be seen as fair and just for all. There were certain cases, though, that could be transferred to the tribes. In this case, when a werewolf from one pack coordinated the murder of a werewolf in another pack—especially if the murdered werewolf was an alpha prime—then the transfer was almost automatic. Rafe Woodland was proving a hard lycan to catch, though. He'd refused to acknowledge the charges and refused to turn himself in to Alpine.

So now they were working on plan B, perving on—er, no, scouting out the enemy. He eyed the woman below.

The sunlight filtered through the trees, picking out copper highlights in her braided brown hair. He wished he could see her eyes, but they were too far off. She turned away, her back to them, and Matthias couldn't help noticing the indentation of her slender waist, the sexy curve of her hips, the way her jeans cupped her trim butt. She had an athletic figure that drew his attention, and he grew hard as he eyed her lean grace as she walked around the clearing, instructing her charges.

A cool breeze washed over him, a sign that the chill

snows of winter were just around the corner. It teased the back of his neck, and he could almost imagine it was her fingers caressing him, playing with him, teasing him. Tempting him. He watched her hands as she spoke, the smooth, rolling gestures hypnotic and innately sensual. He wanted those hands on him. The lust he felt now was at first uncomfortable, then painful, and wholly surprising and unwelcome.

His eyes narrowed. He didn't like the rise of desire within. Didn't like it at all. He told himself he was merely surveying the enemy, that his intense interest— not lust—was completely warranted. She was undeniably sexy, moving with a lithe fluidity that called to a part of him he'd trapped and buried. His senses sharpened. His body throbbed in time with the slow, languid thump of his heart. The leaves in the surrounding trees rustled, whispering encouragement. He took a deep breath to calm his body's reaction, and breathed in the loamy richness of the earth, the rock on which they lay hard and unrelenting. He caught the whiff of a scent, something he knew by instinct was hers, a delicate trail of spice amidst the fragrant forest. He dug his fingers into the stone outcrop as he battled the sensuality that was flooding him. He wanted to leap down, grab her and carry her off. The beast within him unfurled, awakened by his reactions, stretching, arching.

This was not the time to lose himself in an attraction, damn it. He was tempted, though. Tempted to ignore his goal, the reason he was spying on the enemy, to abandon his friend and surrender to the lust that was licking at his defenses, like a bushfire consuming the land.

The woman commanded the attention of several adolescents as she spoke with them quietly. Matthias felt a smile tease at the corners of his mouth as he watched a little boy of maybe five years old standing next to her. Once again, his reaction surprised him as much as it displeased him. The kid mimicked her stance, nodding and frowning as she spoke to the group. A man stood behind the class, and Matthias wondered briefly who he was and what his connection was to the woman. Something deep, dark and possessive rose within him, and yes, so did a hint of jealousy, of envy, that this man was within her trusted circle. The man nodded, then jogged away into the undergrowth.

The woman held up her hands, calling their focus back to her as she assigned partners within the group. Her back was to him, but her movement raised her shirt and jacket, calling his attention back to her butt, her waist. This reaction he had to her was new. Alien. The kid started to wander off, but she grabbed hold of the back of the younger kid's hooded pullover, not once breaking her focus from the adolescents as she gently pulled the child back to her side. Matthias sucked in a breath as, just for a moment, the scene below merged with a memory he'd ruthlessly ignored and never thought to revisit, of another woman, another boy... another time.

The kid frowned up at her, folding his arms as his lips pouted, but the woman ruffled his hair absently as she kept talking. After a few more minutes of instructions, she clapped her hands and gestured to the edge of the clearing, and the pairs of adolescents took off in multiple directions.

"That must be the Woodland Tracker Prime," Zane murmured. "I've heard she's good. One of the best."

Matthias raised his eyebrows briefly at his friend's remarks. The guardian had a knack for acquiring intel. So far he'd been quite valuable in getting information on the Woodland pack. Although he had to admit, even he'd heard of the Woodland Tracker Prime.

"Hmm." Matthias didn't take his gaze off the woman as she finally turned her attention to the boy. She folded her arms and tipped her head to the side. Her brown braid slid forward over her shoulder, and his body tightened. He wanted to touch that hair, unravel the braid and watch it slide through his fingers. He wondered if it was as silky as it looked. Again, he was stunned by his curiosity—no, his need—to know more of this woman.

She was tall, he could tell, despite their angle of viewing. Damn, she had great legs. Long, slender and encased in denim, her coltish frame had just enough curves to catch and hold his attention. Those legs… wrapped around his waist…

He clenched his teeth. This was not the time to get horny over a she-wolf, for God's sake—no matter how long it'd been since he'd looked at another woman as more than just a pack mate. The woman below was Woodland. The enemy. Her family—hell, maybe even she, had been responsible for Jared's death. The pack was systematically thumbing its collective nose at the rest of the lycan tribe. They had killed his friend, his mentor, his alpha prime.

And she was one of *them*.

Everyone at Woodland would pay for what they'd done to Alpine. Just the thought that she was part of the enemy pack—and in a trusted position, if she was training juveniles—was enough to snap everything back into perspective. He wasn't there to ogle. He was there to gather information, maybe even hunt.

From this distance, he couldn't make out what was being said. The kid dragged his toe in the dirt, and she squatted down so that her eyes were level with his. Her jeans tightened around her butt, although it was the sight of the woman leaning in to the little boy that brought a tightness to his throat, the emotion taking him by surprise. He shifted, trying to shrug the moment off. She looked nothing like Cara.

"One would almost think Woodland care for their young, too," Zane commented in a rough whisper.

"They're still lycans," Matthias murmured. And as such, had similar weaknesses to the rest of the lycan tribe, weaknesses that could be exploited. "They'll still value life." The young were to be protected, nurtured. Loved.

Whatever the woman said cheered up the kid, as he started to strut about the clearing. He'd point at something, and she'd either shake her head or shrug, walking behind him with her hands clasped behind her back. She was relaxed, patiently answering the questions the boy asked. Eventually he reached the point where the man had stood, and looked up at his instructor. She smiled and nodded, giving him a high five, then knelt beside him, tracing something in the dirt. The kid nodded, took a few steps, then pointed. She gave him a thumbs-up, rising to her feet to follow.

Zane started to shuffle back from the edge, but Matthias's hand shot out, clutching his forearm. They both froze. The woman halted at the edge of the clearing and cocked her head to the side. She turned to slowly scan the area. Matthias didn't move. His muscles clenched tight, and his breath caught in his chest. The reason they'd picked this vantage point was because they couldn't be seen from below, yet the woman's gaze remained glued to the ridge for a moment, before finally drifting on. The boy must have asked her something, for she turned to him, a reassuring smile on her face as she held her arms out. He ran up to her, and she grasped his wrists, swinging him up and over her shoulders until he could wrap his arms around her neck. She carried him, piggyback-style, into the woods, furtively glancing over her shoulder as she went.

Matthias relaxed once she was out of sight.

"Did she see us?" Zane asked as he retreated from the ridge.

Matthias shook his head. "I don't think so."

"Should we go after her? She could prove valuable."

He shook his head. "No." He kept scanning the trees, but it was as though the brown-haired woman had melted into the forest, disappearing like a wisp of mist. He smiled. They wouldn't go after her, not now.

Maybe later.

Trinity Caldwell slung her backpack over her shoulder as she stepped into the great hall. Fires burned from the wall sconces bolted into the stone, casting flickering shadows down the walls and across the dirt floor as members of her pack went about their daily business. Not many spoke, though, and most walked with their eyes downcast as they went about their tasks. The hall had almost returned to normal, although there were still some repair areas cordoned off. Just over a month ago an explosion had ripped through the hall and some of the main corridors, and there were still some ongoing issues as a result. At least Rafe had acceded to her request for routine structural inspections.

She sighed as she stepped brusquely along. They still weren't quite sure how the explosion had occurred. One moment Rafe was interrogating a half-blood vampire lawyer and her client, Ryder Galen, a dentist accused of murdering the alpha prime from a neighboring pack, and in the next, Galen had somehow managed to trigger an explosion that knocked all those in the hall unconscious. Thankfully, nobody died. Not from the explosion, anyway. One lycan had lost his teeth, courtesy of the dentist, and two guardians had died in the forest on their way to returning the vampire lawyer to the nearby vampire colony. Well, at least that was what she and her pack had thought at the time. It turned out Rafe, her pack's alpha prime, had subtly instructed the guardians to permanently remove the vampire lawyer. She'd killed those guardians in self-defense. All deaths that could have been avoided, damn it. She thought of Jax. His father had been one of the guardians slain in the forest—a guardian prime, no less. Her pack was still reeling from the death of a highly respected, highly valued warrior. His partner, dealing with a young son and the death of her mate, was struggling to cope.

Trinity sighed. She knew how it felt, losing one parent and having another swept away in a tide of mourning. Well, she'd keep an eye on the kid. At least Jax would know he wasn't invisible. Not around Trinity, anyway. She'd taken him out on one of the juvenile training sessions, and the kid had done well. He needed a short leash, though, she'd noticed. He had a tendency to wander off and get into mischief. She smiled. He was a good kid.

She made her way toward a little-used corridor that would lead her deeper into the mountain and then out the other side. She skirted along the rim of the great hall, nodding occasionally to friends and family as she passed them. Some acknowledged her. Others acted as though they didn't see her—but that was a reasonable reaction, she kept telling herself. She wasn't going to let it hurt her, not like it had when she was a teen. The great hall was a large, long cave, and along the rim the stone wall had natural pockets of space used for storage or as alcoves used for sundry tasks and private conversations.

A roar echoed down the main corridor, and instinctively she ducked behind a stone column as her alpha prime, Rafe Woodland, stalked into the long stone cavern. She'd learned that disappearing was always the best option in her dealings with the lycan.

"What do you mean, you can't?" he shouted, arms out.

Dion, the recently appointed Woodland Guardian Prime, strode alongside him. "The supplies have been stopped beyond Summercliffe—Alpine have made a blockade."

Rafe took a deep breath as he clenched and unclenched his fingers, and Trinity drew deeper into the shadows. Some of the others in the hall paused. Everyone knew the warning signs.

"We need those supplies," he grated, his teeth visible.

"We can't get them."

Rafe picked up a cup and hurled it at the wall, and Trinity flinched as the ceramic shattered into small pieces.

Those close enough in the hall to witness the display rose to their feet, and Trinity watched as some of the men exchanged wary looks. A child huddling under one of the tables closest to Rafe caught Trinity's eye, and she sighed. Jax. The pup looked scared, and Trinity glanced around for his mom. The woman was nowhere to be seen; she was probably back in her den staring at a dirt wall as she pined for her dead mate.

Meanwhile, their alpha was having a temper tantrum, and the pack was keeping its distance. Like she should.

Jax's anxious gaze met hers, and her breath escaped in a frustrated gust. She knew what it was like to be the lost kid hiding under the table. Damn it. She should mind her own business. Pretend she didn't hear or see anything. One more look at the kid cowering beneath the table and she pursed her lips. Ah, hell.

She stepped out from behind the pillar, trying to do it slowly, without calling attention to herself.

"You had one job—get the supplies and come back." Rafe backhanded his guardian, sending him crashing against the table under which Jax cowered, and Trinity frowned. Dion reared up, his fists clenched, but forced himself to lower his gaze beneath the angry glare of his alpha prime. Dion's predecessor had died at the hands of the vampire lawyer in the woods, and Dion was still trying to prove himself to the pack leader. It wasn't Dion's fault the border was closed. He didn't deserve that kind of treatment. He was a guardian prime now, too, and should be treated with the respect due his station, especially in front of the rest of the pack.

"What did you expect, Rafe?" Trinity asked coolly as she stepped farther into the hall, wending her way through the small cluster of people, all attempts at blending into the background set aside. She tried to hide the tension in her fists by clutching onto the straps of her backpack. He was being unfair to her pack mate—and she hated unfair. "We've antagonized them." She was still trying to understand the strategic benefit of killing the Alpine Alpha Prime, and she knew other pack members struggled with Rafe's rationale. If she'd known Rafe's intention of killing another pack's alpha prime, she would have tried to stop him. Which was probably why she hadn't known until Rafe had sent guardians into Nightwing, the neighboring vampire territory, to abduct a half-blood vampire and the human accused of the Alpine pack leader's murder in an effort to bury the truth with them. No wonder Alpine were blocking them. They'd killed an *alpha prime*.

Rafe turned to face her, and his eyes narrowed when he recognized her.

"Trinity. This doesn't concern you."

Despite the knot in her stomach, she raised her eyebrows. "Well, if we can't get anything into Woodland, it concerns me. It concerns the whole pack." Nightwing was their most direct route from Irondell, the capital city of Metriz. After the time of Resolution, and during Reformation, each breed was assigned territory, and there were strict rules for governance, travel and trade that had to be observed. Irondell was the engine for it all, home to a blending of all breeds, including humans, and the seat for the Reform Council.

While they had other options like going through the River, Glen and Alpine territories, as well as the Plains, each alternative presented its own issues. They were already low on some of the medical supplies, and they needed to restock their food before the first snows of winter.

Rafe put his hands on his hips as he strolled toward her. His movements were casual, but his posture was intimidating. The ring on his finger glinted in the torchlight from the wall sconces. It bore the Woodland crest, and was only worn by the Woodland Alpha Prime. The sight of that ring would normally make a pack member bow their head in submission.

She lifted her chin. She was a former Scion. She wouldn't allow herself to be intimidated. As he stepped closer, she recognized the ire in his green eyes, such a bright contrast against the fall of dark, scruffy hair, the tanned skin and dark shadow of a beard, and she locked her knees into place. Nope. Not intimidated. He was tall and broad-shouldered, his size as imposing as the mountain they lived within, but she knew him well enough to see past the darkly handsome looks to the even darker personality within. They'd lived as pack mates all her life, yet she could honestly say she didn't know this lycan. He'd been normal, once. Hell, they'd been friends. Then over the course of one winter he'd visited his father in another pack and returned a born-again douche. She barely recognized this angry, bitter stranger. The man who'd taken over her father's position. Her grip tightened on the straps of her backpack.

"Don't push it," he said, his voice low in warning.

"Rafe—we've just received a request," a voice called out, and Trinity turned, as did Rafe. Channing, the head of tech, jogged into the hall.

Rafe frowned, visibly annoyed by the interruption. "For what? From whom?"

Channing came to a stop in front of his alpha, his expression earnest. "Alpine Pack request parley."

Trinity's eyes widened, and she could sense the growing trepidation from her pack mates behind her, yet she felt a relief at the distraction, no longer under the steely regard of her alpha prime.

"Oh, do they just?" Rafe murmured.

"'Matthias, Alpine Guardian Prime, formally requests parley with Rafe, Alpha Prime of Woodland Pack,'" Channing quoted, then dropped his gaze.

Dion swore softly, and the guardians who were in the hall rose to their feet. Trinity stepped closer, and her movement drew Rafe's attention.

"This doesn't concern you, either." His tone was implacable.

Parley from Alpine didn't concern her? Didn't concern pack? Woodland had killed the Alpine Alpha Prime. Alpine were coordinating blockages to supplies and services, and now wanted to discuss a resolution under truce. This concerned all of Woodland Pack. She opened her mouth to tell him so, but Rafe put a finger to his lips.

"Remember, you're no longer part of the Family Prime." He cocked his head to the side, and flashed his teeth in a smile. Trinity eyed his incisors. Those darn teeth. Even now, he lengthened them for effect, for intimidation. This whole debacle had started when he'd visited the Armstrong shadow breed medical clinic in Irondell for a fang enhancement. Now he didn't need to shift in order to use his fangs. Those new fangs also came with an aggressive attitude and a thirst for power. Arthur Armstrong had a lot to answer for. "Unless you'd like to discuss your position?"

He leaned against the table and folded his arms, waiting for her response. Jax paled, and looked about frantically for an escape route.

She maintained eye contact as she stepped closer and leaned down to reach under the table. "No, I'm good, thanks," she said, and felt a small hand slide into her own.

She tugged, and the little boy crawled out, his eyes wide as he glanced up at his fearsome alpha. She pulled him behind her as she started to back away from Rafe. He watched her, his gaze shifting between her and the boy.

"Are you sure?" he asked silkily. "You seem to have an opinion on everything." She shook her head. "Then stay out of my business," he said, his voice louder as he straightened from his position. He glanced around the crowd in the hall. "I'm calling a guardian meeting. Everyone else, clear the hall." He glanced back at Trinity. "I'll deal with you later."

Trinity swallowed as everyone except the Woodland guardians cleared the hall, the low hush of conversation gradually quieting. She nudged Jax in the direction of one of the corridors. She didn't want to be "dealt with" later, particularly not by Rafe. She should have just kept her mouth shut and disappeared into the background.

"Go back to your den. Help out your mother. I'll see you tomorrow for class."

Jax nodded, all too pleased to escape the tension of the great hall.

Trinity hurried from the cavern. She didn't look back, but she could feel the heavy weight of Rafe's stare as she left. Next time, she really would keep her mouth shut.

She knew what he was asking. Hell, pretty much everyone within earshot knew what he was asking, but she couldn't bring herself to do it. The price was too high.

Chapter 2

"I still don't think this is a good idea."

Matthias spared his friend a brief glance. Zane's brown gaze scanned the forest terrain around them. Late-afternoon sunlight filtered through the trees, casting light and shadow in dappled patterns across the forest floor.

"Relax, Zane, we'll be fine," Matthias said, his arms at his sides as he gazed down the trail.

"I don't trust Rafe Woodland as far as I can throw him," the guardian muttered, folding his arms.

Matthias's lips twitched. "Neither do I." He'd been surprised that Woodland had agreed to parley. Surprised and suspicious.

"We should be doing this in Nightwing. Neutral territory."

Matthias glanced over his shoulder, looking for any giveaway movement in the underbrush. Nightwing was the home territory for a colony of vampires, spearheaded by the Marchetta family. Well, Vivianne Marchetta. There was a brother, Lucien, but he hadn't been in the area for years as he headed up the family's interests on the west coast. "Our deal with Marchetta is for thoroughfare only. If we held this meeting in Nightwing, we'd have a whole bunch of vampires raining down on us."

"As opposed to a rival pack," Zane said drily.

Matthias grinned. "You sound scared, Zane." His grin broadened when his sergeant shot him a dark look. "Besides, I don't trust Marchetta that much, either." It had been annoying enough having to enter into talks with Nightwing's vampire prime, but he didn't want to further indebt the Alpine pack to the vampires. They could use the Nightwing territory as a shortcut between Alpine and Woodland, but they were to use it as a thoroughfare, not a stopover. He'd agreed readily enough. He didn't know any wolf who wanted to hang around with a bunch of bats. Besides, their argument was with the Woodland Alpha Prime, not the vamps. If they gave him and his lycans a wide berth, he could do the same.

"I don't see why we don't just storm the den." Zane walked for a couple of steps, then wandered back to him. "The others are ready for it. Hell, they want his blood."

Matthias's lips tightened, and he clasped his friend's shoulder. "Firstly, we have no idea where their den is. Secondly, we all want his blood. Jared was my friend, Zane, as well as my alpha. I hate that he died on my watch, and I'll do everything in my power to avenge his death. That's a promise." He needed the pack to know that.

Zane tilted his head. "Jared's death wasn't your fault, Matt. He went out on his own."

Matthias's arm dropped back to his side. "He was my alpha. I was his guardian, and he was murdered." He glanced away. "I let him down."

In his mind, there was no doubt. Yet again, someone he loved had died on his watch. This time, though, there would be payback.

Zane shook his head as he turned back to the forest. "Nobody blames you for it. Not even Samantha."

He winced. Samantha Alpine was pregnant with Jared's baby. That was possibly the hardest part, knowing his good friend wouldn't be there for the birth of his son, would never hold the babe in his arms, smell his scent, nuzzle noses with him, see him take his first steps, show him how to hunt or talk to him about girls. He wasn't sure what was worse: having some of those moments and knowing what you were missing out on, or missing out on them altogether.

"I appreciate that," he said softly. He did, but nothing could erase his own sense of guilt at the murder of his friend. A sound in the distance alerted him, and farther down the track he heard the rustle of wings as birds were startled into flight.

"They're here," he murmured.

"I say we kill him now."

Matthias shook his head. "Diplomacy first." He shrugged. "Then we kill."

Rafe Woodland came into view, striding along the track with his shoulders back. His expression was dark, fierce—not in the least contrite or remorseful, Matthias noted. Rafe was followed by four guardians.

"I count six in the fringe," Zane murmured. Matthias hid his nod by looking down as he casually folded his arms.

"There will be more," he muttered beneath his breath, before glancing up to meet Rafe's gaze. He'd expected the alpha prime to stock the forest glade with his supporters, but was mildly impressed by the numbers. Pity. Obviously the alpha prime wasn't that interested in a peaceful resolution.

Matthias smiled grimly. He was going to enjoy this.

"You're trespassing," Rafe said brusquely as he stopped in front of him.

"We're here under parley." The very nature of the discussion implied permission to be on the land, from time of entry, for the duration of the talks and until the time of exit.

"Then hurry up and state your terms." Rafe glanced off into the trees behind Matthias. "What is it you want?"

"Oh, that's simple," Matthias answered. "We want you."

Rafe arched an eyebrow. "Then this is a waste of time. Not happening." He started to turn away.

Matthias placed his hands on his hips and bent a leg in a relaxed pose. He puffed his cheeks out as he exhaled. "Well, that's a shame. For you, and for Woodland."

Rafe paused, then glanced over his shoulder. "What do you mean?"

"You conspired with Arthur Armstrong to kill Jared Gray. Armstrong is being handled through Reform Court, but you—your ass is mine."

Rafe turned. "What if I said I don't remember? What if I told you I have no recollection of the events leading up to Jared Gray's death?"

Matthias shook his head. Nothing could excuse what this lycan had done, siding with a human against another of his own kind. "I'd say you were lying to avoid facing punishment."

Rafe chuckled. "Punishment? You're not looking for punishment. You're looking for blood. My blood."

Matthias nodded. "It's a start."

Rafe shook his head. "Thanks, but I'll pass."

Matthias stepped closer to the alpha prime to look him straight in the eye. "I'm offering you a limited-time deal. You come with us. Now. We leave Woodland territory, and nobody else needs to get hurt."

Rafe arched an eyebrow. "Or?"

"Or you hide behind your pack mates, and instigate a pack war. Who knows how many lycans will die?" He was prepared to offer the alpha prime an honorable out. But if the lycan didn't take it, he was prepared to make the whole pack take responsibility for the tragedy wrought against the Alpine pack.

"On both sides," Rafe pointed out.

Matthias smiled. "Ah, but you did us wrong, Woodland, and you pissed us off in the process. We will come at you from every angle, with everything we've got. Do you really think you'll win? How are your stocks going? Got enough to feed your pack for the winter?" He knew they were running low. He'd managed to close a number of their borders with neighboring packs, preventing the delivery of much-needed supplies.

Rafe bared his teeth, and Matthias was surprised to see the lycan's incisors lengthen with a vampiric grace. "You threaten me, and you threaten my pack, under the guise of parley?"

Matthias wouldn't back down, despite the fangs gleaming in his direction. The audacity of the man angered him. Rafe stood there, and his close friend was in the ground, lifeless, because of this lycan's selfish ambition.

"I'm telling you how it is," Matthias rasped, the words emerging from deep within his throat. "And how it will be. Woodland will pay for murdering Jared Gray." He put all his sincerity and determination behind the vow, leaving the alpha prime in no doubt that he meant what he said.

Rafe smiled, his eyes glittering as he removed the Woodland crest ring he wore on the third finger of his right hand, the symbol of his rank within the pack, and slipped it into his jeans pocket. "Well, I guess that's the end of parley, then, isn't it?"

The alpha prime sprang at him, and Matthias grabbed his shoulders, using the momentum to pull him over and hurl him into a giant redwood behind him.

Matthias's guardians rose from their hiding places, teeth bared, and the forest rumbled with the growls of a dozen lycan warriors as they shifted into beast form and attacked.

Rafe rolled to his feet, glaring at Matthias, who grinned back. Woodland wasn't the only one to attend parley with backup. Rafe morphed into his beast form, a wolf with jet-black fur, and Matthias did the same, surrendering to his beast, his white fur almost a beacon in the dark forest. The lycans shrugged the remnants of clothes from their bodies as they launched at each other.

Rafe caught him in the shoulder with a meaty paw. Matthias fell back. He snapped at the black wolf, catching him in the chest with a sharp nip before the Woodland Alpha Prime leaped away. Two wolves bounded into the clearing to aid the Woodland pack leader. Matthias whirled and snapped, relinquishing his control to the rage he always carried within. It started low, but rose in a red-hot wave of fury, power coursing through his muscles, through his very blood. He hunkered down, prepared to take on the three large lycans. One charged at him, and Matthias neatly sidestepped, shredding the wolf's side with his claws as he barreled past.

His heart rate throbbed within his ears, within his chest, as his muscles bunched. A thump on his back propelled him forward, and he rolled, hearing the snap of jaws in his ear as he dodged a nasty bite. He kicked at the attacking wolf with force, sending him back awkwardly against a large boulder, and he heard the crack of the wolf's head against stone.

The large black wolf charged, and they both rolled in the dirt and pine needles, snapping and growling. Matthias jerked his head back from the alpha prime's jaws, and the wolf ended up biting on the chain around his neck instead. Instantly Matthias morphed, grabbing the snout of the lycan to prevent the chain from snapping. For a moment they glared at each other, man to wolf. As realization dawned in the lycan's eyes, Matthias moved. A series of quick, hard jabs to the wolf's soft belly, and the Woodland Alpha Prime was forced to open his mouth to suck in tortured gasps.

Matthias rescued the chain, morphing back into his beast form. He glanced around the clearing. His men were vastly outnumbered, although they held their own against the Woodland guardians. He turned to face the black wolf. Woodland lifted his head and howled. Matthias gritted his teeth. It was a call for reinforcements.

Trinity froze as the call of the lycans echoed through the forest. She glanced about, trying to gauge the direction of the alarm. Another howl echoed through the forest, a voice she didn't recognize.

A trespasser. Someone else was in the forest, someone other than Woodland.

"What's that?" Jax asked, his young eyes wide as he came bounding out of the underbrush.

"Time to go home." She'd had to clear this excursion with Rafe himself. All trips into the forest were assessed with care, so the noises startled her out of her relaxed state, her heart pounding at the rude shock.

She whistled, and one by one, her class of juniors came running through the forest toward her. Her fists clenched as she counted them off on return, nodding with relief when she had full attendance. Their tracking exercise had just been cut drastically short.

She beckoned them into a huddle. "Follow me. Do not stray. Do not wander off. Do not make a sound, okay?"

The young children nodded, eyes wide in pale faces and she gave them all a reassuring smile. "It's okay, guys. This is just a drill—but we do drills exactly like the real thing, don't we?" She tried to make the lie as convincing as possible. They'd never had a drill for anything like this, with the sounds of fighting echoing through the forest.

The kids still looked a little anxious, so she tried again. "First one back to the hall gets a treat." She started jogging cross-country, checking over her shoulder to ensure each of her wards were following closely. Ducking under ferns, leaping over logs, the children ran silently through the forest.

Trinity could hear the grunts and growls in the distance, and her heart hammered in her chest. The kids. She had to get the kids to safety. There would be time enough later to find out what had made hell break loose in the woods.

She skidded to a stop at the foot of the mountain and heaved against a massive boulder. It shifted slowly to reveal a dark hole, one that would just fit her if she bent over double.

"Go here," she ordered to the first child who reached her.

"But it's dark," the girl whispered, shrinking back.

Trinity winked. "It's okay, Mia. The dark can be your friend," she whispered back. "It can hug you and hide you. Don't worry, it's only dark until the first intersection." She'd learned that the dark could protect, could hide, could reveal all sorts of secrets.

"What if we get lost?" Mia whimpered.

"You won't. Keep turning right, and you'll end up in the laundry." She knew all of the tunnels within the mountain like the back of her hand, knew exactly the quickest, shortest route to safety for her pups. "When you're all inside, go and wait for me in the great hall. Now go."

She put her hand over the child's head, guiding her through the opening so that she wouldn't bump into the rock face, then helped the next child, then the next. Seven. Eight. Trinity frowned. Where was number nine?

"Who's missing?" she grabbed the disappearing ankle of the last child in the line as she mentally reviewed the names of the children who'd passed. "Jax. Where's Jax?"

The little boy shrugged. "He saw a trail."

Trinity swore under her breath. Great. The too-curious kid was wandering into a battle zone. "Go on," she muttered. "Get back to the others, and stick together in the great hall until your parents come and collect you, okay?"

The boy nodded, then started crawling again, and Trinity pushed against the boulder until it concealed the bolt-hole, then took off running up the path, her eyes scanning the undergrowth for signs of Jax's trail. When she got her hands on that kid...

She spied a branch that was snapped but not fallen. It had caught on another branch, indicating the direction the boy had taken. She skidded a little as she changed direction, following the slight indentation in the loamy soil here, the break of a branch there, the gap in a bush further along. Her heart pounding, she jumped over fallen logs, ducked under branches, and sprinted along paths that weren't really paths at all, merely vague impressions of a little boy's passing. Little trails worn by smaller creatures through the forest that unfolded at the same breakneck pace she ran. She had a skill for spying tracks and trails, no matter how faint, how old, how unused—or how newly trodden by a five-year-old pup.

Birds screeched and flew overhead, and she almost tripped over a rabbit as it bounded across her path. Something was going on, something big. She tucked her elbows in against her sides, fingers straight and rigid as she pumped her legs faster. Trees whizzed past her in a blur. She catalogued each little sign of Jax's trail, then skidded to a stop, her chest heaving, her eyes wide.

Jax stood on the tips of his toes by a tree, his hooded sweatshirt clutched by a tall, bearded lycan. The man wore only a pair of camouflage pants. No shirt, no shoes. He was streaked with dirt and blood, and his expression was fierce as he gazed back at her.

"Let him go," she said, her voice low. Despite the panic, the fear, her words came out dead calm. She stepped closer, just once, and the man backed away, pulling Jax along with him. Anger flared inside her. Jax was a pup, damn it. A Woodland pup. Nobody threatened her pups.

The boy whimpered, his eyes round with fear.

"It's okay, sweetie," she said in a soothing voice, although her gaze didn't shift from the lycan. "You will not hurt him," she said, her tone low and heavy with warning. If he so much as hurt a hair on Jax's head, she would kill him. Or at least try to. Her skills weren't in fighting. Her eyes narrowed. There was only one of him, and although he was big and obviously a warrior while she was neither, she was prepared to try and take him down, if only to give Jax an opportunity to escape.

"I'm going to count to three, and you're going to release him," she said, edging closer. The lycan narrowed his eyes.

"One," she said slowly, then launched herself at him, using the element of surprise as an advantage.

A heavy body slammed into her side and she was caught in midair and knocked off target. She rolled in the dirt, trying to escape the weight, fists and feet lashing out, cursing herself for her mistake. He wasn't alone. Flashes of tanned skin and white-blond hair made brief impressions as she tried to keep some momentum, to roll away. She heard a muffled *oof* as her fist connected with something firm and warm, then she grunted as her back was slammed against the dirt, and something hard, muscled and strong slammed against her front. Her wrists were grasped and shoved above her head, and she shook her hair out of her eyes as she glared at the shirtless lycan lying on top of her.

"Someone can't count," he commented drily, staring down at her, a grin sliding over his lips.

Chapter 3

Blue eyes. She had blue eyes. Matthias stared down at the woman lying beneath him, the ring on his necklace a hard, unrelenting circle between them. He and Zane had barely retrieved their stash of spare clothing before they'd heard the boy thrashing through the bush, and now—well, now *she* was beneath him. His heart thundered from the fight, from the retreat, adrenaline pulsing through his body. Arousal, hot and heavy, flooded him instantly, his system already on high sensory alert.

"Get off me," she said through gritted teeth, her voice low and husky. She glared up at him, and his heart stuttered, just for a moment. Those eyes, so dark, so stormy blue, yet with slivers of silver that caught and held his gaze. Her nose was narrow, her cheeks flushed, the bones of her cheeks and jaws so defined, her lips luscious. That voice, that breathy, sexy voice that curled and teased at his ears and hardened his arousal. He was bombarded with sensory information. And oh, hell, her scent.

He lowered his head into the cradle of her neck and inhaled, closing his eyes as her scent filled him, washed over him, aroused him. Wild honeysuckle, vanilla and something that was uniquely her, something that drove all sense and inhibition away, something that called to his beast, that had him slowly relaxing into her.

"Ge-get off me," she said, although this time she didn't sound half so ferocious. She tried to buck him off her, and he exhaled blissfully at the thrust of her body against his. He skimmed his nose up her neck, to the little indent behind her ear. She smelled like...home.

The word opened his eyes, and he paused. *Home?* He blinked, lifting his chest off her, but still pressing her into the ground with the weight of his lower body. Focus.

"You have a choice," he murmured, then moaned as she tried to roll, to lift him off her with the strength of those legs he wanted wrapped around his waist. He relaxed, pressing his arousal into the valley between her legs, and her blue eyes widened as she felt his erection.

She swallowed, and he watched the movement of her throat, saw the flutter of the pulse in the indentation of her neck. Her cheeks flushed, and her scent changed, drifting into something darker, sexier, spicier. Arousal. It flowed between them, though by the shock in her eyes, it wasn't exactly welcome.

"What?" her voice came out as a husky rasp.

"Take me to your den," he said, and waited for her reaction.

Her chin lowered. Her eyes narrowed as she gazed up at him, taking in his hair, every feature of his face. He didn't think she meant it, but the intensity with which she stared at him made each glance feel like a caress.

"Alpine?" she whispered, a growing awareness darkening her eyes.

He nodded. "Take me to your den."

She shook her head, pine needles rustling beneath her. "No."

He smiled. He liked that she wasn't a pushover, that she was prepared to stand up to him. Hell, she'd been prepared to attack Zane, a lycan half a head taller than her and a good deal heavier. The thought reminded him of his friend, and he lifted his gaze.

Zane stood off to the side, one hand holding the hooded sweatshirt of the boy, the other hand on his hip, his head tilted. His friend arched an eyebrow as he stared down at the couple lying entangled in the dirt.

"Don't mind us," his friend commented with a casual wave of his hand toward them.

"Take him," Matthias said brusquely.

"No," she cried out, trying to struggle against him. He watched as Zane turned and gently pulled the youngster along with him.

"No, wait."

Matthias glanced down at her. Her concern, her worry for the child, was clearly stamped on her face, and he smiled with satisfaction.

"What do you want?" she looked up at him, then back at the lad. Zane had halted, his head inclined as he listened to their conversation.

"Take me to your alpha prime, and we will release the boy."

"And if I don't?"

"Then we'll take him back to Alpine."

"And what?"

He dipped his head so that his lips were close to her mouth. "What do you think?" he whispered, making sure the boy couldn't hear them. He didn't want the lad scared any more than he already was. He had no idea what Woodland wolves thought they did back home, but imagination could be a good weapon.

Anger flared like blue fire within her eyes. He was surprised by her reaction. Surprised and impressed. Not fear. Not worry, or horror, or distaste. Anger. She was a fighter, one ready to risk her life to protect the boy. Did she have any idea how easy it was to use him as leverage? He certainly wasn't about to clue her in. He smiled.

"Your choice," he whispered against her lips.

Her frown deepened. "That's not a choice," she said, her eyes flashing.

He grinned. "I'm glad you see it my way. Take him back to camp," he called to Zane, not removing his gaze from the woman.

"Trinity," Jax called out, his uncertainty clear.

He tilted his head, and she growled softly, then turned her head to look back at the boy. "It's okay, Jax. We're going to be fine." She gave the lad a reassuring smile, and Matthias was caught by the light in her eyes, the glow of confidence.

He listened as the guardian walked away through the forest. When they turned down the trail, she dropped the smile and turned back to fix him with a steely glare. Not just a fighter, she had the ferocious spirit of a warrior, he realized, intrigued by the visible resolve as her eyes shifted to a steely blue.

"You've got what you want, now get off me," she snapped. She moved under him, trying to pull her wrists out of his grasp.

He relaxed, his chest lowering to press against hers.

Her gaze flicked up to him, and he could feel her heart pounding against his. There was something in her eyes… It wasn't fear; it was an awareness, a flare of something warmer. Desire. He could see it, he could smell it. He could feel it as her breasts swelled beneath him, her nipples a sweet torment as they peaked against his chest.

"Oh, honey, you have no idea what I want," he murmured as he inhaled her sweet essence again. It was pure seduction, her scent. He trailed his nose along her jaw, and smiled when she rolled her head, arching her neck to give him better access. He sank into her, relishing the feel of her body against his. Her body was lithe and toned, but she was soft and curvy where it counted, and undeniably feminine.

Luscious. He wanted to dive into her, and not come up for air. He slid his hands down her arms, feeling the shape of her limbs through her lightweight jacket. She sighed, then inhaled, her breasts pressing firmer against his chest, against the chain he wore. He smiled as her legs widened, and he rolled his hips against hers. Her hands dropped to his shoulders, then delved into his hair, her short nails scoring in a delicious, sensual massage against his scalp. He was as hard as granite, utterly consumed by the need to have this woman.

He trailed his hands down to cup her breasts, and she moaned, flexing her hips against his in response. His need to have her grew. He molded the soft flesh in his hands, taking his time to learn their weight, their shape, her nipples pressing into his palms like hard little studs. He was about to combust. She dragged her nails down his back, and he shuddered in ecstasy.

"Trinity." That's what the boy had called her. *Trinity.* He tasted the name on his lips. He liked it. He rubbed his erection against her, trying to alleviate the pressure, the ache, but her heat increased, as did his need for her. She stiffened beneath him.

"God, what am I doing?" she rasped.

"Getting to know me," he said as he nuzzled her neck.

"No."

"Are you sure? It damn well feels like it. Your hands are in my pants."

Her hands clenched, her nails digging into his buttocks where they'd slid beneath the band of his trousers. Then she pulled them out as though they were burning. "Holy smoke," she whispered.

He groaned. He was burning. A molten mess of burning need. For her. For Trinity. He couldn't remember ever feeling this intense desire, this consuming drive to become part of another lycan. Not even with Cara.

He rose to his feet, grasping the tracker and dragging her up to stand. He held her close, peering into her eyes. They weren't cold and steely anymore; they were dark and turbulent, full of stunned dismay and smoking-hot desire. His eyes narrowed. She'd made him burn, damn it.

Nobody made him burn. He took pride in his self-control, in his self-imposed punishment, and all it took was one tackle with this she-wolf and he was ready to forget everything, forget his plans, forget Jared, forget the rest of the pack that looked to him to avenge their alpha prime's death. All for a roll with the enemy.

He nudged her in the direction Zane had taken with the boy. "Let's go."

Trin resisted, turning back to face him again. She stared at the muscled figure for a moment, her body humming. Holy smoke, indeed. Like his friend, this lycan wore only a pair of low-riding camouflage pants, the button undone, revealing a tantalizing patch of golden skin before the fabric covered a noticeable bulge that seemed to match in scale the rest of him. She'd thought the other lycan was big. Good grief. This lycan towered over her, his shoulders so broad and thickly roped with muscle. Smudges of dirt and blood covered him, his short white-blond hair a stark contrast against the tanned skin and dirt. His eyes, staring back at her so solemnly, were a beautiful green.

He was beautiful. She should have been grossed out by the gore and filth, but there was something so magnetic, so charismatic, that all she could see were those beautiful green eyes, that stunning chest. He wore a gold chain around his neck, a ring resting in the dip between his chest muscles. Perspiration slicked his skin, turning his pectoral muscles and deeply-ridged six-pack into a shiny playground begging for a woman's fingers. Her fingers. Her gaze dipped. He had an old scar that slashed across his abdomen, yet it only added to the sexy, dangerous air about him. He was muscled and toned everywhere, no spare fat. She sucked in her breath. She'd seen some good-looking lycans, but she'd never had such a bone-deep, compelling reaction to anyone before. At least, not in her pack.

But he was Alpine, and he was here, in Woodland territory. She wasn't quite sure of the details, but she wasn't stupid. That howl to war had everything to do with the man in front of her. She released her breath, letting it out slowly, grabbing on to some measure of calm.

"Who are you?" She took a step back, trying to put some distance, some perspective, between them. Good grief, he was *Alpine*. She should be howling to the skies, calling her pack—not that any would be racing to rescue her, with her current standing within the group, but still, she should be raising an alarm, and doing her utmost to fight him. Although, he was such a massive unit, and she was just a tracker; she didn't like the odds of facing him down. Jax. She had to get back to Jax, get him to the safety of their den, such as it was with Rafe in charge.

"Matthias Marshall," he said, inclining his head.

Cold crept over her shoulders, despite the jacket and the heat generated from their physical tussle.

"You're Alpine's guardian prime," she said, eyeing the woods. Of all the damn lycans to run into, this one had to be the worst. The calm she'd so carefully manufactured now fled. She knew of his reputation—hell, all of Woodland had been talking of nothing else since that communication came through yesterday. He'd sworn vengeance against Woodland Pack for their part in the murder of his alpha prime, Jared Gray. He'd successfully applied to enforce tribal law against Woodland, and so far he'd made their lives difficult. Uncomfortable. Borderline hell. She swallowed. And now he stood before her, all six feet three inches of vengeful, ruthless, sexy—no, damn it—relentless and pumped-up guardian.

"And you're the infamous Woodland tracker," he commented, folding his arms.

She swallowed again. He knew who she was. She didn't really want him to know who she was. She lived a largely anonymous life within her pack, had gotten used to being ignored. He wasn't ignoring her, though. He tilted his head to the side, eyeing her closely.

"I'm surprised they let you out unguarded," he murmured.

She frowned. "Why wouldn't they? I'm a tracker." Her position within the pack implied a certain level of competency with looking after herself. Of course, when faced with this hulking guardian prime, she wasn't sure if even Woodland's first-tier guardians could match him. "Besides, we're not expecting Alpine to trespass," she said pointedly as she folded her arms, mimicking his stance. "You and your men need to leave." With the current tensions between the packs, their presence would start a fight that would quickly escalate, considering her alpha prime's easy-to-fire temper.

She lifted her chin. "It's not safe for you here. Let the boy go, leave the area and I'll allow you the opportunity to retreat." Rafe would probably have her hide for letting them go, but her goal was to protect the rest of the pack. Having these lycans in Woodland territory—especially this guardian prime—would result in a fight, perhaps even a war, and she didn't want her pack hurt. Judging by the size of this lycan, there would be many casualties.

Matthias arched an eyebrow. "You'll *allow* me the opportunity to retreat?" His breathless chuckle was incredulous, then he stopped laughing. He unfolded his arms and strode toward her, stalking her as she tried to back away. She halted when her back bumped into a tree. "I'm not trespassing," he grated as he came up close to her, bracing his hands against the trunk, enclosing her in a confined space within his arms. His broad chest pressed against hers, trapping her against the tree. This lycan had no concept of personal space. She lifted her gaze from the muscled shoulders, the defined biceps that cut off any avenue of escape. She took a deep breath, and was surprised by how pleasing his scent was, all mossy and pine, with a hint of something deeper, a musk that was all encingly male. His expression was harsh as he glared down at her.

"My men and I came here under parley," he growled, his eyes flashing. "We came to talk. Your alpha prime broke parley and attacked."

She shook her head, a frown pinching her forehead. "We wouldn't…" her voice trailed off. Actually, knowing Rafe, he probably would. His impetuous actions were what had gotten them into this mess in the first place. But to break parley, to violate discussions under truce—that was an act of dishonor. She couldn't accept that her pack would behave like that. "No…" she said, shaking her head.

He nodded. "Yes. And you know what that means, don't you, Tracker?"

She swallowed. It meant pack war. It meant that borders would not be respected. It meant attacks and assaults, until one pack submitted to the other. It meant many lives were at risk.

He'd already managed to halt their supplies, and winter was coming. How long would they be able to hold out? They would grow hungry, they would weaken, but her pack would fight to the death before they surrendered. Rafe would see to it.

"You can stop this," she said, striving for calm in the face of his brutal intention. "We are the same tribe. We have young, we have old—just like Alpine. What you have planned… This will ruin our pack, and it could ruin yours. Is that what you want? To kill families?"

Something flickered in his gaze, something dark, pained and sad, but then it was gone as he blinked. He shook his head as he leaned closer. "You've brought this upon yourselves."

He was so big he loomed over her, crowding her. All

glorious golden skin and brittle eyes. But she was a former Scion, damn it. The daughter of an alpha prime. She would not be cowed. She shoved at him, with the result of him moving not at all. She didn't think her effort even registered with him. She tilted her head back against the rough bark of the tree.

"What happened to your alpha prime—I'm sorry," she said, and meant it. "It wasn't—nice." No. It wasn't nice at all. Jared Gray's murder in a dentist's chair had sent shock waves throughout the tribes, for a leader to be killed that way. But the dentist had maintained his innocence, and it wasn't until her own alpha prime had coordinated the abduction of the dentist and his half-blood vampire lawyer from Nightwing territory that she and most of her pack learned of their involvement in the event.

Matthias's eyes rounded. "Not nice? Well, that's one way of putting it. Not nice." He shook his head, then tugged on her belt and hauled her close to him. "Your pack wounded mine. Your pack killed my alpha prime, and now your pack will pay for it."

She tried to wriggle away from him, but he started to unbuckle her belt. Panic shot through her, and she shook her head. "No," she gasped, trying to halt his efforts. He was so big, so strong, and she could feel the anger roiling beneath him, as though all it would take was the faintest spark to unleash the fire of his fury. "Please, no." She tried to escape, but he pulled her back. She felt the tug on her belt, then the release as the clasp was undone, and the leather slid out of the loops of her jeans. Her heart hammered in her chest.

"Rape won't solve anything," she gasped as he grabbed her wrists.

He froze, then lifted his gaze from where he clasped

her, the surprise in his face dissolving into an exasperation tinged with hurt.

"I'm not— I wouldn't—" He snapped his lips shut for a moment, his eyebrows golden slashes pulling into the center of his forehead. She could see he'd taken offense to her words. She gaped at him. Was that...was that a blush?

"I don't force myself onto women," he said with a quiet dignity. He wrapped the belt around her left wrist, his pec muscles rippling with the movement, then looped it around his right wrist, securing it so that they were belted together. He held their bound wrists up between them. "But I will do whatever it takes to make Woodland pay for what they did to us, and you're going to help."

He tugged her farther into the forest. If they didn't have Jax, she would have fought. As it was, the thought of the young boy had her reluctantly following him.

Chapter 4

Matthias looked to the opposite side of the fire, watching the tracker offer the boy some cooked rabbit. She'd followed him without resistance, but he didn't fool himself. The reason she'd been so cooperative was currently sitting right beside her, her arm curled protectively around him.

The firelight glimmered against the copper strands in her hair, bathing her features in a soft glow as she said something that made the boy laugh. She smiled, but her smile didn't reach her eyes, and she glanced about the campsite, her gaze assessing. For a brief moment their eyes met, and then she looked away. He frowned. He was still stunned, and slightly abashed, that she'd thought he'd force himself on her. That had hurt. That and the fact that she now tried to shield the boy from him and his lycans. The young pup shot him a curious glance, and he winked. He was rewarded with a tentative smile.

He knew what she thought, what she feared, and was willing to use it to his advantage. But there was no way he would ever hurt a pup. Nor would he hurt a woman. Sure, his physical reaction to her was…intense, but he'd never physically force a woman to submit to him. Hell, he hadn't been remotely interested in a woman since—well, not in a long time. Something about this tracker, though, made him forget his control, forget his own rules, forget that which drove him hardest. He glanced around the campsite, at the lycans who had accepted him into their den, into their pack, and who now looked to him for leadership. When Jared had adopted him into Alpine Pack, nobody could have guessed he would one day become their guardian prime, but in the three years he'd lived with them, he had. He'd earned their trust and loyalty. He wouldn't let them down. Not again.

Night had fallen, and he and his lycans had gathered at the meeting point. They were still in Woodland territory, but very close to the Nightwing border, and there was little chance of the Woodland shifters tracking them here, tonight. Woodland would have to tend to their injured and ensure their home den was secure before setting out to hunt for the Alpine guardians. He'd planned for a scattered retreat, and he and his guardians had laid plenty of false trails before finally descending upon their rendezvous point. He eyed the woman across the campsite. Holding the Woodland Tracker Prime would restrict their enemy's ability to locate them—at least for a while.

Smokey rabbit and pine scented the air, along with the stringent scent of medicinal body rubs and antiseptic creams as the Alpine lycans tended to their injured. Fortunately that nose-burning smell masked the hypnotic fragrance of the woman who even now he couldn't dislodge from his thoughts. She was delectable. He could lose himself in her scent, in her body—and that made him equal parts angry and scared as a day-old pup caught in a summer storm.

A movement caught his eye, and he looked up. Zane was trying to catch his attention. He walked around to his second-in-command, stopping to chat with some of the injured guardians. Fortunately there were no deaths in today's skirmish—but it wasn't for lack of trying on Woodland's part. Today, Alpine had retreated. His lips pressed into a firm line. His expectations for the out-come of talks hadn't been high, but damn, things had gone haywire. He didn't think highly of Rafe Wood-land, yet had still been surprised when the alpha prime had attacked under parley. He smiled. He didn't mind. They now had just cause to launch attack after attack on the enemy pack.

Zane beckoned him over to the pickup truck parked a short distance away from the camp. Matthias caught the eye of Kai, one of his guardians, and gestured toward the tracker. He didn't want her to think this was an op-portunity to escape. Kai nodded and casually strolled to take up a position behind Trinity and the boy.

"What's up?" he asked Zane as he met him and Nate Baxter, another first-tier guardian and valued sergeant, at the pickup.

Zane rolled out a map onto the hood of the car, and clicked on his flashlight. "You were right. Woodland has gone to ground. Nate and a couple of the others tried to track them, but they've disappeared."

Nate sighed. "Like ghosts. Poof."

Matthias took the flashlight and scanned the map, then frowned. He shook his head. "Are you sure this is the most current map?"

Zane nodded, his lips pursed. "Yeah. I know all the packs like to keep some of their trails hidden, but Woodland takes secrecy to a new level."

"I even cross-checked with satellite imagery," Nate said. "The trees effectively mask many of their trails. This is the best we can get."

Matt's eyes narrowed as he surveyed the document. "Rafe Woodland doesn't trust easily."

"Rafe Woodland doesn't trust at all," Zane muttered. "We'd do well to remember that. Someone who doesn't trust easily isn't trustworthy, as he proved today. Although that tracker could prove useful…" His voice trailed off in suggestion.

Matthias kept his eyes glued to the map, and merely grunted a response. He'd been thinking of little else since he'd dragged her into camp late that afternoon. That woman, that…she-wolf. Her long legs, narrow waist, and gentle swell of hip and breast—she was beautiful, in a lithe, natural kind of way. There was something about her that called to him, that stirred his beast, that tightened his body with a need he didn't appreciate and could barely control.

"You two certainly had an—intimate—connection," Zane drawled, leaning his hip against the truck.

"Oh, really?" Nate inquired. Matthias fought the inclination to growl at his pack mates. He wasn't in the mood for any of their teasing.

Zane nodded. "Oh, yeah. Thought he was going to imprint on her," he admitted in a stage whisper to Nate.

"Is that so?"

"Yep."

"Well, that's more than he's done with any of our pack," Nate murmured.

This time Matthias did growl, the sound low and soft yet nonetheless clear in its warning.

Nate folded his arms and looked expectantly at Matthias. "You say so much when you say nothing, Matt."

Matthias shook his head, his lips tight. "She's Woodland." That pretty much said it all. Her pack had conspired to kill his friend.

Zane shrugged. "She's hot."

"That she is," Nate commented, his tone light with interest, and it was all Matthias could do to stop the snarl forming in his throat.

Zane nodded, then glanced back at Matthias. "Two months ago you were the guardian to stop us all going on a pack hunt, Matt—no matter how much I tried to convince you. I would have thought you, of all people, would be prepared to overlook her…shortcomings."

This time Matthias did look up at his friend. Zane had this knack for making him feel ancient. His friend liked to act now, and think through things later. Maybe. Matthias had never thought he'd be the cautious one, the voice of reason, but he'd learned his lessons the hard way. Sometimes it paid to do the homework.

"I stopped the pack hunt because we didn't know what we were up against—we still don't know," he said in a low voice. "Woodland haven't welcomed visitors in years, not since their previous alpha prime died. We have no idea how strong they are, how many there are or how they act. Hell, we can't even get an accurate map of their territory. We learned today that observing the normal rules of engagement won't work with Woodland. We'll fight, but we'll be smart about it."

Zane frowned. "They killed Jared. They all deserve to die."

"And that's why I'm guardian prime, and you're not,"

Matthias said shortly, then leaned forward, crossing his arms over the hood of the pickup. "Just a minute ago you were commenting on the sexy Woodland tracker, now you want me to kill her? What about the pups? Would you kill them? The juveniles? The elders?"

Zane looked down at the toes of his boots. "Of course not."

"We want them to pay, though," Nate said quietly.

Matthias nodded. "Hell, yeah. Jared was a good man, and a great alpha. He didn't deserve to die, not that way."

When the conspiracy between Woodland Pack and one of Irondell's so-called pillars of society, Arthur Armstrong, was revealed, it had been all he could do to keep the Alpine pack from wreaking revenge on Woodland, Nightwing and Irondell—an act that would have cost them dearly.

Armstrong was currently rotting in a prison cell, but Woodland Pack's involvement meant a crime was committed by lycan against lycan, and justice came under tribal jurisdiction. It was Alpine's privilege—and duty—to serve justice to those within the pack responsible for the murder of their alpha.

So it didn't matter how hot, how sexy, how damn desirable their tracker was, she was the enemy. If she was in any way involved, she would pay, along with the rest of her pack.

"I'll be the first one to admit I want blood for blood for Jared's death," he said in a low voice. He shifted his gaze between Zane and Nate. "And I'll do whatever it takes, but no justice is served if we kill any innocents. It wouldn't honor Jared."

Both men dropped their gazes, but he could see he was getting through to them.

"For the record, I said she was hot. You're the one that came up with sexy," Zane grumbled.

Matthias decided to ignore that. He turned to Nate. "You saw the numbers Rafe Woodland had at his disposal. We're going to need reinforcements. Go back home and call up another guardian squad, but make sure there are still some left behind at Alpine. I don't want Samantha left vulnerable."

As Jared's pregnant widowed mate, Samantha Alpine had stepped into the alpha prime role in Alpine Pack when her partner was killed. Not many knew of the discussion she'd had with him prior to doing so. Nobody else knew she'd offered him the prime position. He clenched his teeth. He couldn't accept, though. He had been Jared's guardian prime, and Jared had died under his service. He wasn't fit to be an alpha prime, but he sure as hell wasn't about to leave Samantha defenseless while he avenged his alpha's death.

"Do you think a squad is enough?" Zane asked, his brow furrowing.

Matthias grinned. "Sometimes you need a better weapon than sheer brawn," he said, and glanced over his shoulder at Trinity, now playing a game in the dirt with the pup.

Zane sighed. "Fine. So we have the Woodland tracker— what if we use her as a bargaining chip? Exchange the tracker for the alpha prime?"

Matthias had to clamp down on his instinctive refusal. It was reflexive and purely selfish. He wanted to spend more time with the tracker, although Zane's proposition had merit. If Woodland's alpha prime agreed, then it would mean limiting the risk of casualties and deaths on both sides. And it meant that the alpha prime could save face. He'd be saving one of his own, an honorable surrender.

He sighed. "Fine. Send a message through to Woodland proposing the exchange. In the meantime, let's get those extra guardians down here." He glanced at Nate, who nodded.

"How are we going to get the squad through Summercliffe? That's Nightwing territory. I know Marchetta's granted us access, but don't you think she'll balk at the number of wolves going through her zone?"

"I've already negotiated with Vivianne," he stated, and didn't hide his distaste. The woman was a shrewd bloodsucker, as powerful as she was coldly beautiful, but his skin had crawled at having to do business with the vamp. "She'll let you through."

Nate grimaced. "What's the deal?"

"Nightwing are allowing us safe access, on the condition that none of their vamps are harmed by any werewolf. In return they get one percent of the iron mine's royalties for the next one hundred years."

Zane shook his head. "I'd prefer to just bite them."

Matthias smiled grimly. "Well, I did offer that, too. We don't have the manpower to wage a war against Woodland and the vamps. Let's keep it friendly with our neighbors for as long as we can."

"One percent, huh?" Nate shook his head. "I hate doing business with the bloodsuckers, but even I can see that's pretty reasonable for them to allow us through—considering all we'd have to do is bite them and it's lights-out for the vampires. What's the catch?"

Matthias shook his head. "There's no catch. That dentist and his lawyer were snatched by Woodland guardians from Nightwing territory. Either Marchetta is slipping and her borders are getting lax, or she gave them access so they could try and cover up Jared's murder. Either way, she owes us."

Zane chuckled. "I would have loved to be a fly on the wall when you told her that."

Matthias shuddered. "Ugh, no. Trust me. Marchetta is definitely a cold-blooded bitch. Fortunately, not all of the Nightwing vamps are so difficult to deal with. Vassi Verity was part of the negotiations."

"Verity? Isn't she that vamp lawyer who defended the dentist?" Nate asked, frowning.

Matthias nodded. "Yeah, she and Ryder Galen uncovered Rafe's part in Jared's murder. She works for Marchetta now."

Zane shook his head. "Pity. I thought she was half-decent. Now she's one of the devil's minions."

Matthias shook his head. He'd met Vassi in her efforts to clear her client's name. She might be a vamp, but she was a decent one. "Vassi is fair. She'll do her best to keep the devil honest."

"Didn't she and the dentist end up together?" Nate asked, rubbing his chin.

Matthias nodded. "Yep. She reminded me that his offer to assist us still stands. I think we can manage, though."

He jerked his chin back to the map. "We need to find the den. The best way to stop this war before it starts in earnest is to take Rafe Woodland."

"Then the legendary Woodland tracker will most definitely come in handy," Zane commented.

Matthias nodded as he rolled up the map. "Tomorrow, we'll get her to show us the way."

When a shadow fell over the track she'd drawn in the dirt, Trinity used her boot to scuff the markings she'd drawn for Jax before looking up.

Oh. It was *him*.

She should have known. Her heart was pounding, and she tried to convince herself that it was probably fear and wariness. She would not accept that she was feeling any kind of sexual attraction that was making her senses go on full alert.

"Come with me," he told her brusquely, holding out his hand. He'd cleaned himself up, his chest bearing some slight grazes, and his scar that slashed across his abdomen shone silver against his golden skin. The chain he wore glinted with each movement, drawing her gaze to his chest. Darn it. For once a bare-chested lycan caused her to feel self-conscious—and incredibly conscious of said lycan. She rose to her feet, brushing the dust off her jeans and ignoring the outstretched hand. He'd returned her belt as soon as they'd reached camp, and hadn't come close to her since, a fact that she'd noted with something that bordered on disappointment. She folded her arms. No. She couldn't be disappointed, shouldn't be disappointed. She knew she'd offended him with her remark, but she'd been taken by surprise. Lycans liked to get physical. Touching, stroking, wrestling…but she hadn't been touched, stroked or wrestled with by another adult lycan in what seemed like an age.

His contact, and her reaction, had stunned her. Her lips pressed together tightly. She hadn't realized how long it had been since she'd shared contact with her pack, or how desperate and vulnerable their not-so-subtle shunning had made her. But she was stronger than most thought, and she wasn't about to let the guardian prime of an enemy pack turn her head. Nope.

"Where are we going?" she asked, trying to match his brusque tone. She wasn't about to leave Jax alone. She had no doubt that he was physically safe, and the kid was treating this somewhat like an unplanned adventure. But she wasn't about to surrender him to Alpine. She would protect him until she could get him home to his mom.

Matthias indicated one of the makeshift tents that had been set up a distance from the fire. "The boy is tired. It's time he retired for the night."

She glanced down at Jax, who shook his head. "I'm not tir—" he was interrupted by a large yawn "—tired."

Matthias's lips lifted in a smile, and she was surprised by the gentle humor she saw in his expression.

"You've had a big day, pup, and tomorrow will be even bigger when your tracker shows us the way to your home," he stated, his green eyes flicking up to her with grim intent before his gaze returned to the young boy. "You're going to need some rest."

Trinity dropped her gaze. She was expected to save the boy by betraying her pack. Like that was going to happen. The guardian prime didn't need to know he'd chosen the wrong she-wolf to abandon her family. She knew what her pack mates thought, but despite everything, she would not break trust with Woodland. She had a lot to make up for.

Matthias led them over to the tent and lifted the flap, gesturing inside. She eyed him. "Where are you sleeping?" If he thought he could pull some more of that alpha woo-hoo on her and have her panting for him, he had another think coming. There were always alphas in a pack, mostly serving the alpha prime as a guardian, and she'd dealt with her fair share of them. He may be the most charismatic alpha she'd ever met, but she could control herself. She could—would—resist.

His lips lifted in a wickedly sensual grin. "Oh, you are not leaving my sight, tracker." She kept telling herself she would resist. He leaned down to wink at Jax. "We'll keep her safe, won't we?"

Jax nodded, a smile on his face as he darted behind the tent flap. Trinity's brows dipped. Since they'd arrived in camp, Jax had actually relaxed. The other guardians had treated him kindly, gently. She was surprised. She didn't want to think how her own alpha prime would have behaved under similar circumstances.

"After you," Matthias said, extending his hand toward the tent flap. Her eyes narrowed, and she shot him a steely glare in warning. If he tried anything...

As though reading her mind, he frowned. "I won't touch you. We all need to sleep, and I don't want to have to set guardians to watching you when they could be resting." He folded his arms, and the action added bulk to his shoulders. "For what it's worth, my pack didn't kill another's alpha prime, nor did we break parley. Woodland are the ones who act without honor, not Alpine."

Trinity's cheeks warmed at the words, and she ducked her head and entered the tent to hide her embarrassment. All her life, she'd been taught to take pride in her pack, to be loyal, and to walk with honor. Matthias's words brought shame on her pack, shame on her. She didn't raise her head once she was inside the tent. She hadn't thought she could possibly live with more shame but, well, Matthias had proved there was always room for more.

She hustled over to the far side of the tent, around the curled-up figure of Jax. He smiled at her sleepily, then his smile broadened when Matthias swept into the tent. She made herself comfortable, scooting as far away as she could from the large alpha as he took up a position lying across the front of the tent—effectively blocking any attempt to leave it.

He lay on his side, his arm pillowing his head, and for a moment she couldn't help herself. She stared at him, at the bunched biceps, broad shoulders and muscled chest, his pants loose and comfortable and low on his hips.

When her gaze rose to his face, she realized he was staring at her, and the smoldering heat in his eyes called to an answering warmth deep within her. His regard was unsettling, patient and dark with sensual intent. She swallowed and lay down, rolling to face away from him. Even though she closed her eyes and had her back to him, she could still feel his gaze on her. The knowledge that he was prepared to watch her sleep set her heart pumping, and the muscles in her arm tightened with tension. She didn't think she'd be getting much sleep at all tonight. She sucked in her breath as she heard him shift position behind her.

She was attracted to the guardian.

Chapter 5

Matthias stiffened, his senses on alert as he awoke to the eerie sensation of someone watching him.

He slowly opened his eyes, then blinked, rearing his head back a little to allow his eyes to focus. Two blue eyes, innocent and watchful, hovered an inch from his face.

"I need to pee," Jax whispered.

Matthias blinked again, then nodded. "Okay," he whispered back.

He rolled to a sitting position, and looked at the other side of the tent. It was still dimly lit inside, but he could make out her form. The tracker lay curled up on her side, as though she was trying to roll into herself. Her chest rose and fell in a regular rhythm, and his lips tilted at the softest snore she emitted. She'd turned over during the night, and now lay facing him, her face softened and flushed with sleep.

Something unfurled deep inside him, a warmth that battled momentarily between lust and protectiveness, and he was surprised when his urge to safeguard won. He didn't want to care. It felt wrong, to Alpine, but most of all to Cara. He backed out of the tent without his usual grace, anxious to get away from the threat to his peace of mind. Outside, the night sky was lightening to a golden gray, and most of his guardians still slept.

"Come on," Matthias said to the kid, jerking his head toward a trail. He walked toward the ring of trees, and startled when a little hand slid in to hold his own. For a moment, something hard and brittle rose within, but when he looked down, that brittleness shattered when Jax looked up at him and smiled.

"Can we go hunt?" the boy asked.

Matthias arched an eyebrow. "I thought you needed to pee."

"Then can we hunt?" Jax asked eagerly. He dodged a branch, pulling down on Matthias's hand as he jumped over it. "I didn't break it," he told Matthias proudly.

He frowned. He had no idea what the kid was going on about. "Didn't break what?"

"The branch." Jax ducked around another one. "Trin says the less you break, the harder it is to track you."

"Really? What else does Trin say?" He kept his tone casual as he led the boy over to a tree, and gestured, turning his back to go and relieve himself a little distance away. He couldn't deny that he was fascinated by the tracker.

"She says the forest can be your friend."

"Uh-huh." He supposed a tracker would see it like that.

"She says not to hit Mia, even if she's asking for it."

Matthias finished zipping up his pants and waited for the boy to join him. "Who's Mia?"

Jax frowned. "She's in my class, but she's mean. She's always going on about her dad."

"Why is that a problem?" Matthias asked as he led the boy through some more trees, until he reached the bank of a river. He could smell the sweet scent of the water, and they both knelt down. Matthias leaned forward to wash his hands.

"She's always rubbing it in, that's all," Jax muttered, his lips turned down in a pout. An air of sadness crept over the little boy, one that Matthias didn't fully understand but could easily recognize.

"What does your dad say about it?" he asked quietly, and found himself thinking for the first time what the boy's parents must be going through, with their pup held by a warring pack, what Trinity's family would be experiencing. He could easily remember that panic, that agonizing, gut-wrenching dread that could be so consuming as to drive all rational thought out of a parent's mind.

"My dad's dead," Jax said quietly.

Matthias paused, then sank back on his haunches. "How long?"

Jax shrugged. "Not long."

"And your mother?" Matthias found himself asking, a little knot of tension solidifying like a stone deep in his gut.

Jax blinked and ducked his head. "She's sad."

Relief, slow and cool, swamped the stone to bury it. At least he still had his mom. "I'm sorry," he said, looking down at the sandy-haired boy. "It's hard when you lose family." He almost rolled his eyes. What a damned understatement. He tried again. "I mean, I get it."

Jax lifted his head to look at him, his eyes luminous with unshed tears. Something passed between them, a recognition of shared misery that traversed ages.

Jax nodded, then blinked furiously as he looked down at the rippling waters of the river. Matthias didn't know what made him do it, but he flicked a small amount of water at the boy. Jax squealed as he leaned back, gasping at the chill of the water, and Matthias smiled.

"This river comes down from my territory," he told the boy. "It tastes good, too."

He leaned over to scoop some water up in his hand and took a few sips. Jax watched for a moment, then tried to do the same. Matthias's arm flashed out and caught the back of his sweater as the boy nearly toppled into the river. "Like this," he said, and showed the boy where to plant his feet, then nodded approvingly when Jax successfully sipped water from his own cupped hands. "Good job."

He sat back against the sandy bank, drawing his legs up and resting his arms loosely across the tops of his knees. The river flowed quietly past, with an occasional gurgle as it tumbled over rocks. The sky was turning a peachy orange as the sun began to creep over the tops of the mountains in the distance, and birds twittered as they swooped down for a drink.

Matthias sighed. He enjoyed this time of the day, so peaceful. So tranquil. It gave him a chance to breathe, to thin—

"Oof," he wheezed as a little body launched at his back. Jax held on with his legs, his hands covering Matthias's eyes from behind.

"Gotcha," the boy chortled.

Matthias twisted, pulling the boy up over his shoulders and flipping him over, making sure he landed on his feet. For a few moments they wrestled, and Matthias enjoyed hearing the boy's giggles. The memories they brought forth were bittersweet, but today, they were bearable.

He smelled her before he heard her, turning around as Trinity burst through the reeds that lined the river. Her panicked gaze subsided into relief when she saw Jax was safe and sound and doing his best to trip Matthias over. Zane crashed through the undergrowth behind her, his gaze fierce until he saw his guardian prime. Matthias set the boy back a little, and adopted a stern expression. Jax grinned back as he turned to face his teacher, breathless.

"Good morning," Matthias said smoothly, folding his arms.

"Hey, Trin," Jax said, giving her a little wave.

"Jax, I was worried about you," she said, and Matthias could hear the edge in her voice. He arched his brow.

"He was with me," he told her. That should have soothed her fears. She glanced away, toward the river, as though trying to hide her reaction.

"I needed to pee," Jax told her.

She nodded, holding up her hand. "Fine. Just—just don't go anywhere without telling me, okay, Jax?" He nodded, running over to hug her. She sighed as she bent down to enfold her arms around him, and smiled at the lad. "You are giving me gray hairs, boy," she said, and ruffled his sandy-blond hair.

"Jax, go back to camp with Zane. He'll get you something to eat," Matthias said, and Zane nodded, then reached out to take the boy's hand. Trinity turned to follow, but Matthias shook his head. "No, you can stay."

She halted, gazing after the boy for a moment. Jax started asking Zane questions, and Matthias had to fight the smile as he heard them chattering back to camp. Well, Jax was chattering, and Zane was responding with monosyllabic grunts. When Trinity turned to face him, he quickly masked his smile beneath a determined frown.

"We need to talk."

Trinity gazed back out over the river, for once not really noticing the beauty of the unfolding sunrise. She scanned the opposite side of the river. The ground rose sharply into a craggy bluff. On the other side lay Nightwing, and just beyond that, the rising rain forest that gave way to the Alpine territory. The ridge dipped and rose, a natural border between werewolves and vampires. And yet, their enemy had still managed to camp in Woodland.

She hugged herself tightly before turning to face Matthias. "What?" she asked, impatient. She didn't care how rude she sounded. She wanted to go back to Jax. She'd been so worried for him when she'd awoken alone in the tent. To find him playing with the guardian prime—well, she was still trying to process that one. He stared at her with that green, enigmatic gaze, the one that seemed to elevate her heart rate, curl her toes and reach in and stir the ashes of arousal. He was so intense, so unashamed by his curiosity of her. He didn't try to hide his keen interest at all, as he tilted his head, surveying her.

"You really were worried for him," he said slowly, his eyes narrowed.

She frowned. "Of course I was. I had no idea where he was, where you were."

"Your concern is like that of a parent, yet you're not his mother," he observed. The muscles in her shoulders tightened.

"Jax has had a rough time lately."

Matthias nodded. "He told me. How did his father die?"

Sadness fluttered around her. Jax's father's death was unnecessary and avoidable, and marked one of those times when her pack didn't behave nicely. "He was killed by the dentist," she admitted quietly. The man wrongly accused of killing his alpha, the one Rafe had used to hide his own involvement in the crime.

Matthias dipped his head, and the sun peeked over the edge of the ridge, bathing him in a golden light tinged with rose. He was silent for a moment, then grimaced. "His mother isn't coping?"

Trinity shook her head, surprised at his interest. "She's pining." She leaned down and picked a flat stone off the sandy bank, hefting it in her hand. "She's got an adoring son, and she's locking herself up in her room." Trinity hurled the stone and it landed in the river with a distinct *plunk*. She'd seen it before. Some lycans never recovered from the loss of their mate, gradually fading into the shadows until they finally passed, joining their loved one on the Other Side.

"She's mourning," Matthias said, and picked up a stone.

"Well, she should get over it," Trinity muttered as she located another rock to hurl. She knew she sounded harsh, but she didn't care. The old anger and frustration rose swiftly, and her fingers tightened around the unforgiving stone in her hand.

Matthias frowned at her. "Sometimes it's not that easy, especially if they were mates." He threw the stone, and it skipped a few times across the river before falling below the surface.

Trinity cursed softly as she turned on her side and flung the stone. "The amount of times I've heard that as an excuse for giving up." Tears itched below her eyelids, and she blinked. Damn it, she was over it now. That was all water under the bridge. "Losing a mate shouldn't have to mean losing yourself, especially if a child is depending on you."

He laughed, but she couldn't hear any humor in the sound. "Says someone who has never had a mate, obviously."

"Why would you want one?" she exclaimed softly, and her shoulders sagged. "Jax has lost his father, and his mother doesn't see him." She shook her head. No pup should feel invisible.

"Maybe you should cut her some slack," Matthias suggested, his tone dark. "You can't know what she's going through. Give her some time."

Anger seared through her. She'd heard that before, too. And all her teenage years hadn't been enough time for healing. Trinity frowned as she faced him. "Why are you defending her? Why do you care? She's the enemy, remember. You're Alpine."

Matthias placed his hands on his hips as he faced her, his frown harsh. "And yet I'm not the one who sounds heartless right now."

Shock at his words snapped at her heart. Heartless? He had no idea what he was talking about. She cared. She cared deeply; she cared so much it damn well hurt. She'd seen loss, she'd felt so much stupid, cruel loss, and she'd seen senseless loss. Pining was senseless to her. It was a slow, painful form of suicide. The ring against his chest glinted as he turned to face the river, the muscles in his jaw flickering as he bit down. *He* was angry?

She shook her head. "Is this what you wanted to talk

about? Jax's parents?" Surely the big, ruthless guardian prime had more important issues to involve himself with than a pup from the enemy pack.

He tightened his lips as though biting off a retort, then took a calming breath before he turned his head to look at her. Even now she could see the anger blazing in those green depths.

"How many day's trek is it from here to the den?"

She sucked in a breath. Great. Now they were back to that. She almost preferred talking about that old chestnut, parents giving up on their children.

She gazed about the peaceful scene, so at odds with the turmoil inside her. Hell, what to tell him? She didn't want to take him to the den—she couldn't take him to the den. Not only because it would put her pack at risk, and she never wanted to do something like that, but also because her pack would never forgive her. She already had one sin, one shame darkening her standing within the pack. She lived in hope that one day they'd forgive her, that one day they would look at her, really look at her, and smile kindly.

But if she did this she'd be cast out of the pack, if any of them remained after a skirmish with the Alpine guardians.

"With Jax, and your wounded guardians, about three days trekking," she lied.

His eyebrows rose. "That far? Why were you training the pups so far from home?"

Oops. Good point. It had only taken them a few hours yesterday to reach the Alpine camp. "It's a Woodland tradition. When they turn four we do a training mission." Well, that sounded lame, even to her own ears.

Matthias looked at her for a moment. *Please buy it.*

Please buy it. He finally nodded. "Fine. We'll head out after breakfast."

He'd bought it. Great. Now she just had to figure out how to lose them.

Matthias trudged alongside Trinity. She'd set a grueling pace, and they'd been walking along the base of the ridge.

"When we get to the break in the hills, we'll set up camp," he told her, eyeing his guardians. Some were helping the injured, and while they were all fit, he didn't want them tired if they met up with any Woodland guardians. They'd set up camp early and continue the next day after a full night's rest. Like in the mountainous Alpine territory, the sun set early here in the Woodland mountains. It was already getting dark, although not once had Trinity complained about the hours they'd spent walking through the forest. It was almost as though she was used to day-long hikes in the woods.

She nodded and kept on walking, her eyes on the trail ahead. Well, he couldn't see a trail, but somehow she managed to follow one through the trees. He looked back at Zane. His second-in-command looked pained as Jax chattered along beside him. The boy hadn't stopped talking all day, unless it was to eat or drink. They'd each taken turns carrying the child, and the boy wasn't shy with any of them. Matthias hid his smile. Hearing the young boy's chirpy comments made him realize how much he missed the babble of a curious kid. His lips drooped. He couldn't think along those lines, though. There was too much pain.

Speaking of pain…he glanced sideways at the tracker. She'd seemed so caring, so nurturing with the boy, yet her harsh remarks that morning about Jax's mother had surprised him. He frowned. Could she really be that young, that inexperienced that she could think one could easily get over the death of a mate? Her words had ripped open old wounds for him. He could totally understand the desolation, the heartbreaking loneliness Jax's mother must be feeling, the emptiness that had taken root in her soul at the death of her mate. How could Trinity not understand? Or at least empathize?

He frowned. Since when did he care about caring, for crud's sake? What did it matter to him how naive and foolish the tracker seemed? He wondered, though, if she would have said the same things to him if she'd known of his history. He glanced around the guardians who marched along with him. Most of them knew, but even so, none of them knew all of the details, all of the tragic consequences. Even Jared hadn't known the full story.

Would they view him differently if they knew? Would they still follow him so loyally, trust in him so blindly? He ducked his head. Would they think he wasn't fit to be one of them?

Trinity stumbled a little, and cried out in pain. In a flash he reached for her, clasping her arm, and she startled, looking at him over her shoulder.

"Are you okay?" he asked, trying to keep the concern, the *care* out of his voice.

"Uh, yeah. I, uh, I have a rock in my shoe." She waved him on. "You go on. I'll catch up. I just need to take my shoe off and tip it out." She sat down on a fallen tree and slowly started to unlace her boot. He hesitated, and she raised an eyebrow. She gestured to the group of guardians following. "I'm not going to run, not with all you guys around."

He shot her an exasperated look, then turned to lead on. Jax ran up to the tracker, his expression curious, and Zane tilted his head in relief as he caught up to Matthias.

"That kid is exhausting. He talks, and talks, and, well, talks."

Matthias nodded as they approached a rocky outcropping. "It's good that he feels comfortable to do that," he told his guardian quietly.

Zane sighed. "Yeah, I guess. He's so young, though. He wants to play a lot."

"He's a pup. That's what they do." He remembered a pup just like Jax, with sandy hair and a cheeky grin. They rounded the rocky edge, stepping into the gloom cast by the mountain's shadow. Night was coming. A movement caught his eye, and Matthias put his hand out, halting Zane.

Deep in the shadows cast by the trees and the mountain behind them stood four men. All tall, all wearing dark clothes, with pale skin and the faint yet unmistakable scent of death.

Matthias's lips curled. *Vamps.*

Chapter 6

Matthias narrowed his eyes as one of the vampires stepped forward.

"You're trespassing," the vamp said, baring his teeth. His incisors lengthened, and Matthias clenched his teeth as he looked up at the sky. The sun was setting, but here, in the shadows of the mountains, the night had already crept in.

"This is Woodland territory," he growled at the vampire. "You're the ones trespassing."

The vampire smiled, his pale blue eyes lightening with satisfaction. "Actually, no. Woodland ends about two miles back that way, near that great big line of Douglas firs," he said, waving toward the curve of the ridge. "After that, it's Nightwing."

Matthias glanced over his shoulder, frowning. But Trinity... There was no sign of the tracker, or Jax, and his lips tightened. That damned she-wolf. She'd led them into an ambush. They were trespassing. He hadn't trusted her, and had suspected she was leading them astray, but he hadn't expected her to employ such an effective strategy.

Zane growled next to him, and Matthias shook his head, holding up his hands in a nonthreatening manner. They were in the wrong, but they could salvage this, and walk away. Hopefully.

"Apologies. We thought we were still on Woodland. Don't worry, we won't stay. We'll get out of your hair."

He took a step back, but the lead vampire shook his head, making a tsking sound.

"You think that's going to finish this? A bunch of mutts march through Nightwing, and you think you can just...walk away?" He gestured casually, rolling his wrist. His smile widened. "I don't think so."

Matthias frowned. "Well, I don't care what you think, that's the way it's going to happen. Marchetta and I have an agreement. We don't camp, but we have safe access."

The vampire's eyes narrowed, and he tilted his head. "I don't recall agreeing to that at all."

"Are you going to bail on a deal?" Zane growled from deep in his throat, taking a step forward.

The vampire sprang across the clearing, landing lightly and silently so that he stood toe-to-toe with Zane. "I made no deal." He lashed out, catching Zane on the cheek with his fist.

His movement was like a signal to the three vampires standing behind him, and they launched themselves at the first row of guardians.

Matthias ducked a kick from one vampire, then flung his arm up to brace himself against the punch aimed at his head. Moving like lightning, and with exceptional strength, the vampires were formidable foes on a bad day. This seemed to be a good day.

Matthias grunted as a leg kicked him in the gut, but he stopped and grabbed the next kick to his head. "Don't bite them," he roared to his guardians, fury at limiting his lycans in such a way adding a brutality to his own actions. He twisted the leg in his grip, turning and yanking, grunting in satisfaction at the resulting snap of bone. He heard the grunts and cries of lycan and vampire alike as they fought in the glade.

He sprang at the lead vampire who had Zane's neck twisted at an alarming angle. He used his full body weight to knock the vampire and Zane off their feet. Zane rolled and rose to his feet, stretching his neck. His friend bared his teeth, and Matthias gave the vampire a quick jab to the face before turning to hold his friend back.

"Let me at him," Zane snarled, trying to force his way past Matthias.

"We can't hurt them," Matthias grated back calmly, then lifted his leg to strike out at an advancing vampire, catching him savagely in the groin before spinning and thrusting his foot into the vampire's solar plexus, sending him flying back to hit the rock face behind them.

A hand grabbed onto his hair, but couldn't find purchase in the short military cut. Matthias grabbed the hand and spun, dragging the vampire off his feet and over his shoulder. The lead vampire hit the ground with a loud thud, and his eyes flashed from pale blue to bloodred in the blink of an eye.

Matthias bared his teeth and lowered his head until he and the lead vampire were nose to nose. "I could bite you now and end this," he grated, "but that would be going back on my deal I struck with Vivianne Marchetta, Vampire Prime, and as such is to be honored by all Nightwing vampires and Alpine lycans." He glared at the vampire in warning.

The vampire's eyelids flickered, and his lips curled in a sneer. "My sister is letting the dogs out?" He shook his head in disgust. "She wouldn't," he said through gritted teeth, his incisors gleaming white in the encroaching darkness. "My sister would not make a pact with the dogs."

Matthias nodded. "She did. Alpine are allowed safe access through Nightwing until we resolve a little dispute with your neighbors. During that time, we don't bite the dead." He snapped his teeth in warning, then tilted his head to the side. "Lucien, I presume? You should pay your sister a visit." He waited until the vampire nodded. "Yeah, you'll find there have been a few changes since your last visit."

He levered himself up and off the vampire, stepping back to allow him to gain his feet.

The vampire arched his back, leaping to his feet with a stealthy grace. "I'll talk to my sister, mutt, but trust me, this little arrangement of yours—it's not going to last. I don't know what the hell she was thinking, letting the dogs stink up our land."

Zane's stalked forward, fists clenched. "You think *we* stink?"

Matthias edged between the two, not taking his eyes off the vamp. "Go talk to your sister. I'm sure she'll explain everything. You might want to tell her you nearly started a war with the wolves," he added. "Somehow I don't think she'd appreciate your meddling." He lifted his chin. "And the agreement stands until Vivianne says otherwise—in person."

Lucien Marchetta glared first at him, then at Zane.

"This isn't over." He beckoned his vampires. Two of them had to be helped, and Lucien tucked the arm of one of his injured comrades around his neck. "Now that I'm back in town, things are going to change," he said, his voice low and menacing. Then as a group they jumped, landing lightly on the ridge above them, and then disappeared into the night.

Matthias turned to his guardians, surveying them. Apart from some scratches and bruises, they looked more pissed than hurt.

"Let's go find the tracker." He stormed past them to scan the forest. She was out there somewhere, the traitorous little tracker. He ignored the voice inside his head that reminded him she was doing what any other lycan would do to protect her pack, using every weapon at her disposal. Even though he'd suspected she was somehow trying to trick them, she'd lied to him, which made him angry—but he wasn't sure if he was angry at her for lying to him, or at himself for not detecting it. She'd played him smart, and he could appreciate that, even respect it—but she'd risked his men, the lycans he was responsible for, and that made him angry. Okay, fine, he was maybe a little pissed she didn't trust him, although God only knew why he thought she would… and therein lay that tiny little sting. She didn't trust him, and he wanted her to. So yes, he was hurt, but anger was always a better way to get over it.

But damn it, if things had escalated with Lucien Marchetta, then he'd be facing a war with the vamps as well as Woodland. They jogged back the way they'd come, right up to that fallen tree she'd parked her butt on as she watched them walk into a trap. He'd had no idea there was a curve in the border here, or that they'd be venturing into Nightwing territory. He had to give credit where it was due, though; she was clever.

Zane came up beside him. "She did it on purpose."

"Of course she did it on purpose. She doesn't want us anywhere near her pack." Damn it, the forest was dark, and as they all spread out and peered at the ground, looking for signs of their trail, he realized they were trying to find someone who was very adept at covering her tracks.

"I can't find any sign of her or the boy," Zane said, jogging up to him.

Matthias stood there for a moment, thinking. "We have no idea where the den is," he murmured, "so no clue as to which direction they might be headed in."

He closed his eyes, trying to concentrate on the immediate area. With the sense of sight removed, his other senses deepened. He could hear the rustle of the leaves in the tree, the slight ruffle of wings in the branches above. A cool breeze caressed his shoulders, and something small and four-footed scampered away from his group.

There. Honeysuckle and vanilla. He lifted his nose, sniffing at the air. Yep. It was faint, and it was laced with pine, as though she'd tried to mask her scent, but he would sniff her out if she dosed herself in pepper.

"There," he said, opening his eyes and pointing forward and slightly to the right.

Zane frowned. "How can you tell?"

"Can't you smell her?" Even now, her fragrance curled inside him, arousing him, and stirring his beast.

Zane sniffed the air, then shook his head. "Nope. All I've got is pine."

Matthias smiled grimly. "Then follow me." He turned

to the group. "The rest of you, set up camp near that dip in the ridge."

He and Zane loped off into the forest. They'd gone maybe two hundred yards when Zane tripped over something on the ground. He swore and picked it up, leaning back so the muted moonlight could illuminate the object.

A boot. Her boot.

Three steps later, Matthias found its mate, and narrowing his eyes, he could see the dark shadow of a pair of jeans dumped at the base of a tree.

He toed off his shoes, his hands lowering his fly. "She's shifted." He pulled his pants off and handed them to his friend. "Follow the trail. They're going to need their clothes." Matthias turned and started to jog into the darkness, shifting into wolf form as he ran.

Trin raced through the undergrowth, silently urging Jax to keep up with her. Her heart pounding, she kept changing direction, trying to make it as hard as possible for anyone to follow their trail. She'd used a pine sweeper to start, but once she shifted she couldn't hold on to the sprig of pine to mask their scent. Hopefully it had been enough to prevent the Alpine guardians from picking up their trail.

She wasn't quite sure what kind of start they had, but she was determined to take advantage of it. Jax tripped and rolled, a soft growl emitting from the little pup. He had a coat that consisted of sandy and brown patches, and she winced. His light colors weren't exactly blending into the night forest. She paused until he got to his feet, then nudged him with her nose. They wouldn't be able to get very far, not with Jax's little legs and low stamina, but she hoped to get him to one of the tunnel entrances. Once there, they could hide and take their time to return to the den.

She thought of Matthias, and a faint sense of guilt rose within her. It had been low, leading them into the Nightwing corner. Low, but desperate. She knew there were always sentries there. It was close to the western border of their territory, and was one of the main thoroughfares east–west for the vampires wanting to avoid the lycan mountain ranges. It was always heavily guarded, and served almost as a stopover for traveling vamps.

How else was she supposed to get her and Jax away from them? Because there was no way she could do what Matthias wanted. The hackles on her back rose. *No.* Her heart pounding, she fought the instinct to increase her speed—that would leave Jax unprotected, and damn it, *he* was close by. She could sense him. She didn't know why, didn't understand this awareness she had of him, she just knew he was out there, hunting her down in the dark.

She spied a log in the short distance, and started to run for it. She could hide Jax in—

A flash of white was all the warning she had before she was hit in the side and sent rolling across the pine needles.

Jax skidded to a stop and barked as she found her feet, shaking her head. What the—

The white wolf growled, his green eyes flashing in the moonlight, head down. Instinct told her to lower her head, to sink to the ground and submit, and it took all her courage to deny it.

He was beautiful in wolf form, so fierce and graceful, his paws plodding with a lithe agility as he closed the distance between them. His coat was white, glistening like snow-flecked silver in the moonlight.

Jax scampered toward her, but the wolf growled in warning. The pup stopped and sat on his haunches, his head tilted to the side.

Trinity bared her teeth and growled back, lifting her chin. She wasn't going to make this easy for him, damn it. How had he found them so quickly? He stalked past her, walking between her and the pup, and she had to pace to try and keep the pup in her sight.

The white wolf stepped forward, his lips curled back. She planted her feet and tried to catch Jax's eye, but the pup was focused on the guardian.

She stepped one way, he mirrored it. To get to the pup, she would have to go through him, and he was that pissed she didn't like her chances.

There was some thrashing in the underbrush to her left, and Zane emerged from behind a tree. Her eyes narrowed. He carried their clothing, a dark bundle in his arms. He paused when he saw the standoff, then dumped most of the clothes on the ground.

The guardian held up Jax's clothing and whistled to the pup. "Come on, Jax, you're coming with me. We'll let these two sort it out."

She paced, a growl low in her throat as Jax shuddered, shifting from his wolf form back to human, then took the clothing Zane handed him. When he was dressed, he raised his arms and Zane lifted him, hoisting him onto his hip. Trinity bound to her left in a last-ditch effort as he walked back into the darkness, but the white wolf sprang in front of her, ears erect and forward. He snarled at her. She snarled back.

He started walking around her, the gold necklace glinting against the white-silver coat, getting closer to her until his shoulder brushed against her in a not-so-gentle shove. She lashed out with a paw, teeth bared. He circled behind her, and she pranced about to face him.

It took her a moment to realize he was herding her back toward the fallen log. It bent at an angle on the forest floor, and he was effectively backing her into a corner.

She snapped her teeth in warning. She wasn't going to be backed into anything.

He stared at her for a moment, so close she could feel his breath across her lips. Then he dipped his head and sniffed.

For a moment she was stunned, then she did the same. Oh, he smelled heavenly. Pine, moss and that sexy, alluring musk that was him and him alone. He moved, his body brushing against hers, and she dropped to her haunches. He wasn't going to bite her. He wasn't going to attack her. She could still sense his anger, but he'd calmed down. She rose to her feet and crossed to the pile of clothing, shifting as she went.

She felt the shift in air currents behind her, and knew he did the same. He was naked, and so was she. She grabbed up her clothes and turned to face him.

He was…stunning. All muscle, he stood there in the moonlight, a perfectly formed warrior. And he was staring at her.

Lycans always shifted naked. They couldn't control their clothes, and most of the time stripped before a shift to save on the cost of their wardrobe. The Woodland forest and tunnels were peppered with stashes of clothing for the use of any lycan who needed it. So the naked form was nothing new to her. She'd seen others, and others had seen her, but for the first time, she was vitally aware of her body, as well as another's.

She stood tall, her shoulders back. The cool wind played with her hair, the tendrils caressing her bare shoulders, making her shiver at the teasing sensation. His gaze skittered over her, from the top of her head, halting briefly at her lips before scanning downward. His gaze paused at her breasts, and they grew heavy under his scrutiny, before he lazily toured over the rest of her body, the indent at her waist, the flare of her hips, and lower past the delta between her thighs and down her legs. It was a while before he raised his gaze to hers, and she sucked in her breath at the clear and visible hunger in his eyes.

She couldn't ever remember anyone staring at her so openly, so intently, so freely displaying his desire. She stared back at him for a moment, taking in his broad shoulders, wide and deeply muscled chest, narrow hips, and the erection that told her his desire wasn't her imagination. She swallowed. He was…big. Powerful. Strong. The ring on the chain glinted in the moonlight.

And he bore the brand of another woman.

She turned away from him and dragged on her jeans. He had no business staring at her like that, getting her all hot and hopeful, when he wore the ring of another. She dragged on her bra and snapped it quickly, then pulled her long-sleeve T-shirt on over her head. She scooped up her jacket and turned back to him, her composure in place.

Until she realized he was only now reaching for his pants. The moonlight played over the muscular curve of his butt, and he eyed her closely as he slipped one foot into his pants, then the other. He slid the pants up over his legs, never once looking away from her. She swallowed. How the hell did a guy make getting dressed so damn sexy? It was like watching a stripper in reverse, yet just as provocative.

She slid her arms into her jacket, shrugging it up over her shoulders. She was about to lift her hair free from the collar, but suddenly he was there beside her, his large hand sliding to cup the back of her head, lifting her tresses free of the garment.

He watched the dark curls tumble down her back, and slid his fingers beneath a tendril of hair, rubbing it between his fingers. For a moment he was so focused, so intent on the feel of the hair between his fingertips. Then his gaze shifted to hers, and it was almost a shock when her gaze met his, so close was his face, so blatant was his arousal. He twisted the hair around his fist and gently tugged her closer.

Chapter 7

This woman, this she-wolf, tied him up so tight in knots Matthias didn't know which way was up and which way down. Moments ago he'd been so damn angry, so *hurt* that she would willingly lead him into a vampire's trap, and put the rest of his group at risk. Now just her scent had the ability to drive the anger out of him, and replace that emotion with something just as hot, just as consuming, and far more satisfying.

Using her hair to pull her closer, he kept his gaze on hers. Her eyes were so luminous, so wary, yet so hungry for him. It felt like an aphrodisiac, making him throb in time to the pulse that beat strong and regular in the sweet indentation at the base of her throat.

He touched his lips to hers, heard the delicious gasp from her lips, felt the heat from her body and gave himself up to the experience. He cupped her face, her skin so soft beneath the rough pads of his fingertips. With the slightest pressure, her mouth opened beneath his, and his tongue slid in to stroke against hers. For a moment, that was their contact, mouth to mouth, his hands cupping her head. Then her hands grasped his arms, and instead of pushing him away, they slid up over his biceps to his shoulders. Her fingernails scraped up his neck and through his short hair in that way that instantly set a match to the passion he was trying to control.

Licking, gliding, caressing, the heat built between them as they exchanged long, drugging kisses. He trailed his hands down to her chest, his gaze flickering briefly over her shoulder. He wanted to explore her body, wanted to learn all her secrets. He walked her backward until they reached the broad trunk of a tree, and she leaned back against it, her nails scraping over his scalp as she tugged him closer.

He bent down and lifted her, resting her hips at the same level as his. God, she was amazing. Beautiful. Intoxicating. Again and again, their tongues dueled in a carnal battle. She made him feel so hot, so achy, his arousal so damn tight against his pants. He pressed his hips into hers, feeling her heat through their clothing, craving it. His hand lowered to her breast, and she moaned. He drank in the sound, his mouth gliding over hers, tasting her like a fine wine. She arched into his caress, and he molded his hand over her breast, cupping it, his thumb strumming over that perky little tip.

Rolling his hips in a hypnotic rhythm, his heart pounded in time to the pulse throbbing in his cock. He stroked the rounded curve of her hips, slid his hand under her buttocks and lifted her against him. He sank into that sweet spot between her thighs that seemed just as hot for him as he was for her. He pumped his hips against her, hearing the catch in her throat at each press of the hips, each slide. Matthias wanted their clothes gone. Now.

He dragged his lips from her mouth and kissed his way down her neck as he carefully lowered her legs to the ground. Leaning back with his hips still pressed to hers, Matthias tugged at her jacket. She leaned forward, and he slid it off her shoulders and down her arms.

"Yes," she whispered, her hands caressing his back roughly, as though her urgency matched his.

He kissed her again, tongue licking at hers, then parted from her just long enough to whip the T-shirt she'd just donned up and over her head. She grabbed him and pulled him close again, kissing him frantically now, moaning as he cupped her breasts, the lacy bra a frustrating barrier to the bounty he knew she concealed.

Her hands trailed down from his shoulders, sliding over his chest, and he shuddered at the feel of her hands on his body.

And then she stopped.

She pulled her mouth from his, looking up at him before her gaze dropped to the chain under her hands. Then she pushed him away.

"You skunk," she exclaimed, and punched him on the chest. He backed up, not because that paltry blow made any real impact, but because he was so stunned by her change in mood.

He gaped at her as she shoved at him, and he backed up farther, his hands palm out. "What?"

She bent and retrieved her T-shirt, pulling it on so quickly, so brutally, it looked like she was boxing with the fabric. She finally stuck her head through the right hole and glared at him.

"You skunk," she repeated, contempt lacing her tone. "We are so not doing this."

"But I liked doing this. So did you." What the hell? How had they gone from trying to get into one another's pants to this?

She waved her finger at him, apparently lost for words for a moment, then she clenched her hand into a fist. "There is something really wrong with you," she snapped, and started to storm off.

Her words hit him like a shower of glass slicing through his heart. So hot, so fierce was the pain, he actually staggered back a little. She knew. Somehow, just with a kiss, she knew. He swallowed, dragging a hand over his face as she stomped between the trees. How? How had she sensed what none of his pack had? He sucked in a breath. Well, obviously knowing was a turnoff. Her rejection stung, an effective cold wash over his desire. His lips firmed. See, this was why he never got involved with the opposite sex. It just hurt too damn much.

He would have liked for them to just keep walking in opposite directions, and never come into contact again, but even though he was humiliated, hurt and ever so angry, he couldn't let her walk off. At least, not in that direction.

"The camp is back that way," he yelled, pointing off to his right. She glanced over her shoulder, frowned, then changed direction. He stayed where he was. If he wasn't so angry, so humiliated, he'd tell her that her shirt was on inside out.

Trin sat under a tree, tying an elastic on the end of her braid as she watched Matthias speaking with his lycans. Jax was playing some sort of hand-slapping game with one of the guardians. The lycan winced every now and then, and even from here Trinity could tell he was letting the pup win a few rounds. Finished with her braid, she idly lifted a twig that lay next to her boot. Upon his return to the camp last night, Matthias had ordered them to sleep apart. He'd lain down near the pup, and some guardian named Kai had taken up watch over her. Dawn had finally broken after a sleepless night, and the sunlight shone through the branches of the Douglas firs. She watched as Zane asked a question, and Matthias shook his head, his short hair a golden cap in the sunlight.

But not the least angelic. Trin snapped the twig she'd been playing with, anger and shame still thrumming through her veins. She wasn't stupid. That was a wedding ring he wore around his neck. It wasn't common, but it wasn't unheard of for mates to exchange rings. The problem was hanging on to them through a shift. She picked up another twig. Her father had worn a ring, as had her mother. Her mother's ring was lying in a box padded with cotton wool back in her homely little cave. Her father's ring—well, that had disappeared, probably swept away when he...died. Her vision blurred.

She knew the significance of that ring. She knew the commitment, the loyalty, the fidelity that was supposed to go along with it. The twig snapped again, and she tossed the broken wood over her shoulder. She reached for something else, something stronger. Her father had loved her mother to the point of distraction. It had been a legend in her pack, the alpha prime tamed by his she-wolf. She sniffed. The ring symbolized love. Devotion. It was a promise, a vow, a pledge—love without end.

And Matthias had pledged that to another woman. The stick in her hand snapped, and she dropped it at her feet. How could he kiss her like that, when his heart belonged to another? How could he make her feel like they were the only two on earth, that he was solely focused on her, when he had a she-wolf warming his den?

And why the hell did she care so damn much? She rubbed at her forehead, trying to ease the tension. He was Alpine. A.L.P.I.N.E. She was Woodland. He wanted to annihilate her pack. She'd tried to have him and his guardians killed. It wasn't a good basis for any kind of relationship.

There was a general hubbub as the guardians gathered nodded in agreement over something, and Zane and Matthias made their way over to her.

She looked up, squinting against the sun as the guardians stood in front of her. Matthias lowered himself to one knee beside her and spread out a large document at her feet. A map. Her anger cooled in her veins. *Here we go*, she thought.

His gaze was brittle, cold, remote—such a contrast to the heat and desire of the night before.

"Show us where your den is," he said, his hand holding down the map, his tone cool.

She shook her head. There was no prevarication, no attempt to coax the information out of her, but even if there was, she wouldn't give him that information.

"No."

He rested his arm across his knee, his eyes narrowed as he stared at her, assessing her. "Why not?"

She laughed at his question, then realized he was being serious. "Uh, because I'm not going to get my pack killed."

He tilted his head. "There doesn't need to be any killing. We'll go in peacefully."

She tilted her head, mirroring his angle. "Seriously? You think I'd trust you?" She'd be ten times a fool if she did.

"You have my word," he responded simply. "We will only act to defend ourselves. We're only interested in Rafe."

"And what about the Woodland guardians? So many like your own?" she asked sharply. "What of them? They will do everything in their power to protect our alpha prime. You go in there and they will react to an attack, and lycans will die."

"Rafe killed another alpha prime. Do you realize how disrespectful, how offensive that is?" Matthias asked, his tone silky soft. "Samantha Alpine is pregnant with his pup. She's lost her partner, a child has lost his father and he lost our leader. He will pay. Do you condone what he did?"

Trinity dropped her gaze. No, she didn't. What Rafe had done—well, it was abhorrent to her, and she knew most of her pack felt the same. Primes held a position of honor, of respect, and killing one was the highest of insults. But Rafe was a strong alpha prime. He had loyal guardians who would protect him at the risk of their own lives, purely because he was their alpha prime, and they'd sworn allegiance. The rest—well, they were probably more scared than loyal. Rafe was a formidable enemy, and if you were insubordinate or rebellious, then he made it clear you were his enemy. She'd had to learn that lesson the hard way. He didn't act with the same code of honor as her father when he had been alpha prime. She still had to respect him as her leader, no matter how distasteful. "I'm loyal to my pack."

Matthias looked up at Zane and shrugged. "Take the boy."

Her eyes widened. "What are you doing?"

"I told you, my word is my bond. If you don't help me, I told you I'd have young Jax taken back to Alpine."

Panic rose, and she met his gaze. "You can't," she said quietly.

"Ah, but I can." He started to roll the map up.

"But—you're taking him away from his family," she argued.

He shrugged as he rose. "From what you tell me, it's not much of a life for him, what with his mother pining and all."

"Is Alpine going to be any improvement?" she asked sharply as she gained her feet. He handed the map to Zane and folded his arms, his muscles bunching with the movement. Damn it, none of these lycans seemed interested in wearing shirts, despite the cool autumn air.

"I won't lie to you. There are some at Alpine who want all of Woodland dead for what happened to Jared, and a Woodland pup would be a focus for their anger." He shrugged. "Or else he'll be largely shunned—but not my problem. I'm here to get Rafe."

Tears burned beneath her eyelids at his words, and she looked away. To be abused for a crime you didn't commit was unfair, unjust and unacceptable, but to be shunned—to be ignored, to be made to feel like you're invisible, like you don't matter, that people would be happier if you were just *gone*—that was something she couldn't abide. She knew how that felt, and wouldn't wish it on anyone, let alone a curious, happy little pup like Jax. She lifted her gaze, watching as Zane beckoned the little pup over, took his hand, and started walking off into the forest, toward the Nightwing border.

"It's up to you, Trinity," Matthias said, tilting his head to the side. "Jax or Rafe. I know which one I'd choose."

"This isn't fair," she whispered as Jax disappeared from view, so innocent, so naive, so vulnerable and defenseless against a pack that would hate him on principle.

"Tell that to Samantha Alpine," Matthias responded roughly. "Better yet, tell that to the pup that will grow up without a father." He laughed softly, the sound so bitter, so cold in its humorless tone. "There you go, Jax and Jared's pup have something in common—they'll both grow up without a father because of Rafe Woodland's actions. Interesting that death is the common thread between our packs."

Trinity hugged herself, goose bumps chilling her at his insight. This wasn't fair. This wasn't how it was supposed to be. Why the hell had Rafe not told the trackers that there was going to be a parley in the forest? If she'd known, she would have taken them on a training run through the Woodland den's tunnels, not out into danger.

But what choice did she have? Jax was sweet and innocent, and should be playing in his home forest with his pack mates. Rafe was big enough and mean enough to look after himself. Sure, the pack would never forgive her for leading the Alpine guardians to the home den—but they wouldn't forgive her if she let one of their young be taken. She sucked in a breath. She couldn't allow Jax to be abducted, but just like laying a false trail, she could convince Matthias she was doing as he wanted—and hopefully give Woodland some warning in the progress. Did they even know there was a squad of Alpine guardians on Woodland territory?

"Call him back," she whispered, her eyes still on the spot in the forest where Jax and Zane had disappeared.

"Sorry, not sure I heard you. Do you agree to my terms?"

"I will take you into Woodland," she said, choosing her words carefully. "Bring Jax back." She turned to look at Matthias, her eyes somber. She understood why he was doing what he was doing. She still kind of hated him for it.

He must have read something in her glare, because he stepped closer. "I'll call Jax back as soon as I have your word—no more stunts like yesterday afternoon."

Trinity's lips twisted into a half smile. "What makes you think I'll keep my word?"

Matthias's eyes sharpened, and he moved even closer, as though to make sure she heard what he had to say. "Because I have to hope that not all of Woodland is dishonorable," he said quietly, intently. "Prove me wrong, Trinity. Prove to me that there is still some decency in your pack."

She refused to respond to his challenge. "Call Jax back."

"Your word," he insisted smoothly.

"Fine. No more vampires," she muttered, and her eyelids fluttered. "Please," she whispered, "call him back."

Something flickered in his gaze, an awareness, a curiosity, and he slowly nodded. Pursing his lips, he whistled. It sounded like a bird call, but not one that she recognized. An answering trill was heard in response, and her shoulders relaxed. They were on their way back.

"I might be doing this under protest, but let's get some things straight," she said, needing to show some resistance, just so that he knew she wasn't completely submissive. "Number one, I shouldn't be kissing you. Number two, you *so* shouldn't be kissing me. Number three, the sooner we remember we want each other dead, the happier everyone will be that order is restored in the world."

Matthias's eyes gleamed. "Deal. But just so there is

no repeat of yesterday, you and Jax will remain separated."

"No, please don't," she said, shaking her head as she hugged herself. She needed to hug the boy, reassure both of them that he was here. Safe. Cared for.

Matthias smiled grimly. "Don't worry, he'll be safe enough with me."

She shook her head. An Alpine guardian, even a guardian prime, wasn't the same as family. Sure, Matthias would make sure Jax was physically safe, but it wasn't his physical safety that now concerned her.

"He's with a rival pack, Matthias. He's a kid. He can't be ignored, or merely tolerated. Someone needs to watch him."

"I'll watch him."

"No, he's—he's a curious kid. He'll wander off, he'll get up to mischief, especially if he feels he's being ignored, or like nobody is watching him. Like he's invisible…" her last word trailed off, and she bit her lip. She didn't want Jax to feel invisible, or that he wasn't cared for.

Matthias's eyes narrowed, and he gazed at her intently for a moment. "I'll take care of him," he told her quietly.

She shook her head. "You don't unders—"

"I know how to look after a pup, Trinity," Matthias interrupted, almost roughly, then turned and stalked away.

Trinity blinked at his retreating back. She'd touched a sore point, she realized belatedly, although what the hell it was, she had no idea.

Chapter 8

"I'm pretty sure I've walked past that boulder twice already," Zane muttered.

"Three times, actually," Matthias commented as he walked the trail that apparently Trinity could clearly see, but they could not—although it was becoming clearer each time they completed a circuit.

"Nine times," chirped Jax from atop Matthias's shoulders. Matthias couldn't help the smile that spread across his lips.

"Can you count to ten, Jax?"

"Uh-huh. One, two, nine, four, eleventy—"

"Eleventy?" Matthias's smile morphed into a grin.

"Now you made me lose count," Jax grumbled, tugging on the guardian's hair, and Matthias chuckled.

"It's okay, Jax. You can count just fine. We might need to work on it just a little, though."

"You know she's walking us in circles, right?" Zane grumbled, and kicked a stick out of his way.

"I know."

"And you're okay with that?"

Matthias paused, sensing his friend's frustration. "Yeah, I am. Because I understand." Other guardians continued to trudge past them.

Zane moved his hands in a rolling motion. "Oh, please, share your wisdom, Guardian Prime. Lay it on me." Zane stopped to face him, and Matthias stood on one foot, casually placing his other on the oh-so-familiar boulder. Jax leaned on his head, as though he was interested to hear this, as well.

"She's trying to protect her pack," Matthias said quietly. "She doesn't want any of them hurt." Despite his emotional distance that morning, he'd learned a few things about Trinity from their conversation. Like how much she cared for this pup, and how she wanted to make sure that the pup knew someone cared. That was very important to her, but anything important could always be used against you. He'd felt no guilt at employing her emotional need as a weapon. But he had to admit, her care for the lad was…sweet. She was also faithful to her pack. Painfully so. "She is loyal to a fault. She may not agree with—" he hesitated, tilting his head back. Jax met his gaze, openly curious.

"With what someone has done," he continued. He didn't like Rafe—would love to spit on his grave, frankly—but he was aware he was discussing the boy's alpha prime. "She may not like it, but she is determined to protect her pack." He shrugged, gaining a giggle from the boy sitting on his shoulders and more tugs on the hair. "It's almost admirable." And didn't it suck to have to admit it?

Zane shook his head and waved his hand. "No. No,

no, no, *no*." He turned and walked away for a moment, then came back. "Don't."

Matthias frowned. "Don't?"

"Don't—don't get sucked in by the she-wolf," Zane snapped. "She's Woodland. They're the bad guys, remember?" Zane glanced up at Jax and winced. "No offense, Jax. You're all right." He wagged his finger at Matthias. "But you know what I mean, Matt."

Matthias shook his head. "I'm not getting sucked in by the she-wolf," he stated. Just because he liked to go for long runs in the moonlight, exchange hot kisses and basically try to get into her pants at every opportunity did not mean he was getting sucked in by the she-wolf.

Zane sighed. "Look, I'd be the first person who would be absolutely delighted for you to find someone you're attracted to. Hell, I've tried fixing you up, Nate's tried fixing you up—half the Alpine she-wolves have been trying to get your attention so frankly, it would be nice if you could just finally pick one so that the rest of us have a chance with the females, but—" Zane gestured in the general direction of the tracker leading the guardians on a bush walk "—she's one of *them*."

"I'm confused," Matt said, perplexed. "The other night you were suggesting I ignore her—what was it you called it? Her shortcomings?"

"That was before she led us into an ambush with vampires and dragged us across the butt-end of Woodland, over and over and over again. Now you're cozying up to her, and I don't think we can trust her as far as we can pee."

"I want to get Rafe and make him pay for Jared's death," he said quietly. "That's all there is, that's all it can be."

Zane looked to the sky as though praying for an intervention, then started walking again. "Uh-huh. That's exactly what it looked like last night."

Warmth bloomed in Matthias's cheeks, and he resumed walking. "I didn't realize you saw that." To have one of his guardians witness Trinity's rejection—well, he thought last night was humiliating. Now it appeared he could top it.

Zane looked over his shoulder. "Of course I saw it. I was there, remember? I brought Jax home."

Matthias pretended he was watching where he was putting his feet, and Zane stopped again. Matthias almost plowed into him, and Jax giggled as he swayed forward at the abrupt halt.

"Aw, hell. You're not talking about that, are you?" Zane folded his arms and sighed. "I don't get it. The whole three years you've been with us, I've never seen you so much as look at another wolf. What gives?"

Matthias surveyed his friend. Zane didn't appear angry. He couldn't blame his friend if he had felt anger at what must seem an obvious attraction to the wrong woman. Hell, he was angry at himself for feeling it. Zane was right, he hadn't so much as looked at another woman, not since Cara. Actually, he'd thought, after that night, that maybe he simply *couldn't* experience those emotions again, but this woman... For some reason his libido had woken up and would not let go.

But she'd made it clear. She thought he was a... skunk. He pursed his lips. A damn skunk. Had she smelled something on him? Or was it just a deep sensing that revealed his secret?

"Nothing gives." Like, literally, nothing. He would shut this off, this compelling attraction. He'd managed so long without it, he could keep going, keep functioning. Okay, so maybe it was taking a little more effort these days, but he had practice. He could do it. He'd just keep on keeping on. His focus shouldn't be on Trinity, anyway. His focus, his mission, was to get Rafe. That simple.

He lowered Jax to the ground, despite the boy's protests, "See that guy over there?" he pointed to Warwick, one of the guardians who had just walked past them. "He likes to play tag."

Jax ran off and smacked the large dark-haired guardian in the butt. "You're it," the boy cried excitedly, before dashing off into the forest.

The surprised guardian turned back, and Matthias lifted his chin in the direction of the pup. Warwick rolled his eyes and then loped off after him as Zane muffled a chuckle behind his hand, then sighed as they started walking again.

"I *know* I've been here before," Zane commented as they clambered down a beaten path of mossy green grass.

"She's scared we'll kill her whole pack," Matthias told him.

Zane rolled his eyes. "As tempting as that sounds, you won't let us."

Matthias tilted his head. "Does it? Sound tempting? To wipe out an entire pack?" He halted. "I've seen that happen, and it's not pretty. It's horrific, it's evil and it leaves a stain that you'll never recover from. Annihilation isn't the answer to anything. You're talking about the slaughter of an entire bloodline."

Zane looked at him closely. "You never talk about what happened."

Matthias shook his head and started walking. "No, I don't," he responded simply.

"If you ever want to—"

"I won't."

"Okay, then."

"Okay."

"So what do we do about this tracker leading us on a wild-goose chase?"

"We let her. At the moment, she's our best bet, until Nate comes back with a response from Woodland about the trade. Until then, we just let her lead us where she will. Eventually she'll have to trust us."

"If you're so fantastic at tracking, why haven't we got to the den yet?"

Trinity's eyebrows rose at the question drawled from behind. She glanced briefly over her shoulder at the russet-haired guardian. Kai. Her shadow.

"It talks," she responded drily as she strode on. He'd been her silent watchdog since she began leading them around the northern perimeter.

"And it's wondering if you're really as good as everyone says you are." He lengthened his stride so that he walked alongside her.

She glanced up at him in open curiosity. "How good do they say I am?"

He shrugged. "There's a story of how you saved six of your pack mates after a cave-in. Nobody knew exactly where they were, but you found them."

She ducked her head. "That was quite a while ago. And it was seven, by the way."

"There's also a story about how they buried a T-shirt in the forest and then got you to find it three weeks later."

She nodded. "True." That had been one of her trials, although she hadn't known it at the time. To achieve tracker prime status, there were a number of tests to pass that were set by the alpha prime. Her mouth turned down at the corners. She'd had to track a deer Rafe had injured, purposely letting it go, in great pain, for her to track. She'd also been dumped blindfolded in River Pack territory, and had had to trek her way out, without any of River Pack becoming aware of her presence. She'd hated those four days, hiding, covering tracks, subsisting on berries and bushes to avoid leaving evidence of a kill. That had been three nights of sleeping in trees and constantly living with all senses on high alert.

"So how is it you can find lycans and T-shirts buried under the earth, but you can't find your home den?"

"I know exactly where it is," she commented lightly.

"But we can't be anywhere near it, otherwise we would have run into Woodland guardians by now. Or do they not patrol their territory?" Kai's tone was deliberately challenging.

"Oh, they do," she assured him, lifting her chin. "Trust me, Woodland have their territory covered." Largely, they did. But since Rafe had pissed off the River pack, he'd had to double up patrols along that border. There was a long-standing feud between River and Woodland, so long she wasn't sure if anyone actually remembered how it had started. She only knew their border was constantly in dispute, and there was the occasional flare-up of tension, more so now that Rafe was alpha prime.

Up here in the northern quadrant, where the land rose and fell sharply and the natural landscape deterred intruders, the likelihood of them running into a Woodland team was extremely low—and that's the way she wanted to keep it. That way neither Woodland nor Alpine needed to get hurt. Besides, some of Woodland thought this area was cursed. Her mouth turned down. For those, it was easier to believe than the truth.

She looked up at the tall guardian, and the cut on his biceps caught her eye. Kai caught her gaze and his eyebrows rose at her wince. She gestured to his arm.

"That, uh, that looks painful."

He glanced at it briefly, then shook his head. "Nah, I've had worse."

"Is that—is that from yesterday?" she asked tentatively.

He looked at her directly. "You mean, when you lead us into that cozy little powwow with the vamps? Yes."

She looked away. Kai was young, good-looking, with his russet brown hair and blue-green eyes. Although he was supposed to be guarding her, she'd never sensed any malevolence from him. Yet, he was hurt from the confrontation she'd sensed would occur. He could have died. She'd seen some mild bruising on both Matthias and Zane, as well. More could have died.

"Sorry about that," she said roughly, clambering over some rocks.

Kai chuckled. "Don't sweat it. It was fun. I should be thanking you—a wrestle with vamps was just what I needed."

She shook her head in amazement. This lycan was chatting with her so comfortably, so relaxed—something she found hard to process, after what she'd done, but also because lycans didn't normally chat with her. At least, not from her pack.

"You should hate me," she said quietly. He was so casual with her, making conversation as though they were companions out on a walk, not members of enemy packs who were plotting each other's elimination.

Kai chuckled. "What for? That run-in with the vamps?" He gave a derisive snort. "Hardly worth the effort, that lot. It would take a lot more than that to make me hate someone."

"But it could have been worse." She felt she needed to point that out, to really put her actions into perspective for the young guardian. "I suspected there may be vamps, but I had no idea how many—there could have been a squad there, for all I knew. And I led you into it, knowing you would be attacked."

He shrugged. "All's well that ends well," he said nonchalantly.

She blinked. "But—but we killed your alpha prime." She couldn't understand how this lycan could stomach his babysitting duties, but the fact that they were talking like this, with no animosity—it completely stumped her.

"Did you?" Kai looked at her intently, then ducked under the branch of a tree as they continued their journey. "The way we hear it, the dentist dealt with the lycans directly responsible with handling the poison, that psycho Arthur Armstrong is stinking up a prison cell somewhere deep in a Reform pen and the only person left who hasn't been brought to justice for Jared's death is your alpha prime."

"When…when an alpha prime acts, it's in the name of the pack," she said quietly, quoting her father. "They are the chief representative of the family."

Kai shrugged. "Sure, but if my brother acts like a Class-A dick, does that make me a Class-A dick? Similarly, if I acted like a dick, I wouldn't necessarily want my whole pack blamed for it." He grimaced. "And let's face it, your alpha prime acted like a royal dick."

Trinity trudged on silently after that, mulling over his words. A pack that didn't blame you for the sins of your father? That sounded weird. It also sounded like nirvana.

* * *

Matthias looked up from the campfire as more lycans entered the clearing. Nate had arrived with backup. He rose and went over to greet the guardians. Male and female, they were the fittest, toughest guardians, and he was proud to train them and fight alongside them.

Nate shook his hand, but there was something in the lycan's gaze, a seriousness, that had Matthias raising an eyebrow.

"What's up?" he asked.

Nate jerked his chin, and Matthias followed him, along with Zane, as the current squad welcomed their brothers- and sisters-at-arms.

"I have a message from Vivianne," Nate said, his hands on his hips. "We still have access through Nightwing, but we'll be escorted. No free access."

Matthias pursed his lips. "So Lucien got to her. Darn. Well, it limits us a little, but not much." He shrugged. "Fine, we'll deal with it."

Nate rubbed his chin, hesitating, and Matthias frowned. "What?"

"We, uh, we got a response from Woodland about the exchange."

There was something in Nate's tone that had him straightening his shoulders. "And?"

"When we offered to exchange their tracker prime for their alpha prime, Rafe's response was—and I quote—'You can keep her.'"

Matthias raised his eyebrows. "What?" He couldn't contain his disbelief, his shock. A tracker, especially one with the status of tracker prime, was a valuable resource for a pack. The tracker was the one to call in times of natural disasters, to find safe routes and sites, and to help rescue and recover lost ones. Trackers were also critical for locating new food sources, hunting sites and trespassers. Especially in a time of war, trackers were indispensable.

"That doesn't make sense," Zane muttered. "He could have surrendered with dignity, and his pack would have still flourished with the help of their primes, including the tracker prime. Sure, an alpha prime outranks a tracker prime, but under the circumstances, I'm, well, stunned."

"You and me both," Matthias said, looking back toward the fire. Trinity had finagled a seat next to Jax, and was sharing food out of her bowl. "Sure, Rafe seems to be quite the selfish prick—but he's an alpha prime. Pack comes first." If he'd found himself in the same position, he would have taken the exchange—with a plan to escape, of course, but still…you didn't leave a pack member in the hands of your enemy.

"What about the pup?"

Nate shook his head. "Same deal. Keep the pup, the mother is almost dead, anyway."

Matthias almost reeled backward. Rafe Woodland didn't value his young. He didn't value his tracker prime. Did he value his pack at all? Or would he be prepared to risk them all to save his own skin, his own ego? Having that kind of enemy changed the strategy of battle.

He eyed the little boy sitting next to Trinity. He had a cheeky grin as he told her something, and Matthias could see the smile blossom on her mouth, hear the tinkle of her laughter. The boy yawned, and she picked him up to nestle him on her knees, her arms embracing him as she kissed the top of his head. A lump formed in his throat at the easy display of affection, of love and trust, between the two. Trinity's gaze lifted, and her smile faltered as she found his eyes on hers. A line appeared between her eyebrows as she looked at him and his men.

He turned back to Zane and Nate. "We say nothing of this in front of the pup. He must never know." To be abandoned by one's pack was, in most cases, a fate worse than death. He knew from painful experience. For a kid so young it would be humiliating, terrifying and possibly the harshest punishment ever devised— and this kid had done nothing but scamper through the forest.

Zane and Nate nodded immediately. No pup deserved that kind of treatment.

Matthias shook his head. He was slowly forming a picture in his mind of his enemy. Rafe Woodland was self-serving, ruthless and fierce. The normal leverages wouldn't work with the lycan, and Matthias wanted to get out of this battle with as few casualties as possible. To do that, he needed to understand Rafe better—starting with why the alpha prime didn't seem to care for his tracker.

He strode toward Trinity.

Chapter 9

Matthias beckoned Kai and Warwick over, and Jax's eyes lit up when he saw his playmate from earlier in the day. Matthias lifted the pup from Trinity's lap, shaking his head to still her protests, and hoisted the boy until their eyes were on level.

"Wanna play with the big boys?" he asked.

Jax nodded. "Yes, yes, yes," he chanted.

Matthias nodded. "Okay, but just for a little while, and then it's time for bed." He handed the kid over to Warwick, who winced when Jax grabbed hold of his hair as he climbed up the big man's body to his shoulders.

He bent down and grasped Trinity's arm, gently pulling her to her feet. "We need to talk." He walked her away from the light of the fire, into the enveloping darkness of trees and night.

"What? Why?" she asked, breathless, the sound tightening his groin as he stopped a good distance from the camp, ensuring no others could overhear their conversation. He couldn't help noticing that she hadn't tried to pull away. He didn't know what that meant, what he could read into it, if anything. He glanced back toward the camp. There was a faint glow between the trees, but that was it. They couldn't see any detail of fire, of folks sitting around—which meant those folks couldn't see Trinity's reaction when he told her the news. He wanted to give Trinity some privacy to hear what he had to tell her, a chance for her to hold on to some dignity.

He faced her and folded his arms, trying not to touch her, reach out to her, hold her. She'd made it quite clear she didn't want anything to do with him. Although, the way her eyes followed the movement of his arms and chest, the hot and hungry look in her eyes, had him re-thinking his position.

"Aren't you cold?" she asked, frowning. "Don't any of you own a shirt?" She tugged at the collar of her jacket.

"We're Alpine. We're used to snow and ice. This is balmy in comparison to our home."

Her gaze kept flicking between his chest and his eyes, and all thoughts of dignity flew out the window. He couldn't help himself. He unfolded his arms and placed his hands on his hips, and her eyes dropped to stare at his chest. Then she squeezed her eyes shut for a moment before opening them to meet his gaze. Yeah, she tried to act so damn cool, but there was nothing cool about the heated desire in her eyes that she tried to hide from him.

Okay, so now he was confused. He stunk like a skunk, but it looked like the tracker was attracted to... skunks?

She stared at him with a composed yet mildly curious expression. Oh, now, she was all business. "You wanted to talk?"

No. He wanted to kiss her, but he still remembered the sting of her rejection the night before. A perverse need to make her see him as something more than a skunk prodded him, and he decided to test how deep her cool reserve went.

"Yeah, I did," he said, and flexed his right pec. Her gaze faltered only slightly, not quite dipping below his chin. "Mind telling me what your relationship is with Rafe Woodland?" This time he flexed his left pec. This time her gaze did drop, and he was fascinated by the rosy bloom in her cheeks when she snapped her gaze back up to his. *Yeah. Not that cool.*

"Uh, what?" she asked licking her lips, then she frowned. "My relationship with Rafe? What do you mean?"

"What kind of relationship do you have with Rafe Woodland?" he repeated carefully. He could see the confusion in her gaze, the flicker in her eyes as she tried to guess his goal.

"Uh, he's alpha prime, and I'm tracker prime," she said, shrugging.

He tilted his head to the side, and tried to look at her through the eyes of her alpha. What he saw was a naturally beautiful woman, her brown hair framing her face with soft curls. Her blue gaze could change from nearly a dark slate blue, to steely silver, and every combination in between. He'd discovered he liked looking into her eyes, just to see what shade they were at the time. Her luscious lips, her oval face... It was a very attractive face. And her body... His gaze drifted down, skimming the slight curves of her breasts that he knew were a pleasant weight in his hands, that narrow waist and the legs that were toned with feminine strength. She was gorgeous.

He frowned. "Did you and Rafe have a relationship that was more than just an alpha and his tracker?"

Those luscious lips parted, and she blinked. "Uh, no. Not…really." The rosy hue deepened in her cheeks, and she shifted on her feet.

His eyes narrowed. "Define 'not really.'" Suspicion flared as he guessed at the origin of Rafe's attitude to his tracker prime.

She shrugged. "He asked me once to become his partner. I politely declined."

His eyebrows rose. Well. There it was. "You declined an offer from your alpha prime," he repeated. He tried to ignore the satisfaction and triumph, the possessiveness that rose within him at those words. Rafe had wanted her. She'd said no.

She frowned. "Yes, as is my right. It wasn't a serious offer, anyway."

He blinked. "What do you mean it wasn't a serious offer?" Anytime a lycan made an offer, it was serious. It was never done lightly, picking a life partner. There was always the hope that a life partner could become more…could become a mate.

"He only wanted me because—" she hesitated, then took a deep breath. "He only made an offer because he wanted to be alpha prime, and he thought marrying me would help him. I knew he didn't really have feelings for me, and that he didn't need my help." She folded her arms and lifted her chin. "And I was right. On both counts. He became alpha prime easily enough without my help."

"You don't think he wasn't a little hurt or angered

by your rejection?" He had been, and that was without the weight of an offer behind it. He was surprised by the dry smile that curled her lips.

"Trust me, Rafe wasn't really that into me. My declining his offer probably made him relieved, more than anything."

He frowned. Any lycan who could walk away from Trinity feeling relieved at losing her was a bloody idiot. But then, he was beginning to suspect Rafe Woodland might not be completely sane. This might just confirm it.

"Why are you asking me all this?" she asked.

He bit the inside of his cheek. He had to get Rafe Woodland, and with the information Trinity had just given him, he could possibly use this whole scenario to his advantage—and feel like a royal jerk doing it.

Maybe, though, just maybe if Trinity knew her pack had abandoned her, perhaps she'd help them?

And he'd feel like a schmuck.

But Jared's murder would be avenged.

Yet Trinity would be shattered.

The Alpine pack could move on then, knowing justice had been served.

And he'd still feel like a schmuck.

But Jared's murder would be avenged.

Ah, hell. "We suggested a trade to Woodland Pack. You for Rafe."

She started to laugh, then her eyes widened, and the throaty sound was cut off in a hiccup. "Oh, you're actually serious. He won't go for that."

"He said we could keep you."

For a moment her expression remained the same, then she blinked. Stilled.

"What?" The tone that came out of those luscious

lips was raw, as though all emotion had been ripped out of it.

"He said we could keep you. And Jax."

Her mouth opened, as though she was trying to inhale and wasn't feeling the oxygen. She blinked and turned away, and he could hear it, the wounded, tortured gasping sounds as she tried to breathe past the pain. He reached for her.

"I'm sorry," he said softly.

She flinched, shaking her head. "No. They—they wouldn't. Not—not Jax."

"Trin…" He could feel her pain, it was so obvious, so overwhelming, that it was touching him as well, clawing at him.

She shook her head again, and took a few steps away from him. "I don't believe you," she said hoarsely. "They wouldn't…"

Tears welled in her eyes as she continued to shake her head, unable to speak.

"I wouldn't lie to you, Trin. Not about this," he said quietly, saddened by the hurt he'd inflicted. It may not have come from him, but he'd dealt the blow.

She backed away, boots scuffing through the leaves and branches on the ground, then she spun and took off into the darkness.

"Trin!"

Trinity raced through the dark forest, the branches tugging at her hair, her clothes. Heart racing, feet thudding, she ran. And she ran. And she ran. Tears blurred her vision as she tried to escape the pain, the agonizing slice as though her pack were physically dissecting themselves away from her heart. Each member, one slice at a time. They didn't want her. They truly didn't want her.

No. Please, please, no. She hurled herself along, no care, and no consideration for where she was running, where she put her feet. It was pure instinct. Hot, compulsive, frightening. Flinging her arms up sometimes to protect her face, sometimes not, she catapulted through the night. Creatures fled from her path, and branches that didn't bend before her wound up broken behind her.

Eventually she lurched, hauling herself along from tree to tree, her lungs on fire, until her legs gave out. She fell to her knees, sobbing, trying to gasp, trying to cry and just heaving these big, raw, dragging breaths. She wrapped her arms around herself, rocking in a futile effort to comfort herself, to soothe away the pain.

Oh, God. They didn't want her. They didn't want Jax. They had cast them away.

"Shhh," a deep voice whispered, and she jumped as strong arms enveloped her, pulling her back against a broad chest.

Matthias. He was also panting, trying to catch his breath, his skin hot against her back as he joined her in her rocking. "Shhh," he murmured. "It's okay, I've got you."

He was the one who had started this. He was the one to take her and Jax, and start them on this track. Matthias was the one who had dealt her the most painful blow. Yet those words, those three simple words, they were the words she hadn't realized she most needed to hear.

I've got you.

He had her back. He was there with her, right in the midst of her pain, and he wasn't letting her go. She should have been horrified, humiliated, for her enemy to witness her moment of pain, of vulnerability, but right now Matthias didn't feel like the enemy. He felt like the only one in the world who actually gave a damn—and he wasn't letting her go. She had gone so long without so much as a casual touch, and this contact, this shared embrace was almost too much to bear—but he wasn't letting her go.

She closed her eyes and leaned against him, collapsing into his embrace, into his heat, into his strength, and she let the tears fall.

They sat there, Trinity on her knees, nestled between Matthias's thighs, his arms around her, rocking gently from side to side.

Trinity blinked slowly. She had no idea how much time had passed. Her knees ached from bearing her weight for so long. Her cheek rested against his chest, his heart thudding, calm and steady, in her ear, and her hands held his arms around her.

"How are you doing?" he asked, his voice deep and tender above her in the darkness. She gazed out through the dark shadows of the trees.

"Fine," she whispered, and his chest moved with his silent laugh.

"Liar."

She slid onto her bottom, and stretched her legs out, wincing as her knees protested with the movement. They sat there silently, staring into the darkness. Then Trinity looked down. Matthias's broad muscled thighs were braced either side of her own. She thought one of his legs was roughly the circumference of nearly both of hers, so clearly visible was his strength. His legs were also longer than hers. The man was big, and he was completely wrapped around her, enfolding her. This was the longest she'd had sustained body-to-body contact since before her father died. A lone tear rolled down her cheek, which surprised her. She didn't think she had any tears left in her. Ever.

"They must really h-hate me," she whispered past her hiccups. She felt Matthias move behind her, as though he was leaning forward.

"Why would they hate you?" His voice held a hint of disbelief, and her lips almost lifted at the sound of it.

"I did something wrong." She frowned. "Or I didn't do something right." She blinked, then shook her head. "Whatever. But it really hurt my pack." And now, here was their chance to finally be rid of her.

"What happened?"

Trinity looked down at their boots. His boots were so much bigger than hers. She was tall for a she-wolf. She'd never had petite feet, yet this lycan made her feel almost delicate in comparison.

"Trinity? What happened?"

She'd never really spoken of it to anyone. Not for years, anyway. It was something her pack had decided should never be spoken of again. Now, though, she wanted to talk, *needed* to talk. About some of it, anyway.

"My father—my father was well liked and respected in our pack," she began in a soft voice. "And then he did something that was unforgivable." What an understatement.

Matthias remained silent, as though he sensed how difficult this was for her. She appreciated that, appreciated the patience to let her tell her story. "When he—when he died, it was both a relief and a torture."

His arms tightened around her, and she clung to his strength. "My pack blamed me for his death." She laughed softly, but for once, without the bitterness, just a sad acceptance. "I became their curse."

"How old were you?"

"Fourteen."

"What about your mother?"

Her eyelids flickered, and she was surprised by the current of pain that curled through her at the thought of her mother. "She died when I was four. Cave-in."

It was the risk a lot of the shifters faced, living underground. She'd heard even some of the vampire colonies occasionally suffered the same fate within their own caverns and tunnel systems. Maybe that explained why some of the big cat tribes toward the southwest preferred to build their homes in the trees.

She sniffed, then tried to run her hand through her tangled hair, pulling at snags as she went. His hand covered hers, stilling her, then he took over, combing the knots free with gentle fingers.

"I can understand their response to me," she said quietly. "But Jax… He doesn't deserve this. What about his mother? Why isn't she fighting them on this?"

"She may not be able to," Matthias answered, and his rhythmic tugs on her hair soothed her, his fingers delving into her hair and relieving the tension that had clamped on to her scalp.

Trinity realized the truth in his words and closed her eyes. Poor Jax. His mother was giving herself up to the mourning, allowing the pining to slowly take her away from all of her pain.

"It's not fair," she whispered. "Jax deserves better than this."

"So do you," Matthias said, and she stilled.

Did she? Did she really? After her father's death she'd felt numb, and then she'd felt pain and sorrow, and then the anger had set in. She'd resisted accepting blame. She'd resisted accepting the shame, but over time, she couldn't help but think: Did she have some responsibility there? And then after a while longer, when everyone had slowly stopped talking to her, stopped smiling at her, when she realized that whether she accepted it or not, those she loved believed she did have a share in it, she'd started to wonder. And then, perhaps, after so many years, a small part of her had started to believe. How could she have not seen what was going on?

"Maybe not," she said.

Matthias's other hand rose to her chin, gently nudging her to face him. She peered up at him, his handsome features ragged and worn, as though he'd also suffered. His eyes glittered in the darkness.

"Maybe so," he countered.

She tried to shake her head, but he wouldn't let her budge, one hand cupping the back of her head, the other cupping her chin. "You don't know." He didn't know everything, didn't really know her.

He gazed at her intently for a moment. "I know that I told you your pack had cast you out, and your first thought was for a pup." His smiled, a sincere curling of the lips that transformed the fatigue in his face into something that was warm, admiring and attractive. "I know."

He dipped his head, his gaze intent on hers. "I know," he whispered, one moment before he lowered his lips to hers.

Chapter 10

Matthias was only trying to comfort her, he swore it. Just a kiss to ease her pain, to show her that not everyone had abandoned her, that she wasn't some monster who deserved any of the crap Rafe was sending her way. She was torturing herself, and he couldn't stand it. His intention was just to give her a gentle kiss. Promise.

It started off gentle, for all of about two seconds. Maybe not even.

She tasted delicious. Matthias opened his mouth, delighted when she did the same, and slid his tongue in to tangle with hers. It went from gentle to carnal in the blink of an eye, and his hands tangled in her dark hair as he angled her head, deepening the kiss. Her hands clasped his wrists, and he drew back, his hot gaze meeting hers. Did she want to stop?

Her blue gaze stared back up at him, little shards of silver glistening as confusion and hurt gave way to hunger. She slid her hands along his arms, reaching for him. She tugged him back to her, her lips and tongue tangling with his as she twisted around to face him, rising to her knees.

He dragged one hand down her back to press her close against him. Her scent, that sexy vanilla honeysuckle, was intoxicating, and he paused to breathe her in. She arched against him. He could feel the rougher fabric of her jacket part, the soft fabric of her T-shirt a delicious abrasion against his sensitized nipples. Desire, hot, engrossing and languid, flooded through him, and his pants became an uncomfortable fit over his arousal. He deepened the kiss, a soft growl deep in his throat rumbling through his chest, and her breasts pressed against him, her nipples tight and hard through the fabric of her bra and shirt.

Too many damn clothes.

He tugged her jacket, and she arched against him as she helped him shrug it off her arms. She rose on her knees and shifted slightly, her legs straddling his hips. She moaned as she lowered herself to embrace him, her core so hungry for him, he could feel her damp heat through their layers of clothing.

He dragged his lips down her neck, kissing the exposed skin, and he smiled when she offered her neck, angling her head to the side to give him better access. He closed his eyes and inhaled.

Her scent curled inside him, an intoxicating fragrance of languorous honeysuckle, decadent vanilla and the sexy musk that was her feminine arousal. His cock hardened, and he groaned as she rubbed herself along his ridge.

"You're driving me crazy," he whispered, and licked along her neck, satisfied at the delicious shudder that racked her body, the tightening of her nipples against his chest. She liked that. He did it again, and was rewarded when she writhed against him, rocking her hips against his. She was sexy fire and all-consuming lust, a heady combination that had him breaking a sweat as he tried for some control.

He wrapped her hair around his wrist, angling her head for another kiss, something to slow down the raging fire of arousal that was robbing him of control. He miscalculated.

She nipped and licked at his lips, and the hungry heat clawed at him. He drew back just long enough to drag her T-shirt over her head before pulling her back for another wet, languid kiss.

His hands slid down her back, caressing the smooth skin as her hands glided over his shoulders, scoring at his back before sliding back down again, as though she was ruffling him, then petting him.

He loved it.

"This is so wrong," she gasped as he undid the back fastening of her bra, and he dragged the straps down her arms, discarding the garment.

He stared at her breasts, twin mounds dusted silver by the waxing moonlight, their rosy nipples darker in the night. Beautiful. He shook his head as he clasped the flesh. "No, this is so right."

He lifted one rosy peak to his lips, sucking it into his mouth, and she moaned, her nails digging into his shoulders, delicious little pinpricks of pleasure-pain. He growled low in his throat, and could feel her tremble against him in response.

"Oh, yes," she gasped, and then moaned, her head tilting back as he switched his attention to her other breast, thumbing the first, loving the scent of her, the feel of her, the taste of her.

She writhed against him, her hips riding his, and his pants became uncomfortably tight. He needed her. Now. The heat, the hunger... It was all driving him to one end. To claim her.

He swept up her garments, holding them against her back as he rolled her over, making sure the fabric cushioned her against the floor of the forest. She gasped as he pressed down against her, rolling his hips against hers as he kissed, again and again, the hunger hardening him against her.

He kissed his way down her neck, stopping to lick at the pulse that fluttered at the base of her throat, before touring his lips over her body. She arched beneath him, sexy gasps and moans filling the night air as he tried to taste all of her.

Matthias fumbled with her belt and the clasp of her jeans, pausing to kiss her navel, the soft swell of her stomach. His blood pulsed through him. He had to have her; he would go mad if he didn't. He'd never had this all-consuming drive to mate with a woman. He sucked in a deep breath. He had to get a grip, had to grab on to some control, otherwise he'd explode like a juvenile and neither of them would be satisfied with that. He wanted to feel pleasure with this woman, but more than anything, his thoughts were on her, on her pleasure, on her satisfaction.

He slid the zipper down on her jeans and suddenly she stilled. Those fantastic blue eyes, all molten silver now, caught his gaze as his fingers slid beneath the denim, beneath the cotton and lace of her panties, to the womanly folds beneath.

He groaned when he discovered her slick heat, the

fragrant spice of her arousal teasing his senses, threatening to destroy the thin facade of control he was trying to maintain. His cock throbbed in time with his heartbeat as his fingers slid through the curls and entered her channel.

She gasped, her eyes on his, and he smiled in satisfaction at her oh-so-obvious arousal. For him. She was as hot and ready for him as he was for her, and the knowledge was exhilarating. He played with her, delving inside her, and she arched beneath him, hungry for his touch.

He bent down and took one of her rosy peaks into his mouth, tugging on it with the same rhythm with which he stroked her. He could feel her heat intensify, her heart hammering in her chest, and then he heard her inhale, and her muscles convulsed, clenching his fingers. Her nails dug into his scalp as her body spasmed in his arms. He kept sucking, kept caressing, kept the shudders coming, until he couldn't stand it anymore.

Withdrawing his hand, he tugged at her jeans, pulling off one boot and throwing it over his shoulder, then the other, and dragging her clothing from her body. She sat up a little, the muscles in her stomach flexing as she reached for his own belt buckle, and his fingers met hers, helping her, hurrying her. He shoved his pants down and freed his cock.

She gasped, reaching for it, and he bore her back down onto the crushed jacket, pressing his hips against hers, and lifting her leg a little as he readied himself. His eyes met hers as he slowly slid home. He shuddered as she encased him with her heat, and she gasped, her back arching as he withdrew, then slid home again.

She felt like she was made for him, so perfectly did they fit together. He groaned as he flexed his hips, the blood roaring through him now, his pulse pounding with the rhythm he set as his woman met him, thrust for thrust. Awareness drifted away, until there was nothing but Trinity, her heat, her scent, her taste. Only Trinity. He gave himself up to the beckoning bliss, a freedom taking over that was breathtaking, dizzying, joyous. Her eyes closed, her head thrown back, Trinity's neck was like a silver curve, begging for his kiss, for his bite. He could feel her tightening around him. He braced his elbows on either side of her head as his release roared through him. He sank into her as he exploded, his teeth sinking into the soft skin of her throat as he pumped into her. She screamed as she also found her pleasure, convulsing around him, beneath him, embracing him.

He opened his eyes, awareness of the woman beneath him, of her panting breath against the curve of his neck, her pulse beating against his breast. Her scent filled his nose, his brain, everywhere until he could taste her in his mouth. His fingers caressed her, and he listened to the sexy pants as she calmed, watching her chest rise and fall with each breath. Sight, smell, sound, touch, taste… His awareness narrowed until there was only Trinity. His pulse slowed as realization hit.

He'd imprinted on Trinity.

"That was…" Trinity swallowed, trying to catch her breath. "Er, wow. What was that?"

She'd had sex before—good grief, it felt like another lifetime ago…hell, all shifters were so tactile, so sensual, it was a natural way of life—but what she and Matthias had done kind of transcended the normal bump and grind.

Her heartbeat was racing, although even now it was beginning to slow. She tingled—everywhere. Her fingers, her toes…down there. It was wicked; it was delicious. Had he short-circuited her senses? Maybe so. It had been so long since she'd been touched, even casually, by any of her pack members, maybe a concentrated dose of Matthias was like a megajolt of tactile sensuality in one hit, enough to fill the emptiness inside created by the subtle shunning of her pack.

Matthias sat up, lifting his hips to drag on his trousers that hadn't quite fully made it off him and she pouted when his muscular thighs and buttocks were covered. Then her lips quirked. He'd made love with his boots on.

Her smile died. Made love. Was that what it felt like? No, it couldn't. They'd had sex. Lycans did it all the time, indulging their animal instincts. Sure, she didn't indulge anywhere near as often as she liked. Okay, pretty much after the first three times, never. Still, her previous though limited experience had never prepared her for anything like this. It was great sex. Fantastic sex. She frowned. Maybe it was too-good-to-be-true sex.

Matthias rose to his feet, zipping his fly, his broad shoulders and back covered with dirt and leaves from when he'd rolled off her. She rose to her feet and scooped up her jeans. She scanned the darkness, squinting. Where the hell were her panties? She finally spied them and scooped them up, then dragged on her clothes. She winced as she shook some leaves and twigs out of the cups of her bra. Now that her system was calming down, rational thought was returning, along with the memory of their discussion beforehand. She wasn't ready to revisit the seriousness of that conversation, of being cast out by her pack. She still had to process that a little more. She wanted to hold on to this carefree, joyous sensation for as long as possible, and block out that stark, mind-twisting, heartbreaking reality.

"I have to say, that was, uh, fun." *Keep it light.* She clipped her bra on and pulled her shirt on over her head, almost missing the sharp twist as Matthias looked away.

"Fun, huh?" he muttered, and she frowned as he folded his arms and looked off into the distance, his biceps and pectoral muscles bulging with the movement. Hunger rose within her again, and she was stunned that she could want to touch that chest, stroke those arms, so soon after having her sensory circuits blown.

She slid her arms into her jacket. "Wasn't it?" she asked, and humiliating warmth filled her cheeks. Oh, good grief. What if only she felt this titillating exhilaration coursing through her veins? She felt like she could go on a three-day hike up to the western boundary. Or else have another bout of that great, fantastic sex. Was she that starved, that desperate for affection that she would read so much into what could have been a mundane and ordinary experience for Matthias?

He met her gaze, and it was almost like an electric shock ran through her, setting that previous tingling awake again. Her fingers, her toes, her nipples—her core. It was as though just his eyes were enough to stoke her engine. She swallowed. What was happening to her?

His gaze drifted over her, and she resisted the temptation to pull at the twig caught in her hair. Everywhere his gaze landed, it was like a caress, hot and silky. He nodded finally. "Yeah, it was fun."

Still, there was no levity in his gaze, just an intent, hot, almost angry stare. She dropped her eyes, and her gaze landed on his chest again, and the glint of his chain caught her eye.

Cool horror swamped what had previously been a

lethargic heat stirring within her, and she covered her mouth with her hand. "Oh, my God," she whispered, shaking her head. She hadn't. She didn't. She couldn't.

His blond eyebrows slashed across his forehead as she hugged herself, bending over at the waist as something that burned like cold fire flared in her gut. "What's wrong?"

She had. She did. Apparently she could. She'd lain with another she-wolf's lycan. No wonder he was angry, and...cool. Tears pricked her eyelids. He'd followed her, he'd tried to comfort her, and then...well, things had gotten very intense, for both of them.

"What have we done?" she wailed softly. No, that just wasn't right. How could she not have focused on that ring, on that symbol of another's love? How could she disregard another she-wolf's brand on her territory? It was dishonorable, disrespectful and offensive to that anonymous she-wolf. Despite his obvious involvement and enjoyment, it was an insult to Matthias as well, to not respect his relationship with his woman. Of course, he was also ten times worse than the stinky pond scum for his part, too.

She shook her head as he stepped toward her, his frown quickly changing to concern. "Trinity, what's wrong?"

"We are," she whispered, hugging herself. "What we did—that was so wrong. I'm so sorry." She shook her head as she backed away from him, ashamed and horrified at effectively poaching in another she-wolf's territory.

"You're sorry?" he repeated softly in disbelief. "You're *sorry*?"

"God, no wonder my pack cast me out," she raised

a trembling hand to her forehead. "Look at what I'm capable of, lying with you."

"What is that supposed to mean?" It came out like a growl, and she frowned. He was angry. Sure, he had a right to be angry—what they'd done could cost him his relationship with his mate, but hell, he was part of this, too. It wasn't all her fault.

She stalked up to him, her shock and self-disgust rolling into a far more practical wave of anger. "I mean," she growled back at him, and reached for the ring resting against that smooth, gorgeous, traitorous chest, "that while you wear this, you and I can never be together. Never."

His fingers clasped around her wrist, and they stared at each other for a moment. "It's too late," he murmured silkily, his eyes flashing golden green. "We are together."

She shook her head as she released the ring as though burned, and tried to wrench her arm out of his grip. "No. I won't break up a home. I won't lie with a man wearing another woman's ring."

His cheek flexed, as though he was grinding his teeth, striving for patience. "It's not what you think," he muttered finally, slowly releasing her wrist.

She arched an eyebrow. "Is that your wife's ring?"

"Yes." He said it as a matter of course, as though there wasn't a whole wealth of meaning tied up in that one little word.

"If I asked you, would you take it off?"

Sadness and dismay entered his gaze as he slowly shook his head. "I can't."

Those words pierced her heart, so painful was it to hear that he wouldn't relinquish his link with another woman, if she'd ever ask.

"It's a good thing I'll never ask, then," she stated calmly, coldly. She tried to step around him, but he blocked her, his mouth working as though he was trying to find the right words. But there were no right words for this. Nothing could make the shameful situation right.

"I'm going back to camp. I need to sleep, and I need to wash," she snarled at him, and he flinched as if she'd slapped him.

Funnily enough, she felt like she'd been slapped, too. She frowned as she trudged back to camp, hit with an overwhelming sense of shared desperation. But that didn't make any sense.

Matthias sagged against a tree trunk as he again watched Trinity walk away from him. He didn't like that this was becoming a habit. He had to fight the natural instinct to growl, to howl after the woman who seemed determined to ignore their connection. His beast arched and flexed inside, as though wanting to chase after the woman who twisted him in knots yet set his heart racing, his joy free. He lifted the ring on the chain and stared at it in frustration. For the first time ever he hated the damn thing.

How could Trinity think he was capable of being able to form a commitment with another and then make love with her? He swallowed. Although it wasn't just making love, was it? He growled softly. He should have felt guilty for what he'd done. It should have felt like a betrayal to Cara, but he was unable to see it that way. He'd loved his wife, and since her death he'd never really looked at another female as a potential partner, let alone a mate. Instinct had taken over, and truthfully, still gripped his body.

Matthias thumped the tree trunk. Damn it. She thought he was some sort of lying, cheating, dishonorable man whore. Yet if she knew the truth, she'd find out he was much, much worse.

Maybe he should leave it as is? Let her keep thinking what she was thinking? No. He shook his head. She'd stared at him from dismayed eyes, and although he'd seen disgust, he'd also seen the self-contempt. He couldn't let his woman continue to beat herself up over something that was nonexistent. But he couldn't tell her the truth, either.

His fingers tightened on the ring. When he'd chosen to wear it, being with another lycan had been the furthest thing from his mind. In all that time since, not once had it ever been the problem it was now. He'd been wild in his youth, had indulged in physical relationships just like any other shifter. Then he'd met Cara, and his feelings for her, before and after her death, meant he'd never felt the need for another woman.

Until Trinity.

Aw, hell. He'd never once thought he'd initiate a mating bond. His body tightened as he looked down at that patch of dirt they'd lain on. Even now, he could smell them, smell their musk, the evidence of their new connection. He straightened his shoulders. No lycan walked away after imprinting on another. It was the first stage of a lifelong connection. He'd found his mate.

Now he had to seduce her.

Chapter 11

Matthias hauled himself up over the rock and halted as Zane leaned against a boulder, catching his breath, Nate by his side. Jax was farther ahead, having swapped from Matthias's back to Warwick's only a short while ago.

"She's doing it again—you know that, right?" Zane panted.

Matthias nodded. They'd scaled this rock face earlier in the day. She hadn't come near him, had just waited for the guardians to pack up camp, and then had started tramping toward a low-lying part of the mountain range. They'd been climbing steadily ever since—unless they'd descended to repeat the trip.

Nate frowned. "What is she doing?" He slid his back-pack off his back and leaned his butt against the stone wall. They were all sweaty from their exertions, and Matthias decided the rigorous climb was good conditioning for his guardians.

Zane moved his finger in a circle. "She's leading us in a loop."

Nate frowned as he stood to survey the wall, his eyes widening as realization dawned. "She is, too."

Zane looked up at Matthias. "You told her, right?"

He nodded. Yes, he'd told her; he'd hurt his mate in such a profound way. Her alpha prime had discarded her. He would find a way to make it up to her, though.

"That wasn't all you did," Nate said as he pulled a water bottle out of his pack and twisted the lid.

He nodded. "I imprinted on her." He wasn't going to hide it. Hell, he wanted to yell it from the mountaintop. Fortunately, his scent on her body was doing exactly the same thing to his pack. He'd marked her, and his guardians were becoming aware. They took more notice of her, and although they hadn't mistreated her before this, there was a definite increase in respect in their dealings with her now. She was his lover, whether she was prepared to admit it or not, and he would look after her. His pack would now know that she was under his protection, his care.

"Maybe that explains it," Zane said as he snagged the water bottle from Nate before he could drink from it, and tilted it to his lips, taking a long swallow before finally lowering it and wiping his mouth.

"Explains what?" Nate asked, frowning as he dug out another water bottle.

"Well, yesterday, it was a nice little ramble among the woods, in and out of shade. Quite pleasant, really, as she led us around and around," Zane told him. He cast his eye up the mountain they were all scaling. "Today, I think she's pissed, and that's why we're doing this trek."

Nate's eyebrow rose. "She's pissed because our guardian prime imprinted on her?" He grinned. "Maybe he's not doing it right." He pulled out a third bottle and undid the cap.

Matthias frowned. "I don't think she realizes," he admitted. Ever since he'd returned to camp, he'd been aware of her. He knew where she was sitting, who she was talking to—his body was attuned to finding her, to protecting her. His senses focused on her. And nearly every time he'd looked over to her, he'd met her gaze. He could see the wariness and anger, but he could also see the confusion, the curiosity, just before she looked away.

"She doesn't know?" Zane straightened, shaking his head. "Okay, so then you're really not doing it right."

"No, I mean I don't think she understands an imprint," he said slowly, and took the bottle that Nate had just opened. Nate's lips tightened, and then he started rifling through his bag for another one. Matthias tilted it back and sipped the cool, refreshing liquid. He'd been thinking of nothing else since the night before. Trinity's nonreaction to the imprint had hurt at first, but he'd come to suspect it wasn't an act. She seemed honestly unaware of the fact—although she seemed to be feeling some of the consequences, if those covert glances of hers that touched him like a silent caress were anything to go by.

"How can she not know?" Zane wondered. "We're all taught as soon as we become sexually active."

Matthias nodded. "True. I was told before I left for my first wandering." As juveniles matured into young adults, it was natural to want to assert independence, to strike out and hunt, to spread one's wings, so to speak. It was called wandering, the time a lycan spent away from his pack as he exercised his independence and newfound strength and maturity. It was also the time of exploration: physical, emotional, sexual.

"Same here," Nate commented. He frowned. "How can Woodland not educate their young like that? Which brings me to another point—Woodland? Of all the she-wolves, you had to imprint on a *Woodland* one?"

Matthias shrugged as he took another sip from the water bottle. "We all know there's no control over an imprint." There had been many a humorous tale told around a dinner table about unlikely pairings. If anything, the fact that he'd imprinted on her made it a more palatable outcome than if he'd simply chosen her as a partner. It would be hard for Alpine to accept her as a choice, but as a mate—well, that was simply fate. Unavoidable, inescapable fate.

Well, fate was a bitch with a nasty sense of humor.

"I knew it," Zane muttered as he turned back to the rocky climb. "This torture is your fault. You'll have to have the talk with her."

Matthias frowned. "I think I'll let her work it out on her own." How did you have the talk with a grown woman? He'd prefer to let things run their natural course. In other words, pretend everything was hunky-dory.

Nate shook his head. "No, Zane's right, as much as it hurts to admit it. You've started the process. She's going to need to understand what's going on, before she gets to the next stage." He shook his head. "Otherwise you're both going to be in for a hell of a time." He shuddered. "Can you imagine an angry mate at bonding? Say goodbye to your gonads—at least, for a while. That's if she completes the bond."

Matthias's stomach roiled. He felt sick. Physically ill. If a male imprinted, and a female didn't accept the bond, then the rejection could kill him. It was worse than pining. He started climbing, and a short while later he peered over the top of the mountain for the second time that day, only this time there was a different view.

Despite the heat of their exertions, her collar was high, and he realized she was trying to hide the bite mark on her neck. From the look in her smoldering blue eyes, he also realized Zane was right.

Trinity was pissed.

He hoisted himself up and over the edge, and she backed up, giving the other guardians enough space to pass.

"What the hell did you do to me?" she hissed.

Trinity watched as he hoisted himself over the ledge, his muscles bunching and straining across his shoulders and arms, his abdomen rippling with his movement. His chest was glistening with perspiration from the climb, and as he stood a droplet started a lazy slide down over his left pectoral muscle, rolling over each swell and dip of his golden torso, that sexy silver scar, until it disappeared beneath his belt.

She swallowed. Mercy. The skunk was glorious, and as he stood on top of the rocky outcrop, looked the quintessential alpha. Strong, powerful, lord of all he surveyed. Right now, though, he was surveying her intently.

Well, he damn well wasn't lord of her. She tightened her lips. "What did you do?"

He gestured to his two sergeants-at-arms who followed him up, their expressions openly curious. "Keep the squads moving."

He grasped her arm and walked her through the trees that topped the rocky outcrop. "We need to talk in private," he muttered.

She cringed inwardly. She was beginning to learn

that whenever Matthias used the words *we need to talk*, it usually meant she was going to hear something she wasn't going to like.

"What, you don't want your guardians to know you shagged the enemy while you've got a wife waiting for you at home?" she snapped.

He hauled her to a stop and leaned down toward her, his green gaze full of determination. "One, I don't have a wife waiting for me at home, and two, I'm pretty sure they all know we shagged."

She blinked. "What?" His words stunned her, sucking her anger out like a fire denied oxygen.

He frowned. "What what? What to the wife, or what to everyone knowing we shagged?"

"What to the wife. Wait—everyone knows?" Mortification bloomed hot and fast in her cheeks. She tugged at her arm, and he let her go.

"Okay, start talking," she ordered, holding up a hand.

"What do you want to know first?" He folded his arms in that cocky, confident way of his, his head tilted to the side, a knowing gleam in his eye.

She wanted to know everything—now—but decided to start with what was currently driving her nuts.

"Why—why can't I get rid of you?" she asked, waving her hand to cool herself down. Ever since they'd… shagged…she could smell him. Everywhere. Around her. On her. In her. He was everywhere, to the extent that she couldn't think of much else.

"You mean my scent?" he clarified drily.

She nodded. That would be a start. His scent was pervasive, so pleasant and so damn distracting. She had this knowing, this awareness of him. Where he was, what he was doing, it was as though she'd lost all independent thought and could only focus on him. It had taken every ounce of strength she could muster to stalk ahead of him and lead his pack on this ridiculous hike.

Even now, she wanted to tug his head down and plant her lips on his, press her body to his, rub up against him.

"We-ell," he began slowly, as though searching for the right words. "We shared an intense experience. Something—" he unfolded his arms, his hands gesturing between them "—happened."

Intense. She bit her lip, trying not to smile in pleased satisfaction. He'd called it an intense experience. She frowned. She shouldn't be feeling satisfaction that he'd felt to the same degree what she had. There was still the matter of his wife.

"What about your wife?" she asked abruptly, pulling at her collar. The climb had made her hot. She must be out of shape. She hadn't attempted that particular climb in years, and now she'd done it twice in one day.

His eyebrows rose at the switch in topics. "Uh, my wife is dead," he said in a quiet, reverent tone.

She closed her eyes for a moment. Oh, God, she was a bitch. "Dead?" She opened her eyes in a squint as she peered up at him. He nodded.

"Five years ago."

"I'm so sorry, Matthias," she said in a whisper, and blinked away tears. Now she understood his defense of pining mates.

He placed a finger under her chin and nudged gently until she met his gaze. His brow creased. "You're trying not to cry?"

She shook her head, freeing her chin as she rubbed her nose. "No. I mean, maybe." She sucked in a breath. "I'm sorry to hear that you loved a woman, and you lost her. I feel sad when I hear stuff like that." She gestured to the chain around his neck. "You obviously loved her a great deal, to keep wearing her ring."

His gaze became shuttered as he clasped the ring, covering it with his large hand. "I did love her," he admitted.

Heat washed over her briefly, then it was gone. She pressed the back of her hand to her forehead, patting at the beads of perspiration there. "Uh, well, I'm so ashamed of what I said to you, what I called you," she said, finally meeting his gaze. "I'm truly sorry."

He shook his head. "You have nothing to apologize for," he said softly, then reached up to brush a curl that had escaped her braid behind her ear. He closely scanned her face. "Are you okay, Trinity?"

"I'm fine," she said, this time succeeding with a smile. No. No, she wasn't. Her heart was sore, and damned if she knew why. The first man she'd lain with in years was technically free, but forever bound to his wife's ghost. She was beginning to feel things, weird things, wonderful things, for this lycan she shouldn't be having feelings for, and she'd just learned those feelings would never be returned. He still wore his wife's ring. It was obvious his heart was still bound to her. He might kiss Trinity and more but it seemed his heart would never be free of the woman he'd married.

They hadn't known each other long enough to develop much of anything, but discovering that Matthias was available, yet not, was like showing a pup a bone and tossing it across a vamp border. Available, but unattainable—and yet their families were at war, so it shouldn't matter if he was attainable; he was automatically out of bounds. Even if they had shared the best sex of her life, and all she could think about was sharing more great, fantastic, too-good-to-be-true sex.

Damned if the shame of it all wasn't burning in her like a humiliating fever.

"Now I want to ask you a question," he said, his hands on his hips. Damn it, she wasn't going to stare at his chest. She smiled again as she waited for his query, but even she could tell it was a brittle effort. She forced her focus to those intent eyes of his.

"What?" He'd been decent with her. She'd accused him of cheating on his mate when he hadn't. He'd just been enjoying the moment. A free agent. Just like her. Although maybe when she got out of this mess she'd focus her attentions on a Woodland male, or at least one from a friendly pack—if Rafe hadn't turned all of Irondell against them between now and then. Strangely, the idea of lying with another lycan held no appeal for her.

"Why are you taking us on this roundabout tour of Woodland?"

Oh. He'd noticed. "Uh…"

He stepped closer. "Take me to Rafe, Trinity. Please."

She blinked, but this time she couldn't hold the tears back. "I can't."

He swiped the tear that rolled down her cheek, his confusion evident in his gaze. "Why not?"

"Because I can't betray my pack," she whispered.

His eyes rounded in surprise, and he slid his hand around to cup the back of her head. She closed her eyes briefly, leaning into the caress, before finally meeting the disappointment she knew she'd see.

Matthias was frowning. "Rafe laughed when we suggested the trade, Trinity," he said. "He told us we could keep you, for all he cared. Woodland cast you out." He swallowed. "They hurt you." His expression showed pain, anger—for her? "Why do you still feel loyal to them?"

"They're my family."

"No, family honor you. Family respect you. Family will lay down their lives for you. Woodland has done none of those."

Her eyes narrowed against the hurt, and the truth in his words. "Sometimes family does stupid, annoying, heartbreaking things, Matthias. You have to love them anyway, and hope. And forgive. You can choose your friends, but you can't choose your family."

"I did," he muttered. "You can choose, too, Trinity."

Her eyes widened. "You're not an Alpine genuine?" This was news to her. This lycan defended his pack so devoutly, so assuredly, she would never have guessed he wasn't Alpine by blood.

"I chose to belong to Alpine." His lips curled, and the desire that flared within her was almost a painful yearning. "Actually, it was more like they chose me. Jared welcomed me when I had no family. So you see, Trinity, you *can* choose your family."

"You want me to choose Alpine over my family? My pack?" She shook her head. "You know better than that, Matthias. Werewolves—we are a noble breed. Honor. Family. Commitment. Loyalty. This is what sets us apart from the vampires, no matter how much they might like to argue the point. Woodland is my family. I will not betray them."

He shook his head in disbelief. "Your determination to adhere to an ideal that no longer exists astounds me. Woodland not only cast you aside, they left you in the hands of their enemy. Yet you are steadfast in your commitment to a pack that doesn't even acknowledge you. That's not loyalty, that's—" he bit off the rest of his sentence, shaking his head.

"That's what, Matthias? Naïveté? Stupidity?" she shot back, another wave of heat rising inside her. She didn't know if it was hurt, or anger, or desire. She had no anchor to her emotions around this lycan.

"I was going to say desperate. I don't believe for a second that you back the decisions Rafe made, yet you stubbornly cling to the hope that your pack will want you back. They probably think you're already leading us to them as we speak."

She shook her head. "Despite everything you think you know about me, there are still some in Woodland who know me, and know I would never desert them." One in particular. Dalton had been her only friend, and he'd made her life bearable. She wasn't her father, and she had to believe that somewhere in Woodland, others knew that. That some of them trusted in her good faith. Dalton believed in her, she knew that. If he could, then perhaps the rest could, too. In time. She had hope. She clung to it. Otherwise the last thirteen years would have been a waste of time, craving something she'd never have—and that really would make her her father's daughter.

She glanced up at the sun. It was so hot, so much warmer than a normal autumn day. She shrugged out of her jacket and tied it around her waist, then lifted her braid off the back of her neck and fanned herself. Her heart was thudding in her chest, and she took a deep breath to calm herself.

Damn it, there it was again, his scent. Threading inside her, curling up in all her darkest, most secret places. She growled softly. "I have washed twice before starting out today, and still, all I can smell is you," she muttered. "I think I need to go sniff some smoke."

He blinked. "Sorry?"

"Smoke. It clears the nasal passages," she explained. "That's how I focus on a single scent, if I have to. Wave a smoldering stick under my nose, and then focus." She nodded. Yes, focus. She glanced back at Matthias.

He really was beautiful. The short length of his hair drew her attention to his face, to the line of his jaw, the slash of his nose, those firm, sensuous lips. His skin was so smooth, so golden. Her heart thudded in her chest, and she placed a hand over it.

He frowned as he came closer. "Are you sure you're okay, Trinity?"

She fanned herself, trying to cool herself down, trying dismally to focus on something other than the sexy guardian in front of her, the one who wanted her to cross to the dark side, to commit the ultimate betrayal against her pack.

She couldn't lie. She was tempted. And that knowledge flushed her with shame. He'd held her, he'd stroked her and caressed her, he'd given her ultimate joy—an *intense experience*. She craved his touch again, the driving need to have him pet her, stroke her...

"I, uh, feel a little warm," she confessed.

A knowing crept into his eyes, an acceptance, a carnal satisfaction, but also a tender concern. "I might know why."

She lifted her eyebrows as he approached her, a warm sympathy edging into his eyes, turning them a deeper, darker green. Yeah, he looked like he knew, and whatever it was, it didn't look like she was going to like it. But if she knew, perhaps she could get some relief from this almost unbearable flush. It spread from her core outward, drenching her in a strange, consuming heat. Her body throbbed—her heart, her core, her nipples... Even her ears.

Oh, dear. She must be sick. It was rare for a shifter to get sick, so whatever was wrong with her, it must be serious. She licked her lips. Maybe there was some sort of Alpine virus, and Woodland lycans were susceptible to it.

"When a male and a female, uh…" Matthias winced, and tried to communicate with his hands. She frowned. When they roll over each other? No, when they become a V?

"When a male and female…lie together," he said, trying again, "sometimes something happens…"

She closed her eyes. Good grief. He was trying to have the talk with her.

"Oh, God, please stop. I know where babies come from," she muttered. "And pregnancy doesn't start from a fever." She shook her head. "What the hell do they teach you at Alpine? What, you sneeze and, hello, there's a pup?"

Matthias shook his head, closing his eyes briefly. "God, no. I was trying to say that sometimes when a male and female lie together, something—"

"Yes, something happens. It's called sex, Matthias."

"It's called imprinting," he stated bluntly.

She blinked. "What?"

He cleared his throat. "Imprinting. It's when the male marks his female."

She frowned and stepped away for a moment, her hands on her hips as she pondered his words. When a male marks a… Her hands rose to the bite mark on her neck. He hadn't drawn blood, but there was a definite bruise there.

"You bit me," she said as she turned to face him, rubbing her neck. "Is that what you mean?" She bit her lip. "Did you—did you give me something, when you bit me? Like a virus?" Oh, God, she was going to die.

His expression grew pained, and he grimaced. "Not quite. I marked you, with a bite, and with my scent."

She wrinkled her nose. "That's why I can't get your fragrance out of my nose," she said. She had to admit, if she was going to get a scent stuck up her nose, it could be worse. His was...sexy. Another wave of liquid warmth rose inside her as he reached for her. His large hands settled on her hips, and he pulled her just a little closer, so that they were almost, but not quite, touching chest to chest. His hands were strong as he gripped her. She couldn't help remembering what his hands had felt like, gliding over her, caressing inside her. Hell, she was melting just at the thought.

"I've marked you as mine," he said in a low voice, a rumble from deep inside that broad, muscled chest. There was a possessiveness in his tone, a dominance that sent secret thrills through her, even though her beast arched inside her, as though wanting him to know she wasn't easily dominated.

This time there was no mistaking the flush in her cheeks, the beads of perspiration, and the fire of desire in her core. She sucked in a breath. "I don't understand," she murmured. She was hot, so hot. For him.

"I've marked you as mine, and you are reacting like a female lycan. Your senses go on overdrive, and you have an increased drive to..."

"To what?" she whispered, her gaze meeting his, and she saw the golden glow of the wolf flash in his eyes. She shuddered in response, as a woman, as wolf—as a female.

"To mate."

She licked her lips, then froze. She blinked, then tilted her head back to look at him carefully. Her eyes narrowed.

"Are you saying I'm in *heat*?"

Chapter 12

The earth shook as Trinity's fist connected with his chin, and Matthias stumbled backward. Trinity fell to the ground, her surprised expression mirroring his, as she sat up to look at him.

"Was—was that me?" she queried, shocked.

He gingerly touched his jaw as he gained his feet. His she-wolf could pack quite the punch. Still, it took more than that to throw him to the ground. "I—I think there was a little more to it than you."

She frowned as she scrambled to her feet. "Sorry. Seeing as you're the resident expert on bitches in heat, I thought I'd raise the question," she snapped, and he winced. "Then what was it?"

"I don't know. It might have been an earthquake. We used to have them occasionally on the west coast—but I've never felt one here, in the east," he had to admit.

If he thought Trinity was pissed before, it wasn't a

patch on what she was now. She was angry. Very, very angry.

"So give it to me straight, this imprinting—I see you, I smell you, all I can think about is you and…sex? You did this to me?"

He frowned. "How is it that you don't know this stuff? This is Lycanthropy one-oh-one. All of us learn it before our first wandering. It doesn't just affect the females. A connection is formed, and males have a similar preoccupation with the female and…sex."

"Apologies. Must have missed that particular lecture."

It slowly dawned on him. "Your parents weren't around to give it to you." His lips tightened. "Who looked after you after your father died?"

She blinked, her eyes luminous, as she folded her arms around herself. "I became a ward of the pack."

In other words, everybody and nobody. Damn it, if he could get his hands on Rafe now, he'd do it for the lack of care shown to this lycan. *His* lycan. "You were just a juvenile," he muttered.

She lifted her chin. "I could look after myself."

"You shouldn't have had to, not inside your pack," he snapped, and regretted his outburst at her flinch. He'd tried to be good, to maintain a distance while he told her what had happened. Well, most of what had happened, and what it meant, but learning that she'd basically been abandoned, and had missed out on some critical lycan training angered him, and he hurt. He hurt for his she-wolf. He ached for her. He was through being good. Right now she needed a mate.

He reached for her, but they both froze at an earsplitting scream. Trinity's wide eyes met his for a moment, then she took off running.

"Jax," she cried.

* * *

He sprinted after her, his long legs overtaking her and racing through the underbrush. His heart hammered in his chest as his stride ate up the distance. Adrenaline calmed the effects of the imprint, and he was able to sniff the air, hunting down the pup. "Jax!"

He heard a faint, answering cry, and swiftly changed direction, jumping over logs and boulders, even a babbling creek, until he reached the limit of the rocky ridge. He skidded to a stop, gravel falling over the edge as he peered over the rock.

Jax clung to an exposed tree root, his face white with terror. The ridge dropped away sharply, a thirty-foot drop to the valley below. Cascading water from the creek above fell, creating a cool mist as it tumbled down the rocks to a frothy pool below.

Trinity came racing out of the undergrowth, and he flung out his arm to prevent her from going over. "Jax," she gasped.

"Trinity," the little boy cried.

"It's okay, Jax," Matthias called out to the boy. "I need you to stay calm. Can you do that for me? Brave and calm."

Jax nodded, although his lip trembled. Matthias turned to Trinity. Her face was pale, but her expression was determined, calm. He couldn't help but admire her fortitude.

Jax was just out of his reach. He'd need to climb down.

"Maybe I should climb down to him," she suggested.

"No. I won't risk your life." He wasn't going to put his she-wolf in danger. If anyone was going to climb down the rock face, it would be him. He sat down and slid his legs over the edge.

"Matthias," she gasped in protest. "Please, be careful."

He grinned at her as he twisted onto his belly and carefully slid farther down, bracing himself on the edge. "Anyone would think you cared," he said, winking.

She gaped, then snapped her mouth shut. "I don't actually want you hurt," she finally muttered, and his wolf inside howled in pleasure. She wasn't happy about it, and it might take her a while to calm down, to fully accept what was happening between them, but something was definitely there. He glanced over his shoulder, and thoughts of the boy took his focus. He scaled down the rock face, digging the toes of his boots into any crack or crevice he could find before moving his hands down. He braced himself for a moment, eyeing the terrain. The lower he went, the gloomier it became. The sun had already dipped below the top of the mountain behind them, and a purple dusk was beginning to settle.

There were a number of roots and branches that he could grab onto. The earthquake had upended a few trees on this ledge. His muscles tightened for a moment, then he sprang, catching hold of a thick root. He heard Trinity's soft wail from above, but didn't look up, his concentration purely on the brave little boy who clung to an exposed root that even now was shifting under his weight.

He worked his way down the root, hand over hand. There was a ledge about four feet below them. He winked at Jax as he came closer.

"Hey, Jax, you're doing great. See that ledge? That's where we're going, okay?"

Jax looked down, and his eyes widened.

"Hey, Jax, it's okay, look at me." He waited until the boy's blue gaze met his, and he smiled in encouragement. "Good boy. Can you reach out to me?"

He stretched his arm out, and Jax did the same. There was a gap of about four inches between their fingertips. Matthias gritted his teeth, sweat trickling down his side. He needed to bridge the gap.

He nodded. "No problem, Jax."

He'd need to climb down just a little farther. He braced his feet against the rock face and looked for something, a bump, a ridge, a crack—anywhere he could find purchase with his feet.

There was a soft creak, and Jax cried out. Matthias whipped his head around. The root was giving way. Jax screamed. Matthias dived, catching the boy around the waist and holding him high as they fell to the ledge below. Jax landed on top of him, and his breath wheezed out of his lungs.

Jax clung to him, crying softly, and Matthias rubbed the boy's back. "It's okay, Jax, I've got you." He looked up, and Trinity was peering down at them, a worried look on her face. He gave her a thumbs-up, and she closed her eyes in relief. He continued to make soothing, nonsensical noises as he inhaled, held his breath for a moment, then exhaled, slowly patting the pup. After a while, Jax started doing the same, and eventually his tears died down to faint hiccups.

Matthias winced as he sat up, hugging the boy, and looked around. They were on a ledge, but he could see an indentation in the rock, almost like a half-pipe. He glanced about, seeing the waterfall that roared not too far from their position, and the bird's-eye view of Woodland. He frowned. There was something about the view, magnificent though it was, that bothered him, although he couldn't quite put his finger on what.

Whatever it was, it was secondary to his need to get him and Jax off the mountain.

"Any ideas how to get out of here?" he called up to Trinity.

She pointed to the half-pipe. "If you can climb down there, you'll be able to make your way down to the valley. I'll meet you down there."

"Don't climb down the cliff," he shouted.

"No, I figure I'll take the trail," came her sassy reply, and he grinned. He leaned back to look down at Jax, placing a finger under his chin to meet the boy's gaze. "You all right?"

Jax nodded, then hugged him again. Something tight unfurled inside him as the little arms stole around his neck, and the boy pressed his face against his chest.

Over his heart.

Matthias raised a hand to smooth the boy's tangled hair, the movement triggering memories that were both painful and poignant, and he squeezed his eyes shut as he hugged the boy back.

"I'm glad you're all right," he whispered against Jax's head.

Jax hugged him tighter. "Thank you for saving me, Matt." His voice sounded so young, so vulnerable. That tight, dark place cracked open, letting in the light, the warmth that was threatening to burst from his chest, and he took a deep, shuddering breath.

"I'll always be there for you, Jax," he whispered softly, his vow an unshakable force, an unbreakable promise from guardian to pup. He cleared his throat. "Come on, let's beat Trinity down to the bottom."

Trinity pushed past the branches, stumbling into the clearing. Zane, Nate and Warwick followed her. They'd come racing through trees, and had sagged in relief when they realized Jax was safe. They'd heard his cries and had come bolting, and Trinity was grateful for their action. They'd insisted on following her down to meet their guardian prime, and to check on the little pup. The rest of the guardians were waiting back at the top. Nate had ordered them to set up a camp.

Zane whistled as he entered the clearing. "This is beautiful," he breathed. She nodded as she turned around. She hadn't been here for years, had almost forgotten the illusion of tranquillity the setting offered. The sky above was bathed in rich oranges and purples as dusk began to give way to evening, and the clearing took on an ethereal look, darkening the grass and trees, yet not quite casting it in dark shadows. At the base of the waterfall was a pool that eventually formed the mouth of the river that flowed along the western boundary between Woodland and River Pack. Right now it looked a grayish purple, slithering through the darkening fields, each ripple reflecting the golden orange of the sunset. She didn't care about the picturesque view, though. She spied Matthias sitting on a rock, Jax sitting on his lap, as he pointed to something in the water.

"Jax," she called, her heart swelling with relief when she realized the boy was fine.

Jax jolted, then peered over Matthias's shoulder. His eyes lit up when he saw her, and he wriggled down from Matthias's lap and started running toward her.

She jogged, her arms open, and swept the pup up into a tight embrace, his little body so warm and precious, heart thumping against her own. "Oh, I'm so happy you're okay," she said, trying to hold back her tears. She'd felt a real and palpable fear when first she'd heard his panicked cry, which had only increased when she'd seen him clinging to the tree root. She couldn't lose him. She couldn't lose Jax. "I was so worried about you," she admitted to the little boy, tugging at his hair playfully.

"You took years off my life. Don't do it again." She tilted her head back. "What were you doing?"

"I was playing hide-and-seek," Jax responded, as though it was obvious. Warwick came up to her, his face pale.

"He was playing with me. It was my turn to look." The big guardian looked like he was about to cry. Or throw up.

She reached out and touched him on the arm. "He's okay," she said, trying to reassure him.

Warwick nodded, then pointed at the pup. "Found you. Your turn."

Jax giggled and thrashed, trying to get to the ground. Trinity placed him carefully on his feet, then tried to hide her trembling fingers behind her back as she turned to Matthias.

He was sauntering toward her, a smile on his lips. She took a deep, steadying breath. Just the sight of him had those unfamiliar feelings rushing to overwhelm her, and she battled for control. She couldn't give in to this, couldn't give in to the wild longing, the craving he'd created in her.

"You had me worried there for a moment," she told him, frowning. She could understand Warwick's need to cry or puke. When Matthias had leaped like that, her heart had jumped to her throat. She'd been so scared for him. Terrified. She lifted her chin. And he'd had the audacity to prevent her from climbing down. *Arrogant bastard.* He had a glint in his eye as he stood in front of her, silent.

"How is it not safe for me, but you think it's all right fo—"

He bent forward and kissed her. His mouth opened, pressing her lips open in return, and she gasped as his tongue flicked against hers. That heat, that desire swamped her again and drove out thoughts of everything but him. His arm stole around her waist, and he tugged her to him, his hand cradling her face as he kissed her thoroughly, sensually. Her heart rate flared, and that hidden place between her thighs grew warm and damp. This man had an unnatural ability in demanding sensual responses from her body, to the extent that his scent, and now his lips, could drive out all thought and protest from her mind.

Eventually Jax's giggles broke into her consciousness, and she braced a hand against that broad, golden chest.

He lifted his head, then rubbed his nose against hers, and she trembled. He smiled, a wicked, sensual curl of his lips. Someone cleared his throat, and Trinity blinked. She glanced over her shoulder. Warwick had covered Jax's eyes, and stared at them both in stunned shock. Nate was trying to look anywhere else but at them, and Zane crossed to cover Warwick's eyes with the palm of his hand. Warwick slapped his hand away, frowning at his pack mate.

"You shouldn't do that—"

Matthias kissed her again, and she heard Nate groan and Jax giggled some more. She clung to him, swept away yet again with a desire to press herself against him, and try to drive him as crazy as he so easily drove her.

"Ew, that's disgusting," the boy cried out, and she finally had the strength to push against Matthias's chest. He lifted his head, his eyes twinkling.

She tried to frown at him. "Stop it." She managed to take a step back, but that was all the distance he was allowing her to put between them.

Matthias looked over at his men. "Where are the others?" he asked, and his voice sounded serious, despite the goofy smile on his face. Then Trinity realized she wore a similar goofy smile, and frowned.

Nate gestured to the top of the mountain. "We've told them to set up camp. Any idea what happened?"

Matthias shrugged, and Trinity realized that she still had her hand on his chest, could feel the ripple of muscle beneath her skin. She couldn't quite convince her hand to move. "It could have been an earthquake, but I'm not sure."

He stiffened, and she looked up, twisting to follow his gaze. Sadness filled her when she realized what he saw.

"What is that?" he asked quietly.

Chapter 13

The woman in his arms stiffened, and it was incredible, the change in her body temperature, from captivating heat to a controlled coldness.

"It's nothing," she said.

He shook his head. "No, it's pretty clear it's something." The sun glinting off glass was what had initially caught his eye, but now upon a second look, there appeared to be a roof, some windows. "Who lives up here?"

"Nobody."

The way Trinity shut down, her cool expression, even the languid sensuality in her limbs just moments before had leeched out to be replaced by a tightness in her muscles, a rigidity in her spine. Could this be Rafe's safe haven?

"Show me."

"I'd rather not." Her tone was cool, emphatic, yet reservedly polite.

"Yeah, well, I'd rather be doing other things right now, namely with you, but we don't always get what we want. Come on." He urged her forward, and it was like moving a mummy, so stiff were her movements. He cast a look over at Zane and Nate, who both shrugged, yet grew wary, eyeing the surrounds as they approached the cabin tucked in tightly against the valley wall.

Matthias glanced around. This place was so picturesque, with the waterfall and its pool, the meadow with the river running through it and a log cabin that was almost perfectly camouflaged against the stone wall, ringed by trees. He couldn't believe that nobody lived in this little slice of heaven.

"What is this place?" he asked quietly.

Trinity swallowed. "It's cursed."

Matthias eyed her. "You're a curse, this place is cursed. Your pack really love their curses, don't they?"

She didn't answer, her eyes glued to the cabin.

They walked through the trees, and it was almost as though Trinity's feet grew heavier with each step as they got closer. She dragged her boots through the dirt, and as they entered the shadow cast by the towering pines, she untied her jacket from around her waist and slid her arms into the sleeves.

He gestured to Nate, Zane and Warwick to surround the house, and he looked down at Jax. "Stay with Trin. Promise me."

Jax nodded at the alpha's demand, his hand sliding into Trinity's. Matthias eyed Trinity closely. She looked at the cabin with sadness, and perhaps a tinge of fear. He cocked his head, although he couldn't hear anything untoward. Was this a trap? Would Trinity allow him to walk into an ambush? She'd done it before, with the vamps, and she was obviously reluctant to be anywhere near this place, but he didn't sense danger lurking in the shadows…

He stepped quietly up the short flight of stairs from the ground to the deck, his attention on the cabin.

Rustic, it was built in a conventional style, with a deck running along the front of the house and the sides. It looked charming, yet he sensed a tiredness to it, a slight dilapidation. Cobwebs stretched across the corners of windows that looked like they hadn't seen a cleaning cloth in years. Dirt and dust coated the railing and deck in a thick layer. His own boots were the only disturbance to the dust. No footprints near the doorway—even the door handle looked coated in years of grime and dirt. He frowned, turning to look at Trinity, and was almost taken aback by her expression.

She looked so pale, so forlorn, so vulnerable, and she gathered Jax closer. Matthias beckoned to her, and she shook her head. She wasn't coming any closer. Jax watched with wide, curious eyes, and his eyebrows rose as he met Matthias's stare. Matthias waggled his eyebrows for the benefit of the kid as he reached for the doorknob, and Jax smiled.

Matthias twisted the knob. It creaked, but turned. Matthias frowned. The door wasn't even locked. He let the door swing inward, and paused on the threshold, peering in.

It was darker inside, but he could still make out some features in the gloom. There was a living room with what might have once been comfy couches, but now looked like critters had made their home in the cushions. He stepped inside. Apart from the occasional animal droppings, the place looked relatively undisturbed. A large patterned rug lay on the wooden floorboards, giving the cabin a homely feel. Red-checked curtains were tied back from the windows, their folds coated with dust.

Beyond the living area was a simple kitchen setup. Sink, cabinets and a large, scarred kitchen table. Movement caught his eye, and he stiffened, only to relax when he realized Nate was peering through the window of the back door. Nate rattled the doorknob, and then there was a similar creak, and the door opened. Nate filled the doorway, eyeing the interior with open curiosity.

Matthias turned his attention to the three doorways that led off from the living area. One was open, and he could see the white-tiled floor and vanity of a bathroom. He opened one door, letting it swing inward.

The master bedroom. A king-size bed stood backed up against the far wall, and he could see Trinity and Jax out the window. The bed was covered in a crocheted blanket, and there were similar homely touches around the room, a lacy doily covering the bedside table, a spare blanket folded over the rocking chair in the corner.

He backed out. He didn't sense any evil or malevolence here, nothing that would back up Trinity's claim of a cursed location. He eyed the second door, planted his palm against the timber and pushed.

The door swung open to reveal a quaint little bedroom. A single bed, wooden frame painted white, a pink crocheted blanket folded neatly across the end of the bed. A little dollhouse sat on the floor against the wall, and he could see tiny figures, whittled from wood, propped up against the hand-carved furniture. A child's room. A girl's room at that. His eyebrows rose at the bow leaning against the corner, a quiver full of arrows next to it. Perhaps a tomboy.

"Matt, you should see this," Nate called from the living area. Matthias left the kid's room, and walked over to Nate. Zane and Warwick had since entered the cabin, and were prowling around, looking into cupboards. Nate held a photo frame in his hand, and a clear streak on the glass showed where he'd wiped his hand over it to better see the image it held. He handed it to Matthias.

The photo had been taken in the meadow, the waterfall a bright sheath of white water behind the couple. The man and woman hugged a small child, a little girl, with long dark braids and blue eyes that he instantly recognized.

Trinity and her parents.

He looked at her mother for a moment. She was beautiful, and her eyes matched her daughter's, although her hair was more of a red-brown. Trinity's father was a handsome man, with dark hair that was echoed in his daughter's braids, and an easygoing smile. They were the picture of a loving family, literally, and his stomach tightened. It looked like his she-wolf had once had everything—parents who loved and doted on her. He looked around the room. So what the hell had happened?

"Interesting," he murmured.

"Did you see his ring?"

Matthias searched the photograph. Both of Trinity's parents carried her on their shoulders, and her father had a protective hand on her knee to ensure the safety of her perch. His eyes widened. The man bore the Woodland crest.

"He was an alpha prime," Matthias said softly. Trinity was not only a tracker prime, she was also part of the prime family. A Scion, no less. Pack royalty. "I think it's time my she-wolf and I had a chat."

Woodland had closed themselves off after the death

of this alpha prime. He vaguely remembered hearing about an orphaned Scion, but the pack had largely kept to themselves. Over time, the stories had softened to the occasional whisper around a campfire.

He left the cabin and took the steps from the deck to the ground in one stride. Trinity had picked up Jax, and the boy lay his head against her shoulder, his eyelids drooping. The sight clutched at Matthias's heart, squeezing it to the point of pain. He halted, just for a moment, then continued.

"We need to talk," he said, his tone sharper than he'd intended. She looked at him with resignation, and nodded. A sadness cloaked his she-wolf, something he didn't like to see, and wanted to dispel, but that could only happen if she opened up to him. He suspected there was much more to the story than she'd first told, and he couldn't help the curiosity, the compelling fascination he had for this one woman. He wanted—no, he *needed* to know more about her. He believed, though, that he could know her for a thousand years and still be surprised by her.

Jax blinked and sat up, yawning. Matthias turned to the guardians who followed him. "Go join the camp. Take Jax with you. Don't let him out of your sight."

Warwick nodded, stepping forward, his arms raised. Jax went to him without argument, nestling into the warrior's shoulder. Warwick withstood the temptation for two seconds before dipping his head to rest his chin on the boy's hair. He gave a little nod to Matthias, and Matthias relaxed. Warwick wouldn't let any harm come to the boy. Not ever again.

The three guardians trudged off into the encroaching night, and Matthias turned to face Trinity. She looked tired. Morose.

He tilted his head to the side. "What is this place, Trin?"

She shifted, hugging herself tightly round her waist. "It used to be the vacation lodge for the alpha prime and his family." She cleared her throat. "The former alpha prime."

"Your father."

She flinched, then spied the frame in his hand, and nodded. She held her hand out, and he gave her the frame. Her lips curled as she traced the faces of her parents.

"What happened, Trinity?"

She shook her head, and he could see the tears shimmering in her eyes. "There's nothing much to tell. They died. End of story."

He could almost feel her pain, and regretted prodding her, but this was like a still-bleeding cut for his she-wolf, and he couldn't stand her heartache. He didn't know how, but he wanted to help her. Needed to help her.

"Tell me about it."

She laughed, a harsh sound unfamiliar to her throat. "Sure. Let's open up old wounds. I'll tell you about my family's pathetic story, and you can tell me what happened to your wife. We'll toast marshmallows. It'll be fun."

He took her hand and led her to sit on the steps of the cabin. For a moment she resisted, but he clasped her hand with both of his, as though pleading with her. She reluctantly sank to sit beside him.

For a while they looked at the vista. Trees gave the little cabin a sense of intimacy, of seclusion, but through the trees there was a stretch of dark, and then the glitter of a thousand stars reflected by the river. They sat there for a while, and despite the words unsaid, Matthias found some contentment sitting next to Trinity in the silence and beauty of the night.

"I forgot how beautiful this place can be," Trinity whispered after a while.

"Did you come here often?" He was curious about his she-wolf, about her childhood, her family—what formed the brave, frustratingly loyal woman who sat next to him tonight.

She nodded, and her braid slid over her shoulder. "Every chance we could. After my mother died, not so much, but we still got up here occasionally." She gazed out into the darkness, and he could sense the unease in her. "Dad loved this place."

"Is he buried near here?"

She shook her head, raising her legs to the next step so she could rest her chin against her knees. "No. He was burned. He has no grave."

Matthias's eyebrows rose. It was unusual for a lycan to be cremated. Most preferred to become part of the earth, to help provide nourishment for future generations. "What about your mother?"

Trinity shook her head, and rose to her feet. "Buried in a cave-in. Her body was never recovered. She's part of the mountain now."

He watched as she jammed her hands into the back pockets of her jeans. It drew his eye to her butt, the long line of her slender legs, and he felt the draw of her yet again. He shook his head. It was unlike anything he'd felt before, this compulsion to make sure his she-wolf was safe, protected. Happy.

At the moment, she most definitely wasn't happy, and that made his heart ache as much as hers. He realized, though, that he couldn't very well expect her to share if he didn't show that he was prepared to meet her halfway.

"My wife and son died five years ago," he said quietly into the night. It had been so long since he'd talked about them, his voice felt a little rusty on the subject.

Trinity turned to him. "Your son? Oh, Matthias, I'm so sorry."

He smiled sadly. "I was out doing a border run one night." He stood, too, nervous energy coursing through him as memories resurfaced. "A coven of witches visited. One of my pack had fed on one of their witches." He grimaced. The woman had died a grisly death. "Tore her up pretty bad before he killed her." He cleared his throat. It was still difficult to speak of, all these years later, but for some reason, the pain didn't feel quite so raw as when he'd told Jared the same story three years earlier.

He walked a short distance, and Trinity fell into step with him. They left the dark shadows of the cabin, and the painful memories, and strolled through the stand of trees in the direction of the river.

"What happened?" Trinity asked quietly.

"They killed my pack."

She halted, but he kept walking.

"Wait, they what?" she ran to take her place at his side.

"They killed my pack. Every single one of them that they could find. They cast a spell—it killed them from the inside out, attacking our beast first." He still occasionally had nightmares about that night, but admittedly they were becoming less frequent. He remembered waking up in the woods, naked, sensing that something was wrong. He remembered the sheer panic when he couldn't shift, the sensation of his wolf's claws shredding him from the inside out, frustrated at not being let loose. He'd run. He'd run so damn hard and fast, but he'd still been too late. He'd found the bodies of his family, his wife and young son dead in their sleep, his parents, killed just outside their cave. His brothers were all murdered, too, although it looked like they'd at least managed to put up a fight, and had been slain instead of dying from the inside. All of them gone in one night.

"The Marshlands Massacre," she whispered in shock. "I remember hearing about it. All of the wolf tribes were in shock." She drew in a ragged breath.

"You lost everyone you loved," Trinity said in a whisper, and he turned to look at her. In the light of the waxing gibbous moon, her eyes looked like dark, luminous pools, and he could see she was trying to hold back the tears. She was so sensitive, this one. So empathetic, so caring. He could see a deep recognition, though, a complex understanding. She wasn't merely uttering platitudes. She understood, her eyes sharing his loss, his pain.

"My father killed himself," she told him, her voice full of the sorrow she wasn't permitted to speak of any other time. "Reid Caldwell-Woodland killed himself."

His eyes widened at her confession, and she almost wished she could un-utter the words. She couldn't remember ever saying them before.

He cupped her chin, his gaze sad yet tender. Maybe it was the tenderness that gave her the courage to continue. She blinked. But she wouldn't cry. No. She'd wasted enough tears on that sad chapter of her life.

She turned her head, and immediately missed the warmth of his touch, but it was that touch, the gentleness, that could be her undoing. She wasn't used to touch. Even now she struggled to stand upright and not hurl herself into his arms, have their bodies touch from neck to knee.

"My father loved my mother so much," she began, "When she died, he pined for her." For several months, he'd sat in relative silence, occasionally giving Trinity a distant smile when she tried to draw his attention. She remembered she used to climb up onto his lap and chatter away for hours, then would be called away by one of the elders. She didn't think her presence even registered with him. "He was grieving so much, he kind of lost himself for a while."

She cleared her throat, trying to get rid of the sandpaper that felt like it had lodged there. "I was nearly six when he finally started to take notice of things. His guardians had kept the pack going, had tried to step in to help pick up the slack." She eyed him. "Ten months, Matthias. For ten months my father pretty much forgot he had a daughter, a daughter who loved him, and who'd just lost her mother."

She shook her head when he stepped toward her. "No, I get it. The heart wants what the heart wants, right? You can't control mates—they're a law of nature. Even when he 'returned,'" she said, using her fingers to parenthesize the air, "he put all his energy into governing his pack." She'd shared a cave with a man who largely ignored her. Whatever energy he had, he devoted to running the pack. When he came home it was to sit in silence and stare at the stone wall.

"I tried to be so good for him, to make him proud," she whispered. "I tried to talk with him, to accompany him. That didn't seem to work. Then I tried to give him some space, some time to heal. That didn't work, either—although, toward the end, I thought maybe there was some life, there. It was so gradual, like a fog lifting. He'd started to smile again. He let me sit in on some of the leadership meetings." In increments, he'd warmed. There were times where she'd almost thought he was trying to make up for lost time. And then there were the darker times, when he slid back into that black hole of grief. She thought he was getting better, though, She remembered coming home from exploring the caves, and he'd waited for her. They'd played cards. "There was one night… I remember thinking, hurray, he's back. He's *really* back. We chatted. He could see me, like really see me, and he was talking to me." Her smile stuttered. "Then a few weeks later he came up here for a break. Said he had some serious thinking to do about the pack."

"Trinity…" Matthias said, reaching for her. He grasped her hand. The contact was like a hijack to her brain, flipping her from sadness to an awareness of her senses. The feel of his skin, rougher than her own, against her hand, his clean, heavenly male scent, the silvery play of light and shadow as it danced across the muscles on his chest. Her heart rate kicked up a gear, a steady, regular throb that echoed through her body. She tried to focus on the conversation—tried to use the customary pain of her father's death to quell the awakening.

"He was supposed to be here only for two days. After four, Rafe came up and found him floating in the pool. He'd jumped from the ledge halfway up the waterfall."

Matthias made a rough sound in his throat, a rumble that she could almost feel, trembling through her system. Oh, God. Not now. "There's no chance he fell?" Matthias asked softly. Hopefully.

She shook her head. "Rafe also found a note. It was apparently pretty clear." She'd never read it, though. Rafe believed it would be too painful, and possibly send her into her own spiral. She sighed. "For a werewolf to take his own life, that's serious. When an alpha prime does it, it's like he's abandoned his pack. He betrayed them. He left them—willingly." She winced. "The pack was hurt by that."

"Is that when they closed access to Woodland?"

She nodded. "A suicide by an alpha prime would make the pack look weak. My father's death was covered up, and Rafe successfully fought for the Primary."

"What happened to you?"

She sucked in a breath, caught his scent and held it for a moment, letting the mossy, pine and sexy male musk coil up inside her, then exhaled. *Concentrate, damn it.* That mysterious warmth from earlier was spiraling from her core outward, and she refused to surrender to the heat Matthias had mentioned earlier.

"You have to realize, Matthias, my pack were grieving. Their alpha prime had discarded them. I had been living with them. They didn't know if maybe there were some mental health issues in the bloodline, if suicide ran in the family. They were battling shame. And if I didn't succumb to whatever melancholy had struck my father, how could I share living quarters with him and not notice his decline? And if I did notice, why did I not alert anyone?" Her teeth gnawed at her lip. "When you lose someone like that, you go over everything in your head—what did I miss? How could I have missed it? How could I not know how my father was feeling, or what he was planning?" She lived with the guilt every single day. If she did manage to push it from her mind, even for a little while, the accusatory glances and cold shoulders of her family quickly reminded her.

"My God, is that what they've been telling you?" he breathed, incredulous. "They would put the suicide of a grown man at the feet of his fourteen-year-old daughter?"

"They were afraid, Matthias."

"How can you forgive them for their neglect? You lost both your parents, and they shunned you. No wonder you didn't know about imprinting. Nobody guided you into adulthood. They deserve to die for that, for the pain they caused you. What did your new alpha prime do for you?"

"He allowed me to stay," she whispered, trying to make him understand. "But it wasn't all bad. There's one pack mate, Dalton. He still talks to me—possibly to his detriment. Rafe won't let him promote to a first-tier guardian on account of his relationship with me." She tucked a strand of hair behind her hear. "So you see, some have still made the effort. Matthias, they are my family, and they were hurting. They still are."

Matthias put his hands on his hips, his mouth a harsh slash as he tried to control his rage. His green eyes showed shreds of gold as anger flared inside him. Anger for her. "What they did was cruel, Trinity. Woodland's barbaric behavior has to stop, surely you can see that? Assassinating alpha primes, neglecting their young— as a lycan, it pains me to see a pack behave this way."

"They don't need war," she said, anger rising in her, along with that delicious heat. How could she possibly feel this outrage, this fury, and yet, this attraction, this desire? "Can't you see? They are wounded, Matthias. When their alpha prime killed himself, it was as though he broke the pack. He betrayed their trust. He left them vulnerable. He made them feel unworthy. I know how that feels—can you imagine what it's like on a pack scale? He left them weak. For thirteen years, we've been hiding that from the world." No matter how much they fought, or how much territory they gained, nothing quite got rid of that shame, that toxic belief that they hadn't been valued by their alpha prime. For an individual, it was demoralizing. On a pack level, that effect was amplified, and it took so much longer to heal.

"So...killing another pack's alpha prime is what? Overcompensation? Acting out?"

She pressed her fingers to her forehead. "No, it's self-preservation."

Matthias turned away for a moment, his broad shoulders tense in the moonlight. "You still defend them." He shook his head, and for the first time she recognized disappointment in his tone, and it nearly crushed her.

"What about your pack, Matthias?" she argued.

"Alpine have done nothing to deserve this from Woodland," he snapped.

"I didn't mean Alpine. A member of your pack mistreated a witch. Did you cast that pack mate out? Did you hate him for it? Or did you forgive him?"

Matthias whirled around, and she saw the rage flare in his eyes. "Do not dare to compare Woodland to my pack," he said fiercely.

"Why? It doesn't sound like they were perfect," she snapped.

He stepped toward her. "Leave my family out of this," he said succinctly.

"I'm just trying to point out that my loyalty to my family is not weird, it's not born from desperation. I love them, and I forgive them, and I have hope for them."

Matthias strode up to her, his anger and exasperation so evident, with his fisted hands, the muscles in his neck and arms flexing as he gathered control around him. He stood there, his chest rising and falling with his breaths, then he sighed roughly, pulling her to him, his arms wrapping around her.

"You're too damn good for them," he said in a low voice, and kissed her.

Chapter 14

All the emotion, all the turmoil, all that bundled up energy Matthias had whenever he was around Trinity exploded, sucking away his restraint. He nipped at her lips, growling softly. Her hands rose to his chest and he sighed in pleasure at her touch.

She melted into him, her mouth opening beneath his. His tongue swept in to play with hers, sliding and sucking. He cradled her head, frustrated that he couldn't run his hands through her locks. He traced the end of her braid and tugged at the elastic, removing it from her hair.

He moaned in satisfaction as he threaded his fingers through her curls, gently destroying the braid. Trinity arched her back, breathlessly kissing him back. He loved the feel of her body against his. He covered her hands, encouraging her to touch him, stroke him.

She responded, caressing his chest, cupping his pectoral muscles. He gritted his teeth. Her touch on his skin was arousing, every stroke of her fingertips ratcheting up the tension, testing his control. He started to tug at her shirt, drawing away from her lips to pull the garment up over her head.

"I'm so going to need some new clothes," she panted as he dropped her shirt to the ground.

"Baby, don't ever feel the need to cover up around me," he murmured, his gaze dropping down to her bra. She was a sexy woman, so damn attractive in her underwear— but he'd discovered she looked so much better out of it.

He unclasped her bra, dragging the straps down her arms and dropping it to the grass at their feet.

"I don't understand what's happening to me," she whispered as she leaned forward to kiss his chest. He closed his eyes briefly, indulging in the contact.

"I can't stop thinking about you. Even when I'm frustrated with you, I want you," she said, then flicked her tongue over his nipple, and need, hot and hard, tightened in his cock. He ran his hands up her back, around her sides to cup her breasts.

"It's the imprint," he explained, leaning down to kiss the length of her neck, inhaling the scent. Forever on, he knew he'd always associate honeysuckle with a hard-on. "I have the same problem."

"I don't want it, I want to control all this—but then I don't. I want to give in to it, to let it run its course." She dropped to her knees and fumbled with his belt, his fly.

He should tell her. He should tell her the rest of it. She succeeded in freeing him from his pants, and her breath on him was almost his undoing. Then she took him into her mouth. *Oh, God.* Later. He'd tell her later. Right now, she was driving him crazy.

She kissed him, playing those same, sexy dangerous

games with her tongue, and the pressure built in him, tension tightening in his gut, his groin.

He pulled away from her. "Your turn." He wanted to drive her as crazy and hot for him as he was for her. He toed off his boots and discarded the rest of his clothing as Trinity quickly did the same.

She was so beautiful, standing there naked, her body bathed in the silver light of the moon. He lifted her up in his arms, his mouth latching onto her breast as she wrapped her legs around his waist. She was so warm, so damp, he wanted to be inside her. He bore her down to the ground, gently lying her on top of their wrinkled clothing. He kissed one breast as he fondled the other, then kissed his way down her body, tasting her, reveling in her.

When he reached the apex of her thighs, he paused. He took a deep breath, and her fragrance—musky, feminine, wild—twisted inside him, trailing through all his dark places. It was like a fog to his brain.

Mine.

He kissed her, and she moaned her pleasure to the night, her body his personal playground as he brought her to orgasm, her body trembling from the pleasure he alone could give her.

Mine.

He was blindsided by the streak of possessiveness that tore through him, but he welcomed it. He rose up over her, sheathing himself in her in one smooth glide as her ecstasy still shuddered through her. He met her gaze as he moved inside her.

He was tormenting her. Trinity flexed her hips. He bent down to kiss her, hot and hungry, and she didn't think she could dissolve any more, but she could. She melted. That's what he did to her. Made her a hot puddle of need. His tongue rubbed against hers as he flexed his hips, his arms braced on either side of her body, his massive shoulders blocking out the moonlight, creating a dark place for them. He rocked slowly against her, her body still trying to find some calm after the storm he'd just wreaked on her senses, but there was no respite. She pushed at him gently, and he grinned as he rolled with her, helping her straddle him.

Her eyes widened. Oh, good grief. Now he was deeper. It was so delicious, so wicked, just so...*much*. She writhed against him, and this time it was he who moaned. Her lips curled in satisfaction, knowing she could give him the same pleasure he gave her, and then she couldn't really think much more as he cupped her breasts, the muscles in his shoulders and chest rippling as he moved beneath her. He played with her, thrust underneath her and she convulsed as another wave of ecstasy washed over her. He roared his pleasure, his eyes startled as he met her gaze, both swept away in a tide of bliss neither had known existed.

Matthias lazily trailed a finger down Trinity's arm as he gazed up at the stars. It looked like someone had thrown a dark carpet of diamonds over the world. He brushed his hand up her back, enjoying the tickle of her hair against his arm.

The glimpse she'd given him into her life had been saddening, frustrating, infuriating, awe-inspiring. Shifters were a tactile bunch; they liked to touch and be touched. Trinity had been denied touch contact with her pack for so long, he wanted to make up for it—he wanted to make sure she never went without physical contact, that she never craved another's touch. From now on, he'd fill that need for her. Always.

"What are you thinking about?" Trinity whispered to him as she rolled over to face him.

He smiled. "I'm thinking we should try this in a bed sometime." He looked over to her, and was surprised by her intent gaze. "What?"

"You talk like there's going to be more of this." Her hand waved between them.

He eyed her carefully. "There will be more of this."

Trinity raised an eyebrow. "You sound really sure of yourself. How do you think this is going to work after you've killed my alpha prime, my pack?"

He opened his mouth, then closed it. He didn't know what he should address first, his confidence in them coming together, which involved a longer talk on the subject of imprints—and after her reaction on top of the mountain, he wasn't that eager to revisit the subject— or her assumption that he'd kill her pack. Okay, so he hadn't really given her any reason to think otherwise, but this was his she-wolf. He was her lycan—whether she was prepared to admit it or not. He had to set the record straight.

"Trin, if at all possible, I don't want to kill your pack," he said as he rolled over to face her. "I saw a pack get wiped out. That kind of massacre—I'd never want that visited on another family. Ever. I want Rafe, yes, and I'll do everything within my power to get him, but not at the cost of innocent lives. I lost my wife. I lost my son. There's been enough death."

Her gaze dropped to his chest, and she reached out to touch the ring on his chain. Instinctively, he covered her hand with his own, and she looked up at him, her gaze flicking between their clasped hands and his eyes.

"Would you ever consider taking this off?" she whispered, her eyes so charged with a need he couldn't quite identify.

"No," he whispered back. "I can't."

Her eyelids flickered with a flash of pain so raw it took his breath away, and then her expression became shuttered, and she let go of his chain. Her lips rolled in, and she nodded.

"Okay, then."

She rolled over, and he closed his eyes at the stiffness of her shoulders, the rigidity of her spine.

He pulled her closer, despite her resistance, needing to offer comfort although he couldn't quite remove the cause of her pain. He'd caused that pain, and he felt like a heel for doing it.

"I can't explain—"

"You don't have to," she whispered without turning.

"Trin—"

"It's fine, Matthias. I understand. You loved her. You should never feel guilty for loving your wife."

His lips tightened. He wanted to tell her, he wanted to explain everything, but only one other person knew, and he couldn't risk his secret getting out, not with the task he'd set for himself. He cuddled up next to his she-wolf and closed his eyes, trying his best to absorb her pain.

Trinity woke slowly, squinting. The sun was well above the ridgeline, and a cool wind blew across the meadow. A flock of birds flew in formation overhead, stragglers before the winter snows hit. She didn't have to worry about the cold, though. There was a thermal generator pressed up against her back, his light snore ruffling the hair at the nape of her neck and sending tingling sensations down her spine.

A muscled arm lay across her waist, a broad thigh

resting between her own, and something hard and long jutting against her backside.

Just the realization that he lay there behind her, his body curled around hers, was enough to nudge her system into overdrive.

She swallowed. How could her body betray her like this? The man was in love with his wife's ghost. He couldn't bear to be separated from the symbol of their love, yet she was ready to give her body to him? Was she so desperate for affection, so needy for attention, for love?

Her lips firmed. She was a former Scion, damn it. Even though her father died a shameful death, there were lessons he did instill in her, about loyalty. Protection. Pride.

She slid out from beneath Matthias's arm, biting her lip at the instant yearning that filled her body when she was without his touch. The need flared within her, and she strode over to the pool and dived in, trying to cool the heat in her body. She almost swallowed water, so chilled was the temperature of the pool. Instantly, she gained some relief from the heat.

She swam, diving and kicking, breaking the surface for air and diving again. The water felt glorious against her skin, cooling her, cleansing her. Several minutes later she heard a splash and kicked to the top, slicking back her hair.

Matthias treaded water two yards away from her, a lazy, sexy grin on his face. My, the man was a wickedly gorgeous sight, his broad shoulders and arms glistening with the water, sunshine gleaming down on him, his muscles bunching and rippling with his movement.

"Good morning," he said. His voice was deep, delicious, like water tumbling over rocks. It had the ability to lull her, seduce her. She sank into the water and rose again, sluicing her hair back. She wasn't going to be lulled, or seduced. Not again. And yet, he looked so gorgeous, all tanned and smiling, and the water was so sensual, lapping at her breasts, her thighs as he swam toward her. He was so damn sexy she wanted to— She closed her eyes to try and block the temptation. No, damn it. That ring still glinted around his neck.

"Good morning," she responded, swimming toward the bank. Her knees bumped against the muddy bottom, and she brought her feet up to stand. She turned back to face him, saw the hungry look on his face, the gleam in his eye. He was so…potent. All it would take would be a wink and a grin, and she'd be diving back in again. She turned and strode out of the water, heading toward her clothes.

She grimaced. It felt wonderful to be clean again, but these clothes were getting gross.

She pulled on her jeans. She wondered what Dalton's response had been when Rafe cast her and Jax out. Not that it mattered. Dalton versus Rafe would be a short debate. She heard rustling behind her, realized Matthias was getting dressed, also.

Despite all they'd shared, both about their past history and their physical relationship—whatever the hell that was—this morning felt…awkward.

"Trinity," Matthias began, coming up behind her.

"We should get back to the camp. I want to make sure Jax is okay," she interrupted. She pulled her hair back. What she wouldn't give for a brush right about now. A hand covered hers.

"Leave it. I like it down." His voice was so close to her ear, and it was as if she hadn't been swimming in a natural pool at the base of a constantly flowing, constantly chilled waterfall.

She shook her head and continued to plait her hair. "I'm too hot. I think I might be coming down with something, or else that imprint business is really doing a number on me." She glanced over her shoulder to look at him as her fingers entwined the lengths of her hair. "When is it supposed to go?"

Matthias grimaced, and scratched his head. Her gaze was drawn to the bunching of his biceps. "Uh, about that…" he began, "there's something—"

A loud explosion rent the air, followed by a rumble.

Trinity's eyes widened, and met Matthias's frown. She knew that sound. Blood drained from her face, and she took off running toward the base of the rock face.

"Trin, what is it?" Matthias said, catching up with her.

"I need to get to high ground," she said, hauling herself up, double time. His hand on her arm halted her.

"Careful. We have no ropes here, no support. I don't want you to fall."

She frowned, the need for action pumping through her. "I have climbed these walls a hundred times, Matthias. I'm not some delicate flower. Knowing every inch of my territory is part of my job, now move."

She dug her toe into a crack, pushed and grabbed onto a ledge. She had to see. God, she hoped she was wrong, but she had to get up high and see.

"What is it, Trin?"

She firmed her lips as she climbed. "My worst nightmare."

Chapter 15

Matthias nodded at his squads as he hauled himself up over the ridge. Warwick was giving Jax a piggyback. They were all waiting for them at the top. He leaned over to catch his breath as Trinity jogged across to look south, her hand covering her mouth. His tracker had set a hard pace up the rock wall. She sheltered her eyes from the sun as she stared out at the panorama.

He saw it the same time she did. Now he realized what had bothered him yesterday. One of the mountains had changed shape. Now a brown cloud rose like a hazy dust storm above it.

"Oh, my God," she gasped, then took off running.

Matthias took off after her. She reached the edge, and he skidded to a halt at the rim of the ridge.

Matthias gaped as she jumped. Trinity landed on a trail, rolled over and gained her feet, all in one smooth movement, then took off running again. She left the trail and cut through the trees, skidding on her side down an incline.

"Holy crap. She's like a mountain goat on Ursula's wacky weed," Zane gasped, referring to the Alpine medic.

"Come on," Matthias muttered. He took a few steps back, then ran at the edge and jumped. He landed, rolled and was on his feet, bolting through the forest after his she-wolf. He could hear his guardians following. He glanced over his shoulder. Warwick was running, Jax under his arm, laughing wildly at what must have seemed like a fun ride.

He lengthened his stride, eventually catching up to Trinity. Her arms were pumping at her sides as she ran, her breath coming in controlled pants. He had no idea where she was running. He couldn't see a trail, so remained behind her, happy to let her lead the way.

"What is going on, Trinity?" he panted. This time he wanted answers, damn it.

"The den," she answered in a ragged voice.

She led them at a breakneck pace for an hour and a half, until she reached the base of a mountain.

"No, no, no," she gasped, looking up at a pile of rubble. It took him a moment to realize it was the entrance to a tunnel, effectively sealed.

A cave-in.

"We had an…incident…a little while ago. It weakened the structure of the hall." Trinity rubbed her chin, her fingers trembling. Her lips firmed, and then she climbed up some of the rocks, stopping to sniff the air every now and then. Matthias started to climb up, but she held up her hand.

"Hold," she said in a low voice, but the command in it carried to him and his men, and they froze. She scrambled over some more boulders, bending low to squint at the dirt and rocks, and then sniff. It took a while, but eventually she nodded. "Here. Start here."

Matthias climbed up to her and started shifting the stones. His guardians formed a chain, and rock by rock, they began removing the rubble. In a short time there was an opening wide enough to peer through.

"Hello?" Trinity cried. "Is anybody there? Can you hear me?"

Everyone fell silent, listening. After a few minutes, Trinity repeated the call. Again they waited a few minutes, and still there was silence. Trinity nodded. "Okay, let's keep going."

They made the hole wide enough to fit even Warwick, and Trinity started to climb through. Matthias grasped her arm. "Wait, let us do this," he said.

Trinity looked up at him, her blue eyes filled with purpose. Her cheeks were flushed from her exertions, her dark hair a tangled mess that stubbornly clung to a braid. "This is my job, Matthias. This is what I do—what I'm meant to do. This is our main entrance. This is where most of them would come to escape."

He stared at her for moment, and read the fierce determination in her gaze. She would do everything within her power to protect and rescue her pack mates. He could appreciate that sentiment. He nodded, just once.

"Fine, but I'm going first to make sure it's safe." He turned back to his men, dividing them up into teams. He left Zane to help Warwick and the others to keep clearing the entrance, and Nate and a couple of guardians joined him.

He slid his legs through first, slowly lowering himself into the dark cavity. When his eyes grew accustomed to the darkness, he was able to make out the dimensions of the space he was working with. As a lycan who lived in a cavern system, his eyesight was exceptional, but even he had to blink a few times to adjust to the floating cloud of dust. He dropped down the three feet to the tunnel floor, then turned to help Trinity through the hole.

She stood there for a moment, getting her bearings, then started to prowl around. She found a torch in a wall sconce. She pulled it down, feeling within the sconce until she found the matches. She flicked one, then held it to the head of the torch until it caught fire. She pocketed the rest of the matches.

Matthias watched her as she placed her hand on the dirt wall, cocking her head to listen. She started to walk down the tunnel, sidestepping any rubble, and stopping occasionally to sniff the air and listen.

Matthias did the same, but he mostly got dirt up his nose. Nate sneezed, and Trinity frowned over her shoulder.

"Sorry," Nate whispered.

She started to run up a bend in the corridor. "Here, help me," she cried. Matthias sniffed, but couldn't smell anything other than the rich dirt and maybe granite. She started digging at the wall, and he realized the bend was actually more rubble. A shoe appeared, a sneaker, and he started to pull away at the rocks. The shoe was attached to a foot, which was attached to a leg, and eventually they were able to reveal the body of a teenage girl. Matthias checked her pulse, and was relieved to feel a slight thump against the pads of his fingers.

"She's alive. Let's get her out."

Nate leaned over and scooped her up, then backtracked up the corridor, gently passing her through the hole to some waiting guardians. Matthias turned around, only to find Trinity was already moving.

He and his men followed her, assisting her wherever she stopped. She was calm, practical, efficient, but he could see the tenseness in her muscles, the tightening of her lips, the shadows under her eyes. This had to be bringing back memories of her mother's death, yet she forged on, concentrating on rescuing her family. After locating three more pack members, they rounded a corner into what Matthias could only surmise had once been the great hall.

Tears filled Trinity's eyes as she looked down at the cavern. Much of it was buried under dirt and rocks.

"We have some dead in here," she whispered sadly.

He eyed her. Her sense of smell was uncanny. She brushed at the tears on her cheeks. "But we have some alive, as well. Come on."

The first person they uncovered was a little girl, who coughed as she was pulled out of the rubble. Trinity hugged her. "Hey, Mia. It's okay, you're safe now." She smoothed the child's hair back from her face. "Can you tell me what happened?"

Mia stared up at her, tears making lighter streaks through the dirt on her face. "We—we had a meeting. Rafe wanted us to wait here for him."

"How many were you?" Trinity asked gently.

Mia shrugged. "Lots. All the pups and elders."

Matthias frowned, and Mia shrank back when she noticed. "Who is he?"

"He's a friend, and he's here to help. All these lycans are here to help." Trinity met his gaze for a moment, then smiled down at the little girl. "You go with him now. I've got to find your classmates, okay?"

Mia eyed Matthias with suspicion, and he tried to

gentle his expression. He knelt down so that he wasn't looming over her.

"Hey, Mia. Let's get you out of here, okay?" he held out his arms.

Mia stared at him for a moment, then slowly raised her arms to him. He picked her up and carried her out, holding her trembling body secure in his arms. He shook his head when Nate approached him. He'd take this little one out himself.

Trinity watched as Matthias retreated with little Mia, then glanced around. There was so much destruction. She went to work, sniffing out her family and directing Matthias's guardians in the rescue. Sadly, some of it became a recovery mission, and Trinity fought back tears as they uncovered one of the pups, who had clung to an elder as they'd both perished beneath the rubble. She couldn't afford tears. Not yet. Tears made the nose run, made it difficult to catch a scent. She'd have to mourn the death of her family later.

She found Dion next; the guardian prime was unconscious, but breathing. Nate and a couple of other Alpine guardians carried him carefully to safety.

They managed to dig their way to one of the main corridors, and Trinity sighed in relief when they broke through. There would be many branching tunnels off this one, and hopefully she could get deeper into the mountain, find more of her family.

They worked steadily throughout the day, carrying out several members who clung to life, and some who had lost the battle. She paused at one family den, and Matthias, bearing the flaming torch, didn't miss her hesitation. She could smell death, but more than that, she could smell decay. The lycan in there had been dead for at least three days.

"Do you want me to do this one, Trin?" he asked gently. "Even I can smell this."

She shook her head, then pushed the door open. The woman lay on the bed, her skin mottled, her eyes staring sightlessly to the ceiling. Trinity could see, though, the frailty of the limbs, the tightness of the skin as it stretched over bone. Trinity went over and brushed her hand over the dead woman's face, closing her eyelids, and gently brought the blanket up to cover her head.

She folded her arms and stared at the covered figure, sadness and frustration, and yes, a little anger, washing over her. She pulled a small bag out from beneath the bed. It was a child's bag, like the humans used for school, and she started to pack toys that lay in a box near a smaller bed.

"Trinity?" Matthias said, his voice low as he watched her movements in confusion. She opened some drawers. She knew the woman had kept some keepsakes, some mementos in the top drawer. She scooped them all into the bag, and pulled the photo frames from the top of the dresser to do the same. She zipped up the bag and faced Matthias.

"Jax will want some of his things, and the rest— well, it will give him something of his family when he's older," she said quietly.

Understanding dawned in Matthias's expression, and he closed his eyes, but not before she saw the sadness.

"Come on. There will be others." She wanted to collapse in a heap and sob, but she had family in the den, buried, scared, hurt. She needed to focus on what was really important right now.

They checked other family dens, little pockets within the mountain that each family unit made their own. Curiously, all were empty.

Trinity paused at the door of her own den. "Wait, I—I need a minute." She stepped into her home, the single-sized cave she'd been assigned after her father's death. It was cramped, and it had been well away from the others, but it had been hers. She went over to the nightstand and picked up the trinket box. There was only one thing she really wanted—although she didn't understand why. She reached in and pulled out the simple gold band, then held it up to show Matthias.

"It was my mother's." She laughed softly. "I don't know why I want to keep it. It symbolizes death and grief to me, but I can't seem to let it go. People put such stock into a damn loop of metal."

Matthias stepped in close to her, and she caught sight of the ring resting against his chest. She winced. "Sorry, I don't mean to disparage the memories or emotions for those who do believe in its symbolism."

Matthias eyed her closely. "Do you really see it as a symbol of death and grief?" he inquired. The intensity of his gaze surprised her, as though her answer was important to him. She decided to be brutally honest.

"My mother and father were bonded mates. They loved each other, they wore their rings and when one died, the other didn't fully live. When Jax's father died, his mother starved herself to death. You wear a ring," she said, gesturing to his chest, "as a reminder of the love you had for your wife—now dead." She spoke softly, trying to lighten her words. "You see a symbol of love. I see a death sentence. That's not to say you're wrong and I'm right, or vice versa, it's just a different way of looking at the same thing." She shrugged.

His eyes narrowed. "You see love as a death sentence?"

She considered his words for a moment, then shook

her head. "No. Not at all. I love my students. I love Jax. I loved my parents, and I know they loved me—in their own way. I also love my pack. But I do know with great love comes great pain, and unimaginable sorrow. Love, on its own, is fine. It's more the mate bond that I have a problem with." She made a face. "Like I said, bonding with a mate is just a death sentence temporarily on hold."

Matthias blanched. "Not all mates pine, Trinity. Some mourn, and then learn to live again."

"Is that what happened with you, Matthias?"

His eyes took on a glazed look, as though he was looking internally, remembering. Then those beautiful green eyes sharpened as he met her gaze. "Cara and I loved each other, yes. And I definitely mourned her death. For a while, I lost myself. But I came back. I found a new home." He looked at her meaningfully. She frowned. He was looking at her as though...as though there was something more than there ever could be between them. Would that it were possible...but the evidence that it wasn't hung around his neck.

She reached out and patted him on the chest, taking just a momentary pleasure in among the seriousness of the moment. "And yet you won't take off her ring," she said softly. "Yeah, you've totally moved on." She walked out of her little cave, sliding the ring into the front pocket of her jeans. Matthias followed her, his expression thoughtful in the flickering light of the torch.

Trinity did a sweep of the den, but there weren't many more to be found. She frowned as she returned to what had once been the great hall. Those who had been rescued that were still able to move had joined in the efforts, and for a moment she watched Woodland and Alpine work together.

Their faces were grim, their eyes red with unshed tears, and she went over to join them. There were other tunnels to uncover, more searches to be conducted. So far only the pups and elders had been located—and Jax's mother. Where were the rest of them?

They worked tirelessly. Torches had been lit to shed some more light, and Matthias organized everyone into teams so that work still carried on while others rested. She got to one end of the cavern, the section that had seen the most damage, when an acrid scent caught her attention.

She frowned. It triggered a memory, but it was like the wings of a bird fluttering against a window—not quite substantial enough to break through. She followed the scent, shifting some of the rocks, occasionally getting a whiff of Rafe interlaced among the astringent fragrance, until she reached a pile of dirt. Scooping it out like a dog digging a hole for its bone, she moved the dirt, stopping occasionally to sniff. She grimaced. It was like…like…damn it, what was it? She knew this, but hadn't smelled it in years.

She heaved against a rock, and eventually it rolled down the pile.

Her blood ran cold in her veins when she saw the thin white cable, and recognition hit her. Woodland used to mine copper, and there were these charges her father used to store in one of the locked units farther below…

She pulled at the cable, twining it around her hand until she had it free. She stared at it for a moment, trying to make sense, then startled when she heard the low whistle.

"We've found another tunnel," Nate called softly, waving, and she rose to her feet, stuffing the cable into her jeans pocket as she scrambled toward the hole Nate, Kai and the others had revealed.

Another scent teased her nostrils, one that was instantly recognizable and sent fear and trepidation coursing through her. *Please, please...* As soon as she crept through the hole, she paused, sniffing the air. Matthias followed her, twisting sideways to get through the space.

"Is there someone in here?" he asked, and she nodded.

"Yes, yes there is." And fortunately, the stench of death didn't cling to him.

"Trin!" A faint cry echoed from farther down the tunnel, and she took off running.

"Dalton!"

"Over here, Trin," her friend called, and she stopped when she found the mound. Wooden trusses from the tunnel had collapsed amid the rock and dirt, and she could just make out a tuft of hair, caked in dirt. She started digging at the earth, and in a moment Matthias was by her side. A grimy face was slowly revealed, and her friend coughed as the soil was cleared away.

Dalton blinked, his gray eyes finally focusing on her, and his teeth flashed white against the dirty background of his features. "Took you long enough."

Matthias watched his she-wolf patch up her friend, his expression dour. They'd set up camp a short distance away from the entrance to the den, in case of any more cave-ins. Nate stepped over the log he was sitting on and sat down next to him.

"How many?" Matthias asked.

"Twelve dead. Thirty-two alive, sixteen injured, four of those critical."

Matthias swore. "What the hell happened?" Packs

made their home underground, and by necessity they picked the strongest structural point in their cavern system for their home site. A cave-in on this scale should never have occurred.

"Not sure. I'm no engineer, but it looks like the initial collapse happened when one of the primary structural supports behind the main hall fell, and there was a domino effect throughout the main den area."

"Something must have happened—dens don't just collapse," Matthias said brusquely. "And they'll want a reason for why so many have died."

"True. They're raw at the moment, and they're confused, afraid. They don't know who to blame, but they want to blame someone."

"I'm surprised they're not trying to blame us."

Nate chuckled. "Every lycan knows not to bite the hand that feeds them. Which brings up another point." He shuffled across as Zane joined them.

"What point?" Zane asked. "The point that some Woodland lycan is cozying up to our guardian prime's she-wolf?"

"He's just a friend," Matthias said through gritted teeth, though he did nothing to hide his displeasure. He should be happy that Trinity's friend had survived the cavern collapse, and perhaps even grateful to the man who had been his she-wolf's only friend in a pack of emotionally distant shifters. Instead all he could feel was a ridiculous jealousy that his she-wolf had her hands on another lycan. Her earlier words haunted him. She thought the mating bond was a death sentence. To say that made things a little more challenging for him was an understatement.

"As entertaining and frankly, hysterical, as Matt's newly awakened love life is, I was referring to a lack of medical supplies and food for our new dependents," Nate said drily. "We were more successful than we imagined when we set up that blockade in Summercliffe. They're running low on pretty much everything, and whatever we've been able to scavenge from the wreckage of their pack den won't suffice."

They'd been able to retrieve clothing, blankets and sundry items to set up a camp kitchen, but Matthias had already recognized that what they had was woefully inadequate.

Zane swore. "We're supposed to be killing them, not nursing them," he muttered. He held up a hand when Matthias turned to him. "I know, I know, we're not actually going to kill them," he said, brooding. "But we came here for vengeance. Now we've semi-adopted a pup, our guardian prime is panting after their tracker—" he met Matthias's gaze "—sorry, but you are—and now we're setting up a triage for Woodland's pups and elders. This vengeance kick has no meat in it."

Matthias folded his arms, and tilted his head to look at his impetuous guardian. "What would you have us do, Zane?" He was curious to see what the younger man would suggest.

Zane sighed. "Of course we have to tend to them. They're still our tribe—although it sucks to admit it. I just wish we could do something that had more…" Zane made a face. "I don't know, more grrr in it." His voice roughened on the growl.

Matthias arched an eyebrow. "More grrr?"

Zane nodded, as though his choice of words perfectly communicated his sentiment. "Exactly, more get up and grrr. I want to be a badass with these guys, but they're not in any shape for it."

"Sometimes mercy is the greater display of strength,"

he said quietly. "Understanding that your enemy is weak, and that fighting them in this state has no real honor or pleasure… That's quite a noble lesson to learn."

Zane grimaced. "Yeah, well, being noble sucks. I'd rather smash some skulls."

Matthias grinned. "We haven't abandoned our mission, Zane. We've just got to put it on hold until we deal with this latest development."

"Which brings me back to the supplies," Nate interjected. "We need to make a supply run if we're going to be able to help these werewolves. We'll also need more food, as our camp has nearly tripled in size.

"I'll go," Zane offered.

"No, I'll go," Nate stated.

Zane stood. "You don't think I can do a simple supply run?"

Nate stood to meet his gaze. "You'll have to go through Nightwing. Can you honestly say that if you bump into Lucien Marchetta, you're not going to want to rough him up, maybe even bite him?"

Zane glared at him for a moment, then nodded, just once. "Good point. You go."

Matthias looked at Nate. He'd been interested to see how the power play would pan out, and had been content to sit back and watch. Sometimes Nate's insight surprised him. He'd make a good guardian prime, one day. Maybe even an alpha prime. "Then it's settled," he said as he stood. "We'll set up a more permanent camp here—these wolves are going to need shelter until their den is cleared, or a new den is created, and winter is just around the corner. Nate, you go back to Alpine, explain the situation to Samantha." His alpha prime wasn't going to be happy to learn they were actually helping their enemy, but once she was apprised of the situation, she'd understand and would agree with his actions, he was confident of that. He looked around the camp. These were kids, elders… They were vulnerable and in need of help. The kids deserved protection, and the elders deserved respect, no matter what pack they belonged to.

"Ah, I'm not sure what's going on with your she-wolf," Zane commented, "but that does not look like her happy face."

Matthias turned. Trinity and Dalton were engaged in a serious conversation, and neither looked pleased.

Chapter 16

"Thanks for coming back," Dalton said quietly as Trinity pressed a cloth soaked in witch hazel to a cut on his brow, and he hissed. "I think." He sat on the ground, a ripped and wet cot sheet wrapped around his knee to help reduce the swelling there. Even so, he was about the same size as Zane, so she'd pulled up a piece of cut wood to sit on. She made sure the bowl of water next to her was balanced properly on the rough ground, a small pile of clean bandages next to it.

She smiled. "I was always coming back," she murmured, as she gingerly dabbed at the cut. "You're a shifter. This won't take long to heal." She glanced toward Dion. He'd already gained consciousness and was sitting up. One good thing about being a shifter, she thought, you mended fast. Dalton grasped her hand, and she met his gray gaze, surprised by the sincerity that had replaced his normal mischievous glint.

"I mean it, Trin. I found out about Rafe's message after it was sent. I'd never have allowed it otherwise."

She arched an eyebrow. "Oh, you would have stood up to our alpha prime, huh? That would have been a worthy bout of what, three seconds?" There was a reason Rafe was alpha prime. He was the biggest, strongest lycan out of the lot of them, and he now had new fangs that didn't require a shift to be dangerous.

He shook his head. "No, I would have called a council."

Her eyes widened. "You would have done that, for me?" An alpha prime had an infallible right to rule, but the pack wasn't without democracy. A council could be called to hear an appeal, and the alpha prime would be forced to consider all arguments. Normally it would be to ensure pack justice, but Rafe would have seen it as a challenge to his authority. "That would take you off Rafe's Christmas card list."

"You know I'd always look out for you." He gave her an exasperated look, then grimaced. "Although it seems my protective services are no longer needed."

She pressed the cloth to his forehead again, frowning. "What do you mean?"

"You know, you and that mountain of a guardian prime over there," he said, lifting his chin in the direction of Matthias.

She glanced briefly over her shoulder. Matthias sat on a log, talking with Zane and Nate, but he didn't look at his guardians. No, he was glaring at them.

"Ignore him."

"Please, he looks like he wants to pull my arms out of my sockets and shove them down my throat for talking to his woman."

"Here, hold that," she said, grabbing his hand and

pressing it to the cloth against his head. "Your face is an absolute mess." She grabbed one of the cloths and dipped it into the water. "And I'm not his woman," she muttered. She would never pledge herself to a man who loved another. No matter how gorgeous, ripped or possessive he seemed. She cast a quick glance over her shoulder and frowned at Matthias. He was glaring at her with a hunger that would be obvious and unacceptable to her pack mates, yet created an echoing desire within herself. His brows pulled together when he saw her expression.

"Hey, you'll get no judgement from me, Trin," Dalton said, and tried to dodge the wet cloth she wiped across his cheek. "Trin, please, you're ruining my tough-guy vibe."

"I think that was lost with the pink bunnies wrapped around your knee, now hold still, you big pup." She wiped at the streaks of dirt across his chin. "What do you mean, you're not judging me?"

Dalton's gray gaze shifted from hers. "Look, I know they grabbed you, and I know you had to do whatever you had to, to survive. And really, if fate has that kind of wicked sense of humor, it's okay with me."

She frowned. "What are you talking about?"

Dalton shrugged. "I get it. The pack cast you out, you've forged a new bond with a new pack. Sure, I'd prefer any other pack than Alpine, but I'll get used to it. So will the others."

She gaped at him for a moment, then started to attack the dirt on the other side of his face. "I have not joined Alpine, for crying out loud. I haven't abandoned Woodland, and I don't intend to. No matter how obstinate they are, my family will eventually accept me."

Dalton winced, and she wasn't sure it was from her

cleaning efforts, or her words. "That's going to be a little harder for them to do, considering."

Trinity dropped her hands in her lap. "Considering what?"

Dalton shifted. "Do I have to keep holding this?" he asked, indicating the cloth to his forehead.

"Yes," she snapped, "now don't try to change the subject. Considering what?"

"Considering…" Dalton tilted his head in the direction of Matthias, his eyes widening. "You know."

"No, I don't know. What?" God help her, she was going to strangle her friend if he didn't just spit out whatever it was he was trying to say.

Dalton rolled his eyes. "Fine. You don't know, but I do, Trin. I know," he said meaningfully, tilting his head at Matthias.

She gasped, her cheeks warming. "How do you know?" she whispered, looking about the camp. Her pack members were either lying down or sitting, some being tended to by the Alpine guardians, others looking after themselves. If they knew she'd lain with Matthias, it would be yet another mark against her, another crime against her family.

"How do I—" Dalton's eyes bugged for a moment. "How do I know? I can smell him on you, Trin. I can smell him. I can smell you…" He shook his head. "It's obvious."

She closed her eyes. *Oh. Dear. Lord.* How embarrassing. She covered her face. "I bathed this morning," she muttered. She thought she was the only one who could smell Matthias. He smelled delicious. Potent, powerful, exciting. All through the day, digging out her family, sniffing the air, his scent had teased her, and it had taken a lot of energy to separate his scent, his temptation, from the task at hand. To know her family could smell him on her… "I'll have to go swim in the river," she stated.

Dalton chuckled. "That ain't gonna work, darlin'."

She peered up at him through her fingers. "Why not?"

"Because his scent is all over you. He's marked you as his. That's what happens with imprinting."

She flung her hands up. "God, what does that even mean?" she cried in frustration.

"It means he imprinted on you," Dalton stated, as though it was obvious.

She leaned forward, her eyes meeting his. "What does that mean?" she repeated, pleading with him for something that would help her understand what the hell was going on.

Dalton frowned. "You know, impri—" his eyes widened in understanding. "You don't know," he whispered. "Oh. Hell."

"Tell me," she pleaded again.

He closed his eyes and shuddered. "Being buried alive is beginning to look really good." He opened his eyes, and despite his obvious embarrassment, she saw the sympathy in her friend's gaze. "I thought one of the elders had had the talk with you…"

"Well, obviously there is a gap in my education. Spill it."

Dalton bit his lip, then finally nodded. He held up a finger. "Let me preface this by saying that once this discussion is over, we are going to pretend it never happened, okay?"

She nodded. *It must be bad.* "Okay."

Dalton exhaled, then lowered the cloth from his head.

"Imprinting is when a male marks a female with his scent."

Trinity nodded. "Got it."

"Wait, let me finish. When he marks her, he claims her—"

"Whoa, what? I'm not claimed." Nothing had been discussed; she hadn't agreed to anything. She may not know everything about relationships but she knew enough to be aware that claiming was a two-phase process. One had to claim, and one had to accept the claim. She hadn't accepted any damn claim.

Dalton gave her a warning look. "Will you stop interrupting me and just listen? This conversation is already awkward enough as it is. Let's not drag it out any longer than necessary, okay?"

She clutched her hands in her lap. "Sure. Sorry. Go ahead."

"Thank you. So the male establishes a claim on the female with a bite and his scent." Dalton took a deep breath. Looked at her. Trinity narrowed her eyes. Was he...?

"You're blushing."

"Shut up. I just need a minute." Dalton sucked in another breath.

"You're going to hyperventilate if you keep that up."

"God, Trin, please—shut up," he groaned. He held up a hand to halt her next question. "During..." he rolled his hand. Trinity tilted her head. What was this, some sort of universal body language among men? Matthias had used something similar. She'd almost feel awkward, but Dalton was embarrassed enough for the both of them.

"Sex," she supplied in exasperation.

Dalton's eyes closed and his shoulders sagged. "During sex," he said through gritted teeth, "when—at the point where everyone is feeling good—"

She frowned. "Everyone? How many people do you have sex with at one time?"

His eyelids slowly opened and he glared at her. He didn't need to say a word. "Sorry," she whispered. "I promise, I'll shut up now."

"When the *couple* are most enjoying themselves, certain chemicals are released. Pheromones." He waved a hand. "Whatever. Anyway, they mingle, they mix and then voilà, you have created a bonded scent. This scent acts as a marker to any other males that the female is, uh, taken, if you like."

Trinity opened her mouth to protest, but Dalton shook his head as he continued. "This scent is like a primal connection. The male becomes attached to the female. He has this need to protect her, to nourish her, to keep her safe and to…copulate with her." Dalton swallowed, and an embarrassed heat began to bloom in her own cheeks. "The female recognizes the scent of her partner, and it will affect her…" He dragged a hand over his face. "God, kill me now."

Trinity lowered her gaze. She suspected where he might be headed with this and he was right, it was decidedly awkward.

"The female has the urge to…consort. Repeatedly."

She closed her eyes. *Yep. Awkward.* A wave of heat washed over her, but she could tell it wasn't an effect of the imprint. No, this was pure mortification.

"It's the first stage of the mating bond ritual."

Her muscles tightened, and she slowly opened her eyes. "I beg your pardon?"

Dalton gave her a miserable look. "A claim has been made. For the female to accept the claim and complete the ritual, she has to…" He made that same rolling motion with his hand.

"For God's sake, just spit it out," she whispered.

"She has to bite the male back, when they're both feeling really, really good," he said in a small voice. "If you get my drift."

She nodded.

"I mean, when the couple is being inti—"

"I get it," she said quickly, to try to stop any further embarrassment. Her gaze flicked over to Matthias, who was now listening intently to his guardians. He'd marked her. He'd scented her. He'd started to mate with her. She hadn't agreed to any of this.

"How do you, uh, stop it?" she asked.

"Well, you have two choices. You accept the claim, go ahead with the mating, or you…don't. If you don't, you don't get any, uh—relief from the heat," Dalton said, looking down at his feet. "Not until another male decides to try and mark you, which would be difficult if you're wearing another's scent."

"And the male? What happens to him if the mating isn't completed?" she bit out. "Or does he get off scot-free?"

Dalton winced. "Uh, he doesn't get…off." He lifted his hand and she grabbed it.

"So help me, do not roll your hand again. Use your words, Dalton," she muttered.

"If a mating ritual is not completed, you'll both be frustrated until another potential mate is discovered. If you don't find a new mate, then the, uh, frustration, drains you of energy, and you can both die."

"You mean we pine for each other?" she gasped, horrified.

Dalton pursed his lips, then nodded. "Yeah." His face

lightened. "Or if one of you dies first. If one dies before the mating bond is completed, the other is released."

"That skunk," Trinity gasped, gazing back at Matthias.

"Uh, to be fair, Trinity, sometimes imprinting is a decision, but most of the time, when a male finds a mate, it's a natural instinct. He doesn't necessarily have control over it."

"Have you ever imprinted?"

Dalton gulped. "Uh, no. I haven't met my mate."

"So you do have some control. You can choose not to," Trinity pointed out.

"Sort of. I haven't met my mate, so I don't know how I'll react."

Trinity leaned forward. "Here's a tip. Make sure you get her permission, first."

Dalton rolled his eyes. "This is so not a conversation I ever wanted to have with you."

"So let me get this straight," Trinity said, holding up a finger, frowning as she tried to grapple with the information she'd just received. "I can either shag Matthias and bite him, or else live out the rest of my days in a constant state of horny frustration until I pathetically starve myself and die, or I could kill him. Is that about right?"

Dalton gave her a tight-lipped nod. "Yep."

She sat there in dismayed shock as she processed her friend's news.

"Got it?"

"Got it."

Dalton nodded, then looked away. "So glad we never had this conversation."

Trinity nodded, the muscles tight in her jaw. "Me, too." She looked toward the other side of the campsite, and Matthias watched her warily. "Option three is looking pretty good at the moment…"

She dropped the cloth back into the bowl and rose to her feet, her eyes fixed on a particular heat-inducing lycan.

Matthias wandered away from the campsite, knowing Trinity would follow him. He guessed she was upset, and wanted any discussions they had to be in private. Once they were far enough away from the encampment, he turned to face his she-wolf.

Crack! The fist to his jaw actually made him turn his head this time.

"You weasel," she snarled, her fist pulled back for another punch.

"Weasel? Well, it's better than skunk, I guess," he muttered, rubbing his face. "I take it you heard," he caught her fist as she swung at him. "Okay, granted, I deserved that one, but I only let my she-wolf hit me once a day."

"Oh," she exclaimed in a growl as she lowered her fist. She stalked away, then came back at him, eyes flashing. "I am not your she-wolf."

He mock grimaced. "Well, a certain little bite says otherwise." He had to admit that while he regretted the way it had come about, he couldn't regret the fact that the mate he'd chosen—or that fate had chosen for him—was spectacular.

"Don't I get a say in this?" she rasped. "Where is my choice in the matter?"

He dragged her to him, grasping her hand to place it on the front of his trousers. His arousal was obvious. "Do you think I have a choice in this?" The words came out in a growl. "Did your friend not tell you that sometimes, the male doesn't get a say, either? It just happens?"

Her mouth opened for a moment, and her gaze dropped to his chest, and farther, before finally drifting up to meet his eyes again. "But I don't want a mate," she cried. He closed his eyes briefly at the pain that lanced through him at her words.

His hands rose to rest on her shoulders. "Trust me, I wasn't expecting to find a mate," he muttered.

"Then why did you imprint?" she wailed.

"Fate has a twisted sense of humor," he sighed. He lifted a dark curl from her shoulder. "I had a wife once, Trinity. And I loved her. I grieved for her when she died, and I never thought in a million years I'd find another to share my life with. But Cara—Cara was my wife. She was never a mate."

She looked up at him, her eyes wide. "What are you saying?"

"I'm saying that this is new for me, too." He wrapped the curl around his finger, and tugged playfully at it. She might want to deny their imprint connection, but she couldn't deny their shared physical attraction. That had been clear since the moment he'd tackled her in the forest. Before, if he admitted it to himself. "But I'm not resisting this," he whispered, as he leaned forward. "I'm accepting it."

He covered her mouth with his, running his hand through the thick dark silk of her hair as he pulled her warm, supple body close to him. There was no resistance from her, just an immediate acceptance of his kiss. She opened to him, and his tongue slid inside. The familiar, raging arousal flared within him, and he sighed when he felt her hands slide up his arms and wrap around his neck.

Like every other moment he'd spent with her, he was consumed with an awareness of her. The honeyed taste of her lips, the pounding of her heart against his...the soft yet firm curve of her butt as he pulled her even closer, the heat generated between them almost painful, but always exquisitely pleasurable.

He lifted his lips from hers. "Can you really deny this? Can you walk away from this?"

Her hands flattened along his shoulders to slide down his chest, until they bracketed the ring that rested over his heart.

"Can you walk away from this?" she asked, gesturing to the ring. "I can't commit myself to a man who loves a ghost. I won't share his attention with the memory of another." She shook her head. "I don't mean that to sound harsh, although I know it probably does. I understand you loved your wife, and I'd never want you to forget her. I'd never want to force anyone to let go of something so precious—and after seeing what my father went through, I don't know if that's actually possible." She lifted her gaze to his. "But I won't share my bed with a ghost, Matthias."

"It's not like that," he said, drawing her closer, enjoying the press of her breasts against his chest, the long length of her legs against his.

"Then take off the chain."

That was challenge he couldn't take up, and the fact chafed him. He wanted her to know that what they had was truly special. He'd never had these feelings for another woman, not even the wife he'd loved. Yet he couldn't give Trinity the one thing she needed.

"I can't."

She shook her head. "You won't," she corrected him. She masked her pain behind a tight smile. "You know,

Matthias, I don't know what would be worse, living in a state of perpetual need until I died a slow, miserable death, or committing myself to a man who couldn't fully give of himself, who couldn't move past the love he shared for another."

She turned to leave, and he raised his hand, but grasped at air. He couldn't let her walk away, couldn't let her abandon them, abandon this.

"I can't," he argued. She shook her head as she started to walk away. "I can't," he called softly to her. "I can't shift without it."

Chapter 17

"What?" Trinity asked, stunned.

He put his hands on his hips and looked at a point over her shoulder, the muscles in the strong column of his throat moving as he swallowed. "You once told me you were a curse to your pack. Well, I guess I'm the real thing. I am cursed. I can't shift without the chain. Well, technically it's the ring on the chain."

She took a step closer, her brow wrinkled. "Explain," she said hoarsely.

He nodded, his gaze still not meeting hers. "The spell the witches cast attacked our beast and prevented our ability to shift. An inability to shift strangles our wolf, and as it struggles, it shreds from within. Essentially, we were killed by our own lycans."

She approached him slowly. "How did you survive?"

He smiled weakly. "I was the firstborn of our family, but I wasn't my father's son. My mother was married previously. Apparently there is a null somewhere in my real father's bloodline. Distantly related, though. The connection wasn't strong enough to stop the spell from working altogether, but it did mute the effects." He dropped his gaze to hers, and she saw the blaze of grief in his eyes. "Unfortunately my son wasn't so lucky, with the bloodline further diluted by his birth."

She slid her hand into his. "Tell me everything."

He blinked, and looked down at their clasped hands. "I couldn't shift. I wandered for two years," he whispered, and she bit her lip.

"You were a stray," Trinity said, saddened by the realization. Strays were the lycans who wandered, packless. They were touch-starved, love-starved, wounded. Homeless.

He nodded, his gaze stark with the remembered loneliness. "I don't recommend the experience," he said hoarsely. "To not have the familiarity and support of a pack—I now know why strays don't live long," he said quietly. "For a pack animal, it's hell." He stroked her hair, and she realized why he touched so much, why he was so physical. She could relate to that. She remembered being surrounded by family, their chatter relaxing her, comforting her. Their presence a soothing balm to the soul, providing a sense of contentment and peace. And she'd also had a friend. To not have touch, but to always be surrounded by silence, by a lack of warmth, of shelter and comfort—that truly did sound like a form of hell to a breed accustomed to sharing their lives with others.

"I couldn't shift. No pack would take me, trapped in a human form, unable to change. I was half a lycan— and the weaker half, at that."

"You couldn't shift for two years?" she couldn't

begin to imagine what denying your lycan's freedom would feel like, not being able to let your true nature loose.

"Yeah. I eventually managed to find a witch who could help me." Matthias lifted the ring off his chest, the chain falling in a relaxed loop between them. "He bespelled my wife's ring—seeing as the curse was born from hate, and the ring symbolized the love we shared while tainted with blood and death—don't ask me to explain it, it's all mumbo jumbo to me. The only thing I need to know is that it works. That's when I found Jared—or really, he found me. He didn't care about the ring, didn't care if I could or couldn't shift. He just knew I needed a home."

For the first time, she felt something deep flare at the mention of the Alpine alpha's name. Not quite love, but a respect that eclipsed any such consideration she had for her own alpha prime. To welcome, to love uncon-ditionally, to forgive, to heal—those were traits she'd always associated with family, and what she aspired to see prevail in her own pack. One day.

He cleared his throat, then looked at her intently. "So you see, Trinity, I don't wear this ring to honor my dead wife's memory. I wear this ring as a talisman to help me be whole again."

She digested his words for a moment, then cocked her head as she looked up at him. "Can I ask you a question?"

His eyebrows rose. "Okay. Shoot." His expression was wary.

"This terrible deed that was done to you, and to your pack—it was done by witches. Why did you go to a witch for help?"

He shrugged. "You fight magic with magic. I figured the only way to be able to shift again was to get a witch to break the spell. Unfortunately, as it was a coven who created it, one witch couldn't break it—but he could…change it."

"He sounds like a good witch," she commented, grateful for the expertise of this unknown helper.

Matthias shook his head. "I don't think you could call him a good witch," he said slowly. "Unique, maybe. He runs a tattoo parlor in Irondell, wears leathers and sunglasses all the time, including at night, and rides a motorcycle."

She shook her head, frowning. "Not your usual witch, I guess." She'd come across some during her wanderings, so she wasn't actually sure there was a "usual" type.

"He answers to no coven, but he did me a good deed. He's good at what he does and I respect the man. If he hadn't helped me…" Matthias shook his head, leaving the rest of the sentence unsaid, but she could extrapolate. Strays were well-known for their short life cycles, their nomadic and lonely existences. Some even went crazy, and struck out with extreme violence which usually ended in their deaths. She couldn't imagine a lycan so good at leading people, so gentle with children, and so, well, so good at lovemaking being without that community contact.

"How many people know?" she asked quietly.

Matthias shook his head. "Only Jared and Samantha. And now you." During those wandering, aimless, homeless years, he'd discovered that not many packs would welcome someone who couldn't contribute fully to their family. As a man who couldn't shift into his wolf form, he'd been ridiculed, shunned and had even been attacked. He'd learned to defend himself, and to fight brutally, to try to compensate for his failing. He couldn't face this reaction from his adopted family. Jared and Samantha were special, but he just didn't know how the rest of the pack would react. Anything that involved witches was always bad news. "This curse—it's costly. I don't want it to cost me my family."

She looked down at their clasped hands. As secrets went, his was a big one. She couldn't truly comprehend what it must be like for him, to keep this secret from his pack, and still hold a position of leadership as guardian prime. It was a true testament to his character, his strength.

She looked up at him and smiled gently. "Thank you for trusting me." She realized he'd taken such a risk, telling her about his vulnerability. "I won't share your secret, I promise." Trust given deserved trust in return.

He placed a finger under her chin. "If we're to be mates, there should be no secrets between us." His voice was a gentle rumble, and it set that tide of heat rising again.

"How can you say that? We hardly know each other, and I'm really not happy about this imprinting thing."

He leaned forward and kissed her, his thumb resting with subtle pressure in the corner of her mouth, opening her to him. He kissed her thoroughly, so that she was panting and trembling by the time he finished. He drew back and eyed her.

"You'll get over it," he told her.

"No, it's not a matter of me gett—"

His lips cut her words off, and it was a long time before he lifted his head. This time they were both panting.

"You have to stop doing that," she rasped, then tilted her head to the side as his lips trailed along her jaw to her ear.

"But I like doing it," he murmured, his breath hot against her ear. He playfully nipped her earlobe, and she trembled, the sensation zinging molten heat straight to her core.

"Matthias, we can't. We have to go back to camp, and my pack members—" She had to catch her breath as he nipped and licked his way down her throat.

"Uh-huh...?" He encouraged her to speak, lifting his head.

"My pack members are already wary around me," she tried again, and had to shut her eyes to concentrate as he transferred his kisses to the other side of her neck. "If they knew about us, about what we've done..."

"Maybe we should tell them what I'd like to do... Kiss you, taste you, wrap your legs around my—"

"And that is why we have to stop. You're scent is all over me, damn it." It was already mortifying that Dalton had noticed.

Pride and satisfaction curled his lips. "And you wear it very nicely."

"What if others in my pack notice? They'll see this as a betrayal," she cried.

He frowned. "Perhaps you shouldn't worry so much about what they'll think, and just live," he suggested.

"Says the man who hasn't told his pack he can't shift without a talisman," she pointed out in a hiss, and stomped back to camp.

Of course she worried about what they'd think. She'd spent the last thirteen years trying to make up for what her father had done. She'd tried to be the best that she could be, in the hopes of earning their approval. This thing with Matthias, though, this imprinting—it could risk her family's acceptance. Forever.

Hell. A mate. She bit her lip. She didn't want a mate.

A mate meant vulnerability, losing yourself to another. Matthias was a guardian prime—if this mess with Rafe just went away, she'd still be mated with a warrior. A warrior's chances of dying were greater than the average wolf's. What then? She didn't want to die from a lost love. She shook her head as she reentered the camp. No, she had to figure a way out of this mess.

The Woodland pack were a suspicious lot. Matthias observed them, Jax curled up by his side, tears streaking the dirt across his cheeks as he slid into the sweet escape of sleep. He and Trinity had had to tell the boy of his mother's passing, and since then he was either at his side, or Trinity's. The other children were scared, understandably. He could only guess at the tales that had been told to them of the mean warriors from the north, the Alpine guardians—and they were young and away from their families—and that struck him as curious. It was highly unusual for parents to leave their young like this, especially during a pack war. The young were never left unprotected. No wonder the pups were frightened. Trinity's friend Dalton—well he liked to give the impression of being relaxed, but he watched the activity around the camp with an intent eye. There was another warrior, one who was found unconscious but had since roused. He was one who definitely required watching, judging by the resentment in his gaze as he observed the Alpine guardians go about their business. The elders… They were different. They sat silently, noticing every move he and his men made. He wasn't sure if they were curious, or anticipating an attack.

Matthias pursed his lips. As if he or his men would attack them, the stewards of the pack—or the young. His gaze followed Trinity as she gathered the bowls from the injured, and brought them over to the camp kitchen to help wash. It was sunset, and the dying light of the day bathed her in the warmest of glows, gilding the copper streaks in her hair like spun gold, and giving her skin a warmth and color that was entrancing.

He wanted her. He couldn't help it. She was noble, loyal, strong. Despite everything that had happened in her life, she had a lot of love in her heart to give. She was especially good with the children, soothing their fears, coaxing a smile and a giggle from them. For a moment, he wondered what children with her would be like. Would they have her dark hair, or his blond hair? Green eyes or blue? Son or daughter? However they came, he knew she would ensure they felt the love of their mother, especially after her own experience. His gut still burned over that.

He glanced down at Jax, and brushed the boy's sandy hair off his forehead. This boy was alone in the world, now. Neither mother nor father, and no siblings. He knew what that felt like; he knew the abject loneliness that came with not having family. Like Trinity, he was determined to make sure this boy knew he had a place in the world. His gaze returned to Trinity. She was amazing. She had the biggest heart of anyone he'd ever met. Despite their withdrawal, she'd raced through the forest to come to her pack's aide when they'd needed it most.

She might still be a little mad at him about the imprinting, but he'd seen the compassion in her eyes when he'd told her about his curse. He was still surprised he'd shared that. Not even Zane or Nate were aware of the circumstances of his inability to shift.

For so long, he'd felt…incomplete. Ever since that night when he'd awoken in agony with his wolf clawing at him from the inside, unable to set his lycan free, he'd felt…wrong. Unnatural, as though the body he inhabited wasn't truly his. In the darkest hours of night, alone in his bed, when the insecurity of his deficiencies plagued him the most, he did feel unworthy, as though he was living a charade as Alpine's guardian prime. He wasn't a full lycan. He needed a trigger to shift. He'd striven to prove himself, and Jared had promoted him to guardian prime; it was almost unheard of for a nongenuine to achieve such a rank. Yet he still felt that no matter how hard he worked, he was unfit, and it was just a matter of time before that was exposed.

But when he'd told Trinity, she hadn't looked at him as though she found him disgusting, or contemptible, or as though he were lacking. In fact, she'd looked at him with a tenderness and a softness, an empathy. She knew what it felt like to be lonely, to feel shame—although in her case it was completely unwarranted—and she judged him not.

What a pair they were. He may have lost his family. He may have lost his pack, but he'd never doubted their love and acceptance of him. Trinity, though, had managed to grow up without the loving embrace of her family, yet still gave her heart to those she loved in the hope that they would accept her. Which was ironic, because he could only hope that she would ultimately accept him as her mate.

"Get away from me." The now-conscious guardian slapped the bowl out of Trinity's hand.

Matthias frowned as Trinity stepped back in shock.

"You're a traitor," the guardian hissed, and more Woodland folk turned at the exchange. Dalton hobbled to his feet, his expression wary.

Trinity leaned down to pick up the bowl from the

ground, then glanced at the angry guardian. "I'm not a traitor, Dion."

"You've shacked up with Alpine, I can smell it on you."

Trinity's cheeks glowed with a warmth that even across the campsite, Matthias could see. He gained his feet, careful not to wake the sleeping boy. He stepped forward, his brows lowered. Trinity saw him approaching and gave him a quick shake of her head, which he ignored.

"I would never betray Woodland," she stated in a quiet yet firm voice.

"You already have." Dion rose to his feet to tower over the woman in a move clearly intended to intimidate. Matthias reacted. Moving in a blur, he caught the guardian by his torn shirt and threw him to the ground.

"Matthias," Trinity cried in protest.

"No," he shook his head, placing his foot over the throat of the lycan who dared threaten his she-wolf. He leaned down, ignoring the gurgling noises the guardian uttered. "You should be thanking her," he growled. "Everything she's done, it's been to protect your sorry lot."

The guardian's eyes flashed in anger as he tried to shift the foot pressing against his throat. Matthias added a little more pressure. With a little more push, he could crush the lycan's neck.

"Matthias, please, no." Trinity stepped closer, and Matthias wouldn't look at her. "I swear, Matthias, if you hurt him, so help me I will make your life a living hell, and you know I can do it."

Her words were uttered so ferociously, so fervently, her need to defend her people so frustrating yet so beautifully savage that fierce pride flooded him. He'd thought her desperate need to protect was a weakness, and now he realized it was her strength. Matthias kept his expression impassive as he turned to look at her.

"Even now, when he insults you, you wish to protect him?" He glanced back to the guardian at his feet. "Your alpha prime calls for a parley in the woods at the same time as pups are training. He breaks the conditions of parley. It's your tracker who sees to the safety of the young." He lifted his finger to point to Trinity. "This so-called traitor risked her life to protect Woodland. She's led us everywhere else but the den—she even tried to lead us into a trap with your vamp neighbors. The only reason we're here, you moron, is because she heard the cave-in and came running to pull your sorry ass out from the dirt. And now you have the audacity to turn on the one person who would lay down her life to save you?" He shook his head. "You are so sure we'll kill all of you without a second thought, I may as well do it now."

"Matthias," Trin's voice was low in warning, and he smiled at the guardian.

"Fine, but thank your tracker for saving your life. And if I ever hear you talk like that again, it will be the last thing you say."

He pressed down a little bit, just because it was the only satisfaction he was going to get out of the whole confrontation, then lifted his foot. "Your alpha prime is your true traitor. If you're going to bitch about anyone, bitch about him."

He held out his hand to the guardian, who glared at him with suspicion before accepting the silent offer of assistance. Matthias hauled him to his feet.

"What is that supposed to mean?" the guardian rasped.

Matthias narrowed his eyes. "You don't think it's

odd that the rest of the pack has disappeared, but only the elders and the pups remain?"

"Matthias," Trinity whispered, and he glanced over at her. Her eyes were dark, the shadows under them obvious. Little lines appeared to bracket her mouth, and suddenly, he knew. He had suspected, but Trinity's haunted expression confirmed it. She knew something, and from the looks of it, and it was possibly worse than he'd initially thought. Damn, that Rafe Woodland was a psycho, and needed to be put down.

"What are you saying?" the guardian snapped.

Matthias tilted his head. "It means your alpha prime destroyed your den, Guardian, and took the pack, but left those who would slow him down to perish."

Chapter 18

"You dare to question Rafe Woodland's honor?" Dion grated. Trinity watched as Matthias's eyes widened briefly in disbelief. Zane and Nate started to walk over, and a few of the Alpine guardians shifted closer. Dion was the Woodland Guardian Prime, and he was built beautifully for his role, but even he wouldn't stand a chance against Matthias and his men. The damn guardian was just proud enough to take them on, though. The elders wouldn't be able to sit by and watch that happen, and the elders were no match for guardians in their prime.

"What the hell is in the water, here? Are you all so damn deluded?" Matthias shook his head. "You think *we* are the bad guys. Good grief."

One of the elders, Gilbert Downing, rose from his perch on a log, his gray eyebrows low over his forehead. Agatha, another elder, did the same.

Dion straightened his shoulders, and Trinity could see the determination in his gaze, the clenching of his fists. He would not back down. No guardian prime would let another slur his alpha prime. Matthias smiled grimly as he read the Woodland guardian's stance.

"You seem to forget a little incident of your alpha prime organizing the assassination of my alpha prime— or were you also involved in that?" Matthias stepped forward, his broad shoulders and forbidding expression giving him a menacing air.

Dion's gaze shifted, and he shook his head just once. Matthias's eyes narrowed. "You didn't know, did you?" he breathed. "You didn't know what your alpha prime had planned, what he'd set in motion. Tell me, do you stand by his actions?"

Dion's chin lifted. "I am loyal to my alpha prime," he stated; his gaze flicked briefly to Trinity. "I don't betray my pack."

"Neither do I," she snapped. "In fact, I will do everything in my power to protect it, not put it in danger. Rafe has risked the pack too often."

Dion's eyes widened, but Trinity refused to lower her gaze from the Woodland Guardian Prime. "You turn your back on Woodland?" His voice was low, angry, yet she could hear the undertone of hurt there.

"Trin," Dalton said softly as he limped over to them.

"I'm not the one who evacuated the den," she pointed out softly, saddened by what she'd learned, and for the news she had to deliver to her guardian prime. Dion was a decent guy, when he wasn't acting like a dick. He would have a similar reaction to her.

Dion frowned. "He didn't evacuate. He took all able-bodied family for a combat training session." He lifted his chin toward Matthias and his men. Zane and

Nate now stood shoulder to shoulder with their guardian prime. "We're in the middle of a war, remember," he muttered.

"A war of Rafe's making," Trinity snapped, conscious of Gilbert's and Agatha's shocked reactions. Her words would be considered treasonous by the elders, but for once, she didn't care. Rafe had acted like a monster, and she didn't want to be part of a pack that honored and followed the monster.

"Matthias is right. This all started when Rafe conspired with that human, Armstrong. He didn't trust his pack—he didn't trust *you*, and you're his guardian prime." She knew her words would hurt Dion, but she had to make him see. "He plotted to kill another pack's alpha prime. On *purpose*. If another pack did that, we would shun them." It was such a terrible deed, so full of hateful intent, of insult to another pack.

"He had his reasons," Dion said in a low voice, his blue eyes dark with something that Trinity would almost call sadness.

"And what are they? None of us know," she said, indicating the elders who were gathering behind Dion. "What possible reason would justify the killing of another pack's alpha prime?" She challenged him, finally putting into words the thoughts that had plagued her since this whole situation had flared up. She folded her arms. "He knew I was out in the woods during that parley session. I'd had to clear it with him. He knew there were pups in the woods, and yet he still started a battle that could have harmed them." She shook her head. Assassinating Jared Gray? That was low. Putting the pups at risk? That was low, too, but this time Rafe had outdone himself.

"Tell me, we heard an explosion yesterday. What was that?"

Dion frowned. "One of the tunnels collapsed. You know the structure was weakened. Rafe took everyone out for a session, and the elders were to hold a history class with the pups." He waved a hand toward Dalton, who by now had reached Trinity's side. "Dalton and I remained to work on the tunnel supports."

She slid her hand into her pocket, and pulled out the cable. "I found this beneath the rubble," she said quietly, lifting it for Dion to see. Dion's eyes widened, and the blood drained from his face. He shook his head.

"No."

She nodded. "I smelled traces of the explosives he used, and I smelled him. I had to dig a little, but I found this. You know what this is." Only a select few would know or still remember, but she saw the recognition in Gilbert's eyes, the lowering of his shoulders as he comprehended what she was saying. Remnants from the copper mine they once worked in the mountains. Her father had insured all explosives were locked in a cave deep in the heart of the mountain, away from the den. Only the alpha prime bore a key to those particular supplies. A key that Rafe now carried.

Dion shook his head. "Rafe wouldn't do that, not to his own pack."

Her eyes filled with tears. "But he did."

He'd left behind the ones who would slow him down. Dion rubbed his hands over his face, his disbelief slowly sliding into sorrow, hurt and disappointment.

"No," he said, shaking his head, clinging to the illusion of honor.

Gilbert stepped forward, his expression grim as he placed a hand on Dion's shoulders. "It's time, Dion," Gilbert said quietly, his voice rough with age.

Dion shook his head as Trinity's eyebrows rose. "No.

It's—it's not right," Dion muttered, and Gilbert shook his head.

"No, it's not *easy*," the elder corrected. He looked at Trinity. "Rafe isn't well."

She frowned. It was no excuse for what he'd done, but it could be an explanation. "He's psycho, deranged," she conceded. "Ever since he visited Armstrong's shadow breed medical clinic and had his fangs enhanced, he's been on a *Scary Mary* power trip." She glanced at Matthias. "It's no excuse, but yeah, he's sick."

Matthias arched an eyebrow. "That's an understatement."

"He's my alpha prime," Dion protested.

Trinity stepped forward and reached out for his hand. "He's our alpha prime," she told him sadly. "But he's slowly killing our pack." She indicated Dalton. "He left you two behind. He wanted you both dead," she said quietly.

"And we both would have died in there if Trinity hadn't found us," Dalton pointed out, folding his arms. Then he grimaced. "And if the Alpines hadn't dragged us out." He looked as though that admission was burning a hole in his gut.

"What are we supposed to do?" Dion whispered, glancing over his shoulder at Gilbert.

The elder eyed Matthias.

"That depends," the old lycan said quietly.

Matthias frowned. "On what?"

"On what happens when we find him."

Matthias ran through the woods, following Trinity as she tracked the Woodland pack through their home territory.

So this was how the tracker worked when committed to her task. She was amazing. Her abilities made his look like a juvenile's. He'd lost the trail twice already, but Trinity had followed it unerringly, setting a grueling pace.

They'd decided to pursue Rafe and the pack after a night of rest. Zane ran alongside him, and the Woodland Guardian Prime was just behind him. Matthias shook his head. This was—*weird*. He'd never imagined he'd be running *with* the lycan, but it seemed there was a noble streak buried deep inside this one. It gave him hope for the rest of the pack. He still wasn't about to trust them, though. His gaze fastened on the she-wolf with the stamina of a guardian. All except one, perhaps.

She slowed down and held up her hand. Each of the guardians accompanying them halted at her signal. Matthias had had to split his squads. Some of them remained at the site just outside the Woodland den, tending to the injured and clearing out some of the rubble. Dalton had remained back there; his leg still wasn't healed enough to walk on, let alone run. Nate had left for more supplies, and Kai was there to oversee the elders and the pups, and to supervise any trips into the den. Structural engineers would have to check the integrity of the cave system before the Woodland den could even be considered safe for repairs.

Matthias told himself it wasn't his problem. He was here for Rafe, not for a pack of lycans who should know better than to put their trust and loyalty into a psychotic alpha. He was going to ignore Gilbert and Agatha, and the rest of the elders, their shoulders burdened with the knowledge that their alpha prime was toxic to his pack.

Trinity paced back and forth, surveying the ground. "What's the matter?" he asked her past his panting. She shook her head, her chest rising and falling, but her concentration on the terrain around her, not on catching her breath.

"It's all muddled," she panted. "It's like they got to this point and deliberately scuffed everything. It's a mess."

"Maybe they stopped to catch their breath," he suggested meaningfully. His men were fit, but he still wanted them to have some fuel in the tank for when they finally caught up with the Woodlands.

Trinity shook her head again. "No. See how you guys stand in a spot? You might take a few steps, but where and how you stand," she said pointing to Zane who was leaning over, hands on his knees as though he was going to throw up a lung. "See, that leaves a deeper imprint. You might shift a little, take a step or two, but then off you go. These tracks…" She frowned. "It's almost like—" her eyes widened in realization, and understanding dawned in Matthias at the same time. Her gaze drifted up above them.

"It's a trap," he said, backing up to turn to his men. "Eyes and ears—"

Something thudded onto his back, and he fell to the ground under the weight of it as growls and snarls erupted in the small stretch of woods. He grunted as a fist connected with his back, just below his kidneys. He rolled, pushing against the weight, until he was on his back on top of whoever had dropped on him. Brief impressions of dark figures jumping from the branches above onto his men, the sounds of flesh hitting flesh, the grunts, yells and shouts as attacked and attacker fought, the metallic scent of blood teasing at his senses, stirring his beast. A hand snaked around his throat, and the sunlight glinted on a ring on the man's finger. The Woodland crest.

Rafe.

Jabbing with his elbow several times into the wall of muscle beneath him, he heard the soft grunts with each contact, Rafe's breath gusting past his neck and shoulder.

White-hot pain speared into his neck, his teeth gritting as he realized Rafe was using those weird fangs on him. The damn lycan bit him—in human form. He raised his foot and brought it down hard on Rafe's knee.

Rafe pulled back, yelling in pain. Matthias jerked his head back, head-butting him only hell knew where, and Rafe's grip loosened.

Matthias rolled and was back on his feet instantly, arms out as he faced his nemesis, because that was what Rafe had become to him. The ultimate enemy. For what he'd done to his friend Jared and what he'd done to his own pack, to Trinity.

He scanned the forest, dodging the punches that Rafe threw at him, looking for his she-wolf. He first saw Dion, dodging blows as he tried to talk to his own guardians. The blows aimed at the Woodland Guardian Prime were halfhearted, as though the men were struggling with attacking one of their own. Dion could look after himself. It was Trinity that he was worried about. She was lighter, smaller than the average guardian, and not trained for combat.

There. She was under attack, successfully blocking the strikes of a guardian. He could see her shock, her fear, as she stepped back in an effort to dodge the blows.

Rafe's fist connected with his jaw, and he spun with the momentum, using it to backhand the Woodland Alpha Prime with a sharp crack as hand met cheek. Rafe's eyes flared with anger, and with a strange satisfaction, as he slowly wiped the blood from the resulting cut in his lip.

"You're more of a fool than your alpha was, Marshall, I'll give you that," Rafe said, grinning, his teeth bloody. "No lycan would dare come into my territory uninvited."

Matthias lashed out with a kick, which Rafe dodged, but the alpha didn't dodge the second spin kick Matthias dealt, as he leaped into the air and turned, the sole of his boot connecting with Rafe's jaw.

He landed, braced and centered on his feet, his arms up in a classic defense pose. Matthias grinned. "Well, it looks like I dared. I came, and I'm kicking your ass."

He ducked the punch that Rafe threw, but wasn't quick enough to dodge the next one, Rafe's fist hitting him in the side of his ribs. He sucked in a painful breath.

Rafe grinned, his eyebrows waggling. "I can tell you I had no intention of wiping out a pack's entire prime hierarchy, but the idea is growing on me." He kicked, his foot connecting with Matthias's knee, making him drop to the ground on the injured joint.

Matthias put his arms up, blocking and catching the next kick aimed at his head, then punched Rafe's thigh. He was aiming a little higher, but Rafe tried to jump out of the way. Matthias grabbed Rafe's foot and twisted, but the agile alpha turned with the movement, preventing the snap of his ankle. His other foot caught Matthias on the top of the head and Matthias rolled, briefly stunned.

He rose to his feet, shaking his head to clear the soft cloud of darkness, then raised his arm to block Rafe's punch.

"Give it up, Rafe. I've got your tracker. I've got your

guardian prime. Your elders and pups are being cared for by my men. I've got you."

Rafe's eyes narrowed, and Matthias nodded. "Yeah, you heard me. Your elders didn't die, and they sure are pissed at you." He briefly glanced over his shoulder. Trinity was pinned to the trunk of the tree, a guardian's fist raised against her.

Rafe laughed, although it was more of a breathless chuckle. "You think I care what those old dogs think? They are weak. They can't defend us. They are not strong. They are a waste of space. We are Woodland. We have to be the strongest. The feeble, the frail—the powerless. There is no room in Woodland for that. I have spent my life proving our strength to all of the breeds. Nobody can conquer us. You can have my guardian prime—I don't like traitors. He was working up to a challenge. But the tracker?"

The alpha prime rolled his wrist in an intricate move that turned Matthias and twisted his arm behind his back, all in a blur. Rafe wrapped his other arm around his throat, and held him pinned against him. He turned them so they could watch Trinity shake her head, pleading with the guardian who even now stood over her, ready to deal a violent blow.

"I can smell her on you, Guardian, and I can smell you on her," Rafe rasped. "You will never have her. I'm just trying to make up my mind—should I kill her, and let you live with the burden for the rest of your life that you cost your mate her life? Or should I kill you, and let her pine away, just like her father did for her mother?" His grip tightened. "It has a certain kind of symmetry, don't you think?"

Rage swelled through Matthias at Rafe's words. The threat to his mate was like a shot of adrenaline. He roared in anger, in indignation, and reached behind his head to grasp at Rafe's face, pressing his thumb into the soft, fleshy part of the eye socket.

Rafe reacted instantly, jerking his head back, his grip around Matthias's throat loosening. Matthias brought his foot down, raking the heel of his boot down the alpha prime's shin and stomping on his foot. He used Rafe's natural bend reflex to his advantage, also bending. He stepped out, grimacing at the wrench in his shoulder. He straightened his arm, although Rafe still held it at an angle behind his back. The alpha prime applied pressure, forcing Matthias toward the ground.

Matthias dropped and rolled forward in a somersault, going with the natural movement as opposed to resisting and getting his arm snapped out of its joint. The move surprised the Woodland alpha. Matthias jerked him off his feet, rolling with him, and they wrestled on the ground, striking, kicking and punching where possible.

Matthias roared when he felt Rafe's fangs pierce his forearm, and pulled away. He levered himself up, his fist raised to smash into the alpha's face.

Trinity's cry halted him, and he looked back over his shoulder in time to see her held by the guardian, her neck pulled to an uncomfortable angle. Just the slightest pressure, and that guardian could snap his she-wolf's neck. He turned to end it with the alpha, and his blood chilled in his veins as Rafe smiled up at him, his fist curled around his chain.

"What's it going to be, Guardian? Save your mate, or save this ring and whatever hold it has over you?"

Chapter 19

Behind him, Trinity whimpered in pain, and Matthias made his decision, accepting the full consequences in that split-second rationale. He let go of Rafe, and felt the small tug around his neck as the chain broke. Hatred, hot and heavy, churned in his gut as he raced over to Trinity, tackling the guardian who dared threaten his mate. His teeth were bared as all three fell to the ground, and he wrenched the guardian's arm, freeing Trinity.

He raised his arm, intent on smashing his fist into the ground via this guardian's face.

"No, Matthias," Trinity cried, and she moved into his field of vision, her tear-streaked face catching his attention as nothing else could. Seeing her pain, the stricken expression on her face, grounded him. He couldn't be the source of that pain, but his rage hummed through his veins.

"He was going to kill you," he grated, turning his

gaze to the guardian beneath him. The lycan wore a resigned look, as though waiting for the fist to fall.

"He was following orders," she told him, clutching her hands in front of her.

"He was going to kill you," he repeated. There was no excuse. Harming one of his own, and a female, at that. The guardian's gaze flicked between him and Trinity, wary puzzlement edging into the resignation. He could relate. He didn't know why the guardian was still breathing, either.

"Please don't hurt him," Trinity whispered. "His name is Roscoe. He's Mia's father, and he's just found out what happened to his daughter."

"That doesn't mean he can take it out on you," Matthias stated in a low voice.

"But he didn't. He could have killed me, but he didn't. He's a good man, Matt."

She'd called him Matt. He wondered if she realized her slip. She gazed up at him imploringly. She didn't look at him like a Woodland Tracker Prime trying to defend a guardian against the Alpine Guardian Prime. No, it was personal, it was vulnerable, honest and…intimate. A part of him was still amazed she would defend these guys. Another part of him rejoiced at her growing familiarity with him.

Matthias threw the punch, knocking the guardian unconscious. Trinity gasped. He levered himself to his feet. "He's not dead," he muttered, although he really did want to kill the man. It was clear Trinity wanted him alive, and he wanted what Trinity wanted. At least this way the guardian learned a lesson, and he got a small measure of satisfaction. He reached out to Trinity, assessing her face. There was a dark bloom on her cheek, and bruising on her throat, her arms. She'd put up a hell of a fight.

He pulled her to him, hugging her tight, careful of any injuries. "He hurt you," he murmured into her dark hair. She shook as she chuckled.

"I hurt him back. Trust me. Don't worry—I'll heal fast."

He closed his eyes. He wasn't ready to see the humor in it. Wasn't sure if he ever would. She laid her head against his chest, and it was a moment before she reared back, eyeing his torso.

"Your chain—where is it?" she whispered harshly.

He met her gaze with a calm he didn't feel, his lycan writhing inside, impatient and frustrated, at its inability to shift. "Rafe has it."

Trinity walked among the trees. A lot of Woodland guardians lay unconscious on the ground. The rest had retreated with their alpha prime. Dion sagged against a tree, his lip bloody, along with his bruised knuckles. He'd had to fight his own men, and weariness and defeat lined his face.

"Don't kill them, he says," Zane muttered as he passed Dion. "Do you know how hard it is to resist the compulsion to choke the ever-loving crap out of someone when they're trying to kill you?"

Dion rolled his head to look at the Alpine guardian, as though even that expended too much energy, and she realized he was still recovering from the cave-in.

"They don't deserve to die for their loyalty," Dion said, then winced, his fingers gently touching his lip.

"They do if they're on the wrong side," Zane argued. "What are we supposed to do, wait for them to wake up and then start all over again?"

Dion shook his head tiredly. "Hell, no. Tie them up," he said, gesturing to his unconscious guardians. "When they come to, they're going to be mega pissed. I need—" Dion closed his eyes briefly, then opened them to look at Matthias. "I need to talk to them. I need to explain a few things. When they come to, they'll fight. I just need to hold them long enough to talk to them."

Matthias stood slightly apart from the group, his gaze brooding as he eyed the guardian prime. Despite Dion's original antipathy, he'd actually fought with the Alpines, and now Dion was trying to fight the men who had battled alongside him and who now perceived his alliance as a betrayal of his pack. Trinity hoped Matthias wouldn't ignore that, couldn't ignore the strain it would have put on the lycan, to fight his own, to essentially betray them far more overtly than his accusations to her. Matthias surveyed the fallen guardians, then finally nodded.

"Fine. You have your time. When I return, if there are still guardians true to the Woodland Alpha Prime, then they will have to face the consequences alongside Rafe."

Zane frowned. "When you return?"

Matthias nodded. "I'm going after Rafe. Alone."

"What are we supposed to do in the interim? Babysit these guys?"

"You wait, yes." Matthias said quietly, his arms folded. Trinity eyed him. He was outwardly so calm, so poised, yet she could see the inner turmoil in his eyes. Her heart ached for him. She couldn't imagine what he must be thinking, what he must be feeling, knowing his lycan was caged within him. He'd told her the constrained lycans wound up attacking from within in their effort to gain freedom, something that had ultimately lead to the death of his family. How long did Matthias have before the same happened to him?

"When they stir, let Dion talk to them. Then take them back to the Woodland den. Their elders are there, as well as their pups. These guardians should help them, and while they're at it, they could possibly work on the main entrance to the den."

"You'd let them go home? Rebuild?" Zane said, incredulous.

Matthias was silent for a moment, then nodded. "Yeah. This whole mission is to find those responsible for Jared's death, and to make them pay. These guys," he said, lifting his chin toward the heap of unconscious Woodland guardians, "they're just like you and me. From what I can gather, Rafe Woodland kept his little assassination project largely to himself, but these guys are now in a position where they have to defend him, purely because he's their alpha prime and he demands it." He eyed Zane squarely. "We would do the same for Jared, and now Samantha." He glanced over at Dion. "Not all Woodland wolves are complete dicks."

Zane's gaze flicked between Trinity and Dion, then he sighed. "Fine. We babysit. We build. Got it." He held up a finger toward Dion. "This doesn't mean I like you, or trust you."

Dion nodded wearily. "The feeling is mutual."

Matthias smiled, albeit grimly. "Good." He let his arms drop. "I'm off."

"But wait, you can't go up against Rafe alone," Trinity protested. "He's still got some guardians, he's got the rest of the pack, wherever they are... You'll need help."

Matthias strolled over to her, his shoulders rolling in a smooth, rhythmic motion. He dipped his head forward to gaze into her eyes. "This is something I have to do."

"At least wait for Nate to return," she pleaded. "You're outnumbered, you're—" she glanced briefly over his shoulder to the men who watched their exchange with poorly disguised curiosity. She couldn't expose his secret, his vulnerability. "You're—limited," she finished, wincing. "You can't go up against him and expect to win."

Matthias smoothed her hair back from her cheek, tucking it behind her ear. "The cracks are beginning to show for Rafe," he said. "He's lost his elders, his pups, and now a considerable number of guardians. When word gets back to the rest that his guardian prime is no longer supporting him, it will raise questions. His pack is disintegrating around him."

"And that will just make him angry, and when he's angry, he's mean," she pointed out to him.

His lips curled in a half smile. "I think you underestimate me, Trin," he told her quietly. "There are not enough guardians, not a mean enough alpha, who can kill my friend, who can hurt my mate and escape my vengeance. When I face him, no matter how many wolves he has around him, it will never be enough."

"But why do it by yourself?" she protested softly.

"Because I don't want more lycans hurt," he told her simply. "This has gone on long enough. The elders, the pups—Jax…" Sadness entered his eyes at the mention of the young pup they'd left back at camp. Jax had cried as they'd left, and she'd felt as though she'd left a part of her heart behind with that little boy.

Matthias's words were noble, but she didn't believe them. Well, she did, because she'd learned that while Matthias could be dangerous, lethal and ruthless, he could also be gentle, merciful and caring. This whole thing had been to get Rafe, and she believed him when he said the whole pack didn't have to pay for the sins of the alpha prime. She could also understand his reluctance to risk his own men. No leader willingly sacrificed those under his charge. Well, not unless that leader was Rafe. She eyed the fallen Woodland guardians. So, perhaps he had a point.

"I'm going with you," she said.

He frowned. "No, you're not."

"Yes. You'll need a tracker."

He shook his head. "No, I won't. Trust me, I have a gut feeling about this," he said meaningfully.

She lifted her chin. "I'm not going to let you do this on your own."

His eyebrows rose. "You're not going to *let* me?" His head lifted, as though someone had shocked him with a slap. He blinked rapidly, then his eyebrows drew down in a deep V across his forehead. "Since when do I take instruction from you, Tracker?"

Now Trinity felt like she was the one to be slapped in the face. The change in his manner was disconcerting, and she stared up at him in confusion.

"I am Guardian Prime of Alpine Pack," he told her fiercely, his voice rising ever so slightly. Zane stopped trying to hide his curiosity and stared at them openly, as did the rest of the Alpine guardians. Dion straightened.

"I do not need to justify myself to a lowly little tracker from an enemy pack. I will do as I see fit, when I see fit. This thing between you and me?" He gestured between them. "This doesn't give you license to issue orders to *me*. You are a tracker. You can't go up against a guardian, or an alpha. You are of no use for me in this—you are a liability."

"But, Matthias, you can't face him by yourself," she argued, trying to ignore the hurt that bloomed at his words. She had to make him see sense. He couldn't shift. Rafe wasn't so restricted. In human form lycans possessed more strength than the average human, but even a lycan in human form couldn't beat one in full wolf form.

"You have so little faith, Tracker," he said harshly. "Don't make the mistake of miscalculating me as you did your father." He glared down at her, so fierce, so proud. So remote.

She stepped back, recoiling at the blow of his words. He knew her weak spot, and he had struck, unflinchingly, causing a deep pain reminiscent of the agony she'd endured when Rafe had told her the news of her father.

Her mouth opened, but words failed her, so breathtaking was the hurt. For a moment, his gaze softened, and she thought she saw a glimmer of regret, but he blinked. She realized it must have been her imagination, a desire that he couldn't have meant what he said, that this glorious warrior who stirred her heart and embodied honor and integrity could be so mean.

He nodded, satisfied he'd terminated any further argument. "Now, if we've finished all this hand-holding, I have something more pressing to deal with."

He turned and loped out of the clearing. She stared after him, stunned at what had just transpired. Zane approached her cautiously, frowning after his guardian prime, but it was Dion's hand on her shoulder that pulled her out of her shock. She turned to look at her pack mate, his gaze full of compassion. His reaction, his reaching out to comfort her, should have been a surprise. But she realized she couldn't feel anything beyond the overwhelming world of hurt Matthias had just delivered to her feet.

* * *

Matthias jogged through the forest, away from his men. Away from Trinity… The muscles in his jaw tightened. He'd done what had to be done. His gut roiled. It was for the best, but damn, it sucked.

He paused, sniffed the air, then shifted direction ever so slightly to follow Rafe's scent. He would track the alpha prime down. He hadn't lied in that regard. He'd lied about everything else, but not this. The ring—it called to his beast, and the wolf within was determined to locate it. Even now, he could feel his muscles rippling as his beast struggled to shirk the coil of his human skin, the claws digging underneath the skin of his fingertips, unable to penetrate, unable to gain freedom. His beast was angry—angry at the constraint, but also angry with the way he'd dealt with his she-wolf.

He gritted his teeth. He couldn't shift. The witch had told him: if he and the ring were to ever part ways, he would be forever trapped in the form in which he'd last had contact with the talisman. If he'd been in wolf-form, he wouldn't have been able to communicate quite so effectively with Trinity to prevent her coming with him.

What he'd done was cruel. He dragged in a deep breath. He'd hit her where it hurt, using her own guilt about her father's suicide as a weapon against her. That, in itself, was unconscionable. Knowing she was his mate, and still using that weapon—well, that was dishonest, barbaric, underhanded, unethical and any other contemptuous word he could think of. But it had been necessary.

He paused at a tree to catch his breath. He was at a considerable disadvantage in a fight against another lycan. He could no longer lead the guardians of Alpine Pack. They deserved a strong leader, one who could fight with them, fight for them—not a half wolf, half man unable to commit fully to either sense of self.

And Trinity… She deserved a fully capable lycan to look after her, to keep her safe. He loved her. He couldn't deny it. If faced again with a decision to save the woman he loved or the ring that completed him, he would pick his mate, every time. That didn't mean, though, that a broken mate was worthy of her.

He could not protect her from Rafe if he attacked. He couldn't protect her from any threat, and that was a driving need for a male mate—to protect his she-wolf, his family.

He could do neither.

His hand clenched into a fist against the rough bark of the tree. There was one saving grace—the mating bond hadn't been completed. He would go after Rafe Woodland with every ounce of strength he could muster—and if he failed, then Trinity would be released from his imprint, and free to love another. He would free her from her "death sentence," and that was his priority.

He was prepared to die, so that she could live.

Chapter 20

Trinity watched as Jax and Mia played, dangling a twig in her hand. The boy had clung to her for seemingly hours, and she'd let him, also taking comfort in the embrace. Now, though, he'd ventured from her arms to do what kids should—play. She forced a smile to her face as he cheered, holding up his handful of rocks.

Dion was talking to Roscoe, who sat a few feet away, ever watchful over his young daughter, his expression becoming harder than granite the longer he listened to his guardian prime. Every now and then, his gaze would flick to the entrance of the den, the rubble and destruction still clearly visible. The other Woodland guardians were either bound, or talking quietly with the elders. Two sat at the mouth of the tunnel, their expressions drawn as they realized that some of their pack were gone forever.

Dalton approached her side. His limp was much less pronounced, although he still wasn't quite mended. He sat down next to her. "Dion told me what happened," he said quietly.

She blinked, her sight blurry with the tears she was trying not to shed, her throat tight with the yells she wanted to release. All the way back, and now, sitting in the camp, she could smell him, so conscious of his essence, of his trail, it was almost as if they were somehow linked by scent, a natural, instinctive awareness that pulled at her. She rubbed her lips together. Dion's reaction had surprised her. He'd given her several consolatory pats on the shoulder on the long hike home. He had reached out to her like a pack mate consoling his family, gentle and tender. It was the first time he'd ever behaved in such a way with her. As though he considered her family. She blinked rapidly. It was ironic that being shunned by the man she loved would bring about the acceptance she'd so craved from her pack. A bittersweet side effect of having your heart trampled.

Dalton sighed. "I have to say, I'm surprised. I mean, I know he's Alpine, and some of them can be tools…" Her friend eyed Zane as he folded his arms, standing over a Woodland guardian with a glare that had as much warmth in it as one of the glaciers from the Alpine guardian's home territory. "But Matthias struck me as, well, decent."

"He is," she whispered.

"No, he's a tool. Dion told me what he said." Dalton's lips firmed. "You don't say that to a woman you've…" He rolled his hand and Trinity rolled her eyes. "You know, who you've been with. In *that* way."

"He's dealing with a lot at the moment." She glanced down at the twig she held. Rafe had taken his talisman. Did the Woodland Alpha Prime even know the blow he'd dealt his enemy? She lifted her gaze to the trees.

Matthias was out there, alone. He was at his most vulnerable. Unable to shift. Rafe could rip him to shreds within seconds. She frowned. What the hell was Matthias thinking? Just the thought of not seeing him anymore, of not having him around to tempt her, tease her, frustrate her, challenge her, inspire her... In the brief time she'd known him, she'd already grown accustomed to his presence, his touch. Without him, there was just a cold, lonely darkness, worse than anything she'd ever experienced in the quiet shunning of her pack. For the first time in her life, she understood the nature of a pining mate, of walking the earth without that special one to fall into step with, whose stride matched yours, whose shoulders shared your burdens. The yawning emptiness that would be her life without him made her heart crave him.

"We're all dealing with a lot. But he's imprinted on you. Any male who does that cherishes his she-wolf, and protects her from harm—even from him."

Dalton's words broke her out of her reverie. She blinked. "What?"

"It shouldn't matter how much he has to deal with, he imprinted on you. You're practically his mate. He should be treating you better."

She nodded. Dalton was right. They were practically mates; she didn't want to go through life without him, and for whatever reason, he was off fighting a battle he couldn't win on his own. She had to accept it. She loved the Alpine Guardian Prime. She actually wanted to be his mate—despite what he'd said. Her eyes narrowed. Well, she couldn't just sit here and play with sticks while he faced down her own alpha prime. Mates stuck together, through trials and triumphs. She was going to drill that into his thick skull when she caught up with him.

"You're so right, and I think it's time I tell him so," she said to her friend, and rose to her feet. Dalton frowned, then stood, wincing as he put weight on his knee.

"No." He shook his head emphatically.

"Yes," Trinity said succinctly. "He needs me." Whether he was willing to admit it or not.

"It's ludicrous, Trin. Whatever you're thinking, stop it."

"What's the matter?" Softly spoken, there was no mistaking the curiosity and sternness in the deep baritone. Trinity turned. She hadn't heard Zane's approach. She put her hands on her hips. "I'm going after Matthias."

Zane frowned, and glanced at Dalton. "She can't."

"I know she can't, but try telling her that."

"*She* can hear you quite clearly." Trinity turned toward Jax. She would have to say goodbye to the boy. He'd worry, he'd get anxious, there would be tears from both of them. Under normal circumstances she wouldn't even consider leaving him so soon after he'd lost his mother, but this was something she had to do. Zane dodged so that he again stood in front of her. "Matthias wants to do this on his own."

"Yes, well, Matthias isn't my guardian prime," she pointed out sweetly. "As such, I don't have to take orders from him."

Zane tilted his head. "Did you ever wonder how a non-genuine became our guardian prime?" he asked quietly. She paused, listening. "It's because he's the best. He fought hardest, out of the lot of us. I've seen him fight, and I've seen him battle against all odds.

Hell, none of us have ever beaten him, individually or in a group. He's smart, he's strong—he's the best damn lycan I've ever seen. If he has a plan involving just him and Rafe, believe me, he knows what he's doing."

She'd promised Matthias that she'd never reveal his secret, and that promise now chafed. "What if something happens to him?" She tried a different tack. "We wouldn't even know. He's going to be outnumbered, Zane, and we all know Rafe doesn't fight fair."

For a moment, Zane wavered, then he shook his head. "Nice try. My money's on Matthias."

Every second she wasted arguing was another step closer to danger for Matthias. She couldn't leave him to face this on his own. "Fine. You stay here and baby-sit. I'm going."

Zane sighed and glanced at Dalton, who shrugged. "And do what, Trinity? You're a tracker, not a guardian. Rafe believes you've betrayed him. You're as good as dead as soon as he sees you, and if you're not, it's because Matthias has had to stop whatever he's doing to save your butt. Stay out of his way."

She put her hands on her hips, and eyed each of them in turn. "You can't tell me that if that was your mate out there you wouldn't be doing the same thing. I'm going."

Dalton's eyebrows rose. "Wow. That's the first time you've called him your mate."

"Close enough." They may not have completed the mating bond, but she knew now. She didn't want to lose him, and she'd do everything she could to save him. She just hoped she wasn't too late.

Matthias crouched behind the tree, watching the activity near the yawning mouth of a cave. Woodland Pack members strolled about, talking quietly if at all. There was a pall over the large group. He didn't know if they were aware of the cave-in, but from what he could see, they weren't happy.

A smaller group of guardians were training off to the side, their grunts and yells audible as they sparred with each other. The juveniles sat in a sizable group, whispering among themselves. He eyed the rest of the terrain. Rafe had set more guardians in two perimeters, and he couldn't see how many were inside the cave and beyond, nor could he see the alpha prime.

The guardians were placed too far apart, he realized. Some were in blind spots to the others, and he mentally marked their positions. There were a lot of Woodland here. He needed to trim the numbers.

It was as he gently lowered the fourth guardian he'd knocked unconscious that he heard the whisper-soft crunch of pine needles behind him. He whipped around, but wasn't fast enough to dodge the branch swinging toward his head. He heard the crack, felt the pain and then his beast howled inside his mind, the last sound he registered as he slid into the darkness.

Chapter 21

Trinity trudged through the woods, her arms swinging as she walked the trail they'd left from that morning. She was following Matthias's scent, not resisting the pull of the pine, moss and sexy male. She hadn't been walking long, not even an hour, when she heard the crack of a twig to her right. She whirled, arms up in a defensive pose, her stance balanced.

Nate raised an eyebrow, and the two men he was with halted. Her shoulders sagged when she recognized Matthias's sergeant.

"You startled me," she muttered.

He nodded. "So I see." He gazed beyond her, then frowned. "You're out here alone?"

"You haven't been back to camp, yet?"

He shook his head, and her gaze turned to his companions. One seemed familiar, and she narrowed her eyes as she stared at him. Tall and broad-shouldered, his dark hair and silver-blue eyes teased at her memory, and her eyes widened when recognition finally hit.

"You're the dentist," she breathed. He was big, nearly as big as Matthias, with the proud lift of his chin she automatically associated with a warrior.

Ryder Galen tilted his head as he slowly stepped forward. He wagged a finger at her. "I know you," he said softly in his deep voice, eyes narrowed. "You're Woodland."

She swallowed. Her pack had done a terrible thing to him, and he had the ability to somehow render them all unconscious—she still couldn't remember how that had actually happened. She eyed him warily, and he held up a hand.

"Relax. I remember you—you tried to stop your alpha prime."

She was surprised he remembered that. She'd tried to put a stop to the farce of a pack trial that Rafe had conducted, and then the dentist had spotted the lycan who had delivered the tainted supplies to his surgery that had killed Jared Gray, and all hell had broken loose.

She nodded cautiously, and Ryder smiled grimly. "I have no quarrel with you."

She looked toward the other man, and didn't know whether to run or cry, hide or fight. Nate was a lycan, and Ryder Galen was obviously more than just a dentist, and they each gave an impression of strength, of danger. This other guy, well, he had an air of imposing menace that eclipsed even Rafe's. Taller than the other two, his shoulders were massive, his legs long and thickly toned with muscle beneath the leather pants he wore. Boots, black T-shirt and a black leather jacket added to the overall lethal vibe. She had no idea what color his eyes were, hidden as they were behind very dark sunglasses.

Realization dawned. "You're the witch," she said. She swallowed. "I need you."

His light brown eyebrow rose above the dark frame of his sunglasses. "Darlin', I hear that a lot." His lips lifted in a cocky half smile.

"Uh, I mean, you're the witch who helped Matthias, aren't you?"

This time his eyebrows lowered in a deep V on his forehead. "Who are you?"

She swallowed, trying to get rid of the lump in her throat as she took a step forward, hand outstretched. "I'm—I'm his mate."

The witch stared down at her hand for a moment before he finally reached to envelop her hand in his. He tilted his head, and despite the sunglasses she could feel his intent gaze upon her. He shook her hand, just once, then nodded. "I'm that witch." He waggled his eyebrows. "But you can call me Dave."

She sighed with relief. "Uh, Matthias is in trouble."

"What kind of trouble?" Nate asked abruptly, stepping forward.

"He's gone after Rafe. Alone."

Nate frowned. "Why?"

"I don't fully understand, myself," she admitted. "We were tracking Rafe, and he and some of the Woodland guardians ambushed us. There was a skirmish, and then Rafe retreated." She glanced at the witch. "He took Matthias's ring."

Nate swore, and her eyes widened in surprise at his reaction. He put his hands on his hips, his lips tight with frustration. "Hell. We have to go after him."

"That's what I've been trying to tell Zane, but he's determined to follow his guardian prime's orders."

"That's because he doesn't know," Nate stated.

Her eyes narrowed. "But you do…" she said slowly.

The Alpine guardian nodded. "Yeah. Jared mentioned it once."

She frowned. "You never told Matthias?"

Nate shrugged. "It didn't concern me. He's my guardian prime, and he's the best lycan for the job. That was all that mattered."

"He's ashamed of it," she told him, her frown deepening. "He sees this as a curse, as a stigma—he will put himself into harm's way to protect that secret from his pack."

Hell. If he'd known that Nate knew, would he have gone after Rafe by himself, or would he have trusted his second-in-command? Looking at Nate, they both realized the answer at the same time.

"Can you track him?" Nate asked.

"Of course." Even now, his scent pervaded her senses, but she could easily give herself over to it. She'd track that stubborn mate of hers until the end of time, if necessary.

"Let's go, then."

"Wait. Does someone want to tell me what's going on?" Ryder Galen inquired.

Trinity frowned. This would just waste more time. "I don't mean to be rude, but why are you here?"

Ryder put his hands on his hips. "I once told Matthias I wanted to help him take down Rafe Woodland. I was in Nightwing with my fiancée when Lucien Marchetta told us there was an Alpine presence in Woodland, so I thought I'd come and offer assistance."

Her gaze slid to the witch. He smiled and shrugged. "I came for the bonfire and the beer."

"So what's this about Matthias?" Ryder asked again.

She bit her lip. It was generous of the dentist to offer his help, but she had sworn she wouldn't reveal Matthias's secret.

Dave sighed. "Okay, here's the abridged version. Matthias's pack was cursed by a coven of witches, and he's the sole survivor. Side effect of the curse is that he can't shift. I made him a talisman to allow him to shift, and now Rafe Woodland has stolen the talisman." He turned briefly to Trinity. "That about right?"

She nodded, impressed with his efficiency. "Yes."

Dave tilted his head. "So what exactly do you want me to do?"

"Can you break the curse?" she asked, hope flaring within her.

Dave barked with laughter, his shoulders moving, then shook his head. "No. That spell was cast by a large coven, with the ashes of a dead witch. I'm good, baby, but I'm not that good."

She frowned. "Well, can you do something?"

Dave folded his arms, his brows dipping as he gave her query some consideration. "There was so much hate built into that spell, I had to use something that symbolized love to try and counteract it. You'd need something just as powerful to create something that has any chance of offsetting the initial curse."

Nate rolled his eyes in frustration. "Where are we going to find something like that?"

Trinity's eyes widened, and she dug into her jeans pocket, pulling out her mother's ring. "Will this do?" She held it in the palm of her hand, offering it to the witch.

Dave reached out and carefully picked it up, his fingers handling it with more care than she thought the big guy was capable of. He nodded slowly. "It's a start." He grimaced. "But the original talisman was stained with the blood of Matthias's wife, as well as his."

"You can take my blood. Let's go find Matthias," she said, and started down the trail, the three men falling in step behind her.

Matthias awoke to a painful throbbing in his head, and a burning sting around his wrists and ankles.

"Ah, Sleeping Beauty awakens," a deep voice intoned, and Matthias winced as he turned his head toward the sound. It took a couple of blinks for his vision to clear, but eventually he was able to make out the figure of the Woodland Alpha Prime, sitting on a boulder. He tried to sit up and hissed at the bite at his wrists and ankles. He glanced down. A silver cord was wrapped around his wrists, another around his ankles, the burns already deep from the kiss of the corrosive metal against his skin.

He glanced around. He was in the middle of the clearing in front of the mouth of the cave, and Woodland Pack members surrounded him in a neat circle. *Great.* They all looked at him as though he was something that needed putting down. He couldn't begin to imagine the lies Rafe had told them to explain the decrease in returning Woodland guardians.

"I presume you're here to fetch this," Rafe remarked, and Matthias looked up at him. The Woodland Alpha Prime dangled Cara's ring from the chain held between two fingers. "You know, I never saw you as the type to really love his jewelry, but I must say, I'm impressed that you're so determined to reclaim it." The alpha prime's green eyes narrowed. "I do wonder why it is so important to you?"

Matthias lifted his chin. "It's mine, and I keep what is mine."

Rafe arched an eyebrow. "Like our tracker?" He turned to the group at large. "She'll pay for her betrayal, so I wouldn't get too attached, if I were you." He pursed his lips. "Oh, wait, too late, isn't it?"

Matthias looked around the group. The adults wore bitter expressions, although the adolescents and juveniles looked uncomfortable. Trinity's students.

"She's weak," Rafe stated brusquely. "We can't have weakness in our pack. She's betrayed us, and we're better off without her."

A deep, dark suspicion uncurled within Matthias as he remembered this alpha prime's comments from their fight in the forest. His eyes narrowed. Could it be?

"She has not betrayed you," Matthias stated clearly. "She refused to give up the location of your den, and only led us there when we heard the explosions."

The man he was looking at directly frowned, confusion entering his gaze. Matthias realized they didn't know about the cave-in, about the survivors...their children.

Rafe chuckled. "Lies, but I suppose you'll say anything at the moment to save your skin, and that of your mate."

Matthias sat up, ignoring the painful cut of silver into his skin. "I'm not the liar, here, Rafe. I'm not the one who lied to my pack and assassinated another's alpha prime. I'm not the one who broke parley, and I'm not the one who planted explosives in your den and left your elders and pups to die."

He could see the consternation, the shock, enter the

faces of the Woodland pack as they looked to their alpha prime. "Where is your guardian prime? Where are the guardians your alpha prime left with today?" He challenged the group standing around him.

"They're dead," Rafe said bluntly. "At least, they're dead to me."

"No. They're back at your home den, looking after those who didn't die in the cave-in Rafe created." He wasn't going to use Rafe's title anymore; he no longer deserved it. He glared up at the lycan. "Your pack are deserting you."

Rafe smiled, but it was brittle. "And yet you come here alone. Are you sure it's not your pack deserting you?" He angled his head. "Or have you deserted them?"

Matthias jerked against the silver cord, and hissed. This lycan angered him as no other did.

"I know that you are prepared to risk everything, and everyone, to save yourself," Matthias growled. "But I don't want any more lycans hurt in this."

"Oh, that's so sweet," Rafe said. "But how do you propose we end this? Your pack is coming after mine— in our own territory, I might add. Of course we will defend ourselves." He glanced around the enclosed group, and several Woodland members nodded.

"I challenge you, Rafe Woodland," Matthias said loudly, ensuring his voice carried.

Rafe's eyes narrowed. "I beg your pardon?"

"I challenge you to a fight. You and me. Nobody else." A challenge was serious in a pack, and an alpha prime didn't have the luxury of being able to decline a challenge. One thing he'd learned, though, in this campaign against Rafe, was his ego trumped everything.

Rafe tilted his head. "You dare challenge me? You're not even a Woodland."

"Well, then, you've got nothing left to lose, have you?" Matthias asked silkily.

Rafe stared at him for a moment, then glanced from beneath lowered eyelids at the gathered Woodland crowd. He finally looked down at the chain in his hand, then nodded. "I accept."

Chapter 22

"Quick, we have to hurry," Trinity urged as she rose to her feet.

Nate and Ryder both dragged her back down. "Are you crazy?" Nate hissed.

"You heard them," she whispered, gesturing toward the clearing. They'd been scouting the new den and had heard Matthias's challenge from the copse of trees that concealed them.

"We have to stop this," she whispered back fiercely.

"Let Dave do his thing," Ryder instructed. She turned back to the witch, who was crouching, drawing a circle in the dirt with a twig.

Trinity frowned. "Are you sure this transfer thing will work?"

Dave didn't look up. "Of course."

He'd explained that he could perform a transfer spell, shifting the power of Matthias's wife's ring to the one worn by Trinity's mother. A thought occurred to her, and she crawled over to him, her hand on his leather sleeve halting him.

"Can you—can you transfer the subject, as well?" she asked.

Dave faced her fully. "What do you mean?"

"Well, if you can transfer the power from Cara's ring to my mother's, can you also transfer it to another lycan?"

Nate frowned. "Like who?"

Trinity swallowed, not taking her eyes off the witch. "Like…me?"

Dave stilled. "You don't know what you ask, Tracker."

She grimaced. "I do. I understand that I will need that ring for the rest of my life in order to shift, and if I lose it, I'll be trapped in whatever form I'm in. I understand my beast won't like that and try to claw its way out, and I'd eventually die." She firmed her lips. "So I'll just make sure I'll never lose the ring."

Dave nodded. "Okay, so you do know, but do you *know*?" he said. "You're leashing your beast. Do you think you can live with that?"

Trinity glanced over her shoulder, peering through the trees. Matthias had lived with it, for years. She knew it couldn't have been easy, but he'd done so with dignity. And she'd learned she was prepared to do anything to keep the man she loved alive. She turned back to the witch, her face composed. "For him, I would do it."

"Trinity, you can't. Think of what your pack will do if they find out," Nate protested. "And Matthias will kill me for letting you do it."

"You're exaggerating, Nate. Matthias isn't going to kill you," she argued, then smiled sadly. "But you said it yourself. My pack already consider me a traitor. They won't take me back, especially if I'm helping with this. I've already lost them." Her lips tightened. She wasn't going to cry. It hurt, but losing Matthias would hurt more.

"You would sacrifice your beast for Matthias?" Dave asked softly. "Are you sure?"

She nodded. "Do it."

Fist hit flesh, and Matthias spun with the force of Rafe's punch. He staggered for a moment, then gritted his teeth, turning to face the Woodland lycan, his arms raised to block the next punch, and the next. The Woodland pack gathered close, shouting encouragement to their alpha prime.

Matthias pivoted on his feet, using the movement to add to the force of his own strike. Rafe's head whipped around, drops of blood flying from the cut in his lip. The Woodland lycan lowered his head, snarling as he charged, his fangs exposed. He caught Matthias, carrying him backward until Matthias tripped. He wheezed as the Woodland lycan's shoulder pounded into his stomach as they both fell to the ground.

They wrestled, and Matthias grunted at the jabs Rafe aimed at his side, the bites into his shoulder. Matthias arched his back to avoid a blow to his kidneys, then heaved against the lycan. Rafe fell back, and Matthias braced his hands against the dirt, then arched his back again, flipping up onto his feet.

Rafe was rising to his feet, and Matthias took the opportunity to lash out with this feet. Rafe fell to the ground again and Matthias pounced, his hand digging into the lycan's jeans pocket to retrieve his chain.

Rafe's eyes glowed with a realization, and he bared his teeth, his fangs dripping bloody saliva, the growl that emerged from his throat low and deep. He gripped Matthias's hand and twisted. Matthias quickly turned, gaining release from Rafe's grip.

Rafe wiped at the trail of blood dripping down his chin and glanced briefly at his fingers. He smiled, then slid his hand inside his pocket. Matthias's eyes narrowed as he watched the lycan pull the chain out.

"You are jonesing for this pretty bad," Rafe rasped. He held it up, dangling it before him. "Why? What is so damn important about this piece of metal?"

Matthias spat the blood out of his mouth. "It's got sentimental value," he said roughly.

Rafe laughed, then shook his head. "No, I think there's more to it than that, Guardian." He shrugged. "I'm sure I'll learn its secret." He tossed it to the side of the ring, and Matthias's gaze followed it, cold fear slicing through him. One of the Woodland guardians caught it, but that was as much as he saw before Rafe tackled him to the ground. He rolled, trying to keep the chain in his sight, but Rafe struck him across the face.

The uncertainty, the very real fear of losing his talisman completely, the anger of having to fight for it, spurred him on, giving him a zeal, a focus that eliminated everything but conquering this lycan.

He let fly with a series of punches, jabs and kicks, rolling, twigs and stones scratching his bare back. He rolled to his feet, then faced Rafe, who had done the same. He didn't give the lycan a chance to catch his breath. He raced at Rafe, pummeling him, putting every ounce of hate into his strikes. The Woodland lycan swung, ducked and dipped, but couldn't avoid Matthias's fury. Matthias swung his leg around in a roundhouse kick, and Rafe fell back against his guardians, who caught him.

He decided to see if his suspicions were correct. "Oh, did that hurt, Rafe?"

He bounced a little on his toes, his fists raised to block any attack. "You're not as strong as you think you are. I guess your old alpha prime was right."

Rafe wiped the blood from his chin. "What?" His voice was deep, laced with hatred.

"You know, when you went up to talk to Trinity's father at the cabin."

Anger flashed in Rafe's eyes as he straightened. "You don't know anything."

The rage in the other man's eyes was enough encouragement for Matthias. It was a long shot, and he had nothing to prove it, but Rafe was obsessed with being seen as the strongest. With an alpha prime prone to bouts of depression and pining, would he consider that a weakness that had to be culled from the pack? Trinity had said Rafe had been the one to find him, the one to decree the alpha prime's death a suicide. What if it wasn't? Matthias was not Woodland—he didn't have to believe this alpha prime, and he questioned every fact that came from this particular source.

"Sure I do. He was your alpha prime, but he was depressed. He pined after his mate. You didn't think he was strong enough to lead your pack."

Rafe's eyes narrowed. "He wasn't."

"He didn't jump off the cliff, did he?"

Matthias could hear the whispers, the rumblings from the crowd surrounding them.

Rafe bared his teeth. "He fell."

"Fell? Not jumped? Or…pushed?"

Rafe glanced around the crowd. His pack's expressions were a combination of shock, horror, fear and dismay.

"He fought *me*," he roared. "I challenged him. You all saw it, yet none of you were prepared to do anything about it. He was a shell of a man, and he didn't deserve to be Woodland's alpha prime. He fought me, and he lost." He raised his thumb to his chest, his chin jutting forward with pride. "I won. I showed him. I showed him that I was strong enough to be Woodland Pack's alpha prime—not him."

Matthias noticed he couldn't even say the man's name. He also noticed the shock in the surrounding pack.

Rafe glanced around, seeing the censure, the dismay. He clenched his fists, the tendons in his arms, shoulders and neck standing out as he roared deep from his chest. He tore the Woodland crest from his finger and tossed it to the same guardian. Matthias backed up as the Woodland lycan shifted, his bones snapping, claws extending, his eyes full of anger and hate, his clothes and shoes tearing as the larger frame of the lycan emerged.

The black wolf lowered his head, fangs bared, chest heaving. Matthias clenched his fists. Okay. This wasn't so good.

The wolf tilted his head, and Matthias glimpsed brief confusion in the lycan's eyes when Matthias remained in his human form, then realization bloomed, and the wolf's lips pulled back in what looked like a smile.

Matthias's blood chilled as he brought his arms up, fists clenched, ready to strike at the wolf. He knew. Rafe knew he couldn't shift.

"Oh, God, please hurry," Trinity whispered, glancing from the fight in the clearing to the witch kneeling inside the ring. Dave rose to his feet and beckoned her into the circle.

"I need one more ingredient," he said quietly, calmly. He reached for her hand and held it, palm up.

The knife appeared so quickly, she barely registered his movement, then she hissed softly as the blade was drawn across her palm. Dave turned her hand over, letting drops of blood drip onto the ring that lay on the ground on a black bandanna Dave had pulled from his back pocket. He lifted his chin to the men who watched the ritual with curiosity. "It's time."

"This isn't going to hurt, is it?" Nate asked, stepping slowly toward the drawn circle, his expression suspicious.

Dave arched an eyebrow. "This woman is preparing to leash her beast and sacrifice her blood, and it's the guardian who's concerned about getting hurt…?"

Nate shot him a dark look. "Remind me why I'm letting you do this."

"Because Matthias needs our help," Ryder said simply, "and we're getting justice for Jared Gray's death."

"Fine. But this better not shrivel me up or stop me from shifting or turn me into a frog, all right?"

"Stop you're bitching and get in here. I'm not putting a hex on you—I'm channeling your energy," Dave muttered. "Now, hold hands."

Nate stood to her right, Ryder to her left, and Dave faced her. Once they'd linked their hands, Dave took a deep, calming breath. "Okay, so the curse was cast by a coven—it's too strong for just me to break, but we can shift it to this object."

Trinity frowned. "How are we going to get Matthias's blood onto it?"

Dave leaned to the side to look beyond her to the fight in the clearing. "Somehow, I don't think that's going to be a problem," he said, then straightened. Trinity flinched when she heard the snarl of the wolf, and Matthias's bellow of pain.

"Hurry," she urged, the burn of unshed tears itching at her eyelids.

"Close your eyes," Dave said, "just relax, and close your eyes."

Trinity closed her eyes. Her fear and worry were slowly replaced by a dangerous calm as she listened to Dave's whispered chanting. He spoke in a strange language, and no matter how hard she tried to concentrate, she couldn't quite catch the full sound of the words, let alone their meaning. It was almost as though the words themselves were shrouded in mystery.

A wind stirred around them, but she kept her eyes closed, twigs and leaves brushing by her as though caught in a gentle tornado.

Dave's voice grew ever so louder, and then suddenly he stopped. The wind dropped.

"It's done."

She opened her eyes slowly, then gaped. Her mother's ring floated directly in front of her, held up by an invisible force.

Dave nodded. "Take it, and then get it to Matthias. As soon as his blood comes in contact with this ring, it will anchor the transfer."

Trinity grabbed the ring, turned and sprinted toward the man she loved, who was even now fighting for his life against a powerful werewolf.

Chapter 23

Matthias recoiled, clutching at his left biceps. Rafe's claws and teeth had ripped him open, and Matthias bled from a number of wounds.

He swallowed. Rafe was enjoying this, drawing it out, toying with him, inflicting as much pain as possible. It wouldn't be long, though. His vision was graying at the edges, and his stomach roiled.

He raised his arms in a defensive block, his chest heaving, and lowered his chin. He extended one arm, palm raised, then raised his fingers in a beckoning gesture. *Bring it on.* He was going down, but he would be damned if Rafe was going to survive this without significant, permanent injury.

The wolf lowered his head, his legs splaying, getting ready to pounce.

"Matthias!"

He snapped his head around, his eyes wide. *No.* She shouldn't be here.

Trinity raced through the outer rim of trees. The Woodland pack members closest to her growled, turning to face her. She didn't stop.

"Matthias!" She tried to barrel through her pack, but was easily stopped by the guardians. Her eyes wide, her face pale, she glanced over their shoulders. The pained look on her face as she met his eyes was nearly his undoing, as though she shared his agony, his heartache.

"You're not supposed to be here," he cried.

The black wolf turned, then growled. Trinity's gaze focused on her alpha prime, and anger gave color to her cheeks. "You bastard," she yelled. Silence fell over the pack.

"You tried to kill our pups. You're sick, Rafe. Sick."

The guardian who held her back glanced over his shoulder, a frown appearing on his brow.

"It's true," Matthias called, although it came out more as a croak. "Trinity is right. Rafe tried to kill your young. He tried to kill your elders, your alpha prime."

The black wolf snarled as he glanced between Trinity and himself. Matthias pointed at the lycan. "You committed a crime against the werewolf tribe, Rafe Woodland," he bellowed. "You plotted the death of a fellow alpha prime. You tried to kill members of your own pack." He glanced over at his she-wolf, before glaring at the lycan. "And you killed your former alpha prime. Under tribal jurisdiction, I demand justice."

Trinity stopped struggling, as did the guardian, and she looked at him, stunned.

"What did you say?" Trinity's voice was hoarse with shock.

"He just admitted it," Matthias said, his arms dropping to his sides. He didn't have the strength to brace for impact. "He threw your father over the falls."

The lycan bared his teeth, eyes wild. A murmur grew as the pack talked among themselves, and Trinity stepped forward with no opposition from her guardian.

"You killed my father?" she asked in disbelief, approaching the wolf. He growled at her, and she shook her head. "All this time, you let me believe he'd killed himself. You let our pack believe their alpha prime had abandoned them." Her voice rose with each word. "You sick, miserable bastard. I was shunned by my own pack, all because of your power-hungry ego," she cried through gritted teeth. She shook her head. "The elders are right. You are sick, and you do not deserve your position."

The black wolf hunkered low, then launched at Trinity, knocking her off her feet. The crowd gasped, some screamed. Trinity screamed in pain as Rafe's fangs sank into her shoulder.

Matthias roared, bolting across the clearing, rage governing his actions. His beast bellowed, the sound echoing inside his mind, until there was nothing but his lycan and his anger driving him.

He tackled the wolf and bit him in the neck, regardless of the fact that he was man and Rafe was lycan. The wolf yelped, flinching as Matthias used all of his weight to throw him off his beloved she-wolf. Like a man possessed, he attacked the wolf, a red haze descending over him. The wolf howled, thrashing, claws and teeth scraping against his skin, until Matthias fell. The lycan stood over him, nose to nose, their breaths gusting.

Matthias dropped his head back to the ground. He was going to die. He'd failed. He'd done this to protect Trinity. Now, though, he would die, and Rafe would turn on her as he had on Matthias.

Not if he could help it, damn it. He would fight until

his last breath, and he would rip Rafe's throat out with his bare hands, if need be.

But he didn't want the last words he'd said to Trinity to be his last words to the woman he loved. He rolled his head to the side. Trinity lay a short distance from him, tears streaking her face, her left shoulder torn and bloody.

"I'm sorry," he gasped, ignoring briefly the lycan intent on ending his life. Sorry for the pain he'd caused her in their last exchange. Sorry for hurting her in a way no lycan should harm his mate. "I release you."

Trinity's brow furrowed, then comprehension dawned, and fresh tears rolled down her cheeks. "Not yet." She reached out to him with her right arm, crying out with pain at the resulting movement in her injured shoulder, and her fingers unclenched. A glint of gold caught his eye, and he looked at her hand in confusion. Resting on her palm was a bloodstained ring. Her mother's. She swallowed. "Catch."

The movement was weak, subtle, but he watched as though caught in a time warp, the ring turning over and over as it sailed through the air, and he caught it in his bloodied fist.

Power coursed through him, and his beast lifted his head and roared inside him.

Trinity's head lolled back as Matthias's eyes glowed briefly, then the fist he'd used to catch the ring flashed through the air, smashing into the black wolf's snout.

The lycan yelped, thrown backward from the brutal force. Matthias rolled, his face tight with fury, and he pounded into the wolf.

"You want to know my secret?" he roared, and Trinity tried to roll to her side. Matthias fumbled as he tried to slide the ring onto his pinkie, his fingers slick with blood, with sweat. The black wolf snapped, his jaws closing around Matthias's hand.

Matthias roared, and Trinity saw the rage bloom in his eyes. He pried the wolf's mouth open, ignoring the nips the wolf tried to take. "You want it that bad," he yelled, and clasped his hands around the lycan's snout, and Trinity wanted to scream in frustration when she saw his bare finger. Rafe had bitten off the ring.

"You can have it," Matthias gritted. He forced the lycan's head back, then jabbed the wolf in the neck. The lycan coughed, his body writhing as he made choking sounds, then he swallowed. He bucked. He writhed. Matthias flung him away from him, then scooted back toward Trinity. She heard a commotion behind her, but she couldn't take her eyes off her alpha prime.

The black wolf staggered, harsh coughs heaving his back. He shuddered, his fur rippling as though something was moving beneath the skin. The wolf's eyes widened, startled. He stood up briefly on his hind legs, his forelegs pawing the air. The muscles on his stomach rippled and writhed, then he fell to all fours again, fear creeping into his gaze as he turned to look at Matthias and Trinity. The wolf coughed, then lifted his head to the skies and howled.

The sound was so agonized, so heart-wrenching, so mournful, it gave Trinity goose bumps. Rafe turned to Matthias, his head low, his tail between his legs. He surveyed the crowd surrounding them, staggering in one direction, then turning to pad in another, as though seeking help. The guardians stared at him, then as one, folded their arms. He would get no help from them. The wolf paused, looking at Matthias and Trinity over his shoulder, his eyes stark with a horrific understanding, then he turned and sprinted off into the forest.

Trinity sagged, and Matthias reached her just before she lay back on the ground again. "I've got you," he said, his tone ragged yet tender.

"You rat fink," she rasped, lifting her gaze to meet his.

"Love you, too, honeybun."

Emotions battled within her, relief, love, anger, sadness—she wasn't quite sure which direction she should be pulled, but one thing had become crystal clear in her mind. He'd known he couldn't face Rafe as an equal, had even banked on it, all to release her from his imprint. Dalton had told her that a male will risk his life to protect his mate, and that's what Matthias had been doing, in his own stubborn, wrong and completely flawed, exquisitely beautiful way.

He gazed down at her, holding her gently in his arms. "I couldn't protect you," he said softly. "I thought to release you from your death sentence."

She bit her lip when she heard her own words in his voice, realizing how deeply they must have cut him. She smiled weakly. "I learned that living without you, however you came to me, would be a death sentence." She took a ragged breath. "I accept your claim, Matthias Marshall—and from what I understand, there are no take-backs."

He smiled, dipping his head to press his lips gently against hers. "No, there aren't. You're stuck with me, now."

She sagged against him, then glanced beyond him. Her pack were gathered. The younger members, the juveniles and adolescents, were stunned, perhaps even a little fearful and uncertain. The older members were milling about a group that had just emerged from the forest. Nate, Ryder and Dave were at the forefront, but it was the group behind them that caught her eye. Zane, Dion and Dalton led them. Kai trooped behind, and Roscoe helped Gilbert up the slight incline, followed by Agatha and the rest of the elders as Warwick herded the pups.

Zane surveyed the scene, eyeing the Woodland pack warily. Both Woodland and Alpine faced each other, the tension so thick it was suffocating. Matthias staggered to his feet and reached down to gently lift Trinity to hers. She leaned against him, grateful for his power, his strength. His hand on the small of her back, they faced the large group.

Matthias's green gaze met Trinity's, confusion tinged with gratitude, before he looked over at Dave. He held up his hand, claws poking through his skin. "What happened? I can feel it—my beast and I are completely in synch. I can shift—I can control it."

Trinity frowned. She didn't feel any different, either. She glanced down at her good hand, and tried a subtle shift. Her claws poked through her skin. She gaped. She could still shift, too.

"Your darling wolf asked me to create a transfer spell, and we shifted the curse from your wife's ring to her mother's. She also asked to transfer the curse from you to her."

"Trin," Matthias murmured in shock as he looked at her, sadness making his expression bleak. "No, what were you thinking?"

She shook her head and held up her hand, revealing her claws in an effort to reassure him. "I'm fine—and I was trying to help you." She turned to Dave, puzzled. He'd been so confident. "Your spell didn't work."

His eyebrow rose above his sunglasses. "Oh, but it did, darlin'. I just made a few minor adjustments. Oh, and I didn't transfer it to you." He tilted his head in the direction the black wolf had taken. "As soon as Matthias's blood bound the spell, the curse shifted to that lycan, and the talisman he now carries within him will prevent him from shifting. Ever."

"We should go after him," Zane said.

Matthias shook his head. "No." He straightened his shoulders, wincing at the pain from all of his wounds. "Rafe Woodland is bound in his wolf form forever. I can tell you from experience, that is hell on earth. He's now a stray." He eyed the group. "He's forfeited his pack, his family, and can no longer plot, or lead. If he isn't driven mad by the loneliness, he won't survive for long on his own. I think that is punishment enough."

Trinity blinked. That was generous. She leaned her head against his chest. She still wanted to kill the bastard for everything he'd done, new rage born from learning of her father's murder, but if Matthias could show mercy, maybe she could, too.

Matthias looked down at her. "Alpine has its justice. Rafe will continue to pay for Jared's death, until he dies. We Alpine guardians can go home."

Her mouth opened, and she surveyed the group she'd called family. She was committed to the Alpine guardian prime, now. Her home was with Matthias. It was bittersweet, knowing that she would be leaving Woodland, the only home she'd ever known.

Gilbert hobbled forward. "You can't," the elder said. The old man looked at Dion, who nodded and then crossed to the guardian who had caught the jewelry Rafe had tossed to him.

Dion then approached Matthias, and Trinity watched him with curiosity. Understanding dawned when Dion held out the broken chain and ring in the palm of his hand, and she smiled at the Woodland Guardian Prime, touched by his respect by returning Matthias's ring. Matthias stared at it for a moment, then tilted his head. "Keep it," he told the guardian. "I don't need it anymore."

Happiness warmed Trinity, almost overwhelming the painful throb in her shoulder. Dion's eyebrows rose in surprise, then he shrugged, pocketing the ring and chain. The guardian prime glanced over his shoulder, his intent gaze meeting each of his pack members, before he turned to Gilbert.

"Elder Prime, would you do the honor?" Dion asked in a formal tone.

Gilbert nodded, stepping forward, his gaze alternating between Trinity and Matthias. Trinity straightened. She'd always respected Gilbert; he'd been a good adviser to her father. She chewed her lip. He was looking at her so seriously. Matthias's hand stroked her back, and she took comfort in his touch. She wasn't quite sure what was going to happen. Perhaps they were to address the matter of her "betrayal."

"Alpine Guardian Prime," Gilbert said in a clear voice that resonated throughout the clearing. "Woodland Pack apologizes for its part in your alpha prime's death. We seek to offer recompense, and will send a representative to negotiate with Samantha, Alpine Alpha Prime."

Matthias inclined his head. "Alpine accepts."

Trinity closed her eyes briefly in relief. It was over. Alpine would move forward, and Woodland would, as well. Her pack would pay for the sins of its alpha prime, but it could now walk in honor. No more lycans needed to die over this. Justice was done.

Gilbert then lifted his chin. "There is a small matter of a challenge," he stated. "A challenge to Woodland Alpha Prime was made and accepted. You have defeated the alpha prime. Tribal law will be accepted and enforced." He offered Matthias the ring bearing the Woodland crest in the customary ritual, one hand cupping the other, the ring resting on his uplifted palm, his head bowed. "Will you accept the position of Woodland Alpha Prime?"

Trinity's eyes widened, and she flicked her glance up at her lycan. Matthias's expression was stunned.

"What?"

Dion's lips curved in a smile at his reaction. "You conquered our alpha prime." He gestured to the group surrounding them. "You've freed us. You've shown us your strength—and that was only the half of you. In all of this, despite what was done to your pack, you treated us with honor and dignity, and we respect that. You deserve this, and we honor you." Simply spoken, the words carried the dignity and esteem of a pack. The guardian prime shifted so that he stood shoulder to shoulder with Woodland's elder prime. "Will you accept the position of Woodland Alpha Prime?"

Trinity met Matthias's gaze, and his eyebrows rose, as though asking her a question. She gave a tiny shrug. It was his decision. Matthias swallowed, his gaze wandering over the crowd gathered before them.

Dalton was the first to move, lowering himself to one knee, head bowed in submission. The guardian next to him did the same, and one by one, throughout the crowd, each followed suit. The elders, the guardians, the entire pack—they all knelt on one knee, head bowed, in acceptance of a new alpha prime.

Matthias's throat worked, and his hand slid up to

gently rest on Trinity's shoulder. He nodded, reaching out. "I accept," he stated in a firm voice.

Gilbert slid the ring on his finger, and then he and the guardian prime knelt briefly on one knee, head bowed, then rose and leaned over to kiss the ring.

Dion then turned, claimed Trinity's hand, bent over and kissed the back of her hand. She swallowed. It was a mark of respect, of acceptance, of loyalty. Gilbert stepped forward to do the same, and she sucked in a breath. It was the formal acceptance of a consort prime from the pack's guardian and elder primes.

Her pack accepted her.

Chapter 24

Matthias stared at the group gathered around the fire. Light flickered over the makeshift camp village they'd set up at the cave entrance that led to the original den, dancing with the shadows. The mood was slightly somber, once the rest of the pack saw the destruction of their home den. None of them had been aware of the cave-in, nor the lost lives, so there was a sense of sadness and shock about the camp. The Alpine guardians remained, deciding to return to the Alpine den the following morning.

The pups were sleeping in the tents, and he had to fight the urge to go check on Jax. He wanted to hold the boy, reassure himself that he was safe. He ducked his head. *Let the boy sleep.* Tomorrow would be a brand-new day, and he had a list building of all the things he wanted to take care of—like hugging Jax, showing his she-wolf she meant the world to him, starting the official cleanup process for the den and getting to know his pack.

He sighed. He couldn't believe what had transpired. Never in those haunted midnight dreams did he ever believe he would be chosen to lead a pack. He hadn't thought he could, with his limitations, but the battle with Rafe had taught him something. Love could give you strength. When Trinity had been injured, it was as though a match had been dropped in a pool of lighter fluid. The sparks, the heat, the all-consuming desire for destruction, for vengeance and retribution, had given him a strength, a toughness that would have annihilated his enemy, despite the odds.

If he couldn't shift, he would have still accepted their offer, because at that moment, after that battle—with the risks far more than just to himself—he'd proved his strength to himself. Now, he finally felt like his insides matched his skin. He was strong. He was powerful, and he was in complete harmony with his beast, and he reveled in it.

He turned to the she-wolf at his side. And it was all because of Trinity. He gently pulled her to him, careful of her injuries. He was already healing, as was she, but she'd been ripped pretty bad. He would cosset her and cherish her for as long as she would let him.

"I can't believe you were willing to sacrifice your ability to shift for me," he told her quietly in her ear, then nipped gently at her lobe. He smiled when she trembled.

"And I can't believe you were prepared to die to get me out of this imprint thing," she shot back, and despite her cheeky smile, he could see the shadows deep in her eyes.

"I didn't want to trap you into something you clearly didn't want, especially if I couldn't keep you safe."

She threaded her fingers through his and leaned her head against his shoulder. "Like I said, I'll take you any way I can."

He closed his eyes, so humbled by her big heart. He leaned down to nuzzle the back of her neck. "Speaking of taking me…"

She laughed softly. "I have a feeling your pack want your attention just a little longer on your first night as alpha prime."

He shook his head. Alpha prime. He was still trying to get used to that. "Doesn't an alpha prime get certain…privileges?" He bit gently, and was rewarded with her muffled groan and the tremble that shook her body against his.

Her grip tightened on his hand. "Let's go."

They rose, nodding to the elders and some of the guardians. Nate and Zane gave a casual wave of their hands, deep in conversation with Dion and Dalton. Ryder stepped forward, and Matthias pulled up. Dave reclined against a log, a beer in one hand, a pretty Woodland werewolf in the other, his sunglasses shielding his eyes. As eager as Matthias was to have some alone time with his she-wolf, he owed these men a debt of gratitude.

"Trinity told me what you did for me," he said to them. "I appreciate that." When he'd first heard of Jared's death, he'd wanted to rip this man to shreds. Discovering the truth, though, had made him rethink his position. Ryder Galen was a stand-up guy. He tilted his head to the side.

"I wish you well," Ryder said, accepting the hand Matthias extended, shaking it briefly. "I've made a list of some of the medical supplies you still need, and I'll organize for them to be sent through."

Matthias's eyes narrowed. "I forgot you were running your family's medical clinic now." Ryder was a dentist, but his father, Arthur Armstrong, and brother, Hunter, provided medical treatment to all forms of the shadow breeds in Irondell. With Arthur sitting in a Reform jail cell awaiting trial for his part in the conspiracy to murder Jared Gray, and his brother missing, Ryder had stepped in, sourcing staff in order to keep the clinic open to serve the shadow breed population. "Thanks for that. How's it going?"

Ryder grimaced. "It keeps me busy."

"Have you heard from your brother?" He valued family, valued pack. If you were lucky enough to have family, you kept in touch.

"No," Ryder muttered, and shot a dark look at Dave, who held his hands up in a defensive gesture.

"It's not my fault," he said, then took a swig of his beer. "Blame your brother."

Matthias's eyebrows rose. "You know where he is?"

"I know who he's with," Ryder said slowly in qualification.

"Ah, like that, is it?" He glanced down at Trinity. Disappearing with a woman for a few months held a definite appeal.

Ryder shook his head as Dave choked on his beer. "Not quite."

"Not at all," Dave rasped. "He pissed off the wrong woman, so he's temporarily out of commission."

Matthias tilted his head as he looked down at the witch. "Thank you. Again."

Dave waved a hand. "Don't mention it."

Ryder frowned. "Why do you demand a favor from

me anytime I ask you for help, but Matthias gets your services for free?"

Dave rested his head against the log, and stared at Matthias for a moment. "Because—"

One of the female werewolves cried out, and Matthias turned immediately, hearing the shock, the fear in that sound. There was a general outcry, and Woodland Pack scrambled to their feet. Guardians from both packs shouldered their way through the crowd, and Matthias immediately stepped forward, Trinity right behind him.

The hairs on the back of his neck rose as the strong, metallic scent of blood hit him, along with that faint trace of death.

Woodland Pack members warily stepped out of the way as Lucien Marchetta stalked into the camp, accompanied by four more vampires. Matthias's eyes rounded when he saw the limp body of Lucien's sister in his arms. Vivianne Marchetta was a beautiful woman, but it was hard to see that beauty beneath the blood that now covered her.

"Oh, my God," Trinity gasped, her hand rising to her mouth.

"Luc, what's happened?" Ryder hurried forward. Lucien halted and shook his head when Ryder reached for his sister. "Let me see her, Luc. Let me help."

For a moment Matthias was curious about the friendship that seemed to exist between these two, but then thoughts of friendship fled when he looked into the vampire's eyes.

His pale blue gaze revealed a rage and a bitter desolation that would make a lesser man quail. "You can't help her, Ryder. She's been bitten by a werewolf."

Silence fell over the camp, and Matthias felt the shock hit him like a wave, something that crashed over him and left a slow-building realization of the ramifications in its wake. A werewolf's bite was lethal to a vampire. The victim suffered immense pain, hallucinations and delirium until their death, an event that occurred usually within ten to twelve hours after being bitten.

"How? Who?" He stared down at the woman in the vampire's arms. Her skin was pale, almost alabaster. He could see the perspiration dotting her brow, the slight pull of her eyebrows, as though even unconscious she could still feel the excruciating pain of a werewolf's poison spreading through her system. The vessels in her throat were slowly turning black, radiating out from the bite mark on her shoulder. Another wound was on her thigh, and one on her stomach. The blackening of the blood vessels was a visual symptom that showed the advancement of the toxin. He may not like Vivianne Marchetta overmuch, but he respected the vampire prime. It was a shock to see her so mauled by one of his kind. She was powerful, ruthless, and it was strange to see her in such a weakened state.

Lucien glared at Matthias. "She was getting out of her car when a wolf came out of nowhere and attacked her. She was ambushed." He glanced over to one of the other vampires, who stepped forward, his arms raised to take his sister off his hands. He turned to face Matthias, his fists clenched. "Alpine has reneged on its deal with Nightwing."

Matthias shook his head. "This is not Alpine's doing, Lucien. All my guardians respect and honor that agreement."

Lucien's eyes narrowed to silver slits. "I told my sister it was a mistake to deal with the dogs, but she believed there might be some honor there, somewhere. She was wrong."

"We didn't renege on the deal. We have no quarrel with Nightwing," Matthias said in a low voice. He needed to make the vampire see reason, or else he'd be fighting the clear need for retribution blazing in those cool, pale blue eyes.

Lucien smiled, showing his extended fangs. "I don't care what pack the black wolf belongs to, I'm placing the blame at your feet. The lycans were allowed safe passage through Nightwing. No vampire was to be hurt."

Matthias closed his eyes briefly in realization. Rafe had struck again. He sensed the vampire shifting position, and his eyes snapped open. He could see the battle waging within. This vampire wanted to kill.

"Rafe is the one who harmed your sister." He moved so that his body shielded Trinity from the menace emanating from the vamp. "He is no longer alpha prime of Woodland Pack."

Lucien's eyebrows rose. "Oh, really? And who replaces the mutt?" He glanced around the gathered lycans.

"I do."

"Ah, so not only are you the one who brokered the deal, you now run the pack associated with that renegade wolf."

"He's not associated with any pack," Matthias argued. "He's a stray, loyal and allied to nobody."

"Well, that's unfortunate. I demand justice for my sister's death, and the blood of those responsible is a ripping great start."

Matthias eyed the unconscious woman. She wasn't dead yet, but it wouldn't be long. He folded his arms. "Rafe is no longer in Woodland territory. We can help you track him down—"

Lucien held up his hand. "Please, you and I both know strays don't survive for long, and quite frankly, I don't think I can stomach any help from your kind." He glanced around the group. "No, I believe that in this case, an eye for an eye should do the trick." He tilted his head, eyeing Trinity. "Should I go for the wee little wolf you so obviously wish to protect? She must mean something to you. Not as much as my sister means to me, obviously," Lucien surmised aloud, "but she could be a good start."

Matthias's eyes narrowed, and this time he stepped completely in front of his she-wolf. "You will not harm her."

Lucien pursed his lips. "Hmm, perhaps you're right. I mean, my sister is a vampire prime, after all, and this one," he gestured to Trinity, "well, she's no vampire prime." The vampire nodded. "Yes. Not adequate recompense." He smiled. "Ah, I have it. I'll just kill a prime."

The vampire's eyes flashed red as he launched at Matthias, but before he could react, a tall, familiar figure dived at the vampire. They both fell to the ground.

"Zane," Matthias yelled, but before he could pull his guardian off the vampire, he heard a crack of bone. Zane roared as his arm was twisted behind his back, then groaned as Lucien sank his teeth into his neck. "No!"

He sprang at the couple struggling on the ground, pulling his friend's now limp body away from the vampire. Lucien bared his teeth, ready to attack again, but Ryder blocked him, pushing him back.

"That's enough, Lucien," Ryder yelled, struggling to hold the vampire in check. "Lucien, enough!"

Matthias knelt on the ground, holding his friend in his arms as Zane made a guttural gurgle, his throat torn.

Zane's hand lifted, and Matthias caught it. "I've got you," he whispered, a combination of panic, rage and horror swelling inside as he held his friend. So much blood, the skin torn. He blinked back tears. Zane's life-blood was slowly seeping into the soil.

Trinity raced to his side, her expression horrified as she pulled off her jacket and pressed it to the wound in Zane's neck in an attempt to stem the flow of blood. Matthias choked back the burning emotion that made him want to tear the vampire to shreds. He glanced around. The vampires all glared, fists clenched, teeth bared at the group. They were outnumbered, they were surrounded by lycans whose bite could mean their deaths, but Matthias read their lethal intent. They didn't care. They were hurt, they were enraged and they wanted blood. The Woodland and Alpine guardians shifted forward, their teeth bared as they growled softly. Nate's fists were clenched, his chest rising and falling with his raging emotions. Matthias understood the need to spill blood on behalf of Zane. He felt it, too.

If he attacked, it would be a bloodbath. He couldn't let his emotions risk the lives of the pack who'd chosen him to lead them.

He gazed down at Zane, sadness slowly attacking the anger as the light in his friend's eyes slowly faded. He glanced up at Lucien.

The vampire snarled. "I still believe a debt is owed," he rasped.

"I believe the debt has been more than paid," Matthias gritted. He glanced around. His pack was closing in. He still had to take their measure, still had to build that relationship. If he told them to back off, would they? Or would they ignore his instructions? The number of fatalities would rise, depending on how he handled this.

His gaze landed on a shadowy figure in the back, the flames of the campfire reflecting off sunglass lenses.

"Dave."

The witch pursed his lips, then stepped forward, the crowd parting silently. He halted next to Ryder.

Lucien's eyes narrowed. "You keep questionable company, witch."

Dave smirked. "You haven't met my sister, have you?" He turned his head to face Matthias. "What?"

"Is there anything that can be done?" It galled him to ask on behalf of the vampire, but he needed to prevent a massacre.

Dave lifted his thumb, rubbing it against his lip. He stepped toward the vampire holding Vivianne, and Lucien blocked him. Dave sighed in exasperation. "Your sister isn't dead yet, is she?"

The vampire frowned. "No."

"So there's still a chance you can save her."

Matthias's eyes narrowed, and the lycans turned to each other, frowning.

"There is no cure for a werewolf bite," Lucien pointed out.

Dave held up a finger. "No *known* cure."

"What are you saying?"

"Nature prefers a balance. Life, death, morning, night. Up. Down. Where there is a poison, there must be a cure. You just have to find it."

Lucien pointed to Vivianne. "My sister has only hours to live—where do you presume I'll find this unheard-of cure?"

Dave shrugged. "No idea. But you can delay her death until you do find it."

Matthias gently laid Zane on the ground, then rose to his feet. That sounded…unnatural. "How?"

"A suspension spell will halt the toxin from spreading any further, put her into a deep sleep so she doesn't feel any pain and then we can lift the spell when you find the cure."

Lucien frowned.

"It's like putting her on pause," Dave clarified.

Lucien considered it for a moment, then nodded. "Do it."

Dave leaned forward. "You will owe me a debt."

Ryder's eyes widened, then he leaned forward. "Not a good time, Dave."

Now Matthias understood Ryder's remarks from before.

The witch smiled grimly. "I disagree. He just killed a lycan because he thought Matthias had defaulted on a deal. So he values a promise." Dave folded his arms, the leather of his jacket creaking with the movement. "So do I."

"Why don't I just kill you now?" Lucien queried silkily.

Dave chuckled. "You're welcome to try, but then that won't suspend the toxin in dear sis over there."

"What do you want?" Lucien asked impatiently.

Dave shrugged. "A simple favor."

"What?" The cold tone suggested the vampire was fast losing patience.

"Don't know yet. I'll bank it. But at some time in the future, when I ask a favor of you, you will grant it."

Lucien pursed his lips, and Matthias again sensed the anger radiating from the vampire.

"Come on, tick tock. Your sister's not getting any younger," Dave pointed out.

"Fine. You have a deal. Now do the spell." Lucien

stalked over and gently took hold of his sister's limp form, and held her close to his chest.

Dave placed his palm on Vivianne's forehead and bowed his head, murmuring words in a language Matthias couldn't understand, although he could feel the power in the air, like the electricity in the wind before a storm hit.

After a few minutes, Dave lifted his head.

"Now what?" Lucien asked, frowning.

Dave smiled. "Now we leave."

He started walking off into the darkness. Lucien glared after him for a moment, then turned to Matthias. "All access to Nightwing for any lycan is revoked."

Matthias glared right back. "Consider Woodland a no-go zone for vamps."

He watched as the vampires retreated into the darkness. They made no sound, left no prints. Only Zane's body on the ground and the grim expressions on the lycans showed any evidence of them having been there at all.

Chapter 25

Trinity stood at the mouth of the tunnel, surveying the temporary structural supports. The engineers had cleared the den for activity, and in the ten days since Zane's death, her mate had kept himself and his pack busy.

The rubble had been cleared, extra supports were erected and repairs were being carried out. Matthias had set up a makeshift first aid station with the supplies Ryder had sent through, but was now overseeing the construction of an infirmary within the den. Since Lucien Marchetta's visit, he was determined to care for his pack. As well as the infirmary, he'd ordered Dion to organize appropriate training sessions for all pack, from the elders right down to the pups. Guardians were on a roving security detail, and the border between Woodland and Nightwing was heavily patrolled. It wasn't all doom and gloom, though. Matthias also ensured there was plenty of playtime for the children, and he encouraged the family units to share some quality time.

She sighed. She knew what he was doing. He was making sure his pack was occupied, building for the future and ensuring their defenses were strong in a way Rafe had never done. And by keeping his pack busy, he distracted himself from the death of a good friend.

Jax came barreling up out of the tunnel, squealing with laughter as Matthias caught him and lifted him to perch on his shoulders. Trinity smiled. Jax always managed to bring a smile to Matthias's lips, even in his darkest moments. And her lycan still thought it wasn't cold enough to wear a shirt. She eyed his glorious chest. Not that she was complaining.

"Hey, you two," she said, reaching up to kiss Matthias on the lips. She chuckled when his hand threaded into her hair to hold her still so he could kiss her thoroughly, and she leaned into him.

"Get a room, you two," Dalton called as he walked out of the tunnel, the rest of the pups running and skipping behind him.

She pulled away from him and glanced at her friend. "What are you doing?" Jax held out his arms and leaned forward, and Trinity caught him as he slid from Matthias's shoulders.

"The elders are giving the juveniles a history lesson, the adolescents are helping with the den setup and I am taking the pups out for a run down to the river. We're going to catch some fish stock for winter."

The pups jumped up and down and cheered, and Trinity smiled. She didn't think there would be many fish caught with the racket the kids were making, but they would have some fun, and get some fresh air before the snows came.

"Me, too," Jax cried. "I wanna go, too." He kicked his legs until Trinity gently dropped him to his feet.

"Fine, but do exactly as Dalton tells you, okay?" she said, grinning.

"Catch me something, Jax," Matthias said, ruffling the boy's hair. Jax looked up at Matthias, and the look of hero worship on the little boy's face was unmistakable. She smiled. The last two nights he'd actually slept the night through, without any nightmares. She and Matthias had thoroughly enjoyed catching up on some much-needed sleep.

"Okay, Matt," Jax cried, running off after Dalton, who looked like the Pied Piper marching out of town with the children.

Trinity folded her arms as she watched the boy run off. Matthias slid his arms from behind, and nuzzled her neck.

"What's bothering you?" he asked softly, as though sensing her disquiet. She folded her arms on top of his, relishing their rare moment of solitude.

"We lost so many of our pack," she said, her voice barely above a whisper. "Poor Jax. He's lost his father as well as his mother in such a short time, along with some of his friends."

Matthias rested his chin against the top of her head. "Every time I think of that day, when we were pulling everyone out, it makes me want to fight Rafe all over again."

Trinity took a deep breath. "Jax is going to need a lot of care and attention, a lot of love. When I lost my mother, it was hell, but at least I still had my father—in a way. When Dad—" She hesitated. She still had trouble adjusting from the long-held belief of her father's suicide to the new discovery of his murder. "When Dad died, I felt like that mountain could swallow me whole, and nobody would notice."

She closed her eyes at the memories of lurking in a tunnel to watch her pack eat their evening meal in the great hall, not even noticing she wasn't there with them. Sitting in the dark den, realizing she had run out of batteries for her light, and not having the faintest idea of who to approach for new ones. "I don't want that for Jax. I realize that Rafe is responsible for so much—not just for my father's death, but the way he guided the pack in treating me. He set the standard. I think it's up to us to set a new standard."

Matthias turned her in his arms, his finger lifting her chin so that he could meet her gaze. He smiled gently, his expression tender. "I want us to adopt Jax, too," he told her, his lips curling as she smiled. Warmth flared inside her at his words. This lycan was amazing. He had no idea how much he'd already done to help heal her pack. The care he took to protect, to defend, to ensure the safety—it was already so much more than they'd had in a generation. He brushed his nose against hers. "You're right. I want him to feel love inside his pack. Our pack."

"Oh, thank you, Matthias." She stood on tiptoe to pepper his face with kisses. "Thank you, thank you, thank you. You won't regret it, I promise."

He chuckled, and she realized this was the happiest she'd seen him since Zane's death.

She glanced about the clearing. Dalton and the pups had left them, and the rest of the pack were working in the den. She pulled her shirt out of the waistband of her jeans, and toed off her boots. "Let's go for a run," she suggested. She tugged the shirt over her head.

Matthias's eyebrows rose. "What?" His eyes watched her movements, gleaming golden green in the sunlight.

She grinned up at him, wanting to give him some fun in among the work. "You know what they say about all work and no play."

Matthias arched an eyebrow. She dragged her jeans down over her legs, standing before him in only her bra and panties.

His hands dropped to his belt, and he slowly unbuckled it, toeing off his boots. His eyes meeting hers, he slid down the zipper of his trousers. Her teeth sank into her lip as he slowly peeled back the opening of his pants, the muscles rippling from his shoulders down to the waistline of his trousers and beyond, and the golden V of skin revealed by his opened fly making her fingers itch to touch him. She'd learned that not only did he not wear a shirt, he also liked to go commando. She reached behind her and unhooked her bra, letting it drop to the ground. His eyes flared with heat as he surveyed the swell of her breasts, and she quickly slid her underpants down, stepping out of them. She waggled her eyebrows.

"Catch me if you can," she challenged him, then shifted in midstride as she took off running. She heard him running on two feet, then the pounding paws on the pine needles behind her. She lengthened her stride, enjoying the soft caress of the wind through her fur, her ears back, the crunch of twigs and pine needles beneath her paws, and his scent, curling inside her, teasing her, enthralling her. She could feel him running alongside her, just outside of her peripheral vision. She could feel his breath dancing across the tops of her ears, and she altered direction, grinning as she heard the thud and his frustrated growl as he jumped—and missed. She ran between the trees, letting the exhilaration lend speed to her feet, dodging rays of sunlight, dipping into the shadows of the trees, so that she emerged into a small clearing of twisted oaks.

A heavy body caught her from the side, and she rolled, shifting, laughing as he did the same, until she lay on her back, and he covered her naked body with his, his hands holding hers above her head.

"I've got you," she told him, chuckling.

He cut her laughter off with a hot kiss. Her mouth opened beneath his, and she sighed as his tongue slid in to duel with hers. His fingers entwined with hers. He ravished her mouth, angling his head for better access. She loved the weight of him pressing against her, dominating her. His strength was something her own beast relished.

She sighed, arching her back, their hearts pounding against each other. He freed her hands, sliding down her arms, and goose bumps rose at the sensation. He lifted his chest, his hips pressing into hers, and her core flooded with liquid heat. She could clearly feel his erection throbbing against her lower stomach. He pressed his palm against her sternum and looked her in the eye, those beautiful green eyes so captivating.

"You hold my heart, Trinity." He lowered his head and kissed her again, this time with a tenderness that made her heart melt. He lifted his head, trailing his lips across her jaw to nibble at her ear. She trembled, that liquid heat building between her legs. "I love you. I love the way you smell," he whispered, kissing a scorching trail down her neck. Her breasts swelled, nipples tightening, as her pulse raced.

"I love your smile," he said as his kissed his way down her chest, his hands cupping her breasts. "I love the way you fill my hands." She closed her eyes, head tipping backward as his lips sucked a nipple into his mouth, tugging at the flesh. Her breath escaped in a husky moan, and his hips flexed against hers.

"I love it when you make that sound," he murmured, transferring his kiss from one breast to the other. She made the sound again, seeing as he liked it so much and she didn't have that much control over it when he was driving her mad with delight. He laved her nipple with his tongue, and she shuddered, heat spiraling from her core to the place between her thighs that wept for his touch. "You have such a big heart, Trin," he said, and she could feel the rumble of his voice right down to her core. Her heart thumped in her chest, her desire building with each heartbeat. "I love that you love your family so fiercely, so fervently."

He kissed his way down over her navel, and her nipples tightened in the cool air. She rolled her hips as he worked his way down her body. She wanted him, needed him, inside her, and he was determined to take his time, to shred her control. Her legs shifted as he nestled his broad chest between her thighs. Oh, goodness, he was driving her crazy. He paused, his golden-green gaze meeting hers.

"But most of all," he said, his voice low, deep, his expression determined, "I love that you're mine." He kissed her. Thoroughly, possessively, and she came apart, splintering with pleasure, only to be put back together as a quivering, wanton mess.

He rose up over her, and she caught their scent. Not his, not hers. *Theirs.* Something fired inside her; something that was full of desire, full of love for the man in her arms. She pushed him gently, rolling them over until she straddled his hips. She cradled his face in her hands, meeting his gaze. She loved that even though he possessed great strength, he could be playful, and he could let her take control—just the way her beast liked it.

"Mine," she said simply, bending down to kiss him, tasting her, tasting him. She drew her hands down his chest, gently scoring her nails down his pecs and drawing around and around in ever narrowing circles until her nail flicked his nipple. He sighed, arching his back at her caress. Sunlight embraced his skin, turning it golden and bronze in the dappled shadows from the branches above them.

A fierce possessiveness, a desire to bind him to her, swept over her. "Mine," she whispered, then kissed and licked, nibbled and bit her way down that gorgeous chest, exploring the rise and dip of muscle, the taut silken skin, until she reached his erection. She grasped him, enjoying the tactile strength, the rigid heat of him. Her gaze met his, and she could see the strain on his face, the anticipation.

"Mine," she breathed against him, then took him inside her mouth, kissing him thoroughly until he made that husky moan that she loved to hear. His hands delved into her hair, massaging her scalp, then pulling her up toward his face. She let him, climbing up over his body to settle herself over his hips. He made that husky moan sound again as she took him inside her, his eyes meeting hers as she moved over him.

He reached for her, drawing her down for a kiss as he thrust, and she gasped as she ran her hands up into his short hair. She could feel her body tightening, grasping at him. She kissed the corner of his mouth, then his jaw, her heart racing as she felt the delicious spiraling of tension. Matthias's heart beneath hers, like a sexy rhythm tailored for them. Pulse hammering, her body clenched. Matthias stiffened beneath her, and she clamped her teeth on the stretch of golden skin between neck and shoulder.

Matthias roared, almost unseating her and glorious pleasure unlike she'd ever experienced coursed through her. Her toes curled, her fingers clenched, even her hair follicles spasmed.

She had a brief impression of swirling colors, hazy, sparkling, glimmering, as bliss, hot and ethereal, swept her away on a tide of sensation. She wasn't alone. She could sense Matthias with her, greens and golds rippling around her, melding with blues and silvers, and an awareness, something so pure, so perfect, it was achingly beautiful. She could feel her, and she could feel Matthias, sense his emotions through the bond that warmed between them.

She collapsed on top of him, heart thudding, and his arms wrapped around her. She smiled. She felt complete. Home.

"Mine."

Matthias stroked Trinity's shoulder, gazing up at the canopy of branches above them. His heart rate was slowing to normal, but he didn't think he'd ever be normal again. He took a deep breath. That was—*intense*. Even now, he could feel arousal coursing through his body, his need for the woman in his arms so compelling. He'd never get enough of her, no matter how many lifetimes they shared.

His beast stretched within him, a sense of homecoming, of satisfaction, of possession, thrumming through him.

"Is—is it like that all the time?" Trinity asked, and he smiled at the awe in her voice.

"I sure hope so."

She lifted her head. "Haven't you done this before?"

He chuckled. "I can assure you, I've never done *that* before."

Trinity beamed, and his heart caught. He loved her so much. He'd loved Cara, but that had faded, like the snows melting, receding. The emotion he felt for Trinity, well, it was like the first bloom of spring, the scorching heat of summer and the chaotic blizzards of winter, all rolled up in a love so strong, they were each willing to give up a part of themselves for the other.

She rolled off him, then grimaced as she stretched. "You know, I hear beds are really good for this," she said, rolling her hand between them. He caught her hand and brought it to his mouth, kissing her curled fingers.

"Marry me," he said roughly. It wasn't a question. He wanted to belong to her, and for her to belong to him, every way imaginable. As mates, their connection would be recognized and respected by other shifters. A marriage would be recognized by all.

She smiled. "Definitely."

Four weeks later, with repairs completed on the Woodland den, Matthias stood on the dais, Dion by his side and Gilbert in the center. Matthias eyed the Woodland Guardian Prime. He may have wanted to tear him apart at their first meeting, but he'd discovered Dion had a deep well of integrity, of fairness and honor that was in accordance with his own views. The guardian prime was in full support of Matthias's strategy to protect his new pack, and had some good ideas on strengthening the security of their territory, as well as training the guardians.

Matthias knew he and Dion would make a good team. He glanced down at his clasped hands. He and Trinity would make a better one.

The great hall was packed, filled with Woodland, a considerable number of Alpine Pack members, including a very pregnant Samantha Alpine. He just hoped Nate managed to get her back to the den before Jared's pup decided to make an appearance. The female alpha prime had insisted on coming, as a mark of the new alliance that had been formed between Woodland and Alpine.

Other packs had sent their representatives to witness and celebrate the wedding of the new Woodland Alpha Prime and his mate. Matthias saw it as an opportunity to bridge the rifts created by the previous alpha prime, starting with the River pack.

A violin at the back of the hall struck a chord. There was the sound of chairs scraping as the guests stood, and then the music started. Matthias heard Dion's swift intake of breath, and he turned. His mouth dropped.

Trinity walked down the hall, her dark hair pulled back into an intricate knot at the nape of her neck, a few tendrils escaping to frame her face.

He swallowed. She was—stunning. His mate wore a simple dress, but the effect was anything but. With an ankle-length skirt that flowed around her legs with each step she took, and a lace bodice that managed to look demure and sexy as hell at the same time, she was an enchanting combination of innocence and seduction, with a regal elegance that entranced all within the hall. She was so womanly and feminine, yet the dress also revealed her strength.

She carried no flowers, but instead had one hand on Dalton's arm, and the other clasped within Jax's grip. Matthias winked at the pup, who blinked repeatedly in his effort to wink back.

Gilbert stepped forward, beaming, as Dalton led

Trinity up onto the prime dais, and placed her hand on Matthias's before stepping down to join the gathered crowd. She turned briefly to settle Jax, and Matthias gulped when he saw the back of her dress. The smooth skin of her back was exposed, framed by the scalloped edge of her dress as it lined her sides. She was even sexier from behind. Matthias stared at her, taking in her hair, the face he so loved and the body he wanted next to his for all time.

"You're wearing a dress," he said, not bothering to hide his awe.

Her cheeks colored prettily, and Trinity tilted her head. "And you're wearing a shirt," she commented. He grimaced.

The snows had come, but the caves in Woodland were much warmer than what he was used to up in Alpine. The white-collared shirt was a necessary evil for the occasion. He'd flat out refused the dark jacket.

"You're beautiful," he told his bride solemnly, as he covered her hand with his.

"So are you," she said sincerely, and he smiled as they turned to face Gilbert.

Before the gathered guests, Gilbert married them. They spoke their vows, but Matthias would have to admit later, he hadn't paid that much attention, he was so captivated by his beautiful bride.

"Now the rings," Gilbert stated, but hesitated as both Matthias and Trinity shook their heads.

"No rings," Matthias stated emphatically. Gilbert's eyebrows rose.

"No rings?"

"No rings," Trinity said with a clear certainty, and Matthias winked at his bride. Both of them were very much in agreement on that particular subject.

Gilbert nodded. "All right, then. No rings."

He continued with the ceremony.

"You may now kiss the bride," he finally stated, and Matthias grinned. This was the part he liked.

Trinity stepped closer to him and he leaned down to press his lips against her own. She gasped when she realized he wasn't satisfied with a chaste kiss, and he took advantage, widening her lips with his own as he kissed her thoroughly, enfolding her body in his arms and turning into a dip so that she clung to him. The crowd cheered, and there were several wolf whistles. When it got to the point where he either had to stop or find a private place, he pulled back, and stared down at his she-wolf.

Her blue eyes sparkled with an alluring combination of humor and desire, her cheeks rosy and her lips curling into a happy smile, and he knew. He would protect her with his life. Her happiness was his happiness.

They straightened and turned back to Gilbert, whose eyes widened when he remembered the rest.

"Ah, yes, and one more thing," he said, and the crowd in the hall quieted. Matthias and Trinity drew apart, and she drew Jax closer. Matthias reached out to clasp the boy's other hand, and they stood there, bride, groom, with a child between them. They'd had a talk with Jax, and he now stood, chin up, shoulders back, when Gilbert leaned down to address the boy.

"And you, Jax, do you take Matthias and Trinity as your father and mother?"

"Yes," Jax said, then jumped up and down in excitement. "Yes, yes, yes."

Matthias laughed at his son's exuberance, and just that thought had him blinking back a tear. His *son*.

"And you, Matthias and Trinity, do you take Jax as

your son, to have and to hold, to love and to cherish, for all of time?"

Matthias looked at his wife, and she smiled as they turned back to their elder prime. "We do," they chorused.

Gilbert flung his arms wide. "I pronounce you Family Prime of Woodland Pack."

The crowd erupted into cheers and wild applause. Trinity laughed, her eyes glimmering with tears as all three turned to face the guests. Jax jumped up and down until Matthias lifted him up and rested him on his hip. Trinity's arm stole around to enfold the both of them, and for a moment they stood there in a happy family embrace.

Matthias turned to look at his new family. He had once lost everything, his family, his pack, his ability to lead and a part of himself. Now he had more than he'd ever dreamed possible, and all because of a certain tracker who had shown him that family mattered, above everything.

A short time later, as everyone danced, he held Trinity to his chest. "You make me very happy, Mrs. Woodland," he whispered in her ear, and nipped her in that spot that always made her tremble. He smiled as her body shook delicately against his. She lifted her head to meet his gaze.

"I love you, Mr. Woodland," she told him simply. Her words soothed his beast, who stretched in contentment inside him. She traced the button of his shirt lazily, her gaze darkening with the same desire that was always present in him.

"You can take this off now. If you want…?" she said, and his heart thudded at the suggestive tone, the seductive arch of her eyebrow.

He gazed briefly around the hall. It was one hell of a party. Agatha had already taken Jax and the other pups for a very special sleepover, and the rest of the pack were celebrating as though it had been ages since they'd had something to celebrate. He realized that was probably true, and made a mental vow to give them more reasons for celebration.

He trailed his hand down her back, enjoying the feel of her smooth skin against his fingertips. She inhaled, and he smiled in wicked satisfaction as the swell of her breasts pressed against his chest.

"I'll take off mine if you take off yours," he suggested silkily, and pulled her hips against his, so that she could feel his erection. He was hard already. Had been from the moment she'd walked into the hall. Her eyes widened, then her lips curved in that sexy smile that always promised him pleasure.

She glanced around the hall. "Hmm, it's tempting, but what about our guests? Wouldn't it seem rude if we ditched our own party?"

He smiled at her. He knew he could tempt her. "Well, we do have a bed, now…"

She took hold of his hand, and led him into one of the nearby tunnels. "Follow me."

He eyed her, the swing of her hips, the silky smoothness of her back and the sexy curve of her neck, and grinned. "Always."

* * * * *

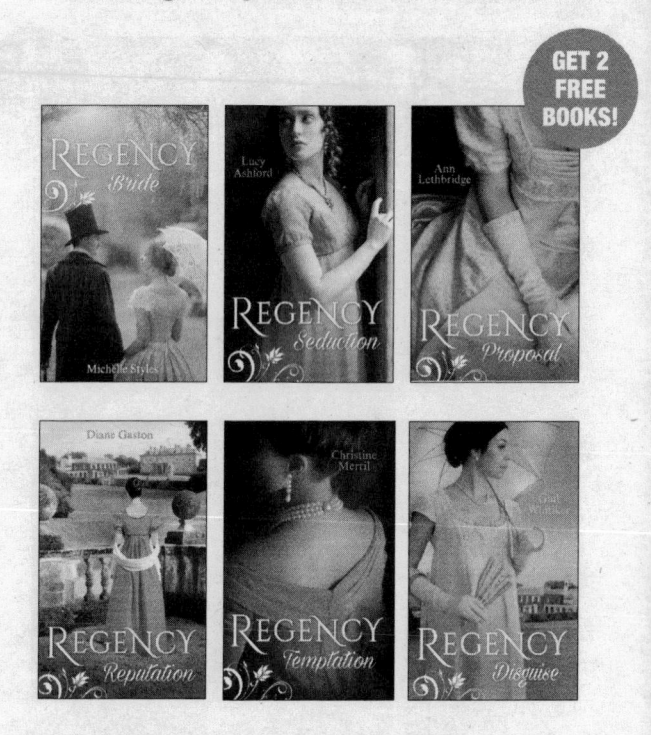

Mat Coward

The Pocket Essential

CLASSIC RADIO COMEDY

www.pocketessentials.com

First published in Great Britain 2003 by
Pocket Essentials, P O Box 394, Harpenden, Herts, AL5 1XJ, UK

Distributed in the USA by Trafalgar Square Publishing,
PO Box 257, Howe Hill Road, North Pomfret, Vermont 05053

Copyright © Mat Coward 2003
Series Editor: David Mathew

A CIP catalogue record for this book is available from the British Library.

ISBN 1-904048-04-8

2 4 6 8 10 9 7 5 3 1

Book typeset by Wordsmith Solutions Ltd
Printed and bound by Cox & Wyman

For Barry Took, funny man.

CONTENTS

Chapter One: The Demob Comics

Have You Ever Been Tickled, Missus:
Introduction

Comedy sticks in the mind.

So do other things, of course - funerals, advertising jingles, phone numbers you haven't rung in twenty years - but comedy is especially sticky. True, we consume vast amounts of comedic matter during our lifetimes, and most of it goes in one ear, pauses briefly to make us smile or chuckle, then drifts out of the other ear, never to be thought of again. But the best of it sticks, and stays stuck, and accompanies us through the rest of our lives, a support in times of trial, a reminder of other days, a restorer of lost perspective, a basis for friendship between strangers. When it comes to affecting, and even shaping our emotions, the only art form that comes near to comedy is music.

Radio, I believe, is the most effective humour delivery system yet devised. Peter Eton, producer of *The Goon Show*, made the astonishing claim that when the BBC invited people to send in drawings of what they imagined the Goons characters looked like, 'ninety-five percent were alike - and corresponded to the Goons' own images of them.' The paradoxically visual nature of radio is often noted; it may be that aural media create fully-realised and lasting images in the mind because the listener is required to take part in the process of creation. A viewer has all the work done for him, so the end result is less personal, and may not penetrate the imagination so profoundly.

I was born in 1960, and am therefore too young to have any first-hand nostalgia for what is generally viewed as the Golden Age of wireless, the 1950s. However, in the early 70s, I began collecting, via birthday and Christmas presents, books of scripts and LP records of classic radio comedies. I was a fan of all forms of comedy, but my favourite was radio comedy, past or present; most of all, I loved the shows which I now recognise as The Big Three, consideration of which makes up the greater part of this book.

I have a clear, scent-filled memory of a high summer day in about 1972, of playing tennis against the back wall of our flat (and losing), with *Just A Minute* floating through an open window. I preferred radio to TV because of the scenery; it's a fairly obvious point, but you don't need to use your eyes when you're listening to the radio. You can look at what you like.

For a child in those days, TV was necessarily communal - it was a large piece of furniture, fixed in position, which families watched *as* families. The wireless could be communal too - at lunchtime on Sunday, for instance, for *Round The Horne* or *The Clitheroe Kid* - but it could also be private. You could take a transistor radio to the bottom of the garden, and it would be just you and *The Men From The Ministry* and next door's lawnmower.

These days while I listen, I'm more likely to be washing-up than playing with my Action Man in the garden, but radio comedy is still a great joy - and there are millions who feel likewise. There's more to radio comedy today than nostalgia for the Golden Age.

The test for greatness in comedy is obvious and simple: does it get funnier each time you hear it? The three shows I've chosen to concentrate on, as living classics in their own right and as major influences on subsequent programmes, really chose themselves.

We Don't Know What It Is, But When It Wants To Go It Screams: Introducing The Goons

The people who revolutionised comedy in the years immediately following World War Two were mostly demobilised servicemen. Young men (and the occasional young woman) who had just won a war against fascism, they'd followed up this not insignificant feat by electing a Labour government to 'win the peace' - that is, abolish the old class system and its inevitable consequences of poverty, ignorance and the certainty that where you ended up in life depended on where you started from. The National Health Service, the welfare state, better housing, more educational opportunities... to many at the time it seemed that a bloodless revolution was occurring in these islands.

Having spent the bulk of their adult lives so far wondering whether they were going to die today, the demob generation faced peacetime with confidence, ambition and determination. They were going to live in a world of their own design - and that included comedy.

Many of the chief players in this story started their showbusiness careers in uniform, found they liked it and wanted to continue it once they were in civvies. This was a new - and unprecedented - generation of

8

comedians, who had little use for timidity, convention or deference. The old world had gone and good riddance to it; post-war comedy should reflect post-war realities. It's easy to imagine them as young people some-what older than their years; they were mostly in their twenties or thirties, but who could deny that their comedy came from a lifetime's experience?

Although by 1951, the year of the first *Goon Show*, disillusionment with Labour's timidity had set in, enormous changes had taken place: Britain was becoming more egalitarian, permissive and diverse. Confor-mity was seen by the young as a character flaw, not a virtue.

Wartime service had a socially broadening effect. People from different regions, classes and backgrounds had met and mixed to an extent that wouldn't have happened otherwise. This influenced not only their voting habits, but also the worldview evident in their comedy.

They despised, above all, pomposity and artificiality. Having seen a good deal of it, they'd come to the conclusion that the British Empire was an anachronistic joke, and that the officer class which it spawned and fed was made up principally of the absurd and the corrupt, the idiotic and the hypocritical, the cowardly and the decadent. Spike Milligan in particular saw the world as being governed by unacknowledged idiots, so he invented his own world, full of *blatant* idiots, as a way of illuminating and ridiculing the original.

The Goon Show was, not surprisingly, a cult success among the young and the dissenting, almost from the off. As much as anything, its sheer energy must have had a revitalising effect on a nation still engloomed with the austerity that came from fighting a total war. One phrase turns up repeatedly in contemporary press notices: that the Goons had 'added a new dimension' to comedy, and even to radio itself. Struggling to describe Goonery, radio critics used terms such as 'visual comedy,' or 'cartoons in sound.'

Although it was not quite as fatherless as is often thought, what some bemused BBC high-ups called *The Go On Show* was a radical programme, exciting because its wholesale departure from ordinary logic, and its almost hysterical determination to laugh at everything that should not be laughed at, was intensely liberating. It has retained that power through the decades since, so that even though the world it was written in is long dead, it remains not only influential as an example of the comedy writer's craft, but also authentically explosive as comedy.

I could waste the whole of this book debating whether the Goons were intellectual terrorists, or just demobbed soldier boys desperate to let off steam after years of fear, discipline and repression - and I'd still not come to any very useful conclusion, other than that they were both. Their weapons were satire and surrealism, their toys were puns, explosions and giant farting noises; or vice versa. For half a century, people in all areas of entertainment - from John Lennon to Mike Myers to Robert Rankin - have acknowledged the influence of the Goons on their own work.

Peter Eton once wrote that the show was 'frankly devoted to man's crazily triumphant return to the trees from which he dropped.'

Oh Look, It's Started Raining: Introducing Hancock

Hancock's Half Hour did so much that was new that it's probably as well to start with something it didn't do. Despite what you may read elsewhere, *HHH* was not the world's first situation comedy. For the record, most authorities list *Myrtle And Bertie* (Radio Luxembourg, 1935), sponsored by Monkey Brand Soap, as the original sitcom.

What is beyond dispute is that *HHH* was the first modern sitcom, and the one that established the template for virtually all future sitcoms. The first episode was broadcast in 1954, but long before it went out its novel characteristics were clear in the minds of its creators - scriptwriters Ray Galton and Alan Simpson, and a young producer, Dennis Main Wilson (a working-class lad from Dulwich, who'd had to add the 'Main' to his name because there was already a Dennis Wilson working at the BBC). Wilson is arguably the single most significant individual in the history of British comedy.

Thirty uninterrupted minutes of dramatic comedy - no variety acts, no musical interludes, no sketches, no patter; a 'non-domestic' or non-cosy situation comedy, in which the humour comes from consistent characters reacting to realistic situations, in the form of a single story, like a short play... this was such a radical idea that some in BBC management didn't believe it could work, even though its protagonist, stand-up comedian Tony Hancock, was already an established star.

Barry Took has written of Galton and Simpson's 'knack of reproducing mundane conversation and lifting it to the level of high art.' They've been compared to the absurdist playwright Eugene Ionesco, for their ability to transmute the banality and tedium of everyday life into something not only very funny, but often painfully insightful. Their relationship with Hancock has frequently been likened to that of composers being interpreted by a musician with perfect pitch.

There's no better example of this than the episode first broadcast on 22nd April 1958, known as *Sunday Afternoon At Home*. In the opinions of many, this is the finest half hour of comedy ever broadcast in any medium - as close to perfection as you're likely to find in a material universe. (It was issued as a record in 1960, and has been in print ever since.)

It's an amazingly sophisticated playlet about ennui, full of pauses and sighs and theatrical repetitions. To allow 'dead air' in a radio show was one of the worst sins a producer could commit. If you're paying for a radio licence, you expect there to be some sound coming out of your radio when you switch it on. But then, Hancock's pauses were as funny, well-timed and expressive as any of his laugh-lines.

Sunday Afternoon is not only fascinating from a technical point of view, it's also wildly funny; it's a glorious coming together of two writers, five actors and one producer all at the height of their powers. It pays the audience the great compliment of assuming that millions of people would sit still and *listen* for half an hour to a meditation on boredom, provided it was done well enough.

From the first line, listeners must have realised that they were being treated to something different. Hancock opens the show with a slow stream of 'Oh dear' and 'Dear me,' culminating in a heartfelt 'Stone me... what a life.'

It's a typical wet, miserable Sunday afternoon, and once you've read the papers, there's nothing to do. The telly's bust, the pubs won't be open for ages, the cinema's only showing ancient films. They can't even play Monopoly because they've lost the board. Imagine that: a day so dull that you're disappointed when you can't play Monopoly. Their one bright moment comes when they realise that they should have put the clocks forward: 'Ah-ha-ha! That'll get rid of another hour!'

Miss Pugh (Hattie Jacques) suggests brightly that the men go for a walk. Hancock - who is finding everything about his companions irritating, and misses no opportunity to snipe at them - isn't impressed. Why doesn't *she* go for a walk instead? 'It'd be one less to look at all day.' He didn't think much of her dinner, either: 'I thought my mother was a bad cook, but at least her gravy used to move about.'

Tony and Sid James pass a little time by swapping platitudes about what a funny old life it is, and gossiping about the barmaid at the local. Tony reckons he can see faces in the wallpaper, but Bill Kerr can't make them out no matter how much he squints. Tony's disgusted: 'You wait till you want *me* to see anything.'

11

For all that, they're still horrified when the old bore next door (Kenneth Williams) pops in for a visit. Hancock is barely civil; when Williams tells him it's raining, Tony comes out with one of the most beautifully delivered lines of his career: 'Oh, so that's what's making the roads wet.'

Having told Tony that his radio show isn't all that good these days - he was at his peak five years ago - the awful neighbour proceeds to run through his repertoire of uncannily unimpressive animal impressions.

Most of the episode is played in real time (it is, after all, a comedy about how slowly time passes), with the exception of a funereal musical link to tell us that Williams has been doing his barnyard noises for seven hours. It's almost midnight, although Hancock feels it must be at least Tuesday. Tony, Bill and Sid are determined that they will never spend another Sunday like this one; they've got to get their lives sorted out. Another round of pauses, inevitably followed by: 'See you next Sunday, then.'

It's probably impossible for anyone born much later than 1970 to understand how deadly Sundays could be in the days when the whole country seemed to close down between chucking-out time on Saturday and clocking-on time on Monday; but you don't need to have lived through an era to appreciate its art. Next time you watch *The Royle Family*, and marvel at its naturalistic style, at the way it creates convincing characters and touching comedy out of almost nothing, remember that what you are marvelling at was invented almost half a century earlier - and on radio, where a pause really is a pause.

We're All Living Under The Shadah Of The Bomb: Introducing Horne

By 1965, the wireless had fallen to the usurper. Television was Britain's main provider of family entertainment. The phenomenal success of Tony Hancock's transfer from radio to TV a decade earlier had started that process.

In pubs and at work, friends now talked about what they'd seen last night - not what they'd heard. Radio continued to play an important part in people's daily lives, but it was no longer at the centre of their imaginations. There were still decent sized audiences available for radio comedies - most notably in the coveted Sunday lunchtime slot - but the idea of a radio show seizing the nation's attention, in the way that had happened so often from the 1930s through the 50s, seemed a vain hope.

If only someone had explained all this to J Peasmold Gruntfuttock, of the Balls Pond Road, we might have been spared some of the most outrageous comedy ever to assail the ears of decent folk.

Round The Horne, the last radio comedy show that the whole nation listened to, or was at least aware of, was not at all radical in format - indeed, coming when it did, it might be called conservative. It was a sketch show, performed in an ensemble style around its star, Kenneth Horne, which paused halfway through its thirty minutes to allow a harmony group to sing a corny song. Its material consisted of film spoofs, recurring outlandish characters, topical gags, bogus ads and comic songs. And if you can listen to it today without wetting yourself laughing, then you need an operation!

RTH was in tune with its times; the social liberalism so long promised or threatened in the post-war world was at last arriving, and the show both celebrated this new mood and took the rise out of it. Its writers, Barry Took and Marty Feldman - and their inspirational producer, John Simmonds - set out to capture something of the spirit of the 60s, a spirit of tolerance, experimentation, and narcissistic poncing about. The programmes were written - in the same week of broadcast - with little thought for posterity, and the scripts are stuffed with topical references to people and events that are now incomprehensible without footnotes. Some of its fans claim that *RTH* hasn't dated at all, which is obvious nonsense; its points of reference have dated but its comedy has ripened.

Its continuing popularity with the young people who buy vast numbers of *Round The Horne* cassettes and CDs is explained by the quality of its writing and performance. Its importance in radio history, and as a direct and indirect influence on comedy ever since, lies in the degree to which its ways and means have sunk into the comic fabric of the nation. Since 1965, it has been almost impossible for any sketch show, on radio or TV, not to show its *RTH* roots - whether consciously or not.

And The Rest Of Us Lie In Bed, Thinking:
Intelligent Comedy

The three shows I've discussed share one crucial and overlooked quality: respect for the audience.

The writers refused to write down to their listeners. They took comedy seriously, and did not view it as a lesser art. They saw themselves in their audience and vice versa - and they were willing to stretch the audience's expectations, confident that listeners would want to keep up. The Goons, for instance, perfected (if they did not actually invent) a new genre of comedy, and deployed it without compromise; they assumed that their listeners shared their own disdain for easy-listening comic pap, and that if faced with something new and strange, would soon catch on to what was happening, and would actually relish the challenge of doing so.

In concentrating my attention on the Big Three, I'm keen to debunk a persistent myth that has inhibited a proper appreciation of the history of radio comedy.

Comedy on the wireless prior to 1951 was certainly different to comedy after 1951, but perhaps not quite as different as people tend to believe. What we could call 'The Legend of the Crazy People' has it that BS - Before Spike - radio schedules were occupied entirely by staid, predictable comedies that did little more than reproduce the stage acts of music hall comedians. Then suddenly there was *The Goon Show* - and lo, the modern age was born in a riot of revolutionary wackiness.

In fact, a quick look at the early history of radio comedy is sufficient to prove that nothing ever comes from nowhere. Charlie Darwin's theories of evolution apply to comedy shows as well as to fish.

To understand what happened to comedy after VE Day, we need to understand what happened before...

Chapter Two: Radio Comedy, 1922-51

Ullo Me Old Ducks: Music Hall On The Air

'John Henry, come here!' has some claim to be British radio comedy's first catchphrase. Henry, a Yorkshire comic who played a hen-pecked husband, was the first comedian to be turned into a national star by his wireless appearances, which began in 1923, and the first to develop a technique and style specifically designed for the new medium. The billing for his first broadcast is an early example of a custom which still continues - that of published programme details gently sending up shows and stars: '9.30: John Henry will try to entertain you,' then at 10.00: 'John Henry will try again.'

According to radio historian Denis Gifford, the first comedian to broadcast in this country was Will Hay on 29th July 1922, and the first to appear solo was Wilfred Liddiatt exactly two months later. Our Lizzie - played by Helena (or Helen, or Helene) Millais from 20th October 1922 - is usually awarded the title of first comedy character created especially for the radio. Another early star was William Rouse (or Rous), who played Wireless Willie from 1924.

The British Broadcasting Company was formed in 1922, about two years after Guglielmo Marconi had made the first public radio broadcast in Britain. (It didn't become the British Broadcasting Corporation, state owned but not state controlled, until 1927). Although comedy played a part in the BBC's output more or less from the off, many successful comics were reluctant to appear on radio - and the same was true of television in the 1940s and early 50s - not least because it used up material far more quickly than touring did. Theatrical managements, meanwhile, were worried by their new rival: why would people pay money to see an act live, if they could hear any number of variety stars for the price of an annual radio licence? Add to this the attitude of much of the BBC high command at the time - that vulgar variety wasn't quite the kind of material they considered most suited for their high-minded new organ - and it's not surprising that it took a while for comedy to become a crucial part of the output.

By the early 30s, it was obvious that radio was here to stay, and that comedians and impresarios would have to learn to live with it - or, better yet, to exploit it. Variety shows were increasingly heard on the air; for instance, *Music Hall* (1932-1952), was just what its name suggests, and was among the first programmes to have a studio audience.

The BBC's Variety Department was formed in 1933 - to the disgust, no doubt, of the corporation's notoriously puritanical director general, Lord Reith. Its was headed by former *Radio Times* editor Eric Maschwitz, who was Hermione Gingold's husband, and writer of the song *These Foolish Things*.

Audience research was already a minor industry (even in those days, the BBC faced competition from overseas stations which could be received in Britain), and it had become clear that variety shows attracted the greatest audiences. In the light of this, what had been planned as yet another run of dance band shows was hastily rejigged - and became the first-ever comedy series on British radio.

Light The Blue Touchpaper And Retire: Band Waggon

Band Waggon (1938-39), written by Vernon Harris, Gordon Crier, and the cast, was set in an imaginary flat at the top of Broadcasting House, shared by two very different characters: titchy Liverpudlian Arthur Askey, an up-and-coming concert party comic with a cheeky, chirpy style; and suave, Cambridge-educated straight man Richard Murdoch, who had worked mainly in revue. It was something quite new: a variety show featuring resident comedians, which was - and this was a radical development, believe it or not - broadcast weekly, at the same time on the same day. (*Band Waggon*, incidentally, seems to be the BBC's preferred spelling, although various forms are used.)

It took a while to catch on - it was almost cancelled six weeks into its scheduled thirteen-week run - but once Murdoch and Askey were given more control over the scripts, it took off swiftly and became a national favourite, turning Murdoch and Askey into huge stars.

The format established in *Band Waggon* is one still to be found on radio and TV today: a mixture of comic patter and sketches with interludes of light music; catchphrases ('Ay thang yew!'; 'Hello playmates!'), regular features and eccentric characters; and, of course, sound effects - it hadn't taken writers long to realise that the new technology offered new comic possibilities. A great pile of tin cans and similar clangy objects was kept in a corner of the studio ready for the crash which ended each episode.

There were only 55 shows in all, during three series; Askey's stage career was thriving, and that's where the money was. The final episode, in which 'Big Hearted' Arthur and 'Stinker' Murdoch left the BH flat, provoked an immense public reaction, adding to the thousands of letters which had already arrived at BH, addressed to the Top Floor Flat.

Delighted with the success of his go-ahead approach - of creating a show for radio, rather than simply adapting stage shows - Maschwitz wondered if the same trick would work with a comedian who was already well-known to radio listeners.

I Don't Mind If I Do: ITMA

It's That Man Again (1939-49), surely the most written about radio series in history, was successful to an extent which is hard to imagine today. Its international audience was measured in the tens of millions.

Its star, Tommy Handley, was undoubtedly the most popular performer, in any field, ever known in Britain. He is said to have received 40,000 fan letters a year, and his funeral in January 1949 was a national day of mourning not matched until Winston Churchill's death in 1965; 10,000 people attended the crematorium, while others lined the hearse's route six deep, for six miles. A radio tribute ended with the *ITMA* door - through which the various characters had made their weekly entrances - being closed for the final time, followed by silence.

Born in Liverpool in 1894, Handley was a concert party comedian in World War One and a music hall comedian in the 1920s, who was soon appearing on radio. During this period, New Zealand-born Ted Kavanagh, who had been a medical student in Edinburgh before the war and since it had worked at various trades, including that of advertising copywriter, heard Handley on the wireless, and sent him a joke. Handley bought it, and so began an association that lasted until the comic's death.

The third element in the creation of *ITMA* was producer Francis Worsley, who had worked with Handley and Kavanagh already. The three men met in the bar of the Langham Hotel, opposite Broadcasting House - in the midst of a convention of clergymen, so the story goes - and came up with what they hoped would be a British version of America's *The Burns And Allen Show*: fast and slick, modern and clever.

Fast, it was. Handley's mastery of microphone technique has never been surpassed; there's no one working today who could match his combination of speed and coherence. But it wasn't very funny; the first few episodes were received by audiences as a somewhat pale imitation of *Band Waggon*. The programme was facing cancellation, when war broke out.

Whether *It's That Man Again* would have been quite such a smash without the assistance of Adolf Hitler's war (the title came from a newspaper catchphrase, referring to the German dictator) is impossible to say; certainly, the recordings don't provoke much laughter from modern audiences, but then they were highly topical.

Evacuated to Bristol, the programme (now known as *ITMA*, in imitation of the wartime mania for acronyms) began to grow into a tension-relieving eruption of crazy humour which mocked - and more importantly humanised - what was happening to Britain, as it stood alone against Nazism. When your country becomes overnight a land of restrictions and regulations, red tape and shortages, swelling bureaucracy and creeping paranoia - and all in vain, since it's pretty bloody obvious that Germany's going to win the war within a few months - what can you do but laugh? Given that the theatres and cinemas were closed for reasons of public safety, radio was for the first time a monopoly supplier of comedy.

As new government departments were announced on what seemed like a daily basis, Handley became Minister of Aggravation and Mysteries at the Office Of Twerps, a ministry which was charged with ensuring that new regulations were as irritating and counter-productive as possible.

The cast from the first series was abandoned along with the old format. In came repertory actor Maurice Denham, as office char Mrs Tickle and Vodkin the Russian inventor. Jack Train, with his great range of voices, played a German spy ('This is Funf speaking'), the civil servant Fusspot ('It's most irregular') and Farmer Jollop; in later series he also delivered Claude ('After you, Cecil'), the toper Colonel Chinstrap ('I don't mind if I do!') and the ancient Mark Time - 'I'll have to ask me dad.' Other regulars over the years included Fred Yule, Dorothy Summers, Horace Percival, Deryck Guyler, Hattie Jacques and Mollie Weir. Kavanagh created more catchphrases for his characters than any writer since Charles Dickens, and before long the whole country was speaking in ITMAese. 'Lovely grub,' 'It's being so cheerful as keeps me going,' 'TTFN - ta-ta for now,' 'I go, I come back'... I'd better stop there, or I'll run out of book. Can I do you now, sir?

The role *ITMA* played in maintaining morale on the Home Front is too well known to warrant repeating here, beyond noting the immeasurable political importance of the flagship comedy show, in a besieged country, being based on dissent, contempt for authoritarianism and disrespect for petty authority. It was as if the BBC was saying, to Britain and to the world, if you want to see the difference between democracy and totalitari-

18

anism, just try to imagine the Office Of Twerps existing, during wartime, in any other country on earth.

What is less often remembered is that much of the programme's humour was of a sort nowadays referred to as 'Goonish,' or 'Pythonesque.' Most significantly, *ITMA* developed into a show which turned its back on radio comedy's music hall roots, and thus became the first fully purpose-built *radio* comedy.

Ee, What A To-do: Robb Wilton

He doesn't really fit into this story very neatly - I suppose because he was genuinely a one-off - but it would be perverse to recount the history of comedy in the 1940s without mentioning a Liverpudlian engineer who became an actor before turning comic in 1903, and was easily the most adored solo comedian of World War Two.

Robb Wilton (1881-1957) is, I reckon, the funniest stand-up there's ever been - though that phrase doesn't quite describe the meandering monologues ('The day war broke out...') which made his voice, a few weeks into the war, the most famous in Britain.

His material concerned the trouble he was having convincing his wife that he was doing his bit. When the Home Guard was formed, he explained to her that he was supposed to stop Hitler's army landing. 'She said, "What, *you*?" I said, "No, not *me*, there's Bob Edwards, Charlie Evans, Billy Brightside... there's seven or eight of us..."'

Wilton's hesitant, henpecked delivery hid gorgeous timing and a sensational ear for a phrase. The role he played - of a middle-aged citizen, bewildered by a frightening new world - and his gentle mockery of his and his country's preparedness for war, is still tremendously funny today. When originally heard, it had the added value of accurately reflecting the nervously determined mood of a large proportion of the country.

Infuriated High Pitched Trumpeting By Single Elephant: The 1940s

ITMA was not alone in its pre-Goon Goonery; funny rather than amusing, tightly written and performed at frenetic speed, full of mad jokes and characters, and noisy sound effects - this was the favoured style of comedy at the heart of the British Empire in its darkest hour.

Danger - Men At Work (1939-47), created by Max Kester and Anthony Hall, introduced 'crazy' humour - which essentially meant the style of the Marx Brothers' films - to the British wireless. Doris Nichols played battle-axe Mrs Ponsonby, and US crosstalk double act Van and Allan were two conmen who, each week, tried a new ruse to rob her of her hotel. In the process, they would insult her with Groucho-like gags delivered at machinegun pace. Getting caught up in their schemes was Jacques Brown as a Greek, Nikolas Ridikoulas, whose beautifully fractured English was echoed decades later by Harry Enfield's Stavros. Jack Train played one of the villains in the second series, after the departure of Van and Allan.

The influence of US popular culture on British comedy around this time was considerable. The restless zaniness of films like Olsen and Johnson's *Hellzapoppin* (1942) had an obvious affect on *Danger* and other shows, and more generally on the everyday humour of the nation's youth. As well as a freer style in comedy, there was a freer style in music; many of the demob comics were jazz fans.

Hi Gang! (1940-49) was American gaggery rather than British silliness. Today's American comedians are mostly bland and inoffensive, their acts founded on sound technique with no spark, but in those days the American style of rapid, wisecracking insult comedy was greeted with enthusiasm by BBC audiences, as something fresh and vigorous. *Hi Gang!* was presented by three Americans: husband and wife Hollywood stars Bebe Daniels and Ben Lyon, and comic and violinist Vic Oliver ('The Old Vic himself'), an Austrian-born aristocrat who was Winston Churchill's son-in-law.

It's best remembered for its extraordinary list of guest stars (from Noel Coward to Tyrone Power, and all points between) and its opening announcement. Most Variety Department shows had been evacuated from the capital by now, but this one really was 'Coming to you from the heart of London,' sticking two fingers up to German propaganda that the city was an uninhabitable ruin. Each episode included a spoof of a film or play - a format still in use today.

Having started on the Overseas Programme in 1942, the lasting importance of *Variety Bandbox* (1944-52), a series of hour-long shows aimed at servicemen, lies in its habit of actively seeking new talent: Frankie Howerd, Tony Hancock, Derek Roy, Dick Emery, Cardew the Cad and Harry Secombe were among many whose careers received an early boost on this immensely popular show.

Not A Word To Bessie: Post-War Comedy

World War Two accelerated social and technological change in many areas, from socialised medicine to the atom bomb. It was also instrumental in creating mass audiences for the BBC. Long before VE Day, the wireless had become part of family life, and the nation's chief purveyor of entertainment. It soon became evident that, even with the many rival attractions which peacetime offered, listening to the radio had become a lasting habit.

Little remembered today, *Merry-Go-Round* (from 1944) consisted of three shows broadcast in rotation, one each for the army, air force and navy - 'Bringing music and fun to boys and girls in khaki and two shades of blue.' The naval version was written by and starred Sub-Lieutenant Eric Barker, with Lieutenant Jon Pertwee and WREN Pearl Hackney - alias Mrs Barker.

Barker was a radio titan in his time. A novelist and short story writer who then became an actor in rep before moving into comedy as an impressionist at the Windmill, he was an established radio performer by the time war broke out; he served five years in the Royal Navy. With *Just Fancy* (1951-62) he changed comic direction entirely, abandoning gags for quiet character sketches. Deryck Guyler joined him to perform his best-loved characters, 'The Two Old Gentlemen,' who talked endlessly at cross-purposes but always ended up agreeing that 'It's only by listening to the other fellow that you get the other fellow's point of view.'

The army edition of *Merry-Go-Round* was written and presented by the music hall comedian and former 'boy yodeller,' Sergeant 'Cheerful' Charlie Chester of the Royal Irish Fusiliers, with his 'happy band of Other Cranks,' such as Arthur Haynes. Representing the flyboys as writers and performers were Flight Lieutenant Richard Murdoch and Wing Commander Kenneth Horne.

After demobilisation, the three strands split into separate series: the navy show became *Waterlogged Spa* (1948-49), the army version turned into *Stand Easy* (1946-49), a high-speed comedy, while Murdoch and Horne, joined by Sam Costa and Maurice Denham, continued in a show which is still considered a minor classic, *Much-Binding-in-The-Marsh* (1947-53).

The settings and styles of all the above suggest that, as far as BBC comedy was concerned, the war hadn't ended at all. It was about to, though.

Wake Up At The Back There: Take It From Here

If any single show began the post-war era of radio comedy, it's *Take It From Here* (1948-60), written by two very tall young men, Frank Muir and Denis Norden.

Norden grew up in north London, where he worked for a while as manager of a cinema and a variety theatre, gaining a lifelong love of the variety form. Muir was born in Kent and left school at 15 following his father's death. Both served in the RAF during the war, and both spent much of their time in uniform writing comedy. After demob, Muir and Norden separately joined a kind of scriptwriter's co-op organised by *ITMA* writer Ted Kavanagh, a legendary encourager of young writers.

In 1947, former Radio Luxembourg producer Charles Maxwell was producing a revival of a forces' show called *Navy Mixture* (1943-47), presented by singer and comic Joy Nichols, who'd been a radio child star in pre-war Australia. Also involved were 'Professor' Jimmy Edwards, and Australian comic Dick Bentley.

Flight Lieutenant Edwards, RAF war hero, ex-public school and Cambridge, drifted into showbusiness, by his own account, through a combination of luck and 'natural laziness.' He'd done a few Footlights revues at college, and some camp concerts in the air force, and after the war he managed to persuade Sid Field's agent to get him some stand-up work at the Windmill. His act centred largely on insulting the audience, and on the props that he continued to use throughout his career: his RAF moustache, schoolmaster's mortarboard, and trombone.

Bentley was a dance band singer when he moved to Britain in 1938, and became a comedian with many radio credits. He spent the war back in Australia, doing forces' broadcasts, and returned to the UK afterwards.

Keen to feature the three in a more up-to-date vehicle, Maxwell approached Muir, who was writing material for Nichols and Edwards, and Norden, who wrote for Bentley.

Early editions of *TIFH* sound fairly ordinary. The programme would start with some jokey chat between the cast, then there'd be a few topical sketches (in which bit parts were played by 'Herbert Mostyn' - respectively, Muir and Norden's middle names) broken by a song, and they'd end up with what was now becoming a radio mainstay - the pastiche playlet.

But already there was something different about the feel of the new show. For a start, it was unapologetically post-war in its atmosphere and concerns. Also, it took a very un-variety-like pride in acknowledging the intelligence of its listeners, not least through a dedication to the joys of language, which revealed itself in agonisingly complex puns and an appreciation of dreadful old jokes redeployed with imaginative relish. In this respect, it can be seen as a direct ancestor of *Round The Horne*; Took and Feldman also shared a passion for wordplay. (Incidentally, the *Carry On* line 'Infamy, infamy - they've all got it in for me!' was originally used in *TIFH*.)

Such intellectual aspirations caused some problems. Writers in those days were used to working under a system of heavy-handed censorship which seemed like a leftover from the previous century (there was to be no mention, for instance, of underclothes, or of the royal family - and *definitely* no mention of the royal family's underclothes), but Muir and Norden may have been the first scriptwriters to be asked to cut a gag about Picasso because 'the audience won't have heard of him.'

Muir and Norden had both done bespoke bits and bobs around the comedy scene, but for their first collaboration they were required to carry the whole burden of a series. They were good writers, with lots of novel ideas, but even so the early shows were not well received. The writers were happy to tinker with the format after receiving responses to each episode - indeed, they'd designed the show to make that possible - but it still took a stroke of luck to save *TIFH*.

(Incidentally, the list of great radio and TV comedies which have nearly been cancelled in their early days because of audience indifference is almost as long as the list of great comedies. Innovation takes time to settle).

Tommy Handley's sudden death from a cerebral haemorrhage - brought on, many believe, by overwork - left a horrible gap in the schedules. *TIFH* was promoted to the Saturday lunchtime slot, previously occupied by one of *ITMA*'s two weekly repeats. Audience figures increased dramatically, and from then on the show was a ratings, critical and award-winning success.

But it wasn't until series six (1953-4) that *TIFH* secured its place in history. Joy Nichols left to resume her theatre career, and her place in the cast was taken by June Whitfield and singer Alma Cogan. A sketch about a 'typically British family,' the Glums, gradually turned into something quite extraordinary - a mini-sitcom, taking over the second half of the show. When you listen to *TIFH* tapes today, you may well find yourself fast forwarding through the first halves, but after the musical break - well, that's different. The Glums are still hilariously, painfully funny.

Far from being a typical British family in the idealised, BBC sense - a stern but kind, pipe-smoking dad, a scatty but loveable, housewifely Mum, and perhaps a slightly naughty teenage child who would see the error of his ways well before the closing announcements - the Glums were the sort of people *The Royle Family* would have looked down on (even though they are clearly descended from them).

Jimmy Edwards as Mr Glum was a boozy, bullying wastrel; Johnny Speight modelled his TV character Alf Garnett partly on Pa Glum. Mr Glum's son Ron (Bentley) was an unemployable moron, and Ron's fiancée Eth (Whitfield) was a girl with a whiny voice, hopeless social aspirations, and a personality derived entirely from reading women's magazines. (Cogan played Mrs Glum - but only with the odd noise off; the character never spoke). It was a wonderful, unfamiliar concept - a family that no one could like, carrying half of a top-rated comedy show.

Many of the biggest laughs came from the straight lines, not from the gags. Nowadays that's a given - from Hancock through Basil Fawlty to Del Boy - but at the time it must have seemed quite adventurous and sophisticated. It was *character* comedy; certainly, it was full of funny lines ('Ron, what do you think of Shanklin?' 'I can't really offer an opinion, Eth. I don't think I've ever shankled') but every joke arose from interactions between faithfully maintained characters.

Sexual frustration was implicit in the Glums - in those days, engaged couples were not expected to embark prematurely on the Great Mystery of Matrimonial Intimacy. More explicitly, the comedy was about the shifting class patterns and expectations of post-war Britain.

Above all, and most astonishingly, the Glums weren't middle-class or even respectable working-class; they weren't nice or cheerful or charmingly roguish; there was nothing cosy about their shabby surroundings or their joyless lives, and it was inconceivable that they would ever encounter a happy ending anywhere this side of the grave. Nothing like them had ever been heard before - yet they were the kind of invention which, once it's revealed, seems so obvious that it's hard to imagine how the world could have existed without it. A bit like the wheel, really. But much funnier.

In 1978, *The Glums* became a TV show (played by Edwards, Patricia Brake and Ian Lavender), which was a slightly silly idea. They belonged on radio. On TV there are too many distractions; on radio, there's just the voice and the words - and the rhythm, made up of pauses and elongations of words, which telly ruins. You can't get proper silences on TV, that's the trouble - the pictures mess them up.

By the beginning of the 1950s, radio comedy had reached adulthood. It had outgrown its origins in the music hall and the revue, it had thrived through a world war and survived peace. Like so many of its creators, it had found that when it took off the khaki for the last time, it had matured into a more confident, less conformist beast than it had been in 1939.

. In short - it was ready for a touch of the old needle-nardle-noo. ('GRAMS: Wallop on back of head. Pop of large pop gun. Set of false teeth hitting inside of bucket.')

Chapter Three: The Goon Show

Lurgi Strikes: The Beginning

There was a pub in London - the Grafton Arms, Victoria - which had been in the Grafton family since 1848. The licencee in the days of demob was Jimmy of that ilk, ex-army, and part-time comedy scriptwriter.

It's impossible to say who entered Grafton's first, or who introduced whom to the place, or in what order. There are many published accounts, and each of them is at variance with all the others; such is the way with human memories, especially - leading scientists suggest - memories concerning events that took place upon licenced premises.

At any rate, Grafton's after the war became a hangout for the younger generation of comedians and comedy writers, especially those working at the nearby Windmill, London's only nude revue venue where comics were employed to fill in the time between the tableaux of naked women. And one by one - or possibly two by two - a particular gang of like-minded funny men coalesced around the beer pumps, and began referring to themselves as 'The Goons,' after the big, idiotic creatures in the *Popeye* strips.

I know it's unwise to become nostalgic about a time before one's own birth, but whoever you talk to or read on the subject, those Grafton's days do sound idyllic; a core of close friends, comrades really, at the centre of a looser alliance of pals, most of them broke most of the time, all of them enjoying the post-war thrill of being young and free and creative and not dead. The atmosphere at Grafton's was fraternal, the various future stars helping each other out financially, and in other ways, depending on who had managed to get a gig that week.

Everyone involved seems to have looked back on Grafton's with pleasure (even Tony Hancock, another made man at the pub, who was a champion non-enjoyer), but none more so than Harry Secombe, who was evidently born to enjoy. In one of his books of memoirs, Secombe remembers spending half the night at a Lyon's Corner House over a cup of coffee and a plate of beans on toast, doing daft voices with Michael Bentine; another time, sitting in a café in Golders Green with Spike Milligan and Norman Vaughan, he buttoned his army surplus duffel coat over his head for a gag, and came up for air after five minutes to discover that he was on his own.

According to some versions, Bentine introduced Secombe to Jimmy Grafton, and the three had an earnest conversation about current radio comedy - agreeing that it was corny and stilted. The next day, Bentine and Secombe returned, and resumed their chat with the man behind the bar - who didn't seem to recognise them. They were talking to Grafton's twin brother.

These days a comedian might plan his career, from A Levels to Perrier Award, with the use of flowcharts, business plans, and bank loans. *The Goon Show* came about as a result of a bunch of nutty boys palling up with a pub landlord. You must admit, it's more romantic.

The Goons existed long before the radio series that carried their name. *The Goon Show* was simply an extension of the Goons. Throughout the story of the show, it's worth keeping in mind that these lads didn't act the Goons - they were the Goons. From the time they assembled in the Grafton Arms until the days of their deaths, they looked, sounded, behaved, thought and lived like Goons. This was the show's greatest strength, and its most serious flaw.

Only In The Mating Season: The Personnel

Terence 'Spike' Milligan was born in India, where his Irish father was a sergeant major in the Indian Army (which was, of course, British). He was educated at convent schools, and grew up observing the 'colonial type' at close quarters; seeing his father have to kowtow to every idiot with a posh voice. He came to Britain in 1934; his father was a keen amateur entertainer in army shows, and Spike's great interest was music. He played in dance bands, before joining the Royal Artillery at the start of the war.

Milligan first met Secombe in north Africa. They met again in a convalescent hospital; Milligan had been severely injured in Italy ('Blown up at Monte Cassino - came down again unaided'). Unsuited for further combat, they ended up in the Central Pool of Artists; Secombe as a comic, Milligan as a musician who got a taste for comedy by clowning between the numbers.

Spike's post-demob career was not going terribly well when he arrived at Grafton's; Secombe, and his friend Peter Sellers, were doing somewhat better. Grafton - who was writing for eminent comedian Derek Roy - rented Milligan a room in the pub attic, and asked him if he'd like to collaborate on some scripts. Milligan immediately became a prolific writer of gags based on loony ideas and inversions of logic - a sort of verbal version of the silent films he'd grown up on in India. Together, landlord and tenant wrote for Roy, Sellers, Bill Kerr, and Secombe, among others.

Milligan's foremost Goon character was Eccles - based largely on Walt Disney's Goofy. Eccles was the original, archetypal Goon, possessed of a single brain cell and a slow, idiotic voice. He would sometimes display an idiot's cunning, and always a unique view of logic. Eccles was simple and happy. And an idiot.

As an unnamed idiot, he first appeared on the air, played by Milligan, in *Hip-Hip-Hoo-Roy* (1949). The Eccles voice was used in *Crazy People*, but not named until show eight; although in show seven, a different character named Eccles had one line, played by Sellers. Grafton, and others, have argued that Eccles and Spike were more or less interchangeable - the happy idiot being the alter ego of the tortured genius.

Eccles's best bits of dialogue were usually opposite Sellers's Bluebottle; the two were great friends, although Bluebottle was always telling him to 'Shut up Eccles!' Eccles was such a friendly idiot that he would often reply 'Shut up Eccles!'

Count Jim Moriarty was usually played by Milligan, though Sellers took over for most of series three, when Milligan was off sick. Originally a master criminal - as in Sherlock Holmes's greatest enemy - as the series proceeded, Moriarty declined to the status of Grytpype-Thynne's sidekick in villainy (and, as Milligan later made clear, partner in life). He was given to going 'Owwwww' or 'Sapristi!'

Another of Milligan's regulars, Minnie Bannister, was the wife - so she said - of Henry Crun. Extremely elderly, and somewhat forgetful, she was once the toast of the Indian Army, and seems to have had a romantic liaison in the distant past with Bloodnok. Addicted to modern, sinful, rhythm-type music, to alcohol and to 'whoopee pills,' she lived in constant fear of molestation - and took all due precautions against it not happening.

Peter Sellers was born into a showbiz family, and started as a drummer and a mimic, before spending most of the war entertaining troops in ENSA and the RAF Gang Show. After demobilisation, he became a comic at the Windmill, where Secombe was also working; he already knew Bentine from the Gang Shows.

It was obvious to everyone that Sellers was an unusually gifted mimic. Many people have spoken of the almost occult way in which he would appear to physically change as he changed character. Secombe's memoirs recall how, during recordings, Sellers would 'Shrink himself for Bluebottle and then seconds later, puff himself out for Bloodnok. It was almost frightening to see it happen.' He goes on to say that when Sellers was asked to do his 'natural' voice he would panic: 'I can't, lads. I don't know what I sound like.'

This has become, in our age when everyone on earth is a fully unqualified psychoanalyst, the universal view of Sellers - that he suffered from some kind of personality disorder that meant that he himself did not really exist, except when taking on roles. There may be something to this; I would only point that out it sounds to me like an extreme form of the condition known to medical science as 'Being an Actor.'

I doubt if anyone has ever played as many characters in a single programme as voice king Sellers did in *The Goon Show*. I won't list them all, or you'll miss your last bus, but they included:

Hercules Grytpype-Thynne. A plausible conman. Posh and educated, his voice was based on that of the actor George Sanders - who generally played suave cads. His attempts to swindle good Ned ('You silly, twisted boy') often formed the basis of the plot. Became a major character during series four.

Major Dennis Bloodnok. Retired from the Indian Army - though 'retired' might be something of a euphemism. Above all else, Bloodnok devoted his life to the cause of cowardice. Despite this, he'd do almost anything, no matter how dangerous, if there was money in it - someone else's money. Suffered dreadfully, and noisily, from digestive problems ('No more curried eggs for me!'). Bloodnok was supposedly modelled on an officer Sellers met during his service in India - but must also, surely, have been the kind of reprehensible creature Milligan came to loath during his Indian childhood.

Henry Crun. An extremely elderly, rather forgetful inventor ('You can't get the wood, you know'), married - so he said - to Min Bannister.

William Cobblers, aka Mate. Developed from a Kenneth Connor character in *Ray's A Laugh* (1949-61), Willium was an elderly, mournful cockney who called everyone 'mate.' Something of a jobsworth, he was sometimes chronically unemployed and sometimes a policeman. And sometimes both.

Bluebottle. Inspired by a large scoutmaster with a bizarre, high-pitched voice, whom Bentine sicced onto Sellers (there are a couple of Internet sites which claim to feature the original 'bottle - but for all I know he might have a brother-in-law who's a libel lawyer, so I won't mention his name here. Worth a quick Google if you're in the mood, though). 'Blune

Bottle' was a schoolboy from Finchley, though in his own mind he was a cardboard cut-out licorice and string hero. Sadly, he tended to die in each episode, which he deeply resented: 'You dirty rotten swine you, you have deaded me! I do not like this game.' He took quite a while to develop into a full character, but eventually became hugely popular with the audience - and with amateur impressionists throughout the Anglophone world.

Michael Bentine was born in Watford to posh Peruvian parents; he was educated at Eton, and did his war service in the RAF. He's described by Grafton as a man of considerable learning who was given to wild invention - it wasn't always easy to tell which of his stories were true. His stage acts were also highly inventive and often fabulously complex. In early episodes, Bentine - the noisiest and most obviously creative of the Goons - played Captain (or sometimes Professor) Osric Pureheart, a mad inventor and adventurer.

Harry Secombe, born in Swansea, worked as a tea boy in a steelworks before the war. In peacetime, touring in variety, he had a comedy act which involved shaving (it was funnier than it sounds, apparently; but then, it would have to be) and comedy singing impressions. He often told of how he was once 'paid off' (i.e., sacked) at the Grand Theatre, Bolton, by a manager who told him 'You'll not shave on my bloody time.'

Everyone who's ever commented on Secombe in public, and in private as far as I know, regards him as rather shy, unusually kind and generous, and irrepressibly - even involuntarily - funny. Even in solemn situations people found it almost impossible to look at him without giggling. He was sharing lodgings with Milligan after the war, and it's likely that he was responsible for introducing Spike to his fellow Windmill worker, Bentine. He met Sellers doing a broadcast for BBC producer Pat Dixon.

Secombe played the protagonist of *The Goon Show* - Neddy Seagoon. Ned of Wales was yet another idiot, but of a more heroic type; a 'true blue British hero and idiot,' in fact. A large fellow - 'a danger to shipping,' even - given to making explosive noises, he was gullible to an almost criminal degree. His catchphrases included 'By Jove, I needed that!' (which is also associated with Ken Dodd); 'Have a gorilla,' (to which the reply would be 'No thanks, I only smoke baboons'), 'Hello folks!' (also claimed by Handley, Askey and Eric Morecambe), and above all: 'What what what what?'

Such was the audience's identification with and passion for the show that almost anything said on air more than once was in danger of becoming a catchphrase. Half the country talked in Goon in the 1950s, and well into the 1980s it was not unusual to hear young people in pubs or work-places greeting each other as 'My Capitaine.' 'And there's more where that came from' is still in everyday use - even if most people couldn't tell you where it came from.

In 1950, Grafton reckoned it was time for the Goons to approach the BBC. He got an old army comrade, BBC announcer Andrew Timothy, to link a demo tape of a Grafton and Milligan script, *Seller's Castle*, which also featured Alfred Marks, Janet Brown, Peter Butterworth and Robert Moreton. The pilot show worked its way through the BBC hierarchy for a while, but never quite made it onto the air.

The Goons, however, had a champion at Broadcasting House; Pat Dixon, an established producer, had already worked with Sellers, Secombe and Bentine. Sellers was by now marked as a radio up-and-comer, through shows like *Variety Bandbox*, and he told Dixon that the three of them, plus a chap called Milligan, would like to do a show together.

Dixon persuaded BBC management to record another pilot, produced by Dennis Main Wilson, who drank at Grafton's with Tony Hancock - where he was known as Dennis Main Drain, for beverage-related reasons. Another friend of Hancock's - ex-commando Larry Stephens - wrote, with Milligan and Grafton, something they called *The Goon Show*. Daft name, said the BBC; let's call it something sensible like... *Crazy People*.

Grafton ensured plenty of pre-publicity for the show, with newspaper articles explaining that anyone who liked the Goons automatically became an 'associate Goon, honorary Goon or Goon follower,' depending on the depth of their fanhood. For all its fame, *The Goon Show* never achieved the giant listening figures of shows designed with a broader appeal; this was a cult series from the word go. Or possibly the word 'owwww.'

Series One

17 episodes, from 28th May 1951 to 20th September 1951. Written by Milligan and Stephens, edited by Grafton. Produced by Dennis Main Wilson (Leslie Bridgmont produced four episodes).

A version of the pantomime *Cinderella* was broadcast on Boxing Day, with Lizbeth Webb as Cinderella and Graham Stark as Prince Charming.

The original aim of the Goons was simply to be as silly as possible after all those very sober years; early shows mostly consisted of gags and short sketches. From the start, Milligan was the main writer. Bentine gave lots of ideas, but the pace and manner of his humour didn't marry easily with Milligan's. Spike didn't perform much in the early shows; he didn't think he could compete with the others, who were far more experienced.

The first series was rather tentative, somewhat self-indulgent, and of variable quality. Some familiar characters emerged early on, but *Crazy People* wasn't yet *The Goon Show*. Secombe had not yet become Seagoon; he was still playing Secombe. However, critical reaction was favourable and listening figures respectable.

Over the years, some scripts or parts of scripts were reworked and reused - sometimes more than once - in subsequent shows. It's hard to imagine modern writers getting away with such fuel efficiency.

Series Two

25 episodes, from 22nd January 1952 to 15th July 1952. All credits as before. Programme billed as *The Goon Show* from now on.

In the second series, the number of sketches per show diminished, but it wasn't until the fourth series that one long story became the usual format.

Episode 8 was *Her* - a spoof of Rider Haggard's *She* - the first of the regular shows to consist of one storyline throughout. There was no show on 12th February, as King George VI chose to ruin everybody's fun by dying.

25 episodes, from 11th November 1952 to 5th May 1953. Produced by Peter Eton (Charles Chilton produced two episodes). A forty-minute Coronation special went out on 3rd June, with Stark. Episode 7 was the 45-minute Boxing Day panto, *Robin Hood*, with Dick Emery and Carole Carr. Other guest stars in this series were Valentine Dyall, and Ellis Powell (in an *Archers* spoof; she was then playing Mrs Dale in *Mrs Dale's Diary*).

Episodes now had three sketches, and this is the first series known to Goonologists by the title of the meatiest sketch (though the shows would not have been announced by title), such as number 19, *Where Do Socks Come From?*

Number 5, *The Expedition For Toothpaste,* is a single-story show; it's believed to have been written by Grafton alone, as Stephens and Milligan were absent that week.

This series was the turning point. Bentine left at the end of series two - it was clear that he and Milligan could not collaborate in harmony - obliging Milligan to take on more of the acting. There was no great falling-out, despite speculation at the time and since; Bentine even made a guest appearance in series four. He left because he believed his solo career was about to take off; because he felt three-man comedy teams worked better than quartets; and because he was, by nature, a comedic loner. All the evidence suggests that all the Goons remained on friendly terms for the rest of their lives.

Meanwhile, Peter Eton took over as producer. He'd been a commercial artist before the war, but - when invalided out of the Royal Navy - joined the BBC. He worked as a drama producer before moving to Variety. He provided the professional discipline which the Goons needed (just as Stephens and Grafton had managed to impose ideas of structure and accessibility on Milligan's chaotic comedy). Eton instituted proper procedures for rehearsal, and cajoled the Goons into approaching the show as if it were a radio programme being broadcast to the nation - not merely a bunch of demobbed mates having fun and corpsing at in-jokes. He also had more technical know-how from his drama days than the rest of them put together and doubled. Here was a producer who could get the inmates of Planet Goon working together, and to a deadline, and as a reward he could translate their ideas into broadcastable form. If you're going to do anarchic, rule-smashing comedy, the first thing you've got to have is iron discipline and a solid adherence to rules. As someone once said, 'A revolutionary must always have clean fingernails.' For all Main Wilson's enthusiasm and supportiveness, it was Eton - himself a keen experimentalist - who managed to bring the Goons under control so as to properly channel their talents.

(It is from Eton, incidentally, that we get the story that the Goons' famous 'raspberry' FX, known as Fred the Oyster, was actually a recording of donkeys farting, slowed down and then speeded up. The tape, that is, not the donkeys.)

In early December, Milligan was admitted to hospital - the first of his 'nervous breakdowns,' as they were then called. The stress of work, and having never recovered from his war injuries, are generally given as the causes. Milligan was a man whose nerve endings, for good and ill, were nearer the surface than most people's. His workload was immense, and relentless; he later said that he habitually wrote from 8am till midnight, and that he 'gave his sanity' for the show. He always blamed *The Goon Show* for the collapse of his first marriage and the poor health he suffered ever after. The show was torture for Milligan, but Sellers and Secombe, in countless interviews, recalled Sundays at the Camden Theatre as the happiest hours of their lives.

Spike wrote some material from his hospital bed, but the next 12 episodes were largely written by Grafton and Stephens. Sellers took over Milligan's voices - seamlessly, like the mimicry equivalent of an invisible mender - and Dick Emery and Graham Stark filled in.

Series Four

30 episodes, from 2nd October 1953 to 19th April 1954. Written by Milligan and Stephens (one episode by Stephens alone, and the last ten by Milligan alone). Produced by Peter Eton (Jacques Brown produced one episode).

Between this series and the next, there were two specials. In June, *Educating Archie* and *The Goon Show* joined up for *Archie In Goonland*, written by Milligan and Eric Sykes and produced by Roy Speer: 'Peter Brough and Archie Andrews enter Goonland via a mousehole,' as *Radio Times* put it. Then in August came *The Starlings*, which was, in production methods and its lack of studio audience or musicians, closer to a radio play than a normal *Goon Show*. In it, Peter Sellers imitated the Queen, which didn't go down well with management; he was eventually stopped from doing impressions of high-ups, after an allegedly disrespectful take off of Sir Winston Churchill, the celebrated war leader and ingester of liquids.

Wallace Greenslade replaced Andrew Timothy as announcer during this series (Timothy leaving, he claimed, because he feared for his sanity); the classic line-up was now in place. Stephens left due to illness, and Grafton left because Spike no longer needed an editor.

The transformation of the show was complete: at Eton's urging, almost all episodes from about halfway through this series consisted of one story.

The characters were in place now, fully fledged - and it's clear that they were very real to the performers; not merely funny voices telling jokes. From this series on, characters were represented in the script by their own names, not by those of the actor. The main parts in each week's story were 'played' by regular characters, rather than directly by the actors. This adds another level of disconcerting fantasy - with characters 'meeting' each other for the first time, again and again. To quote the announcer, 'It's all rather confusing, really.'

The show was now recorded on magnetic tape instead of acetate discs, which meant extensive editing was possible - at last, Milligan and Eton had the tools to make the kind of programme they'd been dreaming of.

Series Five

26 episodes, from 28th September 1954 to 22nd March 1955. Written by Milligan and Sykes (Milligan wrote the first six alone). Guest stars were Dyall, Charlotte Mitchell, and senior announcer John Snagge.

The *Archie* crossover had one good result: the arrival of talented and versatile scriptwriter Eric Sykes. In a recent *Radio Times* interview, Sykes says that he used to write in Milligan's style: 'It's like that old painter, Michelangelo. He didn't paint all of his pictures. His pupils did the choirboys.' He also recalls that when the two of them argued over 'something silly,' he could tell that Spike was getting angry because a rash appeared on his chest. (Rowing over a single word is something all writing teams do occasionally, even if they otherwise live for decades as beloved brothers.)

This series featured the first of what became the best-known episodes, later released on record - for instance, *The Whistling Spy Enigma* and *The Dreaded Batter-Pudding Hurler (Of Bexhill-on-Sea)*. One show, *1985*, an Orwell spoof, was so popular that it was repeated - that is, it was given a second performance, not a second playing of the tape.

From this series onwards, the programme was broadcast by the Transcription Service to various countries, including Australasia and South Africa. BBC radio comedy continues to have a considerable following throughout the English speaking world; the Internet is stiff with American Goons.

Series Six

27 episodes, from 20th September 1955 to 3rd April 1956. Written by Milligan (Milligan and Sykes wrote three, and Milligan and Stephens wrote three). Produced by Peter Eton (Pat Dixon produced the last six). Guests stars were Snagge, Mitchell and Dyall.

Due to a Musicians' Union strike, Spike covered the interval in two shows by singing *I'm Walking Backwards For Christmas*. The first British-made hit record to have the word 'rock' in its title was The Goons' *Bloodnok's Rock'n'Roll Call*, backed with *Ying Tong Song*, which made number eight in the hit parade in September 1956. *I'm Walking Backwards For Christmas* b/w *Bluebottle Blues* got to number five in July 1956; an August 1973 re-release of *Ying Tong Song* only reached number 11 - but then, that was a bloody good summer for pop songs.

Eton left, to work for independent television; Dixon, who had been involved in the events leading up to *Crazy People*, took over.

Highlights of this series included *Napoleon's Piano* and *Foiled by President Fred*.

Series Seven

25 episodes, from 4th October 1956 to 28th March 1957. Written by Milligan and Stephens (Milligan wrote two alone). Produced by Pat Dixon (first two by Peter Eton). Guest stars were Dyall, George Chisholm, Bernard Miles, and Jack Train as Colonel Chinstrap (from *ITMA*), getting drunk with his descendent, Bloodnok. A *Starlings*-style special, *The Reason Why* - about bringing Cleopatra's Needle to London - was broadcast in August.

This series included such classics as *Insurance, The White Man's Burden* and *Wings Over Dagenham*.

Series Eight

26 episodes, from 30th September 1957 to 24th March 1958. Written by Milligan and Stephens; Milligan; Stephens; Milligan and John Antrobus; Stephens & Maurice Wiltshire. Produced by Charles Chilton (Roy Speer produced nine, and Tom Ronald two). Guest stars: Emery, Cecile Chevreau, Chisholm, Snagge, A.E. Matthews.

The quality, and the audience figures, began to drop during this series. Milligan was again under tremendous pressure; along with the series itself, there were fourteen *Vintage Goons* - based on earlier scripts - recorded for the Transcription Service on the same dates as the Home Service recordings. Although many of the best-remembered episodes were still to come, overall the show had peaked.

Series Nine

17 episodes, from 3rd November 1958 to 23rd February 1959. Written by Milligan (Stephens and Wiltshire wrote one). Produced by John Browell. Guest stars: Snagge, Dyall, Stark, Train, Timothy, Chisholm, Kenneth Connor.

Producers had come and gone lately, until at last John Browell - who'd been a studio manager in the show's early days - took over. *I Was Monty's Treble* and *Ned's Atomic Dustbin* went out in this series.

Series Ten

Six episodes, from 24th December 1959 to 28th January 1960. Written by Milligan. Guest stars: Snagge, Dyall.

Series nine had been intended as the last; Milligan wanted to go out at the top, as he could see signs that the show couldn't go for much longer without falling apart. *The Goon Show* was returning to the chaos from which it had emerged. But audience reaction - including a petition and a demo by students from Regent Street Polytechnic - persuaded all concerned that there should be a brief, *final* final series. The last episode was not a particularly good one: *The Last Smoking Seagoon*.

There was talk for some time after of a revival (Milligan wrote six more scripts, which were never recorded, and are said to be entirely surreal and rather dark) but luckily, for once, the irresistible urge to continue flogging horses which are not only dead but have long since been cremated was resisted. It seems clear that if the show had continued it would have become more and more frantic, undisciplined, erratic; the audience would gradually have deserted, fed up with the noise of a bunch of complacent stars laughing at their own jokes. There would have been brilliant moments, no doubt - how could there fail to be? - but at great cost, I can't help feeling, to the legacy of 'radio's own crazy gang.'

There was one reunion. In April 1972, to celebrate the BBC's jubilee, Sellers, Milligan and Secombe, and the musicians Max Geldray and Ray Ellington, recorded, amid great press interest, *The Last Goon Show Of All*, written by Milligan and produced by Browell. It was broadcast on Radio 4 in October, on BBC 1 television at Christmas, and was released as an LP. It wasn't a great show, but it was a good one - and helped bring the Goons to the attention of a new generation. In 2001, Radio 2 marked *The Goon Show*'s 50th anniversary by broadcasting a Goon Night, including a recreation of a lost series three episode performed by Andrew Secombe as his father, Christopher Timothy (famous for playing James Herriott on TV) as his father, Jon Glover as Milligan, Jeffrey Holland as Sellers, and Ray Ellington's son, Lance, providing the music. The producer was Dirk Maggs.

A Time Of Hysteria And Brandy: The End.

At its height, *The Goon Show* was a very funny drama - not just a variety show performed in front of microphones. In some ways it was an *old*-fashioned show; it was close to being a khaki comedy, made by natural civilians who had spent some of their formative years in uniform, and who were now reacting against the absurdities and horrors of service life with irritation, fury, bafflement, delight and even nostalgia. Its thematic roots lie in the pre-*TIFH* age; it wasn't really part of the new comedy revolution. Nonetheless, the show was undeniably groundbreaking, and influential on society at large, and was recognised as such at the time and ever since. I suspect this is largely for the social reasons I've discussed earlier, and because the programme *sounded* so different from everything else. Plenty of radio comics had mocked staidness and humbuggery, but none had ever done it quite so explosively.

Milligan - still relatively new to writing, and to radio - was learning his trade while creating what turned out to be his masterpiece. The programme was painstakingly put together; as with *Round The Horne* in the next decade, there are far fewer adlibs than the listener might think - there is a special skill in writing and performing a line to make it sound as if it's adlibbed, when actually it's part of the script.

As chief writer, Milligan had to fight all the way to get his vision on air. Factions within BBC management were always unhappy with the show. There were frequent attempts at censorship, to which the Goons reacted, predictably, by sneaking in as many forbidden gags as they could. The character Hugh Jampton was not, as they claimed at the time, named in honour of a friend of theirs, but for the rhyming slang expression 'Hampton Wick.'

The Goons enjoyed the protection of a fan club within the BBC establishment, led by senior announcer John Snagge. Unlike the elderly gents who were always trying to take the Goons off the air, some at BH clearly felt that they hadn't fought a war to defend pomposity and censorship.

In later years, Milligan often complained in interviews that his desire to be constantly experimental - a comedic ideology of permanent revolution - was not popular with his bosses. He remembered endless rows, petty and great, with 'part-time Hitlers,' and on the face of it, the BBC in the 1950s (modelled on the Admiralty, via the Civil Service) sounds like the epitome of an organisation that Spike couldn't work with. Ah, but let's not forget: the BBC in the 1950s was in fact the organisation that gave us the Goons, took all the flak, and didn't back down.

The Goon Show was also innovative - though not, in the long run, particularly influential - in its use of music and sound effects, both of which became integral parts of the overall Goonery. There were a lot of musicians involved in the show, during its run: harmonica player Max Geldray, the Ray Ellington Quartet, vocal group The Stargazers, various BBC orchestras, and conductor Wally Stott, who wrote suitably Goonish links. Geldray and Ellington, in particular, could be considered members of the cast.

No series before - and, arguably with the exception of *Hitchhiker's Guide*, none since - employed FX so imaginatively. Milligan was not impressed by the state of the art as he found it at the BBC; by the time he'd finished rummaging in the effects man's cupboard, he had virtually created a new sound language.

Other series had made good use of FX, but Milligan used them without inhibition, without pre-defined limits. The FX were almost another cast member, not just there to fill in the gaps caused by the lack of pictures. With his amazingly detailed requirements written into the scripts, Milligan was never going to be satisfied with a pair of coconut hooves or a pile of tin cans. Secombe has written of the time when a script called for the effect of someone being hit in the face by a sock full of custard. Unable to fake the sound, Milligan asked a BBC dinner lady if she'd make him an egg custard. She must have wondered why she bothered when Milligan turned up to collect the delicacy - and, before her eyes, removed one of his socks and poured the custard into it.

Television is only now beginning to reach a technological level where it's able to compete credibly with radio in the FX department - which is one reason why the TV puppet series *The Telegoons* (1963-4) is of only marginal interest to hardcore Goonists.

In an interview with Philip Oakes, in *Books And Art* (December 1957), Milligan said of the Goons: 'Essentially it is a critical comedy. It is against bureaucracy and on the side of human beings. Its starting point is one man shouting gibberish in the face of authority, and proving by fabricated insanity that nothing could be as mad as what passes for ordinary living.'

People say different things at different times to different audiences. In interviews during the show's run, for instance, Secombe stuck to the line that he and his comrades were just a bunch of loons having a laugh. Later, in autobiographical mode, he remembered the Goons as being comic anarchists, eager to overthrow comedy's established order. It's normal for comedians and humorists to refuse to intellectualise about comedy while they're doing it (though there have been some well-known exceptions, such as Ken Dodd, Douglas Adams, and Tony Hancock), but they often change their minds in their later, more restful years, perhaps fed up with having every clever-dick in the world telling them what they were all about.

Critics are not so hampered, and from the start, they saluted *The Goon Show* as intellectual comedy for ordinary people. In the age of *Friends*, *The Weakest Link* and *Comic Relief* this seems heretical, but there really was a time when popular entertainers, politicians and even journalists believed that if you fed a human brain it would grow.

Because making other people laugh is such a powerful and enviable ability, the term 'genius' is splashed about with abandon by comedy fans. But 'genius' should mean more than just 'unusually good'; it should be reserved for those who do something new, who alter the field in which they work. When discussing Spike Milligan, it's impossible to avoid the word.

The archetypal Goon joke - because it's fast, sharp, hilarious, and it turns you upside down so that you don't know whether to laugh or gasp -

comes in an early episode, in which Sir Isaac Newton is trying to explain gravity to Eccles. 'There - you jumped in the air, but you came back down to earth again. Now, why?' Eccles replies: 'Because I live there.'

Let's face it, there are only two ways of coming up with a joke like that: either be a genius and invent it, or else nick a time machine and go back and patent the joke the day before the genius that invented it invents it.

For all that, the more you look into the matter, the more nonsensical becomes the idea that *The Goon Show* was, creatively, a one-man show; Milligan the genius behind it all, Secombe the loveable straight man (or as near a straight man as you'd get in the Goons), Sellers the brilliant impressionist, and Bentine the irrelevant extra wheel who didn't last long. By all accounts, including Milligan's, the show came about, succeeded and lasted because of the personal and professional chemistry between the cast, the writers, and the production teams. And, of course, because of that pub in Victoria.

One of Peter Eton's most delightful anecdotes tells of how he had to edit out a four-minute laugh from the 1955 episode *The Terrible Revenge Of Fred Fu-Manchu*, which occurred when the cast physically acted out a scene in which Henry, Min and Ned kept locking themselves out of a house. Eton was asked by Ben Lyon, editing at a neighbouring bench, what he was doing, and he replied 'Throwing away laughter.' Lyon said 'We're short of laughter this week, give it to me,' and he spliced it into *Life With The Lyons*. That's the point about *The Goon Show*, I suppose, in the end - it isn't the Goons who are surreal; it's the world.

Chapter Four: Hancock's Half Hour

Rinky Tinky On Purple Grass: The Beginning

When Dennis Main Wilson began planning his new radio show, he knew exactly what he wanted. He wanted Tony Hancock at the centre of it, written for by Ray Galton and Alan Simpson, supported by a strong cast of comedians behaving like actors. What he didn't want was jokes, catchphrases, silly voices, or anything which reeked of variety, or sounded in any way pre-war. He didn't want a comedians' show disguised as a sitcom, like *Life With The Lyons*, or a domestic cosy like *A Life Of Bliss*, or an anarchistic carnival of madness loosely draped across a crazy story, like you-know-who.

He wanted something really new, and really modern. There was to be nothing contrived about it; it was to be as close to real life as comedy could get. Realism was absurd enough on its own; who needed surrealism? Instead of using radio to the full as a technical medium, like the Goons, this would be radio in which the word - precisely written, perfectly delivered - would be everything. The half hour shows would have proper plots, which would be real, truthful, *recognisable* to the audience.

This was what Main Wilson wanted, and he knew it was also what Galton and Simpson wanted, and what Hancock wanted. And you know what? They bloody nearly got it, too.

We Are Not Layabouts - We Are Artists, Mush: The Personnel

Anthony John Hancock was born on 12th May 1924 in Birmingham, to what would have been an impeccably middle-class family if it hadn't been for the eccentricities of Tony's father, Jack. He and his wife, Lily, shared a love of laughter - especially that triggered by absurdity - and he performed comedy turns at Masonic dos and the like. Jack was an office manager by profession, but showbusiness was his real interest, and in 1923 'Jack Hancock (Humorist)' made the first of several broadcasts on the BBC.

The family moved to Bournemouth when Tony was very young, and took over the Railway Hotel, which was popular with show folk appearing in the seaside resort. They made a success of it, and it became widely known throughout the profession.

George Fairweather was a post office worker and semi-pro entertainer. He became friendly with Jack, who he considered a gifted comic; a natural. However, it was Fairweather who eventually turned pro, thanks to Jack Hancock.

Tony grew up in a family where showbusiness - and particularly comedy - was the highest imaginable calling; certainly far more important than lesser matters such as business, money, or family life. Even cancer couldn't stop Jack entertaining his showbiz pals in the bar of the Railway - that is, until it *did* stop him. He died in 1935, aged 47.

Tony was away at boarding school, where he excelled at cricket, and at writing and performing comedy sketches for his classmates, but at little else. In childhood, he showed no particular talent for any branch of the performing arts, but from a very young age he intended to go on the stage.

He left school as soon as he could, at 15, having decided to be a comic. He had already a humorist's view of the world; that much was obvious to all who knew him. He took a course at secretarial college, and serially failed at a few jobs, ending up as a civil servant. His first engagement as a comedian was shortly before his sixteenth birthday, at a smoking concert in a Bournemouth Labour Hall. He had decided on the persona of a 'confidential comic,' dressed like Max Miller, telling blue jokes. It seems likely that the incongruity of mucky stories being told by a thin, painfully shy kid was a lot funnier than the material itself.

His mother asked Fairweather to help, and George tried to persuade Hancock to drop his blue act - which he did, but only after causing a mass walkout at a church hall concert presided over by a Catholic priest. He ditched the smutty gags, and religiously eschewed dirty jokes, or any kind of 'vulgar' humour, for the rest of his life. Through Fairweather's connections, in 1941, 'Tony J. Hancock' made his first radio broadcast, aged 17; a monologue which the two of them wrote. It was not the start of a thrilling career.

Hancock was the middle of three brothers; the eldest, Colin, had been called up for the RAF and in 1942 was reported missing, presumed dead, over the Atlantic; his body was never found. A week later, Tony's own call-up arrived and he reported to RAF Locking, near Weston-super-Mare in Somerset. On the journey there he met another conscript, Slim Miller, who also yearned to be a stand-up comic. Not much use to the war effort as airmen, Miller and Hancock soon became established as entertainers in a comedy double act.

Posted to Bournemouth with Miller after basic training, Hancock, at Fairweather's suggestion, began to develop an act he went on using on stage for the rest of his life - spoofing an amateur impressionist. He was still doing the same impressions two decades later, when the number of people in the audience who knew who he was taking off was rapidly dwindling.

Hancock ended the war as part of Ralph Reader's Gang Show, where he made many friendships and professional associations that would feature throughout his career. It was in the Gang Show that he began to cultivate his pompous, hang-dog persona.

Demobbed, he moved to London, and began the search for an agent, alongside a city full of young men who'd had a taste of the stage in the services, and vowed not to return to ordinary jobs in civilian life. Hancock endured months of unemployment and near poverty, before winning a place in a Ralph Reader variety tour. He got his first properly civilian professional job in a pantomime in Oxford in 1947, where he did well.

It was at this time that Hancock become enamoured of another Birmingham-born comic, Sid Field (1904-50), the last notable performer to emerge from music hall, who had become a West End comedy star. Something about the alcoholic comedian's style appealed enormously to Hancock, who from then on held him up as his model.

The BBC had promised to give auditions to any returning serviceman or woman who asked for one. In charge of sifting the rubbish for the odd sparkling gem was Dennis Main Wilson. He also used to spot talent at the Nuffield Centre, a servicemen's club where any ex-service person could get a try-out - a rather brutal system of instant comic justice, somewhat similar to that employed at the Comedy Store thirty years later. The Nuffield also provided its acts with free grub. Peter Sellers, Harry Secombe, Michael Bentine, Derek Roy, and Jimmy Edwards were all Nuffield graduates. Main Wilson saw Hancock's act there, but thought of him as a face comic, unsuited to radio.

Unemployed again, in 1948 Hancock auditioned for the Windmill, with Derek Scott, an ex-RAF pianist. Although not a place to get laughs, the Windmill was frequented by agents looking out for new clients to feed the post-war comedy boom. Most of the comedians who would dominate light entertainment for the next couple of decades passed through the Windmill's grinder at some stage. Hancock and Scott caught the eye of an agent, Phyllis Rounce.

In September 1948, Hancock and Scott were invited to audition for television. Most agents still refused to handle TV work, or clients who worked on TV, as it was a minor, London-based service seen as a threat to the theatres which made up the main part of their business. Rounce was different - she believed comedy had a big future on the small screen. On that basis, Hancock and his partner signed with her agency. They made their first TV appearance in November 1948. Of course, there was no real money to be made in television, but luckily Tony got a part as an ugly sister in panto in Brighton, part of a cast which included writer and comedian Barry Took.

He wasn't getting as much work as he deserved, however, partly because severe stage fright often robbed him of potential breakthrough jobs. But Rounce believed in her young client, and worked hard on his behalf. She teamed him up with writer Larry Stephens, who shared Hancock's sideways view of humanity, and his commitment to a new, alternative comedy, liberated from the tired gag-spewing of variety. Stephens and Hancock became flatmates and partners.

By 1950, things were starting to happen for Hancock, and in 1951 he got a job on *Happy-Go-Lucky*, playing a scoutmaster in an ongoing sketch called *The Eager Beavers*. His troop included his old Gang Show friend Graham Stark, and Australian comic Bill Kerr. At the same time Hancock was in *Educating Archie*, a show which ran from 1950-59, whose star was a ventriloquist's doll (the vent was Peter Brough), and which is remembered for its record of turning unknowns into stars. One of its writers was Eric Sykes, and Hattie Jacques was in the cast.

Happy-Go-Lucky was a flop. The producer left to have a nervous breakdown - so frequent a malady as to be almost the comedy equivalent of a footballer's groin strain - and Main Wilson was called in to cover for him. He'd seen a couple of likely-looking scripters hanging about the place, and asked them how they fancied writing the rest of the series.

Ray Galton and Alan Simpson had met in 1948, when they were both busy dying of tuberculosis at an isolation hospital in Surrey. A fellow patient (Tony Wallis, unwitting midwife of destiny, innit?) was an enthusiastic radio amateur, and G&S became keen writers and performers of comedy sketches on the sanatorium's own radio 'station'. They were inspired by *TIFH*, and by American sitcoms such as *The Jack Benny Show*. The sanatorium was their equivalent of the forces; they met all kinds of different people, got an education of sorts, broadened their horizons.

Against predictions (and probably regulations), they survived TB, and were eventually discharged. They kept in touch, but didn't really think about writing any more until Simpson was asked to write something for a church concert. They started writing together again, just for fun at first, with every line agreed and perfected between them before Simpson wrote it down. One sketch they were particularly happy with they sent into the BBC, which earned them a meeting with a producer. Making no promises, he encouraged them to keep going and said he'd show their sketch - a *TIFH*-style film skit - to other producers. This led to them being commissioned to provide gags for Derek Roy for his first star vehicle, *Happy-Go-Lucky*, at five shillings per joke used. Under Main Wilson's new regime, they quickly abandoned gags and one-liners, going for more developed sketches.

The first words exchanged between Hancock and G&S have become a comedy legend, and for once all parties seem to agree on what happened. After a recording, Hancock saw G&S and asked them if they had written a particular sketch in that night's show. They admitted it. 'Very funny,' said Hancock. And that was that. But a few weeks later he phoned 'the boys' (as all comedy scriptwriting pairs are known, to this day - unless they're girls), and asked them to do him some five-minute sketches for his variety work. Generously, he offered to pay them half his fee.

The boys were enthusiastic - Hancock was obviously on the way up, and already he had the beginnings of a style that they thought would be interesting to write for. For their part, they were establishing a reputation as good, reliable writers, selling routines to Bill Kerr and Dick Emery as well as Hancock.

Hancock hated being in *Archie*, not least because it was there that he acquired his first catchphrase - 'Flippin' kids' - which haunted him for years. He despised catchphrases, as being for comedians who couldn't manage on talent alone. Besides, always a superstitious man, he came to believe that Archie, the vent's schoolboy doll, was out to get him.

But *Archie* made him a star, gaining him attention in the press and within Broadcasting House. It also involved him working closely with Eric Sykes. The two became friends, and as Sykes got to know him better he began to develop a Hancock character based on the real Hancock's personality. This has always been fundamental to Sykes's approach to scriptwriting; you have to know the actor before you can write for the character (perhaps that's why, over the years, some of Eric Sykes's best writing has been performed by Eric Sykes). Like Hancock, he believed that comedy should put recognisable, consistent characters in situations which, though they might become absurd, are born in workaday frustrations and difficulties. The comedy should be allowed to grow, like a benevolent fungus - not be artificially fertilised by jokes and catchphrases.

G&S were called in to cover for Bob Monkhouse and Dennis Goodwin in 1952, as writers on *Calling All Forces*, again under Main Wilson; Hancock was co-starring with Charlie Chester. In retrospect - and to some extent, Main Wilson and G&S were aware of this at the time - Hancock's work on the show was a kind of dry run for the sitcom they were planning.

Everything in Hancock's career at this time seemed to be nudging him towards situation comedy. In June 1952, he pre-recorded a piece for a children's radio programme. It went very well, and it was suggested to him that he should think about doing a non-audience series. Hancock and Stephens - who had already discussed such ideas between themselves - were enthusiastic. A show recorded without a live audience would be pure radio, dependent entirely on the skills of its creators, and could, potentially, be a comedy of a quite different type - subtle, more sophisticated, with a more natural pace.

They were commissioned to write a pilot of *Welcome To Whelkham* - a situation series based on a pompous, ineffectual, life-like central character, interacting with a support cast of rogues - but the show never quite got through the BBC bureaucracy; most ideas didn't, even in those rather more 'creator-led' days.

Main Wilson continued to lobby the BBC in support of a Hancock sitcom. Management was not keen at first. No musical breaks? No catchphrases? Why would anyone listen to such a show? Nevertheless, Main Wilson finally won approval to start casting the new programme.

Galton and Simpson wanted a conman who would show up a particular aspect of the central character - that he was someone whose vanity and greed made him exceptionally gullible. They'd seen a cockney actor in a film who they thought was perfect. They couldn't remember his name, but they knew the picture - *The Lavender Hill Mob*. They went to see the film again and came out with the name of their ideal Hancock villain: Sidney James. He wasn't a cockney, it transpired, though he usually played one. Born into a showbusiness family in South Africa, he'd worked as a hairdresser, diamond cutter, singer and dancer and amateur boxer. He organised troop entertainments during the war, and arrived in Britain on Christmas Day 1946 in search of an acting career.

James and Hancock had in fact already worked together - in a largely unsatisfactory film, Hancock's first, called *Orders Are Orders* (1954), in which Sellers and Sykes also appeared. James was at first reluctant to join the new show; he was doing very well in films and on stage. He didn't consider himself a natural radio actor, and didn't want to take a wrong turn in his career. Eventually, he agreed to try one or two shows and see how it went.

The programme would also need a versatile character actor, to play all the policemen, bureaucrats, judges and assorted nuisances with whom Hancock would have his run-ins. Main Wilson searched in vain for such a man, until an agent advised him to see the actor playing the Dauphin in a West End production of George Bernard Shaw's *Saint Joan*. Kenneth Williams saw himself as an actor, not a comic; but everyone has to eat. He, too, signed up for Main Wilson's project. His gloriously idiosyncratic delivery immediately and fatally undermined the idea of a 'pure' comedy show, with no funny voices or catchphrases. It's hard to feel sorry for Wilson and G&S though - what on earth did they hire Williams for, if not for him to say 'No, stop messin' about!' and to switch, halfway through a line, from high-falutin' to his patent nasal whine known as 'snide'?

The part of Hancock's chief sidekick went to Bill Kerr - and not, as had been generally assumed, to Tony's dear friend and close associate, Graham Stark. Along with the agent, Phyllis Rounce, Stark was the first major casualty of Hancock's much documented habit of leaving his travelling companions lying in ditches along the roadside.

Kerr had arrived in the UK a few day after Sid James. Also born in South Africa, he'd grown up in Australia, in a theatrical family. In the early series of *Hancock's Half Hour*, Kerr was the second star of the show, a fast-talking patter-merchant who routinely outwitted Hancock - but eventually James and Hancock became something very close to a double act, with Kerr the dim-witted butt of their jokes.

One piece of conservatism that did survive into early series of the show was that the central character had to have a girlfriend. Hancock had worked on *Star Bill* with Moira Lister, yet another South African, who as a child star had worked with Sid James on South African radio. She proved a good choice for the (rather thankless) part, playing a strong character who could stand up to Hancock.

Another frequent cast member was Alan Simpson, who appeared in scores of the radio shows (and a few TV episodes) in small parts for which it wasn't worth getting in an extra actor. Ray Galton was in far fewer episodes, not sharing his partner's enjoyment of acting.

Now they just had to get the music right. The theme tune was composed by Wally Stott. It's a rather ironically cheerful tune, recorded by the BBC Revue Orchestra, but with the tuba sounding an appropriately pompous note. Incidentally, it wasn't written with Hancock in mind - the two men hadn't met - but was simply a piece Stott happened to have lying about.

Series One

16 episodes, from 2nd November 1954 to 15th February 1955.

The first *Hancock's Half Hour* was recorded on October 30th 1954, at the Camden Theatre. For the first time, Hancock gave his breathless, stammering introduction 'H-H-H-Hancock's Half Hour' - a stupid idea of Main Wilson's, he reckoned; far too gimmicky.

Hancock was a caricature of himself in the show; a comedian with a new radio series. (His voice in those early days was noticeably more high-pitched and posher - more actorish - than the half-cockney, half-genteel growl he eventually settled on.) The basic set-up was that Hancock, always trying to do everything on the cheap, would ask his pal, and fellow comic, Kerr for assistance. Kerr would say that his mate Sid would sort it out. 'Not him,' 'Tubs' would object. 'He's a swindler!' But Kerr would persuade him, James would take over, and all would end in disaster.

In other words, it was nothing like the new, gimmickless comedy envisaged. It included silly voices and way-out plots. Most of us, in such circumstances, would probably decide that close enough was good enough - but the perfectionist Hancock must have realised early on that *HHH* was never going to be precisely what he wanted.

Audience reaction to the first series was broadly favourable, though the listening figure was not high; listeners were glad to hear Hancock in his own show at last, but they weren't too impressed by the scripts. The series was picked up straight away by the Transcription Service for use overseas. It was good enough for the BBC, who unhesitatingly commissioned a second series.

12 episodes, from 19th April 1955 to 5th July 1955.

Moira Lister had left to have a baby, so Liverpool-born actress Andrée Melly, sister of the jazzman George Melly, was brought in to replace her, despite never having heard the show, or of its star. The script called for Hancock and Kerr to meet Melly in Paris - saddling her with a strong French accent. This was an uncharacteristically amateurish mistake by G&S and Main Wilson, and the accent gradually faded in subsequent shows.

Otherwise the cast at the start of series two was unchanged. Oh, except for one thing - no Hancock.

Already married, he was in love with his publicist, Freddie Ross, who later became his second wife. He was overworked. He was... well, he was Tony Hancock. For all the professional diagnosing and amateur psycho-analysing that's been done over the years, there's really only one thing that needs to be understood about what went on in that poor sod's head: he couldn't cope. He didn't cope very well with failure, and he certainly couldn't cope with success.

He wasn't the first, or the last, comic to 'go geographical' without warning during a theatrical run. Two days before recording started on the new series, Hancock walked off stage during the first house of his show at the Adelphi, mumbled an apology to co-star Jimmy Edwards, and caught a plane to Rome. He ended up in a pensione in Positano.

Main Wilson phoned Jimmy Grafton - by now Harry Secombe's agent - and it was agreed that Secombe could stand in on *HHH*, largely as a favour among old friends. Secombe has said that the script and supporting cast were so good that he couldn't fail in the part - but he is being, as usual, too modest. The truth is he took over a virtually unmodified script, performed it in his own, raspberry-laden style, and made a great success of it. He covered the next two episodes as well, growing in confidence in the part. If Hancock's career was now over - as seemed likely - the BBC began to think it didn't matter much, they'd found a permanent replacement: change the name of the series to *HHH-Harry's Half Hour*, and a funny-voiced Goon stands revealed as a talented comedy actor...

And then, during the recording of the third show, Hancock reappeared without a word to anyone. He thanked Secombe afterwards, and carried on from episode four as if nothing had happened.

Other than that, the series was settling down nicely, and now had the great boost of a Sunday afternoon repeat. (The first broadcast was at 9.30 on Tuesday evenings).

Series Three

20 episodes, from 19th October 1955 to 29th February 1956.

Guest stars - sportsmen, primarily, playing themselves - appeared in *HHH* from the third series; those episodes tend to be the least satisfactory to listen to now.

Sometimes, G&S admit, they wrote episodes with fantastical plots 'out of sheer desperation because we couldn't think of anything else.' However, by the end of series three, the show was firmly established as a popular success, and was moving towards the style that it's remembered for.

Off stage, James and Hancock were becoming great friends. Hancock and Williams, too, were friends - in as much as two such disturbed, prickly people could ever achieve intimacy. They shared a fascination for philosophy, though inevitably for Hancock it was more of a tortured obsession. Although a superstitious man, he believed that rational philosophy could, or at least should, provide answers to the ultimate questions - life, the universe and everything, to coin a phrase.

Series Four

20 episodes, from 14th October 1956 to 24th February 1957.

In the mid-1950s Hancock was at the peak of his powers. His first read-through of each week's script would be spot on - even though rehearsals made him vomit with nerves and self-doubt. In July 1956, *Hancock's Half Hour* began on television; it was an immediate success, smoothly bridging the radio days and the TV age. He could have gone onto TV earlier, but the money was better on radio; then commercial TV was launched in 1955, and the dosh doubled overnight.

Hancock claimed to find TV much easier to work in than radio, as he considered himself primarily a visual comic. (For the rest of his life he was obsessed with the self-destructive idea that only by becoming a film star could he become an international star). Tony Hancock was the first big star created by radio to become as big, if not bigger, on TV - the biggest, in fact, in both media. For a few, extraordinary years he was not only the king of comedy, he was Britain's best known, and best loved entertainer, with series running on BBC TV and radio, and ITV. (His ITV writers included Sykes and Stephens and, later Terry Nation, creator of the Daleks.)

The presence of a girlfriend never sat comfortably with the emerging 'Ancock character, so when Melly left during this series, bored with her character, experienced radio performer Hattie Jacques joined the cast as Hancock's secretary.

The plots were changing too. At first, 'Ancock was a failed theatrical, but it wasn't clear whether he was a failed comic or a failed ham. Some weeks he had money, some weeks he was on his uppers; now, the setting was edging closer to the realism all concerned were after.

The whole country knew Anthony Aloysius St John Hancock's address: 23 Railway Cuttings, East Cheam. Phyllis Rounce's mother lived in Cheam, a word that Hancock found so funny he would collapse with helpless laughter every time she said it. *East* Cheam, G&S reckoned, was where a failed snob like 'Ancock would end up, while aspiring to Cheam proper.

G&S have described the character as 'a high powered mug.' He exhibited a complex personality, previously unseen in sitcoms. Always keen to improve himself, he was nonetheless at odds with whoever he was talking to - he despised intellectuals to their faces for their phoniness, but ridiculed Sid, Bill and Hattie for their lack of learning.

The show in its definitive form had finally come together. Many of the best episodes were aired in this series: *The Wild Man Of The Woods*, released on record in 1957; *The Diary*, which includes the test-pilot sketch; and *The Old School Reunion*, which sees the Lad humiliated in front of Bill and Sid, as his memories of his grand schooldays turn out to be fantasies.

Series Five

20 episodes, from 21st January 1958 to 3rd June 1958. Producer Tom Ronald (Pat Dixon produced the first show; Wilson had left for a job in TV.). A special, *Bill And Father Christmas*, in which Kerr is traumatised by the discovery that Father Christmas doesn't exist, went out on Christmas Day 1958.

Hancock was by now immensely famous, and earned the wages to match - though he was only allowed a few quid pocket money by his wife and agent, in an attempt to keep him off the booze. Sid Field was a boozer,

Tony reckoned, and it hadn't done him any harm. He had his own celebrity cricket team, Hancock's XI, which, according to Bill Kerr, 'Consisted of every drinking actor you could think of who could stand on his hind legs and hold a piece of willow.'

This fabulous series included *The Scandal Magazine*, a classic Sid-preying-on-Tony story; *The Threatening Letters*, a masterpiece of self-important paranoia; and of course *Sunday Afternoon At Home*, which G&S say was the only time in the radio series that they were actually conscious of 'exploring new ground.'

Away from the microphone, however, things were not so happy. The ease with which Hancock became bored was one of his most serious character faults - and, to be fair, one of the sources of his greatness. (He'd never look at *HHH* radio scripts before the morning of recording, so as to keep his performance fresh.) Now, he reckoned, they'd done East Cheam, it had worked, it was time to dump it and risk trying something better.

Hancock was restless.

Series Six

14 episodes, 29th September 1959 to 29th December 1959.

Williams had been dropped from the TV series - because Hancock, and his writers, didn't consider him part of their continuing master plan to achieve realistic comedy - and was finding the radio show a chore. He resigned after two episodes of series six, believing his role had become pointless and insulting ('To a man of my calibre,' no doubt).

This final radio series contained some of the finest episodes of all. Hattie Jacques had left to have a baby, and perhaps it was the three of them - Hancock, Williams and Kerr - being alone together at last that prompted, for instance, *Hancock In Hospital*, which explored their three-way relationship as never before and is a foretaste of the emotional claustrophobia of Galton and Simpson's TV series, *Steptoe And Son*. Even better was *The Poetry Society*, with Warren Mitchell, Fraser Kerr and Fenella Fielding - a savage and killingly funny assault on arty-farty affectation, which seemed to sum up anything that still needed saying about East Cheam after *Sunday Afternoon*.

And then... it was over. The money wasn't good enough, he was too busy on TV, the radio format was restricting him, and anyway he wanted to be an international film star. Hancock was off, mush.

But The World's Not Entirely To Blame: The End

How did Hancock, a fairly good comic, suddenly become the greatest of his breed? The likeliest explanation is that the four of them - Galton, Simpson, Main Wilson and the Lad Himself - were all highly talented individuals, who, working together, were collectively something much more than that. Of course, G&S and Main Wilson had successes elsewhere, without Hancock. But it was the four of them who invented Anthony Aloysius St John Hancock and thus allowed Tony Hancock to uncover the great performer that was inside him.

Hancock's timing - good on television, miraculously perfect on radio - and his trailblazing use of silence, of the long pause, the aural equivalent of a reaction shot on screen, were extraordinary, and have never been matched by anyone. The pauses built an electric tension, broken when Hancock came back in to hit the laugh line right on its sweet spot and send it, effortlessly it seemed, sailing out of the studio.

Whether Hancock's astonishing ability came from craft or from instinct can only be a matter of opinion. What we do know is that he was serious about comedy, that he studied and analysed it and worked at it; but also that he seems to have been most of the time incapable - literally incapable - of seeing what was best about his own work. Hancock was a perfectionist. This is generally used as a compliment, but in some cases it can describe what is surely an illness. A man who washes his hands 93 times a day is said to be ill - a comic actor who systematically alienates his friends and colleagues through his obsessive search for a self-evidently nonexistent perfection is, it seems obvious with hindsight, far from well.

Contrast with his quest for perfection, the fact that to the end of his life he clung onto ancient, corny material in his stage act - even using it, presumably out of fear, after he'd gone to the trouble and expense of buying new scripts from new writers.

Galton and Simpson did something to Hancock which he had done to others all his life: noted things he said, his reactions to particular situations, salted them away, and used them later in the scripts. The gap between Hancock and 'Ancock was thus progressively narrowed. Creatively, this was wonderful - medically, and again only in hindsight, it might not have been the best thing for Hancock. It can only have magnified his self-loathing to see his own methods of scrutiny - for pomposity, sentimentality, cheapness and so on - turned on himself. Introspection is like alcohol: it's healthy for most of us, but for some it's a killer.

Audiences loved 'Ancock, no matter what idiocies he committed. In real life, too, his intimates loved Hancock no matter how badly he treated them. But eventually, the process of cleansing, purging and paring his comedy, to 'get rid of the rubbish' reached its horribly logical conclusion, and he ditched Galton and Simpson - and that really was pretty much the end.

Hancock's death in 1968, in Sydney where he was making yet another doomed comeback, came as no great surprise to those who knew him. From those who loved him but had never met him, the reaction then and ever since has tended to be exasperation more than anything: 'You were the greatest - we kept *telling* you you were the greatest. Why couldn't you just do the job and enjoy the wages? Was that so much to ask?' The writer J.B. Priestley famously called Hancock 'A comedian with a touch of genius who had no enemy but himself.' But the coroner, as reported in the Australian press, noted in a wise, generous and for its times rather brave statement that 'One can only admire his fortitude in carrying out his work and giving pleasure to people when he himself was beset with problems... Suicide is not a disease, a crime or a sin, but a symptom.'

Chris Bumstead, who for many years ran the Tony Hancock Appreciation Society, was once quoted in a report as saying that Hancock had taught him not to take anything too seriously - not even Hancock himself.

The last period of Tony Hancock's life is well documented - too well documented, even - and makes depressing reading, as a nation's pre-eminent comic talent disintegrates into a stinking, shit-stained, shambling drunk, visibly dying.

Radio had made him and radio was surely where he belonged, this master of the delayed laugh, the precise, teasing timing, of comic foreplay - this great artist who seemed able to perform close-up face comedy through a pictureless medium. But radio wasn't enough. Nothing was enough, for Tony Hancock, and it killed him.

Still, to put it bluntly, that's his problem.

We still have those radio shows available to us - well, the ones the BBC managed not to wipe, at any rate - and they will continue to be enjoyed for generations to come. Everyone has to die sometime, and it's rarely a pretty business; but what they create doesn't have to die.

There's more to Tony Hancock than the sum of his neuroses. After all, stone me - Van Gogh is remembered for more than just cutting off his ear, isn't he?

Chapter Five: Round The Horne

We All Know What 'Hello' Means: The Beginning

At first, Barry Took and Marty Feldman didn't fancy creating a new radio vehicle for Kenneth Horne. They were successful TV writers, and anyway - wasn't radio dying? On the other hand, it was to be produced by John Simmonds, with a terrific cast, so they thought maybe they'd give it a go.

It turned out to be the best thing any of them - cast, producer, writers - were ever involved in. One of Took's happiest memories was of sitting in an enormous traffic jam one Sunday lunchtime, the car windows open in the heat, and realising that everyone around him was listening to *Round The Horne* on their car radios - and laughing out loud.

Be Ye Man Or Be Ye Ghastly Manifestation: The Personnel

Music hall was in its last days in 1955, when two young comics were booked to play the small Empire Theatre in York. Marty Feldman was part of a three-man zany act called Morris, Marty and Mitch, and Barry Took was a stand-up. Took remembers Marty in those days, before his hyperthyroid problems in 1961, as 'quite good looking,' blond, with a goatee beard, and a broken nose from his days boxing with the Jewish Lads' Brigade. Took himself was tall and thin and bespectacled.

The following week, they were on the same bill at Weston-super-Mare, and so began a friendship that lasted for life. They'd both left grammar schools in north London aged 15; they both played the trumpet. Like so many of their generation (albeit, national service rather than war service) they were readers and thinkers, enthusiastic self-educators.

Marty told Barry, in the nicest possible way I'm sure, that he looked funnier in his street clothes than he did in his stage getup; on stage, Barry wore a lounge suit, while off duty he wore a Cheesecutter cap, a tweed jacket and an old school tie. You should go on like that, said Marty. Barry did, and his career as a comic blossomed; he began getting bookings for major variety theatres, and then West End revues.

Business wasn't so good for Feldman. The act had broken up and Marty was working in a bookshop in the Charing Cross Road. The two pals started writing together, inevitably, and before long they were doing

56

well. Like just about every other scriptwriter of the 1950s-80s, they wrote for Frankie Howerd on radio, but their biggest successes were on TV, notably *Bootsie And Snudge*, a spin-off from *The Army Game*.

Feldman was a bona fide comedy neurotic, who had, for instance, a phobia about pigeons. Even so, he was an outgoing, sociable chap, who enjoyed a party (provided there were no pigeons involved). At school, an ex-ENSA teacher had got him interested in playing comedy, and seeing a Sid Field show sealed his ambition. After leaving school, he hung around Soho, playing trumpet, being an arts student, doing paintings, and writing poems; he actually had a few published, after receiving encouragement from a certain Dylan Thomas. Like most other young people, Marty was a fan of *TIFH*, Hancock and the Goons, and decided he wanted to be a comedy writer. He eventually got a job writing and performing on *Educating Archie*.

The son of a manager for the Danish Bacon Company, Took worked as a lad at a Denmark Street music publisher - but he always wanted to be a comedian, and broke into the business through the Carroll Levis Discovery Shows, a nationwide series of locally-based stage talent shows. He subsequently worked as a tour manager for Levis, and from there secured his first radio audition.

In 1958, Took and Eric Merriman (a leading scriptwriter in radio, TV and film for many years) created a vehicle for Kenneth Horne, called *Beyond Our Ken* (1958-64). The cast included Kenneth Williams, Hugh Paddick, Betty Marsden, Ron Moody, Bill Pertwee, Patricia Lancaster, and Stanley Unwin, with announcer Douglas Smith in later series. *BOK* sounds mildly amusing today, but its relationship to *RTH* is that of a caterpillar to a butterfly, or a boil to a carbuncle. It featured some quite funny characters, and some decent puns, but it was relatively unambitious.

Took and Merriman wrote the final series, in 1959-60, of *Take It From Here*, working separately as they had rather different views on comedy writing. Took - with an uncredited Feldman - wrote the Glums.

When Merriman fell out with the BBC in 1964, Took and Feldman were asked to come up with a new show for the *BOK* cast. They refused.

BOK was a popular show, and they weren't sure they could match it. The money on offer was pathetic compared to what they were getting on TV. The boys went back to Barry's flat for lunch with his wife Lyn (a former secretary to Tony Hancock) - and within a couple of hours, to their surprise, had come up with an outline. They returned to the BBC, and said they'd be willing to write six episodes to see how it went. The show's working title was *It's Ken Again*.

Took and Feldman had many shared obsessions, listed by Took as 'music halls, the circus, seaside concert parties, and revolting old men' - all of them (expect perhaps the last-named) being rather old-fashioned by the mid-60s. They wrote *RTH* in longhand because it allowed them to write 'as quickly as we thought.' I've seen some of the original handwritten scripts, and compared them to sound recordings, and it's amazing how little they differ. From 1959-69, Took and Feldman were never out of work, in radio, film and TV.

Their writing seems to have come easily, and to have been fun. Took remembers them writing *RTH* 'doubled up with laughter at the sheer impertinence of what we had written.'

Kenneth Horne was born in 1907. His mother was an Hon, and his father was, among other things, a preacher and a Liberal MP. 'Curly' - he lost the nickname along with his hair early on - was expelled from Cambridge for laziness, despite representing the university at tennis. He had a successful career as a businessman, particularly at Triplex Glass and Chad Valley Toys, but became a semi-pro entertainer during his war service in the RAF. Despite the success of his radio shows with Richard Murdoch, he didn't turn to showbusiness fulltime until forced to retire from his business career following a stroke in 1958.

He was a popular man; even Kenneth Williams, in his notoriously acid diaries, expresses nothing but love and admiration for Horne. As far as can be told - not an enormous amount is known about this private man, except that he was married three times - he wasn't especially neurotic. So what he was doing in comedy is anybody's guess.

Perhaps because of his greater age, or the gravitas he carried from his careers in business, the RAF and radio, or his central position in the show - or maybe just because that's what he was like - it's obvious that all the *RTH* mob viewed him as an almost paternal figure. It's equally obvious that Horne returned their respect and affection. Unlike many of the shows mentioned in this book, *RTH* seems to have been a pleasure for all involved.

Horne, the character, wasn't the kind of father figure who became flustered or annoyed when his young charges misbehaved; rather, he was like a dad or headmaster who believed that children *should* misbehave and mess around and express themselves... just every now and then, when the high spirits threatened to get out of control and cause a breach of the peace, he would reign them in with a quiet word and a friendly wink.

Hancock's Half Hour made Kenneth Williams a radio star, but it wasn't until *BOK* and *RTH* that he found himself properly part of a comedy team - and was revealed, for all his flouncing and showing off, his insecurity and behind-the-back bitching, as a team player. He hated the *Carry On* films, felt oppressed in *HHH*, but when finally given the chance to show his range ('I need stretching! I'm used to enormous parts!') he didn't release his stored-up aggressions and slights in any way except through marvellous performances. The publication of his diaries in 1993 irreversibly changed his public image. Many fans were shocked to discover just how bitter and snobby their beloved funny-voice merchant really was; but I suggest it would behove us, ladies and gentlemen of the comedy jury, to focus on the work, not the life.

Round The Horne was, by a very long way, his best work. In *HHH* he was never asked to do much that he couldn't have done in his sleep, and the same is true of the *Carry-On* films - good as he was in both. His greatest talent as a comic actor was that he was an actor, not a comic; his characterisations achieved depth even in the short span of a sketch - week on week, they achieved reality. Added to this was his famous ability to switch between voices or characters several times in the space of a short speech without losing his rhythm, let alone his place, and somehow have you believing in all of them.

He was the son of a sissy-hating hairdresser in Kings Cross. In the army he was part of a touring concert party with Stanley Baxter, John Schlesinger and Peter Nichols. He turned to acting professionally when demobbed in 1947. A small, dapper man, Williams's body language was painfully fastidious, and his voice, or one of his voices, provocatively cultured (cultured, that is, in much the same way that a yoghurt is cultured - by feeding a borrowed starter with common milk.)

J. Peasmold (the spelling used in the original scripts) Gruntfuttock, Williams's first great *RTH* character, was a disgusting old man - indeed, he was the disgusting old man's disgusting old man. (He was also Feldman's alter ego, as Eccles was Milligan's; working in Hollywood years later, Marty would write letters to Barry as Gruntfuttock). He was the sometime King of Peasmoldia, off the Balls Pond Road, though his independent state wasn't recognised by anyone except the man at the all night chemist: 'He recognised me. 'Oh, it's you, King Gruntfuttock,' he said. 'I've had orders not to serve you with paraffin.''

Fiendish Japanese mastermind Chou En Ginsberg M.A. (Failed) was the perennial enemy of Kenneth Horne, Master Spy. Rambling Syd Rumpo was a thoroughly phoney folk singer, with a nonsensical, but vulgar-sounding, vocabulary ('Three are the times I've lunged my groats, two are my looming thrums'). He began as a send-up of the 1960s fashion for 'ethnic' music; ironically - and wonderfully - he remains probably the only widely known folk singer in Britain.

Julian and Sandy (Hugh Paddick and Williams respectively) were two 'resting' actors working as cleaners; they were very actorish, according to the original script instructions, in which 'J. Behemoth Cadogan' was 'Old, booming actor-laddie,' and 'T. Hamilton Grosvenor' was 'Ageing, sibilant thundering pantaloon.' Producer John Simmonds (another depressive) thought they were depressing, not funny, and suggested changing them to out of work chorus boys. Took and Feldman renamed them after Julian Slade, who wrote *Salad Days*, and Sandy Wilson, who wrote *The Boy Friend*. Jule and Sand also owe something to Williams and Paddick's effeminate *BOK* characters, Rodney and Charles.

It was Jule and Sand who introduced to a wider audience the dialect known as 'Palare,' in which 'bona' means good, a man is an 'omi,' and to 'troll' is to walk in a particular manner. Took and Feldman didn't invent Palare, or 'camp chat'; most of it originated in fairs and circuses, and from there spread to the musical theatre and variety world. In the 1960s, it was also popular among homosexuals - especially those working in showbusiness.

Homosexual acts between men weren't legalised in Britain until 1967, and Jule and Sand's precise relationship was left to the audience's imagination. Mind you, when two unmarried men refer to each other in public as 'presh' and 'heartface,' it's reasonable to suppose that most of the audience would be thinking 'We've all got *your* number, ducky.' (Although once, as very young Boy Scouts, a friend and I did an imitation of 'Julia and Sandy' at a campfire concert, in the belief that our favourite Sunday lunchtime wireless characters were char ladies. We got the loudest laugh of the night, and were thenceforth instructed to sleep in separate tents for the duration.)

Every week, 'that nice Mr Horne' would encounter Jule and Sand in some new setting - running an estate agents, for instance, or working as outfitters for MI5 ('We've been screened. They went into our backgrounds and found that our fides were absolutely bona') - and after a ritualised exchange of greetings ('Hello? Anybody there?' 'Oh hello, I'm

Julian and this is my friend Sandy - how bona to vada your dolly old eek again!') Horne would be subjected to an uncomfortable scrutiny of his butchness, and pelted with comments of questionable decency. Along the way, he'd gamely assay a couple of cheeky quips of his own ('Oh, he's bold! He goes too far!'), but he'd generally emerge worse off, having engaged Julian and Sandy to perform whatever service they were offering (I'm sorry, but *everything* takes on a double meaning under these circumstances). One week, the Bona Private Detective Agency was confident it could put an end to the anonymous phone calls troubling Horne, for a retainer of ten quid a week. How could they be so sure? 'Easy, ducky. We'll stop making them.'

That's actually one of the better punchlines to a Jule and Sand sketch. The tyranny of the punchline was still in place, and Took and Feldman, like most scriptwriters, obviously found achieving that climax to be the hardest part of their job. The next generation of comics - university-bred, confident, arrogant - abandoned punchlines almost entirely, on the grounds that they were anachronistic and artificial. The real reason, of course, is that they just couldn't be bothered to think of any.

Williams also played various parts in which he would claim, against available evidence, to be 'Far from mad. Well, not that far - I commute.'

Many comedy troupes, past and present, have worked around the problem of casting occasional female roles by having men speak in squeaky voices. *RTH* didn't need such subterfuge, as it had wisely secured the services of that indisputably female person, Betty Marsden. Born in Liverpool, educated at the Italia Conti Stage School, and having served in ENSA during the war, Marsden wasn't just there to say 'Mr Horne will see you now, sir,' or 'One lump or two?' An accomplished and protean actress, she shared with Hugh Paddick the ability to conjure laughs from even the smallest part. She also played several recurring characters.

Dame Celia Molestrangler and Binkie Huckaback (Paddick) were a pair of insufferably 'legitimate' actors, who in turn 'played' Fiona and Charles in Noel Coward spoofs: 'I know you know I know.' Daphne Whitethigh was a hoarse-voiced, horse-faced fashion and cookery expert, inspired by the TV cook Fanny Craddock (she'd been Fanny Haddock in *BOK*).

Buttercup was Grunfuttock's wife, who achieved the remarkable distinction of being socially inferior to her appalling husband. In the early shows, Marsden was Lady Beatrice Counterblast (née Clissold), a much married ('Many times... many, many times') ex-gaiety girl who, in retirement, shared her scandalous reminisces. She was served by an octogenarian butler, Spasm (Williams), who was prone to telling visitors 'We be doomed - we're all doomed.'

Hugh Paddick had been destined for a career in law, but become an actor in a touring company instead. He served in the Royal Artillery from 1939; demobbed in 1945, he went straight back to acting, finding success in revue (he did two shows with Took), musical theatre and straight theatre. His profile in *RTH*, and in the memory of many fans, suffers from playing opposite Kenneth Williams - but any lesser talent would have been eclipsed altogether, which in turn would have lessened Williams's impact. He was every bit Williams's equal in the Julian and Sandy sketches, and also played numerous subsidiary parts.

Having started his professional life as a concert party impressionist in 1955, Bill Pertwee was in *BOK* and *RTH* what Kenneth Williams had been for Hancock - the odd-job man, though with less excitingly odd jobs to do. He played the straight parts (and heaven knows, there weren't many of those), and sundry unnamed voices. It was an important role in such a show, but rather an unglamorous one. His only regular character was useless Irish chat-show host Seamus Android ('Well now, we've had our little bit of fun...'), based on Eamonn Andrews.

Sketch shows were still expected to include a musical break. The Fraser Hayes Four did the necessary in *BOK* and *RTH*, singing sweet harmony versions of popular, mostly rather old, songs. This is the one part of *RTH* which comes across now as laughably old-fashioned, although the Four were undoubtedly the cream of their kind. Took always vigorously defended their role in the show, pointing out that, apart from anything, the halftime break gave the studio audience a chance to recharge its laughing muscles. The group also provided some wonderful opportunities for insult gags, as Horne introduced them each week with a cruel comment, my favourite being: 'And now the Fraser Hayes Four - three voices in perfect harmony.'

The excellent house band was Edwin Braden and the Hornblowers; the moustachioed Braden, who replaced Paul Fenoulhet after the first six episodes, was often derided in the scripts by Williams as 'That great 'airy fool!'

The custom of using an announcer as a semi-detached part of a comedy team continues to this day - Charlotte Green is mercilessly ribbed for her sexy voice on *The News Quiz* - but nobody ever did it better than *RTH*, with Douglas Smith, who loved working on the show. His sensible, dignified tones contrasted beautifully with the nonsense he was required to speak - as when he abused his position to advertise Dobbiroids, 'The magic horse rejuvenator with the less fattening centre.' Mostly, he played inanimate objects, such as the sword, Excalibur, in a King Arthur pastiche: 'Swish, swish, snicker - see how the firelight plays on me as I dance in your hand.' His attempts to build up his roles would provoke angry protests from Williams - 'Stop 'anging it out! It's a disgrace!' - or curtness from Horne: 'That'll do, Smith.'

The studio audience was almost an extra character in the show, so involved did it become in proceedings, so diligent was its collective hunt for treble meanings (it was far too sophisticated to be much impressed by double meanings).

Series One

16 episodes, from 7th March 1965 to 20th June 1965.

It took a while to reach its familiar form (this series is comparatively slow and a bit creaky in parts), but the writers had a clear idea from the start of what they wanted to do with *Round The Horne*, structurally. Horne was to be a 'maypole,' a solid, reassuring figure with his deliberate, avuncular delivery, around which all manner of lunacy and naughtiness would cavort. But he wouldn't be a bumbling straight man, overwhelmed by the comedy; rather, he was to be 'master of revels.' Much of the appeal of *RTH* comes from this simple idea, prompting a certain reaction from the listener: 'What the bloody hell is a sensible chap like Mr Horne doing mixed up with that lot? An educated geezer like that, he ought to know better!'

From the start, *RTH* got into trouble. Sir Cyril Black MP complained about a sketch commemorating 'the birth of the crumpet' (episode six), prompting a memo from the Chief of Light Programme to the Head of Light Entertainment (Sound) complaining that the show was 'dirty in parts' and needed to be cleaned up urgently, otherwise it would be impossible to defend against 'a vociferous minority.' The Chief admitted that the programme was very good, and improving, but felt it was undermined by a degree of naughtiness which was inappropriate 'at this time on a Sunday.' He also accused the cast of the unbelievable sin of 'playing for laughs with the studio audience.' The writers responded magnificently, with a closing speech from Horne denouncing 'a tiny minority of killjoys' who had been complaining about the show. 'Evil,' he insisted, 'is in the eye of the beholder, and we believe that you can make anything sound as if it has a double meaning - if you know how.'

Hugh Greene, the director general, staunchly defended the programme from its enemies, internal and external, who soon included Mary Whitehouse - that great champion of Christian values like apartheid. The clean-up campaigners conceded that the scripts contained nothing vile when read (they were wrong!) but argued that, during recordings, the cast were 'putting emphasis on certain words.' Took's response to this Goonish charge is legendary: 'It's called acting,' he said.

John Simmonds produced every edition of *Round The Horne*, with a single exception due to illness.

Series Two

13 episodes, from 13th March 1966 to 5th June 1966.

Horne's health was never terribly good after his stroke. In autumn 1966, he had pleurisy and couldn't appear in the Christmas Day special. The script was reworked without bringing in an extra actor, and the resulting broadcast was well up to standard. Somehow, even in his absence, Horne's presence imbued the show. This was the only absence by a cast member during the show's entire run; by contrast, various Goons were missing from many of their episodes.

The shows were recorded on weekday lunchtimes. The Paris Studio, Lower Regent Street, was always full, with the front row reserved for the writers and cast and their guests - including Williams's mother, who never missed a recording. They were broadcast in the after lunch slot on Sundays, on the Light Programme.

As the show matured, the sketches got sharper and faster. Fewer cuts for time were needed, which helped preserve the rhythm of the writing. Where *BOK* had been a series of discrete sketches, *RTH* was becoming a half hour trip into a world of its own.

Much of Took and Feldman's humour arose from using language which sounded as if it meant something but didn't - so listeners were in a way invited to provide their own jokes, the nonsense gags giving them their raw material. It's that rare comedy - the type that plays in the mind more than in the ear.

Series Three

20 episodes, from 12th February 1967 to 25th June 1967. Christmas special broadcast on Christmas Eve.

Bored with Julian and Sandy's formulaic doings, the writers decided to drop them from this series. The outraged reactions of their *RTH* colleagues quickly persuaded them that they'd better write the Rentachap duo back in.

Every radio show has its moment of peaking, obvious only in hindsight, and series three was *RTH*'s moment. Everything was in place: the film spoofs of 'Armpit Theatre' (*The Plastic Max*); radio's first 'Colour Supplement,' dissecting the swinging London of Carnaby Street and cockney chic; Daphne Whitethigh giving recipes for yak ('Take an ordinary saucepan, the type you use for broiling hippopotamus'); Rambling Syd, keeping alive the tradition of the gander boggler, who 'capers off down the street boggling his gander above his head'; and Seamus Android, interviewing the Earl of Bedlam: 'Well, your grace - ' 'No, you're Grace. I was Grace last night.'

Series Four

16 episodes, from 25th February 1968 to 9th June 1968.

Feldman had decided to leave the show, as his career as a television performer was taking off. He and Took still wrote together, particularly material for Marty's TV and film work.

This final series was largely written by Johnnie Mortimer and Brian Cooke, with, briefly, additional material from actor and writer Donald Webster. Took script-edited, and wrote Rambling Syd and Julian and Sandy. Cooke and Mortimer were newspaper cartoonists who were gradually transmogrifying into comedy writers, notably on *Men From The Ministry*. The standard was as high as ever, and Cooke and Mortimer added a few new characters of their own, including Miss Judy Coolibah, a lovely part for Marsden as a rugged Australian maiden who was convinced that every man she met in sin-soaked London was out to seduce her. Working as a bus conductress, for instance, she threw a passenger off for pushing fourpence into her hand and asking 'How far can I go for that?'

Feldman's defection wasn't total; in a reciprocal arrangement with Took, he wrote two Jule and Sand episodes in this series - though no one now remembers which they were.

A round of budget cuts at the BBC led to the departure of Pertwee and the Fraser Hayes Four, while the Hornblowers were replaced by a smaller outfit, the Max Harris Group. The cast filled in the musical gaps with music hall ditties, such as *The Marrow Song*, with its memorable chorus: 'Oh, what a beauty! I've never seen one as big as that before. Oh, what a beauty! It must be two feet long or even more. It's such a lovely colour, and nice and round and fat, I never thought a marrow could grow as big as that...'

Well, you get the gist.

Cheerio, See You Next Week: The End

On February 14th 1969, Kenneth Horne was co-hosting the BAFTA awards with Earl Mountbatten at the Dorchester Hotel in London. To his delight, he had just given the award for best comedy writing to Took and Feldman for their TV show *Marty*. Suddenly, Horne collapsed on stage; Took and Feldman helped to carry him from the room, but he was already dead. He had suffered a heart attack.

After Horne's death, the series was dead. The BBC tried to carry on with a Kenneth Williams vehicle called *Stop Messing About*, but it didn't last long.

If Horne hadn't died, the show might well have run for years. After all, it had easily survived the departure of Feldman - which seems incredible, but is really a tribute to the firm foundations laid by 'the boys,' by Simmonds and the cast. They had built the thing so soundly that if they'd all gone over the pub half an hour early, you can't help feeling, it wouldn't have mattered; the show was an autonomous organism which would've run on its own, with a little help from the audience.

RTH forms the link between the great days of radio sketch comedy and the next wave, which culminated in *Monty Python*.

It would be impossible to do *RTH* now - the BBC was a more liberal, more talent-driven, more confident organisation back then. *RTH* had plenty of BBC enemies, but it survived - and was championed even - partly because it was one of the few radio shows which still attracted young listeners. It continues to do so, as each new generation discovers *RTH* for itself.

Took always said that the most frequent question he was asked by fans was 'How on earth did you get away with it?' BBC management was not quite so innocent in the 1960s as it had been when the Goons managed to smuggle through such rhyming slang character names as 'Berkley Hunt.' Years after the show ended, Hugh Greene is said to have told Took 'To tell you the truth, I rather like a good dirty joke' - and the dirty jokes in *RTH* were always good; that was the point. It was a combination of outrageous camp, innuendo-laden puns, funny names, non sequiturs taken to a previously unimagined level, madness, cleverness, and the calm but naughty Horne.

This was a powerful cross-fertilisation: the swinging sixties, juxtaposed with echoes of the music hall and the writers' fascination with classic literature. Surrounded by satire, the fashionable comic form of the decade, it provided an alternative to the alternative - yet it never had a nostalgic feel to it.

Round The Horne didn't need to be an overtly revolutionary show; the revolution inside the BBC had largely been won, there was no need to man the barricades against archaic comedy, or for Pure Radio. *RTH*'s manifesto was more to do with winning the peace; now that alternative comedy had become the mainstream, it was time to demonstrate what could be done with it.

Took often said about *RTH*, as Norden has said about *TIFH*, that it was a show which 'recognised the literacy of the listener.' Certainly, in between the camp chat and the cordwangling, *RTH* contained just as many literary allusions and odd pieces of recondite learning as it did double entendres. The average listener, the boys insisted, was bright, open-minded, quite well-informed over a broad area, and ready to receive intelligent entertainment. Intelligent, but - or rather, intelligent *and* - vulgar. Took said that he and Feldman 'tried to write down-market material in an up-market way,' in the belief that all intelligent people contain an erudite and a vulgar part to their characters, and that much laughter could come from the two bumping into each other (most likely in the Marine Commando Club, Paddington, or outside an all night chemists down the Balls Pond Road.)

This idea hasn't entirely died out, but today there is more of a sense that young, metropolitan comedians from the professional classes are telling intelligently vulgar jokes to their own kind. Comedy is more tribal today.

I suspect, too, that staying up all night passionately debating art, life, politics and the nature of being - as the Grafton gang did, as Hancock and Galton and Simpson and Kenneth Williams and Took and Feldman did - would be considered a little *sad* by today's aspirational comics, a little too unironic. To the demob mob, that was a large part of where their comedy came from - an unembarrassed searching and examining of themselves and the world they lived in. They were, after all, people who had survived a war, and doing comedy was to some extent a continuation of that experience - it's no good just fighting, you want to know what you're fighting for. In the 2000s, comedy is for many (and there are plenty of honourable exceptions) a petit-bourgeois career choice rather like accountancy or conveyancing, and that's reflected in the safeness of their material; TV ads, football, and 'Have you ever noticed, yeah, how girls always go to the loo in pairs?'

But, look, you can intellectualise *RTH* forever - analyse the basis of its success, the happy melding of disparate, perfectly complementary talents, the way in which it reflected and even helped to shape the spirit of its times; in the end you just have to accept the overriding fact that it was *incredibly* funny. It was then and it is now. And there's no mystery to that - the best people worked on it, when they were at their best.

Round The Horne was a happy show. Perhaps, in the end, that is the simple secret of its continuing success... it was happy, and it makes you happy. Blimey, did I really need 5,000 thousand words to figure that out? I do apologise.

Chapter Six: The Legacy

Don't Some Mothers Have 'Em:
Other Comedies Of The 1950s And 60s

It's strange how some comedians, illustrious in their prime, seem to vanish from public consciousness the day after their obituaries have been used to line the cat's tray. Al Read (1909-87) is a good example - even though he was on the air as recently as the mid-80s, he scarcely gets a mention today.

Al 'Right Monkey!' Read was the third generation heir of a successful meat-pie making family in the Manchester area, and he began his performing career speaking at trade dinners. While still an amateur he wrote material for comics, including Sid Field, before being talent-spotted by a BBC producer in 1950.

The Al Read Show (1951-68), mostly produced by Ronnie Taylor and sometimes with Jimmy Edwards leading a small support cast, consisted of what we now call observational comedy; 'pages from life,' in Read's phrase. They were essentially monologues (the great American monologist, Bob Newhart, based his driving instructor routine on two of Read's sketches), in which Read performed a wide range of characters. The same format was highly successful on the West End stage, but less so on television.

Frankie Howerd's first solo series was *Fine Goings On*, which began in 1951. Interestingly, it starred the comic as 'himself' in various situations with a supporting cast. It was followed by a variety of formats between then and the mid-60s. The writers over the years included Eric Sykes, Spike Milligan, Galton and Simpson, and Took and Feldman, and actors appearing in Howerd's shows included Hattie Jacques, Tony Hancock (as a guest star), Hugh Paddick, and Dick Bentley.

A real little gem, remembered only by comedy and radio aficionados it seems, was *In All Directions* (1952-55), written and performed by Peter Ustinov and Peter Jones, using a strange method of assembling their material. They would improvise into a tape recorder, transcribe and edit that, learn it - and then chuck it away and improvise again for the actual recording, around their remembered script. The script editors were Muir and Norden.

A Life of Bliss (1953-69), by contrast, must have sounded old-fashioned even when it started; that's not to damn it, though. It was a charming, well-crafted, domestic sitcom that is still enjoyable. Written by Godfrey Harrison, it's about a shy and easily befuddled bachelor, David Alexander Bliss, played for the first few episodes by film actor David Tomlinson, and thereafter by former child star George Cole. His dog, Psyche, was of course played by the most famous of all animal impersonators, Percy Edwards. Actresses playing David's girlfriends included Moira Lister and Petula Clark. *Bliss* is one of my favourite old sitcoms, but it was precisely the sort of thing the Hancock crew were determined to avoid.

The Clitheroe Kid (1958-72) was a typical Sunday lunchtime programme, something the whole family could listen to while smearing horseradish on their roast beef - a chuckle show, rather than one which would interrupt the meal with prolonged laughter. It was hugely successful in ratings terms - while being despised by intellectuals and by many of the writers and performers celebrated in this book. Northern variety comic Jimmy Clitheroe (1922-73) was four foot three inches tall, and had a high voice. In the show, he played a schoolboy who lived with his mum, his Scottish granddad, and his posh sister, Susan. Susan's gormless boyfriend, Alfie, was always being led astray by Jimmy. The basic plot was that Jimmy would set out with good intentions, get himself and Alfie in trouble, make things worse while trying to make them better, and end up being spanked by his granddad.

By the time the show ended, its quality had dropped, its day had passed, and its audience was disappearing. Jimmy died on the day of his mother's funeral, having taken a mixture of barbiturates and alcohol: the verdict of the coroner's court was accidental death. It's hard to imagine, but when I was a child, little Jimmy Clitheroe was one of the most famous comics on earth. The programme employed a number of writers during its long run, but the main talent behind it was James Casey. Over the years, the cast included Peter Sinclair, Renee Houston, Patricia Burke, Diana Day, Peter Goodwright, Danny Ross, Judith Chalmers, Deryck Guyler and Mollie Sugden.

The Navy Lark (1959-77), radio's longest-running sitcom, written by Laurie Wyman (later with George Evans), was created as a vehicle for rising young actor Jon Pertwee (Bill's cousin, who later became even more famous on TV in *Dr Who*). Set aboard HMS Troutbridge, this was a situation comedy in which the situations were daft rather than cosy or realistic. Its other stars included Leslie Phillips ('Left hand down a bit!'), Stephen Murray, and Tenniel Evans - and it made Ronnie Barker famous. It never attempted anything groundbreaking, but was a popular (especially with real life Royal Navy sailors) and thoroughly likeable comedy.

The Men From The Ministry (1962-77) was a gentler forerunner of *Yes Minister* on TV and *Absolute Power* on Radio 4. Set in the civil service, it was slightly satirical about bureaucracy and about an institution that was changing only slowly in a fast-changing society. It sounds positively antique today, but was very popular in its time, and is still able to raise some decent chuckles now. Written by Edward Taylor, with Mortimer and Cooke, and John Graham, and always produced by Edward Taylor, it brought superb performances from Wilfred Hyde-White and Richard Murdoch (later, Deryck Guyler and Murdoch), as Number One and Number Two. The humour was of the farcical, plot-heavy persuasion, with lots of misunderstandings, and to call the show predictable is not to insult it - merely describe it. Its more cynical, more obviously satirical successors are no less formulaic.

I'm Sorry I'll Read That Again (1965-73, with a special on Christmas Day 1989) was hugely influential - but through its personnel, more than its raw, energetic style. *ISIRTA* marked the Coming of the Oxbridge Mafia; people whose pre-radio experience wasn't in variety or theatre, but in student revues, notably the Cambridge Footlights. This tribe has dominated broadcast comedy ever since, although the non-Oxbridge seats of learning have increasingly broken into the circle since the early 1980s. From Footlights beginnings, *ISIRTA* gradually evolved into an assembly point for some young future stars: John Cleese, Tim Brooke-Taylor, Graeme Garden, David Hatch, Jo Kendall, Bill Oddie, Graham Chapman, and producer Humphrey Barclay. It was written by the cast, and by a number of jobbing scripters, including Mortimer & Cooke, John Esmonde and Bob Larbey, Eric Idle, and Clive James. Later series were written principally by Oddie and Garden (who is still one of the cleverest funny men on radio).

Reminiscent of *ITMA* in style, it was a mixture of corny puns, silly songs, satire, wacky sketches and fast patter. It became, perhaps inevitably, a cult - studio audiences felt it their duty to get as involved as possible, and Cleese has spoken of his annoyance at this, with the audience groaning at terrible puns, but not noticing subtler material. It sounds more dated now than many older shows - and, it has to be said, rather amateurish.

When I was a kid, every cool person I knew loved *ISIRTA*, and every prig hated it. (Grannies, generally, thought it rather noisy.) At the time, and for a while thereafter, *ISIRTA* was spoken of as the last of the great radio shows. But radio wasn't finished yet...

There Now Follows A Short Intermission:
The 1970s And 80s

In the late 60s and early 70s things looked a little grim for radio comedy. The money was disappearing into TV - and, naturally, taking the talent with it. Radio budgets were far smaller than they had been, and the shows were frankly unenterprising. Instead of radio programmes moving over to television, during a particularly uninspired phase of scheduling, successful TV sitcoms were being rerecorded as radio shows.

However, while sitcom was struggling, topical comedy thrived. *Week Ending* (1970-98) was created by David Hatch and Simon Brett (producer of the pilots of *Hitchhiker's Guide* and *The News Huddlines*, and now a novelist and sitcom writer), and written by Pete Spence. It evolved into a hard-hitting, often controversial (it was routinely taken off air during general election campaigns) sketch show based on the week's news, largely written by casual writers sending in jokes and sketches on spec. Anyone could attend the weekly writers' meeting and if the producer liked their material, it would go into the programme. It therefore became famous for its almost comically long closing credits, and for starting the careers of just about every comedy writer of note (and many producers, including John Lloyd) during its unprecedentedly long lifetime.

The cast also changed a lot over the years; performers included David Jason, Bill Wallis, David Tate, Sally Grace, Nigel Rees, Sheila Steafel, Tracey Ullman, Jeffrey Holland and Toby Longworth.

The News Huddlines (from 1975) is also a news-based sketch show, but very different from *Week Ending*. It's on Radio 2, rather than Radio 4; it's recorded before a live audience; it gives priority to laughs over making a satirical point (although it often tries to do both), whereas *Week Ending* could sometimes be a little earnest; and it aims at a slightly older audience. The eponymous Roy Hudd (born 1936) is a comic and actor, and an expert on music hall history. He's supported by Chris Emmett and June Whitfield (originally, the female roles were played by Alison Steadman).

The News Huddlines is also written by multiple hands (its credit lists are as long as 'The roll call of the dead in World War One,' according to Hudd), many of whom are amateurs or semi-professionals.

Non-topical sketch comedy in the 1970s covered the gamut, from dull to non-existent - until *The Burkiss Way* (1976-1980), the first radio comedy since *ISIRTA* to get significant press attention, with critics considering it a successor to *The Goon Show*. In 1975, Radio 3 - the classical music channel - did something it doesn't do very often: broadcast a comedy show. *The Half-Open University* was a send up, obviously, of the Open University, written by Andrew Marshall, David Renwick and John Mason, produced by Simon Brett, and performed by Nigel Rees, Chris Emmett, Timothy Davies and Christine Ozanne. From this, came *Burkiss* on Radio 4.

The cast was Rees, Emmett, Fred Harris and Denise Coffey; Jo Kendall took over from Coffey from the second series. The producers were Simon Brett, then John Lloyd, and finally David Hatch. Douglas Adams, a Cambridge buddy of Lloyd's, wrote additional material.

Each episode was presented as if it were a lesson in a correspondence course - 'The Burkiss way to dynamic living' - devised by Professor Burkiss. This led to lengthy programme titles, like *Write Extremely Long Programme Titles The Burkiss Way*, which at least guaranteed the show a decent-sized billing in *Radio Times*. Two consecutive episodes were both called *Repeat Yourself The Burkiss Way*.

Ostensibly a sketch show, *Burkiss* played with form more than any other radio comedy, messing about with reality like a Philip K. Dick novel. Devices used to achieve a fiendishly complex internal structure included false endings, fake continuity announcements, and supposed technical problems leading to the elements of an episode being broadcast in the 'wrong' order. Sketches frequently broke off halfway, to link into other sketches - which would eventually loop back to where they began. (Indeed, I've yet to be convinced that the whole idea of Internet hyperlinks wasn't nicked off *Burkiss*.)

The show had some more familiar elements: spoofs and parodies (especially of other radio programmes), catchphrases, and regular characters, most memorably Eric Pode of Croydon - Gruntfuttock without the charm - who Harris would interview through clenched teeth: 'Isn't he a panic?'

Yet another example of intelligent comedy, the show quickly became the biggest radio cult since *ISIRTA*. After I moved to London in 1978, I rarely missed a recording of Burkiss at the Paris, and not only because the tickets were free. As a live show, it was quite an experience. Its very young, un-Radio 4 studio audience packed the place out, with the overspill sitting on the floor and even on the stage. Many fans would dress up for the occasion, some wearing 'I do it the Burkiss Way' T-shirts - and this wasn't BBC merchandising, people had the shirts made themselves.

The series often attracted controversy, never more so than in its last ever outing, when it mocked celebrations of the Queen Mother's eightieth birthday. Six minutes of the repeat of that episode were cut (and, according to Marshall, wiped from the master tapes) and replaced with music. It would be hard to imagine a more fitting end to a show which, in its determination to use the medium to the full, outgooned *The Goon Show*.

Radio comedy ended the 1970s in triumph, when *The Hitchhiker's Guide To The Galaxy* (1978-80) suddenly exploded out of nowhere, and once again radio was leading the way with a wholly new, cult comedy. I well remember listening to the first episode, at 10.30pm on Wednesday 8th March 1978, and then going into school the next day and trying to explain to people what I'd heard. 'It's sort of science fiction, and it's a comedy, and the world's destroyed, and then...'

I couldn't adequately describe it then, and I won't try now; the show is the subject of a comprehensive book of its own in the Pocket Essentials series. Instead, I'll take a quick look at its roots. *HHG* writer, Douglas Adams (who was subjected to much piss-taking in *The Burkiss Way*), came from the Footlights background which had already produced *ISIRTA* (whose David Hatch was now Controller of Radio 4), and where he had first met John Lloyd. Let's face it, if *HHG* had been written by bloody Martin Smith from Croydon College of Further Education it would never have got on the air.

The most obvious comic influence on *HHG* is *Monty Python* - itself, of course, a child of the Goons, as John Cleese has often acknowledged. In passing, I note that Adams had written gags for *Week Ending*; more importantly, this extraordinary series - which had as much effect on science fiction as it did on comedy - was a fine example of the legacy of the Big Three, with its gloomily pompous Hancockian characters, Goonish logic-stretching, and Horne-like wordplay, catchphrases, silly voices and even sillier names.

On television, the 1980s is remembered by comedy fans mostly for the arrival, and rapid rise to power, of the Comic Strip generation of performers and writers. The 'alternative comedy movement' - as everyone connected with it always insisted it should not be called - was, it has been argued, the comedy wing of the punk rock revolution. The idea of comedy clubs, where anyone could come on and do five minutes, provided they weren't racist, sexist, or booed off by the drunken audience, was inspired by the success of similar venues in the USA, and by the desperately awful state of stand-up comedy in Britain at that time, both at live venues and on TV. It certainly gave a moribund comedy scene a bloody good shake-up, but at first it seemed to bypass radio, and in the early 80s Channel 4 television was comedy's laboratory, not Radio 4.

The main exception to this rule was *The Cabaret Upstairs* in the mid-80s, which introduced any number of stand-ups, both Oxbridge and alternative, to a mass audience (and, just as importantly, to each other). Clive Anderson - warm-up comic, former Frankie Howerd and *Week Ending* writer, and Footlights man of the Douglas Adams and Griff Rhys Jones generation - compeered the show, a job he'd been doing at The Comedy Store. It was on this late-night show that I first heard, separately, the two greatest droll comics of the post-war age: Norman Lovett and Arnold Brown.

Radio Active (1981-88) was the longest-running comedy show of the 1980s. Just for a change, this programme was born at Oxford, not Cambridge. Three college chums - Philip Pope, Angus Deayton and Michael Fenton-Stevens - formed a band called the Heebee Geebees, a lampoon of the Bee Gees. The Heebs' single, *Meaningless Songs In Very High Voices*, one of the cleverest parody songs ever written, was a modest hit and led to the band expanding its cruel repertoire and touring in the UK and Australia. They developed *Radio Active* as a comedy bit to pad out the songs. Naturally, since all Oxbridge graduates are entitled to their own radio series by dint of a tradition or an old charter or something, they were invited to make a pilot, which was broadcast in 1980 and followed by seven series.

The three Heebs were joined in the cast by two more Oxford Revue graduates: Helen Atkinson Wood, and Geoffrey Perkins (who had produced *Hitchhiker's*). Morwenna Banks and Kate Robbins made occasional appearances. Pope was the musician, while Deayton and Perkins wrote most of the scripts; writers of additional material included Richard Curtis. Jimmy Mulville, Jamie Rix, Paul Mayhew-Archer and David Tyler all produced at various times.

A fairly conventional sketch show, *Radio Active* was set apart by the skill with which it was written, presented and produced, and by its gimmick. It was packaged as excerpts from 'Britain's first national local radio station,' and the greater part of its scorn was targeted at the amateurishness then prevalent in local broadcasting. The suggestion that much local radio was only half a step up from hospital radio was underlined in later series with the appearance of Martin Brown (Fenton-Stevens), newly promoted from a hospital station, whose shaky voice and inspired incompetence made him the most irresistible element in a show that was never less than enjoyable, and sometimes achingly so.

Other regular characters included Mike Hunt and Uncle Mike Stand, Nigel Pry and Anna Daptor, and the Norwegian broadcaster, Oivind Vinstra, who was fluent in neither English nor Norwegian. Each episode contained devastatingly accurate musical spoofs, and fake ads - many of which were for services offered by 'Honest Ron, Honest Ron, the others are a con.'

At the centre of the show, in a way representing the listener, was Angus Deayton, busy perfecting the Cleese-like persona - rude, clever, cynical, weary and superior - which has made him so very rich since. He deserves every penny of it, for *Radio Active* alone. In 1990, the show transferred to television, as *KYTV*, where it turned its spite on that embodiment of evil, Sky Television.

The Million Pound Radio Show (mid-80s to 1991, with later specials) was a standard sketch show, written and presented by Andy Hamilton and Nick Revell, with a support cast which included Harry Enfield. It's mainly remembered now for one brilliant sketch, which I'm sure you've heard even if you don't know where it comes from, about a ship of pirates mutinying to demand that their captain grant them a training day, and other such new-age management-speak perks, so that they can 'Compare work methods and prioritise objectives, damn yer eyes!'

Radio 1 suddenly came over all comical with *The Mary Whitehouse Experience* (1989-91), devised by Bill Dare, one of the busiest Light Ent producers of recent years. The main performers were Rob Newman and David Baddiel, and Steve Punt and Hugh Dennis, with various supporters during the four series, including Mark Thomas, Jo Brand, Skint Video, Nick Hancock, Donna MacPhail, Rebecca Front, Doon MacKichan and Jack Dee. Many of the later shows were produced by Armando Iannucci.

Comedy was a new and rare creature on the pop music channel, and this programme (named in honour of the vile old right-wing moraliser and enemy of 'filthy' comedy, who threatened to sue the BBC for misusing her sacred name) was a suitably noisy, punky and youthy mixture of the aggressive and the silly, all done with the atmosphere of a slightly unruly comedy club. Many of the programmes were subsequently repeated on Radio 4, and the *Experience* ultimately span off a quite successful, but very bad, TV series. Comedy, in clubs and on television, became quite frighteningly fashionable during the 1990s, and there's no doubt that this show played its part in that, at least indirectly; whether it convinced millions of teenagers that their wirelesses could be used for comical purposes is debatable. Elements of the *Experience* have survived into the present, with Punt and Dennis's *The Now Show* (Radio 4, from 1998).

Other influential sketch shows of the decade included *Injury Time*, written by Rory McGrath, Jimmy Mulville and Jon Canter, produced by Geoffrey Perkins, and performed by Stephen Fry, Emma Thompson, McGrath, Mulville, Robert Bathurst and Griff Rhys Jones, which was recorded on location before student audiences; *In One Ear* (1983-86), which went out live, starring Helen Lederer, Clive Mantle, Steve Brown and Nick Wilton, and written by the cast with Geoffrey Perkins, Jon Cantor, John Docherty and Moray Hunter; and *Son Of Cliche* (1983-85), written by Rob Grant and Doug Naylor, performed by Chris Barrie, Nick Maloney and Nick Wilton, and produced by Alan Nixon. One of this show's sketches was later expanded by the writers into the first successful SF comedy since *HHG*, the BBC TV show *Red Dwarf*.

My favourite sitcom of the 1980s was *Wrinkles* (1980-1), a slightly surreal series set in an old people's home, starring Anthea Askey (Arthur's daughter), Tom Mennard and Nick Maloney. This was the first comedy series written by Grant and Naylor. Forgotten today, it perhaps displayed more energy than technique, but succeeded in not sounding quite like anything else then being aired.

And What Do Points Mean: Panel Games

So far, I've ignored panel games - mainly because I'm unable to pummel them into any of the main categories of show under consideration here - but since they are some of the most reliable providers of laughter on the air, they demand at least a quick going-over with a damp cloth. The three longest-running (and, perhaps coincidentally, the three best) are, in order of seniority:

Just A Minute (from 1967). Celebrities are required to speak on a given subject for sixty seconds without 'hesitation, repetition or deviation.' The other panelists interrupt them with challenges and if the chairman upholds the challenge, the interrupter takes over the subject. It's a simplified version of *One Minute Please* (1951), chaired by Roy Plomley, and with Kenneth Horne among its panelists, both shows being devised by Ian Messiter. *JAM* is chaired by former straight man Nicholas Parsons, who pretends to take great offence at the insults directed at him by his colleagues, vigorously guards the integrity of the rules, and promotes the show's alleged role in teaching English to remote World Service listeners. The programme's first producer was David Hatch.

Innumerable comedy personalities have appeared on *JAM* over the years - including Barry Took, Betty Marsden, Stephen Fry and the Right Honourable Barbara Castle MP - the longest-serving being Derek Nimmo, Clement Freud, Peter Jones and Kenneth Williams. Williams was the programme's greatest star, and did the best improvised work of his life on *JAM* (or semi-improvised - his diaries suggest that panelists were given advance notice of the subjects; they also suggest that he took the game extremely seriously, and that his outbursts of anger were not entirely theatrical). The format perfectly suited his mixture of erudition and camp ('I'm a cult, I am! I'm the biggest cult going!'), and when he died in 1988 there were fears that *JAM* could not continue. However, a rising comic named Paul Merton wrote to the producer asking if he could appear on the show. Merton - playing the obstreperous, well-informed Williams 'part,' but with less malice - has proved an invigorating addition to the team ever since, and today the programme is as entertaining as ever. Following the deaths of Nimmo, and then Jones, more and more younger comics have appeared on *JAM*, finding room within the old format for their individual styles of wit, invention, and recycling.

I'm Sorry I Haven't A Clue (from 1972). Two teams of two celebrities are 'given silly things to do' by the chairman, Humphrey Lyttleton, jazz musician, cartoonist and former Grenadier Guard. The 'antidote to panel games' was devised by Graeme Garden, and originally featured panelists from *ISIRTA*. For most of its long life, it had a settled team of Garden, Tim Brooke-Taylor, Barry Cryer and the great satirist Willie Rushton, with Colin Sell at the piano.

When Rushton died in 1997, *ISIHAC* took the *JAM* route to survival and began trying out comedians from a younger generation. The most successful of these has been Jeremy Hardy, a quick-thinking comic whose persona is suitably fogeyish. I think it's fair to say that the show has never entirely recovered from Rushton's death, but even so, at its best it is still so funny, clever and fast, that listeners risk asphyxiation. At its worst it's merely very funny (and occasionally obscene, particularly in recent years). The undoubted star is 'Humph,' with his mutters of contempt for the panelists, the games, the audience and the world at large; as long as he is available, *ISIHAC* will run indefinitely.

The News Quiz (from 1977). Created by John Lloyd, chaired originally by Barry Norman, then for many years by Barry Took, and currently by

Simon Hoggart, this is a comedy quiz about the week's news. Comics, journalists and occasionally politicians make up the panel. Some of the most fondly remembered editions featured Richard Ingrams and John Wells, who would affect to know absolutely nothing of what had happened during the past seven days, and not to have been anywhere near a newspaper during that time. Current regulars include Alan Coren, Jeremy Hardy, Andy Hamilton, Francis Wheen, and the funniest woman on radio today, Linda Smith. Inevitably a hit and miss affair - global tragedies involving massive loss of life, for instance, can severely reduce the chuckle quotient - the programme is at its marvellous best when some minor detail of an overlooked story catches the inner eye of one or more of the panelists, allowing them to fly away into worlds of mad fantasy. *Have I Got News For You* is a much less spontaneous TV version.

What Are The Chances Of That Happening: The 1990s And Now

By the end of the 1990s, elements of the ageing alternative comedy movement had intermingled so thoroughly on TV and radio with elements of the Oxbridge mafia, that, as Orwell put it in a slightly different context, 'The creatures outside looked from pig to man, and from man to pig, and from pig to man again; but already it was impossible to say which was which.'

What is clear is that, at the beginning of the twenty-first century, BBC radio has regained its position as the pre-eminent workshop of British comedy. In the late 80s and throughout the 90s, the TV schedules (BBC and commercial) were thick with programmes that had begun on the radio: *Whose Line Is It Anyway?*, *Goodness Gracious Me*, *The League Of Gentlemen*, *Harry Hill's Fruit Fancies*, *The Day Today*, *Knowing Me, Knowing You*, *People Like Us*, *Chambers* and many others; several more are currently in development.

The endless exodus of writers, producers and comedians from sound to vision, in search of bigger money and bigger audiences, annoys some radio fans (and radio tends to produce fans, rather than just listeners, perhaps because of its 'minority' status in the TV age, or what critic Thomas Sutcliffe has called its 'anonymous intimacy' and 'serpentine ability to creep up on us'). But there is a more positive way of looking at the process: as long as the box uses the wireless the way a poacher uses a lord's forest, radio will be forced to continue searching out and developing new talent, and new comic trends. If you want to hear the best comedy - and hear it first, before it starts ponging - you will always have to listen to the radio.

It is proverbially 'too early to tell' what the lasting effects of the French Revolution might be, and it's certainly too early to say which radio shows of the 90s and later will in time be seen as classics. That needn't stop me making a few suggestions, however:

On The Hour (1991-2). Easily the most effective satire ever broadcast, this series is a startling exception to my theme in this book - that modern comedy has its roots in the Big Three. *On The Hour* had no discernible genealogy; one day it wasn't there, the next day it was, and it left listeners gasping at its inventiveness and audacity. *OTH* was a ruthless attack on the values, methods, cliches and self-aggrandising presentation styles of modern news broadcasting. It took the form of a news magazine pro-gramme, and was done so well that anyone tuning in unawares might take a while to realise that they were listening to a comedy, rather than an even more absurd than usual news show. Chris Morris's crazed anchorman was hilarious - but also an accurate send-up. The rest of the cast was Steve Coogan, Rebecca Front, Doon MacKichan, Patrick Marber and David Schneider.

It's impossible to convey how stunningly new this style was when first aired, because *OTH* created a mini-genre of comedy the impact of which, naturally, has become diluted by familiarity. Much of the credit for the show's hideous veracity must go to the technical brilliance of producer Armando Iannucci. The writers, other than the cast, were Iannucci, Rich-ard Herring and Stewart Lee, Steven Wells, Andrew Glover and David Quantick. *OTH* spin-offs included sports reporter (and later chat-show host) Alan Partridge (Coogan), *The Day Today* on BBC 2, and Morris's vicious wind-up phone call campaigns on various channels.

The Mark Steel Solution (from 1992) and *Jeremy Hardy Speaks To The Nation* (from 1993). Kark Marx and Fred Engels were quite chuckly lads in their off-duty hours, but the jokes in their written work come over as a bit heavy these days. How lucky we are, then, to have two Socialist Alli-ance activists who are also very witty comics, able to explore matters of substance from a broadly Marxist viewpoint while illustrating their points with daft jokes. Steel (with co-writer Pete Sinclair) is the more rigorously analytical, while Hardy occasionally veers towards liberal wishy-washi-ness, and a fixation with bottoms and 'front bits,' as befits his comic per-sona, but both are well-informed about history and politics, and both are very funny.

This may be alternative comedy's only abiding effect on radio: the creation of a new form of comedy-as-lecture - or a new method of political education, depending on how you look at it. Its only remote precedent is the series of immensely popular talks on war aims, given by left-wing playwright J.B. Priestley during WW2; Priestley wasn't a comic, of course, but he was a comedy buff, and not above using humour to reinforce a point.

The Masterson Inheritance (1993-95). Improvisational comedy: you either love it or you've got good taste. However, this mock family saga, unrehearsed and unscripted, powered by suggestions from the studio audience, worked very well. The cast of Comedy Store improv veterans was Josie Lawrence, Phelim McDermott, Paul Merton, Caroline Quentin, Lee Simpson (the narrator) and Jim Sweeney; the producer was Phil Clarke. The audience had great fun thinking up prompts which would make life difficult for the performers, while the cast - especially Merton - enjoyed sabotaging each other's attempts to build up to a gag. (The first ever audience suggestion, incidentally, was 'Slaving,' in answer to this request from Lee: 'The first thing that we need is an idea of a hobby or a pastime that a gentleman of the late 18th century might do to pass the time pleasantly...')

Harry Hill's Fruit Corner (1993-97). If ever a man was wasted on television, it's ex-doctor Harry Hill. On TV, his deeply individual and bizarre medley of catchphrases, non sequiturs, odd characters, sound effects, verbal tics and nervous twitches, seemingly random but strangely consistent cultural references, audience participation, doublings-back on himself, snatches of song, music hall mannerisms, pointless celebrity guests and crazed parodies of observational humour is pretty amusing. On radio, it was one of the most uplifting comedy experiences anyone could ever hope to have - like a colonic irrigation for the mind, only without the not-knowing-where-to-look. It was to the 90s what *Burkiss* was to the 70s and *RTH* was to the 60s: liberation through laughter.

TV slows Hill down, and his badgers don't look nearly as funny as they sound. I live in hope that one day he'll return to his natural habitat, and take his rightful place as the Kenneth Horne *and* the Spike Milligan of the 21st century. The support cast consisted variously of Al Murray (great nephew of *The Navy Lark*'s Stephen), Martin Hyder, Matt Bradstock, Edna Doré, Bert Kwuok, Phil Jupitus, Soo Drouet, Phil Nice, Brenda Gilhooley, Joanna Brookes, Peter Serafinowicz and (honestly) the Cliff Ranger Singers. Hill wrote, and Jon Magnusson produced.

People Like Us (1995-97). If I was giving an award for Best Actor In A 1990s Comedy it would go without doubt to Chris Langham as fly-on-the-wall reporter Roy Mallard, in this simply perfect series of spoof documentaries which captured the tone of what was at the time an annoyingly ubiquitous and conceited staple of the TV and radio schedules.

The varying cast never stepped out of character into comedy, while it slowly became clear that everyone Mallard met was mad, or at least incompetent in a peculiarly insane way ('Mr Wilson has returned, Mr Mallard. He'll see you as soon as you're with him'). The supremely inept Mallard wasn't bonkers, he was just not very good at being a reporter; he had trouble with the English language, he tended to rub people up the wrong way, and he was a magnet for mishap and misunderstanding.

Producer Paul Schlesinger edited with split-second precision, so that every joke got *slightly* less reaction time than it needed, and John Morton's scripts were a marvel of comic engineering. Each episode needs to be listened to three or four times before you can be sure you've extracted all its goodness; so many of the laughs come from throwaway lines, and while your head's catching up with one joke, your ears are missing two more.

'At the moment I could be anywhere in the country; in fact, though, I'm here. In the last twenty years light industrial estates like this one in Northampton have sprung up all over Northampton.'

Old Harry's Game (from 1995). Andy Hamilton is His Satanic Majesty in this Hell-set sitcom, produced by Paul Mayhew-Archer, and a splendid radio actor, James Grout, plays the Professor, a thoroughly good man who has been condemned to the fiery pit because he doesn't believe it exists. Andy Hamilton, as writer, relies a little too much on semi-topical references to get easy laughs, but this gently philosophical character comedy still has plenty of very good moments, and fine acting makes it hard to resist.

Goodness Gracious Me! (1996-98). Originally titled *Peter Sellers Is Dead*, on the grounds that one of Sellers's film characters, whose catchphrase was 'Goodness gracious me,' was the best known 'Indian' in British culture. A one-off live show was staged under the *Sellers* title, on the strength of which BBC Television financed the radio series; talk about hedging your bets. In the event, *GGM* was an immediate success, thanks to the high quality acting and, usually, high quality writing. It was an entirely conventional sketch show, with one difference - the main performers were all British Asians: Meera Syal, Sanjeev Bhaskar, Nina

Wadia, Kulvinder Ghir, and Nitin Sawhney. The writers were Sharat Sardana and Richard Pinto, with some contributions from the cast, and the producer was Anil Gupta.

The aim of the series was to present humour about being Asian in the UK (everybody knew black people could be comics - but Asians? They were worthy, hard-working and devout), and to do it in a way which made it funny to mainstream multi-ethnic audiences. The sketch in which a group of Asians in a British restaurant boldly asked the waiter for 'the blandest thing on the menu' was the show's most famous moment, but really that's nothing more than a well executed reversal gag. Some of the recurring characters and their catchphrases, however, were comic creations to rank alongside any of the sketch show greats, and are firmly embedded in the public consciousness. Or I'll eat my chuddies.

Chambers (1996-99). A sitcom about a nest of barristers and their clerk, all of whom are either cynical manipulators or incompetent idiots - or both. A good, old-fashioned workplace comedy, with funny scripts by Clive Coleman, uniformly excellent performances from John Bird, Sarah Lancashire, James Fleet and Jonathan Kydd, and sharp production by Paul Schlesinger.

On The Town With The League Of Gentlemen (1997). Much praised for its originality, this mixture of sketch show and sitcom, produced by Sarah Smith, could best be described as a very sinister, twisted, altogether rather yucky version of the first *Goon Show* series: a tapestry of essentially discrete sketches, featuring a repertory of interlinked recurring characters, almost all of whom were rather horrible; though I think Barbara - a taxi driver with a voice like Milligan's 'Throat,' who was having trouble with her sex change process - probably meant well enough.

The first amazing fact which everyone discovered about the *League* was that the entire population of the dying town of Spent was played by just three men (except for one brief appearance by Sally Phillips as post-op Barbara): Mark Gatiss, Steve Pemberton and Reece Shearsmith. The trio also wrote the series, with Jeremy Dyson. For my taste, it was too creepy to enjoy as a comedy; as a gothic melodrama with catchphrases, on the other hand, it was terrific.

The Very World Of Milton Jones (from 1998). Jones is an actor and stand-up who co-writes this sketch-show-cum-character-comedy with Dan Evans, Jon Holmes and Andy Hurst, Mark Evans and James Bachman, Mike Haskins and Tony Roche; David Tyler produces. Each episode begins with Milton facing certain death, and witnessing events from his life flashing before his eyes. Despite the set-up, this is a thoroughly cheerful show, making great use of puns which manage to conjure, simultaneously, groans and Goonish visions. The small supporting cast has included Alistair McGowan and Sally Grace.

Dead Ringers (from 2000). This impersonation-based sketch show is highly unusual for two reasons: the impressions are generally spot on, and the scripts are inventive and funny. Instead of a failed comic sticking a beret on his head and going 'Oooh, Betty,' this lot think up things for their characters to do or say which are either horribly appropriate, or eye-openingly inappropriate. This isn't mimicry, it is genuine impressionism - the kind that can change forever the way you look at a particular public figure. The impressionists include Alistair McGowan, Kate Robbins, John Culshaw and Simon Lipson; the show was devised by Bill Dare; and the writers' list is of unprintable *Huddlines* proportions, but has included Jon Holmes and Andy Hurst, Simon Blackwell, Nev Fountain and Tom Jamieson, Ivor Baddiel and Ashley Boroda, George Jeffrie and Bert Tyler Moore.

It's All In The Mind, You Know: The Future Of Radio Comedy

With very few exceptions, almost all successful radio and television sitcoms since the 1950s have been centred on an irritable, misanthropic, Hancockian figure; equally, it's hard to think of an example of a modern sketch show which doesn't display a great debt to either the madness of *The Goon Show* or the camp exuberance of *Round The Horne*, or both. The speech patterns of Hancock and Kenneth Williams are echoed by dozens of our favourite contemporary comics (Paul Merton, Linda Smith and Graham Norton, for instance), while Spike Milligan's policy of fighting idiocy with idiocy animates the joyfully baffled irreverence of programmes like *Big Train*, *The Shuttleworths* and *The Small World Of Dominic Holland*.

This is not to suggest that comedy is static; I hope this chapter, particularly, has shown that the opposite is true. Comedy constantly feeds on its own history, and disgorges new ways of telling old jokes, fresh formats built in the ruins of the old. The budgets may be smaller than they used to be - you won't get a full orchestra on a radio show anymore - but even today, when TV comedy is to a depressing extent a corporately-owned, factory-made commodity, radio still finds some space for a more free-range, wholemeal type of humour.

It's generally assumed that the Golden Age of wireless comedy belongs to the long-ago... I'm not so sure. There are growing signs that television's time as the dominant mass medium is coming to an end. The audience figures as a whole have been falling over the last few years, while the growth in channels means that audiences for specific shows are generally much smaller than a decade ago. The biggest regular TV audience today is tiny compared to a decent radio audience of the 1950s, despite population growth.

Britain already spends more hours listening to radio than it does watching TV, and overall radio audience figures are growing. In 2002, the BBC launched BBC7, a digital station which broadcasts several hours of 'classic' comedy every day. Of course, it may be that radio will fall victim to the same forces of deregulation and excessive competition - leading inevitably to plummeting standards - which have undermined TV; on the other hand, seeing what has happened to television, we might all realise what an irreplaceable treasure we have in BBC radio and vow to hold onto it, through violent insurrection if necessary.

Television just doesn't suit the patterns of our lives today the way it once did - but radio does. The great truism of radio - that you don't have to watch it - makes it a flexible survivalist. In the 1940s, entire families would sit and listen to *ITMA*; in the 2000s, commuters listen to its successors in the car, or at home in the bath, or in the office when the boss has buggered off early.

The obituary of radio comedy has been written many times, and no doubt will be written again. It will, I believe, always be premature; the undramatic truth is that the Golden Age of radio comedy never ended - it's been with us all along, and shows no signs of closing. Radio's mass audiences have probably gone forever, but now that we live in a post-mass audience age, does that matter? Radio still provides comedy's heartbeat - thanks in no small part to our Big Three. Today, radio is again the principle source of innovative comedy; there's no reason to suppose that new cult shows will not arise in this century as they did in the last. Surveying the quality and variety available to us now, I can only conclude that radio comedy is more important and more vibrant than it has been at any time since *Round The Horne*.

Welcome to the Golden Age.

Chapter Seven: Resources

The Reunion Party: Tying Up Loose Ends

Here are the subsequent adventures of some of the people mentioned in the preceding chapters. Where details are missing, it's because I don't know them, or can't confirm them. I'd be delighted to receive new information for this section, or corrections to errors of fact in any part of the book; please contact me via Pocket Essentials.

Adams, Douglas (1952-2001): Remained a well-known writer and broadcaster, though not surprisingly he never produced anything to match *Hitchhiker's*. His death in California, from a heart attack, prompted some of the most extravagantly praising and grief-stricken obituaries ever accorded a comedy or science-fiction writer.

Askey, Arthur (1900-82): A star of TV, cinema and pantomime, severe health problems forced his retirement in the late 1970s.

Barker, Eric (1912-90): Moved into television and films, especially the *St Trinian's* and *Carry On* series.

Bentine, Michael (1922-96): Continued to successfully develop his own style of comedy in radio and TV - a style which was, if anything, even more uncompromisingly experimental than Milligan's. He also wrote numerous books on various subjects, including the paranormal. He was decorated by Britain and Peru.

Bentley, Dick (1907-95): Returned to Australia in 1966, and acted in films and television. Retired in 1973.

Brough, Peter (1916-99): His ventriloquism act didn't take on TV (allegedly because the audience could see his lips moving), so when his radio career petered out, he returned to running the family clothing business.

Chester, Charlie (1914-97): His successful career continued, in all media, almost until his death.

Cogan, Alma (1932-66): 'The girl with the laughter in her voice' was a popular singer, with several chart hits in the mid-50s. She died of cancer.

Connor, Kenneth (1916-93): A regular in the *Carry On* films, and the TV sitcom *'allo 'allo*; continued working until days before his death.

Cooke, Brian: After *RTH*, Cooke and Mortimer became one of the top TV comedy writing partnerships, their credits including *Man About The House*.

Daniels, Bebe (1901-71): Settled in London after WW2, with her husband and partner Ben Lyon, and continued to work in TV, radio, films and stage. Outside the UK, they're remembered mostly as silent film stars, and for the story that Lyon, as a talent scout, discovered Marilyn Monroe. After Daniels's death, Lyon remarried and returned to the USA.

Denham, Maurice (1909-2002): One of Britain's busiest character actors, in all media and through several decades, he provided the voices of all the animals in the animated 1955 film of *Animal Farm*.

Dyall, Valentine (1908-85): Acted in all media until shortly before his death; one of his last appearances was in *Blackadder*.

Edwards, Jimmy (1920-88): Appeared in many TV and radio shows, and a few films. Played headmaster in TV sitcom *Whack-O!* from 1956-72.

Emery, Dick (1917-83): One of Britain's principal TV stars of the 60s and 70s, playing multiple characters in his own sketch shows.

Fairweather, George: Died November 1999, aged 89.

Feldman, Marty (1933-82): Became a TV star in the UK and US, and then made a number of Hollywood films, before dying on set, of a heart attack.

Galton, Ray (born 1930): Galton and Simpson wrote *Steptoe And Son* (1962-74), still among the most admired TV sitcoms. Their Hancock and *Steptoe* TV scripts continue to be newly produced around the world; in the mid-90s they updated some of their best scripts for Paul Merton on ITV. Greatly honoured, by the state and by their industry, they no longer write new material together.

Geldray, Max (born 1916): One of the most eminent jazz harmonica players ever, Geldray's life story is too extraordinary to be decently summarised. He has lived in the USA for many years, and retired in the 1990s due to ill health.

Guyler, Deryck (1919-99): Played support roles in many TV series, notably *Sykes*. Emigrated to Australia in 1992.

Hatch, David: For many years a senior manager in BBC radio. Currently presenting a Radio 4 panel game about radio.

Howerd, Frankie (1917-92): Made two comebacks, in the early 60s and the late 80s. Made hundreds of appearances on TV, especially, and on radio and stage. Posthumously recognised as a great comedian.

Jacques, Hattie (1924-80): A regular in the *Carry On* films, but at her best playing Eric Sykes's sister in the TV series *Sykes*.

James, Sid (1913-76): Regular in the *Carry On* films and on TV, he died on stage.

Jones, Peter (1920-2000): Elegantly witty, Jones starred in *The Rag Trade* (1961-63) on TV, and was contributing to *Just A Minute* until shortly before his death.

Kerr, Bill (born 1924): Continued working in British TV before returning to Australia, where he has since worked mainly as a film actor.

Lister, Moira (born 1923): Still a West End and film actress.

Lyon, Ben (1901-79): *see* Daniels, Bebe.

Marsden, Betty (1919-98): After *RTH*, she resumed her theatrical career, and was acting in all media until shortly before her death.

Marshall, Andrew: Wrote some TV series with David Renwick, then created long-running family sitcom *2 Point 4 Children* (from 1991) for BBC TV.

Maschwitz, Eric (1901-69): An extraordinary career included writing the screenplay for the film *Goodbye Mr Chips* and the lyrics for *A Nightingale Sang In Berkeley Square*, being Head of Light Ent for the BBC, and a lifelong involvement in professional and amateur musical theatre.

Melly, Andrée (born 1932). Stage, TV, radio and film actress. Her many films roles include *The Brides Of Dracula*.

Milligan, Spike (1918-2002): Went on to write novels, TV shows, volumes of memoirs, poetry and children's books, and to campaign for many causes, including animal welfare and children's rights. In 1994, he endeared himself to yet another generation when he called Goons fan Prince Charles a 'little grovelling bastard' on live television. He had a triple heart bypass ('I couldn't afford any more'), and in 2000 was given an honorary knighthood. On a day of political crises, international conflict and sensational court cases, the death of 'The last of the Goons' - an elderly man, who'd been ill for some years - still made headlines, and dominated the next day's front pages.

Mortimer, Johnnie (died 1992): *see* Cooke, Brian.

Muir, Frank (1920-98): Worked as a very influential Light Ent manager, as a panelist on radio and TV panel games, as a broadcaster and book writer.

Murdoch, Richard (1907-90): Continued acting on TV; appeared in an episode of *Blackadder* which Valentine Dyall was also in.

Norden, Dennis (born 1922): Worked on panel games with Muir; in 1977 created, and still presents, TV outtakes show *It'll be Alright On The Night*. In 2000 Norden, and Muir's family, donated over 600 of their scripts to the University of Sussex, which described the collection as 'profoundly important.'

Paddick, Hugh (1915-2000): Continued working on TV and stage, and in films including *The Killing Of Sister George*. He lived privately and would perhaps have been surprised by how widely he was mourned.

Perkins, Geoffrey: After some years as BBC TV's Head of Comedy, in 2001 he left the BBC to become creative director for an independent production company.

Pertwee, Bill (born 1926): A film and TV actor, his most famous role being ARP Warden Hodges in *Dad's Army*.

Rees, Nigel (born 1944): Chairman since 1976 of Radio 4 panel game *Quote... Unquote*, which he also devised.

Renwick, David: In 1990 created one of the most popular and acclaimed of all TV sitcoms, *One Foot In The Grave*.

Rounce, Phyllis (1912-2001): Remained an agent with her company International Artistes, until retiring late in life.

Secombe, Harry (1921-2001): Knighted in 1981, Ned of Wales probably had the most fulfilling post-Goon career of all of them; he was celebrated as a singer, writer of memoirs and fiction, stage and film actor, charity worker, and latterly religious broadcaster. He retired in 1999. The international outpouring of affection for him at the time of his death was remarkable. He once said that he hoped his obituary would read 'He suffered fools gladly because he was one of them.'

Sellers, Peter (1925-80): An international film star of the 1950s, 60s and 70s, in pictures like *Dr Strangelove* and *Being There*. Caused hilarity among fellow Goons from beyond the grave, by having *In The Mood* played at his funeral; they knew it was the tune he hated most.

Simpson, Alan (born 1929): *see* Galton, Ray.

Stephens, Larry: Died in January 1959, of a brain haemorrhage, while dining with Spike Milligan.

Stott, Wally (born 1924): A leading conductor, arranger and composer in TV and films in the 1950s-80s. Underwent a sex change in the 1970s, and continued working as Angela Morley. Lives in the USA.

Sykes, Eric (born 1923): Still working as a scriptwriter and stage actor, although more or less blind and deaf; still, he claims, 'hoping to be discovered.' Frequently interviewed by journalists as the last active survivor of an extraordinary comic generation, he will be best remembered for his TV series *Sykes* and its predecessors (1960-79).

Took, Barry (1928-2002): Continued writing comedy scripts, in Britain and the USA, and took up management duties in television light entertainment, where his most famous achievement was the creation of *Monty Python's Flying Circus* (given the working title by Cleese et al of *Baron Von Took's Flying Circus*). He also worked as a presenter on TV and radio. Ill-health forced his retirement in 2001.

Williams, Kenneth (1926-88): In later years, Williams's best performances were as an anecdotal guest on chat shows, and as a panelist on *Just A Minute*.

Wilson, Dennis Main (1924-97): In 1957 Wilson moved to TV, where he was responsible for *Six Five-Special*, the first TV pop show, and many great comedy shows including *The Rag Trade* and *Till Death Us Do Part*. He was also the man who gave John Sullivan, writer of *Citizen Smith* and *Only Fools And Horses*, his first break. He left the BBC in 1983, believing that producers no longer had enough creative control.

Many of the books listed here are out of print, but since they haven't been replaced by equally good in-print books they're worth the effort of tracking down.

Books about particular shows and artistes:

The Goon Show Companion by Roger Wilmut (Sphere, 1977). A detailed history of the show by Britain's foremost historian of comedy, with a long memoir by Jimmy Grafton.

Hancock by Freddie Hancock and David Nathan (new edition, Ariel Books, 1986). The first weighty biography of the Lad, co-written by his widow.

The Illustrated Tony Hancock by Roger Wilmut (Queen Anne Press, 1986). Lavish collection of annotated photographs.

The Kenneth Williams Diaries edited by Russell Davies (HarperCollins, 1993).

The Pocket Essential Hitchhiker's Guide by MJ Simpson (Pocket Essentials, 2001).

Round The Horne, The Complete And Utter History by Barry Took (Boxtree, 1998).

Tony Hancock by Philip Oakes (Woburn-Futura, 1975). Memoir by one of Hancock's later collaborators.

Tony Hancock 'Artiste' by Roger Wilmut (Eyre Methuen, 1978). A Hancock companion.

When The Wind Changed, The Life And Death Of Tony Hancock by Cliff Goodwin (Century, 1999). By far the most thorough and detailed study of his life and work yet undertaken.

Books about comedy:

From Fringe To Flying Circus by Roger Wilmut (Methuen, 1980). Marvellous study of the 1960-80 Oxbridge comedy generation.

The Golden Age Of Radio by Denis Gifford (Batsford, 1985). Comprehensive; covers radio generally, not just comedy.

Grace, Beauty And Banjos by Michael Kilgarriff (Oberon Books, 1998). Unique; a study of music hall bill matter.

The Laughtermakers by David Nathan (Peter Owen, 1971). An intellectual study of the nature of popular comedy; sophisticated and highly entertaining.

Radio Comedy 1938-68 by Andy Foster and Steve Furst (Virgin, 1996). A superbly detailed and interesting show-by-show guide; indispensable. (If only the publishers had thought to commission an index!)

Radio: The Great Years by Derek Parker (David & Charles, 1977). A valuable 'Golden Age' history.

Radio Times Guide To TV Comedy by Mark Lewisohn (BBC, 1988). Impressive work of scholarship, with much material of interest to radio fans.

Very Interesting... But Stupid by Nigel Rees (Unwin, 1980). Pioneering collection of catchphrases.

The Wireless Stars by George Nobbs (Wensum Books, 1972). From pre-*Band Waggon* to post-Hancock.

Books of scripts:

The Best Of Round The Horne by Barry Took with Mat Coward (Boxtree, 2000). Selected scripts, with introductions and annotations.

The Book Of The Goons by Spike Milligan (Robson Books, 1974). Includes essay by Peter Eton, and facsimiles of inter-Goon correspondence.

The Goon Show Scripts by Spike Milligan (Woburn Press, 1972).

Hancock's Half Hour by Ray Galton and Alan Simpson, compiled by Chris Bumstead (BBC, 1987). Eight radio scripts; there have been several collections of *HHH* television scripts.

The ITMA Years by Ted Kavanagh (Woburn Press, 1974). Includes reminiscences by various people connected with the show.

More Goon Show Scripts by Spike Milligan (Woburn Press, 1973).

Round The Horne by Barry Took and Marty Feldman (Woburn Press, 1974).

Books of particular shows:

Bestseller! The Life & Death Of Eric Pode of Croydon by Andrew Marshall & David Renwick (Allen & Unwin, 1981).

Radio Active Times by Angus Deayton and Geoffrey Perkins (Sphere, 1986).

Also worth looking out for:

Hancock's Last Half Hour by Heathcote Williams; the script of this biographical play, first produced at The Almost Free Theatre in London in 1977, has been published in book form.

In 1955, Chad Valley Toys issued a *Hancock's Half Hour* board game. I once saw it for sale in a London comics shop in the late 1980s; unfortunately I didn't have £50 on me. Or off me, come to that. Speaking of comics, *Film Fun* carried a Hancock strip for four years from 1958. And next time you're in Birmingham, don't forget to visit Old Square, to have your picture taken next to the 12ft square bronze statue of The Lad Himself.

I haven't included a discography, for a happy reason; after decades of casual neglect, the BBC in recent years has learned to exploit the seemingly bottomless market for commercial audio releases of comedy shows. As well as the Big Three, most of the other titles discussed in this book are now available. For a catalogue, phone 01672 562255, or go to http://www.bbcworldwide.com/spokenword/

For anything you can't buy, get in touch with the Old-Time Radio Show Collector's Association (www.eurekanet.com/~orca/), which Barry Hill founded in Leeds in the 1980s, and now runs from RT1, Box 197, Belpre, OH 45714, USA. ORCA has a tape lending library the size of a planet.

Hello Folks Of World (And In That Order):
Fandom And The Internet.

Radio comedy fandom is almost as old as radio comedy, but it's never been as organised and influential as it is today. Details change rapidly - due to burn-out among organisers, for instance, or even splits between factions - so the best way of getting in touch is through the Internet. A quick flick of the old search-engine will uncover great riches, but here are a few choice sites to get you started, some of which include audio clips:

http://www.britishcomedy.org.uk/comedy/comedy.htm - details of dozens of radio and TV shows.

http://www.transdiffusion.org/rmc/index.asp - lots of pages about radio history, including excellent sites on *The Burkiss Way* and *Radio Active*.

http://www.goonshow.org.uk/ - the Goon Show Preservation Society homepage.

http://www.petersellerssociety.net/ - the Peter Sellers Appreciation Society homepage.

http://www.whirligig-tv.co.uk/radio/index.htm - radio nostalgia site.

http://www.laughradio.com.au/more3.htm - a huge bibliography of comedy-related titles.

http://www.kennethwilliams.org.uk/ - home page of the Kenneth Williams Appreciation Society.

http://www.tonyhancock.co.uk/ - one of many Hancock sites, this one allows you to hear the poems from *The Poetry Society*.

http://www.tonyhancock.org.uk/ - homepage of the Tony Hancock Appreciation Society.

http://www.zz9.org/ - the Official Hitchhiker's Guide to the Galaxy Appreciation Society, ZZ9 Plural Z Alpha, has existed since 1980.

http://www.rethink.demon.co.uk/laugh.html - some *On The Hour* clips.

www.angelfire.com/pq/radiohaha - 'The online encyclopaedia of contemporary British radio comedy' is a wonderful resource for anyone interested in shows from the 1980s to the present; elegant, insightful writing, full of facts and dripping with links.

The Essential Library: Film Best-Sellers

Build up your library with new titles every month

Stanley Kubrick by Paul Duncan

Kubrick's work, like all masterpieces, has a timeless quality. His vision is so complete, the detail so meticulous, that you believe you are in a three-dimensional space displayed on a two-dimensional screen. He was commercially successful because he embraced traditional genres like War (*Paths Of Glory*, *Full Metal Jacket*), Crime (*The Killing*), Science Fiction (*2001*), Horror (*The Shining*) and Love (*Barry Lyndon*). At the same time, he stretched the boundaries of film with controversial themes: underage sex (*Lolita*); ultra violence (*A Clockwork Orange*); and erotica (*Eyes Wide Shut*).

Film Noir by Paul Duncan

The laconic private eye, the corrupt cop, the heist that goes wrong, the femme fatale with the rich husband and the dim lover - these are the trademark characters of Film Noir. This book charts the progression of the Noir style as a vehicle for film-makers who wanted to record the darkness at the heart of American society as it emerged from World War to the Cold War. As well as an introduction explaining the origins of Film Noir, seven films are examined in detail and an exhaustive list of over 500 Films Noirs are listed.

Alfred Hitchcock by Paul Duncan

More than 20 years after his death, Alfred Hitchcock is still a household name, most people in the Western world have seen at least one of his films, and he popularised the action movie format we see every week on the cinema screen. He was both a great artist and dynamite at the box office. This book examines the genius and enduring popularity of one of the most influential figures in the history of the cinema!

Orson Welles (Revised & Updated Edition) by Martin Fitzgerald

The popular myth is that after the artistic success of *Citizen Kane* it all went downhill for Orson Welles, that he was some kind of fallen genius. Yet, despite overwhelming odds, he went on to make great Films Noirs like *The Lady From Shanghai* and *Touch Of Evil*. He translated Shakespeare's work into films with heart and soul (*Othello*, *Chimes At Midnight*, *Macbeth*), and he gave voice to bitterness, regret and desperation in *The Magnificent Ambersons* and *The Trial*. Far from being down and out, Welles became one of the first cutting-edge independent film-makers.

Woody Allen (Revised & Updated Edition) by Martin Fitzgerald

Woody Allen: Neurotic. Jewish. Funny. Inept. Loser. A man with problems. Or so you would think from the characters he plays in his movies. But hold on. Allen has written and directed 30 films. He may be a funny man, but he is also one of the most serious American film-makers of his generation. This revised and updated edition includes *Sweet And Lowdown* and *Small Time Crooks*.

The Essential Library: Currently Available

Film Directors:

Woody Allen (2nd)	Tim Burton	Ang Lee
Jane Campion*	John Carpenter	Joel & Ethan Coen (2nd)
Jackie Chan	Steven Soderbergh	Clint Eastwood
David Cronenberg	Terry Gilliam*	Michael Mann
Alfred Hitchcock (2nd)	Krzysztof Kieslowski*	Roman Polanski
Stanley Kubrick (2nd)	Sergio Leone	Oliver Stone
David Lynch (2nd)	Brian De Palma*	George Lucas
Sam Peckinpah*	Ridley Scott (2nd)	James Cameron
Orson Welles (2nd)	Billy Wilder	Roger Corman
Steven Spielberg	Mike Hodges	Spike Lee
Hal Hartley		

Film Genres:

Blaxploitation Films	Bollywood	French New Wave
Horror Films	Spaghetti Westerns	Vietnam War Movies
Slasher Movies	Film Noir	Hammer Films
Vampire Films*	Heroic Bloodshed*	Carry On Films
German Expressionist Films		

Film Subjects:

Laurel & Hardy	Marx Brothers	Film Music
Steve McQueen*	Marilyn Monroe	The Oscars® (2nd)
Filming On A Microbudget	Bruce Lee	Writing A Screenplay
Film Studies		

Music:

The Madchester Scene	Beastie Boys	Jethro Tull
How To Succeed In The Music Business		The Beatles

Literature:

Cyberpunk	Philip K Dick	The Beat Generation
Agatha Christie	Sherlock Holmes	Noir Fiction
Terry Pratchett	Hitchhiker's Guide (2nd)	Alan Moore
William Shakespeare	Creative Writing	Tintin
Georges Simenon		

Ideas:

Conspiracy Theories	Nietzsche	UFOs
Feminism	Freud & Psychoanalysis	Bisexuality

History:

Alchemy & Alchemists	The Crusades	The Black Death
Jack The Ripper	The Rise Of New Labour	Ancient Greece
American Civil War	American Indian Wars	Witchcraft
Globalisation	Who Shot JFK?	

Miscellaneous:

Stock Market Essentials	How To Succeed As A Sports Agent	Doctor Who
Classic Radio Comedy		

Available at bookstores or send a cheque (payable to 'Oldcastle Books') to: **Pocket Essentials (Dept CRC), P O Box 394, Harpenden, Herts, AL5 1XJ, UK.** £3.99 each (£2.99 if marked with an *). For each book add 50p(UK)/£1 (elsewhere) postage & packing